OXFORD MONOGRAPHS IN
INTERNATIONAL LAW

GENERAL EDITOR: PROFESSOR IAN BROWNLIE CBE, QC, FBA
Chichele Professor of Public International Law in the University of
Oxford and Fellow of All Souls College, Oxford.

RECOGNITION OF GOVERNMENTS IN INTERNATIONAL LAW: WITH PARTICULAR REFERENCE TO GOVERNMENTS IN EXILE

OXFORD MONOGRAPHS IN
INTERNATIONAL LAW

The aim of this series of monographs is to publish important and original pieces of research on all aspects of public international law. Topics which are given particular prominence are those which, while of interest to the academic lawyer, also have important bearing on issues which touch the actual conduct of international relations. None the less the series is wide in scope and includes monographs on the history and philosophical foundations of international law.

RECENT TITLES IN THIS SERIES

The Regime of Straits in International Law

B.B. JIA

The Concept of International Obligations
Erga Omnes

M. RAGAZZI

The Termination and Revision of Treaties
in the Light of New Customary International Law

N. KONTOU

Land and Martime Zones of Peace
in International Law

S. P. SUBEDI

International Management of Hazardous Wastes:
The Basel Convention and Related legal Rules

K. KUMMER

Human Rights in the Private Sphere

A. CLAPHAM

Self-Determination and National Minorities

T. D. MUSGRAVE

Recognition of Governments in International Law: With Particular Reference to Governments in Exile

STEFAN TALMON

CLARENDON PRESS · OXFORD
1998

Oxford University Press, Great Clarendon Street, Oxford OX2 6DP

Oxford New York
Athens Auckland Bangkok Bogota Bombay Buenos Aires
Calcutta Cape Town Dar es Salaam Delhi Florence Hong Kong
Istanbul Karachi Kuala Lumpur Madras Madrid Melbourne
Mexico City Nairobi Paris Singapore Taipei Tokyo Toronto Warsaw

and associated companies in
Berlin Ibadan

Oxford is a trade mark of Oxford University Press

Published in the United States by
Oxford University Press Inc., New York

A catalogue record for this book is available from the British Library

Library of Congress Cataloging-in-Publication Data
Talmon, Stefan.
Recognition of governments in international law : with particular reference to governments in exile / Stefan Talmon.
p. cm.—(Oxford monographs in international law)
Includes bibliographical references (p.).
1. Governments in exile. 2. Recognition (International law)
I. Title. II. Series.
KZ4041.T35 1997
341.26–dc21 97-24351
ISBN 0-19-826573-5

Typeset by Best-set Typesetter Ltd., Hong Kong
Printed in Great Britain
on acid-free paper by
Bookcraft Ltd., Midsomer Norton, Somerset

General Editor's Preface

The recognition of governments remains one of the most important and also most difficult topics within public international law. Dr. Talmon's work is a masterpiece of exposition both of the general issues of recognition and of the special department of governments in exile, the problems of which illuminate the subject in general.

The particular strengths of the study are the independence of mind of the writer, and his ability to analyse the conduct of States and tribunals in respect of recognition. In addition, in contrast to the existing monographs, the work is based upon a most impressive assemblage of the practice of States. The outcome will be of great value both to academic experts and to practitioners.

The monograph derives from Dr. Talmon's doctoral thesis prepared in Oxford under my supervision. Consequently, this preface might seem to be self-serving, were it not for the fact that the work is very much the product of the writer's own scholarly persistence and toughness of mind. His Supervisor, the pilot, so to speak, of the vessel, left the bridge at an early stage of the voyage.

Oxford.
10th April 1997. IAN BROWNLIE.

Preface

This work does not purport to be a comprehensive study of all the questions connected with the recognition of governments in international law, save that it refers to aspects of them where appropriate, nor does it intend to be yet another contribution to the eternal debate on the theories of recognition and their related questions: is recognition a legal or a (purely) political act? Is recognition declaratory in character or rather constitutive? Is there a right to recognition (and a correlative duty to recognize) once certain (minimum) criteria are fulfilled or is recognition purely discretionary? Does recognition produce retroactive effects? etc. The short answer to all these questions is: that depends!—on the factual and legal circumstances of each individual case. As Professor Brownlie has rightly pointed out:

> in the case of 'recognition', theory has not only failed to enhance the subject but has created a *tertium quid* which stands, like a bank of fog on a still day, between the observer and the contours of the ground which call for investigation. With rare exceptions the theories on recognition have not only failed to improve the quality of thought but have deflected lawyers from the application of ordinary methods of legal analysis.[1]

Rather than attempting to confront (and refute) the various theories of recognition on their own terms this study more modestly attempts to apply what Professor Brownlie called 'ordinary methods of legal analysis' to two questions of the recognition of governments in international law: what are the meanings of recognition of governments and its variants such as *de facto*, *de jure*, and diplomatic recognition, and, closely connected herewith, what is the effect of such recognition on the legal status of governments and, here in particular, of governments in exile. The answers to these questions may also shed some light on the above-mentioned theoretical questions. Along the lines of these questions the study is organized in a general introduction and two main parts which are followed by three appendices: (i) replies received from various States in response to a questionnaire on the recognition of governments, (ii) short profiles of authorities in exile claiming to be 'governments', and (iii) a list of treaties concluded by authorities in exile recognized as governments.

The treatment of the recognition of governments is complicated by the fact that the term 'government' is not a 'registered trademark' and that any individual or body of individuals may call itself a 'government'. The use of the term 'government' by an individual or a body of individuals thus

[1] 'Recognition in Theory and Practice' (1982) 53 *BYBIL* 197–211 at 197.

indicates only its claim to governmental status and need not necessarily denote a government in the sense of international law. Equally, the use of the term 'government' in formal recognition statements need not necessarily express that, in the view of the recognizing State, the individual or body of individuals in question qualifies as a government in international law, but may just refer to its self-given name. Generally, for the purpose of this study, a recognized government, either in exile or *in situ*, means an authority in exile or *in situ* expressly recognized 'as' a government by the recognizing State and, conversely, an unrecognized government means an authority not recognized 'as' a government (but perhaps in some other lesser capacity).

Governments in exile, or better authorities in exile claiming to be governments, have been chosen as an example to show the effect of recognition on legal status for two reasons. First, there are numerous studies of the legal status of unrecognized governments *in situ*, i.e. of authorities exercising effective control over the people and territory of a State but not being recognized as its government,[2] but only few studies, mainly undertaken during and after the Second World War, have explored the legal status of their counterpart: authorities in exile not exercising effective control over the State's people and territory but nevertheless recognized as its government.[3] Secondly, the effect of recognition on legal status is especially obvious in the case of authorities in exile which, unlike authorities *in situ*, lack effective control over people and territory and thus are wholly dependent on their host State and other States in order to function as a government. As governments in exile are not a special category but, like their counterparts *in situ*, are the representative organs of States, the findings reached with respect to governments in exile will also shed some light on the effect of recognition on the legal status of governments *in situ*, at least with respect to governmental functions to be exercised outside their States' own territory. Governments in exile are usually associated with the First and Second

[2] See, e.g., Nedjati, 'Acts of Unrecognized Governments' (1981) 30 *ICLQ* 388–415; Balekjian, *Die Effektivität und die Stellung nichtanerkannter Staaten im Völkerrecht* (1970); Frowein, *Das de facto-Regime im Völkerrecht* (1968); Rösch, *Die Rechtsstellung der nichtanerkannten Regierung vor Gericht* (1968); Erdmann, *Nichtanerkannte Staaten und Regierungen: Formen und Grenzen internationaler Beziehungen* (1966); Viret, *La portée extraterritoriale des actes de souveraineté interne d'un gouvernement non-reconnu* (1951); Stierlin, *Die Rechtsstellung der nichtanerkannten Regierung im Völkerrecht* (1940); Stoupnitzky, *Statut International de l'URRS. Etat Commerçant* (1936), 170–232, 300–31; Dickinson, 'The Unrecognized Government or State in English and American Law' (1923) 22 *Mich. LR* 29–45, 118–34.

[3] See Janke, 'Rechtsnatur und Rechtsstellung der Regierung im Exil', doctoral thesis (University of Hamburg, 1954); Mattern, *Die Exilregierung. Eine historische Betrachtung der internationalen Praxis seit dem Beginne des Ersten Weltkrieges und deren völkerrechtliche Wertung* (1953); Flory, *Le statut international des Gouvernements réfugiés et le cas de la France Libre 1939–1945* (1952); Oppenheimer, 'Governments and Authorities in Exile' (1942) 36 *AJIL* 568–95; Jumeau, *Le Refuge du Gouvernement National à l'Etranger* (1941). For a more recent study in Hebrew, see Shraga, 'Recognition of Governments-in-Exile' (1980) 7 *Iyune Mishpat* 681–702.

World Wars. Since 1914 some seventy authorities in exile have called themselves or claimed to be the 'governments' of certain States, but only nineteen were established during the World Wars. These figures do not include the numerous liberation organizations, national councils or committees, free movements, and other opposition groups in exile which have neither claimed or purported to be governments nor have been recognized as such. Of these seventy 'governments' in exile thirty-nine have received either *de facto* or *de jure* recognition by one or more States.[4] By examining the treatment which recognized governments in exile have received by recognizing States and comparing it with the treatment of authorities in exile claiming to be governments but not being recognized as such, both the status of government (in exile) under international law and the effect of recognition on the legal status of authorities in exile claiming to be governments may be established.

This work also does not purport to be a comprehesive study of all the legal questions connected with the exile of a government and, in particular, does not attempt to establish in each individual case whether or not a recognized government in exile, in fact, qualified as a government under international law, and whether the recognizing State thus acted lawfully when recognizing it. This question, which largely depends on an evaluation of the factual circumstances, must be reserved for individual case studies. For this study on the *recognition* of governments the only question that is relevant is whether an authority in exile has, in fact, been recognized as a government and whether and, if so, to what extent the dealings of States with such recognized governments differ from their dealings with unrecognized authorities in exile.

After having thus both limited and outlined the subject matter of the work, it may be said that it was my principal aim to base my findings, as far as possible, on State practice and the decisions of national and international courts whereby, in Professor Spiropoulos' words, 'I hoped to escape the dangers of subjective-speculative findings and their so questionable results'.[5]

This work is a revised and extended version of a thesis submitted in the Trinity Term 1995 for the degree of Doctor of Philosophy in the University of Oxford. The research on which this book is based was mainly carried out during the tenure of a Rhodes Scholarship from 1991 to 1994 and I wish to express my gratitude to the Trustees of the Rhodes Trust and its Secretary, Sir Anthony Kenny. While at Oxford I was fortunate in having as supervisor Professor Ian Brownlie, QC. My intellectual debt to Professor Brownlie cannot be repaid. All I can do is to put on record my lasting gratitude to him

[4] See the profiles in App. II.
[5] Spiropoulos, *Die de facto-Regierung im Völkerrecht* (1926), p. xvi (translation supplied).

for his guidance and support. The shortcomings of this book I claim as my own; but whatever merits it may possess are due to my having been Professor Brownlie's pupil. I wish to thank my examiners, Professor James Crawford of Jesus College, Cambridge, and Dr Mark Janis, of Exeter College, Oxford, for their valuable comments. I also wish to thank Dr Steffi Arzt, Dr Christine Gray, Dr Phoebe Okowa, Dr Mike Bools, Dr Bing Bing Jia, Professor Benedict Kingsbury, and Dr William (now Lord) Wallace for their friendly interest in my work and their assistance. A special word of thanks must go to Dr Anke Frankenberger for her encouragement and invaluable support. For their assistance in providing materials and translations I wish to thank Professor Mariko Kawano, Dr Manuela Ungureanu, Ms Barbara Hinterwirth, Mr Arno Blehr, Mr Alois Ebner, Dr Rainer Liedtke, and Dr Werner Walk. I must also thank the librarians and staff of the Bodleian, Codrington, and St Antony's College Libraries, Oxford, who have been extremely helpful in meeting a variety of requests. I should further acknowledge the benefit of the use of the libraries of McGill University, Montreal; Eberhard-Karls-University, Tübingen; and Max Planck Institute for Comparative Public Law and International Law, Heidelberg. Finally, my deepest thanks are owed to my parents, to whom this work is also dedicated, for their unfailing encouragement, patience, and love.

Stefan Talmon
Bad Wildbad
January 1997

Contents

Abbreviations

AC	Appeal Cases, Law Reports, United Kingdom, 1891– (House of Lords)
ACR	Africa Contemporary Record
AD	Annual Digest and Reports of Public International Law Cases, 1 (1919–22) – 16 (1949); continued as ILR
AdG	*Keesing's Archiv der Gegenwart*
A&E	Admiralty and Ecclesiastical Division, Law Reports, England
AFDI	*Annuaire français de droit international*
AFPCD	American Foreign Policy. Current Documents
Africa Diary	*Africa Diary*
AHG	Assembly of African Heads of State and Government
AILC	American International Law Cases
AJIL	*American Journal of International Law*
AJHQ	*American Jewish Historical Quarterly*
AJPH	*Australian Journal of Politics and History*
ALI	American Law Institute
ALJ	*Australian Law Journal*
All ER	All England Law Reports
ALR	Australian Law Reports
AMC	American Maritime Cases
Annuaire	*Annuaire de l'Institut de droit international*
Ann. Reg.	*Annual Register*
AöR	*Archiv des öffentlichen Rechts*
APAI	*Annuaire Polonais des Affaires Internationales*
APZ	*Aus Politik und Zeitgeschichte* (Supplement to *Das Parlament*)
ARA	Les archives de la révolution algérienne
ARB	Africa Research Bulletin
ASEAN	Association of South-East Asian Nations
ASIL Proc.	*Proceedings of the American Society of International Law*
Aust. Outlook	*Australian Outlook*
Aust. Quart.	*Australian Quarterly*
AVNOJ	Antifašističko veće narodnog oslobodenja Jugoslavije (Antifascist Council of the National Liberation of Yugoslavia)

AVR	*Archiv des Völkerrechts*
AYBIL	*Australian Year Book of International Law*
Baltic Rev.	*Baltic Review*
BayVGH	Bayerischer Verwaltungsgerichtshof (Bavarian Supreme Administrative Court)
BBC	British Broadcasting Corporation
BDIL	British Digest of International Law
BFSP	British and Foreign State Papers
BGBl.	Bundesgesetzblatt (Germany, Federal Law Gazette)
BGE	Entscheidungen des Schweizerischen Bundesgerichts (Decisions of the Swiss Federal Tribunal)
BGH	Bundesgerichtshof (Federal Court of Justice, Germany)
BGHSt.	Decisions of the BGH in Criminal Matters, Official Reports
BGHZ	Decisions of the BGH in Civil Matters, Official Reports
BILC	British International Law Cases
Bi-Monthly LR	*Bi-Monthly Law Review*
Bohemia	*Bohemia. A Journal of History and Civilization in East Central Europe*
Boston ULR	*Boston University Law Review*
BT-Drs.	Verhandlungen des Deutschen Bundestages. Anlagen zu den Stenographischen Berichten. Drucksachen (Proceedings of the German Federal Parliament. Supplement to the verbatim protocols. Papers)
BT Sten. Ber.	Stenographische Berichte des Deutschen Bundestages (Verbatim protocols of the German Federal Parliament)
Bulletin	*Bulletin*, ed. by the Press and Informationservice of the German Federal Government
Bull. égypt.	Bulletin de législation et de jurisprudence égyptiennes
BVerfGE	Entscheidungen des Bundesverfassungsgerichts (Decisions of the German Federal Constitutional Court, Official Reports)
BVerwGE	Entscheidungen des Bundesverwaltungsgerichts (Decisions of the German Federal Administrative Court, Official Reports)
BYBIL	*British Year Book of International Law*
C.	Command Paper [Paper laid by command of the Crown before Parliament] (2nd ser., 1870–99)

CA	Court of Appeal
Cah. fr.	*Les Cahiers français*
Can. BR	*Canadian Bar Review*
CAR	Central African Republic
Cd.	Command Paper (3rd ser., 1900–18)
CEAFDW	Convention on the Elimination of All Forms of Discrimination against Women 1979
Cent. Europ. Observer	*Central European Observer*
CFLN	Comité Français de la Libération Nationale
CGDK	Coalition Government of Democratic Kampuchea
Ch.	Chancery Division of the High Court of Justice, Reports, Law Reports, England, 1891
CILC	Commonwealth International Law Cases
CLJ	*Cambridge Law Journal*
CLR	Commonwealth Law Reports
CM	(OAU) Council of Ministers
Cm.	Command Paper (6th ser., 1986–)
Cmd.	Command Paper (4th ser., 1918–56)
Cmnd.	Command Paper (5th ser., 1956–86)
CNF	Comité National Français
Col. LR	*Columbia Law Review*
Com. Int.	*Comunità internazionale*
Comm. LR	Commercial Law Reports
Cong. Rec.	United States, Congress, Congressional Record
CPD	South African Law Reports. Cape Provincial Division.
Cranch	Reports of Cases Argued and Adjudged in the Supreme Court of The United States by William Cranch, 1801–15
CSM	Convention on Special Missions 1969
CST	A Calendar of Soviet Treaties, I: 1917–57: II: 1958–73
CWRJIL	*Case Western Reserve Journal of International Law*
CYBIL	*Czechoslovak Year Book of International Law*
CYIL	*Canadian Yearbook of International Law*
DAFP	Documents on Australian Foreign Policy 1937–49
DAFR	Documents on American Foreign Relations
DBFP	Documents on British Foreign Policy 1919–39
DBPO	Documents on British Policy Overseas
DCER	Documents on Canadian External Relations
DCW	*Destiny Can Wait. The Polish Air Force in the Second World War*
DDS	Documents Diplomatiques Suisses 1848–1945
DGFP	Documents on German Foreign Policy 1919–45

DIA	Documents on International Affairs
Dict. Dipl.	*Dictionnaire Diplomatique*
DJZ	*Deutsche Juristen-Zeitung*
DLR	Dominion Law Reports
DPIC	Documents on Pakistan and International Conflicts
DPSR	Documents on Polish–Soviet Relations 1939–45
DR	Decisions and Reports (of the European Commission of Human Rights)
DRVN	Democratic Republic of Viet Nam
DSB	US, Department of State, *Bulletin*
DSD	US, Department of State, *Dispatch*
DUNCIO	Documents of the United Nations Conference on International Organization
DUSPIL	Digest of United States Practice in International Law, 1973–80
EA	*Europa Archiv*
EC Bull.	*Bulletin of the European Communities*
ECJ	Court of Justice of the European Communities
ECHR	European Court of Human Rights
E.Comm. HR	European Commission of Human Rights
ECM/RES.	Resolutions adopted at the Extraordinary Sessions of the Council of Ministers of the OAU
ECR I	European Court Reports. Part I, Court of Justice
Edw.	Edwards, Reports of Cases Argued and Determined in the High Court of Admiralty (England)
EU Bull.	*Bulletin of the European Union*
FAZ	*Frankfurter Allgemeine Zeitung für Deutschland*
Fed.	Federal Reporter, 1st ser.
F.2d	Federal Reporter, 2nd ser.
FEER	*Far Eastern Economic Review*
FLN	Front de Libération Nationale (Algerian National Liberation Front)
FMLN	Farabundo Martí National Liberation Front (El Salvador)
FO	Foreign Office Papers
Fontes	Fontes Juris Gentium (referred to in the order: series, *sectio*, *tomus*, *pars*)
For. Affairs	*Foreign Affairs*
FR	Federal Register (USA)
Free Europe	*Free Europe*
Freies Alg.	*Freies Algerien*
FRG	Federal Republic of Germany (West Germany)

FRUS	Foreign Relations of the United States. Diplomatic Papers and Papers Relating to the Foreign Relations of the United States
FSIA	Foreign Sovereign Immunities Act 1976 (USA)
FUNCINPEC	National United Front for an Independent, Neutral, Peaceful, and Co-operative Cambodia
GA	General Assembly
GAOR	Official Records of the General Assembly
GDK	Government of Democratic Kampuchea
GDR	German Democratic Republic (East Germany)
GMCC	*Guerres Mondiales et Conflits Contemporains*
GP	Gazette du palais
GPRA	Gouvernement Provisoire de la République Algérienne (Provisional Government of the Algerian Republic)
GRAE	Govêrno Revolucionário de Angola no Exílio (Revolutionary Government of Angola in Exile)
GRCC	Geneva Red Cross Convention 1949
Grot. Soc.	*Transactions of the Grotius Society*
GVG	Gerichtsverfassungsgesetz (Judicature Act, Germany)
Harv. ILJ	*Harvard International Law Journal*
HC Debs.	Parliamentary Debates, House of Commons
HKLR	Hong Kong Law Reports
HL	House of Lords
HL Debs.	Parliamentary Debates, House of Lords
HR	Regulations Respecting the Laws and Customs of War on Land. Annex to the Fourth Hague Convention of 18 October 1907
HRuGZ	*Hanseatische Rechts- und Gerichtszeitschrift*
HSC	Geneva Convention on the High Seas, 1958
Hudson	International Legislation, ed. by M. O. Hudson
ICAO	International Civil Aviation Organization
ICCPR	International Covenant on Civil and Political Rights 1966
ICJ	International Court of Justice
ICLQ	*International and Comparative Law Quarterly*
ICO	Islamic Conference Organization
ICESCR	International Covenant on Economic, Social and Cultural Rights 1966
IHT	*International Herald Tribune*
ILC	International Law Commission
ILC Yb.	*Yearbook of the International Law Commission*

ILM	International Legal Materials
ILO	International Labour Organization
ILR	International Law Reports (succeeded AD) (1950–date)
ILTR	Irish Law Times Reports
Indian JPS	*Indian Journal of Political Science*
Ind. Chron.	*Indochina Chronology*
Int. Bus. Lawyer	*International Business Lawyer*
Int. Conc.	*International Conciliation*
Int. Org.	*International Organization*
Int. Stud.	*International Studies*
IR	Irish Reports
IRD	*Internationales Recht und Diplomatie*
Ital. YIL	*Italian Yearbook of International Law*
JAL	*Journal of African Law*
JAIL	*Japanese Annual of International Law*
J. Cent. Europ. Aff.	*Journal of Central European Affairs*
JCL	*Journal of Comparative Legislation and International Law*, 3rd Series, 1 (1919) – 33 (1951)
J. Crim. Law	*The Journal of Criminal Law*
JDI	*Journal du droit international privé et de la jurisprudence comparée*, 1 (1874) – 41 (1914); *Journal du droit international (Clunet)*, 42 (1915)–
JIR	*Jahrbuch für internationales Recht*
JO	Journal Officiel des Communautés Européennes (1958–72)
JORF	Journal Officiel de la République française
JöR	*Jahrbuch des öffentlichen Rechts der Gegenwart*
JR	*Juristische Rundschau*
JRMP	*Jugoslovenska revija za medunarodno pravo*
JW	*Juristische Wochenschrift*
JZ	*Juristen-Zeitung*
KB	King's Bench Reports (England), 1901–51
Keesing's	*Keesing's Contemporary Archives. Record of World Events*, 1 (1931) – 32 (1986) and *Keesing's Record of World Events*, 33 (1987)–
KG	Kammergericht (Berlin Court of Appeal)
Législation en exil	*Législation promulgée par le Gouvernement belge en exil*
LG Rev.	*Lawyers Guild Review*
LG	Landgericht (Regional Court), also sometimes translated as Provincial Court
Lond. Gaz.	London Gazette

Ll.LR	Lloyd's List Law Reports, 1919–50
Lloyd's Rep.	Lloyd's Reports, 1951–
LM	Lindenmaier-Möhrig. Nachschlagewerk des Bundesgerichtshofes
LNOJ	League of Nations Official Journal
LNTS	League of Nations Treaty Series
LQR	*Law Quarterly Review*
LT	*Law Times*
Maghreb Machrek	*Monde arabe. Maghreb Machrek*
MECS	*Middle East Contemporary Survey*
MEED	*Middle East Economic Digest*
MEJ	*Middle East Journal*
Melbourne ULR	*Melbourne University Law Review*
Mich. LR	*Michigan Law Review*
MLR	*Modern Law Review*
MPLA	Movimento Popular de Libertação de Angola (Popular Angolan Liberation Movement)
NATO	North Atlantic Treaty Organization
NCGUB	National Coalition Government of the Union of Burma
NED	Documentation française, Notes et études documentaires
Ned. TIR	*Nederlands Tijdschrift voor International Recht*
NEI	Netherlands East Indies
NGC	National Government of Cambodia
N.Ir.LQ	*Northern Ireland Law Quarterly*
NJ	Nederlandse Jurisprudentie
NJW	Neue Juristische Wochenschrift
Nord. TIR	*Nordisk Tidsskrift for International Ret*
Norsk Ret.	Norsk Retstidende (Norwegian Supreme Court Law Reports)
NRG	Nouveau recueil général de traités et autres actes relatifs aux rapports de droit international
NUFK	National United Front of Kampuchea
NY	New York Reports, 1st ser.
NY2d	New York Reports, 2nd ser.
NYIL	*Netherlands Yearbook of International Law*
NYLJ	*New York Law Journal*
NYLSJICL	*New York Law School Journal of International and Comparative Law*
NYS	New York Supplement
NYS2d	New York Supplement, 2nd ser.
NY Times	*New York Times*

NZZ	*Neue Zürcher Zeitung und schweizerisches Handelsblatt*
OAS	Organization of American States
OAU	Organization of African Unity
OJ	Official Journal of the European Communities (1973–)
OJLS	*Oxford Journal of Legal Studies*
ÖBGBl.	Bundesgesetzblatt der Republik Österreich (Austria, Federal Law Gazette)
ÖZöR	*Österreichische Zeitschrift für öffentliches Recht*
ÖZöRV	*Österreichische Zeitschrift für öffentliches Recht und Völkerrecht*
OGLTR	*Oil and Gas: Law and Taxation Review*
OLG	Oberlandesgericht (Regional Court of Appeal)
P.	Probate Reports (England), 1891–1971
P.2d	Pacific Reporter, 2nd ser.
PAIGC	Partido Africano de Independência da Guiné e do Cabo Verde (African Independence Party of Guinea and Cape Verde)
Parl. Pap.	Parliamentary Papers, United Kingdom
Pas.belge	Pasicrisie belge. Recueil général de la jurisprudence des cours et tribunaux de Belgique en matière civile, commerciale, criminelle et administrative (Brussels, 1841–)
PCIJ	Permanent Court of International Justice Reports, 1923–40
PH	Prentice Hall Weekly Legal Service, South Africa, 1 (1923)–
PLO	Palestine Liberation Organization
PLR	Law Reports of Palestine
Pol. Stud.	*Political Studies*
PR	People's Republic
PRC	People's Republic of China
Pub. L	*Public Law*
QB	Queen's Bench Reports (England), 1891–1900, 1952–date
Qu. BR	Quebec Cour du Banc du Roi
RADIC	*Revue Africaine de Droit International et Comparé*
RBDI	*Revue belge de droit international*
RCDI	*Revue critique de droit international*, 29 (1933) – (succeeded *RDIP*)
RdC	Academie de Droit International, *Recueil des Cours*

RDI	*Revue de Droit International*
RDIP	*Revue de droit international privé*, 1 (1905) – 28 (1933) (continued as *RCDI*)
RDISDPS	*Revue de Droit International, de Sciences Diplomatiques, Politiques et Sociales*
RDILC	*Revue de droit international et de la législation comparé*
Recueil TAM	Recueil des décisions des tribunaux arbitraux mixtes
Res Publica	*Res Publica*
Rev. égypt.	*Revue égyptienne de droit international*
Rev. Roum. Et. Int.	*Revue Roumanie d'Etudes Internationales*
RFH	Reichsfinanzhof (German Supreme Tax Court 1918–45)
RFSP	*Revue Française de Science Politique*
RG	Reichsgericht (German Supreme Court, 1879–1945)
RGBl.	Reichsgesetzblatt (German Law Gazette, 1871–1945)
RGSt	Entscheidungen des Reichsgerichts in Strafsachen (Decision of the RG in Criminal Matters, Official Reports)
RGDIP	*Revue générale de droit international public*
RGNUC	Royal Government of National Union of Cambodia
RHDGM	*Revue d'Histoire de la Deuxième Guerre Mondiale*
RHDI	*Revue Hellénique de Droit International*
RIAA	United Nations Reports of International Arbitral Awards
RIIA	Royal Institute of International Affairs, London
RIW	Recht der internationalen Wirtschaft
Riv. DI	*Rivista di Diritto Internazionale*
RJPUF	*Revue juridique et politique de l'Union Française*
ROC	Republic of China
ROW	*Recht in Ost und West*
RSFSR	Russian Socialist Federal Soviet Republics
RSPI	*Rivista di Studi Politici Internazionali*
RVN	Republic of Viet Nam (South Vietnam)
RZfZuP	*Rheinische Zeitschrift für Zivil- und Prozeßrecht*
RzW	Rechtsprechung zum Wiedergutmachungsrecht. Supplement to NJW, 1 (1949–50) – 32 (1981)
SADR	Saharan Arab Democratic Republic
SALJ	*South African Law Journal*

SALR	South African Law Reports
SC	Session Cases (Scotland)
Sch. JIR	*Schweizerisches Jahrbuch für internationales Recht/ Annuaire suisse de droit international*
S.Ct.	Supreme Court
SCOR	Official Records of the Security Council
SCR	Canada Law Reports. The Supreme and Exchequer Courts of Canada
SLR	Colony of Singapore Law Reports
SNC	Supreme National Council of Cambodia
Sol. Jo.	*Solicitors' Journal & Weekly Reporter*
Soviet For. Pol.	Soviet Foreign Policy during the Patriotic War
S.R. & O.	Statutory Rules and Orders Other Than Those of a Local, Personal or Temporary Character for the Year . . .
SRuSZ	*Saarländische Rechts- und Steuerzeitschrift*
Stanford LR	*Stanford Law Review*
St.R.Qd.	Queensland State Reporter
Survey	*Survey of International Affairs*, RIIA
SVN	State of Viet-Nam (South Vietnam)
SWAPO	South West Africa People's Organzation
SWB	*Summary of World Broadcasts*, BBC Monitoring Service
SZ	*Süddeutsche Zeitung*
TIAS	Treaties and Other International Acts Series (US State Department)
Tibet. Bull.	*Tibetan Bulletin*
TLR	Times Law Reports
TR	*Turkish Review. Quarterly Digest*
UAE	United Arab Emirates
UAR	United Arab Republic (Union of Egypt and Syria, 22 February 1958–28 September 1961), afterwards name for Egypt
U.Chicago LR	*University of Chicago Law Review*
UKMIL	United Kingdom Materials on International Law
UKTS	United Kingdom Treaty Series
UN Doc.	United Nations Document
UNITA	União Naçional para a Independência Total de Angola
UNCLOS	United Nations Convention on the Law of the Sea 1982
UNHCR	(Office of the) United Nations High Commissioner for Refugees

UN Leg. Ser.	United Nations Legislative Series: Multilateral Treaties in Respect of which the Secretary-General Performs Depositary Functions (ST/LEG/SER.D)
UNRRA	United Nations Relief and Rehabilitation Administration
UNTAC	United Nations Transitional Authority in Cambodia
UNTS	United Nations Treaty Series
UNYB	Yearbook of the United Nations
U.Penn. LR	*University of Pennsylvania Law Review*
US	United States Reports
USC	United States Code
USI	United States of Indonesia
VCCR	Vienna Convention on Consular Relations 1963
VCDR	Vienna Convention on Diplomatic Relations 1961
VCLT	Vienna Convention on the Law of Treaties 1969
VLR	Victoria Law Reports
VZG	*Vierteljahreshefte für Zeitgeschichte*
WA	Written Answers
Wheat.	Reports of Cases Argued and Adjudged in the Supreme Court of The United States by Henry Wheaton, 1816–27
WK	Wiedergutmachungskammer der Landgerichte (Restitution Chamber of the Regional Courts)
WLR	Weekly Law Reports
WM	Wertpapier-Mitteilungen
WN	Weekly Notes Reports, New South Wales
World Pol.	*World Politics*
WP	*Washington Post*
WPA	War and Peace Aims of the United Nations, edited L. W. Holborn
WT	*Washington Times*
Yale JWPO	*Yale Journal of World Public Order*
ZaöRV	*Zeitschrift für ausländisches öffentliches Recht und Völkerrecht*
ZfVuB	*Zeitschrift für Völkerrecht und Bundesstaatsrecht*, 1 (1907) – 6 (1913) continued as part of the *ZVR*
ZLR	Zambia Law Reports
ZVR	*Zeitschrift für Völkerrecht* (succeeded the *ZfVuB*)

Table of Cases

Alphabetical Table

Classification According to Countries and Courts

A. International Courts and Tribunals

PERMANENT COURT OF INTERNATIONAL JUSTICE

INTERNATIONAL COURT OF JUSTICE

PERMANENT COURT OF ARBITRATION

ARBITRAL TRIBUNALS AND MIXED CLAIMS COMMISSIONS

Affaire de Guano, Franco-Chilean Arbitral Tribunal, Rapperschwyl, Sentence of 5 July 1901: 15 RIAA 125; (1922) 29 RGDIP 278–80 . . 134

Herwyn v. *Müller*, Tribunal arbitral mixte germano-belge, 27 July 1922: Recueil TAM, 2 (1923), 368–71; Hackworth (ed.), *Digest of International Law* (1943), vi, 398 224

Jansen v. *Mexico*, Mexican-US Claims Commission, 1868: Moore (ed.), *Arbitrations* (1898), iii, 2902 105

Tinoco Arbitration [Aguilar-Amory and Royal Bank of Canada Claims] (*Great Britain* v. *Costa Rica*), Washington, DC, 18 October 1923: 1 RIAA 368; (1924) 18 AJIL 147–74; (1925) 6 BYBIL 199–204; (1923–4) 2 AD No 15, 34–9 . . . . 34, 134, 146

EUROPEAN COURT OF JUSTICE

Judgment of 5 July 1994 - Case C–432/92 (*R.* v. *Minister of Agriculture, Fisheries and Food, ex parte S.P. Anastasiou (Pissouri) Ltd and Others*): [1994] ECR I–3087; 100 ILR 257 32

EUROPEAN COURT OF HUMAN RIGHTS

Judgment of 23 March 1995 (*Loizidou* v. *Turkey (Preliminary Objections)*): Series A no 310; (1995) 16 HRLJ 15–29 134

EUROPEAN COMMISSION OF HUMAN RIGHTS

Application No 8007/77 (*Cyprus* v. *Turkey*, Decision of 10 July 1978): 13 DR 85–156; (1978) 21 YBECHR 101–247 . . . . 32, 115

Applications Nos. 15299/89, 15300/89 and 15318/89 (*Chrysostomos, Papachrysostomou and Loizidou* v. *Turkey*, Decision of 4 March 1991): 68 DR 216–53; (1991) 34 YBECER 35–60; (1992) 51 ZaöRV 156–76; (1991) 18 EuGRZ 254–60 32

B. National Courts and Tribunals

AUSTRALIA

Anglo-Czechoslovak & Prague Credit Bank v. *Janssen*, Supreme Court of Victoria, 23 August 1943: [1943] VLR 185; [1943] ALR 427; (1943–5) 12 AD No 11, 43–7; 3 CILC 1 . . . . 106, 162, 230

Captain Ortoli, Re. Ex parte Charles Lancial, Supreme Court of New South Wales, 26 August 1942: 59 WN 146; (1919–42) 11 AD No 6, 13–6 204

BELGIUM

FRANCE

GERMANY

GREECE

HONG KONG

ITALY

JAPAN

NETHERLANDS

NEW ZEALAND

NORWAY

PALESTINE

PHILIPPINES

POLAND

SINGAPORE

SOUTH AFRICA

SWEDEN

SWITZERLAND

UNITED KINGDOM

UNITED STATES OF AMERICA

ZAMBIA

Table of Treaties

Note: All entries are listed in chronological order in the sequence: year/month/day. Unless otherwise stated, dates are those of signature or those on which an instrument was declared open for signature.

Bilateral Treaties

Multilateral Treaties

Table of National Legislation

ALGERIA

BELGIUM

BURMA

CHINA

EUROPEAN UNION

FRANCE

GERMANY

GREECE

HAITI

INDIA

IRAQ

ITALY

KUWAIT

LUXEMBOURG

NETHERLANDS

NORWAY

PANAMA

POLAND

PORTUGAL

SOUTH AFRICA

SOVIET UNION

SWITZERLAND

UNITED KINGDOM

UNITED STATES

In international law it is true that one generally recognizes the Government which exercises effective control over a territory. But this is not an absolute rule without exceptions. . . .

Credentials of the Kampuchean Delegation
to the 34th UN General Assembly 1979.
Statement of Ambassador T. T. B. Koh
(Singapore), 21 Scptember 1979.
(UN Doc.A/34/PV.3, para. 51)

Introduction

ABOLITION OF RECOGNITION OF GOVERNMENTS?

A study on the recognition of governments in international law may, at first sight, seem rather outdated at a time when more and more States declare that their policy is to recognize States, not governments.[1] However, while the change in recognition policy by the United Kingdom and other Commonwealth countries in the 1980s has received wide coverage[2] and has led some writers to conclude that the recognition of governments has been abolished,[3] it is informative to look at the practice of States that have adopted the policy of recognizing States, not governments, much earlier, some, such as Switzerland, as early as 1945.[4] An examination of the practice of these States and of the statements made by the British and Commonwealth Governments will show that the adoption of this policy signifies only a change in the method of according recognition, not the abolition of the recognition of governments as such.[5] This may be illustrated

[1] A memorandum on the recognition of governments, dated 21 Mar. 1988, supplied to the author by the Ministry of Foreign Affairs and Trade Relations of the Solomon Islands states: 'The practice of most states (70) to-date is to recognize States and not Governments. . . . In fact most Commonwealth countries have adopted this policy and practice.' Notable exceptions are the USA, Russia, and Japan.

[2] For the UK, see Warbrick, 'The New British Policy on Recognition of Governments' (1981) 30 *ICLQ* 568–92; Davidson, 'Beyond Recognition' (1981) 32 *N.Ir.LQ* 22–30; Symmons, 'United Kingdom Abolition of the Doctrine of Recognition of Governments: A Rose by Another Name?' [1982] *Pub.L* 249–62; and Talmon, 'Recognition of Governments: An Analysis of the New British Policy and Practice' (1992) 63 *BYBIL* 231–97. For Australia, see Starke, 'The New Australian Policy of Recognition of Foreign Governments' (1988) 62 *ALJ* 390–1; Bergin, 'The New Australian Policy on Recognition of States Only' (1988) 42 *Aust. Outlook* 150–4; Charlesworth, 'The New Australian Recognition Policy in Comparative Perspective' (1991) 18 *Melbourne ULR* 1–25; and Greig, 'The Effects in Municipal Law of Australia's New Recognition Policy' (1991) 11 *AYBIL* 33–65. For New Zealand, see Davidson, 'Recognition of Foreign Governments in New Zealand' (1991) 40 *ICLQ* 162–70. For general studies of the policy of recognizing States, not governments, see Nomura, 'Recognition of Foreign Governments' (1982) 25 *JAIL* 67–72; Ando, 'The Recognition of Governments Reconsidered' (1985) 28 *JAIL* 29–46; Peterson, 'Political Use of Recognition: The Influence of the International System' (1982) 34 *World Pol.* 324–52 and 'Recognition of Governments Should not be Abolished' (1983) 77 *AJIL* 31–50.

[3] Shaw, *International Law* (3rd edn., 1991), 253; Starke, *Introduction to International Law* (10th edn., 1989), 138–9. See also Ando, 'Recognition', n. 2 above, 29–46, arguing for the abolition of recognition of governments; and Peterson, n. 2 above, 31–50, arguing that recognition of governments should not be abolished.

[4] See App. I, No II.13. On Swiss recognition practice with regard to governments since 1945 in general, see Klarer, *Schweizerische Praxis der völkerrechtlichen Anerkennung* (1981), 278–96.

[5] See Charlesworth, n. 2 above, 1–25: Greig, n. 2 above, 33–65; Talmon, n. 2 above, 231–97.

by an interesting exchange between M. Henri Rolin and the Belgian Minister of Foreign Affairs in the Belgian Parliament on 30 November 1965. In that year the Belgian Government had affirmed that the policy of recognizing States, not governments, was the 'traditional policy of Belgium'.[6] M. Rolin asked:

> Could the Minister distance himself from the well-informed source, who on the occasion of the recent *coup d'état* in the Congo Republic has declared, that Belgium recognizes States and not governments?
>
> It is indeed indispensable when an unconstitutional change of government occurs in a foreign State that the governments of third States have to decide whether or not or when to consider the leaders of the revolution as effectively representing the State, which they purport to control. There was belated recognition on the occasion of the Soviet revolution as well as during Franco's *coup d'état* and only some days ago the Belgian Government refused to recognize Mao Tse-tung instead of Tshiang Kai-shek as the Government of the Chinese State. What is true is that recognition may be implicit and may result from the simple continuation of diplomatic relations.
>
> This is the Belgian practice, according to which no express recognition is accorded when a new government succeeds in effectively seizing power without the deposed government being able to challenge that power. Does one not have to understand the above given information in this way? [Author's translation].

To this the Foreign Minister replied:

> The interpretation given by the Honourable Member of the information which forms the object of his question is correct.
>
> Recognition of a government must not necessarily be the object of an express declaration; it may result from dealings which clearly indicate the intention of considering that government as effectively representing the state which it controls and, in particular, it may result from the simple continuation of diplomatic relations [Author's translation.][7]

Thus, rather than formally announcing their recognition of a new government, States following this policy, as a rule, implicitly recognize a new authority in power as the government of a foreign State by dealing with it *as such*.[8] As some writers have rightly pointed out under the policy of recognizing States, not governments, 'recognition will be more a matter of implication than of express declaration'.[9] Indeed, it has long been established

[6] See App. I, No II.2. [7] (1968) 4 RBDI 541–2.

[8] Cf. App. I, Nos II.2, II.5, II.10. With respect to Swiss practice, see Klarer, n. 4 above, 280. See also the Memorandum on US recognition policy and practice, dated 25 September 1981: 'recognition will . . . be implied by USG [US Government] continuing to deal with the new government' (Nash (ed.), *Cumulative Digest of United States Practice in Internatinoal Law 1981–8* (1994), i, 295–8 at 296).

[9] Jennings and Watts (eds.), *Oppenheim's International Law* (9th edn., 1991), i, 148. See also Harris, *Cases and Materials on International Law* (4th edn., 1991), 144, n. 78; Akehurst, *A Modern Introduction to International Law* (6th edn., 1987), 59.

that a State may recognize a new government without employing the word 'recognition'.[10]

If recognition could really be abolished simply by announcing that from now on a State recognizes only States, not governments, this would raise the question whether for the last 150 years or so States have indulged in a political game without any legal purpose and significance when announcing their recognition or non-recognition of a certain authority *in situ* or in exile. Resolutions of the UN Security Council which called upon States not to recognize a certain authority[11] or even decided that Member States should refrain from recognizing a certain authority[12] would hardly have been necessary if recognition had had no legal meaning. The fundamental question of the recognition of governments and its abolition is thus what States actually meant (and mean) when they formally announced or still announce their 'recognition' or 'non-recognition' of a certain government. Although central to all problems of recognition of governments the question of the meanings of the term 'recognition', used in formal announcements on the recognition of governments, is dealt with by most writers in a single sentence, if at all—a fact which has led to much confusion and is reflected in the view that recognition of governments has been 'abolished'. Part I of the study therefore undertakes, in the words of the British Foreign Secretary, Mr Canning, 'to put on its true ground, and in its just light, the expression of "recognition" which has been so much mistaken'.[13] In doing so, the question of the (continued) recognition of a government cannot always be separated from the related question of the recognition of the sovereignty and independence of a new State or the recognition of the annexation of an existing State, as in both cases the question which regularly arises is: who is to be recognized as the sovereign authority, i.e. the *de jure* government of the territory in question? It will be shown in Part II of the study with respect to governments in exile that, by making a formal announcement of 'recognition', States made (and may still make) public a certain decision from which definite legal consequences follow. The issues which have initially led to the introduction of the concept of recognition do not go away simply by States no longer using the term. States still have to decide whether and from which date they regard a certain authority (in exile or *in situ*) as the government of another State, i.e. as its representative organ

[10] On acts implying recognition in general, see Loudwin, *Die konkludente Anerkennung im Völkerrecht* (1983); Meissner, *Formen stillschweigender Anerkennung im Völkerrecht* (1966); Sir Hersch Lauterpacht, 'Implied Recognition' (1944) 21 *BYBIL* 123–50.

[11] See S/RES/661 of 6 Aug. 1990: 'The Security Council . . . calls upon all States . . . not to recognize any régime [in Kuwait] set up by the [Iraqi] occupying Power.' See also A/RES/3411 (XXX).

[12] See S/RES/277 of 18 Mar. 1970: 'The Security Council . . . decides that Member States shall refrain from recognizing this illegal régime in Southern Rhodesia.'

[13] HC Debs., vol. 11, col. 1398, 15 June 1824.

in international affairs, and whether and, if so, to what extent they want to have dealings with it as such. States making these decisions still 'recognize' or 'do not recognize' an authority in question as a government. It will be shown that the policy of recognizing States, not governments, is only abolishing (or playing down) formal public statements on the recognition of governments but not the concept of recognition of governments as such.

It has been indicated that one of the British Government's reasons for adopting in 1980 the policy of recognizing States, not governments was the criticism of its formal (continued) recognition in cases such as the genocidal Pol Pot Government of Cambodia and the Rawlings Government in Ghana by the public and the media, which considered formal recognition as tantamount to moral approval.[14] However, in such cases the British Government still has to decide, for example, whether it wants to have formal diplomatic relations with that government, whether that government is entitled to the foreign State's property or funds in the United Kingdom, whether that government enjoys jurisdictional immunity and has *locus standi* to act for the foreign State in the British courts, and whether it approves that government's credentials in international or regional organizations. If it decides these questions in the affirmative, then, it is argued, it recognizes that government as the legal government of the foreign State in question—the only thing the British Government probably no longer does is expose itself to public criticism of its recognition decision, as it is more difficult for the media and the public to infer this recognition decision from individual, often not publicized, acts than to take note of a formal announcement of a recognition decision.[15] If anything, the policy frees governments in their conduct of international relations from the constraints of public opinion. What it certainly does not do away with is the element of arbitrary discretion involved in any recognition decision.[16]

That States which have adopted the policy of recognizing States, not governments, still recognize governments also becomes clear from the fact that they have been called upon by third parties to 'recognize' a certain government.[17] These States also have stated that certain dealings with an

[14] See Talmon, n. 2 above, at 241–3.

[15] Cf. Starke, n. 2 above, at 391.

[16] For the government at the receiving end of a recognition decision it does not make any difference whether, for example, the British Government denies it access to its State's property in the UK because (for political reasons) it does not 'recognize' or, to use the new British formula, because (for political reasons) it does not have government-to-government dealings with it.

[17] On 23 Nov. 1989 the European Parliament adopted a resolution calling upon 'the EEC Member States to recognize the *de facto* government of Cambodia.' [1989] OJ No C323/101–2. For a similar resolution calling for the recognition of the new Rwandan Government, see *EU Bull.* 9–1994, 64. By 1994 all EU Member States had adopted the policy of recognizing States, not governments.

authority do not imply its 'recognition' as the government of a State.[18] Furthermore, they have refrained from certain actions, on the ground that they implied 'recognition'.[19] That the diplomatic window-dressing of recognizing only States, not governments, is sometimes difficult to sustain may be illustrated by the following statement of Mr Waldegrave, the British Minister of State for Foreign and Commonwealth Affairs:

> As *we now recognize states, not Governments*, our only judgement is whether there is a Government within a country with which we are able to deal. Obviously the extent of that Government's ability of themselves to control their territory, will be one consideration. So will be the assessment of British interests. *At present, we recognize no Government in Cambodia.*[20]

In the standard situation of recognition of governments, i.e. the replacement of one authority as the government of a State by another in a *coup d'état*, no real recognition problem in the sense of who is the State's government arises and States may simply continue formal diplomatic relations with the new government, thereby implicitly recognizing it as such.[21] There are, however, more complex situations in which even States whose policy it is to recognize only States, not governments, have found (and will find) it necessary, in order to clarify their attitude on the legal status of an authority, or expedient for political reasons to make a formal announcement of their decision to recognize or not to recognize an authority as the government of a certain State. Three different situations may be identified.

First, there is the situation of two or more local *de facto* authorities each claiming to be the only legitimate government of a (recognized) State.[22]

[18] See the joint statement of the European Community (now Union) and its Member States concerning the Iraqi invasion of Kuwait, issued in Rome on 4 Aug. 1990: 'The Community and its Member States . . . will refrain from any act which may be considered as *implicit recognition* of authorities imposed in Kuwait by the invaders' (*EC Bull.* 7/8–1990, 122 (italics supplied)). All members of the EU follow the policy of recognizing States only. After the coup in Gambia on 23 July 1994 a Foreign Office source said the meeting with the junta did not imply British recognition of the new government (*Guardian*, 26 July 1994, 11). For further examples, see also HC Debs. vol. 160, col. 46, 13 Nov. 1989; (1993) 53 *ZaöRV*, 925; *Europe*, 41st Year, No 6088 (n.s.), 18/19 Oct. 1993, 3.

[19] For example, in mid-May 1996 the German Foreign Office asked the Ministry of Economic Co-operation to withdraw a pledge of US $190,000 for a conference on Tibet in Bonn, which was organized by Tibet support groups and the 'Tibetan Government in exile', saying this would imply 'recognition' of the Tibetan Government in exile (*FAZ*, 13 June 1996, 10; *ibid.*, 17 June 1996, 4). Germany since the 1970s has adopted the policy of recognizing States, not governments.

[20] HC Debs., vol. 160, col. 46, 13 Nov. 1989.

[21] See App. I, Nos II.2, II.8.

[22] Cf. Mann, *Foreign Affairs in English Courts* (1986), 44–5, who states with regard to the recognition policy adopted by the UK in 1980 that 'it is not certain whether the Secretary of State's new policy is intended to apply to such cases [where as a result of a revolution or civil war a recognized State is split so that its territory becomes subject to two different regimes], for it seems to envisage only the case in which there is a single government in "effective control of the territory of the State concerned".'

The State of China with its two authorities, i.e. the Government of the Republic of China (on Taiwan) and the Government of the People's Republic of China (in Peking), both claiming to be the government of the whole of China, is a topical case in point.[23] France, which has followed the policy of recognizing States, not governments, since 1965, on 12 January 1994 signed in Peking a Joint Franco-Chinese communiqué on the restoration of friendly relations and traditional co-operation which reads: 'The French party has confirmed that the French Government recognizes the Government of the People's Republic of China as the sole legal government of China and Taiwan as an integral part of the Chinese territory.'[24]

Secondly, there is the situation that the government of a State claims to continue to be the government of a part of the State's territory that has *de facto* seceded. This situation may be illustrated by the case of Cyprus, where the Greek Cypriot Government in the south of the island does not accept the *de facto* secession of the Turkish north, claims to be the government of the whole island of Cyprus, and is recognized as such by the international community with the sole exception of Turkey.[25] The United Kingdom adopted the policy of recognizing States, not governments, in 1980. Nevertheless, the British Foreign Secretary, Mr Hurd, on 20 November 1991 felt compelled to state in Parliament: 'We recognize the Government of the Republic of Cyprus as the Government of the whole of Cyprus.'[26]

Thirdly, there is the situation in which an authority in exile claims to be the government of a State which is under the effective control of a colonial power, a belligerent occupant or its local puppet, or an authority which came to power by *coup d'état* or revolution. Despite its adoption of the policy of recognizing States, not governments, the French Government felt compelled expressly to state its non-recognition of either one or both authorities at times when Cambodia had both an authority in exile and an

[23] Rival or parallel governments also existed in Greece (1916–17), Spain (1936–9), Finland (1939–40), Italy (1943–5), Congo-Léopoldville (1960–3), Laos (1961–2), South Vietnam (1969–75), Lebanon (1988–90), and Afghanistan (1996).

[24] *NY Times*, 13 Jan. 1994, Sec. A, 11; *Le Monde*, 14 Jan. 1994, 3. For a similar statement by Italy which has followed the policy of recognizing States, not governments, since 1946 (see App. I, No II.9), see (1970) 13/46 *PR* 6. For a similar statement in 1990 by Australia, which has followed this policy since 1988, see BBC, *SWB*, 3rd series, FE/0921/A/3, 14 Nov. 1990. See also the statement of French President Mitterand that France 'recognized' neither of the two governments in Zaïre: *Le Monde*, 20 Oct. 1993, 6; *ibid.*, 24–25 Oct. 1993, 6.

[25] See also the cases of Biafra (30 May 1967–12 Jan. 1970) and Katanga (15 July 1960–21 Jan. 1963) which declared independence from Nigeria and Congo (Zaïre), respectively, and for some time succeeded in maintaining a certain *de facto* independence. With regard to the latter a Circular Telegram of the US State Department, dated 21 July 1960, reads: '(1) at present time we do not recognize Katanga . . . and (3) US recognizes Congo Government and hopes stable unified Congo Government can be developed once present crisis is over': [1958–60] XIV FRUS 344–5.

[26] HC Debs., vol. 199, col. 259, 20 Nov. 1991.

authority *in situ* claiming to be the country's government.[27] In the case of the Haitian and Kuwaiti Governments in exile many States which recognize only States, not governments, also announced their non-recognition of the *de facto* authorities *in situ* and their continued recognition of the exiled governments.[28] Canada, which in 1988 adopted the policy of recognizing only States, not governments,[29] is a case in point. On 3 October 1991 Mr Fortier stated in the Security Council that 'the Government of Canada fully supports and unconditionally recognizes President Aristide as the only legitimate head of the Government of Haiti'[30] and, shortly afterwards, the Canadian Prime Minister, Mr Mulroney, stated: 'Under no circumstances have we the intention of recognizing a group of rogues who have seized power in Haiti by overthrowing a democratically elected president and government' [author's translation].[31] Another case that may be added here, but which so far has only produced statements of express non-recognition, is the Tibetan Government in exile. For example, the Foreign Minister of the Federal Republic of Germany, a country which since the 1970s has recognized only States, not governments, declared on 20 June 1996 in the Federal Parliament:

> The Federal Government, as all governments in the world, regards Tibet as part of the Chinese State. From this clear statement of international law it follows that the Federal Government will not recognize a self-styled Government of Tibet in exile. This is not a formality but a question of international law.[32]

[27] On 8 May 1970 the French Foreign Minister, M. Schumann, said in an interview that 'the French Government does not intend to recognize the Government of Prince Sihanouk because it must protect its nationals, but it maintains contacts with it' [author's translation] ([1970] I *La politique étrangère de la France. Textes et documents*, 21). In an interview with *Libération* published on 22 Feb. 1984 the French Foreign Minister M. Claude Cheysson declared: 'We do not and we will not recognize the Phnom Penh Government but we have never stopped supplying aid to the regions which it controls through the EEC and the NGOs [non-governmental organizations] . . . France will never assist the Coalition Government' [author's translation] (*Le Monde*, 23 Feb. 1984, 4; [1984] *AdG* 27534).

[28] For the British statement on the continued recognition of the Government of Kuwait, see HC Debs., vol. 182, WA, *col.* 483, 13 Dec. 1990; *ibid.*, vol. 186, col. 455, 21 Feb. 1991. For the continued recognition by Greece of the Kuwaiti Government, see BBC, *SWB*, 3rd series, ME/0868/A/9–10, 13 Sept. 1990. On Greece's recognition policy, see App. I, No II.7.

[29] See (1989) 27 *CYIL* 387–8.

[30] UN Doc.S/PV.3011, 3 Oct. 1990.

[31] (1992) 30 *CYIL* 366.

[32] BT Sten. Ber., 13th Legislative Period, 113th Session, 20 June 1996, 10096–8 at 10097 (translation provided by the author). Dr Kinkel made the statement in a debate on a Resolution on Tibet adopted by the Federal Parliament. In the resolution the Federal Parliament called 'on the German Government to step up its efforts so that the Government of the PR China reacts positively to the efforts of the Dalai Lama and the Tibetan Government in exile towards a constructive dialogue and negotiates over more rights for the Tibetan people' (BT–Drs. 13/4445). For further statements that the German Government does not recognize the self-styled Tibetan Government in exile, see *Handelsblatt*, 30/31 Aug. 1996, 1 and 10; *Wirtschaftswoche*, Nr. 39/19 Sept. 1996, 20–1 at 21. For British statements of express non-recognition, see HC Debs., vol. 172, WA, *col.* 126, 9 May 1990; HL Debs., vol. 526, col. 963, 26 Feb. 1991.

The common feature of all these situations is that there are two or more rival authorities claiming to be the government of the same State.[33]

On the basis of both principle and State practice it is thus argued that recognition of governments, either as a concept of international law or indeed as a term appearing in official statements, has not been abolished. Moreover, if the recent examples of Panama and Haiti are anything to go by there may even be a tendency, at least in the western hemisphere, to revive as a means to promote and consolidate representative democracy the Tobar and Wilson[34] doctrines of formally denying recognition to governments coming to power by unconstitutional means and combining them with the element of continued recognition of the democratically elected governments forced into exile by *coup d'état* or revolution. While in the case of Panama the United States as yet stood alone in continuing to recognize the Government of ousted President Delvalle and in formally denying recognition to the Noriega-controlled government,[35] in the case of Haiti all members of the Organization of American States (OAS) continued to recognize the government of exiled President Aristide, who had been ousted by a *coup d'état*, as the legitimate Government of Haiti and formally denied recognition to the military-backed governments in Port-au-Prince.[36] Thus, the Canadian representative stated in the UN General Assembly on 11 October 1991 with respect to Haiti that 'all OAS members will refuse to recognize any government set up under these circumstances or any Government elected as a result of these illegal actions'.[37] The basis for this non-recognition coupled with the continued recognition of President Aristide's Government in exile by OAS member-States was OAS General Assembly

[33] Again the Belgian position is informative on this point. See App. I, No II.2.

[34] On the Tobar doctrine, see Heilborn, 'Tobardoktrin' in Strupp (ed.), *Wörterbuch des Völkerrechts und der Diplomatie* (1925), ii, 717–8; Garcia, 'Las Guerras Civiles de Hispano-América y la Doctrina Tobar. Trajo presentado al primer Congreso Cientifico Pan-Americano' (1915) 17 *Revista de Derecho, Historia y Letras* 526–46. On the Wilson doctrine, see also Bartlett (ed.), *The Record of American Diplomacy. Documents and Readings in the History of American Foreign Relations* (2nd edn., 1952), 549–51. On both doctrines, see Hackworth (ed.), *Digest of International Law* (1940), i, 180–6, 188, 234–6.

[35] For details, see App. II.

[36] On the OAS response to the *coup d'état* in Haiti, see Acevedo, 'The Haitian Crisis and the OAS Response: A Test of Effectiveness in Protecting Democrary' in Damrosch (ed.), *Enforcing Restraint. Collective Intervention in Internal Conflicts* (1993), 119–55.

[37] UN Doc.A/46/PV.31, 15 Oct. 1991, 24. See also the statement of Mr Flores Bermudez, Honduras: 'They [the OAS Foreign Ministers] also stated that they would not recognize any government resulting from the illegal situation' (*ibid.*, 15–16), and the statement of Mr Alleyne, Dominica, speaking on behalf of the CARICOM States and Surinam: 'President Aristide is still the legitimate President of Haiti, and we recognize him as such' (*ibid.*, 33). See also the statement of the US representative, Mr Pickering, in the UN Security Council on 3 Oct. 1991: 'The United States does not, and will not, recognize the self-appointed junta which has illegally usurped power in Haiti. . . . This junta is illegitimate. It has no standing in the international community. Until democracy is restored this junta will be treated in this hemisphere as a pariah—without assistance, without friends and without a future' (UN Doc.S/PV.3011, 3 Oct. 1990, 32–3). See further App. I, Nos II.1, II.3, II.4.

Resolution 1080, the 'Santiago Commitment to Democracy and the Renewal of the Inter-American System',[38] which established a mechanism to operate 'in the case of any event giving rise to the sudden or irregular interruption of the democratic political institutional process of the legitimate exercise of power by the democratically elected government in any of the Organization's member States'.[39] That resolution was adopted on the United States' initiative in view of the OAS' failure to restore democracy to Panama in 1988–9 and in recognition, as the December 1990 *coup d'état* in Surinam proved,[40] that violent anti-democratic forces remained a constant threat to the stability, peace, and development of the region. In the case of events constituting a sudden or irregular interruption of the legitimate exercise of power by the democratically elected government of a member State, Resolution 1080 entrusts to an *ad hoc* meeting of the Ministers of Foreign Affairs or a special session of the OAS General Assembly the adoption of 'any measure deemed appropriate, in accordance with the OAS Charter and international law'.[41] In the case of Haiti one of the measures adopted by the *ad hoc* meeting of Ministers of Foreign Affairs thus was the continued recognition of President Aristide's Government in exile and the non-recognition of the various governments installed by the military in Port-au-Prince. On 2 October 1991 the *ad hoc* meeting of Foreign Ministers, considering that events in Haiti 'have compelled President Jean-Bertrand Aristide to leave Haitian territory temporarily and against his will', demanded his 'immediate reinstatement' and recommended, 'with due respect for the policy of each member state on the recognition of states and governments, action to bring about the diplomatic isolation of those who hold power illegally in Haiti'.[42] Upon the election of Judge Joseph Nérette as 'Acting President' by the Haitian Parliament under the pressure

[38] Approved by unanimous vote of the 34 member-States at the twenty-first regular session of the OAS General Assembly, held at Santiago, Chile, on 5 June 1991: AG/RES.1080 (XXI–0/91), reproduced in (1991) 2/40 *DSD* 750. It should be noted that the OAS Charter contains several references in support of democratic institutions. Art. 2.a lists as one of the basic purposes of the Organization 'to promote and consolidate representative democracy'. Furthermore, Art. 3.d reaffirms the principle that 'the solidarity of the American States and the high aims which are sought through it, require the political organization of those States on the basis of the effective exercise of representative democracy'. See also Art. I of the third Protocol of Amendment to the OAS Charter, the Protocol of Washington ((1993) 33 ILM 1005), adopted on 14 Dec. 1992, which provides for the possibility of suspension of member-States whose democratically constituted governments have been overthrown by force. The Protocol has, however, not yet entered into force.

[39] *Ibid.*, para. 1.

[40] On 24 Dec. 1990 democratically elected President Ramsewak Shankar was deposed in a bloodless military *coup*. See [1990] *Keesing's* 37912. See also OAS Permanent Council resolution on the Present Political Situation in Surinam, adopted on 28 Dec. 1990: CP/RES.554.

[41] AG/RES.1080 (XXI–0/91), para. 2.

[42] See Res. MRE/RES.1/91: UN Doc.A/46/231, 3 Oct. 1991. See also the res. of the Permanent Council of the OAS adopted the day of the *coup* (CP/RES.567 (870/91), reproduced in (1991) 2/40 *DSD* 750).

from the military on 7 October 1991 the *ad hoc* meeting of Foreign Ministers on 8 October condemned 'strongly . . . the decision to replace illegally the constitutional President of Haiti, Jean-Bertand Aristide' and declared 'that no government that may result from this illegal situation will be accepted and, consequently, to declare that no representative of such government will be accepted'.[43] Two points should, however, be made in this connection. First, the OAS need not necessarily and will not automatically adopt this measure as the constitutional *coup d'état* of Peruvian President Alberto Fujimori on 5 April 1992 shows.[44] Resolution 1080 expressly provides that 'due respect must be observed for the policies of each member country in regard to the recognition of states and governments'.[45] (Non-)recognition thus is only one, not *the*, measure for the collective defence of democracy at the OAS' disposal and requires the consent of the member States in each individual case. Secondly, the OAS action is not necessarily a generalizable precedent, but must be seen within the special context of the OAS member States' commitment to representative democracy as the (only) form of government of the region. This is reflected in a letter, dated 10 July 1992, from the Secretary-General of the OAS, João Clemente Baena Soares, to UN Secretary General Boutros Boutros-Ghali:

> What is involved is a situation of this region's own making, which is therefore hardly applicable to other situations of regional or universal scope, the defining characteristics of which are necessarily different.
>
> The present crisis in Haiti is of an internal nature; it is a disruption of the democratic process recently initiated in that country and, accordingly, calls for joint action, in accordance with the commitments by which the American countries are bound. . . .

[43] See Res. MRE/RES.2/91: UN Doc.A/46/550–S/23127, 9 Oct. 1991. On 10 Nov. 1992 the OAS Permanent Council adopted resolution CP/RES.594 (923/92) which urged the UN members to adopt the measures specified in the previous OAS resolutions. On 24 Nov. 1992 the UN GA thereupon 'strongly condemns again the attempted illegal replacement of the constitutional President of Haiti . . . reaffirms as unacceptable any entity resulting from that illegal situation and demands the immediate restoration of the legitimate Government of President Jean-Bertrand Aristide' and 'urges the States Members of the UN to renew their support within the framework of the UN Charter and international law by adopting measures in accordance with resolutions MRE/RES.1/91, MRE/RES.2/91 . . . , adopted by the OAS, especially as they relate to the strengthening of representative democracy'. See also para. 7 of A/RES/47/20B of 20 Apr. 1993; and paras. 3, 14 of A/RES/48/27 of 6 Dec. 1993.

[44] President Alberto Fujimori seized power in an army-backed constitutional *coup* on 5 Apr. 1992. He suspended the constitution, dissolved Congress, and dismissed a number of judges. On 21 Apr. the First Vice-President Maximo San Romám Cáceres was sworn in as 'Constitutional President' in front of 200 members of the dissolved Congress ([1992] *Keesing's* 38846). *Ad hoc* meetings of OAS Foreign Ministers, held on 13 Apr. and 18 May 1992, only 'deeply deplored' Fujimori's action. The OAS or its member States, however, did not withdraw recognition of Fujimori in favour of San Román as the legitimate President of Peru. See MRE/RES.1/92, 13 Apr. 1992; MRE/RES.2/92, 18 May 1992. On the OAS' reaction to the constitutional *coup* in Guatemala on 25 May 1993, see (1993) 4/23 *DSD* 409–10.

[45] AG/RES.1080 (XXI–0/91).

> The community of American nations, organized in O.A.S., has therefore characteristics that are peculiar to it, one of the main such characteristics being that relating to the promotion and consolidation of democracy . . . no claim is being made that these distinctive features are universally applicable.[46]

Under the traditional notion of sovereignty every State has the right to choose its form of government without interference in any form by any other State.[47] As has been pointed out by Mr Soares, the governmental crisis in Haiti was 'of an internal nature'. Continued recognition of the deposed government of President Aristide in Washington and non-recognition of the government established in Port-au-Prince on the ground that the one was democratically elected while the other was not would thus have, on principle, constituted interference in the internal affairs of Haiti.[48] Haiti, however, was an exceptional case as the continued recognition of the deposed democratically elected government of President Aristide in exile was the result of a decision of a regional organization on the basis of a commitment to democratic government by the State in question.[49] A State, which is free to decide upon the form of government within its domestic order, is sovereign for the purpose of accepting a limitation of its sovereignty in this field.[50] By their action it becomes clear that OAS member States did regard General Assembly Resolution 1080 not just as a political pledge but as a commitment of a legal nature.[51] It is argued that if States are bound by similar legal commitments to a democratic form of government,[52]

[46] UN Doc.S/24340, 22 July 1992, 7–10 at 7–8.

[47] Cf. the third principle of the Declaration on the Principles of International Law Concerning Friendly Relations and Co-operation among States, which stipulates that 'every State has an inalienable right to choose its political, economic, social and cultural system, without interference in any form by another State': (A/RES/2625 (XXV), 24 Oct. 1970, annex).

[48] In 1824 Sir James Mackintosh stated with respect to the recognition, by Louis XIV, of the exiled son of James II, that 'great wrong is done to the government which exercises authority by the recognition of a pretender who is without actual power, however just his pretentions to it may be believed to be. That recognition was therefore justly resented by England as a wanton insult; as a direct interference in her internal affairs, as an assumption of authority to pronounce against the lawfulness of her government' (HC Debs., vol. 11, cols. 1354–5: 15 June 1824).

[49] For the possibility of States to enter such a commitment, see *Military and Paramilitary Activities Case*, ICJ Rep. 1986, 14 at 131.

[50] Cf. the Court's judgment: *ibid*. See also Jennings and Watts, n. 9 above, 383, n. 4, who point out that membership of an organization may also impose certain restraints upon a State's freedom to adopt whatever form of government it chooses.

[51] This becomes clear from the terminology employed by the OAS Secretary-General, Mr Soares, who speaks of 'commitments by which the American countries are bound' (UN Doc.S/24340, 22 July 1992, 7–10 at 8).

[52] Such a legal commitment may be seen in Art. F.1 of the Treaty of European Union (TEU), signed at Maastricht on 7 Feb. 1992, which provides that the systems of government of the Member States are founded on the principles of democracy. In contrast, the commitment to democratic government in such instruments as the Charter of Paris for a New Europe, adopted on 21 Nov. 1990, or the Helsinki Final Act and subsequent CSCE/OSCE declarations will probably not suffice.

the continued recognition of a deposed democratically elected government in exile coupled with the non-recognition of the government *in situ* will be lawful. As it is important for States in order to discourage *coups d'état* and revolutions to make public their decision to continue to recognize the exiled democratic government and not to recognize the undemocratic government *in situ*, formal recognition of governments may even see, within the limits indicated, a revival as a measure for the protection and consolidation of democratic government.[53]

RECOGNITION OF GOVERNMENTS IN EXILE

The recognition of governments, both in exile and *in situ*, combines a subjective and an objective concept: the subjective concept of recognition[54] and the objective concept of government. This may be illustrated by the following example. State A (and the majority of other States) recognize in September 1962 (and the following months) authority b.1 (*in situ*) as the government of State B. State C (and one other State), on the other hand, continue to recognize authority b.2 (in exile) as the government of State B. Only eight years later, in 1970, State C withdraws its recognition from authority b.2 and recognizes authority b.1 as the government of State B.[55] Relations with State B thus differ according to which authority other States recognize as the government of State B. However, irrespective of which authority, b.1 or b.2, States recognize as the government of State B and when they accord that recognition, once they have recognized an authority as the government of State B, they accord it the treatment attached to the same legal status, i.e. that of a government. Thus, the British Secretary of State for the Home Department, Mr Morrison, stated with respect to the Allied Governments in exile in London during the Second World War: 'we feel that if we recognize these Allied and associated Governments as sovereign Governments, then logically, we must give them the rights of sovereign Governments'.[56] From this statement it becomes clear that once States have

[53] It should be noted however, that in case of the legal commitment to democratic government of a State, the other States may continue to recognize only the exiled democratically elected government but may not, due to the lack of democratic legitimization, recognize a new government formed in exile.

[54] For the subjective character of recognition, see Suy, *Les actes juridiques unilatéraux en droit international public* (1962), 207; Verzijl, *International Law in Historical Perspective* (1969), ii, 581; Friedmann, 'Comment' in Moore (ed.), *Law and Civil War in the Modern World* (1974), 574–81 at 576.

[55] The example is modelled on the British recognition of the Royal and Republican Governments of Yemen from 1962 to 1970. For the facts, see App. II. Other good examples are the recognition of the Nationalist or Communist Government of China (1949 to date), and the recognition of the Republican or Nationalist Government of Spain (1936–9).

[56] HC Debs., vol. 371, col. 1106, 13 May 1941.

recognized an authority, either in exile or *in situ, as a government* they will accord it the treatment due to its governmental status. State practice shows that this is true irrespective of whether the authority in exile has been recognized *as a government* in the context of belligerent occupation, civil war, decolonization, or, more recently, democratization.[57] While it is true that a government, as the organ of a State, by definition requires the existence of a State, writers rejecting recognition of authorities in exile as governments in the context of decolonization[58] have overlooked the fact that States which have recognized an authority in exile as a government in the context of decolonization may simultaneously have recognized the independence of the State in question. For example, the Provisional Government of the Algerian Republic (GPRA) was recognized *de jure* by thrity-one States prior to the factual achievement of independence of Algeria from France on 3 July 1962. Recognition of the GPRA as a government may be explained by the statement of President Kwame Nkrumah of Ghana who, acting as chairman of the day's session at the Belgrade Conference of Heads of State or Government of Non-Aligned Countries, said on 5 September 1961: 'The most significant fact of this conference so far is the presence of the head of the Provisional Government of Algeria. This stresses the fact that we accept Algeria as a free, sovereign and independent State which, in my view, should be admitted to the United Nations.'[59] There may be differences in treatment between recognized governments in exile owing to the factual circumstances but not owing to the context in which they are recognized. Thus, an authority in exile recognized as a State government in the context of decolonization, unlike one in the context of belligerent occupation, civil war, or democratization, will not be able to claim access to State funds abroad, simply because the State for whose independence the recognized government works does not yet possess such funds. As Part II will show, in areas such as treaty-making, diplomatic relations, immunity, privileges, and jurisdiction over nationals States have accorded the same treatment to authorities in exile recognized as governments irrespective of the context in which they were recognized as such.[60]

According to the predominant view in legal literature the term 'government in exile' does not denote special legal status or an independent subject

[57] This was first pointed out with respect to recognized governments in exile in the context of belligerent occupation and *coup d'état* or revolution by Scelle, *Manuel de droit international public* (1948), 174, 175. See also Janke, 'Rechtsnatur und Rechtsstellung der Regierung im Exil' doctoral thesis (University of Hamburg, 1954), 102–3, 136, 142; Strebel, 'Regierung' in Strupp and Schlochauer (eds.), *Wörterbuch des Völkerrechts* (1962), iii, 85–7 at 86–7.

[58] Verhoeven, *La reconnaissance internationale dans la pratique contemporaine. Les relations publiques internationales* (1975), 81.

[59] [1961–2] *Africa Diary* 123. For the fact that some States recognized both the State of Algeria and the GPRA, see also the Report of the Minister for North African Affairs in the GPRA, dated Apr. 1960: ARA no 95, 447–58 at 455.

[60] Cf. Halajczuk, *Los estados conquistados ante el derecho internacional* (1950), 85.

of international law[61] but indicates the domicile of a 'government', i.e. the depository of a State's sovereignty and its representative organ in international relations.[62] This view also finds support in State practice. Thus, the British Lord Chancellor, Viscount Simon, stated on 19 December 1940 that the 'Allied Governments, although forced temporarily to live in exile, are continuing to discharge their functions as the legitimate Governments of their countries.'[63] The hyphenated expression 'government-in-exile' found both in the press and in the recent literature is thus misleading, giving the impression of a body with a legal status distinct from that of a 'government'. It should be noted in this connection that States have never recognized an authority as a 'government in exile' but have recognized various authorities in exile as 'governments'. For instance, France in 1940 recognized the Belgian Government at Angers as 'the only legal government of Belgium'[64] and not as the Belgian Government in exile. The distinction drawn in the literature between so-called 'genuine', 'quasi', and 'fictitious' governments in exile,[65] between 'legitimate', 'illegitimate' and 'incomplete' governments in exile,[66] or between 'genuine', and 'false' governments in exile[67] finds no support in the practice of States.[68] On the contrary, States distinguish in their treatment of authorities in exile only between those recognized as governments and those not recognized as governments (but perhaps in

[61] But see Guggenheim, *Lehrbuch des Völkerrechts* (1951), ii, 787, n. 62. Prof. Guggenheim, however, later partly abandoned his view in his *Traité de Droit international public* (1953), i, 209, n. 1. Cf. also Lagoni, 'Rechtsmängel springen ins Auge', *Der Spiegel*, 42/47 (21 Nov. 1988), 164. According to Sperduti governments in exile are 'provisional fiduciary agents' which in times of crisis represent the people ('Governi in esilio e comitati nazionali all'estero' [1952] *Com. Int.* 404–13 at 409).

[62] Cf., e.g., Clunet, 'La présence des Alliés en France et "l'exterritorialité"' (1918) 45 *JDI* 514–7 at 514; Langenhove, *L'action du Gouvernement belge en matière économique pendant la guerre* (1927), 31; Jumeau, *Le Refuge du Governement National à l'Etranger* (1941), 160; Oppenheimer, 'Governments and Authorities in Exile' (1942) 36 *AJIL* 568–95 at 568; Verdross, Review of *Lehrbuch des Völkerrechts* by Paul Guggenheim (1949–50) 2 *ÖZöR* 144–5 at 144; Brandweiler, 'Zur Lehre von den Exilregierungen' (1950–1) 3 *ÖZöR* 497–519 at 504, 514; Janke, n. 57 above, 16–9, 94–5, and *passim*; Marek, *Identity and Continuity of States in Public International Law* (1954), 87–101; Tommasi di Vignano, 'Note sui governi in esilio' (1958) 25 *RSPI* 479–92 at 480 n. 1, 489; Reut-Nicolussi, 'Exilregierung' in *Staatslexikon* (6th edn., 1959), iii, 209–12 at 209; Jovičić, 'Vlada u izbeglištvu—njen pravni status i ovlašćenja' (1959) 6 *JRMP* 84–104 at 102; Schaumann, 'Exilregierung' in Strupp and Schlochauer (eds.) *Wörterbuch des Völkerrechts* (1960), i, 498–9 at 498; Kelsen, *Principles of International Law* (2nd edn., 1967), 410; Verhoeven, n. 58 above, 78.

[63] HL Debs., vol. 118, col. 194, 19 Dec. 1940. See also the statement of the British Secretary of State for the Home Department, Mr Herbert Morrison: 'the Allied Governments who are enjoying our hospitality are accepted as sovereign Governments' (HC Debs., vol. 371, col. 1106, 13 May 1941).

[64] Scanlon, *European Governments in Exile* (1943), 2.

[65] So Brandweiler, n. 62 above, 497–519 at 502–3. This distinction has also been adopted with qualifications by Tommasi di Vignano, n. 62 above, 479–92 at 479–80, 483–5.

[66] Mattern, *Die Exilregierung* (1953), iii–iv, 65–6.

[67] Guggenheim, n. 61 above, i, 208–9.

[68] For a classification of governments in exile according to their factual situation, see Halajczuk, n. 60 above, 88–9.

some other—lesser—capacity).[69] Thus, the practice of many writers of subsuming all (or most) authorities in exile under the heading 'government in exile', either genuine, quasi, or false, and of just stating that they have been 'recognized' without stating in what capacity, has led to widespread misconceptions. For example, the Free French authorities in London which received some 'recognition' by the Allies are widely regarded as a government in exile.[70] But caveat—neither did the Free French authorities call themselves or claim to be a government nor were they recognized as the Government of France by any State. For example, the French Committee of National Liberation (CFLN) was 'recognized' by most Allies (only) 'as the body qualified to conduct French effort in the war within the framework of inter-allied co-operation'.[71] Similarly, the Palestine Liberation Organization (PLO), while still in exile, was frequently referred to as a 'government-in-exile'.[72] While it is true that the PLO since the 1970s on several occasions had declared its intention to set up a 'Provisional Government of the State of Palestine',[73] it never did so for lack of commitment by Arab and Western States to recognize such a government, and because of disagreement within the PLO over its composition.[74] Consequently, the PLO never received any recognition as a government, but only as the (sole legitimate) 'representative of the Palestinian people'[75]—the most important of those recognitions being that of Israel on 9 September 1993.[76]

[69] Dr Halajczuk has rightly pointed out: 'La prática internacional solamente distingue dos tipos de gobiernos emigrados: reconocidos y no reconocidos' 'International practice only distinguishes between two types of governments in exile: recognized and non-recognized ones' [author's translation] (n. 60 above, 91).

[70] Thus, the Deputy Prime Minister and Foreign Minister of the Kuwaiti Government in exile stated on 15 Aug. 1990: 'Ours is like the French exile Government [during World War II]' (*NY Times*, 16 Aug. 1990, Sec. A, 15). For other statements of politicians, see Misra, 'Recognition of the "Provisional Government of the Algerian Republic": A Study of the Policy of the Government of India' (1962) 10 *Pol. Stud.* 130–45 at 134; (1970) 13/35 *PR* 8–15 at 12. See also Gallagher, 'Toward a Settlement in Algeria' (1960) 38 *For. Affairs* 273–84.

[71] For Australia, see VI *DAFP* no 274, at 505; for Canada, see IX *DCER* no 1403, at 1727; for South Africa, see [1943] *Keesing's* 5971A; for the UK, see Woodward, *British Foreign Policy in the Second World War* (1971), ii, 459.

[72] Cf., e.g., *WP*, 11 Jan. 1990, Sec. A, 28.

[73] For the text of the resolution concerning the Palestinian government, adopted by the PNC at its 19th emergency session on 15 Nov. 1988, see BBC, *SWB*, 3rd series, ME/0312/A/1, 18 Nov. 1988. See also (1988) 12 *MECS* 250.

[74] Cf. [1992] *Keesing's* R144; (1988) 12 *MECS* 245; *Guardian*, 13 Aug. 1988, 5, 15 Sept. 1988, 10, and 11 Oct. 1988, 20.

[75] See the Res. on Palestine adopted by the 7th Arab Summit Conference, Rabat, Morocco, 28 Oct. 1974. For text of the resolution, see Becker, *The United Nations and Israel. From Recognition to Reprehension* (1988), 165–6. The PLO was recognized 'as the sole representative of the Palestinian people', e.g., by Turkey ((1989) 3/13 *TR* 117–27 at 122) and by the USSR (Golan, 'The Soviet Union and the PLO since the War in Lebanon' (1986) 40 *MEJ* 285–305 at 285).

[76] For the text of the letters exchanged between Chairman Arafat and Prime Minister Rabin, see *NY Times*, 10 Sept. 1993, Sec. A, 12; *Independent*, 10 Sept. 1993, 1.

PART I

Meanings of Recognition of Governments in International Law

1

Meanings of 'Recognition'

1 INTRODUCTION

The confusion which characterizes the subject of recognition[1] of governments is due not so much to the unsettled state of the principles involved as to the nebulous nature of the term 'recognition'. The lack of any clear definition of the term has sometimes led even government departments to argue whether they have accorded recognition to a certain government. For example, on 18 June 1919, Lord Curzon of Kedleston, British Acting Foreign Secretary, approved and rephrased a telegramme to Sir Charles Eliot, the British High Commissioner in Siberia, to begin: 'Recognition of Admiral Kolchak's Government has at the same time made clear the policy of the Allied Powers'. Mr Walford Selby, the deputy head of the Foreign Office's Russia Department minuted on a draft of the outgoing telegramme: 'The Allied governments have not "recognized" Admiral Kolchak's Government'. Curzon then scrawled: 'Very well. But if we have not recognized him I don't know what it all means. Everyone knows that it is recognition.'[2] In a telegramme to US President Roosevelt that concerned the recognition of the French Committee of National Liberation (CFLN), the British Prime Minister, Mr Churchill, wrote on 21 July 1943: 'What does recognition mean? One can recognize a man as an Emperor or as a grocer. Recognition is meaningless without a defining formula.'[3]

However, even if a defining formula is added (a practice not always adhered to by States), the meaning of the term will not automatically become clear, as the example of the British recognition of the Czechoslovak National Council shows. In August 1918 the British Government was not prepared to follow the French Government in recognizing the Czechoslovak National Council 'as the first basis of the future Czechoslovak

[1] The act of recognition must be distinguished from the term 'recognition' used in diplomatic correspondence and official declarations. As the act of recognition may be express or implied, states may recognize governments and their analogues without employing the word 'recognition'. However, in order to be able to establish what consists an act of recognition it is necessary to clarify first what States mean by 'recognition'.

[2] Ullman, *Anglo-Soviet Relations, 1917–1920* (1968), ii, 205, n. 1. On the recognition of General Kolchak's Government, see Kettle, *Russia and the Allies* (1992), iii, 370–413. The US State Department said on 29 July 1994 that the USA had formally recognized the new government in Rwanda. The White House disavowed the statement and said it was not yet prepared to announce diplomatic recognition.

[3] Churchill, *The Second World War* (1954), v, 137; and [1943] II FRUS 173.

Government'.[4] The reluctance of the British Foreign Minister, Mr Balfour, to recognize the Council as the Provisional Czechoslovak Government was overcome by the use of a 'mystical' formula recognizing the Council 'as the present trustee of the future Czecho-Slovak Government'.[5] A formula which left not just the Secretary-General of the Czechoslovak National Council, Dr Beneš, puzzled. According to Henry Wickham Steed, a *Times* journalist, who devised the formula, it meant that the Council 'will be recognized as responsible for the faithful expression of the wishes of the Czechoslovak people, if and when they wish to form an independent State and government of their own, but that they will be entitled to get rid of you if they do not want you'.[6] The literature on the topic gives the firm impression that 'recognition' and its congener 'non-recognition' are terms of art with a consistent, uniform legal meaning,[7] but, as Professor Brownlie has pointed out, 'nothing could be further from the truth'.[8] Most textbooks also give the wrong impression that 'recognition' of governments is exclusively concerned with the legal status of governments coming to power by *coup d'état*, revolution, or any other event involving a break in legal continuity.[9] While it is true that normally no formal statement of recognition is made with respect to constitutional governments, recognition will as a matter of fact be implied by States continuing to deal with the newly elected govern-

[4] On the French recognition, see Kolař, 'Edouard Beneš et le Conseil national tchécoslovaque de la rue Bonaparte' (1993) 43/169 *GMCC* 9–15 at 14; *The Birth of Czechoslovakia* (1968), 48–9; Mattern, *Die Exilregierung* (1953), 30–1; Seton-Watson, 'The Liberation of the Nationalities. Part III. The Formation of the Czecho-Slovak State' in Temperley (ed.), *A History of the Peace Conference of Paris* (1921), iv, 237–77 at 261.

[5] [1918] *Ann. Reg.* 217. On British recognition, see also 'The Recognition of the Czecho-Slovak Armies' (1917–18) 62 *Sol. Jo.* 735–6; Masaryk, *The Making of a State: Memories and Observations 1914–1918* (1927), 265, 342–3, and annex.

[6] *Through Thirty Years 1892–1922. A Personal Narrative* (1924), ii, 231–3.

[7] 'Recognition of a government is formal acknowledgement that a particular regime is the effective government of a state and implies a commitment to treat that regime as the government of that state': American Law Institute, *Restatement of the Law (Third). The Foreign Relations Law of the United States* (1987), i, 84. For similar definitions of 'recognition' of governments, see Ruda, 'Recognition of States and Governments' in Bedjaoui (ed.), *International Law: Achievements and Prospects* (1991), 449–65 at 455; Ipsen, *Völkerrecht* (3rd edn., 1990), 242; Rousseau, *Droit international public* (1977), iii, 554.

[8] Brownlie, 'Recognition in Theory and Practice' (1982) 53 *BYBIL* 197–211 at 198 and *Principles of Public International Law* (4th edn., 1990), 91, 93. See also Wengler, *Völkerrecht* (1964), i, 773–80. An earlier attempt to distinguish between different meanings of the term 'recognition' may be seen in Professor Kelsen's distinction between political and legal recognition: 'Recognition in International Law: Theoretical Observations' (1941) 35 *AJIL* 605–17 and *Principles of International Law* (2nd edn., 1967), 389–91, 399–404. First signs of a distinction between different meanings of the term may also be found in Chen, *The International Law of Recognition. With Special Reference to Practice in Great Britain and the United States* (1951), 129.

[9] See, e.g., Jennings and Watts (eds.), *Oppenheim's International Law* (9th edn., 1992), i, 148; Brierly, *The Law of Nations. An Introduction to the International Law of Peace* (6th edn., 1963), 145–6; Mugerwa, 'Subjects of International Law' in Sørensen (ed.), *Manual of Public International Law* (1968), 271; Dahm, Delbrück, Wolfrum, *Völkerrecht* (2nd edn., 1989), I/1, 186–7; and Nguyen Quoc, Daillier, Pellet, *Droit international public* (3rd edn., 1987), 502–3.

ment.[10] That recognition is not restricted to unconstitutional governments becomes clear from the fact that in certain circumstances States have both expressly recognized and refused to recognize elected governments.[11] The practice of States shows that the term 'recognition' has been employed in a variety of different meanings depending on the factual and legal circumstances of the case. Already in 1824, the British Foreign Secretary, Mr Canning, referring to the recognition of the independence of the Spanish colonies in South America, stressed that 'it [recognition] has clearly two senses, in which it is to be differently understood'.[12] This is equally true for the recognition of governments, as will be shown in the following.

2 INDICATION OF WILLINGNESS TO ENTER INTO OFFICIAL RELATIONS

By the term 'recognition' or 'non-recognition' may be meant an indication of willingness or unwillingness on the part of the recognizing government to establish or maintain official, but not necessarily intimate,[13] relations[14] with the government in question.[15] Especially in cases of prolonged official non-recognition of established governments States frequently speak of their willingness to 'normalize' their relations with the Government in question.[16]

[10] So also Scelle, *Manuel de droit international public* (1948), 177. Cf. also 'Recognition of Governments' (1917–18) 62 *Sol. Jo.* 359–60 at 360; (1968) 4 *RBDI* 541–2.

[11] See League of Nations, *Records of the First Assembly. Plenary Meetings* (1920), 598, 606; DBFP, 1st ser., XII, no 449, 528; [1945] *Keesing's* 7600, 7618A; DBPO, 1st ser., V, no 96, and no 73, 349, n. 7; (1962) 47 *DSB* 560.

[12] HC Debs., vol. 11, col. 1397, 15 June 1824. For an elaboration of the two different meanings of the term 'recognition' see the speech of Sir James Mackintosh urging the British Government to 'recognize' the States of Spanish America: *ibid.*, cols. 1347–50, 15 June 1824.

[13] See the address of US Secretary of State Acheson to the Pan American Society of the USA, New York, 19 Sept. 1949: 'our long-range objectives . . . may, in fact, be best served by recognizing it [the new government] and thus maintaining a channel of communication with the country involved. . . . our act of recognition need not necessarily be understood as the forerunner of a policy of intimate cooperation with the government concerned' (Whiteman (ed.), *Digest of International Law* (1963), ii, 5).

[14] The term 'relations' comprises communications, negotiations, and other political and legal transactions. It has been used interchangeably with 'business', 'intercourse', and 'dealings'.

[15] Compare, e.g., Schwarzenberger and Brown, *A Manual of International Law* (6th edn., 1976), 70; Rolin, 'Conditions and Methods of Recognition of New Governments' in Bisshop (ed.), *International Law Conference London, 10th–12th July 1943* (1944), 40–7 at 42; Guggenheim, *Lehrbuch des Völkerrechts* (1948), i, 189; Heydte, *Völkerrecht. Ein Lehrbuch* (1958), 204; Akehurst, *A Modern Introduction to International Law* (6th edn., 1987), 58; and also Cassese, *International Law in a Divided World* (1986), 79, with respect to recognition of States.

[16] For the 'normalization of relations' between the Government of the USA and the Government of the PR China, see the messages, dated 31 Dec. 1978 and 1 Jan. 1979: BBC, *SWB*, 2nd series, FE/6006/C/1–3, 3 Jan. 1979.

This meaning of the term is given expression, for example, in a memorandum dated 17 May 1933 of the Legal Adviser to the US Department of State, Mr Hackworth, which reads in the relevant part as follows: 'By the term "recognition", used in the sense of recognition of new governments, is meant the establishment of normal official relations by the recognizing government with the government recognized, or an indication of readiness to do so.'[17] While in most cases recognition of a government will lead to the establishment of normal official relations, this is not necessarily so, as the establishment of bilateral relations requires the consent of both parties.[18] In view of the fact that recognition is only a unilateral act,[19] it is therefore more precise to speak of an indication of readiness to establish normal official relations than to speak of the establishment of the same. Mr Hackworth was probably thinking of cases in which 'recognition' by the United States was in response to an official act of the government to be recognized, such as a formal note announcing the formation of the new government and expressing the desire to continue the existing friendly relations with the US Government. In such cases recognition may be compared to the acceptance of an existing offer thereby concluding a fictitious 'agreement' on the establishment of official relations.

[17] Whiteman, n. 13 above, 48. See also another memorandum by the same author of 8 Feb. 1934: *ibid.*, 535. In vol. I of his *Digest* Mr Hackworth wrote: '[Recognition] is evidenced, in the case of a new state or government, by an act officially . . . *indicating a readiness* on the part of the recognizing state *to enter into formal relations* with it' (*Digest of International Law* (1940), i, 161), and 'In order that recognition may be implied from any act short of explicit recognition, the act must be of such unequivocal character as to leave no doubt of the *intention . . . to deal with the new . . . government officially as such*' (*ibid.*, 327, italics supplied). See further the statement of US Secretary of State Hughes on 19 July 1923: 'Recognition is an invitation to intercourse' (*ibid.*, 178); and the instruction of 8 Sept. 1900 sent by Acting Secretary of State Hill to Mr Hart, US minister at Bogota: '[a foreign government] is recognized by directing the United States representative formally to notify its proper minister of his *readiness to enter into relations* with it' (Moore (ed.), *A Digest of International Law* (1906), i, 139, italics supplied). See also the despatch of the German Chancellor Bismarck to Count Bernstorff, dated 15/16 Jan. 1862: 'recognition only means that we think that the new government is adequately secure in order to establish *regular relations* with it in the interest of our citizens' (Fontes, B.I.I.1, 150, italics and translation supplied).

[18] See Art. 2 of the VCDR (500 UNTS 95). On 13 Oct. 1944 the Swiss envoy in London presented an Aide-Mémoire to the Soviet Embassy there expressing the Swiss federal Government's recognition of the Soviet Government, i.e. its desire to re-establish normal diplomatic relations. The offer to re-establish normal diplomatic relations was rejected by the Soviet Government in a Memorandum of 1 Nov. 1944: DDS XV, nos 257, 277; Klarer, *Schweizerische Praxis der völkerrechtlichen Anerkennung* (1981), 127–9. See also the statement of the People's Commissariat for Foreign Affairs of the USSR of 5 Nov. 1944: Soviet For. Pol. II, 174–5. For further illustrations that the establishment of bilateral relations requires the consent of both parties see the survey of the status of relations between the USA and 11 governments with which the USA did not maintain relations in 1977: (1977) 77 *DSB* 463.

[19] See Suy, *Les actes juridiques unilatéraux en droit international public* (1969), 191–201; Rohr, 'El reconocimiento como acto unilateral' (1978) 2 *Derecho Comparado* 107–35 and (1979) 3 *Derecho Comparado* 92–124; Jennings and Watts, n. 9 above, 1188; Verdross and Simma, *Universelles Völkerrecht. Theorie und Praxis* (3rd edn., 1984), §666. *Contra* Verzijl, *International Law in Historical Perspective* (1969), ii, 578–9. For an example of 'unilateral diplomatic recognition', see [1972] *Keesing's* 25624B.

It should be noted that 'recognition' itself says nothing about the nature, i.e. the extent, form, and content, of the official relations which the recognizing government is willing to enter into with the authority recognized. While there is a presumption that recognition of a 'government' indicates the readiness to enter into 'normal', i.e. diplomatic, relations, this is not the case with non-governmental authorities. It is, *inter alia*, for this reason that Mr Churchill called for a defining formula relating to the term when discussing the recognition of the CFLN with US President Roosevelt. By recognizing an authority 'as something', i.e. in a certain capacity, the recognizing government may indicate the nature of the official relations which it is willing to have with the authority recognized. Recognition 'as something' will thus usually mean that the recognizing government is willing to enter into official relations with the authority recognized in the capacity, and only in the capacity, set out in the defining formula. Thus, when on 26 August 1943 the United States recognized the CFLN 'as administering those French overseas territories which acknowledge its authority', it was pointed out that 'this statement does not constitute recognition of a government of France or of the French Empire by the United States. It does constitute recognition of the French Committee of National Liberation as functioning within specific limitations during the war.'[20] The recognition by the French, Italian, and British Governments in June 1918 of the Czecho-Slovak National Council '*as the supreme organ of the Czechoslovak movement in Allied countries*' must thus be interpreted as indicating the willingness of these governments to enter into official relations with the Czecho-Slovak National Council on all matters concerning that movement and nothing more.[21] This also becomes clear from a statement of Professor Masaryk, the President of the Czecho-Slovak National Council and later the President of Czechoslovakia, who writes in his memoirs that 'the negotiations with the Allied governments for recognition were often long and difficult. There is, for instance, . . . a certain difference between the recognition of our National Council and the subsequent recognition of it as a Provisional Government.'[22]

Recognizing States have been very creative in devising such formulae. For instance, General de Gaulle was recognized by the United Kingdom on 28 June 1940, when it was still maintaining diplomatic relations with the French Government at Bordeaux, 'as the leader of all free Frenchmen wherever they may be who rally to him in support of the Allied

[20] At the end of Aug. 1943 the State Department instructed the American Ambassador to London that the establishment by the Government of the USA 'of official relations with the French Committee of National Liberation at Algiers . . . render obsolete the liaison arrangements set up in London' (Whiteman, n. 13 above, ii, 370–1).

[21] For the British recognition statement of 3 June 1918, see Beneš , *My War Memoirs* (1928), 376.

[22] Masaryk, n. 5 above, 342–3.

cause'.[23] The Polish National Committee at Paris was recognized by the French Government on 20 September 1917 'as official national Polish organization'.[24] The Dutch representative in the UN General Assembly stated on 4 November 1977: 'The Netherlands recognizes SWAPO as a major political force in Namibia'.[25] Similarly, France and Mexico on 28 August 1981 announced their recognition of the FMLN–FDR alliance in El Salvador as a 'representative political force', while stating that this did not imply a break with the Government of El Salvador.[26] However, while some formulae have been used only once to define a special relationship, others such as 'government', '*de facto* government', '*de jure* government', 'legal or legitimate government', and (sole) 'representative of a people' have become standard formulae which, it is suggested, define a certain (but not necessarily different) nature of official relations. The use of these terms as a defining formula of the term 'recognition' indicating a certain nature of official relations must be distinguished from their descriptive usage.[27] For example, a government may exist in fact, that is to say, it may be described as a '*de facto* government', long before it is recognized as such, i.e. long before the recognizing government indicates its willingness to enter into official relations with it in that capacity. Thus, the Soviet Russian Government was referred to by the British Government as a '*de facto* Government' long before it was recognized as the *de facto* Government of Russia on 16 March 1921.[28] The defining formulae used by recognizing States with respect to a certain authority may vary, as may the nature of the relations which they are willing to have with it. For instance, the CFLN was recognized by the United States on 26 August 1943 'as administering those French overseas territories which acknowledge its authority' while it was recognized by the USSR on 27 August 1943 'as representing the State

[23] HC Debs., vol. 362, col. 815, 3 July 1940.

[24] Blociszewski, 'La restauration de la Pologne et la diplomatie européenne' (1921) 28 *RGDIP* 1–83 at 68. The British, Italian, and US Governments followed the French example on 15 and 30 Oct. and 1 Dec. 1917, respectively (Roth, *Die Entstehung des polnischen Staates. Eine völkerrechtlich-politische Untersuchung* (1926), 132–3). See also the statement of the British Assistant Secretary of State for Foreign Affairs, Lord Robert Cecil, in the House of Commons on 2 July 1918: 'The Polish National Committee, which has been recognized by all the Allied Governments as the most practicable channel through which to deal with Polish communities and interests in each country' (HC Debs., vol. 107, cols. 1552, 2 July 1918).

[25] (1979) 10 *NYIL* 322.

[26] [1981] *Keesing's* 30572A, 31174. A Dutch Foreign Ministry spokesman stated on 29 Sept. 1981: 'We now recognize the Front [FMLN–FDR] as one of the political forces in the conflict. This step is in accord with the Franco-Mexican agreement' (*ibid.*). On 22 Sept. 1981 the US State Department announced that the USA was ready, if the Salvadorean Government wished, to help initiate 'contacts and discussions with the legally recognized parties on the holding of elections' (*ibid.*, 31175).

[27] Cf. Jennings and Watts, n. 9 above, 155, n. 3.

[28] See, e.g., HC Debs., vol. 104, col. 22, 11 Mar. 1918 (Mr Balfour). Cf. also *ibid.*, vol. 106, cols. 940–1, 30 May 1918 and DBFP, 1st ser., XX, no 357, 648–9.

interests of the French Republic, and as leading all French patriots fighting Hitlerite tyranny'.[29] It is of interest to note in this connection the remark of Mr Bogomolov, the Soviet Ambassador to London, that 'the USSR . . . has recognized the Committee far more fully than the other powers have'.[30] The recognizing government may also indicate its willingness to change the nature of its relations with a government or a non-governmental authority by changing the defining formula, i.e. by recognizing it in a different capacity. For example, the British Government 'recognized' the Bolshevik Government 'as the *de facto* Government of Russia' on 16 March 1921 when it concluded a Trade Agreement with it.[31] The Agreement provided, *inter alia*, for the exchange of official agents without diplomatic status, and its preamble declared that the agreement was merely preliminary to the conclusion of a formal general Peace Treaty covering both political and economic relations between the two countries.[32] The Agreement was repeatedly referred to in Parliament as a 'trade agreement' to promote commercial relations, the 'question of political relations being postponed'.[33] On 12 February 1924 the British Prime Minister in reply to a question said: 'His Majesty's Government . . . granted *de jure* recognition to the Soviet Government on 1st February [1924].'[34] On that day, Mr Hodgson, the British representative in Moscow under the Trade Agreement, stated in a note to the Soviet Government after informing it about his Government's recognition: 'I have been given the status of Chargé d'affaires pending the appointment of an Ambassador; and I am to state that his Majesty's Government will be glad similarly to receive a Russian Chargé d'affaires representing the Government of the Union at the Court of St James.'[35]

In the majority of cases, however, no defining formula is added to the term 'recognition' and the recognizing government simply states that it recognizes or that it does not recognize a certain government or authority. In these cases, the nature of the official relations must be determined by looking at the factual and legal context in which the 'recognition' statement is made. The case of the British recognition of the Czechoslovak National Committee may serve as an example. On 23 July 1940, the British Prime

[29] [1943] *Keesing's* 5971A.

[30] De Gaulle, *War Memoirs. Documents* (1959), ii, 331.

[31] HC Debs., vol. 139, col. 2506, 22 Mar. 1921 (Mr Lloyd George); *A.M. Luther* v. *James Sagor and Company* [1921] 3 KB 532 at 536 (CA).

[32] 114 BFSP 373. On the history of the Trade Agreement, see Ullman, n. 2 above, (1972), iii.

[33] HC Debs., vol. 139, col. 2198, 21 Mar. 1921. On the only limited relations between the British and the Soviet Government prior to *de jure* recognition, see HC Debs., vol. 149, WA, *col.* 302, 16 Dec. 1921.

[34] HC Debs., vol. 174, col. 534 12 Feb. 1924.

[35] Wilson, 'British Recognition De Facto and De Jure of the USSR' (1934) 28 *AJIL* 99–101 at 100. On the question whether there was a difference in the factual or legal character of the Soviet Government in 1921 and 1924, see Lauterpacht, *Recognition in International Law* (1947), 337, 338–9; and Chen, n. 8 above, 274, 275.

Minister, Mr Churchill, read out in the House of Commons a letter, dated 21 July 1940, from Lord Halifax to Dr Beneš:

> *In the light of exchanges of view which have taken place between us*, I have the honour to inform you, that in response to the request of the Czechoslovak National Committee, His Majesty's Government in the United Kingdom are happy to recognize and enter into relations with the Provisional Government established by the Czechoslovak National Committee to function in this country.[36]

In the exchange of view which the letter refers to, Lord Halifax had 'taken notice of the fact that this Provisional Government is to be a representative Government of the Czech and Slovak people' (in contrast to a Provisional Government of the Czechoslovak Republic), had reserved the British Government's 'attitude concerning the legal continuity of the Czechoslovak Republic' and had set out certain questions which had to be settled between His Majesty's Government and the Provisional Czechoslovak Government.[37] It should be noted in this connection that Mr Churchill, when asked about the position of the Czechoslovak Government in relation to the Polish and other Governments, stated that '*there may be certain differences of form*, but in principle there is no difference'. The Foreign Office, pointing to the lack of legal continuity of the Provisional Czechoslovak Government, had suggested answering that there are '*certain technical distinctions*'.[38] It took the British Government until 18 July 1941 to even out these 'differences of form' and 'to accord full recognition to the Czechoslovak Government and . . . to accredit an Envoy Extraordinary and Minister Plenipotentiary to Dr Beneš as President of the Czechoslovak Republic'.[39]

Recognition used in the context of recognition of a *de facto* government of a recognized State,[40] as a rule, indicates a willingness on the part of the recognizing State to enter into normal official, i.e. diplomatic, relations with the government in question. In fact, most examples given under the heading 'Recognition of [new] Governments' in digests and compilations of State practice concern the question whether or not to enter into or re-establish diplomatic relations with a certain *de facto* government. This view is sup-

[36] HC Debs., vol. 363, col. 615, 23 July 1940 (italics added).

[37] For the correspondence between Dr Beneš and Lord Halifax preceding the above 'recognition' statement, see Beneš, *Memoirs of Dr Eduard Beneš* (1954), 106–10.

[38] FO 371, vol. 26394, quoted in Brügel, 'Die Anerkennung der tschechoslowakischen Auslandsregierung 1940–1942' (1983) 24 *Bohemia*, 335–47 at 343.

[39] [1942] *CYBIL* 231.

[40] The term is used here in its descriptive meaning. It is interesting to note in this connection that, e.g., the USA in prevailing practice speaks of recognition of a *de facto* government rather than of recognition 'as' a government, thereby implying that the terms 'recognition' and 'non-recognition' both refer to an existing government and not to whether or not a government exists. See Whiteman, n. 13 above, i, 157–8; ii, 72, and the references in that *Digest* to the 'US Position on Recognition of *de facto* Governments, First Meeting of the Inter-American Council of Jurists, Rio de Janeiro, 1950'.

ported by statements of Assistant Legal Adviser to the US Department of State, Dr Whiteman, and others,[41] the former writing in Volume II of her *Digest* in 1963: 'Recognition of a government indicates a willingness on the part of the recognizing state to carry on diplomatic relations with that government.'[42] This is reflected by the fact that the United States in modern practice increasingly uses the term 'diplomatic recognition' or 'full diplomatic recognition' instead of 'recognition'.[43] However, it must be pointed out that recognizing governments need not add the adjective 'diplomatic' in order to indicate their readiness to enter into this kind of official relations. It is argued that when a government speaks of 'full', 'partial', or 'limited' recognition of a *de facto* government it uses the term 'recognition' in the meaning of an indication of readiness to enter into official relations, as these qualifying terms are incompatible with the idea of both factual existence of and legal status as a government. A government either exists (and fulfils the criteria for its legal status) or it does not. There is no 'halfway house'. Such a rigid dichotomy does not apply to official relations which may be graded.[44] It must be emphasized, however, that the use of the term 'recognition' in this meaning is not restricted to cases in which such qualifiers are added. On the contrary, as will be seen in the further course of this study recognition, with or without qualifier, is mainly, although not exclusively, used in this mode.

3 MANIFESTATION OF AN OPINION ON LEGAL STATUS

By the term 'recognition' or 'non-recognition' may also be meant the manifestation of the recognizing government's opinion on the legal status of the government in question. It must be emphasized that recognition does not

[41] Mr Aldrich, Acting Legal Adviser to the US Department of State, said before the Senate Foreign Relations Committee on 17 June 1969: 'recognition is generally conceived to be something which can be negotiated and I think the Chinese Communists have certainly negotiated about the terms of *recognition in terms of exchange of diplomatic representatives* about as hard as any country I know' (Congress, Senate, Committee on Foreign Relations, *United States Recognition of Foreign Governments* (1969), 8–17 at 12, italics supplied). In 1919 the British Under-Secretary of State for Foreign Affairs, Mr Harmsworth, stated in somewhat similar terms: 'His Majesty's Government are not disposed, in view of the Mexican Government, to *accord the recognition implied by the resumption of diplomatic relations*' (HC Debs., vol. 115, WA, *col.* 1472, 13 May 1919, italics added). See further HL Debs., vol. 233, col. 908, 25 July 1961.

[42] Whiteman, n. 13 above, ii, 29.

[43] *Ibid.*, *passim*. On 'diplomatic recognition' generally, see also Ch. 2 sect. 3(6) below.

[44] Sir Hersch Lauterpacht, examining the distinction between *de facto* and *de jure* recognition, writes: 'It may be maintained that so long as those other conditions [of recognition] have not been complied with there can be no recognition at all, and that full recognition or complete refusal of recognition are the only alternatives. But the necessities of international intercourse do not favour any such rigid dichotomy' (n. 35 above, 340).

objectively establish the legal status of a government, but that it simply constitutes a subjective (relative) statement on that status. The British Foreign Secretary Canning already in 1824 pointed out that by 'recognizing' the independence of the Spanish colonies in South America the 'other state simply acknowledges the fact, or rather *its opinion on the fact* [of independence]'.[45] Comparing the different meanings of the term 'recognition', Mr Hackworth, the Legal Adviser to the US Department of State, stated in a memorandum dated 13 December 1940: 'There is a difference between recognition of a government in this sense of the word [i.e. in the sense of establishing normal official relations with a government] and recognition or admission that a government *exists*.'[46] Similarly, Dr Whiteman, the Assistant Legal Adviser to the US Department of State, wrote in 1963 in Volume II of her *Digest*: 'The character of the object recognized may be recognized as "*de facto*" in existence or control. . . . The United States may . . . , should it so desire, recognize a . . . government; that is to say, recognize that the . . . government . . . in fact exists.'[47]

Recognition or non-recognition of a government may thus manifest whether or not, in the opinion of the recognizing authority, the government in question exists *as such*, that is to say whether or not it fulfils the criteria prescribed by international law[48] for the status of government.[49] By recognizing or not recognizing an authority 'as something', i.e. in a certain capacity, the recognizing government may indicate the legal status which, in its opinion, the authority in question qualifies, or does not qualify, for. Thus, when on 14 November 1966 the Protocol for the Further Prolongation of the International Sugar Agreement of 1958 was signed on behalf of China by the Nationalist Chinese Government, the British Foreign Secretary de-

[45] HC Debs., vol. 11, col. 1397, 15 June 1824, italics added. On the subjectivity of recognition, see *German Interests in Polish Upper Silesia* (1926), PCIJ, Series A, No 7, 28. See also Suy, n. 19 above, 207.

[46] Whiteman, n. 13 above, ii, 48, italics supplied.

[47] *Ibid.*, 3. For the distinction between recognition of the fact that the State of the Vatican City exists as an international entity and formal recognition of the State of the Vatican City or of its Government by the USA: see *ibid.*, 542–3. See also the distinction between '*de facto* recognition of the existence of the new régime' in Manchuria and the 'general principles in practice in the recognition of new states and new governments' (*ibid.*, 596).

[48] It must be noted that the criteria of a certain status need not necessarily be prescribed by international law. For example, in 1963 the OAU Co-ordinating Committee for the Liberation of Africa laid down conditions for the financial and moral assistance of liberation movements. By 'recognizing' a liberation movement the Co-ordinating Committee determines only that, in its opinion, the movement in question fulfils the criteria for assistance. Cf. Jennings and Watts, n. 9 above, 163, n. 6; Ginther, 'Die völkerrechtliche Stellung nationaler Befreiungsbewegungen im südlichen Afrika' (1982) 32 *ÖZöRV* 131–57 at 140–5; Červenka, *The Unfinished Quest for Unity. Africa and the OAU* (1977), 46–50; and Wilson, *International Law and the Use of Force by National Liberation Movements* (1988), 142–6.

[49] This seems to be the meaning attributed to the term 'recognition' by most textbook writers. Professor Kelsen describes this meaning as the 'legal act of recognition' (n. 8 above, at 606–7).

clared 'that since the Government of the United Kingdom *do not recognize* the Nationalist Government *as the competent Government of China*, they cannot regard signature of the Protocol by a Nationalist Chinese representative as a valid signature on behalf of China'.[50] Express non-recognition of a (government or non-governmental) authority 'as something', however, does not exclude tacit 'recognition as something else', that is to say that, in the recognizing government's view, the authority in question fulfils the criteria for another legal status. The express manifestation of that opinion in the form of a recognition statement may be inopportune for political reasons. For example, the certificate issued by the British Foreign and Commonwealth Office in *Hesperides Hotels Ltd* v. *Aegean Turkish Holidays Ltd* (1977)[51] reads as follows: 'Her Majesty's Government in the United Kingdom do not recognize the administration established under the name of the "Turkish Federated State of Cyprus" . . . Her Majesty's Government do not recognize such administration *as being the government of an independent de facto sovereign state*.'[52] In this certificate the Foreign Office specified the British non-recognition of the Turkish Cypriot administration as non-recognition as 'the government of an independent *de facto* sovereign state'.[53] This, however, does not rule out HM Government tacitly recognizing the administration as, for example, the local *de facto* government of the Turkish (occupied) part of Cyprus or a subordinate body of the Turkish occupation authorities. In order to establish in what form the Turkish Cypriot administration may have been recognized, other manifestations of the British Government's opinion on its legal status will have to be examined. In this connection one may take into account that the British Government in parliamentary statements regularly refers to 'Turkish Cypriot authorities'.[54] The British Government's opinion on the legal status of the Turkish Cypriot authorities may also be manifested in the nature of the

[50] UKTS No 28 (1966), Cmnd. 3001, 35 (italics added). See in this connection the statement of the Joint Under-Secretary of State for Foreign Affairs in the House of Lords: 'Her Majesty's Government, of course, *recognize* the Government of the People's Republic of China *as the Government of China*' (HL Debs., vol. 206, col. 190, 7 Nov. 1957, italics supplied). See also the statement of the British Foreign Secretary, Mr Hurd, in Nov. 1991: 'We recognize the Government of the Republic of Cyprus as the Government of the whole of Cyprus' (HC Debs., vol. 199, col. 259, 20 Nov. 1991).

[51] [1978] 1 QB 205. For a discussion of the 'recognition' question in this case, see Crawford (1978) 49 *BYBIL* 259–61; Lloyd Jones (1978) 37 *CLJ* 48–51; and Merrills (1979) 28 *ICLQ* 523–5.

[52] [1978] 1 QB 205 at 216 (italics supplied).

[53] This non-recognition as the 'government of an independent *de facto* sovereign State' has, for example, the consequence that the authorities of the Turkish part of Cyprus will not enjoy sovereign immunity in the British courts. Cf. *The Arantzazu Mendi* [1939] AC 256 (HL).

[54] HC Debs., vol. 957, WA, *col.* 247, 8 Nov. 1978; *ibid.*, vol. 50, WA, *col.* 219, 8 Dec. 1983. Cf. Jennings and Watts, n. 9 above, 190, who speculate whether the UN Security Council by referring to the 'Turkish Cypriot authorities' accorded some undefined degree of recognition.

relations with these authorities. For example, there have been 'operational contacts between British police forces and the Turkish Cypriot police'.[55] The British Government has presented claims for compensation for loss and damage suffered by British citizens during the fighting in 1974 to the Turkish Cypriot authorities,[56] has maintained a general informal dialogue with them through the British High Commission in Nicosia,[57] and has maintained a 'residual presence' of the British High Commission in the Turkish sector of Nicosia in order to deal with inquiries from individual Turkish Cypriots and British nationals.[58] The Foreign Office also sent the British High Commissioner in Cyprus to lodge an official appeal with the Turkish Cypriot authorities for the return of the fugitive businessman Asil Nadir.[59] Furthermore, the British Government had accepted export documentation for citrus and other produce issued by the Turkish Cypriot authorities, a practice which was later declared by the European Court of Justice to be not in conformity with EC law.[60] On the other hand, the British Government does not recognize travel documents issued by the Turkish Cypriot authorities and does not endorse them with entrance clearances.[61] It accepts the authority of the (Greek) Cypriot Government in matters of air traffic and telecommunication over the whole island of Cyprus.[62] From these dealings it may be concluded that, in the opinion of the British Government, the Turkish Cypriot authorities qualify as the *de facto* government of the (occupied) northern part of Cyprus.[63]

Recognition in the sense of a manifestation of an opinion on legal status seems to suggest itself in cases in which the legal status of an authority is uncertain or controversial and the authority in question is expressly recognized 'as something'. Such cases may arise, for example, when competing authorities claim to be the government of the same State, when questions of

[55] HC Debs., vol. 175, WA, *cols.* 15–16, 25 June 1990.

[56] HC Debs., vol. 154, WA, *col.* 474, 14 June 1989.

[57] HC Debs., vol. 46, WA, *col.* 246, 22 July 1983; *ibid.*, vol. 56, WA, *col.* 178, 14 Mar. 1984.

[58] HC Debs., vol. 102, WA, *col.* 256, 23 July 1986.

[59] *The Times*, 6 May 1993, 1.

[60] Case C–432/92 *R.* v. *Minister of Agriculture, Fisheries and Food, ex parte Anastasiou* [1994] ECR I–3116.

[61] HC Debs., vol. 49, WA, *col.* 257, 24 Nov. 1983.

[62] HC Debs., vol. 56, WA, *col.* 221, 15 Mar. 1984; HL Debs., vol. 489, col. 528, 27 Oct. 1987.

[63] Thus, Scott LJ held in *Polly Peck International* v. *Nadir (No 2)*: 'Northern Cyprus is not recognized by Her Majesty's government but none the less has had *de facto* control over its territory since about 1974': [1992] 4 All ER 769 at 773 (CA). Glidewell LJ in his judgment in *Polly Peck International* v. *Nadir (No 3)* even referred to 'the government of Northern Cyprus' (*The Times*, 22 Mar. 1993). On the status of the Turkish Cypriot authorities, see also the decisions of the E. Comm. HR in App. No 8007/77 (*Cyprus* v. *Turkey*, 10 July 1978) 13 DR 85 at 148–50 and Apps. Nos 15299/89, 15300/89, and 15318/89 (*Chrysostomos and Others* v. *Turkey*, 4 Mar. 1991) 68 DR 216 at 246–8. On the question of statehood of Northern Cyprus, see Blay, 'Self-Determination in Cyprus: The New Dimension of an Old Conflict' (1987) 10 *AYBIL* 67–100 at 89–97, and Necatigil, *The Cyprus Question and the Turkish Position in International Law* (2nd edn., 1993), 317–30.

statehood and government status are linked, when the factual situation within a State is unclear owing to civil war, when a government is established by outside intervention, or when an authority claims 'unusual' legal status. However, this meaning of the term 'recognition' is not restricted to such cases and to the use of a defining formula ('as something'). Even if the legal status of an authority is evident, recognition may still manifest the recognizing government's opinion on it. But in this instance, recognition will very rarely be used in this meaning alone.

4 RELATIONSHIP BETWEEN THE TWO MEANINGS

In general, the two meanings of the term 'recognition' will coincide, that is to say, recognition of a government will express both the recognizing government's willingness to enter into official relations with it and its opinion that the government recognized exists *as such*. This coincidence may be based on the recognizing government's understanding that it should enter into official (but not necessarily diplomatic) relations with an authority when the same fulfils the criteria prescribed by international law for the status of government, and that it should not enter into such relations when the criteria are not fulfilled.[64] However, the two meanings of the term need not always coincide. Recognizing governments may make their willingness to enter into official relations with a government dependent on criteria other than its legal status. Thus non-recognition of, for example, a government need not necessarily mean that, in the opinion of the recognizing government, the unrecognized government does not exist as a government in the sense of international law. It may mean only that the recognizing government is unwilling to enter into normal official, i.e. diplomatic, relations with it.[65] Some of the 'famous' non-recognition cases may serve as examples for this proposition.

[64] Great Britain generally seems to have followed this approach since 1924. See the statement of the British Foreign Secretary, Mr Morrison, in 1951: 'His Majesty's Government consider that recognition should be accorded when the conditions specified by international law [for government status] are, in fact, fulfilled and that recognition should not be given when these conditions are not fulfilled' (HC Debs., vol. 485, col. 2411, 21 Mar. 1951), and the speech on the British viewpoint on 'diplomatic recognition' delivered by the British Ambassador to the USA, Sir Roger Makins, at the Catholic University of America on 13 May 1954 (Whiteman, n. 13 above, ii, 110–11).

[65] See Wengler, n. 8 above, i, 778. After the military *coup d'état* in Bolivia on 17 July 1980 the German Government declared that it did not 'recognize' the new Bolivian Government. On this 'non-recognition' Minister of State Dr Hamm-Brücher declared in the Bundestag on 6 October 1980: 'contact between the German embassy and the Bolivian Government is restricted to humanitarian, human rights and consular questions. It is neither our nor the Bolivian view that this means that we maintain normal diplomatic relations' ((1982) 42 *ZaöRV* 538–9, translation supplied). It is of interest to note in this connection that governments and courts regularly refer to unrecognized '*governments*', thereby implying that it is not the status of government that is in question.

The Tinoco Government of Costa Rica. Great Britain refused to recognize the Government of Frederico Tinoco in Costa Rica (January 1917–August 1919). However, this did not prevent the British Government from contending in an arbitration between Great Britain and Costa Rica in 1923 that 'the Tinoco Government was the only government of Costa Rica *de facto* and *de jure* for two years and nine months [and] that it was in peaceful administration of the whole country, with the acquiescence of its people'.[66] Arbitrator Taft tried to reconcile these apparently conflicting statements by assuming a change in the British Government's position on the question of the legal status of the Tinoco Government.[67] Looking at the British practice prior to 1924, and especially the case of prolonged non-recognition of successive (elected) Mexican Governments for political reasons, it seems more likely that by not recognizing the Tinoco Government the British Government expressed its unwillingness to enter into official relations with an authority, which, in its opinion, qualified as the *de jure* and *de facto* government of Costa Rica. It is of interest to note in this connection that Mr Harmsworth, British Under-Secretary of State for Foreign Affairs, stated on 6 August 1919 in reply to a question in the House of Commons concerning British relations with the Spanish-American Republics: 'The two latter posts [of Minister and Consul-General in Costa Rica] are at present in abeyance, as His Majesty's Government have not recognized the *present Government of Costa Rica.*'[68] The Tinoco Government had been recognized in 1917 by twenty States. Only the United States, Great Britain, France, and Italy refused to accord recognition. Arbitrator Taft speculated that 'probably because of the leadership of the United States . . . her then Allies in the war . . . declined to recognize the Tinoco Government'.[69] US non-recognition, however, was motivated by political rather than legal reasons, as becomes clear from a Department of State instruction to the American Minister in Costa Rica. On 17 February 1917 the State Department instructed him that, by authorization of President Wilson, he should inform General Tinoco 'that even if he is elected he will not be given recognition by the United States'.[70]

The Bolshevik Government of Russia.[71] The Bolsheviks seized power in

[66] *Tinoco Arbitration* (1923), 1 RIAA 369 at 377. [67] *Ibid.*, 382.

[68] HC Debs., vol. 119, col. 348, 6 Aug. 1919, italics supplied.

[69] *Tinoco Arbitration*, n. 66 above, 381.

[70] On US non-recognition policy towards 'the *de facto* government of General Tinoco', see Hackworth, n. 17 above, i, 233–7, Baker, 'Woodrow Wilson's Use of the Non-Recognition Policy in Costa Rica' (1965) 22 *Americas* 3–15; and Murillo-Jimenez, 'Wilson and Tinoco. The United States and the Policy of Non-Recognition in Costa Rica, 1917–1919', Ph.D. thesis (San Diego: University of California, 1978).

[71] Russia became the Russian Socialist Federative Soviet Republic (RSFSR) in Mar. 1918. On 30 Dec. 1922 the RSFSR formally became part of the Union of Soviet Socialist Republics (USSR) which also included the White Russian, the Ukrainian, and the Trans-Caucasian Soviet Socialist Republics.

Russia by *coup d'état* on 25 October/7 November 1917. In 1923 only seventeen States had extended either *de facto* or *de jure* recognition to the Soviet Government.[72] This number rose to twenty-two in August 1926[73] and stood at twenty-eight[74] by 16 November 1933 when the United States accorded recognition.[75] Mr Hackworth, the Legal Adviser to the US State Department, wrote in 1940 with respect to this 'recognition': 'We recognized or, to state it in a different way, realized that a Soviet Government existed long before we extended [political] recognition.'[76] This statement shows that the recognition extended by the United States in 1933, and the same is probably true for the belated recognition of other States, expressed willingness to enter into normal official (diplomatic) relations with the Soviet Government rather than an opinion on its existence as a government. This view is also supported by the fact that the notes exchanged between the Soviet and US Governments on 16 November 1933 do not mention the word 'recognition' but state the mutual decision of the two Governments to establish normal diplomatic relations. In the letter to the President of the All Union Central Executive Committee of the USSR, which initiated the process leading to 'recognition' of the Soviet Government, President Roosevelt wrote on 10 October 1933: 'Since the beginning of my Administration, I have contemplated the desirability of an effort to end the present abnormal relations. . . . It is most regrettable that these great peoples . . . should now be without a practical method of communicating directly with each other.'[77] In this connection it is also of interest to note that proposed Senate

[72] According to the British Government, by May 1923 the following countries had 'extended *de jure* recognition to the Soviet Government: Afghanistan, Esthonia, Finland, Germany, Latvia, Lithuania, Persia, Poland, Turkey (Government of the Grand National Assembly). *De facto* recognition is understood to have been given by the following countries in addition to Great Britain: Austria, Czecho-Slovakia, Denmark, Italy, Norway' (HC Debs., vol. 164, col. 22, 14 May 1923). To this list must be added Hungary and Mongolia. For the former, see Makarov, 'Aufnahme der diplomatischen Beziehungen zwischen Ungarn und der Sowjetunion' (1934) 4 *ZaöRV* 315–19 at 315. For the latter, see Makarov, 'Die Anerkennung der Sowjetregierung durch die Vereinigten Staaten' (1934) 4 *ZaöRV* 1–24, at 7, n. 41.

[73] See the list in Houghton, 'Policy of the United States and Other Nations with Respect to the Recognition of the Russian Soviet Government, 1917–1929' *Int. Conc.* no 247 (1929), 83–108 at 105, n. 99. See also the table in *Int. Conc.* no 217 (1926), 114.

[74] See 'Recognition of Soviet Union (List furnished by [US] Department of State)' (1934) 28 *AJIL* 97–8, and Makarov, 'Anerkennung', n. 72 above, at 4–8. In addition to the countries mentioned in n. 72, these were: Greece, Sweden, China, Denmark, Mexico, France, the Kingdom of the Hejaz and Nejd [Saudi Arabia], Japan, Iceland, Uruguay, Yemen, and Spain. See, generally, Noulens, 'La reconnaissance du gouvernement soviétique de l'URSS', *Dict. Dipl.* (1933), ii, 532–8.

[75] On US 'recognition' of the Soviet Government, see Hackworth, n. 17 above, i, 194–5, 299–305. For the correspondence between the USA and the USSR concerning the 'recognition' of the Soviet Government, see US Department of State, *Establishment of Diplomatic Relations with the Union of Soviet Socialist Republics* (1933).

[76] Department of State, memorandum, 13 Dec. 1940: Whiteman, n. 13 above, ii, 48. For actions implying 'political recognition' Mr Hackworth mentioned the 'exchange of diplomatic and consular officers' and the 'negotiation of a treaty'.

[77] Hackworth, n. 17 above, i, 303.

Concurrent Resolution 7, which was introduced in the Senate on 21 January 1935, stated: 'That it is the sense of the Senate and the House of Representatives of the United States that the *diplomatic recognition* by the Government of the United States of the Union of Soviet Socialist Republics should be withdrawn.'[78] That the prolonged non-recognition of the Soviet Government was only the expression of the unwillingness of the non-recognizing State to enter into normal diplomatic relations with it is also supported by the reasons most commonly given by States for not recognizing the Soviet Government. Non-recognition of the Soviet Government was not based on a lack of effective control, stability, or independence, as becomes clear from the statement of the British Prime Minister, Lloyd George, in the House of Commons on 22 March 1921 that the Soviet Government 'have as complete control over that vast territory as any Government could possibly have under present conditions'.[79] And the US Secretary of State's Office stated on the 'status of the Soviet Government' in *Salimoff* v. *Standard Oil Co.* (1933):

> 2. The Department of State is cognizant of the fact that the Soviet regime is exercising control and power in territory of the former Russian Empire . . . 3. The refusal of the Government of the United States to accord recognition to the Soviet regime is not based on the ground that the regime does not exercise control and authority in territory of the former Russian Empire, but on other facts.[80]

These other fact were, *inter alia*, the unwillingness of the Soviet Government to accept the liabilities of its predecessors[81] and, above all, the fear of propaganda by diplomatic agents aimed at the overthrow of the recognizing government. Thus, US President Wilson wrote in a note on Russian affairs, delivered to the Italian Embassy in Washington on 10 August 1920, that:

[78] Whiteman, n. 13 above, ii, 45, italics added. See further the Annex, 'Illustrative Instances of Recognition in the History of the United States', to the Memorandum on 'Recognition of New States and Governments in Palestine' by Ernest A. Gross, Legal Adviser to the US State Department, dated 11 May 1948 (Cohen (ed.), *The Rise of Israel. A Documentary Record from the Nineteenth Century to 1948* (1987), xxxix, 149–50 at 149).

[79] HC Debs., vol. 139, col. 2506, 22 Mar. 1921.

[80] 262 NY 220 at 224 (CA NY 1933).

[81] M. Millerand, the French Prime Minister and Foreign Minister, speaking in the Chamber of Deputies on 20 July 1920 recalled the fact that it only depended upon the Soviet Government itself to *resume diplomatic relations* with the French Republic. M. Millerand repeated his offer that France would at once change her attitude when the Soviet Government had really behaved like a Government and *recognized the liabilities of its predecessors* (*The Times*, 21 July 1920, 13, italics added). See also US President Coolidge's annual message to Congress on 6 Dec. 1923 in which he stated the reasons for the continued refusal to recognize the Soviet Government: 'Our Government does not propose, however, to enter into relations with another régime which refuses to recognize the sanctity of international obligations' (Hackworth, n. 17 above, i, 302).

it is not possible for the Government of the United States to recognize the present rulers of Russia as a government with which the relations common to friendly Governments can be maintained. . . . Indeed upon numerous occasions responsible spokesmen of this power and its official agencies have declared that it is their understanding that the very existence of Bolshevism in Russia, the maintenance of their own rule, depends, and must continue to depend, upon the occurrence of revolutions in all other great civilized nations, including the United States, which will overthrow and destroy their Governments and set up Bolshevist rule in their stead. They have made it quite plain that they intend to use every means, including, of course, diplomatic agencies, to promote such revolutionary movements in other countries. . . . We cannot *recognize, hold official relations with,* or give friendly reception to the agents of a Government which is determined and bound to conspire against our institutions, whose diplomats will be the agitators of dangerous revolt.[82]

'Such conduct', the Court of Appeals of New York said, 'may lead to governmental refusal to recognize Russia as a country with which the United States may have diplomatic dealings. . . . The Government may be objectionable in a political sense. It is not unrecognizable as a real governmental power'.[83] That prolonged non-recognition in the case of the Soviet Government expressed an unwillingness to enter into normal official (diplomatic) relations with it rather than a denial of governmental status also becomes clear in the case of Switzerland. As one of the last countries to recognize the Soviet Government, it extended 'full recognition' on 10 October 1944 when the Swiss envoy to London handed an Aide-Mémoire to the Russian Embassy there which stated: 'Switzerland has the sincere desire to entertain normal relations based on the rules of international law and customs with all powers. Switzerland of course regrets circumstances which may have interrupted this general and normal intercourse. The Swiss Government and people are desirous of reestablishing normal relations with the USSR.'[84] That, in the opinion of Switzerland, the Soviet Government qualified as a government in international law long before its 'full recognition' in 1944 is evidenced by the Berlin Declaration which had been issued by the two Governments on 16 April 1927 and which started: 'In view of the desire of the Governments of the USSR and of the Swiss Confederation, to end the conflict existing between the two States' (author's translation).[85]

[82] *The Times*, 13 Aug. 1920, 9, italics added. It is interesting to note that President Wilson uses 'recognize' and 'hold official relations with' as synonyms. For a similar explanation given by the Swiss Federal Council on 24 June 1927, see Klarer, n. 18 above, 119.

[83] *Salimoff* v. *Standard Oil Co.*, 262 NY 220 at 227 (CA NY 1933).

[84] DDS XV, no 257; Klarer, n. 18 above, 127–8 at 128. Switzerland regarded the '*de jure* or full recognition' of the Soviet Government always as a question of re-establishment of diplomatic relations and not of governmental status of the Soviet Government. See Klarer, *ibid.*, 104–34; LNOJ Spec. Supp. No 130, 15; and Feldmann, *Die Schweiz und Sowjetrußland* (1944).

[85] Klarer, n. 18 above, 117.

The MPLA Government of Angola. The Popular Movement for the Liberation of Angola (MPLA), one of the three Angolan liberation movements, seized power with Cuban and Soviet backing in Angola on 11 November 1975 when the country became independent of Portugal. The MPLA established the People's Republic of Angola, which on 11 February 1976 became a member of the OAU and on 1 December 1976 a member of the UN. By 1980 the MPLA Government had expressly or tacitly been recognized by all States except the United States and South Africa. After withholding recognition for over seventeen years, the United States on 19 May 1993 finally recognized the (MPLA) Government of the People's Republic of Angola and established diplomatic relations with it.[86] Despite this non-recognition the US Department of State *Dispatch* had recorded, for example, in September 1991 the accession of Angola to the Vienna Convention on Diplomatic Relations 1961, and to the Convention on the Privileges and Immunities of the United Nations 1946, on 9 August 1990.[87] As States can act only through their government and through their government exclusively[88] it seems that 'non-recognition' did not connote that, in the opinion of the United States, the Angolan (MPLA) Government which declared the accession to these treaties did not qualify in international law as the Government of Angola.[89] It rather expressed the United States' unwillingness to enter into normal diplomatic relations with the MPLA Government. This becomes clear in a letter of Alfredo Salvaterra, Alternative Permanent Observer of the Republic of Angola to the OAS, to the *Washington Post*, published on 16 February 1993: 'Finally, as to a fully normalized relationship with the United States, it is the view of my country, as expressed recently in a letter to President Clinton from

[86] See 'US Recognition of Angolan Government', Statement by President Clinton, Washington, DC, 19 May 1993: (1993) 4/21 *DSD* 375. On recognition of the Angolan Government, see also HL Debs., vol. 545, WA, *col.* 71, 13 May 1993. On US–Angolan relations during the years of non-recognition, see Nash (ed.), *Cumulative Digest of United States Practice in International Law 1981–8* (1994), i, 277–99.

[87] (1991) 2/36 *DSD* 677: 'Treaty Actions'. It is also interesting to note in this connection that since Jan. 1992 Angola maintained with the Permanent Observer Mission to the OAS a diplomatic mission in Washington (*WP*, 16 Feb. 1993, Sec. OP/ED, 13). The US was represented in Luanda by a 'Liaison Office' (*WP*, 26 Jan. 1993, Sec. A, 14).

[88] See Bin Cheng, *General Principles of Law as applied by International Courts and Tribunals* (1953), 183–4.

[89] It should be noted that access to US courts, which according to 'a long-standing principle' has ordinarily been denied to unrecognized governments (*Republic of Vietnam* v. *Pfizer*, 556 F.2d 892 at 894 (8th Cir. 1977), and American Law Institute, n. 7 above, §205), in the case of the unrecognized MPLA Government was regarded by the State Department as 'consistent with the foreign policy interests of the United States'. See *Transportes Aereos de Angola* v. *Ronair, Inc.*, 544 F.Supp. 858 at 861 (D. Del. 1982); and *TAAG Linhas Aereas de Angola* v. *Transamerica Airlines* (ND Cal. 1988), reported in Nash, n. 86 above, i, 298–9; and 915 F.2d 1351 (9th Cir. 1990).

President dos Santos, that it is in the interest of both the United States and Angola to have *full diplomatic recognition*.'[90]

Angola is a good illustration that both the meaning and the purpose of non-recognition may change over the years. At the beginning of the Angolan civil war between MPLA and UNITA the communist-oriented MPLA Government was armed by the Soviet Union and had thousands of Cuban troops fighting for it. US non-recognition was initially based on the Cuban and Soviet involvement in the civil war, and may be regarded as an expression of concern about the independence of the MPLA Government and thus about its governmental status. Thus Dr Kissinger, the US Secretary of State, declared in March 1976 that 'there is every prospect of our dealing with the MPLA in Angola once it is clear that they are indeed an African government and not totally beholden of foreign input'.[91] Later, after the withdrawal of the Cuban military presence, the United States withheld recognition, in the sense of formal diplomatic relations, in order to achieve national reconciliation between MPLA and UNITA.[92] Thus, President Clinton declared on the occasion of US recognition of the MPLA Government on 19 May 1993 that he had 'tried to use the possibility of U.S. recognition as a leverage toward promoting an end to the civil war and hostilities and, hopefully, the participation of all relevant political groups in the Government of Angola'.[93]

While non-recognition may only express the recognizing governments's unwillingness to enter into normal official (diplomatic) relations, recognition may only express the recognizing government's willingness to enter into such relations. Recognition of a 'government', while establishing a presumption that a government exists, need not necessarily mean that, in the opinion of the recognizing government, the recognized 'government' is,

[90] *WP*, 16 Feb. 1993, Sec. OP/ED, 13 (italics added). See also the consideration of 101 H. Con. Res. 203 expressing the sense of Congress that the USA should normalize relations with Angola by the Foreign Affairs Committee of the House of Representatives (Congress, House of Representatives, Committee on Foreign Affairs, *Review of US Policy Toward Political Negotiations in Angola* (1989), 110–13. See also the joint resolution adopted by the US Congress on 25 Mar. 1993 calling upon the administration immediately to grant 'diplomatic recognition' to the MPLA Government of Angola (*Guardian*, 26 Mar. 1993, 15).

[91] *West Africa*, no. 3064 (22 Mar. 1976), 395. The withdrawal of the Cuban troops was made a public precondition for US recognition of the MPLA Government (*ibid.*, no 3078 (28 June 1976), 934). See also Nash, n. 86 above, i, 277. On the early stages of US non-recognition of the MPLA Government, see also Galloway, *Recognizing Foreign Governments: The Practice of the United States* (1978), 121–3.

[92] (1989) 89/2153 *DSB* 31–2 at 31; (1991) 2/52 *DSD* 912–22 at 919. On US non-recognition, i.e. unwillingness to maintain diplomatic relations, see also [1990] AFPCD no 563, 769; and Nash, n. 86 above, i, 277–99.

[93] (1993) 4/21 *DSD* 375. On the reasons for US recognition and non-recognition over the years, see also *NY Times*, 19 May 1993, Sec. A, 1; *ibid.*, 20 May 1993, Sec. A, 9; *WP*, 20 May 1993, Sec. A, 28.

in fact, a government in the sense of international law. Being no 'registered trade mark', the term 'government', used in 'recognition' statements, need not denote a government in the sense of international law. It may just refer to the (self-given) name of an individual or a body of individuals.[94] Thus recognition of the 'Government of the Republic of . . .' may mean only that the recognizing government is ready to enter into official relations with an individual or a group of individuals calling itself the 'Government of the Republic of . . .'. For example, on 7 October 1960 the Soviet Prime Minister, Mr Khrushchev, stated at a press conference in New York:

> It may be taken that our meetings and conversations with the representatives of the Algerian Provisional Government indicate[95] *de facto* recognition of that Government. I would like to add it is not we alone who give *de facto* recognition to the Algerian Provisional Government, but the whole world beginning with the President of the French Republic, General de Gaulle, because he has begun negotiations with that Government.[96]

In October 1960, however, the Provisional Government of the Algerian Republic (GPRA) did not yet, in the opinion of the Soviet Government, qualify as the government of the State of Algeria.[97] This becomes clear from correspondence between the Soviet Government and the GPRA[98] and the subsequent Soviet *de jure* recognition of the GPRA on 19 March 1962, connected with the offer to establish formal diplomatic relations.[99]

The distinction between recognition '*of*' and recognition '*as*' something seems to be an indication for the recognizing State's intention regarding the

[94] Compare the judgment of Sir John Donaldson MR in *Gur Corporation* v. *Trust Bank of Africa Ltd.* (1986), [1987] 1 QB 599 at 617, which concerned the standing of the ('unrecognized') 'Government of the Republic of Ciskei' in the English courts: 'The mere fact that a party to litigation chooses to describe itself as "The Government of the Republic of . . ." does not of itself create any problem of *locus standi*. This may be a trade name, a firm name, the title of an incorporated or unincorporated association, a description of what is known in the travel industry as an "affinity group" or simply an example of what I venture to call the "Pimlico Syndrome", after the classic film "Passport to Pimlico".'

[95] Other sources read: 'constitute' or 'can be regarded as signifying' instead of 'indicate'.

[96] Bedjaoui, *Law and the Algerian Revolution* (1961), 139 and 114. See also *The Times*, 8 Oct. 1960, 5; and [1958–60] XIII FRUS 706. Mr Khrushchev added: 'The Soviet people has always shown its sympathy for colonial peoples who are struggling for their independence. How can we exclude the people of Algeria? We whole-heartedly salute their struggle and will always give them the maximum aid which will help them to win their freedom' ([1960] *Keesing's* 17832A).

[97] On the GPRA, see App. II. For the basic document of the Algerian Republic, the *Institutions provisoires de L'Etat algérien*, see *Die Algerische Revolution* (1963), 87–90. On the GPRA's legal status, see Charpentier, 'La reconnaissance du GPRA' (1959) 5 *AFDI* 799–816 at 801–10; Flory, 'Algérie et le droit international' (1959) 5 *AFDI* 817–44 at 835–9; Oppermann, 'Die Endphase des Algerienkonfliktes 1959–1962' (1963) 23 *ZaöRV* 1–20 at 2; and Belkherroubi, *La naissance et la reconnaissance de la République algérienne* (1972), 85–98.

[98] See e.g. the telegram of Mr Khrushchev to the 'Prime Minister' of the GPRA, dated 1 Nov. 1961: [1961–2] *Africa Diary* 233.

[99] *Ibid.*, 473; [1962] *Keesing's* 18808.

meaning of recognition. It seems that if a State speaks of the recognition of an authority '*as something*' (i.e. 'as the government of a particular State') it intends to say that, in its opinion, the authority *so* recognized qualifies for that particular status. On the other hand, if a State speaks of the recognition '*of something*' (i.e. a group of exiles calling themselves the government of a particular State) it seems that it intends, especially if the 'something' recognized is not a *de facto* government, to express only its willingness to enter into official relations with the 'something'. The same is true if a State recognizes only the 'existence' or 'constitution'[100] of a government rather than the government *as such*. This view is supported by the fact that whenever the legal status of an authority is in question recognition statements speak of the recognition of the authority 'as something'. This may sometimes lead to strange statements such as 'We recognize the "Government of X" as the Government of X'. For example, the so-called 'Foreign Offices certificates' supplied to the British courts, when the British Government still formally accorded recognition, always spoke of the recognition of the authority in question 'as something'. Under the new British policy of 'recognizing States, not governments', the Foreign Office certificate may state whether the British Government has dealings with the authority in question 'as something'. Thus in *Re an Application by Ernst Jaakson and Aarand Roos* (1990) the Foreign Office stated that 'Her Majesty's Government do not have dealings with Mr Ernst Jaakson or Dr Aarand Roos as the representatives of Estonia or the Government thereof.'[101] However, it must be emphasized that these are only general guidelines on the meaning of 'recognition' which do not absolve people from investigating the meaning in which the term is used in each individual case. In exceptional cases this investigation may even reveal that 'recognition' bears neither of the these two meanings and is simply understood to express moral support. The Omani recognition of the 'State of Palestine' is a good example for this. In a statement issued on 12 December 1988 the Omani Foreign Ministry said that Oman had decided to grant 'official and legal recognition to the Palestinian State'.[102] Referring to the timing and nature of the recognition Sultan Quabus, the Omani ruler, explained in an interview with the Kuwaiti newspaper AL-SIYASA, published on 17 December 1988, that:

> the desire to establish the state of Palestine has been declared, but the state itself has not yet been established. Hence, what has actually taken place was the decision to establish this state. . . . The Palestinian brothers have explained to us the nature

[100] The French National Commissariat of Foreign Affairs announced on 31 Oct. 1941 that the Belgian, Czechoslovak, and Polish Governments in London had recognized the constitution of the French National Committee ([1941] *Keesing's* 4855C).

[101] 85 ILR 53 at 57. See also the Foreign Office certificate in this case: UKMIL 1990 (1990) 61 *BYBIL* 499–502.

[102] BBC, *SWB*, 3rd series, ME/0334/i, 14 Dec. 1988.

of recognition which has moral dimensions, so we immediately announced our recognition.

In January 1989 the Omani Minister of State for Foreign Affairs, Yusuf Ibn Alawi Ibn Abdallah, declared with respect to the issue of opening a PLO office in Muscat that Oman preferred to maintain relations with States that conducted their affairs in an orderly manner, rather than with organizations that tended to be irresponsible. While noting that there were Palestinian elements whose interest was incompatible with that of Oman, Alawi further emphasized that Oman would establish links with the Palestinian state when it was established.[103] The value of newspaper reports that, for example, the PLO (or the State of Palestine) 'won the recognition of 117 nations'[104] must thus be assessed in the light of the above example.[105] The examples given above show that the meaning of the term 'recognition' depends entirely on the intention of the State using it within the factual and legal context of a particular case.[106] Recognition statements alone are seldom a safe guide to the intention of the recognizing State. It will rather have to be ascertained from all the available evidence: diplomatic correspondence, communiqués, statements in international organizations, declarations in national assemblies, interviews by government officials, and so forth. Finally, one should beware of the assumption that a certain State always uses the term 'recognition' in the same meaning, something to be proved. The British Government in particular has liked to portray its recognition policy since 1924 as consistent and principled. Prior to 1924 the British Government decided on a case-by-case basis whether it was in its political interest to enter into official (diplomatic) relations with a certain government.[107] From 1924 onwards the view seems to have been that it is generally in the British interest to have official (but not necessarily diplomatic) relations with all new régimes that fulfil the criteria for government status.[108] The prolonged non-recognition, together with the absence of diplomatic

[103] (1988) 12 *MECS* 452.

[104] *IHT*, 2 June 1992, 1.

[105] For recognition 'as a gesture of solidarity', see the Canadian memorandum on the recognition of the Czechoslovak National Committee, dated 31 May 1940: VII DCER 26–7. On the idea, expressed as early as 1866, of recognition as 'a mere demonstration of moral support', see Wheaton, *Elements of International Law* (8th edn., 1866), 29, n. 15.

[106] While all textbook writers mention that implied recognition is a matter of intention, it seems that only Prof. Brownlie has pointed out that the meaning of the term 'recognition' itself depends on the intention of the government using it. See Brownlie, 'Recognition in Theory and Practice' (1982) 53 *BYBIL* 197–211 at 199. See also, more general, Schwarzenberger and Brown, n. 15 above, 55.

[107] On the distinction between British pre- and post-1924 practice see Whiteman, n. 13 above, ii, 110–12.

[108] Cf. the statement made by Foreign Secretary Morrison in 1951: 'recognition [of a government] should be accorded when the conditions by international law are, in fact, fulfilled and that recognition should not be given when these conditions are not fulfilled' (HC Debs., vol. 485, col. 2411, 21 Mar. 1951).

relations, with the Soviet Government and its adverse effects may have served as a 'catalyst' for this change in British recognition policy. It must however be noted that this policy of 'universality of relations' has not always been strictly adhered to as the initial non-recognition of the Farrell Government in Argentina and the Villaroel Government in Bolivia during the Second World War and the prolonged non-recognition of the Republican Government in the Yemen (27 September 1962–29 July 1970) show.[109]

[109] For a detailed examination of the British recognition policy, see Pattison, 'The International Law of Recognition in Contemporary British Foreign Policy', Ph.D. thesis (University of Virginia, 1981).

2

Recognition and its Variants

1 VARIANTS AND THEIR MEANINGS

The investigation into the meaning of the term 'recognition', as used in a certain case, has not been facilitated by the introduction of several variations of the term. A distinction between '*de facto* recognition', 'diplomatic recognition', and '*de jure* recognition' may be traced back to the secession of the Spanish provinces in South America in the first quarter of the nineteenth century.[1] A Memorandum, dated 8 August 1822, drawn up by the British Foreign Secretary Lord Castlereagh, reads with respect to the recognition of the 'actual governments of South America':

> it is material to distinguish the following descriptions of Recognition:
>
> 1st. The Recognition, *de facto*, which now substantially subsists.
>
> 2ndly. The more formal recognition by diplomatick agents.
>
> 3rdly. The Recognition, *de jure*, which professes to decide upon the title and thereby to create a certain impediment to the assertion of the rights of the former occupant.[2]

[1] According to Prof. Larnaude the term '*de facto* government' was first used, although not in connection with recognition, by Vicomte de Chateaubriand in an article published on 2 July 1819: 'The Revolutionaries, the Partisans of the National Convention [1792–5], the supporters of the *de facto* government; would they claim that regicide is not a crime?' (Chateaubriand, *Œuvres complètes* (1862), vii, 487 (author's translation)). Vicomte de Chateaubriand used the term with respect to domestic affairs in order to describe 'the usurper' in contrast to 'the legitimate prince' or 'legitimate authority' (cf. Chateaubriand, *De Buonaparte, des Bourbons, et de la nécessité de se rallier à nos princes légitimes, pour le bonheur de la France et celui de l'Europe* (1814), 40, 44). In the same sense the term Head of State 'de Facto tho' not de Jure' had already been used by Sir James Marriott in a Legal Opinion for the British Government, dated 30 Nov. 1764. See McNair, *The Law of Treaties* (1961), 671. The notion of *de facto* and *de jure* government in municipal law may be traced back to the Wars of the Roses in England. In 1495 Parliament enacted the so-called *Rex de facto* statute (11 Henry VII, cap. 1) which provides that no one shall be convicted of high treason who serves a usurper who is in effective occupation of the throne or of any part of the country. On this statute, which is still the law, see '*De facto* and *De Jure* Governments' (1916–17) 61 *Sol. Jo.* 739–40; and '*Rex de facto* and *Rex de jure*' (1919–20) 64 *Sol. Jo.* 631. On *de facto* governments in general see Larnaude, 'Les gouvernements de fait' (1921) 28 *RGDIP* 457–503; Spiropoulos, *Die de facto-Regierung im Völkerrecht* (1926); Frowein, *Das de facto-Regime im Völkerrecht* (1968).

[2] The Memorandum formed part of the Instructions given by the Earl of Bathurst, the British Acting Foreign Secretary, to the Duke of Wellington, the British Plenipotentiary at the Congress of Verona, dated 14 Sept. 1822: Webster (ed.), *Britain and the Independence of Latin America 1812–1830. Select Documents from the Foreign Office Archives* (1938), ii, 71–2 at 72. On the Memorandum generally, see Temperley, *The Foreign Policy of Canning 1822–1827* (1925), 53–5.

The *de facto* recognition which, according to the Memorandum, substantially subsisted had been effected by the statute 3 Geo. IV, c. 43, passed on 24 June 1822, section 3, of which provided:

> That from and after the passing of this Act, any Goods and Merchandise being the Growth, Production or Manufacture of any Country or Place in *America* or the *West Indies*, being or having been a Part of the Dominions of the King of Spain . . . may be imported into the United Kingdom . . . in ships or Vessels of the Built of the Country or Place of which such Goods or Merchandise may be the Growth, Production or Manufacture.

This becomes clear from a speech of Lord Castlereagh's successor as Foreign Secretary, George Canning, who in the debate on the London Petition for the Recognition of the Independence of South America in June 1824 stated that:

> in the year 1822, the extent of the commerce then existing between this country and the colonies of Spain, led to another *de facto* recognition of their separate political existence: we recognized their commercial flag, which was admitted to the same advantages as the flags of independent states in amity with England.[3]

The 'more formal recognition by diplomatick agent' is to be understood as 'diplomatic recognition'. This is evidenced by the following statements. Thus, Lord Castlereagh himself asked: 'How long should the *de facto* system of Recognition be maintained to the exclusion of the diplomatick, and when should the latter be adopted?',[4] and Canning wrote in a dispatch to Bosanquet at Madrid, dated 31 December 1824, that 'the effect of such [Commercial] Treaties, when severally ratified by His Majesty, will be a Diplomatick Recognition of the *"De facto"* Governments of those three Countries [Mexico, Columbia, and Buenos Aires]'.[5] Since Lord Castlereagh's days, 'official recognition', 'formal recognition', 'political recognition', 'full recognition', and 'full diplomatic recognition' have been added to the list of variants. Surprisingly enough, however, only '*de*

[3] HC Debs., vol. 11, col. 1395, 15 June 1824; Canning, *The Speeches of the Right Honourable George Canning With a Memoir of His Life* (1828), v, 291–304 at 296. See also Smith (ed.), *Great Britain and the Law of Nations* (1932), i, 122. On the recognition of the governments in Latin America in general, see Gibbs, *Recognition: A Chapter from the History of the North American & South American States* (1863), 18–46; Paxson, *The Independence of the South-American Republics* (1970); Robertson, *France and Latin-American Independence* (1939); and Temperley, n. 2 above, 131–56, 496–505.

[4] Webster, n. 2 above, ii, 72.

[5] Smith, n. 3 above, 149–51 at 150. Compare also Bourquin, *Histoire de la Sainte Alliance* (1954), 402, n. 1; and Reibstein, *Völkerrecht* (1963), ii, 527 who, with regard to Lord Castlereagh's second description, speak of *reconnaissance diplomatique* and *diplomatische Anerkennung*, respectively. For some early examples of the use of 'diplomatic recognition' see Fontes B.I.I.1, no 541, 172; and the despatch of the German Chancellor Bismarck to Minister of State von Roon, dated 5 Sept. 1867, in which he insisted on the necessity of avoiding any neglect of 'international courtesy which is not dependent upon the diplomatic recognition of the respective government' (*ibid.*, no 553, at 176, translation provided).

facto recognition'[6] and '*de jure* recognition', terms nowadays rarely used by States in formal declarations of recognition, are dealt with in textbooks and relevant articles.[7] The concentration on this pair of opposites, it seems, has brought about much confusion of thought in modern literature.

Some writers, assuming that these terms are 'probably not capable of literal analysis',[8] have concentrated on the terms' (allegedly) distinctive features. Thus it has been stated that *de facto* recognition is provisional, conditional, implied, incomplete, and/or (more easily) revokable recognition, while *de jure* recognition is final, unconditional, express, full, and/or irrevocable recognition.[9] Several objections may be raised against this argument. First of all it amounts to a *petitio principii* in so far as writers have argued that '*de facto* recognition is the provisional, revokable recognition of a State or government' as 'the term *de facto* recognition is characterized by the features of provisionality, revocability, and conditionality'.[10] While these attributes might characterize *de facto* recognition in a particular case, they leave open the question of the actual meaning of the term. Furthermore, the question of what is meant, for example, by limited recognition or why *de facto* recognition is limited can be answered only on the basis of the meaning of the term '*de facto* recognition'. One may also ask whether the adjectives '*de facto*' and '*de jure*' stand for all or only for one and, if so, for which of the listed attributes. Apart from these theoretical objections, practice shows that States have made express declarations of *de facto* recognition,[11]

[6] '*De facto* recognition' must not be confused with 'factual recognition' (*faktičeskoe priznanie*), a term predominantly used in the writings of socialist international lawyers. On the meaning of 'factual recognition' (a term not used by States), see Frenzke, 'De-jure-, De-facto- und faktische Anerkennung in der Völkerrechtslehre der DDR und der UdSSR' (1970) 14 *ROW* 181–90; Loudwin, *Die konkludente Anerkennung im Völkerrecht* (1983), 68–70, 184–5.

[7] For notable exceptions, see Brownlie, *Principles of Public International Law* (4th edn., 1990), 91 ('full diplomatic recognition', 'formal recognition'); Berber, *Lehrbuch des Völkerrechts* (1975), i, 234 ('volle Anerkennung'); Mössner, *Einführung in das Völkerrecht* (1977), 64 ('diplomatische Anerkennung').

[8] Jennings and Watts (eds.), *Oppenheim's International Law* (9th edn., 1992), i, 155.

[9] For a selection of the older literature on the distinctive features of *de facto* and *de jure* recognition, see Lauterpacht, *Recognition in International Law* (1947), 329, n. 2. For more recent expositions of the distinctive features, see Nguyen Quoc, Daillier, and Pellet, *Droit international public* (3rd edn., 1987), 505–6 and 499–500; Dahm, Delbrück, and Wolfrum, *Völkerrecht* (2nd edn., 1989), I/1, 209–13. For a critical discussion of these distinctive features, see Chen, *The International Law of Recognition* (1951), 277–90; Verhoeven, *La reconnaissance internationale dans la pratique contemporaine* (1975), 624–48.

[10] Schlüter, *De-facto Anerkennung im Völkerrecht* (1936), 4.

[11] For an example of express '*de facto* recognition' see the message of 24 Dec. 1948 from the Canadian Secretary of State for External Affairs, Mr Pearson, to Mr Mohame Shertale, Foreign Secretary of the Provisional Government of Israel: 'I have the honour to inform you, on behalf of the Government of Canada, that Canada recognizes *de facto* the authority of the Provisional Government of Israel' (Binavince, 'Canadian Perspectives in Matters of Recognition' in Macdonald, Morris, and Johnston (eds.), *Canadian Perspectives on International Law and Organization* (1974), 153–83 at 162). In this connection it may be noted that it was at the request of Prof. Brierly that the Institut de Droit International in 1936 added to the original text of Art. 14 that: '*De facto* recognition of a new government finds its expression: 1. either in

have granted *de jure* recognition on certain conditions[12] and have withdrawn *de jure* recognition.[13] The replacing of one adjective with another thus does not contribute much to the clarification of the meaning of the terms '*de facto*' and '*de jure* recognition'.

Other writers have completely sidestepped the question of the meaning of the terms by arguing that, in law, *de facto* recognition does not seem to be distinguishable from *de jure* recognition. According to these writers the distinction lies merely in the political sphere.[14] This view was also taken by

an *express declaration*' (Institute of International Law, 'La reconnaissance des nouveaux Etats et des nouveaux gouvernements' (1936) 39–II, *Annuaire* 244, italics added, translation supplied).

[12] Great Britain and other Allied Powers in 1922 made *de jure* recognition of Lithuania conditional on the Lithuanian Government accepting the stipulations of the Treaty of Versailles regarding the freedom of navigation on the Niemen. On 26 Aug. 1922 Lord Hardinge sent the following draft resolution to Lord Curzon: 'It is decided by the conference of ambassadors to inform the Lithuanian government in reply to their note of the 4th August, that the French, British, Italian and Japanese governments take note of the fact that the above letter does not constitute a full acceptation of the conditions attached by these governments to their recognition *de jure* of the Lithuanian government and they consider therefore that the above recognition cannot be considered effective' (DBFP, 1st ser., XXIII, no 447, at 554). See also *ibid.*, no 425, at 521, n. 2; *ibid.*, no 427, at 523–4; *ibid.*, no 500, at 617. On German conditional *de jure* recognition of Latvia, see League of Nations, *Records of the First Assembly. Plenary Meetings* (1920), 636–7 at 637. For further examples, see HC Debs., vol. 427, WA, *col.* 53, 9 Oct. 1946; II *DPSR* 827.

[13] See, e.g., *Azazh Kebbeda Tesema* v. *Italian Government* (1940) 7 PLR 597–9 at 599, in which the High Commissioner for Palestine informed Trusted CJ: 'I have been acquainted by the Secretary of State for the Colonies that the *de jure* recognition by His Majesty's Government of the Italian conquest of Ethiopia has been withdrawn.' On 13 Aug. 1974 the Australian Foreign Affairs Minister, Senator Willesee, announced that in July the Australian Government had decided to accord *de jure* recognition of the incorporation of the Baltic States into the Soviet Union. (Suter, 'The Australian Government's Policy of Recognition and Diplomatic Relations' (1975) 47/3 *Aust. Quart.* 67–79 at 73). Following the election of a new Government on 4 Dec. 1975, the new Government decided to withdraw *de jure* recognition of the incorporation of the Baltic States into the Soviet Union. ((1983) 8 *AYBIL* 278). On Egypt's withdrawal of recognition from President Kyprianou as President of Cyprus on 22 Feb. 1978, see *The Times*, 23 Feb. 1978, 1; and *SZ*, 23 Feb. 1978, 1, 2. On the withdrawal of recognition by Tunisia and Jordan from the Sallal Government in Yemen on 11 and 18 Feb. 1967, respectively, see [1967] *Keesing's* 21894. In both cases the initial recognition had been *de jure* and not *de facto*. On the withdrawal of recognition from the North Korean Government in Nov. 1983 by Burma, see [1983] *Keesing's* 32567. On this last case, see also Chang, 'International Law in a Divided World: Recent Korean Experiences' in Böckstiegel, Folz, Mössner, and Zemanek (eds.), *Völkerrecht, Recht der Internationalen Organisationen, Weltwirtschaftsrecht* (1988), 509–25 at 511–14. In the cases of Cyprus, Yemen, and North Korea de-recognition followed the severance of diplomatic relations and was regarded as a separate additional act.

[14] See e.g. Anzilotti, *Lehrbuch des Völkerrechts* (3rd edn., 1929), 127; Briggs, 'De Facto and De Jure Recognition: The Arantzazu Mendi' (1939) 33 *AJIL* 689–99 at 690; McNair, 'Municipal Effects of Belligerent Occupation' (1941) 57 *LQR* 33–73 at 66; Hütten, 'Zur Frage der Anerkennung von Staaten und Regierungen im modernen Völkerrecht' (1951) 3 *SRuSZ* 6–8 at 7; Chen, n. 9 above, 288–9; Patel, *Recognition in the Law of Nations* (1959), 53; Blix, 'Contemporary Aspects of Recognition' (1970-II) 130 *RdC* 587–704 at 603; Heydte, 'Einige Aspekte der Anerkennung im Völkerrecht' in Marcic, Mosler, Suy, and Zemanek (eds.), *Internationale Festschrift für Alfred Verdross zum 80. Geburtstag* (1971), 129–51 at 140; Loudwin, n. 6 above, 34. With qualifications see also Brownlie, n. 7 above, 94.

General Romulo, the representative of the Philippines in the Security Council, who stated on 15 August 1947 that 'while publicists may quibble about the difference in essence between *de jure* and *de facto* recognition it seems settled that as far as legal effects are concerned, there is no appreciable difference between the two modes of recognition, at least while the *de facto* recognition subsists.'[15] One might wonder why, in that case, the Security Council debated the question on several occasions in August 1947. Indeed, recognition, and especially the distinction between *de facto* and *de jure* recognition, has given rise to debates in international organizations on several occasions. One may recall in this connection Lord Halifax's speech in the Council of the League of Nations on 12 May 1938 that 'His Majesty's Government has no desire to embark on a discussion of legal points, such as the distinction between *de facto* and *de jure* recognition, and what action in a particular case can be held to amount to one or the other'.[16]

It is suggested that, like 'recognition', these terms can be given meaning by establishing the intention of the authority using them within the factual and legal context of each individual case.[17] The meaning of *de facto* and *de jure* recognition as well as of the other variants is therefore to be determined by an analysis of the cases in which these terms have actually been employed by States. Such an analysis must encompass the *de jure* and *de facto* recognition of both States and governments. This is necessary as States, especially when they recognize the governments of newly established States, often do not distinguish between the institutions of government and State. The following examples may illustrate this:

> (i) *Latvia*. The official record of the session of the Swiss Federal Council on 28 January 1921 reads as follows: 'The Government of Latvia has desired for some time to be recognized *de facto* by Switzerland. . . . It is decided: . . . to recognize Latvia *de facto*.'[18]
>
> (ii) *Indonesia*. On 31 March 1947 the British Prime Minister, Mr Attlee, declared: 'His Majesty's Government will extend to the Indonesian Republic the *de facto* recognition accorded by the Netherlands under Article I of the Agreement [of Linggadjati].'[19] Article 1 of the Linggadjati Agreement of 25 March 1947 however reads: 'The Nether-

[15] SCOR, 2nd Year, No 77, 185th Meeting, 15 Aug. 1947, 2021–2.

[16] [1938] LNOJ 334.

[17] Cf. Brownlie, 'Recognition in Theory and Practice' (1982) 53 *BYBIL* 197–211 at 207. See also the comment of the US Department of State that 'intent is an important factor in the question of *de facto* recognition' ([1950] IV FRUS 942–4 at 943).

[18] Guggenheim, *Répertoire suisse de droit international public* (1975), i, 439, 441 (translation supplied). No distinction was made in 1922 between British *de jure* recognition of Lithuania and the Lithuanian Government. See DBFP, 1st ser., XXIII, no 447, at 554 and no 425, at 521. The same was true in the case of Georgia and the Georgian Government: *ibid.*, XII, no 652, at 664.

[19] HC Debs., vol. 435, col. 1657, 31 Mar. 1947.

lands Government recognizes the Government of the Republic of Indonesia as exercising *de facto* authority over Java, Madura, and Sumatra.'[20]

(iii) *Israel.* On 27 April 1950 the Minister of State, Mr Kenneth Younger, announced in the House of Commons: 'His Majesty's Government have also decided to accord *de jure* recognition to the State of Israel'.[21] However, the King's Speech of 26 October 1950 said: 'My Government have taken two important steps towards peace and stability in the Middle East. In April they granted *de jure* recognition to the Government of Israel'.[22]

2 EARLY USAGE OF *DE FACTO*, DIPLOMATIC, AND *DE JURE* RECOGNITION: THE RECOGNITION OF THE NEW STATES IN AMERICA

(1) Original Meanings of the Variants

A convenient starting point for this analysis may be Lord Castlereagh's threefold division in 1822 into *de facto*, diplomatic, and *de jure* recognition which, according to Professor Bourquin 'has played an important role in the formation of the theory of recognition' (author's translation).[23] According to Lord Castlereagh and his immediate successor as Foreign Secretary, George Canning, the first two descriptions of recognition, *de facto* and diplomatic, concerned the practical question of 'the mode of our relations' with the Spanish Provinces in South America, while the last description of recognition, *de jure*, concerned the question of 'title'[24] or 'right'.[25] By title

[20] [1946] *Keesing's* 8272A.

[21] HC Debs., vol. 474, cols. 1138–9, 27 Apr. 1950.

[22] HL Debs., vol. 168, col. 1418, 26 Oct. 1950.

[23] Bourquin, n. 5 above, 402, n. 1. See also the oral argument of M. Basdevant, the representative of France, in the public hearing on 4 Aug. 1931 in *Customs Régime between Germany and Austria* (1931): 'The case [of the recognition of the independence of the South American Republics] is indeed very important, because it has determined the direction of modern international law as far as recognition of States is concerned' (PCIJ, Ser. C, No 53, 570 (author's translation)).

[24] Webster, n. 2 above, 71–2 at 72.

[25] In a dispatch to the Spanish Minister in London, Chevalier de Los Rios, Mr Canning wrote on 25 Mar. 1825: 'we admit that no question of right is decided by our recognition of the New States of America' (Smith, n. 3 above, 162–70 at 169). See also the notes of a Foreign Office Official [probably Lord Francis Conyngham] on a letter received from the Spanish Foreign Minister, dated 21 Jan. 1825, containing a formal protest against the British decision to recognize the governments *de facto* established in Spanish America: 'We do not now judge the question of right. This remains were it was placed . . . by the instructions to the Duke of Wellington at Verona [i.e. with the mother country].' (Smith, n. 3 above, at 161). For the instructions to the Duke of Wellington, see Webster, n. 2 above, 71–2.

or right Mr Canning and his contemporaries understood the title or right of sovereignty. While reference was also sometimes made to 'independence' or 'independence and sovereignty', it is submitted that it is at least imprecise to use sovereignty as a synonym for independence[26] as sovereignty denotes a legal right or status while independence denotes a factual situation. A sovereign State may (temporarily) lose its factual independence while retaining its sovereignty as, for example, the Baltic States during their illegal incorporation into the Soviet Union from 1940 to 1991. That sovereignty is a legal right distinct from independence also becomes clear from the fact that it is transferable, a notion not applicable to independence.[27] It should also be noted that Vietnam, Laos, and Cambodia acquired formal sovereignty long before they achieved factual independence.[28] That title refers to sovereignty rather than to independence becomes clear in a statement of Sir James Mackintosh in the House of Commons on 15 June 1824. Referring to *de jure* recognition, he said:

> the true and legitimate sense of the word 'Recognition' as a technical term of international law, is that in which it denotes the explicit acknowledgement of the independence of a country by a state which formerly exercised sovereignty over it. . . . Such recognitions are renunciations of sovereignty. They are a surrender of the power or of the claim to govern. They are of the utmost importance, as quieting possession and extinguishing a foreign pretension to authority: they free a nation from the evils of a disputed sovereignty.[29]

The view that recognition, *de jure*, professes to decide upon a State's or ruler's (right of) sovereignty is also reflected in the diplomatic correspond-

[26] But, for the synonymous use of sovereignty and independence see, e.g., Oppenheim, *International Law. A Treatise* (8th edn., 1955), i, 118–19, 286; Verdross and Simma, *Universelles Völkerrecht* (3rd edn., 1984), 29–30; Brownlie, n. 7 above, 78. See also the award of Max Huber in the *Island of Palmas Arbitration* (1928), 2 RIAA 829 at 838, and the Separate Opinion of Judge Anzilotti in *Customs Régime between Germany and Austria* (1931), PCIJ, Ser. A/B, No 41 at 57).

[27] For example, in the Peace Treaties after the First World War Germany and Bulgaria renounced their sovereignty over Memel and Western Thrace, respectively, in favour of the Allied and Associated Powers.

[28] By ratifying the treaties which it had concluded with Viet Nam (8 Mar. 1949), Laos (19 July 1949) and Cambodia (8 Nov. 1949) France on 2 Feb. 1950 recognized the sovereignty and independence of these States. However, under these treaties France was to continue to exercise most of their sovereign rights, the exercise of which was only gradually to be transferred to the governments of these States. This transfer was completed only on 29 Dec. 1954. For the text of the treaties, see 155 BFSP 158, 405, 472; Kiss, *Répertoire de la Pratique française en matière de droit international public* (1965), iii, nos 1, 51, 375. See also Lacharrière, 'Le changement du statut de la Cochinchine', *RJPUF* (April–June 1949), 146–73.

[29] HC Debs., vol. 11, col. 1347, 15 June 1824. For the endorsement of Sir James' opinion by Foreign Secretary Canning, see *ibid.*, col. 1397. See also Mr Canning's Notes on a Despatch from M. de Chateaubriand to the Prince de Polignac [French Ambassador at London], 26 Jan. 1824, printed in Temperley, n. 2 above, 543–8.

ence,[30] the legal opinions,[31] and the writings of international lawyers of that time.[32] The question then is what is to be understood by sovereignty in this context. Some of the English cases concerning the recognition of the new States in America may give an answer. For the purpose of an examination of these cases it should be recalled that the terms 'sovereignty' and 'dominion' may and have been used interchangeably.[33] In 1804 the native inhabitants of St Domingo rose against the French colonial power and established an Empire in parts of the island. In 1807 Orders in Council were published to the effect that: 'British vessels are permitted to go to such parts and places in the island of St Domingo as are not or shall not be under the dominion and in the actual possession of His Majesty's enemies [the Governments of France and Spain]'. In his judgment in *The 'Manilla'* (1808) Sir William Scott (later Lord Stowell) said: 'The words "*dominion and actual possession*" must mean something more than the mere fact of possession. What is the legal meaning of *dominion*? Its legal meaning implies rightful possession and authority: . . . as applied to public possession it is the right of legal authority.'[34] In *Yrissari* v. *Clement* (1826), Best CJ stated that for communities to be considered sovereign states it must be shown *inter alia* that they are 'associations . . . who acknowledge no other authority but that of their own government'.[35] Sovereignty, used in this context, may thus be

[30] The French Foreign Minister, M. Talleyrand, wrote in his instructions for the royal ambassadors to the Congress of Vienna in 1815: 'that any title of sovereignty, and consequently the right which it supposes, is only in existence for the other States as far as they have recongized it.' (Talleyrand, *Mémoires* (1891), ii, 214–54 at 218 author's translation). In a despatch, dated 6 July 1825, Prince Esterházy, the Austrian Ambassador to London, wrote to Prince Metternich, the Austrian Chancellor and Foreign Minister. 'the establishment of [British] consuls [in Mexico] is not a political act, they are not of a diplomatic character—they represent no English sovereignty, they attest no acknowledgement of the Mexican sovereignty' (Temperley, n. 2 above, 502–3). See also the message of the Acting President of Colombia to the Congress of that State on 2 Jan. 1826: 'the French Government . . . will finally recognize our sovereignty in imitation of other great powers' (Robertson, n. 3 above, 350).

[31] On 22 Feb. 1823 Sir Christopher Robinson, the King's Advocate, wrote to Secretary of State Canning concerning the wording of the commissions for the commercial Agents or Consuls to be sent to new States in Latin America: 'I have omitted any reference to . . . terms which may seem to imply in some degree the relations of recognized Sovereignty' (McNair, *International Law Opinions* (1956), i, 133).

[32] See e.g. Klüber, *Droit des gens moderne de l'Europe* (1819), i, §§ 23, 45; Wildman, *Institutes of International Law* (1849), i, 57; Wheaton, *Elements of International Law* (8th edn., 1866), §§ 21, 23 and especially § 26: 'where a revolted province or colony has declared and shown its ability to maintain independence, the recognition of its sovereignty by other foreign States is a question of policy and prudence only', and Mr Dana's note No 16.

[33] Compare 'dominion' in *The Oxford English Dictionary* (2nd edn., 1989).

[34] Edw. 1 at 4–5. See also the judgment of the Court of Appeal in *The 'Pelikan'* (1809), Edw. (App.) iv. On the legal status of the Island of St Domingo prior to the Orders in Council see the opinion of the Law Officers of the Crown of 22 Mar. 1806: McNair, n. 31 above, 132.

[35] 3 Bing. 432 at 438. For cases concerning the recognition of the South American States and Governments, see Bushe-Fox, 'Unrecognized States: Cases in the Admiralty and Common Law Courts 1805–26' (1932) 13 *BYBIL* 39–48; and 'The Court of Chancery and Recognition 1804–31' (1931) 12 *BYBIL* 63–75.

defined as legal authority[36] which is not, in law, dependent upon any other authority and which is defined by international law.[37] Sovereignty, in this sense, is not to be confused with the exercise of sovereign rights, i.e. rights normally stemming from sovereignty. Thus, in the case concerning the *Lighthouses in Crete and Samos* (1937), the Permanent Court of International Justice held that sovereignty over the island of Crete had not ceased to belong to the Ottoman Empire, although by Article 4 of the Treaty of London 1899 the Sultan had ceded to the Allied Sovereigns 'all rights of sovereignty and all other rights which he possessed over that island'.[38] The (former) Spanish Provinces in America exercised sovereign rights long before their sovereignty was recognized. Equally, States may continue to recognize the sovereignty of a state even though some or all of its sovereign rights are exercised by another State (or other States) as in the case of military occupation, (illegal) annexation, or international administration. For example, France, Great Britain, the USA, and the USSR in the Declaration of Berlin of 5 June 1945[39] assumed supreme authority with respect to Germany, including all the powers possessed by the German Government and any state, municipal, or local government or authority while maintaining that Germany continued to exist as a sovereign State. Thus, the State of Germany (as distinct from the GDR or the FRG) in 1985 qualified for sovereign immunity under the United Kingdom State Immunity Act 1978 (SIA).[40] Sovereignty, as an abstract legal concept, may thus, in the most extreme case, be reduced to (and indeed survive as) a *nudum ius*.[41] Sover-

[36] Legal authority may be understood in the sense of the German *Hoheitsgewalt*.

[37] For a similar definition, see Jennings and Watts, n. 8 above, 122. On the meanings of sovereignty in general, see Oppenheim, n. 26 above, 120–3; Verdross and Simma, n. 26 above, 25–33; Steinberger, 'Sovereignty' in Bernhardt (ed.), *Encyclopedia of Public International Law* (1987), x, 397–418; Dahm, Delbrück, and Wolfrum, n. 9 above, 214–28.

[38] PCIJ, Ser. A./B., No 71, 92 at 103. For criticism of this view, see Judge Hudson: *ibid.*, at 127. For observations on the distinction between the exercise of sovereign rights or powers and sovereignty in a national law context, see also *Trustees of Phillips Exeter Academy* v. *Exeter*, 27 A.2d 569 at 580–1 (S.Ct. NH 1942). See further Sir Hersch Lauterpacht, 'Règles générales du droit de la paix' (1937–IV) 62 *RdC* 99–422 at 325–6; and Crawford, *The Creation of States in International Law* (1979), 27. Cf. also Vattel, *The Law of Nations or the Principles of Natural Law* (1758), Bk. IV, Ch. V, § 59, who speaks of the 'rights whose assemblage constitutes the plenitude of sovereignty'.

[39] 145 BFSP 796.

[40] See *R.* v. *Secretary of State for Foreign and Commonwealth Affairs, ex parte Trawnik* [1985] TLR 18 April 1985 (QBD), and [1986] TLR 21 February 1986 (CA). Under Art. 49 of the Treaty of Peace, concluded at Versailles on 28 June 1919 (112 BFSP 1), Germany renounced in favour of the League of Nations, in the capacity of trustee, the government of the Saar Basin but retained sovereignty over the territory. See [1920–3] *Survey* 76–85; Crawford, n. 38 above, 160–1. See further the case of Bosnia-Herzegowina, which, according to Art. 25 of the Treaty of Berlin of 13 July 1878 (69 BFSP 749), was administered by Austria-Hungary until its annexation on 5 Oct. 1908 while nominally remaining under the sovereignty of the Ottoman Empire.

[41] On 2 Sept. 1991 the USA, which had never recognized the incorporation of the Baltic States into the Soviet Union, did not recognize Estonia, Latvia, and Lithuania as sovereign

eignty, in this sense, is also not to be confused with statehood. This becomes clear from the fact that a distinction is usually drawn between 'sovereign States' and 'semi-sovereign States' or 'part-sovereign States'.[42] It should also be noted that States, as a rule, have recognized not new States but their 'sovereignty' or have recognized them as 'sovereign States'.[43] Reference is frequently made in British diplomatic correspondence during 1822–4 to the 'States' or the 'New States' of America.[44] Thus, recognition, *de jure*, as used by Lord Castlereagh, does not profess to decide upon the question of statehood but upon the question of the State's sovereignty.[45] Starting out from the two different meanings of recognition developed above it is therefore suggested that the term *de jure* recognition, as used by Lord Castlereagh and his successor, indicates that, in the opinion of the recognizing State, the recognized State is a sovereign State and/or indicates the recognizing State's willingness to deal with it as such, i.e. to enter into relations with it on the basis of sovereign equality.[46] In contrast, *de facto* and

independent States but recognized only their governments, taking the view that it had already recognized the Baltic States on 28 July 1922. See [1990] AFPCD no 209, at 376; (1991) 2/36 *DSD* 667; *WP*, 3 Sept. 1991, Sec. A, 1. The Soviet Union, on the other hand, on 6 Sept. 1991 recognized the Baltic States as sovereign nations (*WP*, 7 Sept. 1991, Sec. A, 14).

[42] See e.g. Liszt, *Das Völkerrecht* (12th edn., 1925), 94–5; Lawrence, *The Principles of International Law* (7th edn., 1925), 47–56; Jennings and Watts, n. 8 above, 123–4.

[43] Most recently, for example, Iraq declared on 10 Nov. 1994 that it 'recognizes the sovereignty of the State of Kuwait' (*Daily Telegraph*, 11 Nov. 1994, 1, 13), and on 21 Oct. 1993 it was announced that Belgium had formally recognized the ex-Yugoslav Republic of Macedonia as a 'sovereign and independent state' (*Europe*, 41st Year, No 6091 (n.s.), 22 Oct. 1993, 3).

[44] See e.g. the dispatches of Mr Canning printed in Smith, n. 3 above, 129, 132, 140, 142. See also the Duke of Wellington's *Observations* on Notes on a Dispatch from M. Chateaubriand (26 Jan. 1824) to the prince of Polignac: Webster, n. 2 above, 141, n. 1.

[45] The Duke of Wellington in his *Observations* wrote: 'The existence of these countries . . . are matters of fact' (Webster, n. 2 above, 141, n. 1). For the distinction between statehood and sovereignty in modern literature see e.g. Erich, 'La naissance et reconnaissance des Etats' (1926–III) 13 *RdC* 431–507 at 432–5; Raestad, 'La reconnaissance internationale des nouveaux Etats et des nouveaux gouvernements' (1936) 17 *RDILC* 257–313 at 283–7; Heydte, n. 14 above, 128–51 at 133, 134. For the distinction between 'state' and 'sovereign and independent state', see also the speech of Mr van Kleffens, the Dutch representative in the Security Council, on 12 Aug. 1947: SCOR, 2nd Year, No 74, 181st Meeting, 12 Aug. 1947, 1921–3. *Contra* Lauterpacht, n. 9 above, 28, who sees the possession of sovereignty as the 'primary requirement of statehood'.

[46] It is of interest to note that the Netherlands, which had proclaimed their independence from Spain in 1581, stated in the negotiations preceding the Peace of Westphalia of 1648: 'The Dutch did not want their representatives to turn up there differently from the Ambassadors of a Sovereign Republic, equal to those of other sovereigns' (author's translation). The Emperor, however, decided in 1646 that the ambassadors of the Netherlands should not be received on an equal footing and should not be given the title of 'Excellency' as long as it was not granted to them by Spain. This controversy was only resolved by the treaty of 30 Jan. 1648 between Spain and the Netherlands in which the Spanish King 'recognizes that the said States-General of the United Netherlands are free and sovereign States' (author's translation). See Frowein, 'Transfer or Recognition of Sovereignty—Some Early Problems in Connection with Dependent Territories' (1971) 65 *AJIL* 568–71 at 568–9 and 'Die Entwicklung der Anerkennung von Staaten und Regierungen im Völkerrecht' (1972) 11 *Der Staat* 145–59 at 146–7.

diplomatic recognition, according to Lord Castlereagh and his successor, do not manifest an attitude on the question of sovereignty but simply indicate a willingness to have a certain mode of relations. *De facto* recognition of a new State is thereby identified with the recognition of its commercial flag, the appointment of consuls, the acceptance of its *exequatur*, and the sending of diplomatic or political agents to it,[47] while diplomatic recognition is identified with regular diplomatic relations evidenced in the accrediting of a *chargé d'affaires*, Minister, or Ambassador.[48]

(2) Reason for the Introduction of the Variants

It seems that Lord Castlereagh introduced the hitherto unknown distinction between *de facto*, diplomatic, and *de jure* recognition in response to the attempts of the Powers of the Holy Alliance at the beginning of the nineteenth century to establish the principle of dynastic legitimacy in international law. The principle of dynastic legitimacy may be defined as the inalienable right of sovereignty of the legitimate ruling dynasty, which can be lost only by voluntary renunciation (transfer) or extinction of the dynasty.[49] As a consequence of the principle of dynastic legitimacy the members of the Holy Alliance would not recognize the independence of a new State or a new Sovereign before the former Sovereign had renounced his sovereignty.[50] Thus the Austrian delegate at the Conference of Verona

[47] See the Duke of Wellington's *Observations*: Webster, n. 2 above, 141, n. 1; and Mr Canning's speech: HC Debs., vol. 11, col. 1395, 15 June 1824. See also Phillimore, *Commentaries upon International Law* (3rd edn., 1882), ii, 23.

[48] In a dispatch to Mr Bosanquet, the British *chargé* at Madrid, dated 31 Dec. 1824, the British Foreign Secretary, Mr Canning, wrote that 'The *effect* of such Treaties [of Amity, Commerce, and Navigation], when severally ratified by His Majesty, will be a Diplomatick Recognition of the "*De facto*" Governments of those three Countries [Buenos Aires, Colombia, and Mexico]' (Smith, n. 3 above, 149–51 at 150, italics added). For the Treaty of Amity, Commerce, and Navigation, between Great Britain and the United Provinces of Rio de la Plata, signed at Buenos Aires on 2 Feb. 1825, see 12 BFSP 29. Ratification documents of the treaty were exchanged on 11 May 1825 and on 26 July 1825, as a result of the treaty, Sir J. Woodbine Parish formally presented himself as the first British *chargé d'affaires* to Buenos Aires. The Treaties with Colombia and Mexico were signed on 18 Apr. 1825 and 26 Dec. 1826 and ratification documents exchanged on 7 Nov. 1825 and 19 July 1827, respectively. On (diplomatic) recognition and diplomatic relations, see also the speech of Sir James Mackintosh in the House of Commons: HC Debs., vol. 11, cols. 1366–70, 15 June 1824.

[49] Cf. Heffter, *Das europäische Völkerrecht der Gegenwart auf den bisherigen Grundlagen* (4th edn., 1861), 97; Held, *Über Legitimität, Legitimitätsprincip* (1859), 43, 44; Gauland, *Das Legitimitätsprinzip in der Staatenpraxis seit dem Wiener Kongreß* (1971), 30. On the Holy Alliance and the principle of dynastic legitimacy in general see *ibid.*, 29–50, and Bourquin, n. 5 above; Pflügl, 'Sainte-Alliance', *Dict.Dipl.* (1933), ii, 629–30.

[50] For an example of recognition in accordance with the principle of dynastic legitimacy, see Art. I of the Treaty between His Most Faithful Majesty (John VI, King of Portugal) and His Imperial Majesty (Dom Pedro), concerning the Recognition of the Empire of Brazil, signed at Rio de Janeiro, 29 Aug. 1825: 'His Most Faithful Majesty recognizes Brazil as an Empire independent and separate from the Kingdom of Portugal and Algarve; and His most beloved and esteemed Son Dom Pedro as Emperor; ceding and transferring, of his own free will, the

stated in reply to a British Memorandum concerning the recognition of the Spanish Colonies of America:

His Imperial Majesty, always true to the grand principles on which the social order and the preservation of the legitimate governments is based, will never recognize the independence of the Spanish Provinces in America, as long as His Catholic Majesty will not have renounced freely and formally his rights of Sovereignty which he has hitherto exercised over these provinces [author's translation].[51]

The secession of the Spanish Provinces in America confronted Great Britain with the problem of reconciling the necessities of commercial and political intercourse with these new States with the principle of dynastic legitimacy.[52] Although not a member of the Holy Alliance[53] Great Britain was, as the US Minister to London, Mr Adams, put it, not uninfluenced by 'the mystic Virtues of Legitimacy'[54] and it seems that she regarded the principle of dynastic legitimacy as a legal obstacle to recognition of the independence of the Spanish Colonies in America.[55] Lord Castlereagh and his successor, Mr Canning,[56] tried to surmount this obstacle by introducing the distinction

Sovereignty of the said Empire to His Son and to His legitimate successors' (12 BFSP 674 at 675–6).

[51] Declaration of the Austrian Cabinet in response to that of the British Cabinet, 24 Nov. 1822: Webster, n. 2 above, 80. It must however be noted that Austria, while declining to recognize the independence of the new States, felt free 'equally to adopt *vis-à-vis* the Spanish Colonies this *de facto* attitude which considerations of interest and general utility may have suggested to it' (author's translation) (*ibid.*).

[52] It should be remembered that the driving force behind British recognition of the new States in America was powerful commercial interests. For one of several Petitions for the Recognition of the Independence of South America by the merchants of the city of London, see HC Debs., vol. 11, cols. 1392–4, 15 June 1824. See also Smith, n. 3 above, 122. It may be noted in passing that the Foreign Secretary, Mr Canning, sat in Parliament for Liverpool, the centre of British trading interests at that time. On British commercial and political relations with Spanish America generally, see Paxson, n. 3 above, 178–252. Compare also the 'Third Cabinet Memo on Recognition, December 1824': Temperley, n. 2 above, 550–4 at 552.

[53] The Holy Alliance originally consisted of Austria, Prussia, and Russia. It was later joined by all European States with the exception of Great Britain, the Papal States, and Turkey.

[54] Mr Adams to Secretary of State Monroe, 22 Jan. 1816: Manning (ed.), *Diplomatic Correspondence of the United States Concerning the Independence of the Latin American Nations* (1926), iii, 1433. The USA, true to her revolutionary origin, had no sympathy for the principle of legitimacy. President Monroe declared in his message of 2 Dec. 1823 (containing the so-called Monroe Doctrine) that the policy of the USA in regard to Europe was 'not to interfere in the internal concerns of any of its powers; to consider the government *de facto* as the legitimate government for us' (Perkins, *A History of the Monroe Doctrine* (1941), 391–3 at 393). This position was reiterated by the US Secretary of State, Mr Buchanan, in his instructions for Mr Rush, the US Minister at Paris, on 31 Mar. 1848: 'In its intercourse with foreign nations the Government of the United States has, from its origin, always recognized *de facto* governments. . . . We do not go behind the existing Government to involve ourselves in the question of legitimacy' (Moore (ed.), *A Digest of International Law* (1906), i, 124). On the attitude of the USA towards the question of legitimacy, see also *ibid.*, at 142.

[55] To the same effect see Chen, n. 9 above, 106.

[56] According to Professor Temperley Mr Canning's view was 'not sympathetic with Legitimacy'. He writes: 'Canning equally objected to the "natural law" doctrine of [US Secretary of

between *de facto*, diplomatic, and *de jure* recognition, of which only the last was to decide upon the question of sovereignty and was therefore to belong exclusively to the former sovereign. Lord Castlereagh declared with respect to *de jure* recognition that 'there can be no fair pretence for calling upon this country to commit herself by its adoption. It is for the two contending parties themselves to settle the question of title, not for third parties to interfere'.[57] Mr Canning wrote on the same lines in a letter to Mr Ward, the British Commissioner in Mexico, on 9 September 1825:

There is one condition . . . which it belongs to Spain *alone* to grant,—the Recognition *de jure* of Mexican Independence. When any third Power acknowledges the Independence of the Mexican Republick, it does that which may be very agreeable to Mexico, but which neither constitutes the fact which it acknowledges, nor makes any surrender of right of interest in that acknowledgement: Spain would do both.—She would surrender a right, and (as She supposes) a Great interest; and by her simple admission that Mexico was independent, would constitute the Independence which she admitted.[58]

The distinction between *de jure* recognition, belonging to the former sovereign, and *de facto* and diplomatic recognition, belonging to other States, was thus designed to enable Great Britain to enter into comprehensive commercial and diplomatic relations with the new States in America while pretending not to decide upon the question of the sovereignty of these States.

(3) Distinction Between de jure *Recognition by the Former Sovereign and Recognition by Other States*

In December 1824 the French Foreign Minister, Baron Damas, wrote in reply to the question by the French Ambassador to St Petersburg, M. de la

State] Adams that all nations ought to be free who wished to be, and to the Legitimist doctrine of Alexander [I, Czar of Russia] that no nation could ever be free without the leave of a monarch. Canning's doctrine was the *via media*. . . . His main point, throughout, was that a *de facto* government ought eventually to be recognized, and that England's commercial interests ought not to be sacrificed to vague political theories, whether despotic or democratic' (n. 2 above, 497). On Mr Canning's policy towards South America generally, see *ibid.*, at 131–56, 499–504. See also Perkins, *The Monroe Doctrine 1823–1826* (1932), 57.

[57] See the Memorandum of Lord Castlereagh: Webster, n. 2 above, 71–2 at 72. See also Phillimore, n. 47 above, 23: 'There is no proposition of law upon which there exists a more universal agreement of all jurists than upon this, viz., that this virtual and *de facto* Recognition of a new State gives no just cause of offence to the old State, inasmuch as it decides nothing concerning the asserted rights of the latter.'

[58] Smith, n. 3 above, 126. For the distinction between recognition by the mother country and recognition by other States, see also Mr Canning's dispatch to Sir William à Court, the British Minister to Spain, dated 30 Nov. 1822: *ibid.*, at 131–3. Mr Canning distinguished between 'recognition in the major sense', settling the question of title and being for the incumbent sovereign alone to grant, and 'recognition in the minor sense', concerning the question of relations and being for third parties to grant (cf. HC Debs., vol. 11, col. 1397, 15 June 1824). For the notion of 'recognition in the minor sense', see also Martens, *Précis du droit des gens moderne de l'Europe fondé sur les traités et l'usage* (3rd edn., 1821), Bk. III, Ch. II, s. 80.

Ferronays, whether France, like England, acknowledged a recognition of fact independent of law:

There cannot be recognition *de facto* independent of recognition *de jure*. A nation can admit as a fact that a state exists and may even enter into relations of commerce or other relations with it which do not necessitate arranging political transactions. From the moment, however, that by a formal and explicit act a nation recognizes the existence of another state, the right is joined to the fact which has been acknowledged.[59]

In other words, the question of relations cannot always be separated from the question of sovereignty. Certain transactions require, and therefore implicitly recognize, sovereignty. For example, when in 1818 the United Provinces of South America requested the United States to issue the exequatur for a Consul-General the request was refused, as prematurely involving recognition of the United Provinces 'as a Sovereign and Independent Power'. Mr John Quincy Adams, the US Secretary of State, wrote in a report to President James Monroe, dated 28 January 1819: 'Consuls are, indeed, received by the Government of The United States from acknowledged Sovereign Powers. . . . But the Exequatur for a Consul-General, can obviously not be granted, without recognizing the Authority, from whom his Appointment proceeds, as Sovereign.'[60] Similarly, during the Portuguese Civil War (1830–4) the question arose whether the British Government should grant an exequatur to a Consul appointed by one of the claimants to the Portuguese throne.[61] On 18 September 1832 Mr Jenner, a Law Officer of the Crown, wrote to Viscount Palmerston, the British Foreign Secretary, that 'the appointment of a Consul is an act of Sovereignty, and consequently that the admission of an Individual to act in that capacity, is an acknowledgement that the *right of Sovereignty* is in the party, by whom he is appointed'.[62] Furthermore, as certain rights and duties under international and municipal law depend on the question whether a State is sovereign or a government is the depository of the State's sovereignty, other States are regularly called upon to decide the question of sovereignty. Thus in September 1870 Count Bismarck, the Chancellor of the North German Confederation, was confronted with the question whether the newly

[59] Robertson, n. 3 above, 352–3 at 353.
[60] 6 BFSP 1060 at 1063.
[61] For the historical background see Smith, n. 3 above, 176–8.
[62] McNair, n. 31 above, i, 134–5 at 135, italics added. See in this connection also a despatch of 26 Apr. 1811 in which Lord Castlereagh asked Sir Henry Wellesley, the British Ambassador at Madrid to 'procure from the Spanish Government the necessary Exequatur for Mr Robert Staples's Commission as His Majesty's Consul at Buenos Aires'. He continued: 'Indeed the best practical proof that Great Britain does not thereby [by the appointment of a Consul] acknowledge the sovereignty or independence of the Junta of Buenos Aires is that you are hereby instructed to request the orders and authority of the Regency to be exerted in favour of Mr Staples' (Smith, n. 3 above, 117–18).

established 'Gouvernement de la Défense Nationale'[63] could be regarded as the bearer of French sovereignty legally entitled to bind France in an armistice and peace agreement.[64] A similar question of the sovereignty of a government arose in 1873 with regard to the Khedive of Egypt, who claimed sovereign immunity in the English courts. Sir Robert Phillimore J put himself in communication with the Foreign Office which replied to his question 'that the Khedive has not been and is not now recognized by her Majesty as reigning sovereign of the state of Egypt'.[65] These examples show that the former sovereign and other States equally decide upon the question of sovereignty, if not by their express pronouncements so, at least, by their actions. The distinction between recognition by the former sovereign and recognition by other States was therefore rightly regarded as a matter of legal window-dressing in order to appease the legitimist Powers of the Holy Alliance. The Austrian Chancellor, Prince Metternich, on 18 July 1824 thus directed Prince Esterházy, the Austrian Ambassador to London, secretly to inform the Duke of Wellington and King George IV that everything in Canning's words was 'reprehensible and false' and that no minister of a king ought to distinguish between recognition *de facto* and *de jure*.[66] Mr Canning himself came close to admitting this in a letter to Sir William à Court, dated

[63] During the Franco-Prussian War (1870–1) Emperor Napoleon III was taken prisoner on 1 Sept. 1870. On 4 Sept. 1870 the 3rd Republic was proclaimed and a Provisional Government of National Defence was established.

[64] See the telegram from Count Bismarck to Count Bernstorff, dated 12 Sept. 1870: '[you] cannot attach to the overtures of the Government now acting in Paris the importance of an overture of the Government of France, because it is not yet recognized by France, and the Emperor Napoleon is still formally, for foreign Powers, the bearer of the sovereignty. . . . What guarantee can the present Government, or one of those which will probably follow it in Paris, give that agreements with it would be recognized by France' ([1871] *Ann. Reg.* 250–1; 61 BFSP 770). For other dispatches of Count Bismarck on the representative character of the French Government of National Defence, see: Fontes B.I.I.1, no 526, at 166; no 556, at 177; no 1496, at 603; no 1499, at 604; no 1500, at 604–5. See in this connection also the Dispatch of the British Foreign Secretary, Lord Granville, to HM Ambassador to Paris, of 1 Oct. 1870, quoted (without reference) by Professor Rolin: 'The new Government of National Defence cannot be recognized *de jure* for the voice of France speaking in a Constitutional Assembly could alone determine the form and character of the Government to whom the destinies of France should be finally committed' (Rolin, 'Conditions and Methods of Recognition of New Governments' in Bisshop (ed.), *International Law Conference London. 10th–12th July 1943* (1944), 40–7 at 43). It must however be noted that the dispatch from Lord Granville to Lord Lyons, the British Ambassador to Paris, dated 1 Oct. 1870, printed in 61 BFSP 802–3, does not contain the passage quoted by Prof. Rolin.

[65] *The Charkieh* (1873), 4 LR A&E 59 at 86. The Khedive was recognized by HM's Government only 'as the hereditary ruler of the province of Egypt under the supremacy of the Sultan of Turkey' (*ibid.*). It is of interest to note that Sir Robert Phillimore uses the terms '*de facto* recognition' and '*de jure* recognition' but seems to equate them with recognition by factual conduct and recognition by formal Foreign Office certificate (*ibid.*). See in this connection also the speech of Lord Atkin in *The Arantzazu Mendi* [1939] AC 256 at 264 (HL): 'Our Sovereign has to decide whom he will recognize as a fellow sovereign in the family of States; and the relations of the foreign States with ours in the matter of State immunities must flow from that decision alone.'

[66] See Temperley, n. 2 above, 142.

31 March 1824, in which he wrote: 'If the Recognition by Spain of the Independence of Mexico should be much longer withholden, it may become utterly valueless, by the progress which the new States will have made in obtaining through the Recognition of other Powers, an undisputed place among independent States.'[67] Consequently, the, in effect, purely nominal distinction between recognition by the former sovereign and recognition by other States did not survive the age of the Holy Alliance, while the distinction between *de facto*, diplomatic, and *de jure* recognition did.[68] The question then is in what meaning the terms survived.

3 MODERN USAGE OF *DE FACTO* AND *DE JURE* RECOGNITION

(1) Relationship Between de jure/de facto *Recognition and Recognition of or as a* de jure/de facto *Government*

States have used not only the term '*de facto* recognition' but also such expressions as 'recognition as a *de facto* government (authority or ruler)',[69] 'recognition of a *de facto* government (authority or ruler)', and 'recognition

[67] Smith, n. 3 above, 139–42 at 140. See also Mr Canning's dispatch of 12 Jan. 1825 to Mr Chamberlain, the British Consul General in Brazil: 'What would our situation be, if Brazil were acknowledged by us as an independent State, without the concurrence of the Mother Country, and if, after such acknowledgement, Brazil were to make War upon Portugal? Whatever may be the construction of our Treaties [of Mutual Assistance with Portugal] as applied to the unforseen case of a contest between two parts of the Portuguese Monarchy, those Treaties unquestionably bind us to defend Portugal against any Foreign Power; and Brazil would have been made a Foreign Power, in respect to Portugal, by our Act, and, therefore, of necessity, in our view the instant that we had recognized her entire Independence. We could not reasonably declare Brazil, in despite of Portugal, a separate and substantive Power; and at the same time deny to Portugal that assistance against an aggression from Brazil which we should be bound to afford to her against every other Power in the World' (*ibid.*, 189–96 at 192–3).

[68] The principle of legitimacy was abandoned for the first time in 1830 when the European Powers recognized King Louis Philippes of France. Cf. Gauland, n. 49 above, 43–4. See also the statement of British Foreign Secretary, Lord Malmesbury, in the House of Lords on 6 Dec. 1852: 'It has been . . . our usual policy for a period of 22 years—since the Revolution of 1830 in Paris—to acknowledge the constitutional doctrine that the people of every country have the right to choose their own sovereign without any foreign interference; and that a sovereign having freely been chosen by them, that sovereign, or ruler, or whatever he may be called, being *de facto* the ruler of that country, should be recognized by the sovereign of this' (HL Debs., vol. 123, col. 971, 6 Dec. 1852).

[69] With respect to the Spanish Republican Government which assumed power after the resignation of King Amadeo on 12 Feb. 1873, M. Thiers, the French President, on 26 Mar. 1873 wrote to M. de Bouillé, the French Minister at Madrid: 'before the Spanish Government could be recognized as *de facto* government, that factual capacity had to be established by a certain period of time' (author's translation) (Fontes, B.I.II.1, no 212, at 100). On recognition of the French Government of National Defence 'as the *de facto* rulers' of France by Austria, see the despatch of Earl Granville to Lord Bloomfield, 12 Oct. 1870: 61 BFSP 847 at 849.

as a *de facto* independent body'.[70] Similarly, States have spoken of '*de jure* recognition' and of 'recognition as a *de jure* government (authority or ruler)'. Before continuing the investigation into the meaning of the terms *de facto* and *de jure* recognition it is necessary to clarify the relationship in which the terms stand to these expressions. When doing this, it is well to remember at the outset that the term '*de facto* government' in particular has been used by States and writers in more than one sense. Thus, the term *de facto* government has been used to describe (1) an effective government, i.e. a government wielding effective control over people and territory, (2) an unconstitutional government, (3) a government fulfilling some but not all the conditions of a government in international law, (4) a partially successful government, i.e. a belligerent community or a military occupant, (5) a government without sovereign authority, and (6) an illegal government under international law. In order to understand the literature on recognition it is therefore essential first to establish the meaning in which a writer is using the term. Seemingly contradictory statements often stem from the fact that writers are using the term in different meanings. It has been maintained by some writers that '*de facto* recognition' and 'recognition as a *de facto* government' belong to 'entirely different categories of ideas' and that 'to say that a *de facto* recognition is recognition as a *de facto* government is an obvious contradiction in terms'.[71] This view, however, has no foundation in State practice. On the contrary, States have regularly used the terms '*de facto* recognition' and 'recognition "as" a *de facto* government, authority or independent body' as synonyms.[72] This may be illustrated by the following cases:

(i) *Spanish Colonies*. The Duke of Wellington, the British Plenipotentiary at the Congress of Verona, in a letter to Foreign Secretary Canning, dated 26 November 1822, referred to 'the first Instructions which I received upon the subject, viz., the Recognition of the Govern-

[70] 'Recognition as a *de facto* independent body' was granted, for example, to the Estonian National Council by Great Britain (3 May 1918), France (13 May 1918), and Italy (29 May 1918). See [1918] II FRUS. Russia 829. For the French recognition statement, see Visscher, 'Les gouvernements étrangers en justice. Reconnaissance internationale et immunités' (1922) 50 *RDILC* 149–70 at 152. Recognition in similar terms was extended to the Latvian and Lithuanian National Councils.

[71] Chen, n. 9 above, 273, 274. For other writers advocating a strict distinction between *de facto* and *de jure* recognition and recognition as a *de facto/de jure* government, see Kunz, 'Staatsgewalt de facto' in Strupp (ed.), *Wörterbuch des Völkerrechts und der Diplomatic* (1925), ii, 605–15 at 609; Spiropoulos, n. 1 above, 18; Strupp, *Grundzüge des positiven Völkerrechts* (5th edn., 1932), 79, n. 3. This view is a consequence of the writers' definition of the term *de facto* government.

[72] For the view that '*de facto* recognition' and '*de jure* recognition' are convenient abbreviations for 'recognition as a *de facto* government' and 'recognition as a *de jure* government', see Lauterpacht, n. 9 above, 330; McNair with Watts, *The Legal Effects of War* (4th edn., 1966), 407, n. 2; O'Connell, *International Law* (2nd edn., 1970), i, 160; Ruda, 'Recognition of States and Governments' in Bedjaoui (ed.), *International Law: Achievements and Prospects* (1991), 449–65 at 459; Brierly, *The Law of Nations* (6th edn., 1963), 147.

ments of those [Spanish] Colonies in which all contest had ceased as Governments *de facto*'.[73] The instructions the Duke of Wellington was referring to, i.e. Lord Castlereagh's Memorandum, spoke of 'Recognition, *de facto*' and the '*de facto* system of Recognition'.[74]

(ii) *South Russia.* In a letter to the *chargé d'affaires* of Russia, M. Basily, the French Prime Minister and Foreign Minister, M. Millerand, wrote on 10 August 1920: 'I have the honour to inform you that the Government of the Republic has decided to accord *de facto* recognition to the Government of South Russia[75] and to send a diplomatic agent to Sebastopol, in conformity with your suggestions' (author's translation).[76] The official announcement issued the following day, however, reads: 'The French Government, taking into consideration the military successes and the growing strength of the Government of General Wrangel . . . , has decided to recognize as a *de facto* Government the Government of South Russia.'[77]

(iii) *Caucasian States.* The Allied Foreign Ministers decided at their Paris meeting on 10 January 1920 'that the Principal Allied and Associated Powers should together recognize the Governments of Georgia and Azerbaijan as *de facto* Governments'.[78] With reference to the above decision the British Under-Secretary of State for Foreign Affairs, Mr Harmsworth, stated on 19 December 1921 in Parliament that 'His Majesty's' Government accorded *de facto* recognition to the Republic of Georgia in January 1920' and that 'similar recognition was granted by the Governments of the Allied and other Powers'.[79]

(iv) *Baltic States.* With respect to the British recognition of the Estonian and Latvian National Councils as '*de facto* independent

[73] Webster, n. 2 above, 78.

[74] *Ibid.*, 71–2.

[75] The Government of General Wrangel.

[76] (1938) 39 *Bull. de l'Institute Juridique International* 474, n. 1.

[77] *The Times*, 12 Aug. 1920, 10.

[78] DBFP, 1st ser., II, no 65, at 797. It is of interest to note that the participants in the meeting spoke of '*de facto* recognition' while the decision itself speaks of 'recognition as *de facto* Governments'. The *de facto* recognition of the Governments of Georgia and Azerbaijan was also referred to as 'recognition of *de facto* independence' (*ibid.*, III, no 635, at 751–2). On the recognition of the Government of the Armenian State as a *de facto* Government, see *ibid.*, II, no 77, at 922–5; *ibid.*, III, no 655, at 768. On the *de facto* recognition of the Armenian Government in general, see Hovanisian, *The Republic of Armenia* (1982), ii, 482–530. For the interchangeable use of '*de facto* recognition' and 'recognition as a *de facto* government' with regard to the recognition of the Armenian Government, see also [1920] III FRUS 775–8.

[79] H.C. Debs., vol. 149, col. 399, 19 Dec. 1921. On the *de facto* recognition of Georgia, see also *ibid.*, vol. 151, col. 552, 2 Mar. 1922. On the *de facto* recognition of Georgia in general, see Avalishvili, *The Independence of Georgia in International Politics 1918–1921* (1940), 216–26. On the interchangeable use of 'recognition as *de facto* government' and '*de facto* recognition' with regard to the recognition of the Soviet Government by Great Britain, see HC Debs., vol. 139, col. 2506, 22 Mar. 1921; *ibid.*, vol. 164, col. 22, 14 May 1923; and the letter of the Foreign Office, dated 20 Apr. 1920, in *A. M. Luther* v. *James Sagor and Company* [1921] 3 KB 532 at 536 (CA).

bodies',[80] Lord Curzon wrote on 18 August 1919 in a letter to Mr Balfour: 'As you are aware the Provisional Governments of Esthonia and Latvia have received *de facto* recognition from His Majesty's Government, and there would seem to be no reason why a similar measure of recognition should not now be extended to the Provisional Government of Lithuania'.[81]

(v) *Israel.* The White House Press Release announcing the recognition of the State of Israel stated that 'The United States recognizes the provisional government as the *de facto* authority of the new State of Israel.'[82] With regard to US recognition of Israel, Dr Jessup, Deputy US Representative in the Security Council, informed the Security Council on 17 December 1948 that 'so far as the Provisional Government of Israel is concerned, the United States did extend *de facto* recognition to that Provisional Government of Israel.'[83] In this connection it is also of interest to note Dr Jessup's telegram of 13 July 1948 to Secretary of State Marshall stating: 'it is our understanding that US recognition of State of Israel is unqualified, that is, *de jure*, while our recognition of PGI [Provisional Government of Israel] was a *de facto* recognition of government [of] that state. Is this interpretation correct?' The Department, on 15 July, stated its agreement with New York's understanding and set forth its belief that 'in case of recognition of new states as distinguished from new governments no question of *de facto* as against *de jure* recognition is involved'.[84] This view, however, was not shared by the British Government. On 24 September 1948 the British Lord Chancellor, Viscount Jowitt, stated with respect to *de jure* and *de facto* recognition of Israel: 'There can be, I think, *de facto* recognition of a Government or of a country'.[85]

Similarly, States have used the term '*de jure* recognition' synonymously with 'recognition "as" a *de jure* government, authority or ruler', as the following examples may show:

(i) *USSR.* On 1 February 1924 the British representative in Moscow under the 1921 Trade Agreement, Mr Hodgson, sent a Note to the

[80] Cf. HC Debs., vol. 116, cols. 813–14, 26 May 1919.

[81] DBFP, 1st ser., III, no 386, at 509. On 23 (15) September 1919 the British Government recognized the provisional Government of Lithuania 'as a *de facto* independent body' (*ibid.*, no 441, at 567) For the Note of the British Commissioner at Kaunas (Ward) to the President of Lithuania, see Rutenberg, 'Die Anerkennung des Litauischen Staates' (1929) 1-II *ZaöRV* 250–63 at 255.

[82] (1948) 18 *DSB* 673.

[83] SCOR, 3rd Year, No 130, 385th Meeting, 17 Dec. 1948, 12.

[84] [1948] V-2 FRUS 1215–16.

[85] HL Debs., vol. 158, col. 319, 24 Sept. 1948. For the interchangeable use of *de facto* recognition and recognition as a *de facto* authority, see also the speech of the Indian representative in the Security Council on 7 Aug. 1947 with respect to the Government of the Republic of Indonesia. (SCOR, 2nd Year, No 72, 178th Meeting, 7 Aug. 1947, 1843).

Soviet Government which read in part: 'I have the honour, by direction of my Government, to inform Your Excellency that they recognize the Union of Soviet Socialist Republics as the *de jure* rulers of those territories of the old Russian Empire which acknowledge their authority'. The Soviet reply of 8 February 1924 stated:

> I have the honour, on behalf of the Government of the Union of Soviet Socialist Republics, to inform your Excellency that my Government has taken cognizance with satisfaction of the contents of the British Note of February 1, 1924, in which the British Government recognizes '*de jure*' the Government of the Union of Soviet Socialist Republics.[86]

(ii) *Angola.* The Congolese Foreign Ministry announced on 29 June 1963 that 'The Republic of the Congo-Léopoldville grants *de jure* recognition to the Revolutionary Government of Angola from this day forward'.[87] Mr Marcel Lengema, the Acting Foreign Minister of the Congo, said in an interview in Léopoldville on 7 January 1964: 'We recognized Mr Holden Roberto's government as the *de jure* government of Angola.'[88]

(iii) *Iraq.* On 11 November 1976, Mr Shamwell, Deputy Assistant Legal Adviser for Management, Department of State, gave a legal opinion to the Visa Office of the Department in which he upheld the eligibility of diplomatic representatives assigned to the Iraqi Interests Section in Washington for A–1 visas under section 1101(a)(15)(A)(i) of the Immigration and Nationality Act. The opinion reads in the relevant part: 'notwithstanding the break of diplomatic relation in 1967, an individual who is assigned to the Iraqi Interests Section and who is in fact a career diplomatic or consular officer is entitled to be issued an A–1 visa since the US has recognized his government as the *de jure* government of Iraq'.[89] The section of the Immigration and Nationality Act to which Mr Shamwell was referring to defines the class of aliens to whom A–1 visas may be issued as follows: 'An ambassador, public minister, or career diplomatic or consular officer who has been accredited by a foreign government, recognized *de jure* by the United States'.[90]

[86] For the full text of the Notes, see Coates and Coates, *A History of Anglo-Soviet Relations* (1943), 133–5. See also Wilson, 'British Recognition De Facto and De Jure of the USSR' (1934) 28 *AJIL* 99–101. See also the statement of British Prime Minister MacDonald on 12 Feb. 1924: 'His Majesty's Government . . . granted *de jure* recognition to the Soviet Government on the 1st of February [1924]' (HC Debs., vol. 169, col. 721, 12 Feb. 1924). On British *de jure* recognition of the Soviet Government in general, see DBFP, 1st ser., XXV, nos 202, 204–7, and LNOJ Spec. Supp. No 23, 158–60.

[87] Marcum, *The Angolan Revolution* (1978), ii, 78–9.

[88] *NY Times*, 8 Jan. 1964, 4.

[89] [1976] DUSPIL 17–18.

[90] 8 USC 1988 ed. § 1101(a)(15)(A)(i).

While '*de facto* recognition' and 'recognition "as" a *de facto* government, ruler, authority, or independent body' are used by States as synonyms this is not normally the case with '*de facto* recognition' and 'recognition "of" a *de facto* government'.[91] Recognition 'of' a *de facto* government seems to differ from recognition 'as' a *de facto* government, in that the former presupposes a *de facto* government in the sense of a government wielding effective control while the latter ascribes to a government which need not necessarily wield effective control the status of *de facto* government. The recognition element in 'recognition "of" a *de facto* government'[92] may be either *de facto* recognition or *de jure* recognition depending on the intention of the recognizing authority. The first alternative seems to be rather the exception. For example, on 23 November 1989 the European Parliament adopted a Resolution on Cambodia which reads in part as follows: 'The European Parliament, . . . 9. Calls upon all EEC Member States to recognize the *de facto* Government of Cambodia'.[93] Mr Alavanos (Greece), speaking on behalf of the groups introducing the joint motion later adopted by the European Parliament, said: 'I therefore believe that the measures proposed by the House, such as . . . the *de facto* recognition of the Government of Cambodia should be immediately advocated both by the Council and the political cooperation.'[94] In most cases 'recognition "of" a *de facto* government' is used in the sense of *de jure* recognition of a government wielding effective control over people and territory. In particular, the various *Digests* of United States Practice in International Law frequently speak of 'recognition "of" *de facto* governments'. With respect to this practice Dr Whiteman, the Assistant Legal Adviser to the US Department of State, wrote in Volume II of her *Digest*: 'In prevailing practice, when the United States extends recognition, it is recognition per se, not *"de facto"* recogni-

[91] No statement has been found announcing the 'recognition "of" a *de jure* government'. However, governments are regularly recognized 'as' *de jure* governments.

[92] The same is true for the granting of 'recognition "to" a *de facto* government' or 'recognizing a *de facto* government'.

[93] [1989] OJ C 323/101–2.

[94] [1989–90] OJ (Annex). Debates of the European Parliament No 3–383/257. On Khmer Rouge charges of UNTAC '*de facto* recognition' of the Hun Sen Government of Cambodia, see *WP*, 19 June 1992, Sec. A, 30. See also the US recognition of 'the *de facto* Government of the Armenian Republic' on 23 Apr. 1920 ([1920] III FRUS 778). From the correspondence between the US Ambassador to France, Mr Wallace, and the Department of State it becomes clear that what was intended was '*de facto* recognition'. Compare *ibid.*, 775–8. See also the circular of the Swiss Political Department of 22 Sept. 1920 which states that Armenia is 'recognized only *de facto* by the Allies': Klarer, *Schweizerische Praxis der völkerrechtlichen Anerkennung* (1981), 74, n. 53. In the meeting of Ministers of Foreign Affairs, held in Paris on 10 Jan. 1920, the British Foreign Secretary, Lord Curzon, advocated the 'recognition of the '*de facto*' Governments of Georgia and Azerbaijan' (DBFP, 1st ser., II, no 65, at 796–7). What was meant was *de facto* recognition. See HC Debs., vol. 149, col. 399, 19 Dec. 1921. For the meaning of the recognition extended by the USA on 19 Oct. 1915 to 'the *de facto* Government of Mexico, of which General Venustiano Carranza is the Chief Executive' ([1915] FRUS 771), see *Oetjen* v. *Central Leather Co.*, 246 US 297 at 301 (1918).

tion.'[95] Clarifying that passage Dr Whiteman stated in 1966: 'I had hoped to make it clear in the *Digest* that in the past the United States has extended *de jure* recognition to both *de jure* and *de facto* governments, as the case may have been. It is the government that is *de facto*, not the US recognition.'[96] This statement seems to be based on the early view of the United States that 'So far as we are concerned, that which is the Government *de facto* is equally so *de jure*.'[97] Other States have interpreted the expression in the same way. Thus British recognition of the 'independence of Finland and the *de facto* Finnish Government' in May 1919[98] was explained to the US Ambassador in Great Britain on 8 December 1919 as having been 'intended to convey *de jure* recognition of the hitherto *de facto* Government'.[99]

As a general rule it may be said that there is a strong presumption that what is meant is *de facto* recognition whenever the term '*de facto*', in whatever combination, is used in an official announcement or notification of recognition in contrast to the use of the term in theoretical statements and diplomatic correspondence.[100] The same is true for the term '*de jure*'.

(2) Meanings of de jure *Recognition*

As shown above, according to Lord Castlereagh and his successor George Canning, States employing *de jure* recognition professed to decide upon the question of sovereignty. In the post-Holy Alliance era the terms '*de jure* recognition' and '*de facto* recognition' were used very rarely indeed.[101] Instead when deciding upon the question of sovereignty, States usually employed only the term recognition, as the following examples may show:

(i) *Confederate States*. Mr Seward, the US Secretary of State, wrote on 21 May 1861 to Mr Adams, the US Minister in London: 'As to the recognition of the so-called Southern Confederacy. . . . It is, of course,

[95] Whiteman (ed.), *Digest of International Law* (1963), ii, 3.

[96] Letter to Professor Cochran, dated 6 Apr. 1966: Cochran, 'De Facto and De Jure Recognition: Is There a Difference?' (1968) 62 *AJIL* 457–60 at 457. See also Reisman and Suzuki, 'Recognition and Social Change in International Law: A Prologue for Decision-making' in McDougal and Reisman (eds.), *International Law Essays* (1981), 493–554 at 531, n. 121.

[97] See the instruction of US Secretary of State Van Buren to Mr Moore, the US diplomatic representative in Colombia, dated 9 June 1829: Moore, n. 54 above, i, 137. For similar pronouncements, see also *ibid.*, 128, 142–3. It must be noted, however, that this view has not always guided US recognition practice. On the meaning of *de facto* government in US practice, see the instruction sent on 6 Sept. 1870 by Mr Davis, the Acting Secretary of State, to Mr Washburne, the US Minister at Paris: *ibid.*, 127.

[98] HC Debs., vol. 115, cols. 760–1, 6 May 1919.

[99] [1919] II FRUS 223–4. However, it was admitted that it was a 'loose statement'.

[100] It is of interest to note in this connection that official announcements of recognition by the USA only very rarely use the term '*de facto*' at all.

[101] In contrast, States always distinguished with regard to recognition between *de facto* and *de jure* governments (rulers, authorities). See Fontes, B.I.I.1, no 444, at 132; no 510, at 158–9.

direct recognition to publish an acknowledgement of the sovereignty and independence of a new power',[102] and Baron Van Zuylen wrote to Mr Pike on 17 September 1861: 'The rights of war cannot, then, in the opinion of the King's government be refused to the Confederate States; but I hasten to add that the recognition of these rights do not import in favour of such States recognition of their sovereignty.'[103]

(ii) *Romania.* M. Kogalniceano, the Romanian Foreign Minister, wrote to Colonel Arion on 2/14 January 1878: 'Formal and absolute recognition of the full and entire independence of Romania. This recognition would secure Romania the position of a sovereign State with regard to both the Ottoman Empire and the Powers' (author's translation).[104]

It was only in the first quarter of the twentieth century that the terms *de facto* and *de jure* recognition experienced a revival. The meaning attributed to them, however, seems to have remained the same. On the occasion of the presentation of his letters of credence to the French President on 10 November 1921 the first Minister of Latvia to France, Mr Grosswald, referred to the French *de jure* recognition of Latvia as 'the definitive and irrevocable confirmation of the sovereignty of the Latvian State' (author's translation).[105] A US Memorandum on the question of *de jure* recognition of Vietnam, drawn up in 1950, stated:

> What we are witnessing in the transfer of power from the French to the state of Viet Nam is in truth a *de jure* solution . . .—perhaps one which is yet to be fully established in fact. With due observance of legal form the French are *handing over sovereignty* to an associated state of the French Union. *De jure* recognition is *therefore* more consistent with the existing triangular relationship among ourselves, Viet Nam and the French.[106]

The relationship between the question of sovereignty and *de jure* recognition is also reflected in the decision *NV Suikerfabriek 'Wono-Aseh'* v. *National Bank of City of New York* (1953), in which the US District Court for the Southern District of New York held that 'The sovereignty of Indonesia has been recognized in both the Netherlands and the United States. The control exercised there is not that of the *de facto* government of an invader. The Republic of Indonesia is a *de jure* government and entitled to

[102] Fontes, B.I.I.1, no 456, at 139.
[103] *Ibid.*, no 468, at 144.
[104] *Ibid.*, no 173, at 83.
[105] Strupp, 'Les Règles Générales du Droit de la Paix' (1934–I) 47 *RdC* 263–593 at 449. Latvia was recognized *de jure* on 26 Jan. 1921. On the recognition of Latvia generally, see Laserson, 'The Recognition of Latvia' (1943) 37 *AJIL* 233–47.
[106] The Memorandum was drawn up on 26 Jan. 1950 by Mr Gullion, a State Department official, who on 7 Feb. 1950 became US *chargé d'affaires ad interim* in Saigon: [1950] VI FRUS 700–2 at 701, italics added.

the recognition accorded such governments.'[107] Similarly, the Joint Declaration of the Portuguese Government and the African Party for the Independence of Guinea-Bissau and Cape Verde Islands (PAIGC) of 26 August 1974 seems to link *de jure* recognition and sovereignty. In this Declaration the parties announced that they had reached complete agreement, *inter alia*, on the following points: 'The *de jure* recognition of the Republic of Guinea-Bissau, as a sovereign nation, by the Portuguese State, will take place September 10, 1974.'[108]

The government of a sovereign State, properly so-called in international law, is the depository of the State's sovereignty, exclusively entitled in international law to represent that State in its international relations and to exercise its sovereign rights.[109] It is therefore suggested that *de jure* recognition, used in the sense of *de jure* recognition of governments, manifests that, in the opinion of the recognizing State, the government so recognized is the government of a sovereign State,[110] i.e. the depository of the State's sovereignty or, in more general terms, a sovereign authority. This view finds support both in the literature and in State practice. For example, Mr Dana's 1866 edition of Wheaton's *Elements of International Law* reads on the question of recognition of governments:

> Where a revolution or forcible change of governments has occurred, a minister who had been accredited to the country, and duly received by the former government, . . . will usually enjoy the immunities of a public minister, although his own State may not have recognized the new government as the real sovereignty.[111]

Professor Rougier even stated in 1903 that 'Recognition is the act by which a foreign State declares that it considers the new government as the depositary of the [State's] sovereign authority' (author's translation).[112] That this view also finds support in State practice throughout history may be shown by the following statements:

(i) *Spanish Central Junta (1808)*. After the setting up of the Napoleonic Government in Spain in May 1808 a Central Junta was established in Seville as a Spanish counter Government. The Chevalier de Onis was sent to the United States as the Junta's diplomatic

[107] 111 F.Supp. 833 at 845 (SDNY 1953). Compare also the decision in *Compania Minera Ygnacio Rodriguez Ramos* v. *Bartlesville Zinc Co.*, 115 Tex. 21 at 31 (S.Ct. Tex. 1924): 'The United States, a sovereign nation, a de jure government, did not recognize'.

[108] (1974) 13 ILM 1244.

[109] Cf. Strebel, 'Der völkerrechtliche Begriff der Regierung' (1956) 7 ÖZöR 309–19 at 313; Bin Cheng, *General Principles of Law as applied by International Courts and Tribunals* (1953), 183–5.

[110] Cf. the counter-mémoire of India in *Right of Passage over Indian Territory (Merits)*, ICJ Pleadings 1960, ii, §§ 353–4, at 152, in which India stated that 'recognition as a *de facto* provisional government' is not 'recognition as a government of a State'.

[111] Wheaton, n. 32 above, note no 21 at 245.

[112] Rougier, *Les guerres civiles et le droit des gens* (1903), 499, italics added.

representative. However, the US President refused to receive him 'while it was not known in whose possession the sovereignty of Spain actually is'. It was stated that the President would not 'by any act whatever evince a disposition prematurely to recognize in either claimant the sovereignty of Spain'.[113]

(ii) *Rival Governments in Chile (1891)*. In *Société des Forges et Chantiers de la Méditerranée* v. *MM. Matte et Ross* (1891) the Paris Court of Appeal was called upon to decide which of two rival authorities, the Government of President Balmaceda or the Provisional Congressionalist Government, was to be regarded as the Government of Chile. During the proceedings on 7 July 1891 the French Advocate-General, M. Sarrut, referring to 'legal recognition', stated: 'Without doubt, from the diplomatic point of view, as far as international relations are concerned, an unrecognized government is not to be considered as vested with sovereignty; it does not belong to the family of governments, the community of States' (author's translation).[114]

(iii) *Government of the USSR*. On 7 February 1924 Italy recognized the Soviet Government *de jure* by concluding a Treaty of Commerce and Navigation with it. Article I of this Treaty reads *inter alia*: 'The power of each of the contracting States is mutually recognized as the sole legal and sovereign of the respective countries, with all the consequences which result from this for the other party according to international law and international custom' (author's translation).[115] After the signing of the Treaty Mr Mussolini addressed a Note to the Soviet Foreign Minister in which he declared that with the conclusion of the treaty he considered 'as resolved the question of the *de jure* recognition by Italy of the Government of the Union of Soviet Republics' (author's translation).[116]

[113] Moore, n. 54 above, i, 131–2. For the claim of the Rivas-Walker Government in Nicaragua in 1855 to 'be in possession of the sovereign authority' of that state, see *ibid.*, at 140. On the status of the French Government of National Defence as the 'representative of [French] sovereign authority', see the despatch of Earl Granville to Lord Lyons, dated 14 Jan. 1871: 61 BFSP 981.

[114] (1891) 18 *JDI* 871–87 at 875. See in this connection also the judgment of the Court of Appeal in *The Arantzazu Mendi* (1938), [1939] P. 37 at 54. With regard to the evidential value of the reply received from the Foreign Office to the question whether His Majesty's Government recognized the Spanish Nationalist Government of General Franco, Goddard LJ stated: 'I have always understood and I believe it to be the law that where a question is raised as to the status of a body of persons who claim to be a government of a sovereign state, where a question is raised as to whether there is sovereignty in that body or not, it is not for the court to decide it. . . . The proper course and the only course is to enquire of the Secretary of State what His Majesty's attitude is pleased to be.' Denning LJ spoke of the 'sovereignty which is involved in recognition' (*Boguslawski* v. *Gdynia-Ameryka Linie* (1950), [1951] 1 KB 162 at 181).

[115] NRG, 3rd ser., XXXIX, 595–615 at 596.

[116] Gemma, 'Les gouvernements de fait' (1924–III) 4 *RdC* 293–413 at 369. On Italian *de facto* and *de jure* recognition of the Soviet Government, see also Fedozzi, *Trattato di Diritto Internazionale* (4th edn., 1940), i, 194–5.

(iv) *East German Authorities*. On 8 April 1954 the Allied High Commissioners in Germany declared in response to the (alleged) transfer of sovereignty by the USSR to the Government of the German Democratic Republic on 25 March 1955 that 'they do not recognize the sovereignty of the East German regime and that they do not intend to treat it as a government' (author's translation).[117] Already on 7 April 1954 the Government of the Federal Republic of Germany had issued a formal declaration on the non-recognition of the 'sovereignty' of the Government in the Soviet occupied part of Germany.[118] It is of interest to note in this connection that the Kammergericht, notwithstanding the non-recognition of the sovereignty of the East German authorities, regarded the two German Governments as being 'mutually recognized *de facto*'.[119]

It could be argued that the view that *de jure* recognition expresses that, in the opinion of the recognizing State, the government so recognized is a sovereign authority conflicts with the decision of the English Court of Appeal in the case of *The Gagara* (1919).[120] In that case the statement made by the Attorney-General on behalf of the Foreign Office that the British Government 'has for the time being provisionally, and with all necessary reservations as to the future, recognized the Estonian National Council as a *de facto* independent body, and accordingly has received a certain gentleman as the informal diplomatic representative of that Provisional Government'[121] was interpreted by the Court as implying that the British Government regarded the Estonian National Council as having the 'status of a foreign independent sovereign'.[122] In view of the factual situation in Estonia and the absence of a final settlement with Russia, it may be doubted whether the British Government really regarded the Estonian National Council as having the status of a sovereign authority. On 3 May 1918, i.e. when the 'recognition statement' was made, Estonia was under German occupation (February–November 1918) and subsequently it was occupied

[117] Kiss, n. 28 above, iii, no 61, at 45.

[118] *Die Bemühungen der Bundesrepublik um Wiederherstellung der Einheit Deutschlands durch Gesamtdeutsche Wahlen. Dokumente und Akten* (1958), ii, 92.

[119] See KG, 2 May 1951, (1951) 5 *JR* 689, and the comment of Prof. Wengler, *ibid.,* 690–1. On the *de facto* recognition of the GDR see also BVerfG, 31 July 1973 [*Grundlagenvertragsurteil*]: BVerfGE 36, 1 at 16.

[120] [1919] P. 95.

[121] *Ibid.*, 103–4. Junior Counsel for the Treasury, at a later stage, added: 'in the present view of His Majesty's Government, and without in any way binding itself as to the future, the Esthonian Government is such a Government as could, if it thought fit, set up a Prize Court.' It should be noted in this connection that insurgents recognized as having the status of a belligerent but not of a sovereign state may set up Prize Courts. Cf. Lawrence, n. 42 above, 64–5, 328–9, 459. See also the opinions of the Law Officers of the British Crown with regard to the right of the Confederate States to set up Prize Courts during the American Civil War (1861–5): McNair, n. 31 above, i, 138–40.

[122] [1919] P. 95 at 102. To the same effect, see Brownlie, n. 7 above, 93.

by the Red Army and a Soviet Government of Estonia was proclaimed on 29 November 1918.[123] One objection which may be put forward against the Court's interpretation of the recognition statement of the British Government is that the Latvian National Council had been recognized in similar terms by the British Government even before it declared the independence of Latvia on 18 November 1918.[124] The US Department of State stated on 23 August 1919, i.e. six months after the decision of the Court of Appeal, that it understood that the Peace Conference, of which Great Britain was a member, did not recognize the independence of Estonia or any of the Baltic provinces, although it considered them as entitled to autonomy and to self-determination short of complete independence.[125] The American view is supported by British Foreign Office Documents. For example, on 1 July 1919 Lord Curzon wrote to Mr Balfour that

> many of these [border] States are *now* putting forward claims to the recognition of their sovereign independence . . . Notwithstanding their present claims, indications are not wanting that several of these border States would be prepared to consolidate their interests with Russia on a federal basis, and it is suggested that an effort might with advantage be made to solve the problem along some such lines.[126]

On 25 September 1919 he wrote to Mr Bosanquet, the British representative at Reval: 'His Majesty's Government have already recognized the *autonomous existence of the Governments* of the Baltic States, and have dealt with them as such. The question of the *de jure* recognition of the independence of the States is one which it is impossible for them to decide upon their own'.[127] From these statements it may be concluded that while the British

[123] Although the Estonian Army Commander reported on 24 Feb. 1919 that the last Soviet troops were driven across the border, fighting continued until the Russian-Estonian Armistice of 31 Dec. 1919, and only in the Peace Treaty of 2 Feb. 1920 did Russia recognize the independence and sovereignty of Estonia. Cf. Jäschke, 'Estland' in Strupp (ed.) *Wörterbuch des Völkerrechts und der Diplomatic* (1924), i, 289.

[124] The British Note of 11 Nov. 1918 stated in part: 'His Majesty's Government . . . are glad to reaffirm their readiness to grant provisional recognition to the Latvian National Council as a *de facto* independent body until such time as the Peace Conference lays its foundations of a new era of freedom and happiness for your people. In the meantime His Majesty's Government will be glad to receive you as the informal diplomatic Representative of the Latvian Provisional Government' (US Congress, House of Representatives, Select Committee on Communist Aggression, *Baltic States: A Study of Their Origin and National Development; Their Seizure and Incorporation into the USSR* (1954), 59).

[125] Telegram to the US Commissioner at Helsingfors: Hackworth (ed.), *Digest of International Law* (1940), i, 199. See also the official explanation given by the Allied Supreme Council to General Denikin that the recognition of the independence of the governments *de facto* is not recognition of the independence of the Border States (Avalishvili, n. 79 above, 226).

[126] DBFP, 1st ser., III, no 288, at 409–10, italics added.

[127] *Ibid.*, no 445, at 569, italics supplied. See also Lord Curzon's letter of 4 Oct. 1919 to Mr Wardrop at Tiflis: 'We have recently addressed a message to the Baltic States pointing out that we have already recognized them as autonomous States' (*ibid.*, no 455, at 578). For further evidence that the British Government by Feb. 1919 had not recognized the Estonian Government as having the status of a 'foreign independent sovereign', see *ibid.*, nos 383, 385, 403, 433,

Government regarded the Estonian National Council Council as the government of an autonomous State it did not regard the Council as the government of an independent sovereign State. It is therefore suggested that the Court of Appeal misinterpreted what the appellants' Counsel called 'deliberate statements of a benevolent character'.[128] It seems that the Foreign Office learned a lesson from the court's interpretation of its certificate in *The Gagara*. Its certificate of 17 February 1919, three days after the judgment in *The Gagara*, on the status of the Provisional Government of Northern Russia, while stating, *inter alia*, that His Majesty's Government was co-operating with the Provisional Government and had exchanged representatives with it, emphasized that it 'has not been formally recognized either by His Majesty's Government or by the Allied Powers as the Government of a sovereign independent state'.[129] As the Government of an independent sovereign State the Estonian Government was regarded by Britain only after the recognition of Estonia on 26 January 1921 'as State *de jure*'.[130]

As has been set out above, recognition may not only manifest an attitude towards the legal status of the government recognized but may also or instead indicate the recognizing government's willingness to enter into official relations with it. Applied to *de jure* recognition of governments this means that the recognizing government expresses its willingness to enter into normal, but not necessarily friendly,[131] government-to-government relations with the government recognized *de jure*, i.e. to enter into relations with it on an equal footing as between one sovereign authority and another. This view also seems to have been underlying the instructions of Mr Hill, the Acting Secretary of State, to Mr Hart, the United States Minister at Bogota, dated 8 September 1900:

> When [the government's] establishment upon such *de facto* basis is ascertained, it is recognized by directing the United States representative formally to notify its proper minister of his readiness to enter into relations with it. . . . Pending such *de facto* entrance into relations, the agents of the United States have the right to

and [1918] II FRUS. Russia 819–20, 841–2. It is also of interest to note that in a Note of 26 May 1919 to Admiral Kolchak the Allied Governments made their assistance to the Kolchak Government dependent on its recognition of 'these territories [i.e. the Baltic and Caucasian territories] as autonomous' while they demanded the recognition of 'the independence of Finland and Poland' ([1919] FRUS. Russia 367–70 at 369). On British–Baltic relations in general, see Anderson, 'The British Policy Toward the Baltic States 1918–1920' (1959) 19 *J. Cent. Europ. Aff.* 276–89.

[128] [1919] P. 95 at 103.

[129] *The Annette; The Dora* [1919] P. 105 at 107.

[130] For the text of the Note of 26 Jan. 1921, addressed by the President of the Inter-Allied Conference at Paris to the President of the Estonian Delegation, see 114 BFSP 558.

[131] See the 'Memorandum on Russia' of 20 Jan. 1924, drawn up by the Head of the Northern Department of the British Foreign Office, Mr Gregory: 'It is now necessary to draw a distinction, which has not always been made clear, between the *de jure* recognition of Soviet Russia and the re-establishment of friendly relations between the two countries. Recognition does not necessarily involve the latter' (DBFP, 1st ser., XXV, no 205, 322–30 at 327).

demand of any local authority assuming to exercise power and control protection of American life and property from injury and damage and respect for all American rights secured by treaty and international law, and their doing so is to be held an act of necessity, without prejudice to *the ulterior question of international relations as between one sovereign government and another.*[132]

Some writers have equated *de jure* recognition with the exchange of diplomatic representatives.[133] At least in this generalized form, this view is not in accord with State practice. Often the announcement of *de jure* recognition and the offer to enter into diplomatic relations are contained in one and the same statement.[134] If the one just meant the other, this would be tautologous. While in the practice of certain States *de jure* recognition may express a willingness to enter into diplomatic relations or to exchange diplomatic representatives this is not generally the case. For example, in US practice *de jure* recognition is regarded as automatically expressing a willingness on the part of the United States to enter into or to maintain diplomatic relations.[135] Statements such as the one by the Acting Secretary of State, Mr Lovett, on 26 May 1948 that 'The establishment of legations and the exchange of accredited diplomatic representatives between Israel and the United States would constitute recognition of the "provisional government" as the government *de jure* of Israel'[136] must thus be interpreted against the background of individual US practice. This becomes clear from the fact that Great Britain accredited a Minister to Israel without regarding this as implying *de jure* recognition.[137] Another case concerning the recognition of Israel is also informative. On 25 January 1964 the Republic of Ireland disclosed that it had granted *de jure* recognition to Israel 'some time ago'.[138] However, it was not until 12 December 1974 that the Irish Republic and Israel announced that they had agreed to establish diplomatic relations[139]

[132] Moore, n. 54 above, i, 138–9 at 139 (italics supplied).

[133] See, e.g., Anzilotti, n. 14 above, i, 126, 127, 134; Smith, n. 3 above, 78.

[134] For example, on 18 July 1958, the Cambodian Premier Prince Sihanouk wrote to Premier Chou En-lai, informing him of the decision of the Cambodian Government to extend *de jure* recognition to the PRC and proposing the establishment of diplomatic relations ((1958) 1/22 *PR* 21).

[135] See e.g. the memorandum of Assistant Legal Adviser to the US State Department Flournoy, dated 3 June 1927: 'recognition of a foreign Government as *de jure* . . . means that this Government intends to carry on formal diplomatic intercourse with the foreign Government in question' (Whiteman, n. 95 above, ii, 527).

[136] [1948] V–2 FRUS 1051–3 at 1502.

[137] Cf. *The Times*, 14 May 1949, 4; HL Debs., vol. 168, col. 1418, 26 Oct. 1950.

[138] *Irish Times*, 25 Jan. 1964, 1. A government spokesman was reported to have said that while *de jure* recognition opened the way for the exchange of diplomatic representation between Ireland and Israel, Ireland had no immediate intention of exchanging missions, though honorary consuls might be appointed. (*ibid.*, and *NY Times*, 26 Jan. 1964, 10). Eire had recognized Israel *de facto* on 12 Feb. 1949.

[139] [1975] *Keesing's* 27020B.

and the Irish Government approved the opening of an Israeli embassy in Dublin only on 14 December 1993.[140] Governments have maintained diplomatic relations and have exchanged accredited representatives with governments without granting them *de jure* recognition.[141] The practice of the following States may illustrate this:

(i) *France*. On 1 April 1864 the French Minister of Foreign Affairs, M. Drouyn de Lhuys, wrote to Vicomte de Méloizes:

> Only an existing government is in a position to designate plenipotentiaries and to enter into relations with other cabinets. It is not absolutely necessary that its independence is recognized *de jure*: its independence must exist in fact, and it must not be disputed by those with whom it is to negotiate [author's translation].[142]

(ii) *United States*. The United States recognized the Government of [General] Carranza as the *de facto* government of the Republic of Mexico, on 19 October 1915, and as the *de jure* government on 31 August 1917.[143] Already on 3 March 1917 US Ambassador Fletcher presented his letters of credence to General Carranza and on 17 April 1917 President Wilson accorded 'formal recognition to Señor Bonillas as Ambassador of the *de facto* Government of Mexico'.[144]

(iii) *United Kingdom*. On 18 April 1921 the Law Officers of the Crown advised the Foreign Secretary, Earl Curzon, on the effect of the *de facto* recognition of the Soviet Government on the relations between His Majesty's Government and the Soviet Government as follows: 'we think it necessarily follows that direct diplomatic relations can be established between representatives of the Soviet Government and the Secretary of State for Foreign Affairs'.[145] The case of

[140] *Independent*, 15 Dec. 1993, 10. On 15 Dec. 1925, Norway recognized the Soviet Government *de jure*, by means of a comprehensive Treaty of Commerce and Navigation. In Art. 1 the High Contracting Parties agreed to accord each other the right to nominate Consuls-General, Consuls, Vice-Consuls and Consular Agents but not diplomatic representatives. See NRG, 3rd ser., XXVI, 460–76 at 461. Diplomatic relations between Norway and the USSR were restored only by agreement of 5 Aug. 1941. See Soviet For.Pol. I, 85.

[141] Cf. also Hyde, *International Law* (2nd edn., 1947), i, 151: 'It has been observed that European and other States have found it possible to maintain diplomatic relations with countries . . . without recognizing them for all purposes as States of international law.'

[142] Kiss, n. 28 above, iii, no 26, at 18. On diplomatic relations between France and the Government of Israel at a time when the latter was recognized *de facto* only, see *ibid.*, no 6, at 6–7. It seems that the announcement on 21 May 1949 of the elevation of the French diplomatic mission in Tel Aviv and the appointment of the first French Minister to Israel was regarded as constituting *de jure* recognition. Cf. [1949] *Keesing's* 10005D.

[143] *Oetjen* v. *Central Leather Co.*, 246 US 297 at 301 (1918).

[144] [1917] FRUS 910–12, 915. *De jure* recognition was effected by a letter from President Wilson to President Carranza on 31 Aug. 1917. See *ibid.*, 943.

[145] DBFP, 1st ser., XX, no 357, at 649, n. 3.

British–Israeli relations prior to *de jure* recognition may be examined in more detail in this connection.[146] On 29 January 1949 the British Foreign Office issued a communiqué stating that 'His Majesty's Government in the United Kingdom have decided to accord *de facto* recognition to the Government of Israel. They hope to arrange with that Government for the early exchange of representatives.'[147] On 5 April 1949 the Israeli envoy Dr Eliash arrived in London and on 7 April called on Mr Mayhew, the Under-Secretary of State for Foreign Affairs, at the Foreign Office and presented his credentials.[148] On 13 May 1949 the Foreign Office announced that 'His Majesty's Government in the United Kingdom and the Government of Israel have agreed to raise the status of their representatives in Tel Aviv and London to that of duly accredited Ministers, and that of their offices to Legations. The two Governments have not discussed any change in the present basis of the relationship between the two countries'.[149] The exchange of Ministers gave rise to the question of implied *de jure* recognition of Israel by the United Kingdom. Mr Bevin, the British Foreign Secretary, on 22 June 1949 replied to a question in Parliament whether the official pronouncement by his Department of 7 November 1921, that 'it is not the practice of the Sovereign to receive the representatives of States which have not been recognized *de jure*',[150] is still a correct statement of the practice in its application to any representative of the State of Israel:

[146] On the recognition of Israel generally, see Eytan, *The First Ten Years: A Diplomatic History of Israel* (1958), 8–16; Brown, 'The Recognition of Israel' (1948) 42 *AJIL* 620–7; Bickerton, 'President Truman's Recognition of Israel' (1968–9) 58 *AJHQ*, 173–240; Baum, 'Full Recognition of Israel' (1948) 8 *LG Rev.* 441–6; Röper, 'Rechtsfragen bei der Entstehung Israels', *APZ*, B18/78 (6 May 1978), 3–21; Cohen (ed.), *The Rise of Israel. A Documentary Record from the Nineteenth Century to 1948* (1987), xxxix; Klieman (ed.), *American Zionism. A Documentary History* (1991), xiii.

[147] *NY Times*, 29 Jan. 1949, 6. On 28 Jan. 1949 the Consultative Council of the Western Union, consisting of the Foreign Ministers of Great Britain, France, Belgium, Holland, and Luxembourg, had announced in a communiqué: 'As regards Palestine, there was general agreement that the stage had now been reached at which *de facto* recognition could be given to the Government of Israel' (*The Times*, 29 Jan. 1949, 4). On the legal status of Israel in 1949, see *Reparations for Injuries Suffered in the Service of the United Nations*, ICJ Rep. 1949, 174; BGH, 23 Oct. 1963: LM—§160 BEG 1956, No 23.

[148] *The Times*, 6 Apr. 1949, 4, and 8 Apr. 1949, 4. On the appointment of a commercial representative to Israel see HC Debs., vol. 462, cols. 2251–2, 17 Mar. 1949; and vol. 463, cols. 3033–4, 14 Apr. 1949.

[149] *The Times*, 14 May 1949, 4. The exchange of accredited Ministers was agreed upon after the Israeli Government had represented that without the legal immunities of a Minister the British envoy might be at some disadvantage in Tel Aviv. Mr Helm, the first British Minister to Israel, arrived in Tel Aviv on 17 May 1949 (*The Times*, 18 May 1949, 3) and presented his letters of credence on 27 May 1949 to President Weizmann (*The Times*, 28 May 1949, 3). Dr Eliash presented his Letters of Credence to King George VI on 5 July 1949 (*The Times*, 6 July 1949, 7).

[150] The questioner, Mr Foster, referred to the reply given by the Foreign Office to a question addressed to it in the course of the proceedings of *Fenton Textile Association* v. *Krassin* (1921), 38 TLR 259 at 260.

> The statement . . . represented the practice at the time it was made. His Majesty's Government are, however, advised that, although it has not been done in this country up till now, there is no reason under international or constitutional law why His Majesty should not receive as a Minister Plenipotentiary the representative of a State which has been recognized *de facto* only.[151]

Accredited Ministers were exchanged almost a year before the United Kingdom accorded *de jure* recognition. On 27 April 1950 the Minister of State, Mr Kenneth Younger, informed the House of Commons:

> His Majesty's Government have . . . decided to accord *de jure* recognition to the State of Israel, subject to explanations on two points. . . . First, that His Majesty's Government are unable to recognize the sovereignty of Israel over that part of Jerusalem which she occupies, though, pending a final determination of the status of the area, they recognize that Israel exercises *de facto* authority in it.[152]

These and other examples[153] show that, while in the practice of certain States *de jure* recognition may express a willingness to exchange diplomatic representatives, it generally cannot be equated with the exchange of diplomatic representation. States may recognize a government *de jure* without having diplomatic relations with it[154] and may have diplomatic relations with a government without recognizing it *de jure*.

Support for the view that *de jure* recognition shows that, in the opinion of the recognizing State, the government so recognized is a sovereign authority may also be found in the statements of the British Government with regard to the recognition of Israel. *De jure* recognition of Israel was granted subject to the explanation that it did not comprise recognition of the 'sovereignty of Israel over the part of Jerusalem which she occupies'. One may therefore argue *e contrario* that *de jure* recognition meant recognition of the sovereignty of Israel in the other parts which she occupied.[155] In its explanation

[151] HC Debs., vol. 466, WA, *cols.* 17–18, 22 June 1949.

[152] HC Debs., vol. 474, cols. 1138–9, 27 Apr. 1950. For the identical statement in the Lords, see HL Debs., vol. 166, cols. 1212–13, 27 Apr. 1950.

[153] For further examples of diplomatic relations prior to official recognition, see Smith, n. 3 above, 139–42 at 141; Fontes, B.I.I.1, no 529, at 167; 61 BFSP 995 at 996. For German–Latvian relations 'by the despatch of duly accredited Plenipotentiaries' prior to *de jure* recognition of Latvia by Germany see Arts. I and II of the Provisional Agreement between Germany and Latvia for the Resumption of Relations between the two countries, signed at Berlin on 15 July 1920: 113 BFSP 1058. On Ukrainian–Romanian diplomatic relations in the absence of *de jure* recognition, see Markus, *L'Ukraine Soviétique dans les Relations Internationales et son statut en Droit International 1918–1923* (1959), 36.

[154] See *Japanese Government* v. *Commercial Cas. Ins. Co.*, 101 F.Supp. 243 at 246 (SDNY 1951): 'Recognition as a sovereign government may, and not infrequently does, exist independently and in the absence of diplomatic representation.' See further the statement of Latchum J in *National Oil Corporation* v. *Libyan Sun Oil Company*, 733 F.Supp. 800 at 806 (D.Del. 1990): 'recognition and the existence of diplomatic relations are not synonymous'.

[155] In *Re Schtraks* (1962), [1963] 1 QB 55 at 74, Lord Parker CJ, giving the judgment of the Divisional Court, endorsed the view that 'territory of Israel means that geographical area over which Israel exercises *sovereignty recognized by Her Majesty's Government*' (italics added).

of the *de jure* recognition of Israel the British Government distinguished between recognition of 'sovereignty' and recognition of '*de facto* authority'. This distinction was discussed by the House of Lords in *R.* v. *Governor of Brixton Prison, ex parte Schtraks* (1962).[156] From the speeches of their Lordships it becomes clear that, in their opinion, *de jure* recognition means that a State or Government so recognized is regarded by Her Majesty's Government as being a sovereign authority.[157] This finding is supported by the decision of the United States Supreme Court in *Banco Nacional de Cuba* v. *Sabbatino* (1964). Considering the difference between the severance of diplomatic relations and non-recognition, the Court held that: 'the refusal to recognize has a unique legal aspect. It signifies this country's unwillingness to acknowledge that the government in question speaks as the sovereign authority for the territory it purports to control'.[158]

In conclusion, it may be said that *de jure* recognition manifests that, in the opinion of the recognizing State, the government so recognized is a sovereign authority, i.e. the government of a sovereign State, and/or indicates the recognizing State's willingness to enter into relations with it on the basis of sovereign equality,[159] i.e. to have normal government-to-government relations with it as between one sovereign authority and another.

[156] [1964] AC 566. The case concerned *inter alia* the question whether the Extradition Agreement of 4 Apr. 1960 between the UK and Israel applied to the part of Jerusalem under Israeli occupation. For the distinction between *de jure* sovereignty and *de facto* control, see also the decision of the Italian Consiglio di Stato of 9 Dec. 1958 in *Re An Inquiry by the Italian Ministry for Foreign Affairs* (1958) 26 ILR 68.

[157] Lord Reid stated that 'the British Government recognizes the *de facto* authority of the Government of Israel [over that part of Jerusalem which she occupies] on the ground that that Government is not recognized as sovereign there' ([1964] AC 566 at 579). Viscount Radcliffe expressly referred to the distinction between *de facto* and *de jure* recognition with respect to the distinction between recognition of *de facto* authority and *de jure* sovereignty (*ibid.*, 586–7). See also the judgment of Roche J in *A.M. Luther* v. *James Sagor and Company* (1920), [1921] 1 KB 456 at 474: 'If a foreign government is recognized by the Government of this country the Court of this country may and must recognize the sovereignty of that foreign government.'

[158] 376 US 398 at 410 (1964). See also *RSFSR* v. *Cibrario*, 235 NY 255 at 260–3 (CA NY 1923). For the view that the severance of diplomatic relations does not constitute a revocation of recognition, see e.g. the statement made by the US Department of State on 28 June 1962 in connection with the severance of US–Cuban diplomatic relations: 'Although the United States has severed diplomatic relations with Cuba, it has not withdrawn recognition from the Castro Government as the government of Cuba '((1963) 57 *AJIL* 409–10). See also *P. & E. Shipping Corpn.* v. *Banco Para el Commercio Exterior de Cuba*, 228 F.Supp. 501 (DC Puerto Rico 1964).

[159] It is of interest to note in this connection that when the British Government announced the exchange of duly accredited Ministers with the *de facto* recognized Government of Israel, it stated that 'The two Governments have not discussed any change in the present *basis of the relationship between the two countries*' (*The Times*, 14 May 1949, 4, italics supplied). On the participation of Lebanon in the International Civil Aviation Conference, held in Chicago from 1 Nov. to 7 Dec. 1944, on the basis of sovereign equality after its recognition by the USA, see [1944] V FRUS 778–9.

(3) Meanings of de facto *Recognition*

It was suggested by Professor Lauterpacht that *de facto* recognition is 'a declaration that the body claiming to be the government of an established or a new State actually wields effective authority [over the State's people and territory] without, however, satisfying other conditions of full, *de jure*, recognition'.[160] Without going into the question of what these 'other conditions' of full, *de jure* recognition may be, it can be said that this view is not in conformity with State practice which shows that *de facto* recognition has been accorded not only to governments wielding effective authority over people and territory but also to governments in exile and other émigré organizations. This may be illustrated by the following examples:

(i) *Czechoslovak National Council.* On 3 September 1918 the United States announced its recognition of the Czechoslovak National Council in Paris 'as a *de facto* belligerent government clothed with proper authority to direct the military and political affairs of the Czecho-Slovaks' and declared that it was 'prepared to enter formally into relations with the *de facto* government thus recognized for the purpose of prosecuting the war against the common enemy, the Empires of Germany and Austria-Hungary'.[161] Similarly, in Article II of the Accord between the French Government and the Czecho-Slovak National Council concerning the status of the Czecho-Slovak nation in France, signed at Paris on 28 September 1918, France recognized the Czecho-Slovak National Council 'as *de facto* government with its seat in France.'[162] These two recognition statements must be interpreted against the historical background of the Czecho-Slovak independence movement abroad during the First World War. The Czecho-Slovak National Council had been constituted in Paris in the course of 1916.

[160] Lauterpacht, n. 9 above, 340. See also Fitzmaurice, 'The General Principles of International Law. Considered from the Standpoint of the Rule of Law' (1957-II) 92 *RdC* 1–223 at 27; Jennings and Watts, n. 8 above, i, 155; and Bedjaoui, *Law and the Algerian Revolution* (1961), 112, according to whom '*de facto* recognition . . . signifies that the government extended such recognition wields effective power'. It should be noted that Prof. Lauterpacht himself expresses doubts about the soundness of his definition of *de facto* recognition. See Lauterpacht, n. 9 above, 340–1. For some of the problems Prof. Lauterpacht faces when applying his definition to State practice, see e.g. *ibid.*, at 334, n. 3.

[161] Hackworth, n. 125 above, i, 203–4 at 204. On US recognition of the Czecho-Slovak National Council, see also [1914–29] II FRUS. The Lansing Papers 139–41, 144–5; Hyde, 'The Recognition of Czecho-Slovaks as Belligerents' (1919) 13 *AJIL* 93–5. See further *Garvin* v. *Diamond Coal & Coke Co.*, where the court interpreted the US recognition of September 1918 as 'recognition of a revolutionary people' (278 Pa. 469 at 473 (S.Ct. Pa. 1924)).

[162] Kiss, n. 28 above, i, no 87, at 49 (translation supplied). See also Mr Beneš' Memoirs: 'In my interviews at the [French] Ministry [of Foreign Affairs] I laid stress upon the following points: . . . 2. The National Council should be not merely the representative basis of a future Government, but an actual provisional Government, which in the agreement was to be recognized as the *de facto* Czechoslovak Government.' (Beneš, *My War Memoirs* (1928), 418).

On 26 September 1918, it was decided to transform the National Council into a Provisional Czecho-Slovak Government. This transformation was formally notified to the Allied Governments on 14 October 1918, and on 18 October 1918 the Provisional Government in Paris issued a declaration of independence. Only on 28 October 1918 the Czech National Committee (not to be confused with the National Council in Paris) seized power in Prague, declared the formation of the Czecho-slovak State, and proclaimed itself as a government 'from this day onwards'.[163] Thus, at the time of both the American and the French *de facto* recognition the Czecho-Slovak National Council, residing in Paris, did not wield effective authority over the territory of Czechoslovakia and a Czechoslovak State had not even been proclaimed. With regard to French recognition it was stated in the Chamber of Deputies on 19 June 1919:

> The Czech State did not exist during the war. The territories which historically and geographically formed it were incorporated as mere provinces in the Austro-Hungarian Empire. . . . The Government of the Republic, being unable to deal with a not yet existing State, dealt with the Czecho-Slovak nation. . . . France, adopting a new practice without precedence in legal history, has taken the initiative of recognizing as a nation a country which it could not recognize as a State, because it lacked a territory and frontiers, i.e. the two essential attributes of sovereignty [author's translation].[164]

[163] For the text of the declaration of independence of 18 Oct. 1918, see (1918–19) 63 *Sol. Jo.* 34. On the recognition of the Czecho-Slovak National Council and Czecho-Slovak State, see Weyr, 'Der Tschechoslowakische Staat. Seine Entstehung und Verfassung' (1922) 11 *JöR*, 351–75; Hobza, 'La république Tchécoslovaque et le droit international' (1922) 29 *RGDIP* 385–409; Rauchberg, 'Tschechoslowakische Republik' in Strupp (ed.), *Wörterbuch des Völkerrechts und der Diplomatie* (1925), ii, 728–36; Buza, 'Die Entstehung der tschechoslowakischen Republik im Lichte des Völkerrechts' (1926) 13 *ZVR* 112–19; Müller, *Die Neuentstehung von Staaten* (1928), 52–61; Klasen, *Die völkerrechtliche Bedeutung der Anerkennung der Tschechoslowaken während des Weltkrieges* (1933); La Pradelle, 'La Tchécoslovaquie de Versailles à Munich—De la Paix de Versailles à l'Auschluss autrichien (11 mars 1938)' (1938) 22 *RDI* 354–76 at 358–60; Steed, 'The Birth of Czechoslovakia' (1943) 8 *Free Europe* 152–3; *The Birth of Czechoslovakia* (1968); Pichlík, 'Die Entstehung der Tschechoslowakei' (1969) 17 *VZG* 160–80; Kolař, 'Edouard Beneš et le Conseil national tchécoslovaque de la rue Bonaparte' (1993) 43/169 *GMCC* 9–15. See also *Appeals from Hungaro-Czechoslovak Mixed Arbitral Tribunal* (1927), PCIJ, Ser. C, No 68, 55–6, 67–71, 71–95; *Jaworzina Case* (1923), PCIJ, Ser. B, No 8, 20; and Ser. C, No 4, 315–16.

[164] Kiss, n. 28 above, iii, no 38, at 26, 28. It is of interest to note that by 7 Jan. 1919 the USA had not yet recognized the Czecho-Slovak Republic. Cf. Hackworth, n. 125 above, i, 207–8 and Whiteman, n. 95 above, ii, 527–8. No formal statement on the recognition of the Czechoslovak State by the USA or other States could be found. However, in the Treaty between the Principal Allied and Associated Powers and Czechoslovakia, signed at Saint-Germain-en-Laye on 10 Sept. 1919, the USA, the British Empire, France, Italy, and Japan confirmed 'their recognition of the Czechoslovak State as a sovereign and independent member of the Family of Nations within the boundaries which have been or may be determined in accordance with the terms of the Treaty of Peace with Austria of even date' ([1919] XIII FRUS. The Paris Peace Conference 808–22 at 809).

Recognition of the Czecho-Slovak National Council as a *de facto* government thus was not intended to mean that France, the United States, and other States[165] regarded the Council as wielding effective authority over an (as yet non-existent) Czechoslovak State.

(ii) *Lettish National Council.* When the British Foreign Minister, Mr Balfour, told the Latvian envoy, Mr Meierovics, on 23 October 1918 that his Government was ready 'to grant provisional recognition to the Lettish National Council as a *de facto* government until such time as the Peace Conference comes to a decision in regard to the future of Lettland',[166] Lettland was still under German occupation.

(iii) *Kolchak Government of Russia.* In a discussion between the Foreign Office and the War Office on the recognition of the Government of Admiral Kolchak at Omsk in October 1919 the Foreign Office suggested that if Admiral Kolchak's regime were accorded any sort of recognition, it should be as a *de facto* All-Russian government, rather than, as the War Office proposal implied, a Siberian government.[167] The control of Admiral Kolchak's Government was however restricted to Siberia and the Ural-Volga area.[168]

(iv) *French Committee of National Liberation.* At a Press conference on 11 July 1944 President Roosevelt announced that the 'United States of America has decided to recognize the French Committee of National Liberation as the *de facto* authority for the government of the liberated area of France pending elections'.[169] At the time of the announcement the French Committee of National Liberation (CFLN), which on 2 June 1944 had adopted the name 'Provisional Government of the French Republic', was still resident in Algiers and did not exercise effective control over French metropolitan territory. Only on 31 August 1944 the 'French Provisional Government' left Algiers for Paris[170] and only on 22 October 1944 it was announced that, in

[165] The Italian Premier Orlando, in a declaration of 3 Oct. 1918, expressly noted that the conclusion on 21 Apr. 1918 of an agreement regarding the situation of the Czecho-Slovak Army in Italy was equivalent to the recognition of the National Council as a *de facto* government (Táborský, *The Czechoslovak Cause* (1944), 87).

[166] *Guardian*, 18 Nov. 1918, 4.

[167] FO 371/4096, quoted in Ullman, *Anglo-Soviet Relations, 1917–1921* (1968), ii, 246.

[168] On the Kolchak Government in general, see Norton, *The Far Eastern Republic of Siberia* (1923).

[169] See Mr Eden's statement in the House of Commons on 12 July 1944: HC Debs., vol. 401, col. 1711, 12 July 1944; [1944] III FRUS 724–5, 726; and *NY Times*, 12 July 1944, 1. See also the statement issued on 25 Aug. 1944, on the occasion of the conclusion of the civil administration agreement between the UK and USA on the one side and the CFLN on the other: 'General Eisenhower as United States Commanding General has been authorized to deal with the French authorities at Algiers as the *de facto* authority in France so long as they continue to receive the support of the majority of Frenchmen who are fighting for the defeat of Germany and the liberation of France' ((1944) 11 *DSB* 205).

[170] [1944] *Keesing's* 6739A.

accordance with the Civil Affairs Agreements of 25 August 1944,[171] administrative control over the larger part of France, including Paris, was transferred from the Supreme Allied Commander, General Eisenhower, to the French 'Provisional Government'.[172]

(v) *GPRA and GRAE.* While Algeria and Angola were still under the (more or less) effective control of their colonial Powers, France and Portugal, several States extended *de facto* recognition to the 'Provisional Government of the Algerian Republic' (GPRA)[173] and to Señor Holden Roberto's 'Revolutionary Angolan Government-in-exile' (GRAE).[174]

(vi) *NCGUB.* A group of candidates elected to Burma's People's Assembly in the May 1990 elections announced at Manerplaw on the border with Thailand on 18 December 1990 the establishment of the 'National Coalition Government of the Union of Burma' (NCGUB) in opposition to the country's ruling military junta, the State Law and Order Restoration Council (SLORC). Although established within Burma, the NCGUB did not exercise any effective control over people and territory.[175] It was reported that in December 1991 Norway, which allows the NCGUB's 'Democratic Voice of Burma' to broadcast over its shortwave radio station, had accorded *de facto* recognition to the NCGUB.[176]

These examples show that the meaning of *de facto* recognition is not necessarily 'a declaration that a body claiming to be the government of a . . . State actually wields effective authority'. The wielding of effective authority may, however, in the practice of individual States, be a/the condition for *de facto* recognition. For example, after the Second World War the United Kingdom regarded effective control as a precondition for *de facto* recognition or recognition as a *de facto* government as the following statements show. In 1951 the British Foreign Secretary, Mr Morrison, set out the British view on recognition of governments in the following terms:

> it is international law which defines the conditions under which a Government should be recognized *de jure* or *de facto*. . . . The conditions under international law

[171] [1944] *Keesing's*, 6635A. On the civil affairs agreement see Woodward, *British Foreign Policy in the Second World War* (1962), 260–8.

[172] [1944] *Keesing's* 6767A. Following the transfer of authority, on 23 Oct. 1944, the USA 'recognized the French *de facto* authority established in Paris under the leadership of General de Gaulle as the Provisional Government of the French Republic': Whiteman, n. 95 above, ii, 376.

[173] States expressly specifying their recognition as '*de facto*' were: Ghana, Liberia, the Soviet Union, Czechoslovakia, India, and Ethiopia. See App. II. The question of *de facto* recognition of the GPRA was also raised in the House of Commons on 26 Apr. 1961: HC Debs., vol. 639, cols. 403–4, 26 Apr. 1961.

[174] Nigeria, Iraq, and Liberia expressly accorded '*de facto* recognition'. See App. II.

[175] Cf. [1990] *Keesing's* 37915.

[176] *FEER*, 26 Dec. 1991/2 Jan. 1992, 12; [1991] *Keesing's* 38681.

for the recognition of a new regime as the *de facto* Government of a State are that the new regime has in fact effective control over most of the State's territory and that this control seems likely to continue.[177]

Similarly, the Parliamentary Under-Secretary of State for Foreign Affairs, the Marquess of Reading, stated in 1953: 'if Her Majesty's Government had not been satisfied that the Government of Egypt were in sufficient control of the country to justify the step taken, *de facto* recognition would not have been extended'.[178] It must be remembered in this connection that the post-Second World War British practice was strongly influenced by Professor Lauterpacht's views on recognition. If a State treats effective control as a precondition of *de facto* recognition then, of course, it may be said that (in the case of that State) *de facto* recognition *in addition* implies that, in the opinion of the recognizing State, the government so recognized actually wields effective authority. The meaning of *de facto* recognition is not however restricted to this additional implication. This becomes clear from the practice of States, including the United Kingdom, sometimes expressly to deny *de facto* recognition of governments which are undoubtedly wielding effective authority[179]—a practice which would be difficult to understand if *de facto* recognition meant only a declaration that the government actually wields effective authority. The question then is what *de facto* recognition means.

It was suggested that *de facto* recognition has no meaning of its own, and that it constitutes only the *negativum* to *de jure* recognition.[180] States, however, have expressly stated that they do not (want to) recognize a certain government or State, either *de jure* 'or' *de facto*. For example, the Italian representative on the Fifth Committee of the League of Nations Assembly stated on 6 December 1920 that 'at the moment the Italian Government has not recognized the Albanian Government either *de jure* or *de facto*'.[181] This

[177] HC Debs., vol. 485, cols. 2410–11, 21 Mar. 1951.

[178] HL Debs. vol. 183, col. 1418, 28 Oct. 1953.

[179] On British non-recognition, '*de jure* or *de facto*', of the Democratic Republic of (North) Vietnam, see HC Debs., vol. 716, col. 1132, 19 July 1965. See also the instructions of US Secretary of State (Colby) to the Chargé in Mexico (Summerlin), 25 May 1920: 'You should therefore be cautious in any necessary dealings with the parties now in possession, not to permit any imputation that the present régime has been even *de facto* recognized by the Government of the United States' ([1920] III FRUS 167).

[180] Cf. Schlüter, *De-facto Anerkennung im Völkerrecht* (1936), 14. For the view that *de lege ferenda* the distinctive feature of *de facto* and *de jure* recognition should be 'consent of the people' expressed either by general acquiescence or free vote, see Art. 2 and 3 of the Resolutions on Recognition of Governments, adopted by the International Law Conference at its Meeting in London on 12 July 1943: Bisschop (ed.), *International Law Conference London. 10th–12th July, 1943* (1943), 157–8 at 157. See also *ibid.*, at 45, 46, 149. For the view that *de facto* recognition is a 'fiction', see Henkin, 'International Law: Politics, Values and Functions: General Course on Public International Law' (1989–IV) 216 *RdC* 9–416 at 31.

[181] League of Nations, n. 12 above, 669. On the British view that 'we must be most careful not to be led into a situation in which recognition *de facto* or *de jure* of any provisional [Austrian] Government is forced upon us', see DBPO, 1st ser., V, no 21, at 94. See also the

shows that *de facto* recognition must have a meaning other than the mere negation of *de jure* recognition.

As shown above, originally, *de facto* recognition, like diplomatic recognition, was used to manifest the recognizing State's willingness to have a certain mode of relations with the recognized government. A similar meaning was attributed to *de facto* recognition by Mr Luis Anderson in 1925, who defined *de facto* recognition of a government as the 'indication of the willingness to cultivate with it practical relations like those relating to protection of nationals, commercial agreements, armistices, peace treaties, etc.' (author's translation).[182] The same view also seems to have been taken by the Institut de droit international. A somehow 'lost' paragraph of the Resolutions concerning the recognition of new States and new governments, adopted by the Institute at Brussels on 23 April 1936 reads: '*De facto* recognition of a new government is the act by which another government expresses its willingness to take notice of its existence in view of maintaining with it relations of mutual benefit' (author's translation).[183] It is in this meaning that *de facto* recognition was used, for example, by the United States. According to a memorandum drawn up in May 1948 by Mr Gross, the Legal Adviser to the US Department of State, the recognition of the Provisional Government of Israel as the *de facto* authority in control of the new State of Israel 'implied that the United States would deal with this *de facto* authority concerning matters of mutual interest to Israel and the United States' and that it 'would, of course, permit a practical working relationship between that regime and the Government of the United States'.[184]

From the US memorandum it becomes clear that *de facto* recognition

instructions to the American *chargé d'affaires* in Mexico 'to be cautious . . . not to permit any imputation that the present régime has been even *de facto* recognized' (Hackworth, n. 125 above, i, 261). For further examples, see HC Debs. vol. 101, col. 294, 16 Jan. 1918; [1938] *Keesing's* 3261A; [1950] IV FRUS 942; (1966) 26 *ZaöRV* 154–5; and the FO certificate in *Carl Zeiss Stiftung* v. *Rayner and Keeler (No 2)* (1966), [1967] 1 AC 853 at 902 (HL).

[182] Anderson, *El gobierno de facto* (1925), 21.

[183] Art. 15(1): (1936) 39–II *Annuaire* 241. The *Annuaire* states: 'The two paragraphs of article 15 are adopted by 29 votes to 3' (author's translation) (at 242) and: 'Articles 11, 12, 13, 14, 15 et 16 are adopted' (at 253). Art. 15 of the Resolutions printed in the *Annuaire* only contains the original para. 2. Compare *ibid.,* 300–5 at 304. No indication has been found in the *Annuaire* that the original vote on Art. 15 was subsequently reversed. It therefore seems that Art. 15(1) has been 'lost' by mistake. Art. 15(1) is identical to Art. 10 of the Resolutions adopted by the Eleventh Committee of the Institut de Droit International at Oslo on 19 Aug. 1932. See (1934) 38 *Annuaire* 342–50 at 346.

[184] Memorandum on the 'Request of Israel for Exchange of Diplomatic Representatives' by the Acting Secretary of State, Mr Lovett, to President Truman, 26 May 1948: [1948] V–2 FRUS 1051–3 at 1052, 1053. In Apr. 1990 President Bush was asked to move toward '*de facto* recognition' of the Lithuanian Government of President Vytautas Landsbergis. It was explained that such a policy, involving meetings with representatives of the Landsbergis Government and other steps, would be an interim move toward official (i.e. diplomatic) recognition. See *WP*, 12 Apr. 1990, Sec. A, 33.

does not express the willingness to enter into a specific kind, mode or scope of relations but rather that it expresses the general willingness to maintain official relations with the government so recognized. This view is supported by Lord Silkin's statement in the House of Lords on 28 March 1962 that '"*De facto*" recognition can mean a great deal; it can mean very little: But it does mean, at any rate, that you are prepared to talk when necessary.'[185] This may also be illustrated by the following examples:

(i) On 10 January 1920 the Supreme Allied Council at Paris gave *de facto* recognition to the Governments of Georgia and Azerbaijan.[186] On 15 January 1920 the meaning of *de facto* recognition was explained to the Georgian and Azerbaijani Delegations to the Paris Peace Conference at the Quai d'Orsay. M. Jules Cambon stated that 'from that moment the Conference could enter into regular relations with the delegations of these Republics, and the delegates, on their part, could present to the Conference the necessary materials, notes, etc.'[187]

(ii) After according *de facto* recognition to the Soviet Government by agreeing on the exchange of 'official agents' in the Trade Agreement of 16 March 1921, the British Government instructed its diplomatic representatives in foreign capitals 'now that trade agreement has been signed . . . not to refuse to transact any business' with Soviet representatives.[188] It is also interesting to note in this connection the Brief for Foreign Secretary Bevin on the *de facto* recognition of Israel, dated 25 January 1949: 'His Majesty's Government consider that the time has come to give *de facto* recognition to the Israeli Government. They are influenced by the importance of entering into direct relations with Israel in order to facilitate day to day transactions . . . with the Israeli Government'.[189]

The characteristic of *de facto* recognition therefore is not that certain relations are maintained but the 'general willingness' on the part of the recognizing government to maintain official relations. This may be illustrated by the fact that States may have a wide range of (informal) relations with a government while expressly declining to recognize it *de facto*. The Australian Foreign Minister, Mr Peacock, said in the House of Representatives on 20 October 1976: 'Non-recognition does not necessarily signify

[185] HC Debs., vol. 238, cols. 1052–3, 28 Mar. 1962. The Greek Prime Minister, Constantine Mitsotakis, refused to hold talks with the Macedonian Government on the ground that this would imply *de facto* recognition of Macedonia (*Guardian*, 31 Mar. 1993, 9). In the practice of Switzerland *de facto* recognition has been regularly equated with *de facto* relations. See Klarer, n. 94 above, 62, 69, 78, 81, 84.

[186] See DBFP, 1st ser., II, no 65, at 797; HC Debs., vol. 149, col. 399, 19 Dec. 1921.

[187] Avalishvili, n. 79 above, 219.

[188] DBFP, 1st ser., XX, no 359, at 651, n. 3.

[189] FO 371/75369, quoted in Pattison, 'The Delayed British Recognition of Israel' (1983) 37 *MEJ* 412–28 at 424.

non-intercourse. There must be a will on the part of the recognizing body. . . . As will be well known there are essentially three stages: Firstly, informal relations on a non-recognition basis, distinct from *de facto* recognition: secondly, *de facto* recognition, and thirdly, *de jure* recognition.'[190] Informal Relations with a government not recognized *de facto* are not based on a general willingness to maintain relations. They are only exceptions to the general unwillingness to have official relations leaving the unrecognized government with no guarantee that its future overtures will even be answered.[191] This situation has been vividly described by Sir Robert Jennings who said:

> if there is an intention that some limited intercourse implies recognition *de facto*, this means that given the inch, you may properly assume that you are entitled to the ell. But informal relations *without* that implication seem to mean that you might enjoy the ell, but you must not imagine that you are entitled thereby to even an inch extra.[192]

That *de facto* recognition expresses the general willingness to maintain official relations rather than the willingness to enter into a specific kind of relations also becomes clear from the fact that the same kind of relations may signify *de facto* recognition in one case but not in another. For example, at a press conference on 8 October 1960 the Soviet Premier, Mr Khrushchev, declared: 'Our meetings and conversations with the representatives of the Algerian Provisional Government [on 3 October 1960] can be regarded as signifying *de facto* recognition of that Government.'[193] In contrast, the British Government in 1920 held conversations with the representatives of the Soviet Government and negotiated agreements with it.[194] Nevertheless, the Foreign Office in a communication to the High Court in *A.M. Luther* v. *James Sagor and Company* (1920) declared: 'His Majesty's Government have never officially recognized the Soviet Government in any

[190] (1981) 7 *AYBIL* 430–2 at 432.

[191] On the practice of the British Government not to answer proposals from the unrecognized authorities in East Germany with whom it had 'a great many practical dealings', see HC Debs., vol. 723, WA, *col.* 253, 2 Feb. 1966. See also *ibid.*, vol. 597, WA, *col.* 5, 8 Dec. 1958. On the dealings with East Germany, see HL Debs., vol. 238, col. 1054, 28 Mar. 1962. But compare also the statement of the British Prime Minister, Mr Wilson, in the course of the foreign affairs debate on 19 July 1965: 'Her Majesty's Government . . . do not recognize *de jure* or *de facto* the DRV [Democratic Republic of Vietnam] . . . there have been occasions—nothing like universal—when [the British Consul General] has been able to transmit messages, and indeed get a reply. But there have been other times when, I must tell the House, the absence of diplomatic recognition has led to refusal to receive an important message' (HC Debs., vol. 716, col. 1132, 19 July 1965).

[192] Jennings, 'Recognition De Jure and De Facto', *Report of the International Law Conference held at London, July 1962* (1962), 21–8 at 27.

[193] Bedjaoui, n. 160 above, 114.

[194] On 12 Feb. 1920 the British Government signed an Agreement with the Soviet Government of Russia for the Exchange of Prisoners (1 LNTS 263) and in May 1920 received its Trade Delegation in London in order to negotiate a Trade Agreement.

way.'[195] As the general willingness to have official relations with a certain government may find expression in all kinds of dealings, from occasional informal meetings between officials to the exchange of permanent representatives, the question whether certain dealings signify *de facto* recognition exclusively depends upon the intention of the government in question. However, the exchange (or sending or receiving) of resident official non-diplomatic representatives, delegates, agents, or commissioners (to whom diplomatic privileges will regularly be accorded as a matter of courtesy or on the basis of a special agreement) will, as a rule, constitute *de facto* recognition.[196] This is confirmed by the fact that States have regarded the exchange of representatives as amounting or being tantamount to *de facto* recognition.[197]

In conclusion, it may be said that *de facto* recognition, while expressing the general willingness to maintain official relations, says nothing about the kind or extent of the official relations actually to be maintained. This is a question for discussion between the recognizing government and the government recognized.[198] *De facto* recognition indicates only that this

[195] [1921] 1 KB 456 at 477. For an overview of Anglo-Soviet relations prior to *de facto* recognition in Mar. 1921, see Degras, *Calendar of Soviet Documents on Foreign Policy 1917–1941* (1948), 10–13.

[196] It will be difficult for a State to argue that it is generally not willing to maintain official relations with a government in the face of the exchange of representatives for that purpose.

[197] For the statement of Count Sforza, the Italian Under-Secretary for Foreign Affairs, that the presence of an Italian Mission at Tiflis and of a Georgian Mission at Rome was tantamount to *de facto* recognition, see DBFP, 1st ser., III, no 524, at 637. For the claim of the Government of Ukraine that it had been recognized *de facto* by Great Britain and France in Jan. 1918, these governments having at that time appointed representatives to the Republic, see League of Nations, n. 12 above, 666. For the German view that the sending of a delegate to General Franco amounted to *de facto* recognition, see Merkes, *Die deutsche Politik gegenüber dem spanischen Bürgerkrieg 1936–1939* (1961), 63. For further examples, see DBFP, 1st ser., XXIII, no 581, at 711; DGFP, ser. D, III, no 109, at 121; [1950] VI FRUS 690, 691, 694; Singh and Nawaz, 'The Contemporary Practice of India in the Field of International Law' (1962–3) 4 *Int. Stud.* 283. See also BVerfG, 31 July 1973 [*Grundlagenvertragsurteil*], where the German Federal Constitutional Court accepted that one might interpret the relations between the FRG and the GDR, and especially the Treaty of Basic Relations between the two countries of 21 Dec. 1972, as *de facto* recognition *sui generis* (BVerfGE 36, 1 at 22–3). In its judgment the Court especially referred to Art. 8 of the Basic Treaty which provides that 'the FRG and the GDR will exchange permanent representative missions. They will be established at the seat of the respective Governments' ([1972] *Keesing's* 25621A).

[198] On the discussion between the *de facto* recognized Provisional Government of Israel and the Government of the USA on the exchange of diplomatic representatives, see [1948] V–2 FRUS 1012–13, 1051–3, 1058–60, 1074–5. The Israeli proposal to establish legations and to exchange accredited diplomatic representatives was declined by the USA on the ground that this would constitute *de jure* recognition of the Provisional Government of Israel. The two Governments agreed instead on the establishment of missions and the exchange of 'Special Representatives' which would have indicated the *de facto* relationship existing between the two Governments ((1948) 19 *DSB* 22; *NY Times*, 23 June 1948, 24). See also Waters, *The Ad Hoc Diplomat: A Study in Municipal and International Law* (1963), 178, who lists the US special representative to Israel, Mr McDonald, as one of the 'special agents who have been sent on foreign missions by the Presidents of the United States'.

discussion may take place. *De facto* and *de jure* recognition thus differ in so far as the former expresses the general willingness to maintain relations while the latter expresses the willingness to maintain a certain kind of relations, viz. normal government-to-government relations. *De jure* recognition thus does not supersede but rather builds on *de facto* recognition.[199]

De facto recognition, however, may not only express the recognizing State's general willingness to maintain official relations, but may also or instead indicate that, in the opinion of the recognizing State, the government so recognized is not (yet) a sovereign authority.[200] The *de facto* recognition of the following authorities may illustrate this:

(i) *Czechoslovak National Council.* On 19 August 1918 US Secretary of State Lansing wrote to President Wilson: 'I do not think that it would be wise to give full recognition of the Czecho-Slovaks *as a sovereign nation.* Without discussing the legal objections a serious embarrassment would be the effect on the Jugo-Slavs'. He therefore proposed the recognition only of the 'belligerency of the Czecho-Slovak revolutionists'. Further, he suggested to 'recognize the Czecho-Slovak Council . . . as a *de facto* Revolutionary Government and give to it such aid as seems expedient'.[201] This course of action was approved by President Wilson and on 3 September 1918 the United States recognized 'the Czecho-Slovak National Council as a *de facto* belligerent Government'.[202]

(ii) *Government of the Republic of Indonesia.* On 17 August 1945 Indonesian Nationalist leaders proclaimed the independence of the 'Republic of Indonesia'. There followed a protracted military and diplomatic conflict between the Netherlands and the new Republic which was formally ended with the transfer of sovereignty over Indonesia from the Netherlands to the Republic of the United States of Indonesia on 27 December 1949. Article 1 of the Charter of Transfer of Sovereignty, signed at The Hague on 2 November 1949 reads: 'The Kingdom

[199] Cf. in this connection the statement on the Canadian policy concerning the recognition of governments made by the Canadian Secretary of State for External Affairs in the House of Commons on 2 Apr. 1964: 'With regard to the recognition of a government we would want to bear in mind the durability of tenure of the government itself. If this were apparent, all other things being considered equal we would extend *de facto* recognition. The question of *de jure* recognition would follow' ((1966) 4 *CYIL* 234).

[200] Compare the explanation for the recognition by the French Government of the Czechoslovak National Council as a *de facto* government: Kiss, n. 28 above, iii, no 38, at 26, 28.

[201] [1914–29] II FRUS. The Lansing Papers 139–41.

[202] *Ibid.*, 144–5. See also Hackworth, n. 125 above, i, 203–8. For the view that the recognition of the Armenian Government as a *de facto* government did not mean recognition of the independence of Armenia, see [1920] III FRUS 775, 777. See also the statement of US Secretary of State Blaine on 18 Mar. 1889: 'No formal recognition of either of the Haitian factions *as a Government* by the Government of the United States had been made subsequent to the downfall of President Salomon. . . . *De facto* relations with the authorities in possession of Power at Port au Prince have been kept up' (Moore, n. 54 above, i, 201).

of the Netherlands unconditionally and irrevocably transfers complete sovereignty over Indonesia to the Republic of the United States of Indonesia, and recognizes the Republic of the United States of Indonesia as an independent and sovereign State'.[203] Prior to the formal transfer of sovereignty the Government of the Republic of Indonesia had been recognized *de facto* by the Netherlands in the Linggadjati Agreement of 25 March 1947.[204] Article I of that Agreement stated: 'The Netherlands Government recognizes the Government of the Republic of Indonesia as exercising *de facto* authority over Java, Madura, and Sumatra.'[205] Some ten States followed the Netherlands' example and accorded *de facto* recognition to the Government of the Republic.[206] For example, the British Prime Minister, Mr Attlee, declared in the House of Commons on 31 March 1947 that 'His Majesty's Government will extend to the Indonesian Republic the *de facto* recognition accorded by the Netherlands under Article I of the [Linggadjati] Agreement. Our contacts with the Republic will, for the present, be maintained through His Majesty's Consul General at

[203] 69 UNTS 200 at 206. On the developments in Indonesia and their legal evaluation, see Sastroamidjojo and Delson, 'The Status of the Republic of Indonesia in International Law' (1949) 49 *Col. LR* 344–61; Hyde, 'The Status of the Republic of Indonesia in International Law', (1949) 49 *Col. LR* 955–66. 955–66; Bünger, 'Dokumente zur Entstehung der Vereinigten Staaten von Indonesien — Vorbemerkung' (1950–1) 13 *ZaöRV* 431–52; Scheuner, 'Die Entstehung des indonesischen Staates' (1951–2) 3 *AVR* 44–67; Taylor, *Indonesian Independence and the United Nations* (1960); Syatauw, *Some Newly Established Asian States and the Development of International Law* (1961), 93–112; Verzijl, *International Law in Historical Perspective* (1969), ii, 82–5.

[204] The Dutch–Indonesian draft agreement was signed on 15 Nov. 1946 at Linggadjati, near Cheribon on Java. The actual Agreement was signed in Batavia on Java on 25 Mar. 1947.

[205] [1946] *Keesing's* 8272A, Taylor, n. 203 above, 464–7.

[206] Colonel Hodgson, the Australian representative on the Security Council, stated on 14 Aug. 1947: '*de facto* recognition was given not by an infinitesimal number of States, but by Egypt, Syria, Iraq, the Netherlands, the United Kingdom, the United States of America and Australia' (SCOR, 2nd Year, No 76, 184th Meeting, 14 Aug. 1947, 1981). On the Australian Government's view on the status of the Republic of Indonesia see also *Van Heyningen* v. *Netherlands-Indies Government* [1949] St.R.Qd. 54. According to Dr Sastroamidjojo, Minister of Education of the Republic of Indonesia, 'the Republic received *de facto* recognition from Australia, Burma, India, the Philippine Islands, the United Kingdom and the United States of America, while Afghanistan, Egypt, Iran, Lebanon, Saudi Arabia and Syria, who had extended *de facto* recognition after the Linggadjati Agreement had been initialled, now [i.e., after the conclusion of the Agreement] granted *de jure* recognition' (Sastroamidjojo and Delson, n. 203 above, 344–61 at 345). Caution must be urged with respect to Dr Sastroamidjojo's list of countries which extended *de jure* recognition. It seems that the author interpreted Treaties of Friendship concluded, for example, with Egypt and Syria on 11(10) June 1947 and 2 July 1947, respectively, as constituting *de jure* recognition. This, however, conflicts with Colonel Hodgson's statement in the Security Council which was not contradicted by Syria which was at that time a non-permanent member of the Council. See also Collins, 'The United Nations and Indonesia', *Int. Conc.*, 459 (Mar. 1950), 115–200 at 124; Wolf, *The Indonesian Story: The Birth, Growth and Structure of the Indonesian Republic* (1948), 113; Taylor, n. 203 above, 349, n. 48.

Batavia.'[207] According to the Netherlands *de facto* recognition meant that the Government of the Republic of Indonesia was not (yet) regarded as a sovereign authority and that the Netherlands retained sovereignty throughout the Netherlands Indies for the time being. Thus Mr van Kleffens, the Dutch representative in the Security Council, stated on 12 August 1947:

> In the hope of strengthening the Government of the Republic, we recognized it in the Linggadjati Agreement as exercising *de facto* authority in Java and Sumatra, neither more nor less. It has not been recognized by us as a *de jure* Government. Still less has the Republic, as contrasted with the Government of the Republic, been recognized by us as a sovereign and independent State.[208]

De facto recognition of the Government of the Republic of Indonesia by other States was based on the same understanding. Thus, for example, a US Aide Mémoire to the Republic of Indonesia, delivered on 27 June 1947, stated that 'From the reading of the Linggadjati Agreement, it is clear that a transition period is envisaged (between now and January 1, 1949) during which the Netherlands is to retain sovereignty and ultimate authority in Indonesia.'[209]

De facto recognition may thus generally be employed in (at least) the following two meanings: it may indicate that, in the opinion of the recognizing State, the government so recognized is not a sovereign authority and/or it may express the recognizing State's general willingness to maintain relations with it. In addition, in the practice of individual States, it has been used in the meaning of a simple acknowledgement that a government exists and wields effective control over people and territory.[210]

[207] HC Debs., vol. 435, col. 1657, 31 Mar. 1947. See also the statement of the Foreign Secretary, Mr Bevin, at the beginning of Oct. 1945 that 'From the political angle, the arguments in favour of non-intervention . . . must be balanced against the very harmful effect of Anglo-Dutch relations which may be produced. . . . I feel that no recognition should be given to any authorities not approved by the Netherlands Government' (Bullock, *Ernest Bevin. Foreign Secretary, 1945–1951* (1983), 153).

[208] SCOR, 2nd Year, No 74, 181st Meeting, 12 Aug. 1947, 1922. See also Mr Kleffens' further explanations of Dutch *de facto* recognition: *ibid.*, 1921–3. See also the first principle of the 'Six Additional Principles for the Negotiation towards a Political Settlement' accepted by the Netherlands and the Republic of Indonesia on 19 Jan. 1948: (1948) 2 *Int. Org.* 407–8 at 407.

[209] Wolf, n. 206 above, 180–1. See also the telegram to the US Legation in Egypt of 29 Apr. 1947, in which the State Department noted that 'US Govt recognizes continuance Neth[erlands] sovereignty over entire NEI [Netherlands East Indies] pending establishment sovereign United States of Indonesia as contemplated Lingga Djati' ([1947] VI FRUS 919, n. 63). For US *de jure* recognition on 28 Dec. 1949, see Whiteman, n. 95 above, ii, 165–7; *NY Times*, 28 Dec. 1949, 1 and 29 Dec. 1949, 1. Great Britain on 27 Dec. 1949 recognized the Republic of the United States of Indonesia (RUSI) 'as an independent sovereign state': HC Debs. vol. 472, col. 37, 6 Mar. 1950. According to Taylor, n. 203 above, 350, 'the evidence would indicate that they [the members of the UN] were awaiting such a transfer [of sovereignty] before according *de jure* recognition to the USI'.

[210] Cf. the interview of the West German Chancellor, Mr Brandt, with the French weekly *L'Express* on 7 Dec. 1970: *Texte zur Deutschlandpolitik* (1971) vi, 251–7 at 254–5.

(4) *Use of the Terms* 'de facto' *and* 'de jure *Recognition*'

It has been pointed out by some writers that 'the terminology is very out of fashion'.[211] While it is true that in modern State practice there have not been many official statements expressly employing the term '*de facto* recognition' or '*de jure* recognition', the terms, and more importantly the acts they describe, have not disappeared.[212] To give but the most recent examples: on 13 July 1995 the European Parliament adopted a resolution on the situation in Tibet in which it reaffirmed that 'before the invasion by China in 1950, Tibet was recognized *de facto* by many countries'.[213] The Report of the Political Affairs Committee of the Parliamentary Assembly of the Council of Europe on the situation in Cyprus, dated 15 December 1994, speaks of the '*de facto* recognition of the entity in the northern part of Cyprus'.[214] On 17 October 1993 the French Ambassador to Djibouti, M. Régis de Bélenet, stated that the delivery of aid to Somaliland 'does not constitute a *de facto* recognition',[215] on 21 May 1990 Greece announced its decision 'to recognize *de jure* the State of Israel',[216] and UN diplomats were reported to have said that the United States had opposed a move by the PLO to address the UN Security Council under Rule 37 of its Rules for fear it would grant *de facto* recognition to the PLO as representative of a Palestinian nation before the Security Council.[217] It should also be remembered that in the history of

[211] Brownlie, n. 17 above, at 207; Menon, 'Some Aspects of the Law of Recognition'. Part V: Modes of Recognition (1991) 69 *RDISDPS* 19–49 at 31.

[212] See e.g. OAU CM/Res.491(XXVII), adopted at Port Louis on 3 July 1976, on the *de jure* recognition of Angola; (1970) 13/35 *PR* 15 on the *de jure* recognition of the RGNUC; HL Debs., vol. 183, cols 1417–18, 28 Oct. 1953 on the *de facto* recognition of the Egyptian Government. For the use of *de facto* recognition, see also GAOR, 17th Sess. 1201st Plenary Meeting, 20 Dec. 1962, 1222.

[213] *Tibet. Bull.*, July–Aug. 1995, 21.

[214] Council of Europe, Parliamentary Assembly, *Documents*, Doc. 7206, 19.

[215] *Le Monde*, 20 Oct. 1993, 5 (translation supplied). The French aid consisted of 45 tons of rice, 800 uniforms, and medicine which were handed over by the French Ambassador to the Vice-President of Somliland, and 5,000 blankets which were delivered by UNHCR. Compare, in this connection, the view taken in 1962 by the British Government that it could not supply 50,000 blankets to the Yemeni Republican Government without recognizing it (HC Debs., vol. 669, cols. 1253–4, 19 Dec. 1962). The British view, however, seems to have been determined by the disapproval of the Sallal Government rather than by legal principle. When on 14 Oct. 1978 the Spanish governing party, the Union of the Democratic Centre (UDC), recognized the Frente POLISARIO as 'the sole legitimate representative of the Sahrawi people', the Spanish Government emphasized that this did not represent a *de facto* recognition of the Frente POLISARIO by Spain itself ([1979] *Keesing's* 29565).

[216] For the full text of the Greek statement, see (1989–90) 42–3 *RHDI* 417–50 at 424. See also the statement of the Greek Prime Minister Constantine Mitsotakis: *NY Times*, 22 May 1990, Sec. A, 12. On the refusal of the Greek Prime Minister Mitsotakis to hold official talks with the Macedonian Government as this would imply *de facto* recognition, see *Guardian*, 31 Mar. 1993, 9.

[217] *WP*, 11 Jan. 1989, Sec. A, 14. On the request by Lithuanian, Estonian, and Latvian Americans to move toward *de facto* recognition of the Lithuanian Government of President Vytautas Landsbergis in Apr. 1990 and the response of the US Government, see *WP*, 12 Apr. 1990, Sec. A, 33.

recognition declarations expressly using the terms '*de facto* recognition' and '*de jure* recognition' have always been the exception and that, if such declarations were made at all, they were normally made for political rather than legal reasons.

The absence of the terms from official statements may also be explained by the following. States generally regard *de facto* recognition as the opposite to 'recognition' properly so called, i.e. *de jure* recognition.[218] When States thus use the term 'recognition' they actually mean *de jure* recognition. This may be illustrated by the following examples:

(i) On 26 May 1948 the US Acting Secretary of State, Mr Lovett, presented a Memorandum to President Truman which stated that 'United States policy in the past, with respect to the according of recognition *de jure*, does not furnish any consistent line of precedent'.[219] For the precedents of *de jure* recognition the Memorandum referred to 'Hackworth, *Digest of International Law*, i, 222–318'. The chapter on 'Recognition of New Governments' referred to in the Memorandum mentions the term *de jure* exactly four times;[220] otherwise it speaks only of 'recognition' or other variants. The Memorandum also stated that 'in the recent case of Pakistan recognition *de jure* was granted on the same day as the new government and state of Pakistan came into existence'.[221] However, the message of recognition which President Truman on 15 August 1947, the day Pakistan became independent, sent to the Governor-General of the Dominion of Pakistan, Mr Jinnah, did not speak of recognition, to say nothing of *de jure* recognition, but simply extended on behalf of the American people the best wishes 'on this auspicious day which marks the emergence among the family of nations of the new Dominion of Pakistan'.[222]

(ii) With regard to the recognition of Transjordan, the Political Department of the Swiss Confederation stated on 25 March 1949: 'As far as Transjordan is concerned, it could be said, that the Federal Council did not have to comment on its [recognition] decision, but that

[218] It was with respect to *de jure* recognition that Sir James Mackintosh in 1824 spoke of 'the true and legitimate sense of the word "Recognition" as a technical term of international law' (HC Debs., vol. 11, col. 1347, 15 June 1824). Compare also Fauchille, *Traité de Droit International Public* (1922), I/1, 323: 'a recognition *de facto* in contrast to recognition in the proper sense which is called *de jure* recognition' (author's translation), and Strupp, n. 105 above, 263–593 at 449: 'The diplomatic language has invented the expression *de facto* recognition in contrast to the normal recognition, which is called *de jure*' (author's translation). See in this connection also *Haile Selassie* v. *Cable and Wireless, Ltd (No 2)* (1938), [1939] 1 Ch. 182 at 196 (CA). On Australian practice, see Suter, n. 13 above, 67–79 at 74.

[219] The memorandum had been drawn up by Mr Gross, the Legal Adviser to the Department of State: [1948] V–2 FRUS 1051–3 at 1053.

[220] See Hackworth, n. 125 above, i, 225, 245, 297, 317.

[221] *Ibid.*

[222] Whiteman, n. 95 above, ii, 210–11.

according to the general principles of international law, a recognition which was not further qualified meant *de jure* recognition.'[223]

(iii) In Volume II of her *Digest* Dr Whiteman, Assistant Legal Adviser to the US State Department, had written in 1963 that 'In prevailing practice, when the United States extends recognition, it is recognition per se, not "*de facto*" recognition.'[224] Clarifying that passage Dr Whiteman stated in 1966: 'I had hoped to make it clear in the *Digest* that in the past the United States has extended *de jure recognition*.... I used the expression recognition "per se" meaning that the recognition was "recognition" not a tenuous or qualified recognition, not a *de facto* recognition.'[225]

(iv) On 19 April 1982 the Foreign and Commonwealth Office wrote in a letter to the Chancery Registrar at the Royal Courts of Justice concerning *Bank Saderat Iran* v. *Seyed Hossein Farshneshani* (1982): 'Her Majesty's Government recognized the Government of the Islamic Republic of Iran *de jure* on 13 February 1979.'[226] The announcement of the British recognition on 14 February 1979, however, said only: 'We have recognized the new Iranian government of Dr Bazargan.'[227]

As governments use 'recognition' and *de jure* recognition as synonyms, what has been said above about the meanings of *de jure* recognition holds good for 'recognition' too.

That governments mean *de jure* recognition when they use the term 'recognition' also becomes clear from the fact that government officials have referred to governments which were recognized *de facto* as 'unrecognized' governments.[228] Thus, Sir Alexander Cadogan, the British representative in the Security Council, stated on 12 August 1947 that 'As representative of a Government which has not recognized the Indonesian

[223] Klarer, n. 94 above, 231 (translation by the author). See also the note of the Political Department with respect to the recognition of the Zaim Government in Syria in Apr. 1949: 'a recognition in the proper sense (*de jure*) in our view is not indispensable' (*ibid.*, 288 (author's translation)). For further examples that in Swiss practice recognition means *de jure* recognition, see *ibid.*, 64, 84, 93.

[224] Whiteman, n. 95 above, ii, 3. For a rare instance of express *de facto* recognition by the USA, see Hackworth, n. 125 above, i, 244 (Ecuador, 1925).

[225] Letter to Professor Cochran, dated 6 Apr. 1966: Cochran, n. 96 above, 457–60 at 457.

[226] UKMIL 1982, (1982) 53 *BYBIL* 355. The case to which the letter refers is briefly reported in [1982] Comm. LR 111.

[227] HC Debs., vol. 962, WA, *col.* 543, 14 Feb. 1979. It should also be noted in this connection that when in the 1960s and 1970s the British Government was asked to state the criteria for recognition, it always set out the criteria for *de jure* recognition. Cf. HC Debs., vol. 969, WA, *cols.* 152–3, 26 June 1979; *ibid.*, vol. 859, cols. 521–2, 4 July 1973; HL Debs., vol. 282, col. 106, 18 Apr. 1967. See further Talmon, 'Recognition of Governments: An Analysis of the New British Policy and Practice' (1992) 63 *BYBIL* 231–97 at 236, 240–1.

[228] English courts on the other hand have, however, often attributed (too) great significance to *de facto* recognition by the executive. See, e.g., *The Gagara* [1919] P. 95; *The Arantzazu Mendi* [1939] AC 256 (HL).

Republic, I cannot vote in favour of inviting it to participate in the proceedings of the Security Council.'[229] On 31 March 1947 the British Prime Minister had announced that 'His Majesty's Government will extend to the Indonesian Republic the *de facto* recognition accorded by the Netherlands under Article I of the [Linggadjati] Agreement.'[230] This shows that an 'unrecognized' government may nevertheless be recognized *de facto*.

States have generally refrained from announcing their *de facto* recognition of a government because often such an announcement is not only unnecessary but politically disadvantageous.[231] Apart from clarifying their opinion on the legal status of a government (which can, of course, also be achieved without employing the term *de facto* recognition), States have used an announcement of *de facto* recognition only in order to express their moral support for or political approval of a 'government' which, for political or legal reasons, they could or would not (yet) recognize *de jure*. Similarly, an announcement of *de facto* recognition 'only' has been used as a means to express the State's disapproval of a government or to express concerns about the sovereignty of an authority. The only reference to (proposed or planned) *de facto* recognition therefore can normally be found in the relevant diplomatic correspondence.[232] It is also of interest to note that even if

[229] SCOR, 2nd Year, No 74, 181st Meeting, 12 Aug. 1947, 1923. See also the statement of the German Minister of State Dr Hamm-Brücher on 9 Nov. 1979 that besides Germany 13 other NATO States had not recognized the annexation of the Baltic States by the Soviet Union. Only the Netherlands would take a special position as it recognized the Soviet Union diplomatically only in 1942 (BT Sten. Ber., 8th Legislative Period, Annex 48 to 184th Session, 14541). However, the UK and Canada had recognized the annexation *de facto*.

[230] HC Debs., vol. 435, col. 1657, 31 Mar. 1947. See also Art. VII of the Preliminary Agreement between Norway and Russia of 2 Sept. 1921 which states: 'Passports, powers of attorney, and similar documents . . . shall be treated . . . *as if they were issued or certified by the authorities of a recognized foreign government*' (NRG., 3rd ser., XVI, 249–53 at 251, italics supplied). For similar provisions, see Art. VIII of the Anglo-Russian Trade Agreement of 16 Mar. 1921 (*ibid.*, XVIII, 684–9 at 687) and Art. VI of the Danish–Russian Preliminary Commercial Agreement of 23 Apr. 1923 (*ibid.*, XIV, 411–17 at 415). These Treaties were regarded as constituting *de facto* recognition of the Soviet Government. Cf. 'Recognition of Soviet Government. List furnished by the Department of State' (1934) 28 *AJIL* 97–8.

[231] For the view of the US State Department that *de facto* recognition of the (Government of the) United Arab Republic (UAR) 'would merely cause irritation and resentment and make it more difficult for [the] state extending *de facto* recognition to transact business with [the] UAR and exert influence upon it. United States, for its part, foresees that there may be occasions when it will wish seek persuade UAR adopt a particular course of action, . . . United States would not wish [to] be hampered in such approaches by self-imposed political disadvantage which in United States view would achieve no significant gain for United States' ([1958–60] XIII FRUS 430–1). On the recognition of the UAR Government, see also *ibid.*, 422–6. The USA finally accorded 'full recognition' on 25 Feb. 1958.

[232] See the confidential telegram of the Acting Secretary of State Acheson to the US Embassy in the Netherlands, dated 24 Apr. 1947: 'Dept issued no statement *de facto* recognition. When queried by several news agencies on stories not originating Dept, officials stated following: a) US had requested Neth FonOff inform Indonesian Republic that it accorded Republic same *de facto* recognition accorded by Neth Govt under Lingga Djati Agreement' ([1947] VI FRUS 919).

de facto recognition has been accorded, such as in the case of US *de facto* recognition of the Government of the Republic of Indonesia, it normally is not mentioned in the official *Digests* and other compilations of State practice.[233] It is suggested that, as a rule, *de facto* recognition is 'practised' rather than 'announced'. This becomes clear from the fact that States have been accused of[234] or warned against the granting of *de facto* recognition[235] although they had not made (or even planned) an announcement to that effect. This view is also supported by a memorandum, dated 4 August 1937, outlining the Swiss relations with the parties in the Spanish Civil War. The Political Department of the Swiss Confederation wrote with respect to the relations with the then still 'unrecognized' Franco Government: 'The Swiss Government is under no obligation to state whether the existence of actual relations includes a *de facto* recognition, as this is a purely theoretical question'.[236] On 3 May 1938 the Swiss Federal Council decided to send an agent to General Franco. A 'Representacion del Estado Espanol' had been tolerated and given certain privileges in Switzerland since 1937. On 24 November 1938 Mr Butler, the British Under-Secretary of State for Foreign Affairs, informed the House of Commons that *inter alia* Switzerland had 'granted *de facto* recognition' and appointed an agent to the Nationalist Spanish Government.[237] While governments are under no

[233] On US *de facto* recognition of the Republic of Indonesia, see [1947] VI FRUS 912, 914–15, 916, 919. See also the report on *de facto* recognition in *NY Times*, 18 Apr. 1947, 17. *De facto* recognition however is not mentioned in Dr Whiteman's *Digest*, n. 95 above, ii, 165–7. The 'List of Governments that have recognized Bangladesh on 15 May 1972', provided by the Bangladesh Ministry of Foreign Affairs (printed in Salmon, 'Naissance et reconnaissance du Bangla-Desh' in Tittel (ed.), *Multitudo legum ius unum* (1973), i, 467–90 at 478) lists several countries as having accorded *de facto* recognition prior to *de jure* recognition. In none of these cases had *de facto* recognition been announced or reported in *Digests*.

[234] In May 1976 the OAU Secretary-General, Mr William Eteki Mboumoua, said: 'Whatever the humanitarian motivations of the UNHCR, it must be clear that its action is tantamount to the *de facto* recognition of the illegitimate South African regime in Namibia' (*West Africa*, no 3071 (10 May 1976), 658). On charges of *de facto* recognition by UNTAC of the Hun Sen Government in Cambodia, see *WP*, 19 June 1992, Sec. A, 30.

[235] On 29 Dec. 1947 the UN Balkan Commission adopted a resolution aimed at Bulgaria and Yugoslavia which stated that 'recognition of [the first provisional democratic Government of free Greece], even *de facto* recognition, and any direct or indirect assistance given to an insurrectional movement against the Government of a member of the United Nations would constitute a grave threat to the maintenance of international peace and security' (*The Times*, 30 Dec. 1947, 4). See also GAOR, 37th Session, 11th Plenary Meeting, 30 Sept. 1982, 158, 159.

[236] Klarer, n. 94 above, 301–2 at 302 (translation by the author).

[237] HC Debs., vol. 341, WA, *col.* 1970, 24 Nov. 1938. In this connection it is interesting to note that prior to the recognition of Bangladesh by Great Britain on 4 Feb. 1972 there was a British mission in Dacca and a Bangladeshi mission in London (cf. HC Debs., vol. 829, cols. 220, 221, 18 Jan. 1972; *ibid.*, vol. 830, col. 823, 4 Feb. 1972) and on 24 Jan. 1972 the British Foreign Secretary, Sir Alec Douglas-Home, declared: 'We are at all levels in working touch with the Bangladesh administration' (*ibid.*, vol. 829, WA, *col.* 306, 24 Jan. 1972). At no time, however, was there an announcement of British *de facto* recognition of the Bangladesh Government. For the evasive answer to the question of *de facto* recognition of Bangladesh, see *ibid.*, vol. 829, WA, *col.* 30, 17 Jan. 1972.

obligation to announce their *de facto* recognition of a government they may be forced by public opinion or foreign policy considerations to announce (against better knowledge) that their relations with an authority do not constitute *de facto* recognition. For example, the British Government, under pressure from the pro-Republican press and the opposition in Parliament, was careful not to give the slightest impression of any kind of recognition of the Franco Government when it exchanged Agents with it in November 1937. On 11 November 1937 a communiqué was issued in London which stated expressly that 'The reception of an Agent in London does not in any way constitute recognition by His Majesty's Government of the authorities of the territory under the control of General Franco'.[238] Pressed by the leader of the opposition, Mr Attlee, whether an exchange of agents did not, 'in effect, mean a *de facto* recognition of the Insurgent Government?', Prime Minster Chamberlain replied: 'No, Sir; I am advised that it makes no difference in the existing situation.'[239] However, this was seen differently by other States. Thus, on 27 November 1937 the German Ambassador to Nationalist Spain, Dr Eberhard von Stohrer, wrote with regard to the exchange of agents between the British Government and the Government of General Franco: 'With the *de facto* recognition of the Franco Government by England a new phase in the relations of Nationalist Spain with the rest of the world has begun',[240] and the US Ambassador to Republican Spain, Mr Bowers, referred to the exchange of Agents as British 'semi-recognition' of the Franco Government.[241] Similarly, while France denied any recognition of the Provisional Government of the Algerian Republic (GPRA), several States regarded the negotiations between the French Government and the GPRA at Evian and Lugrin as amounting to *de facto* recognition. Thus, Pakistan, announcing its formal (*de jure*) recognition of the GPRA, stated that 'by agreeing to enter into negotiations France itself has given de facto recognition of the Provisional Government'.[242]

[238] [1937] *Keesing's* 2817C.

[239] HC Debs., vol. 328, cols. 1125–6, 4 Nov. 1937. See also *ibid.*, vol. 328, cols. 1124–5, 4 Nov. 1937; *ibid.*, vol. 328, cols. 1384–7, 8 Nov. 1937.

[240] DGFP, ser. D, III, no 473, 512–16 at 512.

[241] Bowers, *My Mission to Spain* (1954), 373. See also the memoirs of Sir Robert Hodgson, the British Agent to the Franco Government, *Spain Resurgent* (1953), 78–85. It is of interest to note that Sir Robert Hodgson had also served as 'official agent' to Soviet Russia from 1921 to 1924. In that case the exchange of agents under the Trade Agreement of 16 Mar. 1921 had signified *de facto* recognition. Cf. DBFP, 1st ser., XX, no 357, at 648–9.

[242] [1961–2] *Africa Diary* 64. For a similar statement of the USSR, see Bedjaoui, n. 160 above, 139. On French *de facto* recognition of the GPRA, see also GAOR, First Committee, 1220th Meeting, 14 Dec. 1961, 301 (Yugoslavia); *ibid.*, 1222nd Meeting, 16 Dec. 1961, 315 (Ghana); *ibid.*, 1223rd Meeting, 16 Dec. 1961, 319 (Cambodia).

(5) *Areas of Use of* de facto *and* de jure *Recognition*

When States have expressly announced their *de facto* or *de jure* recognition of a government they have usually done so in order to express their view on the legal status of the government recognized. Four groups of cases may thereby be distinguished.

(a) Secession, Decolonization, or Partition of States

As long as the sovereignty and independence of a (new) State have not been recognized its government cannot be regarded as a sovereign authority, and therefore cannot be recognized *de jure*. Thus, prior to the recognition of the sovereignty of a State its government can be recognized only *de facto*. However, States may indicate that they regard a new State as sovereign and independent by recognizing its government *de jure*.[243]

(i) *Secession*. Some of the governments and other authorities of the new States coming into existence at the end of the First World War as a result of the break up of the Austro-Hungarian and Russian Empires were accorded only *de facto* recognition by the Allied and Associated Powers prior to the recognition of the new States as sovereign independent States. In the case of the Transcaucasian and Baltic States *de facto* recognition was accorded, *inter alia*, in order to give them moral support in their struggle against the Bolsheviks while at the same time postponing a final decision on the question of sovereignty and, thereby, leaving open the possibility of the restoration of the Russian Empire under a non-Bolshevik government.[244] Other reasons for *de facto* recognition only were that the frontiers of these States were not yet settled and doubts about their viability.[245] Based on the assumption that the illegality of the annexation of Austria by Germany on 13 March 1938 had initially been waived by Great Britain through her (at least implicit) recognition of the *Anschluß*,[246] the re-establishment of

[243] According to the Soviet Government the recognition of the Provisional Austrian Government of Dr Renner 'not only makes Austria an independent state but also restores Austrian sovereignty' (DBPO, 1st ser., V, no 53.iv, at 250). The Soviet decision to recognize the Renner Government was conveyed to it on 20 Oct. 1945. See also *ibid.*, no 53.ii, at 249; no 96.i, at 451.

[244] See Kazemzadeh, *The Struggle for Transcaucasia (1917–1921)* (1951), 273; Lauterpacht, n. 9 above, 11, n. 1. For the US view that the turmoil in Russia created by the Bolshevik revolution should not be made the occasion for the alienation of Russian territory without her consent, see [1914–29] II FRUS. The Lansing Papers 349–51; [1919] IV FRUS. The Paris Peace Conference 688; [1919] FRUS. Russia 723, 727–8; and [1920] III FRUS 463–8, 659.

[245] Cf. DBFP, 1st ser., III, no 655, at 768.

[246] On the international legal status of Austria from 1938–46, see Miehsler and Schreuer, 'Austria' in Bernhardt (ed.), *Encyclopedia of Public International Law* (1992), i, 296–301 at 299–300; Crawford, n. 38 above, 310–11; Brownlie, *International Law and the Use of Force by States* (1963), 414–15; and especially Chen, n. 9 above, 67–70, whose analysis of the events seems

Austria in 1946 may also serve as an example for the proposition that a government can be recognized *de jure* only after its State has been recognized as a sovereign State. The British Foreign Office, which seems to have taken the above view on the legal status of Austria, on 13 December 1945 suggested in a memorandum for Foreign Secretary Bevin that the new Austrian Government[247] should be acknowledged 'on a *de facto* basis' until the time when Austria would be 'formally recognized as an independent State' and the 'new President would be recognized as the *de jure* head of State'.[248]

(ii) *Decolonization*. That in the context of decolonization States will not recognize (*de jure*) the government of a former colony before they have recognized the colony as a sovereign independent State may be illustrated by the case of the French *de facto* recognition of the Guinean Government. Following the rejection by the people of Guinea of the new French Constitution in the referendum on 28 September 1958[249] the Guinean territorial assembly on 2 October 1958 proclaimed Guinea a sovereign and independent Republic. On the same day M. Touré, the Prime Minister of the new Republic, sent a telegram to the French President, General de Gaulle, asking for *de jure* recognition of his Government and expressing Guinea's desire for an association between the two countries.[250] While France refused to grant immediate *de jure* recognition to the Republic of Guinea it recognized its Government *de facto*. The French position was set out in a Note of 22 November 1958 which reads in part:

> On the day after the referendum of 28 September the Government of the French Republic has confirmed that it did not hinder the severance of existing ties between

most convincing to the author. On the German annexation of Austria in general, see Kroener, Müller, and Umbreit, *Das Deutsche Reich und der Zweite Weltkrieg* (1988), V/1, 12–4.

[247] A new Austrian Government had been elected on 25 Nov. 1945 and on 7 Dec. 1945 Dr Figl was nominated as Chancellor. On 8 Dec. Dr Figl communicated a list of members of his proposed government to the Allied Council for Austria (ACA) for approval. On 28 Dec. 1945 the ACA approved Dr Figl's Government.

[248] See DBPO, 1st ser., V, no 96, at 448, 449. The memorandum also stated that 'when Austria is recognized as an independent State she should be free (as at present she is not) to exchange diplomatic representatives with other Powers'. On the recognition of the Figl Government and its predecessor, see *ibid.*, nos 7, 21, 35; and HC Debs., vol, 417, cols. 1471–2, 19 Dec. 1945. See also [1945] III FRUS 615–18, 690–6. The Government of Dr Figl was recognized by the four Powers represented on the ACA on 7 Jan. 1946 thereby re-recognizing the independence and sovereignty of Austria. The 're-establishment' of Austria 'as a sovereign, independent and democratic State' was recognized by the four Powers in Art. I of the Austrian State Treaty 1955 (217 UNTS 223). For the Canadian recognition on 30 Jan. 1946 of the existence of an independent Austrian Government, see DCER XII, no 1093, at 1852.

[249] Under the new French Constitution Guinea could have opted to become an autonomous republic within the French Community.

[250] On 9 Oct. 1958 M. Touré sent a second telegram to General de Gaulle repeating his request for *de jure* recognition and his proposal for an association with France.

France and Guinea. It has expressed this *de facto* recognition by sending a representative to the Governing Council of Guinea in order to sort out the principal questions directly posed by the present situation. At the same time the Government of the French Republic has pointed out that the definitive establishment of its relations with Guinea depended on the conclusion of the accords which would eventually be signed. This provisional situation would end with the final result of the negotiations which one could enter into. On the basis of the concluded treaties the question of the *de jure* recognition of the Republic of Guinea would then be resolved [author's translation].[251]

On 7 January 1959 France and Guinea signed three Accords concerning technical and administrative assistance, cultural relations, and the membership of Guinea of the franc zone. These Accords were referred to by a French Foreign Office official on the same day as constituting (*de jure*) recognition of Guinea.[252] French *de jure* recognition was granted at a time when Guinea had already been recognized 'as an independent sovereign State' by some sixty countries and had been admitted as the 82nd Member of the United Nations on 12 December 1958.[253]

(iii) *Partition*. In case of the factual partition of a sovereign State only one government can be recognized (*de jure*) without abandoning the unity of the sovereign State as there can be only one depository of the State's sovereignty. Thus, in 1950 Indian reluctance to recognize the East German Government was explained as follows: 'India look forward to the unification

[251] Touré, *L'Action politique du Parti démocratique de Guinée pour l'emancipation africaine* (1959), ii, 172. See also General de Gaulle's reply of 16 Oct. 1958 to M. Touré's request for *de jure* recognition of the Guinean Government: 'For the Government to follow your desired route, you will surely understand that various conditions must be fulfilled in advance. For the Government it is important to collect evidence that the present Government of Guinea is able, within its abilities, to fulfil effectively the burdens and the obligations of independence and of sovereignty' (author's translation) (*ibid.*, 161).

[252] See *Le Monde*, 8 Jan. 1959, 4; Whiteman, n. 95 above, ii, 156; and [1959] *Keesing's* 16601. See also the general preamble of the Accords: 'The Government of the French Republic and the Government of the Republic of Guinea, conscious of the necessity to establish *legal ties* of co-operation and friendship between the two countries' (author's translation) (Fischer, 'L'indépendance de la Guinée et les accords Franco-Guinéens' (1958) 4 *AFDI* 711–22 at 718, italics added) and the communiqué, issued by the French Government on 15 Jan. 1959, that 'the French Government, having fully recognized the Republic of Guinea, will send a *chargé d'affaires* to Conakry very soon' (*Le Monde*, 17 Jan. 1959, 1 (translation supplied)).

[253] The following is the text of the telegram sent by the British Foreign Secretary on 1 Nov. 1958 to M. Touré: 'I have pleasure in informing you that Her Majesty's Government in the United Kingdom recognize the Republic of Guinea as an independent sovereign state and Your Excellency's Government as the Government of that state. I sincerely reciprocate the desire you have expressed for the establishment in due course of diplomatic relations between our two countries' (E. Lauterpacht, 'The Contemporary Practice of the United Kingdom in the Field of International Law—Survey and Comment' (1959) 8 *ICLQ* 157–8). See also O'Brien and Goebel, 'United States Recognition Policy Toward the New Nations' in O'Brien (ed.), *The Yearbook of World Polity* (1965), iii, 98–228 at 156–9, who argue that the 'formal recognition' of the 'Government' of Guinea (rather than recognition of the independence of Guinea), extended by the US Government on 2 Nov. 1958, was no more than *de facto* recognition.

of Germany and are, therefore, reluctant to take any step which may retard the process of unification. Recognition of the East German Republic would have a certain implication that India have accepted the division of Germany as final.'[254] However, pending a final solution of the partition one government may be recognized *de jure* and the other *de facto* or both governments may be recognized *de facto* for the time being. Recognition (*de jure*) of two governments will manifest that the recognizing State regards the two States as separate sovereign States and consequently regards the sovereignty of the former State as extinct as no two sovereign States can exist on the same territory at the same time. The cases of Vietnam and Germany may illustrate this.

Vietnam. According to the Geneva Agreement on the Cessation of Hostilities in Vietnam, signed on 20 July 1954, and the Final Declaration of the Geneva Conference on Vietnam, dated 21 July 1954,[255] the State of Vietnam, the unity of which was affirmed in principle, was provisionally to be partitioned, the northern part under the control of the Government of the Democratic Republic of Vietnam (DRVN) and the southern part under the Government of the State of Vietnam (SVN).[256] Elections were to be held simultaneously in both parts of Vietnam by 20 July 1956 with the aim of establishing a unified Government of the State of Vietnam. France, which recognized the sovereignty of the Government of the SVN over the entire territory of Vietnam on 21 July 1954 accorded *de facto* recognition to the DRVN Government.[257] Pakistan accorded *de facto* recognition to both North and South Vietnam on 21 December 1954[258] and only on 7 November 1972 announced its 'recognition' of North Vietnam.[259] Similarly, India which had already accorded *de facto* recognition of South Vietnam on 15 December 1954 accorded *de facto* recognition also to North Vietnam.[260] Only after the formal unification of North and South Vietnam in 1976 did India accord 'recognition'.[261] On 6 April 1955 it was announced

[254] Misra, *India's Policy of Recognition of States and Governments* (1966), 81. See also *ibid.*, 81–94; and Mitra, *India and the German Problem. A Case for Recognition of the GDR* (1966).

[255] House of Commons, *Sessional Papers*, 31 (1953–4), Cmd. 9239. On the legal status of Vietnam in general, see Hammerbacher, *Die völkerrechtliche Stellung Vietnams* (1960); Corbett, 'The Vietnam Struggle and International Law' in Falk (ed.), *The International Law of Civil War* (1971), 348–404; Oánh, *Die Wandlung der völkerrechtlichen Stellung Vietnams bis zum Pariser Waffenstillstandsabkommen 1973* (1974); Crawford, n. 38 above, 284–6.

[256] On 26 Oct. 1955 Ngo Dinh Diem (who had deposed Emperor Bao Dai on 20 Oct. 1955) declared the territory south of the 17th parallel the 'Republic of Vietnam' (RVN).

[257] See Thierry, 'La condition juridique du Nord Viet-nam' (1955) 1 *AFDI* 169–74 at 173, 174. See also House of Commons, *Sessional Papers*, 31 (1953–4), Cmd. 9239, 5–9.

[258] [1955] *Keesing's* 14028C.

[259] [1972] *Keesing's* 25601A.

[260] [1954] *Keesing's* 13954C.

[261] See Tripathi, *India's Foreign Policy on Diplomatic Recognition of States and Governments* (1990), 101–2, 124. On the Japanese view that there are two regimes in 'existence *de facto*' in the state of Vietnam of which Japan regarded the Government of the Republic of

that the Indonesian Government had decided to accord *de facto* recognition to the DRVN and the SVN, that Consulates would be established in the capitals of the two States, and that the question of *de jure* recognition would be decided upon after the holding of general elections in Vietnam as provided in the Geneva Agreements.[262] Elections in both parts of Vietnam, however, never materialized. On 21 June 1965 the British Foreign Secretary, Mr Stewart, expressing the at that time still predominant view among States, declared that 'Her Majesty's Government do not recognize the existence of two separate States in Vietnam, which would be inconsistent with the principles generally accepted at the Geneva Conference of 1954.' He declared further that the only Government in Vietnam which Her Majesty's Government recognized was the Government of the Republic of Vietnam and that the present arrangements did not restrict the Government's ability to have contact with the North Vietnamese authorities.[263] When in July 1973 the British Government finally recognized the Government of the DRNV it recognized the existence of a second sovereign State in Vietnam. This becomes clear from the statement of the Parliamentary Under-Secretary of State for Foreign Affairs, Mr Royle, on 17 July 1973 that 'We have now recognized the Government of the Democratic Republic of Vietnam, with its capital at Hanoi, as the Government of a State whose territory lies north of the provisional military demarcation line laid down in the 1954 Geneva Agreement.'[264]

Germany. The view that in the case of partitioned States only one government can be recognized (*de jure*) without abandoning the unity of the sovereign State at first sight seems to conflict with the partition of Germany after the Second World War. The four Allied Powers with special rights and responsibilities with respect to Germany as a whole 'recognized' both the Government of the FRG and the Government of the GDR while at the same time maintaining that Germany as a whole continued to exist as a sovereign State (although without competent German organs to act on its

(South) Vietnam 'as the legitimate government which represents the whole of Vietnam', see Oda and Owada, 'The Practice of Japan in International Law' (1967) 11 *JAIL* 109, and (1982) 25 *JAIL* 74–8.

[262] [1955] *Keesing's* 14231D.

[263] HC Debs., vol. 714, WA, *col.* 136, 21 June 1965. See also *ibid.*, vol. 722, WA, *col.* 363, 20 Dec. 1965; *ibid.*, vol. 684, WA, *col.* 106, 20 Nov. 1963. Great Britain had accorded *de jure* recognition to the Bao Dai Government of the State of Vietnam on 7 Feb. 1950: HL Debs., vol. 166, col. 8, 6 Mar. 1950; HC Debs., vol. 472, cols. 748–9, 13 Mar. 1950. On British recognition of the Bao Dai Government see also Bullock, n. 207 above, 745, 748.

[264] HC Debs., vol. 860, WA, *col.* 93, 17 July 1973. But see also the Act of the International Conference on Vietnam, signed in Paris on 2 Mar. 1973, to which the UK was a party. Art. 4 reads: 'The parties to this Act solemnly recognize and strictly respect the fundamental national rights of the Vietnamese people—i.e. the independence, sovereignty, unity and territorial integrity of Vietnam—as well as the right of the South Vietnamese people to self-determination' ([1973] *Keesing's* 25886).

behalf).[265] However, neither of the two governments was recognized as the *de jure* government of Germany as a whole. For example, the certificate of the British Foreign Office of 6 November 1964 in the case *Carl Zeiss Stiftung* v. *Rayner & Keeler (No 2)* (1966) said: 'This statement does not constitute recognition of the Government of the Federal Republic of Germany as the *de jure* Government of all Germany.'[266] The Government of the Federal Republic of Germany, however, was recognized by the Western Allies 'pending the unification of Germany . . . as the only German Government freely and legitimately constituted and therefore entitled to speak for Germany as the representative of the German people in international affairs.'[267] Furthermore, neither of the two German States was recognized, at least by the Western Powers and probably also by the Soviet Union,[268] as a new sovereign State. France, the United Kingdom, and the United States on 5 May 1955 recognized the FRG not as a sovereign independent State but only as 'having the full authority of a sovereign State over its internal and external affairs'.[269] A similar statement was made by the British Government on 6 February 1973 with respect to the GDR. The Minister of State, Foreign and Commonwealth Office, Baroness Tweedsmuir Belhelvie stated:

[265] US Secretary of State Dulles stated on 18 May 1959: 'under international law the entity known as Germany remains in existence, notwithstanding what has happened since 1945' ((1959) 40 *DSB* 819). See also the Opinion of the Legal Department of the US Military Government in Germany of 17 Mar. 1947 ((1950–1) 13 *ZaöRV* 175–6); and the FO certificate in *R.* v. *Bottrill, ex parte Kuechenmeister* (1946), 62 TLR 374 at 375. On the continuing existence of Germany see also *Trawnik* v. *Lennox* (1984), [1985] 2 All ER 368; *R.* v. *Secretary of State for Foreign and Commonwealth Affairs, ex parte Trawnik* [1985] TLR 18 April 1985 (QBD), [1986] TLR 21 Feb. 1986 (CA). See also Art. 7(2) of the Treaty on the Final Settlement with respect to Germany, signed at Moscow on 12 Sept. 1990 ((1990) 29 ILM 1186). On the legal status of Germany, in general see Jennings and Watts, n. 8 above, 138–9; Crawford, n. 38 above, 273–81.

[266] [1967] 1 AC 853 at 920 (HL). For a similar statement by the US Department of State, see *Carl Zeiss Stiftung* v. *VEB Carl Zeiss, Jena*, 293 F.Supp. 892 at 900 (SDNY 1968). See also BVerfG, 31 July 1973 [*Grundlagenvertragsurteil*], BVerfGE 36, 1 at 16; BVerfG, 21 Oct. 1987 [*Single German Nationality (Teso) Case*], BVerfGE 77, 137 at 143.

[267] See the New York Declaration on Western Germany of 19 Sept. 1950: (1950) 23 *DSB* 530; (1950–1) 13 *ZaöRV* 667. This declaration was reiterated in 1955, 1964, and 1966.

[268] The Soviet Government had declared on 25 Mar. 1954 that '(1) The Soviet Union assumes the same relations with the German Democratic Republic as with other sovereign States. (2) The German Democratic Republic will be at liberty to make its own decisions in internal and external affairs, including the questions of relations with Western Germany' ([1956] *Keesing's* 15271).

[269] See Art. 1(2) of the Convention on the Relations between the Three Powers and the German Federal Republic (of 26 May 1952) in the version of 23 Oct. 1954 ((1963) 23 *ZaöRV* 292). The Convention entered into force on 5 May 1955. Recognition of the FRG by the USSR was effected on 13 Sept. 1955 by an announcement on the establishment of diplomatic relations ([1955] *Keesing's* 14425A). Recognition as 'having the full authority of a sovereign State over its internal and external affairs' was interpreted by the West German Government as being allowed freely to exercise the 'sovereignty of Germany' with regard to the FRG. Cf. the Report of the Legal Committee of the German Parliament of 11 Feb. 1955: (1963) 23 *ZaöRV* 300.

Subject to the rights and responsibilities of the Four Powers in respect of Berlin and Germany as a whole, Her Majesty's Government recognize that the German Democratic Republic has the full authority of a sovereign State over its internal and external affairs. This does not in any way indicate a change in our position on the special situation in Germany as set out in the NATO communiqué of December 8, 1972.[270]

The other Western Allies also did not recognize the sovereignty of the GDR but only 'its existence'[271] and established diplomatic relations with it.[272] It is of interest to note that most (Western) States in the 1970s conspicuously avoided any statement of recognition and simply announced the establishment of diplomatic relations with the GDR. Thus, for example, the Report of the Swiss Federal Council for 1972 stated that 'By recognizing the People's Republic of Bangladesh in March and by establishing diplomatic relations with the German Democratic Republic in December Switzerland undertook a further step towards the universality of her foreign policy.'[273] It may be concluded that the two German governments were not recognized (*de jure*), i.e. as governments of two sovereign States, but rather as authorities competent to act 'like' sovereign authorities with respect to that part of German territory under their control, always subject, of course, to the rights and responsibilities of the four Allied Powers. A memorandum of the British Foreign and Commonwealth Office on 'The Status of the Two German States', dated March 1990, seems to confirm this view. The Memorandum reads in the relevant part:

Her Majesty's Government recognizes both the Federal Republic of Germany and the German Democratic Republic *as having the full authority of sovereign States* [but not as sovereign States] over their external and internal affairs, subject only to Allied rights and responsibilities. Germany as a whole continues to exist as a State in international law.[274]

[270] HL Debs., vol. 338, col. 959, 6 Feb. 1973. For the NATO communiqué of 8 Dec. 1972, see [1973] *Keesing's* 25697A.

[271] On 30 Nov. 1972 the French Foreign Minister spoke of the 'recognition of the existence of the GDR' which will take full effect with the establishment of diplomatic relations ((1973) 19 *AFDI* 1069). The French President, M. Pompidou, in a press conference on 9 Jan. 1973 spoke of 'the recognition, more precisely the establishment of diplomatic relations' (*ibid.*, 1070).

[272] The establishment of diplomatic relations with the GDR was announced by the UK and France on 9 Feb. 1973 and by the USA on 4 Sept. 1974 ((1974) 71 *DSB* 423).

[273] Klarer, n. 94 above, 276 (translation supplied). Dr Klarer points out that the report at no point indicates that the establishment of diplomatic relations with the GDR might constitute *de jure* recognition of that State. Japan and the GDR on 15 May 1973 established diplomatic relations. It was reported that 'with its *de facto* recognition of an independent eastern half of Germany, Japan became the eighty-second country to recognize the Democratic Republic of Germany' ((1974) 18 *JAIL* 219).

[274] [1989–90] Parl. Pap., HC Paper 225–i, 3.

(b) Annexation of States

As long as a government has not yet recognized the annexation of a State (i.e. the sovereignty of the annexing State over the annexed territory)[275] it cannot recognize (*de jure*) the annexing State's government as the government of the annexed territory. It may, however, accord *de facto* recognition to the annexing State's government while continuing to recognize *de jure* the annexed State's government in exile or its diplomatic representatives.[276] This may be illustrated by the following cases:

(i) *Ethiopia*. On 3 October 1935 Italy invaded Ethiopia and later formally proclaimed its annexation. Article 1 of the Royal Italian Decree of 9 May 1936 reads in part: 'The territories and peoples that belonged to the Empire of Ethiopia are placed under the full and entire sovereignty of the Kingdom of Italy'.[277] Prior to the recognition of Italian sovereignty over Ethiopia the Italian Government was recognized by some eleven countries,[278] as the Government *de facto* of the parts of Ethiopia which it controlled[279] while the Emperor Haile Selassie (although in exile) continued to be recognized as the *de jure* ruler of Ethiopia. However, once Italian sovereignty over Ethiopia was

[275] That it is the sovereignty of the annexing State over the annexed State rather than the annexation that is recognized by other States was pointed out on several occasions by Switzerland in the case of the Italian annexation of Ethiopia. See Klarer, n. 94 above, 322–33.

[276] *De jure* but not *de facto* recognition of the annexation automatically entails the de-recognition of the annexed State's *de jure* government in exile as such, without a special announcement to this effect being necessary. See HC Debs., vol. 341, cols. 480–1, 14 Nov. 1938.

[277] *The Times*, 13 May 1936, 16. On the Italian annexation of Ethiopia in general, see Strupp, 'Problèmes soulevés à l'occasion de l'annexion par Italie de l'Empire éthiopien (1937) 44 *RGDIP* 43–50; Gernhuber, 'Der italienisch-abessinische Konflikt und das Völkerrecht', doctoral thesis (University of Königsberg, 1937); Nostitz-Wallnitz, 'Die Annexion Abessiniens und die Liquidation des abessinischen Konflikts' (1937) 7 *ZaöRV* 38–66; Rousseau, 'Le conflit italo-éthiopien—La conquête et ses conséquences' (1938) 45 *RGDIP* 53–123; Bentwich, 'Legal Aspects of the Restoration of Ethiopian Sovereignty' (1945) 22 *BYBIL* 275–8.

[278] According to a note of the Italian Government at the beginning of 1938 the following countries accorded it *de facto* recognition: Belgium, Bulgaria, Czechoslovakia, France, Greece, Haiti, Iran, Peru, Romania, Turkey, and the UK ((1938) 38 *Bull. de l'Institute Juridique International* 106–7 at 107). On the *de facto* and *de jure* recognition of the annexation, see Rousseau, n. 277 above, 53–123 at 83–123. For a list of States which accorded recognition, *de jure* and *de facto*, to the Italian annexation of Ethiopia and 'de-recognized' the Emperor Haile Selassie, see HC Debs., vol. 337, col. 1890, 29 June 1938.

[279] Mr Butler, the British Under-Secretary of State for Foreign Affairs, stated in Mar. 1937: 'His Majesty's Government have, since December, 1936, recognized the Italian Government as the Government *de facto* of the parts of Abyssinia which they control' (HC Debs., vol. 333, WA, *col.* 617, 17 Mar. 1938). See also *ibid.*, vol. 335, WA, *cols.* 1608–9, 11 May 1938 and the Foreign Office certificate in *Bank of Ethiopia* v. *National Bank of Egypt and Liguori* [1937] 1 Ch. 513 at 519. On this decision, see Wright, 'The British Courts and Ethiopian Recognition' (1937) 31 *AJIL* 683–8. On the withdrawal of recognition of Italian sovereignty over Ethiopia, see HC Debs., vol. 362, col. 814, 3 July 1940.

recognized, the King of Italy was at the same time recognized as *de jure* Emperor of Ethiopia.[280]

(ii) *Baltic States.* In June 1940, after short ultimata, Soviet forces occupied the Baltic States. Following what were called elections the newly elected national assemblies of these States voted unanimously in favour of union with the Soviet Union. The Supreme Soviet of the USSR resolved to 'admit' Lithuania on 3 August, Latvia on 5 August, and Estonia on 6 August. By a law of 7 August the three States became the fourteenth, fifteenth, and sixteenth constituent republics of the USSR.[281] The majority of States refused to recognize the incorporation of the Baltic States.[282] Consequently, these States recognized the local Governments of the new Soviet Republics either only *de facto* or not at all.[283] Thus, the Canadian Secretary of State for External Affairs stated in the case *Laane and Baltser* v. *Estonian State Cargo & Passenger S.S. Line* (1949):

> The Government of Canada recognizes that Estonia has *de facto* entered the Union of Soviet Socialist Republics but has not recognized this *de jure*. The Government of Canada recognizes the Government of the Estonian Soviet

[280] See the Foreign Office certificate of 30 Nov. 1938 in *Haile Selassie* v. *Cable and Wireless, Ltd (No 2)* (1938), [1939] 1 Ch. 182 at 197 (CA). On British recognition of Italian sovereignty over Ethiopia see e.g. DBFP, 2nd ser., XIX, no 87, at 152; no 115, at 219–27. See also [1938] I *Survey* 144–52.

[281] On the incorporation of the Baltic States and their legal status after 1940, see Makarov, 'Die Eingliederung der baltischen Staaten in die Sowjet-Union' (1940–1) 10 *ZaöRV* 682–707; Congress, House of Representatives, Select Committee on Communist Aggression, n. 124 above; Hough, 'The Annexation of the Baltic States and its Effect on the Development of Law Prohibiting Forcible Seizure of Territory' (1985) 6 *NYLSJICL* 301–533; Meissner, 'Die staatliche Kontinuität und völkerrechtliche Stellung der baltischen Länder' in Meissner (ed.), *Die baltischen Nationen* (1990), 192–218.

[282] One must distinguish in this respect between express non-recognition by the executive and the (limited) 'recognition' of the factual consequences of the annexation by the judiciary. Of the Western countries Sweden, Switzerland, the Netherlands, and for a time Australia (July 1974–Dec. 1975) and New Zealand seem to have recognized the incorporation of the Baltic States *de jure*. Cf. *WP*, 4 Aug. 1993, Sec. A, 17; Klarer, n. 94 above, 336–7; Timmermans, 'The Baltic States, the Soviet Union and the Netherlands: A Historical Note' (1985) 32 *Ned. TIR* 288–94. On Australia's *de jure* recognition, see Suter, n. 13 above, 67–79 at 72–4; Dunsdorfs, *The Baltic Dilemma. The Case of the de jure Recognition by Australia of the Incorporation of the Baltic States into the Soviet Union* (1975).

[283] *De facto* recognition was accorded by the UK, Canada, and probably also France and Italy. The USA, Belgium, (West) Germany, Ireland, Portugal, Spain, and the Vatican accorded neither *de facto* nor *de jure* recognition. Cf. Riismandel, 'The Continued Legal Existence of the Baltic States', *Baltic Rev.*, 12 (7 Nov. 1957), 48–68 at 53–4; Selter, 'Zur Rechtslage der baltischen Staaten' [1956] *IRD* 33–51 at 49; Meissner, *Die Sowjetunion, die baltischen Staaten und das Völkerrecht* (1956), 291–312. For US non-recognition and its practical limitations, see Vitas, *The United States and Lithuania. The Stimson Doctrine of Nonrecognition* (1990); Ambros, 'Nonrecognition: Its Development in International Law and Its Application by the United States with Particular Reference to the Baltic States', Ph.D. thesis (New York, 1965).

Socialist Republic to be the *de facto* government of Estonia but does not recognize it as the *de jure* government of Estonia.[284]

(iii) *Goa.* On 18 December 1961 Indian troops invaded and occupied the Portuguese territories in India—Goa and the enclaves of Damão and Dio—and on 27 March 1962 the Indian Constitution was amended by an Act constituting Goa, Damão and Dio as Indian 'Union Territories' with retrospective effect from 20 December 1961.[285] Until 31 December 1974 Portugal did not recognize Indian sovereignty over the enclaves but regarded them as only temporarily 'withdrawn from the full and effective exercise of Portuguese sovereignty'.[286] When asked in March 1965 'what status Her Majesty's Government accord to the territories of Goa, Damão and Dio', Mr Hughes, the Minister of State for Commonwealth Relations, answered: 'Her Majesty's Government recognize the Government of India as the *de facto* government of Goa, Damão and Dio. The Governments of India and Portugal were informed of this in September, 1963.'[287] Bearing in mind that 'no territorial acquisition resulting from the threat or use of force shall be recognized as legal' and that a majority of the Security Council took the view that the Indian action was illegal,[288] it is suggested that *de facto*

[284] [1949] SCR 530 at 540. See also *Estonian State Cargo and Passenger SS Line* v. *Proceeds of SS Elise* [1948] 4 DLR 247. For Canada's view on the legal status of the Baltic States, see DCER XII, no 989, at 1694; no 1258, at 2064; and Binavince, n. 11 above, 174–5. For similar certificates of the British Foreign Office, see *A/S Tallinna Laevauhisus* v. *Tallinna Shipping Company* (1946) 79 Ll.LR 245 at 251 and *A/S Tallinna Laevauhisus* v. *Estonian State Steamship Line* (1946), (1947) 80 Ll.LR 99 at 101 (CA); *In the Estate of Pikelny* (1955) 22 ILR 97–9 at 99; *In the Matter of 167 Queen's Gate [London] S.W. 7* and *In the Matter of the Trustee Act 1925*, UKMIL 1990, (1990) 61 BYBIL 499–502. On British *de facto* but not *de jure* recognition of the incorporation of the Baltic States, see also HC Debs., vol. 732, WA, *col.* 8, 18 July 1966; *ibid.*, vol. 82, WA, *col.* 273, 5 July 1985; *ibid.*, vol. 131, WA, *col.* 249, 15 Apr. 1988; HL Debs., vol. 525, col. 1264, 6 Feb. 1991. In order to secure the conclusion of the Anglo-Russian Treaty for Mutual Assistance of 26 May 1942 Britain considered even *de jure* recognition of the annexation of the Baltic States. See Woodward, *British Foreign Policy in the Second World War* (1971), ii, 226–34, 237–45. Compare also *Zarine* v. *Owners SS 'Ramava'* (1941) 75 ILTR 153–63 at 158, where the Minister of External Affairs of Eire, which did not recognize the annexation, informed the Court that 'Eire did not officially recognize the USSR as the Sovereign Government of the Republics of Latvia and Estonia'.

[285] See The Constitution (Twelfth Amendment) Act 1962. See also [1962] *Keesing's* 18635A, 18856A. On the invasion and annexation of Goa, see Wright, 'The Goa Incident' (1962) 56 *AJIL* 617–32; Flory, 'Les implications juridiques de l'affaire de Goa' (1962) 8 *AFDI* 476–91; Falk, 'The New States and International Legal Order' (1966–II) 118 *RdC* 7–103 at 53–7; Scholz, *Die Behandlung der Goa-Frage durch die Vereinten Nationen* (1970).

[286] See Law 2112 of 17 Feb. 1962 by which the Portuguese National Assembly established a Goan government-in-exile in Lisbon: Whiteman, n. 95 above, ii, 486, 1144. In Art. 1 of the Treaty between Portugal and India, signed at New Delhi on 31 Dec. 1974, Portugal renounced all claims to her former Indian territories and recognized the full sovereignty of India over these territories with effect from the dates when they became parts of India under the Constitution of India (982 UNTS 153 at 159). See also [1975] *Keesing's* 26922B.

[287] HC Debs., vol. 708, WA, *col.* 31, 8 Mar. 1965.

[288] See Crawford, n. 38 above, 112.

recognition manifested, that in the opinion of the British Government, the Indian Government, by its illegal annexation, had not acquired sovereignty over the Portuguese territories.[289]

(c) Rival Governments of the Same State

There is a long line of precedents that 'there can be but one government in the same State at the same time'.[290] In *New York Chinese TV Programs* v. *UE Enterprises* (1992), the United States Circuit Court of Appeals pointed out that 'because both the PRC and the ROC professed to be the one "China", the United States could not pretend that both governments had sovereignty over all of China. Recognition of the PRC, therefore, necessitated derecognition of the ROC'.[291] As long as one of two rival governments is recognized *de jure* the other can only be recognized *de facto* as there can be only one depository of the State's sovereignty. States may, however, recognize one of the rival governments as the *de jure* government of a new separate State. They may also choose to recognize both rival governments *de facto* only.[292] That States can recognize only one government *de jure* at a time was also stressed by Lord Reid who stated in *Gdynia Ameryka Linie* v. *Boguslawski* (1952) that 'apart from the distinction between recognition *de jure* and recognition *de facto* . . . we cannot recognize two different governments of the same country at the same time'.[293] This was also made clear by the French Prime Minister, M. Blum, in the Chamber of Deputies on 5 December 1936: 'I repeat . . . that for us in Spain, there is only one legal government or, to say it better, only one government. The principles which could be described as democratic law in this respect are identical with the undisputed rules of international law' (author's translation).[294] As *de facto*

[289] Cf. A/RES/2625 (XXV), 24 Oct. 1970; A/RES/3314 (XXIX), 14 Dec. 1974; Art. 5 (3). On the principle of non-recognition of acquisition of territory resulting from the threat or use of force, see Brownlie, n. 246 above, 410–23. See also the decision of the Brussels CA of 20 Jan. 1965 which declared that the annexation of Goa was contrary to the UN Charter and that therefore 'no legal consequence can be recognized as resulting from this act of violence until an international treaty is concluded' (*Estado da India* v. *Société Anonyme Kredietbank et Verbruggen* (1965), [1966] II Pas.belge 19–23 (translation supplied)).

[290] See the decision of the Mex.-US Cl.Comm. in *Jansen* v. *Mexico* (1868): Moore (ed.), *History and Digest of the International Arbitrations to Which the United States Has Been a Party* (1898), iii, 2902 at 2928. See also American Law Institute, *Restatement of the Law (Second). The Foreign Relations Law of the United States* (1965), 323: 'Customarily, recognition of governments is made on a "one or the other" basis.'

[291] 954 F.2d 847 at 850 (2nd Cir. 1992).

[292] This course of action was adopted by some of the Eastern European States with respect to the Lon Nol Government and the Royal Government of National Union (RGNUC), both claiming to be the Government of Cambodia in 1970–5. See [1971] *Keesing's* 24810. States may, of course, also choose to accord *de facto* recognition to only one of several rival governments. See Moore, n. 54 above, i, 201.

[293] [1953] AC 11 at 45 (HL). See also the judgment of Cohen LJ in *Boguslawski* v. *Gdynia-Ameryka Linie* (1950), [1951] 1 KB 162 at 177 (CA).

[294] Kiss, n. 28 above, iii, no 83, at 64. See also the statement of the Swiss Political Department

recognition does not impair the legal status of the incumbent government States can recognize one or more rival governments *de facto* while continuing to recognize the incumbent government *de jure*.[295] This may be illustrated by the recognition practice with respect to the rival governments in the following countries:

(i) *Greece*. During the First World War, in October 1916, Great Britain recognized the pro-Entente Provisional Government of the former Greek Prime Minister Eleuthérios Venizélos at Salonika 'as the *de facto* authority in the districts where it is established' while continuing to recognize the Government of the pro-German King Constantine at Athens as 'the only *de jure* Government in Greece'.[296] The Government at Salonika declared war on Germany and Bulgaria on 24 November 1916 while the *de jure* Government at Athens declared war on Germany only on 25 June 1917. After the War the question arose from what time Greece was at war with the Central Powers and especially with Germany as, by application of Article 232 of the Treaty of Peace signed at Versailles on 28 June 1919,[297] Germany was responsible for all damages caused to the civilian population of the Allied and Associated Powers during the period in which they were at war with Germany. The Reparation Commission which had to determine for each Power the point from which it was at war with Germany adopted the 25 June 1917 as the date from which Greece was at war with Germany as only the *de jure* government of Greece could validly declare war on foreign States.[298]

(ii) *Spain*. Similarly, during the Spanish Civil War (1936–9) several States granted *de facto* recognition to the Government of General Franco while continuing to recognize the incumbent Republican Government *de jure*. On 24 November 1938 Mr Butler, the Under-

of 2 Feb. 1945: 'Simultaneous recognition of a second government [of Yugoslavia] according to principles of international law inconceivable' (DDS XV, no 353, at 877, translation supplied). But see Padelford, *International Law and Diplomacy in the Spanish Civil Strife* (1939), 6, who seems to assume that States can recognize two authorities simultaneously as a *de jure* government of the same State.

[295] In *Anglo Czechoslovak & Prague Credit Bank* v. *Janssen* [1943] VLR 185 at 199, Mann CJ said: 'the recognition of the *de jure* sovereignty of one government is in no wise inconsistent with the contemporaneous admission of *de facto* control by another'.

[296] Cf. the statements of the Under-Secretary of State for Foreign Affairs, Lord Robert Cecil: HC Debs., vol. 86, cols. 1674, 1677, 31 Oct. 1916; *ibid.*, vol. 87, col. 551, 14 Nov. 1916; *ibid.*, vol. 88, cols. 118–19, 27 Nov. 1916. *De facto* recognition was also extended by France. See Rousseau, *Droit international public* (1977), iii, 573. On the Venizélos Government at Salonika (28 Sept. 1916–26 June 1917) and the developments in Greece in general, see Maccas, 'La Grèce et l'Entente (1914–1917)' (1918) 25 *RGDIP* 154–222; Ion, 'The Hellenic Crisis from the Point of View of Constitutional and International Law' (1917) 11 *AJIL* 46–73, 327–57 and (1918) 12 *AJIL* 312–37, 562–88, 796–812; Jumeau, *Le Refuge du Gouvernement National à l'Etranger* (1941), 150–3; and the *Occupation of Cavalla* Case, (1929–30) 5 AD no 292, 496–7.

[297] 112 BFSP 1 at 104–5.

[298] Ténékidès, 'La nature juridique des gouvernements institués par l'occupant en Grèce suivant la jurisprudence hellénique' (1947) 51 *RGDIP* 113–33 at 129.

Secretary of State for Foreign Affairs, informed the House of Commons that the 'following *foreign* countries have granted *de facto* recognition and appointed agents [to the Spanish Nationalist Government]:—Czechoslovakia, Greece, Rumania, Switzerland, Turkey, Bulgaria, Holland, Uruguay, Yugoslavia, Norway, Denmark, Finland, Venezuela.'[299]

(iii) *France.* During the Second World War several States granted *de facto* recognition to the French National Committee (CNF) while they continued to recognize (*de jure*) the Government of Marshal Pétain at Vichy and maintained diplomatic relations with it. For example, Cuba on 29 April 1942 accorded *de facto* recognition to the CNF with respect to Equatorial Africa, the Cameroons, Tahiti, New Caledonia, and the New Hebrides.[300] But, diplomatic relations with the Vichy Government were severed only on 9 November 1942.[301] On 9 July 1942 the US State Department announced the appointment of a representative to the CNF in London.[302] Already on 1 March 1942 the State Department had announced that the US Government:

> recognizes, in particular, that French island possessions in that area [i.e. the Pacific] are under the effective control of the French National Committee established in London, and the United States authorities are co-operating for the defence of these islands with the authorities established by the French National Committee and with no other French authority.[303]

However, only on 8 November 1942 did the United States sever diplomatic relations with the French Government at Vichy.[304]

(d) Effective Governments of States

The granting of express *de facto* recognition 'only' to an effective government has been used by States in order to indicate that in their opinion the regime in power does not qualify as the State's government or that they are unwilling to treat with it as such. Thus, only *de facto* recognition has been given to governments installed by outside intervention.[305] It has also been granted for an intermediate period in which it was established whether or not the government fulfilled the qualifications for recognition or in which States consulted on recognition within the context of regional co-

299 HC Debs., vol. 341, WA, *col.* 1970, 24 Nov. 1938, italics added. To this list the UK must be added.

300 [1942] *Keesing's* 5318A.

301 RIIA, *Chronology of the Second World War* (1947), 152.

302 (1942) 7 *DSB* 613.

303 De Gaulle, *War Memoirs. Documents* (1955), i, 273–4. Similar statements were made with respect to French Equatorial Africa and the Cameroons ((1942) 6 *DSB* 208, 273).

304 Cf. [1943] II FRUS 88. On US *de facto* recognition of the CNF, see DAFR IV, 633–4. See also Cassin, 'Vichy or Free France' (1941) 20 *For. Affairs* 102–12 at 111 and 'La création du Comité national français de Londres, le 24 septembre 1941', *Cah. fr.* (Sept. 1956), 2–5.

305 e.g. on 6 June 1922 Czechoslovakia recognized *de facto* the Soviet Government of Ukraine. See Markus, n. 153 above, 261, n. 12 and 264.

operation.[306] For example, Dahomey (Benin) on 24 January 1963 extended *de facto* recognition to the Grunitzky Government in Togo pending the outcome of the Council meeting of the thirteen-member African-Malagasy Union (UAM) Organization which was to be held in Lagos on 24 to 26 January 1963 to consider the *coup d'état* in Togo. While express *de facto* recognition may, of course, also be used by States simply in order to indicate their disapproval of an effective government this course of action normally is not adopted because it has proved politically more disadvantageous to the recognizing government than to the only *de facto* recognized government. Thus the US Department of State wrote on 21 February 1958 to its Embassy in Baghdad with respect to the Iraqi proposal to recognize the Government of the United Arab Republic (UAR) only *de facto*:

We have noted request of Government of Iraq that Baghdad Pact Governments and United States confine themselves to *de facto* recognition, postponing *de jure* recognition. We believe that this position, half-way between recognition and non-recognition, would not achieve whatever benefits might reside in either of these attitudes, but, by indicating doubt that UAR possessed legal qualifications for recognition, which is not the case in our view, would merely cause irritation and resentment and make it more difficult for state extending *de facto* recognition to transact business with UAR and exert influence upon it.[307]

(6) Meanings of Other Variants

Besides the terms '*de facto*' and '*de jure* recognition' States have employed the terms 'official recognition',[308] 'formal recognition',[309] 'political recogni-

[306] The Togolese Government of President Sylvanus Olympio was overthrown and the President himself killed while trying to gain refuge in the US Embassy in a military rising (*coup*) in Lomé on 13 Jan. 1963. Nigeria and Guinea in particular claimed Ghanese involvement in the *coup* and tried to get other African States not to recognize the new Government formed by M. Grunitzky. Only Ghana and Senegal had accorded *de jure* recognition prior to Dahomey's action ([1963] *West Africa* 59, 85; [1963] *Keesing's* 19249A). See also Akinyemi, 'Organization of African Unity: The Practice of Recognition of Governments' (1975) 36 *Indian JPS* 63–79 at 63–7.

[307] [1958–60] XIII FRUS 430–1. The USA on 25 Feb. 1958 accorded 'full recognition' to the UAR (*ibid.*), as it did not wish to cast doubt on the *de jure* character of the UAR (Whiteman, n. 95 above, ii, 4). Both the USA and the UK treated the recognition of the UAR as a question of recognition of its government. See *ibid.*, at 230–3; and HC Debs., vol. 582, col. 391, 12 Feb. 1958.

[308] On 20 Jan. 1871 Earl Granville, the British Foreign Secretary, wrote to Lord Lyons, the British Ambassador to France, with respect to the request by the French Government of National Defence for official recognition by Her Majesty's Government: 'By official recognition I understand nothing more than the issue of regular credentials on behalf of the British Ambassador in France to the actual head of the Government of that country' (61 BFSP 995). For examples of 'official recognition', see Whiteman, n. 95 above, ii, 41, 217; Moore, n. 54 above, i, 148; Smith, n. 3 above, 230; Wilson, 'The Bolsheviks and Diplomacy' in Temperley (ed.), *A History of the Peace Conference of Paris* (1924), vi, 311–34 at 327–8; Fontes, B.I.I.1, nos 529, 530; *ibid.*, B.I.II.1, nos 214, 245.

[309] For examples of 'formal recognition', see Hackworth, n. 125 above, i, 244–5, 317; 61 BFSP 843, 865; Fontes, B.I.I.1, no 443; *ibid.*, B.I.II.1, at 218.

tion',[310] 'full recognition',[311] and '[full] diplomatic recognition'.[312] These terms are normally used interchangeably with *de jure* recognition.[313] For example, on 1 January 1949 the United States extended 'full recognition to the Government of the Republic of Korea'.[314] On 25 March 1949, on the occasion of the presentation of his letters of credence to President Truman, the newly appointed Korean Ambassador, Dr Chang, referred to that recognition in the following terms: 'We remember particularly, with profound gratitude, your very gracious action in according the first *de jure* recognition to the Republic of Korea on January first of this year.'[315] It is important to note that these variants, like *de jure* recognition, have been used with a double meaning. They may either express the recognizing State's willingness to maintain normal official, i.e. diplomatic, relations, or manifest that in the recognizing State's opinion the recognized government qualifies as such. This may be shown in the case of diplomatic recognition, the variant that has gained most prominence in modern State, and especially United States, practice. In the large majority of cases the variant will express the

[310] For examples of 'political recognition', see Whiteman, n. 95 above, ii, 38, 48, 524, 562, 590, 597; Hackworth, n. 125 above, i, 300 and iv, 37; Moore, n. 54 above, i, 240. Courts have also used the term as meaning recognition by the political branch of government, i.e. the executive, in contrast to 'judicial recognition' by the courts. Cf. *Banco Nacional de Cuba* v. *Sabbatino et al.*, 376 US 398 at 410 (1964).

[311] For examples of 'full recognition', see AHG/RES.18 (I); Whiteman, n. 95 above, ii, 180, 200; [1944] V FRUS 1152; Hackworth, n. 125 above, i, 217, 219; HC Debs., vol. 373, col. 861, 23 July 1941. Full recognition does not necessarily require the appointment of ambassadors. See DBFP, 1st ser., XXV, no 206, at 330–2.

[312] For examples of '[full] diplomatic recognition', see *WP*, 16 Dec. 1991, Sec. A, 1; (1976) 14 *CYIL* 347; [1970] *Keesing's* 23844A and 24050; Whiteman, n. 95 above, ii, 6, 45, 97, 102, 140, 544–5, 548–9, 601, 606; HC Debs., vol. 711, WA, *col.* 218, 6 May 1965; *ibid.*, vol. 714, WA, *col.* 136, 21 June 1965; *ibid.*, vol. 829, col. 218, 18 Jan. 1972; *ibid.*, vol. 977, WA, *col.* 427, 25 Jan. 1980; Czechoslovak Ministry of Foreign Affairs (ed.), *Four Fighting Years* (1943), 186. On US diplomatic recognition in general, see also (1977) 77 *DSB* 462–3.

[313] For examples in which *de jure* recognition has been used in the same statement interchangeably with: (i) political recognition: Whiteman, n. 95 above, ii, 561–2, 172; (ii) formal recognition: Hackworth, n. 125 above, i, 244–5, 317; Klarer, n. 94 above, 70; DBFP, 1st ser., XV, no 6, at 50 and no 8, at 59; and *Murarka et al.* v. *Bachrak Bros., Inc.*, 215 F.2d 547 at 552 (2nd Cir. 1954); (iii) full recognition: Hackworth, n. 125 above, i, 245; 212–13, 297; [1949] VI FRUS 702–3; Klarer, n. 94 above, 85, 82; 332; DBFP, 1st ser., XV, no 6, at 50; *ibid.*, III, no 485, at 604; *ibid.*, XXV, nos 204–7; (iv) official recognition: HL Debs., vol. 234, col. 343, 17 Oct. 1961. But see the statement of Mr Myres that diplomatic recognition is 'obviously different from *de facto*, *de jure* or plain recognition' ('Contemporary Practice of the United States Relating to International Law—Recognition of States' (1961) 55 *AJIL* 703–20 at 714).

[314] (1949) 20 *DSB* 59–60 at 60. On US recognition of Korea, see Myers, n. 313 above, 703–20 at 707–9; O'Brien and Goebel, n. 253 above, iii, 98–228 at 134–9.

[315] Whiteman, n. 95 above, ii, 80. Compare also the statement of US Secretary of State Shultz on 13 June 1986: 'After the fall of Somoza, the United States and Nicaragua's neighbours quickly extended diplomatic recognition to the broadly based revolutionary government in Managua' ((1986) 86/2113 *DSB* 19–22 at 20) and the decision in *OPE Shipping* v. *Allstate Insurance Company*, 521 F.Supp. 342 at 350 (SDNY 1981), in which the court referred to the Sandinista Government as the Government that 'replaced Somoza as the recognized *de jure* government'.

recognizing State's willingness to enter into diplomatic relations.[316] The following cases may illustrate this.

(i) On 22 March 1946 the United Kingdom recognized her former mandate Trans-Jordan 'as a fully independent State and His Highness The Amir as the sovereign thereof'.[317] It was not until 31 January 1949 that the United States Government 'extended *de jure* recognition to the Government of Transjordan'.[318] With respect to the fact that the United States has 'not extended *diplomatic recognition* to the Transjordan Government', the Legal Adviser to the State Department, Mr Gross, wrote on 11 May 1948: 'The United States Government, however, in 1946 and 1947 supported the application of Trans-Jordan for admission to membership in the United Nations, thus implying recognition of the existence of Trans-Jordan as a state'[319] and, one must add, its government,[320] with which the US Government had for some time maintained 'informal and friendly' but not diplomatic relations. These were only established once '*formal recognition*' was extended.[321] The case of Transjordan shows clearly that *de jure*, diplomatic and formal recognition may be used interchangeably and that normally no distinction is drawn between a new State and its government.

(ii) Diplomatic recognition was also used in the sense of diplomatic relations in 1974 by the US Congress House Concurrent Resolution 271 expressed 'the sense of Congress that it shall be the policy of the United States that the Government of the United States shall cease forthwith all consideration of . . . diplomatic recognition . . . with the Democratic Republic of North Vietnam or the Provisional Revolutionary Government (Vietcong)'. Thus, Mr Gilman, who spoke in the House of Representatives on 3 June 1974 for the resolution, stated that the resolution was 'calling for the prohibition of diplomatic relations with these nations'.[322]

[316] Compare (1989) 89/2152 *DSB* 75–9 at 77; (1992) 3/8 *DSD* 125.

[317] See Art. 1 of the Treaty of Alliance between the UK and Trans-Jordan, signed at London on 22 Mar. 1946: 6 UNTS 144.

[318] (1949) 20 *DSB* 205.

[319] Department of State, 867 N.01/5–1048: reprinted in Cohen, n. 146 above, 142–50 at 150, italics added.

[320] Cf. [1948] *Keesing's* 9302.

[321] See the statement of 28 Feb. 1949: 'Pursuant to the formal recognition of the Hashemite Kingdom of Transjordan by the United States on January 31, 1949, the United States Government on February 28 established a Legation in Amman, the capital of Transjordan' ((1949) 20 *DSB* 332). On US recognition of the State and Government of Transjordan see Myres, n. 313 above, 703–20 at 709–11; O'Brien and Goebel, n. 253 above, iii, 98–228 at 125–8; Whiteman, n. 95 above, ii, 171–2.

[322] Cong. Rec., 93rd Cong., 2nd sess., vol. 120, part 13, 17219. See also proposed S.Con.Res. 7, introduced on 21 Jan. 1935, which stated 'that it is the sense of Senate and House of Representatives of the United States that the diplomatic recognition by the Government of the United States of the Union of Soviet Socialist Republics should be withdrawn' (Whiteman, n.

(iii) In 1987 the United States repeatedly criticized the Soviet Union for withholding 'diplomatic recognition' of Israel.[323] Diplomatic recognition in this context referred to the unwillingness of the Soviet Government to re-establish diplomatic relations which had been severed in 1967.[324] The USSR had been the third State, after the USA and Guatemala, to recognize 'officially' the State of Israel and its Provisional Government on 17 May 1948—a recognition which had never been withdrawn.[325]

While in the large majority of cases diplomatic recognition will be used in the meaning of diplomatic relations this must not always be the case. In 1955 Senator McCarthy introduced Senate Resolution 126 which resolved that 'it is the sense of the Senate that the United States should . . . withdraw its diplomatic recognition from the Communist regimes in Bulgaria, Czechoslovakia, Hungary, Poland and Romania'. With regard to the fact that the United States had already broken off diplomatic relations with the Government of Bulgaria on 20 February 1950 and that its interests there were represented by Switzerland,[326] Senator McCarthy stated before the Senate Foreign Relations Committee on 13 July 1955 that he had been 'informed by the Department of State that this suspension of diplomatic relations does not imply withdrawal of diplomatic recognition from the Communist Government of Bulgaria'.[327]

95 above, ii, 45). Secretary of State Hull stated on 9 Feb. 1935 that the only way by which effect could be given to the view expressed in the resolution would be through the severance of diplomatic relations with the Soviet Government' (*ibid.*).

[323] For the statement of Secretary of State Shultz see (1987) 87/2124 *DSB* 7–10 at 9. For statements by other officials, see (1987) 87/2126 *DSB* 45–8 at 47.

[324] The USSR severed diplomatic relations with Israel on 10 June 1967 as a consequence of the 3rd Arab–Israeli (6-Day) War: [1967] *Keesing's* 22105A.

[325] The Soviet note is printed in *NY Times*, 18 May 1948, 1, 5. On 26 May 1948 it was announced that agreement had been reached between the Soviet Union and Israel to establish diplomatic missions in Moscow and Tel Aviv. Ministers were appointed on 25 June 1948.

[326] [1950] *Keesing's* 10557A. The resumption of diplomatic relations was announced on 27 Mar. 1959 ([1959] *Keesing's* 16729A).

[327] US Congress, Senate, Committee on Foreign Relations, *Executive Sessions of the Senate Foreign Relations Committee (Historical Series)* (1978), vii, 677.

Very thorough analysis of meanings + uses of de jure + de facto recognition and of their differences, as well as the meanings + uses of "official", "formal", or "political" or "diplomatic" "recognition".

Of value to academic experts, but I doubt if the analysis will be of much use to practitioners, either governmental or private because, as author acknowledged in his preface in relation to debates on theories of recog., it depends on the factual + legal circumstances of each individual case as to the meanings of recognition, whether de jure, de facto or diplomatic and the subsequent effect on the legal status of governments.

PART II

Legal Status of Authorities in Exile Recognized as Governments

3

Preliminary Considerations

From the fact that States are juridical persons it follows that they must act through organs. In the words of the Permanent Court of International Justice, 'States can act only by and through their agents and representatives.'[1] It is generally agreed that the organ representing the State in international intercourse is its government.[2] But, as Professor Bin Cheng has rightly pointed out, 'States not only act through their government but through their government exclusively'.[3] The government, consequently, possesses the *jus repraesentationis omnimodae*, i.e. the plenary and exclusive competence in international law to represent its State in the international sphere.[4] It is submitted that this is the case irrespective of whether the government is *in situ* or in exile. As has been pointed out above, the rider 'in exile' indicates only the domicile of the government and not special legal status. No case is known in which a State has denied a certain governmental competence to a government on the ground that it was in exile. Thus, in a judgment of 21 July 1918 the Conseil de guerre belge at Le Havre stated: 'France has declared from the outset of the present situation that the exercise of the Belgian sovereign prerogatives would not be impaired by the exile of the government' (author's translation).[5] To question the representative competence of a government which qualifies as such in international law because it is in exile would be to act to the benefit of the illegal authority *in situ*, and would lead to the (at least partial) incapacity to act of the State in question.[6] A qualification of the competence of a government in exile also finds no support in State practice. The US Court of Appeals, for instance, stated in *Delany* v. *Moraitis* (1943) that 'when a territory is

[1] *German Settlers in Poland* (1923), PCIJ, Ser. B, No 6, 1 at 22.

[2] See, e.g., McNair, *International Law Opinions* (1956), i, 131; Strebel, 'Der völkerrechtliche Begriff der Regierung' (1956) 7 *ÖZöR*, 309–19; Blix, 'Contemporary Aspects of Recognition' (1970–II) 130 *RdC* 587–704 at 597–8; Verdross and Simma, *Universelles Völkerrecht* (3rd edn., 1984), §§ 877–9.

[3] Bin Cheng, *General Principles of Law as applied by International Courts and Tribunals* (1953), 184.

[4] This competence may, however, be qualified by the internal law of the State.

[5] Travers, *Le droit pénal international et sa mise en œuvre en temps de paix et en temps de guerre* (1920), i, 241–5 at 244.

[6] Cf. the statement of the Syrian representative to the UN General Assembly: GAOR, 28th Session, 2190th Meeting, 5 Dec. 1973, 7. On the capacity of a government in exile to represent its State, see also the submission of the Republic of Cyprus in the decision of the E.Comm.H.R. on App. No 8007/77 (*Cyprus* v. *Turkey*, 10 July 1978) 13 DR 85 at 116–17.

overrun by its enemies and its government is in exile in the territory of a friendly nation exercising power in international matters in behalf of its nationals . . . the government in exile . . . is the only agency representing the country with which a foreign government can deal'.[7] While the principle that a State is represented by its government in exile is well established, the controversial question is whether a certain authority in exile qualifies as the State's government in international law. It is in this context that recognition comes in.[8] This is well illustrated by a decision of the Kammergericht where the Court held that: 'a government in exile represents an occupied or annexed country wherever . . . *it is recognized as such*'.[9] The statement intimates the importance of recognition *as a government* for the competence of an authority in exile to represent the State in relation to other States. The following examination therefore has two aims: first, to establish the legal effects of recognition, by examining the different treatment accorded to authorities in exile recognized as a government and those not recognized as a government in the various areas of international intercourse not dependent on the exercise of effective control over territory; secondly, as a by-product of this examination, it is hoped to establish the legal status of government in this area of international intercourse. However, one preliminary point must be made. The legal status of a government which it is hoped will emerge from the following examination does not prescribe a certain competence, privileges, and immunities which all authorities in exile must, to be governments, possess; rather it is a presumption that an authority in exile which is recognized as a government possesses that competence as well as those privileges and immunities unless otherwise provided for by the recognizing State.

[7] 136 F.2d 129 at 130–1 (4th Cir. 1943). This statement was endorsed by the US Court of Appeals in *Lee Wei Fang* v. *Kennedy*, 317 F.2d 180 at 185 (D.C.Cir. 1963). See also Sundberg, 'The War of Laws' (1958) 28 *Nord. TIR.* 268–309 at 273. *Contra* Laband, *Die Verwaltung Belgiens während der kriegerischen Besetzung* (1916), 25; and, with qualifications, Guggenheim, *Traité de Droit international public* (1953), i, 209.

[8] Cf. Blix, n. 2 above, 587–704 at 598.

[9] KG, 25 Feb. 1955 [*Republic of Latvia Case*]: (1957) 7 *JIR* 397–400 at 400 (translation by the author (italics added)).

4

International Representation

1 LEGAL TRANSACTIONS

(1) Treaties

(a) Treaty-making Competence

While both recognized governments in exile and authorities in exile not recognized as governments have made treaties and have entered into contracts, only the former, in their character as organs of State, have been regarded as competent to do so on behalf of the State which they purported to represent. The first treaty in modern history which was concluded by a government in exile is probably the Final Act of the Congress of Vienna which on 9 June 1815, during Napoleon's reign of the 100 days, was signed on behalf of France by the representative of King Louis XVIII who had fled to Ghent but continued to be recognized as the legitimate ruler of France.[1]

That only authorities in exile recognized as a government have been regarded as competent legally to bind a State may be shown by the case of the Czechoslovak National Council in Paris. On 2 November 1918 the US State Department wrote with respect to the question whether the financial obligations entered into by the Czechoslovak National Council could be regarded as binding on a State of Czechoslovakia that 'the obligations entered into by President Masaryk . . . will *in honour* bind the present *de facto* belligerent Czechoslovak Government to recognize these obligations as valid and binding internationally and to confirm recognition of them by appropriate legal measure, should the independence of the nation be hereafter established'.[2] That the financial obligations entered into by the Czechoslovak National Committee were not regarded as automatically binding on the (future) State of Czechoslovakia may be explained by the fact that the United States had not recognized the Council as the

[1] For the Final Act, see 2 BFSP 7.

[2] Whiteman (ed.), *Digest of International Law* (1963), ii, 527–8 at 528 (italics added). See also Klasen, *Die völkerrechtliche Bedeutung der Anerkennung der Tschechoslowaken während des Weltkrieges* (1933), 38–9. On the subsidiary personal liability of the members of the Polish National Committee for a loan contracted by the Committee with the French and British Governments, should a future Polish Government not honour the agreement, see Roth, *Die Entstehung des polnischen Staates* (1926), 42.

Government of Czechoslovakia. While the Council in June 1918 had asked for its '*de facto* recognition . . . as constituting the lawful Government of [the Czecho-Slovak] State'[3] the United States on 3 September 1918 recognized the Council only 'as a *de facto* belligerent Government, clothed with proper authority to direct the military and political affairs of the Czecho-Slovaks'[4] which was not to be understood as recognition of the Council as the Government of Czechoslovakia.[5] That recognition of the contracting authority in exile as a government has been regarded as crucial for the creation of a legally binding obligation on the State is also supported by plans for the establishment of a Polish Government in exile in the United States during the First World War. In 1917 US Secretary of State Robert Lansing suggested the 'establishment in this country of a Polish Provisional Government to be recognized by the Government of this country and the Allied Governments as the Government of an independent Poland'. He continued that 'upon such recognition this Government could legally loan the government so set up funds for military purposes secured by Polish bonds underwritten by this country and the Allies'.[6]

Authorities in exile not recognized as governments have been allowed to enter into agreements only in their own name[7] or on behalf of their movement, but not on behalf of the State which they purported to represent.[8] This is well illustrated by the case of the 'Provisional Czechoslovak Government' in London (1940–5) which concluded several agreements prior to its

[3] Hackworth (ed.), *Digest of International Law* (1940), i, 203.

[4] *Ibid.*, at 203–4; Klasen, n. 2 above, 14.

[5] See [1914–29] II FRUS. The Lansing Papers 139–41, 144–5.

[6] [1917] I FRUS Supp. 2, 760–1. See also n. 5 above, 35–6.

[7] Cf. e.g. the Agreement of 3 Sept. 1918 between the British Government and the Czecho-Slovak National Council ([1918] I FRUS Supp. 1, 844–5), and the Modus Vivendi between the USA and the CFLN on Reciprocal Aid in French North and West Africa of 25 Sept. 1943 (76 UNTS 183). While the Preamble to the Final Act of the United Nations Conference on Food and Agriculture, adopted on 3 June 1943, referred to the Governments of the various States participating in the conference, it spoke only of 'the French Representative' ((1943) 37 *AJIL* Supp., 159–92 at 159).

[8] Cf. e.g. the Exchange of Notes Constituting an Agreement between the USA and the CNF (acting on behalf of Fighting France) Relating to the Principles Governing the Provision of Reciprocal Aid in the Prosecution of the War. Done at London, 3 Sept. 1942: 24 UNTS 177. Cf. also Art. 4 of Ordinance 16 of 24 Sept. 1941 on the organization of the public powers of Free France ((1940–5) 67–72 *JDI* 171–3) and Art. 3 of the Ordinance of 3 June 1943 on the constitution of the French Committee of National Liberation (*ibid.*, at 173–4). See also the Accord between the French Government and the Polish National Committee for the repayment of expenses incurred by France for the upkeep of the Autonomous Polish Army during the First World War, signed in Paris on 27 January 1919, which provided. 'The Polish National Committee, speaking on behalf of the Polish nation, which it represents abroad, declares . . .' (Roth, n. 2 above, 48–9, translation supplied). It is of interest to note that the French Government, which did not recognize the Piłsudski Government at Warsaw, concluded the Accord with the National Committee as representative abroad of the *Polish nation* and not as that of the State of Poland, although the latter had already been admitted to the first plenary session of the Paris Peace Conference on 18 Jan. 1919.

full recognition.[9] However, much to its disappointment it was not allowed to conclude those agreements in the name of the Czechoslovak Republic. This led it on 18 April 1941 to present a special memorandum to the British Government in which it requested, *inter alia*, that agreements 'be concluded, as before September, 1938, in the name of the Czechoslovak Republic'.[10] The situation changed only once it was 'placed on the same legal basis as other Allied Governments-in-exile',[11] i.e. when it was accorded full recognition (as the Government of Czechoslovakia in exile).[12] Conveying the British recognition, the Foreign Secretary, Mr Eden, wrote on 18 July 1941: 'His Majesty's Government also accept that agreements concluded in future with your Government shall be negotiated in the name of the Czecho-slovak Republic.'[13] Recognition of an authority in exile as a government, however, affects not only the form but also the substance of the treaties that it is competent to conclude.

As a general rule it may be stated that only an authority in exile recognized as a government, i.e. as a State organ, can validly sign, ratify, or accede to a multilateral inter-State treaty.[14] It was for this reason that the French National Committee (CNF), which the Allies did not recognize as the Government of France,[15] was not invited to sign the Declaration by United Nations done at Washington on 1 January 1942.[16] Instead, the

[9] See App. III. It is interesting in this connection to compare the Military Agreement Regarding the Reconstruction of the Czechoslovak Army in France which was signed on 2 Oct. 1939 by the Czechoslovak Minister in Paris, M. Osusky, in the name of the Provisional Czechoslovak Government ([1942] *CYBIL* 232–4) with the Franco-Polish Military Agreement of 4 Jan. 1940 on the Re-establishment of the Polish Army in France ((1940) 1 *Free Europe* 108).

[10] *Four Fighting Years* (1943), 186; Beneš, *Memoirs of Dr Eduard Beneš* (1954), 125. See also Blix, *Treaty-Making Power* (1960), 163–5; Marek, *Identity and Continuity of States in Public International Law* (1954), 316.

[11] Beneš, n. 10 above, 123. On full recognition of the Czechoslovak Government, see *ibid.*, 123–5.

[12] *Contra* Táborský, *The Czechoslovak Cause* (1944), 93, who fails to recognize that earlier agreements were concluded in the name of the 'Provisional Czechoslovak Government' and not in the name of the Czechoslovak Republic.

[13] Beneš, n. 10 above, 125–6 at 126. See also Táborský, 'The Constitutionality of Official Acts of Allied Governments and International Law' [1942] *CYBIL* 183–6 at 184, and n. 12 above, 95.

[14] For examples of governments in exile signing, ratifying, or acceding to multilateral treaties, see App. III.

[15] See e.g. Manning, 'Le gouvernement néederlandais à Londres et la "France libre"' (1987) 37/146 *GMCC* 41–54 at 45–7; Woodward, *British Foreign Policy in the Second World War* (1971), ii, 302–3. With regard to a possible adherence to the UN Declaration by the CFLN, the successor to the CNF, the US Consul General at Algiers, Mr Murphy Wiley, wrote on 1 June 1943: 'It is recognized that the United Nations Declaration contemplates the adherence of "Governments" and that the new French administration will not be a government' ([1943] II FRUS 128).

[16] For the Declaration, see 204 LNTS 381. On CNF exclusion from signing the Declaration by United Nations, see DAFP V, no 236, at 380; DCER IX, no 130; Woodward, n. 15 above,

Government of the United States, as depositary of the Declaration, on 4 January 1942 issued a statement aimed at the CNF which stated that it would receive 'statements of adherence to its principles from appropriate authorities which are not Governments'.[17] For the same reason, it seems, the British Government in 1960 issued the following statement with regard to the (purported) accession of the Provisional Government of the Algerian Republic (GPRA) to the four Geneva Conventions of 12 August 1949:[18] 'The United Kingdom Government *do not recognize* the so-called "Provisional Government of the Algerian Republic" *as a government* and are unable to accept that this so-called government has the right to accede to these Conventions'.[19] The situation, however, is different if an authority in exile, such as the GPRA, is recognized as a government by some but not by other parties to a multilateral inter-State treaty. In this case the authority in exile will normally be allowed to sign, ratify, or accede to the treaty. For these acts, it seems, it is not necessary that the authority in exile is recognized as a government by the majority of the parties, although an infinitesimal number probably will not suffice. It is submitted that the number of recognizing parties required may vary according to the nature and purpose of the treaty, the threshold for human rights and humanitarian law instruments usually being lower than that for technical or organizational treaties. This may be explained by the fact that the universal application and global observance of treaties of a humanitarian character are in the interest of the international community. The following examples may serve as illustration:

(i) *Algeria*. On 20 June 1960, i.e. at a time when the GPRA was recognized, either *de facto* or *de jure*, by only eighteen of the seventy-

ii, 214–19; De Gaulle, *Mémoires de Guerre* (1954), i, 184. It is of interest to note that as late as 15 Sept. 1944 the British Minister to Syria and Lebanon, Sir Edward Spears, admitted that there was force in the argument that the French regime of General de Gaulle did not possess capacity to conclude treaties on behalf of France with Syria and Lebanon ending the French mandate in the Levant States ([1944] V FRUS 777).

[17] [1942] *Keesing's* 4992E. However, for reasons of wounded pride neither the CNF nor its successor, the CFLN, made use of this chance of adherence. It was only on 1 Jan. 1945 that the (then recognized) Provisional Government of the French Republic signed the Declaration. See (1944) 11 *DSB* 845; and (1945) 12 *DSB* 17. For the unilateral statement of adherence by Mr de Kauffmann, the Danish Minister in Washington, on behalf of the Danish people see Rasmussen, 'Danemark (Royaume de)' *Dict. Dipl.* (1947), iv, 302–4 at 302.

[18] 75 UNTS 31, 85, 135 and 287, respectively.

[19] UKTS No 87 (1960), Cmnd. 1276, 10, italics supplied. Similar statements were made, for instance, by Switzerland, as party to the Conventions, and France (cf. Bedjaoui, *Law and the Algerian Revolution* (1961), 184; Klarer, *Schweizerische Praxis der völkerrechtlichen Anerkennung* (1981), 240). Doubts about the validity of the Algerian accession were also expressed by Pinto, 'Le "GPRA" et les conventions de Genève', *Le Monde*, 13 Apr. 1960, 1; Oppermann, 'Die Anwendbarkeit der Genfer Abkommen zum Schutze der Kriegsopfer im Algerien Konflikt' (1961–2) 9 *AVR* 47–59 at 59, n. 46; Bot, *Nonrecognition and Treaty Relations* (1968), 161–2; and Verhoeven, *La reconnaissance internationale dans la pratique contemporaine* (1975), 151, n. 220.

seven parties to the four Geneva Conventions, the Swiss Federal Council (which did not recognize the GPRA), as depositary, accepted the instruments of accession to the Conventions tendered by the GPRA on behalf of the State of Algeria and communicated its accession to all the parties to the Conventions.[20]

(ii) *Cambodia.* The UN Secretary-General allowed the various Cambodian Governments in exile, the Government of Democratic Kampuchea (GDK) and the Coalition Government of Democratic Kampuchea (CGDK), which were recognized during the 1980s by some eighty States[21] and the United Nations as the Government of Cambodia to sign multilateral treaties for which he was acting as depositary and notified members of the United Nations of their signatures. For example, on 17 October 1980 the GDK was allowed to sign the 1966 International Covenants on Civil and Political Rights (ICCPR)[22] and on Economic, Social, and Cultural Rights (ICESCR)[23] as well as the 1979 Convention on the Elimination of All Forms of Discrimination against Women (CEAFDW).[24] Some of the about thirty States which recognized the Government of the People's Republic of Kampuchea (GPRK) as the Government of Cambodia strongly protested against those signatures. For instance, Mongolia, which had recognized the GPRK on 11 January 1979 'as the legal Government of Kampuchea and genuine spokesman of the sovereign will and aspirations of its people',[25] stated on 5 November 1980 that it

> considers that only the People's Revolutionary Council of Kampuchea as the sole authentic and lawful representative of the Kampuchean people has the right to assume international obligations on behalf of the Kampuchean people. Therefore the Government of the Mongolian People's Republic considers that the signature of the Human Rights Covenants by the representative of the so-

[20] On the Algerian accession to the Geneva Conventions, see Bedjaoui, n. 19 above, 135–7, 189–99, 217–20; (1960) 3/8 *Freies Algerien* 1–2; Klarer, n. 19 above, 240, 307; Algerian Office, New York, *White Paper on the Application of the Geneva Conventions of 1949 to the French-Algerian Conflict* (1960). According to Art. 20(3) of the Provisional Institutions of the Algerian State 'The GPRA is entitled to sign conventions of an international character' (*Die Algerische Revolution* (1963), App.). On the obligations of the depositary of an open multilateral treaty in the case of (purported) accession by an unrecognized State or government in general, see the opinion of the Swiss Federal Political Department of 28 Dec. 1960 on 'Obligations du gouvernement dépositaire d'une convention multilatérale': Guggenheim, 'Pratique Suisse' (1963) 20 *Sch. JIR* 65–120 at 76–83; and Na, *Die völkerrechtliche Stellung Koreas* (1991), 252–3. On the application of the Geneva Conventions to the Algerian conflict by the French courts, see Touscoz, 'Etude de la jurisprudence interne sur les aspects internationaux de l'affaire algérienne' (1963) 9 *AFDI* 953–69 at 957–62.

[21] See App. II.

[22] Cf. Arts. 26, 30 ICCPR (999 UNTS 171).

[23] Cf. Arts. 48, 52 ICESCR (993 UNTS 3).

[24] Cf. Art. 25 CEAFDW (1249 UNTS 13). See (1980) 34 UNYB 859, 910.

[25] BBC, *SWB*, 3rd series, FE/6015/A3/7, 13 Jan. 1979.

called Democratic Kampuchea, a regime that ceased to exist as a result of the people's revolution in Kampuchea, is null and void.[26]

These protests did not prevent the UN Secretary-General from permitting the CGDK on 1 July 1983 to sign the 1982 United Nations Convention on the Law of the Sea (UNCLOS) at the UN Headquarters in New York.[27]

(iii) *Western Sahara.* On 1 July 1989, i.e. at a time when the Saharan Arab Democratic Republic (SADR) had been recognized by sixty-eight of the 165 States parties to the Geneva Conventions,[28] the Foreign Minister of the SADR declared in a letter to the Swiss Federal Council that his Government had decided to accede to the four Geneva Conventions. However, subsequently, the Polisario Front[29] explained that the letter was not to be regarded as an instrument of accession but only as a declaration of intent. As there was thus no formal instrument of accession, the Swiss Federal Council had not to decide whether to reject or to notify such a declaration of accession by the Government of the SADR.[30] On the basis of the above precedents and in view of the fact that by 1996 the number of States recognizing the SADR had risen to seventy-three (while at the same time the number of States parties to the Geneva Conventions had increased to 186) it seems highly probable that the Swiss Federal Council would notify a formal declaration of accession made by the SADR's Government in exile.

While a partially recognized government in exile, as a rule, will be allowed to sign, ratify, or accede to a multilateral inter-State treaty, the role of recognition by the depositary of the treaty must not be underestimated. This may be illustrated by the following example. According to Article 9(2) of the Treaty on the Non-Proliferation of Nuclear Weapons of 1 July 1968,[31] instruments of accession may be deposited with the Governments of the USSR, the United Kingdom, and the USA. On 2 June 1972 the Govern-

[26] UN Doc.ST/LEG/SER.E/11, 120. Similar communications were received from the GDR, Poland, Ukraine, Laos, Hungary, Bulgaria, Russian Federation, Belarus, and Czechoslovakia. See *ibid.* and UN Docs.A/35/660, A/35/679, A/35/781, A/35/784, A/36/63, and A/36/129. It should, however, be noted that although the GDK had signed all three treaties the SNC of Cambodia deposited instruments of *accession* to the ICCPR and ICESCR on 26 May 1992 and to the CEAFDW on 15 Oct. 1992 (UN Doc.ST/LEG/SER.E/11, 114, 123, 162).

[27] Cf. Art. 305(2) of UNCLOS 1982 (UN Doc.A/CONF.62/122, 7 Oct. 1982). See (1983) 37 UNYB 104.

[28] See App. II.

[29] i.e. the Western Sahara liberation movement. On Polisario, see Pazzanita and Hodges, *Historical Dictionary of Western Sahara* (2nd edn., 1994), 162–73.

[30] Letter to the author dated 8 Nov. 1996 from the Swiss Federal Department of External Affairs.

[31] 729 UNTS 161.

ment of the Khmer Republic, which had been recognized by the United States and the United Kingdom but not by the Soviet Union as the Government of Cambodia, deposited the instrument of accession to that Treaty on behalf of Cambodia at Washington.[32] As the USSR had not recognized the Government of the Khmer Republic it did not regard Cambodia as a party to the Non-Proliferation Treaty and thus had no problem in accepting on 10 August 1987 a new instrument of accession to that Treaty on behalf of Cambodia by the Government of the People's Republic of Kampuchea, which[33] on 9 January 1979, it had recognized as the 'sole legitimate Government of Kampuchea'.[34] With a few exceptions such as China, which recognized neither the Government of the Khmer Republic nor the Government of the People's Republic of Kampuchea, but in both cases recognized the respective Cambodian Government in exile, Cambodia should now be a party to the Non-Proliferation Treaty in relation to most other parties.

The signature of or accession to a treaty by an authority in exile recognized as a government by some but not by all parties to the treaty does not, however, create treaty relations between it and the non-recognizing parties, irrespective of whether or not the latter make an express statement to that effect.[35] The possibility of different legal regimes applying simultaneously to individual parties to a multilateral treaty is a fact which has long been accepted in the case of reservations.[36] There is no reason why the same should not be possible as a consequence of recognition. This is supported by a statement of the Swiss Federal Political Department issued in Berne on 27 July 1960. With regard to the accession to the Geneva Conventions of 12 August 1949 by the GPRA, it stated:

> In a statement issued on 23 July the Provisional Government of the Republic of Algeria declared that its accession to the Geneva Convention . . . meant that the Algerian Republic, independent of the French Republic, was a party to the Convention. As depositary of the Conventions Switzerland only has the task to receive declarations of accession and to notify them to the parties. It is for each party to decide whether and, if so, to what extent it considers itself bound by the declaration of accession. . . .

[32] See 830 UNTS 374; [1976] II BGBl. 552 at 553.

[33] See [1987] *AdG* 31349, n. 3; *Munzinger. Zeitarchiv*, Kambodscha, Chronik, 1987.

[34] BBC, *SWB*, 3rd series, FE/6014/A2/3, 12 Jan. 1979.

[35] See BGH, 18 Dec. 1959, BGHZ 31, 374 at 382–3; and Erdmann, *Nichtanerkannte Staaten und Regierungen: Formen und Grenzen internationaler Beziehungen* (1966), 85, 87. *Contra* Bedjaoui, n. 19 above, 136. It is suggested that in the case of accessions to open multilateral treaties the expressed non-recognition by a party of the acceding authority in exile has the effect of an automatic reservation. To such a 'reservation' by States already parties to a treaty Art. 23 of the Vienna Convention on the Law of Treaties (VCLT) 1969 does not apply. Cf. also Art. 2(1)(d) of the Convention.

[36] See the advisory opinion in *Reservations to the Genocide Convention*, ICJ Rep. 1951, 15; and Art. 21 of the VCLT. Cf. also Art. 76 of the Convention, which envisages the situation that 'a treaty has not entered into force between certain of the parties'. On the 'relativity' of multilateral treaty relations, see also Erdmann, n. 35 above, 85.

> For the Governments which have not recognized [the GPRA], the declaration of accession is *without any legal significance* and entails, at best, a *moral* obligation of the Provisional Government to respect the Geneva Conventions. The accession can only create a legal relationship with those parties, which have *recognized* the Provisional Government.[37]

That the accession to a multilateral treaty does not create treaty relations between the non-recognizing parties and the acceding authority in exile should not, however, prevent the latter from exercising general rights under the treaty, such as the right to propose amendments or to participate in a diplomatic conference uniting all the States parties to the treaty for the purpose of changing the text of the treaty.[38] After all, it would be wrong to say that the accession to an open inter-State treaty by a partially recognized authority in exile has no legal effect at all. The accession is to be regarded as not effective only with regard to the non-recognizing parties.

If, as in the case of the Algerian accession to the Geneva Conventions, parties to a multilateral inter-State treaty recognize as a government neither the acceding authority in exile nor the State on whose behalf accession is declared as an independent State, the question arises whether the treaty becomes effective *vis-à-vis* the non-recognizing parties automatically on the achievement of independence by the acceding State, on the recognition of that independence by the non-recognizing parties, or only on the renewed accession or confirmation of accession by the recognized government of the independent State. State practice is not uniform. In the 1960s Switzerland, as depositary of the Conventions, listed in the official register two dates of accession of Algeria, viz., the date of the declaration of accession (20 June 1960) and the date of Algerian independence (3 July 1962).[39] The current list of parties to the Conventions, compiled by Switzerland as depositary, however, gives only 20 June 1960 as the date of accession of Algeria and consequently[40] 20 December 1960 as the date of entry into force of the Conventions for Algeria.[41] But Switzerland as a party to the Conventions

[37] For the full text of the statement 'Algerien und die Genfer Abkommen', see *NZZ*, 28 July 1960, Sheet 3 (translation supplied by the author, italics as in the original). See also Flory, 'Algérie algérienne et droit interational' (1960) 6 *AFDI* 973–98 at 988; and Meissner, *Formen stillschweigender Anerkennung im Völkerrecht* (1966), 41.

[38] Cf. Bedjaoui, n. 19 above, 185. *Contra* with respect to the case of the Algerian accession to the Geneva Conventions: Bot, n. 19 above, 162.

[39] Cf. Schindler and Toman (eds.), *The Laws of Armed Conflict* (3rd revised edn., 1988), 557, n. 2.

[40] Cf. the relevant articles of the four Geneva Red Cross Conventions (GRCC) 1949: Art. 58(2) of GRCC I, Art. 57(2) of GRCC II, Art. 138(2) of GRCC III, and Art. 152(2) of GRCC IV.

[41] See also the list published by the International Committee of the Red Cross on the 'Status of the Four Geneva Conventions and Additional Protocols I and II [As of 31 December 1986]', reproduced in (1987) 26 ILM 553 at 554.

regards Algeria as a party to the Conventions only as from 4 July 1962 when it recognized Algeria as an independent State.[42] The same view is taken by Austria, which lists as the date of entry into force of the Conventions for Algeria 7 July 1962, the date of Austrian recognition of Algeria as an independent State.[43] The United Kingdom[44] and Germany,[45] on the other hand, have recorded the date of Algeria's accession as 14 December 1964. In a note to the Swiss Federal Council of that date, the Government of the Algerian Republic, referring to the statement of accession made by the GPRA on 20 June 1960, declared that it regarded itself bound by the four Geneva Conventions.[46] It is submitted that the latter is the more principled view as it is difficult to understand how States can regard Algeria bound by a declaration made by an authority in exile which they themselves never recognized as the Government of Algeria or in any other capacity. As the non-recognizing States did not regard the GPRA as a party to the Conventions the 'principe de la survivance des anciennes conventions' is also not applicable to the Algerian case. Finally, Algeria expressly ruled out its succession to France in respect of the Conventions.[47] It is of interest to note in this connection that the US Government, which on 3 July 1962 recognized Algeria as an independent State but did not recognize any authority as the Government of Algeria until 29 September 1962,[48] nevertheless had listed in the US State Department publication, *Treaties in Force . . . on January 1, 1962* under 'States which are parties' to the Geneva Conventions the 'Algerian Rep., Provisional Gov't'.[49] As from 1 January 1963 *Treaties in Force* lists under 'States which are parties' to the Geneva Conventions: 'Algeria'.[50]

As a further rule it may be stated that only an authority in exile recognized as a government can validly conclude a treaty that involves the exercise of State sovereignty on its part. This may be illustrated by the following example. In May and July 1944 the United Kingdom, the USA, and the USSR concluded so-called Civil Affairs Agreements with the governments in exile recognized by the United Nations, in which the latter

[42] Letter to the author, dated 8 Nov. 1996, from the Swiss Federal Department of External Affairs.

[43] [1967] ÖBGBl. 607.

[44] UKTS No 72 (1965), Cmnd. 2765, 17.

[45] [1965] II BGBl. 5.

[46] For the text of the note, see *ibid.*

[47] See Goerdeler, *Die Staatensukzession in multilaterale Verträge* (1970), 65.

[48] See (1962) 47 *DSB* 135 and 560.

[49] *Treaties in Force . . . on January 1, 1962*, 272, 275, 282. But in *Treaties in Force . . . on January 1, 1961* neither Algeria nor the GPRA was listed as a party to the Geneva Conventions. Cf. *ibid.*, at 259, 263, 270.

[50] For 1963, see *Treaties in Force*, 300, 303, 309. The State Department does not record the Algerian note of 14 Dec. 1964. Compare the sections on 'Recent Actions Regarding Treaties to Which the United States is a Party' in (1965) 4 ILM.

agreed that the respective Allied Commander-in-Chief 'must *de facto* exercise supreme responsibility and authority to the full extent necessitated by the military situation' in their liberated territories.[51] For example, on 16 May 1944 the United Kingdom, the USA, and the USSR on the one hand and Norway on the other hand signed separate but largely identical Memoranda of Agreement Respecting the Arrangements for Civil Administration and Jurisdiction in Norwegian Territory Liberated by an Allied Expeditionary Force.[52] Similar agreements were signed on 16 May 1944 with Belgium and the Netherlands, on 8 May 1944 with Czechoslovakia, and on 27 July 1944 with Luxembourg.[53] As no State (or its official) may exercise supreme authority within the territory of another State without the latter's consent[54] except as a result of belligerent occupation, such agreements were required if the Allies were not to violate the territorial sovereignty of the liberated States. Notably, no such agreements were concluded with authorities in exile not (or no longer) recognized by the liberating Ally or Allies as a government such as the Polish Government in London[55] and the French Committee of National Liberation (CFLN). As early as 9 September 1943 the latter had submitted to the US State Department a draft Civil Affairs Agreement on the lines of those concluded with the recognized governments in exile. President Roosevelt, however, objected to the conclusion of such an agreement with the CFLN on the ground that it would have the appearance of giving recognition to the CFLN as the Government of France.[56] Only after President Roosevelt's recognition of the CFLN as 'temporary *de facto* authority for civil administration in France' on 10 July 1944[57] a Civil Affairs Agreement was concluded on 25 August 1944 between the United States and the United Kingdom on the one side and the CFLN on the other.[58] This Agreement differed from the Memoranda of Agree-

[51] Norway, for instance, was administered by the Commander-in-Chief of Allied Forces in Norway until 7 June 1945.

[52] For the Agreements, see App. III.

[53] For references to these agreements, see App. III.

[54] See *The Lotus* (1927), PCIJ, Ser. A, No 10, 18–19; and *The Schooner Exchange* v. *M'Faddon* (1812), 7 Cranch 116 at 136. A Memorandum prepared by the US Army and Navy Department, dated 18 Feb. 1944, pointed out that the authority of the military commander in liberated territory of allied States was limited and that agreements with the sovereign authorities of those territories were required ([1944] V FRUS 1190–4 at 1193).

[55] On 25 July 1944 the Soviet Government declared that it viewed the military operations conducted by the Red Army on the territory of Poland as operations on the territory of a sovereign, friendly, Allied State, that it had no intention of establishing on the territory of Poland its own administrative organs, considering that a concern of the Polish people, and that it had, therefore, decided to conclude with the Polish Committee of National Liberation (formed on 23 July 1944) an agreement regarding relations between the Soviet Command and the Polish administration ([1945] *Keesing's* 6637).

[56] See Woodward, *British Foreign Policy in the Second World War* (1962), 261.

[57] [1944] III FRUS 724–5 at 724.

[58] See Woodward n. 56 above, 260–8; Blix, n. 10 above, 180–3. For the Agreement, see TIAS No 2313.

ment signed with the recognized governments in exile in that it contained the consent of the Allied Commander-in-Chief to the limited exercise of authority by the CFLN rather than the consent of the CFLN to the exercise of supreme authority by the Allied Commander-in-Chief. This becomes clear from a statement of the US Government, issued on 25 August 1944, whose final paragraph reads:

> General Eisenhower as United States Commanding General has been authorized to deal with the French authorities at Algiers as the *de facto* authority in France. . . . This authorization is also based on the understanding that as Supreme Allied Commander General Eisenhower must *retain* whatever authority he considers necessary for the unimpeded conduct of military operations.[59]

Treaties which dispose of State territory have also been concluded only with authorities in exile recognized as governments,[60] as only a government may exercise the State's territorial sovereignty. The following examples may illustrate this:

(i) *Ukraine*. On 21 April 1920, at the time when the Directorate of the Ukrainian People's Republic had lost all control over its territory and was established in Polish-occupied territory, the Polish Government and the Directorate signed a Treaty in Warsaw in which Poland 'recognized the Directorate of the independent Ukrainian People's Republic, with Ataman Symon Petliura as the Head of the Government of the Ukrainian People's Republic'[61] and the Directorate in return renounced all claims of the Ukrainian People's Republic to Western Ukraine (Galicia).[62]

(ii) *Algeria*. After Morocco had recognized the GPRA as the Government of Algeria it no longer made any attempt to reach a settlement with France over the Moroccan–Algerian Sahara boundary but, on the

[59] (1944) 11 *DSB* 205, italics added. But according to General de Gaulle General Eisenhower derived his authority, in respect of France, from the Provisional Government of the French Republic (DCER X, no 200, at 161–2). For the prevailing Allied view, however, see *ibid.*, nos 180, 184.

[60] See e.g. the Agreement between the UK and Belgium Respecting Boundaries in East Africa (Mount Sabinio to the Congo–Nile Watershed), signed at London, on 3 Feb. 1915. Ratifications, however, were exchanged only on 20 Oct. 1919 (110 BFSP 487). It should be noted, however, that during the Second World War annual Agreements were concluded between 'France' and India renewing for one year the Convention of 1935 between France and India regarding the Lease of the French Lodge of Balasore (163 LNTS 287): 205 LNTS 214 (for 1940), 215–16 (for 1941–3). These agreements were concluded by the Governor of French India in the name of the 'French Government' although the Governor on 9 Sept. 1940 had declared for Free France.

[61] Horak, *Poland's International Affairs 1919–1960* (1964), 234–5; Twardowski, 'Ukraine' in Strupp (ed.), *Wörterbuch des Völkerrechts und der Diplomatie* (1925), ii, 753–5 at 754.

[62] See Hornykiewicz, *Ereignisse in der Ukraine 1914–1922 deren Bedeutung und historische Hintergründe* (1969), iv, 255–6; Doroshenko, *A Survey of Ukrainian History* (1975), 647; *The Times*, 12 Apr. 1920, 13.

contrary, regarded the GPRA as the rightful authority with which to decide the issue. On 6 July 1961 the Government of Morocco and the GPRA therefore signed a Convention at Rabat in which the GPRA recognized 'the territorial problem created by the delimitation imposed arbitrarily by France on the two countries' and which stated that 'this problem will be resolved through negotiations between the Kingdom of Morocco and the Government of Independent Algeria'.[63] In contrast, Tunisia, despite its recognition of the GPRA, continued to claim certain Algerian territories from France which put a great strain on Algerian–Tunisian relations. A Report of the Algerian Foreign Ministry, dated 6 April 1960, states with respect to Tunisia's territorial claims:

> The territorial claims addressed by President Bourguiba to France . . . , while the GPRA was already recognized by the Tunisian Government, unequivocally confirm that Tunisia recognized the right of France to dispose of a part of Algerian territory. The incompatibility of this position with the recognition of the Algerian Government and State is obvious [author's translation].[64]

Treaties by which the State's rights are relinquished have also been concluded only by and with authorities in exile recognized as a government. Thus, while several of the recognized governments in London in 1943 concluded treaties with the Chinese Government at Chungking by which they formally relinquished the State's extraterritorial rights in China,[65] the CNF promised only to negotiate the abolition of French extraterritorial rights in China after the war.[66] A Treaty on the Renunciation of French Exterritorial Rights in China was finally concluded on 28 February 1946.[67]

Furthermore, only authorities in exile recognized as governments can validly make agreements affecting the legal status of a State's nationals and their property abroad, as only a government is entitled to exercise personal sovereignty over the State's nationals at home and abroad.[68] This is well

[63] Méric, 'Le conflit algéro-marocain' (1965) 15 *RFSP* 743–52 at 744–8; Donelan and Grieve, *International Disputes. Case Histories 1945–1970* (1973), 144; Wild, 'The Organization of African Unity and the Algerian-Moroccan Border Conflict: A Study of New Machinery for Peacekeeping and for Peaceful Settlement of Disputes Among African States' (1966) 20 *Int. Org.* 18–36 at 21.

[64] ARA no 95, 447–58 at 453.

[65] For the treaties concluded by the Governments of Belgium, Luxembourg, and Norway, see App. III.

[66] De Gaulle, *War Memoirs. Documents* (1955), i, 255–6.

[67] (1947) 51 *RGDIP* 328–34.

[68] During the Second World War the USA concluded agreements with the governments in exile relating to the services of nationals of one country in the armed forces of the other country: see App. III. In Great Britain, by the Allied Powers (War Service) Act 1942 (5 & 6 Geo. 6, c. 29), nationals of the Allied Governments in exile were, under certain conditions, made liable for national service in the British Armed Forces under the various Allied Powers (War Service) Orders. It appears that both the Act and the Orders were preceded by agree-

illustrated by the British International Labour Force (Registration of Foreign Nationals) Orders 1941. While in the case of nationals of States whose recognized government resided in Great Britain the Orders provided that the British Government and the government in exile had agreed that it was expedient that provisions should be made for regulating the engagement of its nationals in Great Britain by employers and that for that purpose its nationals should be required to register particulars about themselves,[69] the International Labour Force (Registration of French Nationals) Order 1941 made no such reference to an agreement with the French National Committee although in other respects the Order treated the Committee like the governments in exile.[70]

(b) Limitations upon Treaty-making Competence

It has been suggested that the competence of a government in exile to make treaties on behalf of a State is subject to the State's constitutional requirements for the conclusion of treaties such as parliamentary approval of (certain types of) treaties prior to ratification or ratification by the head of State only.[71] State practice shows that such constitutional, i.e. internal law,

ments made with the various Allied governments in exile concerned. For a statement to that effect, see HC Debs., vol. 380, col. 2176, 25 June 1942. Some of the governments in exile had to pass legislation legalizing the service of their nationals in foreign armed forces. See, e.g. the Polish law of 14 August 1942: (1942) 6 *Free Europe* 78. On the illegality of drafting Greek nationals into the Australian Armed Forces without the consent of the Greek Government in exile, see *Polites* v. *The Commonwealth* and *Kandiliotes* v. *The Commonwealth* (1945) 70 CLR 60 at 70 (*per* Latham CJ). Compare also the Military Service (Conventions with Allied States) Act 1917 (7 & 8 Geo. 5, c. 26). On 30 Nov. 1914 the French Government concluded an agreement with the Belgian Government at Le Havre concerning the search and arrest for Belgian deserters in France by French authorities ((1915) 42 *JDI* 236–7). See also the Exchange of Notes between the British and Belgian Governments concerning the disposal of the property of Belgian and British seamen who die while serving in British and Belgian ships, London, 4 Jan. 1943 (145 BFSP 120).

[69] S. O. & R. 1941 No 719 (Belgian nationals), S.O. & R. 1941 No 720 (Dutch nationals), S.O. & R. 1941 No 721 (Norwegian nationals), S.O. & R. 1941 No 722 (Polish nationals), S.O. & R. 1941 No 723 (Czechoslovak nationals), S.R. & O. 1943 No 1049 (Greek nationals), S.R. & O. 1943 No 1052 (Yugoslav nationals).

[70] S.R. & O. 1941 No 724. See also the International Labour Force (Registration of Danish Nationals) Order 1943: S.R. & O. 1943 No 1048 (vol. II, 606). It is also of interest to note that the Allied Powers (War Service) Act 1942 (5 & 6 Geo. 6, c. 29) was made applicable by the Allied Powers (War Service) Order 1943 to the nationals of the 8 European Governments in exile in London with effect from 1 Apr. 1943 (S.R. & O. 1943 No 381). With regard to French nationals it was made applicable only with effect from 1 Sept. 1944, i.e. after the Allied liberation of Paris. See the Allied Powers (War Service) (No 3) Order 1944 (S.R. & O. 1944 No 992).

[71] Cf. Marek, n. 10 above, 458; Mattern, *Die Exilregierung* (1953), 64. Cf. also McNair and Watts, *The Legal Effects of War* (4th edn., 1966), 426, according to whom the validity of sovereign acts of a government in exile depends upon the requirement that 'its constitutional law contains no insuperable obstacle'. On the problem in general, see Brownlie, *Principles of Public International Law* (4th edn., 1990), 613–14; Verdross and Simma, *Universelles Völkerrecht* (3rd edn., 1984), §§ 689–93; Ibler, 'Unconstitutional Ratifications' (1956) 3 *JRMP* 271–86.

restrictions have had no effect on the treaty-making competence of recognized governments in exile under international law. For example, the Polish Government in London validly concluded treaties despite Article 52(1) of the Constitution of 23 April 1935 which required (for certain treaties) 'before ratification, the agreement of the Legislative Chambers expressed in the form of a law'.[72] Article 68(1) of the Belgian Constitution of 7 February 1831 provides that 'The King . . . makes treaties of peace, alliance and commerce'. King Leopold III, however, surrendered on 28 May 1940 to the German army and became a prisoner of war. The absence of the King did not prevent the Allies from concluding treaties with the Belgian Government in London.[73] In a letter dated 3 December 1940, Mr Dean of the British Foreign Office wrote to Mr Hull of the Department of the Solicitor-General: 'His Majesty's Government do regard the four Belgian Minister composing the Belgian Government in London as the legitimate and constitutional Government of Belgium and competent to exercise *full authority* in the name of the Sovereign State of Belgium.'[74] That a violation of its internal law does not automatically make invalid treaties concluded by governments in exile is also confirmed by the 1969 Vienna Convention on the Law of Treaties (VCLT) which considers certain government officials normally members of a government in exile as generally competent to make treaties on behalf of the State[75] and allows only the State (by way of exception) to invoke the violation of its internal law regarding competence to conclude treaties as a ground for invalidating a treaty if such violation is clear and the violated provision of its internal law of fundamental importance.[76] It may be argued that the conclusion of a treaty contrary to the constitution by a person other than the head of State or the ratification of a treaty without parliamentary approval always constitutes a manifest violation of a rule of fundamental importance. According to Article 45 of the VCLT a State loses its right to invoke a ground for invalidating a treaty if, after becoming aware of the facts, it has expressly agreed that the treaty is valid or must by reason of its conduct be considered as having acquiesced in the validity of the treaty. If, after the government in exile concluding the treaty or its recognized successor has re-established constitutional order

[72] See Blix, n. 10 above, 158–9. For the conclusion of the Polish–Soviet Agreement of 30 July 1941 by Prime Minister Sikorski without the authorization of the President of Poland which is required by Art. 12 of the Polish Constitution, see *Poland in the British Parliament 1939–1945* (1946), i, 469–71. For an overview of the treaty activity of the Polish Government in general, see App. III.

[73] For an overview of the treaties concluded by the Belgian Government in exile, see App. III.

[74] FO 371/24 378, italics added: quoted in Kerchove d'Exaerde, 'Quelques questions en droit international public relatives à la présence et à l'activité du gouvernement belge en exil à Londres (Octobre 1940–Septembre 1944), (1990) 23 *RBDI* 93–151 at 111.

[75] Cf. Art. 7(2)(a) of VCLT.

[76] Cf. Art. 46 of VCLT.

inside the State's territory, it does not invoke the invalidity of the treaty within reasonable time, the State may be considered as having acquiesced in the validity of the treaty. This, however, means that treaties with a government in exile unable to comply with the State's internal law regarding competence to conclude treaties are always concluded under the implicit condition subsequent that after the re-establishment of constitutional order the competent authorities do not invoke the invalidity of the treaty. This view creates legal uncertainty and may even prevent other States from concluding vital treaties with such governments in exile. Further, it discriminates against exiled constitutional governments of existing States as it places them in a worse position than governments formed in exile without constitutional restraints. It is therefore submitted that the better view is that treaties concluded by authorities in exile recognized as a government by the other party or parties to the treaty cannot be invalidated on the ground that the recognized government in exile did not comply with the State's internal law regarding competence to conclude treaties. It may however be declared null and void *ab initio* on the ground that recognition of the authority in exile as the State's government on the part of the other parties was unlawful, as the authority in exile did not qualify as the government of the State under international law.

It has also been suggested that treaties concluded by a recognized government in exile on behalf of a State are binding on its successor *in situ* only if the government in exile succeeds in re-establishing itself within the State or if the treaties are (explicitly or by implication) confirmed by its successor *in situ*.[77] This view fails to take account of the fact that treaties are binding on the contracting States and that, therefore, changes in the government of one of the parties do not, as a general rule, affect the binding force of treaties.[78] This may be illustrated by the treaties concluded by the Polish Government in exile. Despite the fact that this Government did not succeed in re-establishing itself in Poland after the Second World War the treaties concluded by it in the name of Poland were regarded as continuing in force both by the other parties[79] and, with certain qualifications, by the succeeding

[77] See Wengler, *Völkerrecht* (1964), i, 301; Lourie and Meyer, 'Governments-in-Exile and the Effect of Their Expropriatory Decrees' (1943) 11 *U.Chicago LR* 26–48 at 26–7. See also Erdmann, n. 35 above, 50–1; *Contra*, Heydte, *Völkerrecht. Ein Lehrbuch* (1958), i, 141, n. 43.

[78] See Jennings and Watts (eds.), *Oppenheim's International Law* (9th edn., 1992), i, 1253–4; McNair, *The Law of Treaties* (1961), 668–72. Cf. also Art. 42(2) of VCLT.

[79] For the view that the Polish Provisional Government of National Unity was liable for debts incurred by the Polish Government in exile under agreements with the British Government, see the Proposals of the British Delegation to the Potsdam Conference, dated 19 July 1945: DPSR II, no 382, at 632. See also HC Debs., vol. 414, col. 664, 15 Oct. 1945; *ibid.*, vol. 417, col. 1289, 18 Dec. 1945. On the debts incurred by the Polish Government in exile in general, see DBPO, 1st ser., VI, no 8.i, at 30; and [1945] *Keesing's* 7301. For the view that the Lend-Lease Agreement between the USA and Poland continued in force, see [1950] IV FRUS 1040–51 at 1045.

Polish Governments *in situ*.[80] According to Article 3 of the Charter of the United Nations 'original members of the United Nations shall be the States which, having participated in the United Nations Conference on International Organization at San Francisco, or having previously signed the Declaration by United Nations of January 1, 1942, sign the present Charter'. As the four Sponsoring States of the San Francisco Conference[81] recognized different authorities as the Government of Poland, and thus could not agree on which Government should represent Poland, Poland was not represented at the San Francisco Conference at the end of which the UN Charter was signed. However, a space at the end of the Charter was reserved for the signature of Poland as the Polish Government in London had signed the Declaration by United Nations on 1 January 1942. After all Sponsoring States had recognized the Polish Provisional Government of National Unity, it was allowed to sign the Charter on 15 October 1945, thus making Poland one of the fifty-one original Members of the United Nations.[82] The Polish Governments *in situ* also concluded several agreements with the United Kingdom[83] and the United States[84] for the settlement of financial claims arising under treaties made by the Polish Government in London. They, further, ratified multilateral treaties signed by the London Polish Government.[85] They refused, however, to carry out obligations arising from treaties entered into by the Polish Government in exile after the establishment of a Provisional Government in Poland on 31 December 1944.[86] On 12 January 1945 the Prime Minster of that Government, Mr Osóbka-Morawski, had issued the following declaration:

[80] i.e. the Polish Provisional Government of National Unity and the Government of the People's Republic of Poland.

[81] i.e. China, UK, USA, and USSR.

[82] See DUNCIO V, 305. On the participation of Poland in the San Francisco Conference, in general, see *ibid*., I, 168, 346–8; V, 93–6. See also Bierzanek, 'La reconnaissance internationale du Comité Polonais de Libération Nationale et du Gouvernement d'Unité Nationale' (1964–5) 5 *APAI* 41–58 at 50; Gelberg, *Die Entstehung der Volksrepublik Polen* (1972), 45.

[83] See the Agreement between the Government of the UK and the Polish Provisional Government of National Unity for the Settlement of Outstanding Financial Questions, signed at London, on 24 June 1946 (11 UNTS 59); and the Agreement between the Government of the UK and the Government of the Polish People's Republic Relating to a Settlement of Financial Matters, signed at Warsaw, on 11 Nov. 1954 (204 UNTS 137).

[84] See the Agreement between the Government of the USA and the Government of the Polish People's Republic on Settlement for Lend-Lease and Certain Claims, signed at Washington, on 28 June 1956: 273 UNTS 79. The Agreement Relating to the Principles Applying to Mutual Aid in the Prosecution of the War Against Aggression (Lend-Lease Agreement) between the Governments of the USA and Poland had been signed by the Polish Government in exile at Washington on 1 July 1942 ((1942) 7 *DSB*, 577; text: 103 UNTS 266). For the amount of Lend-Lease received by Poland under the Agreement, see DAFR VIII, 154.

[85] On 31 Dec. 1945 the Polish National Council passed a law expressing its consent to the ratification of the Agreements on the International Monetary Fund and the International Bank for Reconstruction and Development, both signed at Bretton Woods, on 22 July 1944. Cf. Gelberg, n. 82 above, 44, n. 101.

[86] See Gelberg, n. 82 above, 48. On the creation of 'the first Provisional Government of Liberated Democratic Poland', see [1945] *Keesing's* 6902A. For treaties signed and ratified after the creation of the 'Provisional Government' in Poland, see App. III.

The Provisional Government of the Republic of Poland hereby notifies all interested States, juridical and natural persons, that, as the only legitimate Government of Poland, which expresses the will of the people in Poland and which bears the burden of the struggle for the liberation of the rest of the country still under German occupation, it will not honour the agreements and contracts entered into by the Polish Government in exile in London or by its subordinate organs. Contrary to the will of the people and with damaging effect on their vital interests, they waste the wealth of the nation at their disposal and abuse the trust of the parties to treaties with them by incurring financial obligations and thereby endangering the interests of these parties.[87]

A similar declaration, made by the Second Assembly of the Antifascist Council of the National Liberation of Yugoslavia (AVNOJ) at Jajce on 29 November 1943, declared that the Royal Yugoslav Government in exile 'is deprived of all the rights of a legal government of Yugoslavia' and 'that all international treaties and obligations entered into by the fugitive Yugoslav government abroad in the name of Yugoslavia shall be re-examined for decision as to whether they should be annulled, renewed or confirmed'. It further declared that 'international treaties or obligations which may in future be contracted by the fugitive Yugoslav Government in the name of Yugoslavia and of her peoples will not be recognized'.[88] However, the united Yugoslav Government under Marshal Tito, which in conformity with the Tito-Šubašić Agreement of 1 December 1944 succeeded the Royal Yugoslav Government in exile on 7 March 1945, did not act on this declaration. Responding to a request by the United States Marshal Tito stated in the Yugoslav National Assembly on 1 April 1946 that the Government of the Federal People's Republic of Yugoslavia accepted the obligations contracted by the former Yugoslav governments towards the United States.[89]

However, neither the formation of an (unrecognized) government *in situ* nor a declaration such as the one by the Polish Provisional Government or the AVNOJ can, as a general rule, deprive a generally recognized government in exile of its competence to conclude treaties on behalf of its State. This was made clear, for instance, to the Government of the People's Republic of Poland by the majority of members of the International Civil Aviation Organization (ICAO) when it tried to adhere to the Convention on International Civil Aviation which had been ratified by the Polish Government in exile on 6 April 1945, i.e. after the above declaration by Mr Osóbka-Morawski.[90] A US Department of State Policy Statement of 27 November 1950 declared:

[87] See Gelberg, n. 82 above, 49 (translation supplied). See also Bierzanek, n. 82 above, at 46.

[88] (1943) 8 *Free Europe* 222; [1939–46] II DIA 334. See also Tomšić, 'The Identity of the Yugoslav State Under International Law' (1956) 3 *JRMP* 15–27 at 18, 25.

[89] Tomšić, n. 88 above, 15–27 at 26, n. 47. See also Whiteman, n. 2 above, ii, 80–1.

[90] The Polish Government in exile had signed the Convention on 7 Dec. 1944 (15 UNTS 295 at 372).

> We regard Poland as a member of the ICAO as a result of the ratification of the Chicago Convention by the Polish Government in exile in London. The present Polish Government, however, has not participated in any of the plenary sessions of ICAO and is delinquent in its dues. We have rejected offers of the present Polish Government to become a member of ICAO since in the view of both the United States and ICAO Poland is already a member.[91]

On the ground that Poland had become a member in 1945 and was delinquent in its dues the ICAO in 1952 deprived Poland of its voting right. The right to vote was only restored upon an agreement, made in 1958, in which Poland agreed to pay some 25 per cent of the arrears from 1945 and onward.[92]

The situation is different if the (revolutionary) authority *in situ* has also been recognized by some States as the *de jure* government of the State.[93] In this case it may be argued that each authority is competent to conclude treaties with those States that have recognized it as the State's government. This view, however, fails to take account of the fact that treaties are binding on the contracting States and that a State can only have one government competent to bind it at a time.[94] In view of the probative value ascribed to recognition by national and international tribunals in deciding the legal status of an authority,[95] it is submitted that an authority in exile will normally be regarded as competent to conclude treaties on behalf of a State, at least by an international tribunal,[96] only if it is recognized by the majority (or at least a substantial number) of States as its government. It is submitted that the ICAO thus acted correctly when it treated Poland as a member of the organization on the ground that the Polish Government in London on 6 April 1945 had validly ratified the Convention on International Civil Aviation. At the time of ratification the London Polish authority was still recognized by the majority of Allied States as the Government of Poland.

[91] [1950] IV FRUS 1040–51 at 1046. See also Whiteman, n. 2 above, ii, 53.

[92] See ICAO Doc. 7888 A11–P/12, 30 June 1958 and Blix, n. 10 above, 155–7.

[93] This must be distinguished from the situation in which the government in exile is recognized as the *de jure* government of the State while the government *in situ* is recognized as the *de facto* government of the State. Cf. *Gdynia Ameryka Linie* v. *Boguslawski* (1952), [1953] AC 11 (HL), which affirmed the decisions of the Court of Appeal (1950), [1951] 1 KB 162, and of Finnemore J (1949), [1950] 1 KB 157, *sub nom. Boguslawski* v. *Gdynia-Ameryka Linie*.

[94] Cf. *Gdynia Ameryka Linie* v. *Boguslawski* (1952), [1953] AC 11 at 29 (*per* Lord Porter); at 45 (*per* Lord Reid). See also the judgment of Cohen LJ in *Boguslawski* v. *Gdynia-Ameryka Linie* (1950), [1951] 1 KB 162 at 177. Cf. also Scelle, *Manuel de droit international public* (1948), 174–5.

[95] For examples of the latter, see e.g. the Awards in the *Tinoco Arbitration* (1923), 1 RIAA 369–99 at 381 and in *French Claims Against Peru* (1921): (1922) 29 *RGDIP* 256–83 at 270, 277. The French Memorial in the latter case referred to the recognitions by the various Powers as 'Pièces justificatives' (*ibid*., at 261, n. 4). See also the Award of the Franco–Chilean Arbitral Tribunal in *Affaire de Guano*, rendered at Rapperschwyl on 5 July 1901: 15 RIAA 125. For a more recent example of recognition being used as evidence of the status of a government, see the judgment of the ECHR in *Loizidou* v. *Turkey* (1995), Series A no. 310, para. 40.

[96] A national court may be bound by the recognition of its executive branch of government.

Only the USSR (4 January 1945), Czechoslovakia (31 January 1945), Bulgaria (3 February 1945) and Yugoslavia (30 March 1945) had accorded *de jure* recognition to the Polish Provisional Government at Warsaw.[97] If the authorities in exile and *in situ* are recognized as government by roughly the same number of States or if they receive only a limited number of recognitions this will normally indicate strong disagreement or doubt about the legal status of these authorities. In these cases the treaty-making competence of the (only partially) recognized government in exile is, to say the least, extremely questionable. Although much will depend on the circumstances of the particular case, there will normally be a presumption that States which conclude treaties with such (partially recognized) governments in exile are not acting in good faith.[98] Governments in exile recognized only by the other party to a treaty will undoubtedly be incompetent to bind the State, especially if the government *in situ* is widely recognized. It is therefore submitted that the Panamanian Government justly refused to pay some US$ 80,000 to the United States for services rendered to Eric Arturo Delvalle after he had been ousted from the presidency on 25 February 1988 by General Noriega. During the rule of Noriega-backed governments in Panama the United States alone continued to recognize ousted President Delvalle as the President of Panama. In 1988 and 1989 President Delvalle was flown several times by US military aircraft from a US military base inside the Panama Canal Zone to different places in the United States. After the US invasion of Panama in December 1989 the United States presented Panama with the bill for these flights.[99]

It has further been suggested that 'in view of the inherent limitations of a government in exile' it is incompetent to make certain treaties, such as treaties effecting the cession of State territory.[100] No reason can be seen why the treaty-making competence of a government in exile should be limited with respect to some subjects but not others. Either a government in exile is the organ of the State competent to bind it or it is not; there is no halfway

[97] On British non-recognition of the Polish Provisional Government at Warsaw, see HC Debs., vol. 408, cols. 1669–70, 1 Mar. 1945; *ibid.*, vol. 409, cols. 1795–6, 11 Apr. 1945; *ibid.*, vol. 411, WA, *col.* 706, 5 June 1945. On continued recognition of the Polish Government in London by the USA, see the statement of Secretary of State Stettinius on 1 Jan. 1945: DPSR II, no. 293, at 505.

[98] Cf. the *Nuclear Tests Cases* 'One of the basic principles governing the creation . . . of legal obligations, whatever their source, is the principle of good faith' (ICJ Rep. 1974, 253 at 268 and 457 at 473). See also principle 7(3) of the Declaration on Principles of International Law concerning Friendly Relations and Co-operation among States in accordance with the Charter of the United Nations, approved by the General Assembly on 24 Oct. 1970 (A/RES/2625 (XXV), annex).

[99] See *FAZ*, 25 May 1993, 5.

[100] Cf. Marek, n. 10 above, 458; Sperduti, 'Governi in esilio e comitati nazionali all'estero' [1952] *Com. Int.* 404–13 at 408. *Contra*, Blix, n. 10 above, 193–4 and 'Contemporary Aspects of Recognition' (1970-II) 130 *RdC* 587–704 at 620; and Rotter, 'Government in Exile' in Bernhardt (ed.), *Encyclopedia of Public International Law* (1987), x, 210–14 at 212.

house. The only inherent limitation of a government in exile is its—presumably temporary—absence from the State territory. This only limits the competence to perform certain treaties and not the competence to conclude them.[101] Governments in exile have regularly concluded treaties to be performed on their return home.[102] As the list of bilateral and multilateral treaties concluded by authorities in exile recognized as governments (Appendix III) suggests there is no difference between the treaty-making competence of governments in exile and that of governments *in situ*. For example, recognized governments in exile have concluded military, defence, economic, trade, loan, aid, extradition, administration, and political agreements, some of them binding their State for up to twenty years. If the treaty-making competence of a recognized government in exile is in question, this is usually the result of doubts about its status as a government under international law and not the result of some general limitations on the treaty-making competence of a government while in exile.

(c) Rights and Duties under Existing Treaties

The absence of a government from its State does not automatically suspend or terminate existing treaties. Thus, the Court of Appeal of The Hague stated in *Valk* v. *Kokes* (1950) that 'the circumstance that the Czechoslovak Government had been prevented by violence from exercising its authority in its own territory [did not] result in any change in its international relations resulting from existing treaties'.[103] The same view was also held in a series of decisions by United States Surrogate's Courts during the Second World War which confirmed that the 1931 Treaty of Friendship, Commerce, and Consular Rights between the United States of America and Poland[104] continued in full force and effect despite the displacement of the legitimate governmental authorities of the Polish Republic.[105] However, the conditions that cause a government to establish itself in exile, such as armed conflict or civil war, may lead to the termination or suspension of individual treaties on grounds of impossibility of performance,[106] fundamental change

[101] For treaties concerning rights to territory concluded by governments in exile, see App. III.

[102] For example, on 5 Sept. 1944 the Governments of Belgium, the Netherlands, and Luxembourg concluded an agreement concerning a Customs Union after liberation. The agreement was to enter into force provisionally immediately on the reinstallation of the contracting governments in their liberated countries. See [1944] *Keesing's* 6679A.

[103] (1950) 17 ILR no. 114, at 358. See also Verhoeven, n. 19 above, 77, and Liszt, *Das Völkerrecht* (12th edn., 1925), 491.

[104] 139 LNTS 395.

[105] See *In re Skewrys' Estate. In re Murika*, 46 NYS2d 942 at 943 (1944); *In re Flaum's Estate*, 42 NYS2d 539 at 540 (1943); *In re Zalewski's Estate*, 30 NYS2d 658 at 661 (1941), affirmed 38 NYS2d 37 (1942), reversed on other grounds 292 NY 332 (1944); *In re Schurz's Estate*, 28 NYS2d 165 at 166 (1941).

[106] Cf. Art. 61(1) of VCLT.

of circumstances,[107] or other grounds.[108] As there is a general presumption of the continuance in force of existing treaties the question arises to what extent authorities in exile may exercise the State's rights and must perform its obligations under those treaties.

State practice shows that only authorities in exile recognized as a government by the other party or, in case of multilateral treaties, by a majority of the other parties to the treaty have been regarded as competent to exercise the State's rights under the treaty. Similarly, the termination of a treaty by an authority in exile not recognized as a government by the other party (or parties) to the treaty has not been treated as effective. This may be illustrated by the following examples:

(i) *Korea.* Article 1(2) of the United States–Korean Treaty of Peace, Amity, Commerce, and Navigation of 22 May 1882 provided: 'If other powers deal unjustly or oppressively with either Government, the other will exert their good offices, on being informed of the case, to bring about an amicable arrangement, thus showing their friendly feelings.'[109] On 27 June 1919 Mr Syngman Rhee, Premier of the unrecognized 'Korean Provisional Government' (KPG) sent an official communication to the US State Department requesting that the US Government 'intervene and use [its] good offices'.[110] All attempts by the KPG to invoke the Treaty were ignored by the United States. In another action with respect to an existing treaty, the KPG, immediately upon its flight into exile, on 23 April 1919 declared invalid the Treaty of 29 August 1910 between Japan and Korea[111] by Article 1 of which the Emperor of Korea had made 'complete and permanent cession to . . . the Emperor of Japan of all rights of sovereignty over the whole of Korea'.[112] In Article 2 of the Treaty of Basic Relations between Japan and the Republic of Korea of 22 June 1965, the invalidity of this treaty was 'confirmed'.[113] According to the Japanese Government the treaty had not lost its legal validity because of the KPG's declaration, but because of either the independence of Korea on 15 August 1948,

[107] Cf. Art. 62 of VCLT.

[108] e.g. if the government's exile is caused by the outbreak of hostilities between States. This question is not prejudged by the VCLT. Cf. Art. 73 of VCLT. See also [1966] *ILC Yb.* 267–8; and [1982] II/2 *ILC Yb.* 68.

[109] Malloy (ed.), *Treaties, Conventions, International Acts, Protocols and Agreements Between the USA and Other Powers 1776–1909* (1910), i, 334–40 at 334–5.

[110] Choong-Sik, *The Politics of Korean Nationalism* (1963), 309, n. 60. For a further communication sent on 14 Mar. 1942 by Mr Syngman Rhee, as Chairman of the Korean Commission in Washington, see Oliver, *Syngman Rhee: The Man Behind the Myth* (1955), 179–80.

[111] On the declaration of the KPG, see Kim, *Die staatliche Einheit Koreas unter Berücksichtigung des Selbstbestimmungsrechts des koreanischen Volkes* (1995), 45–50.

[112] For the text of the Treaty of Annexation, see (1910) 4 *AJIL* Supp., 282–3; (1910) 4 *ZfVuB* 624–5.

[113] See (1966) 10 *JAIL* 263–4.

the Japanese recognition of that independence on 9 September 1951, or the entry into force of the Treaty of Peace with Japan on 24 April 1952.[114]

(ii) *France*. The French National Committee (CNF), which was not recognized by the Allies as the Government of France, on 29 September 1942 only declared that 'they' considered the Munich Agreement of 29 September 1938[115] and its consequences as null and void and did not declare it invalid on behalf of France.[116] This was only done in a joint statement by the Czechoslovak Government and the Provisional Government of the French Republic, signed on 22 August 1944, on the occasion of the Czechoslovak recognition of the Provisional Government as the Government of France.[117] With respect to the treaty character of mandates,[118] it is also of interest to note an Aide Mémoire by the National Commission for Foreign Affairs of Free France, dated 2 October 1941, on the termination of the French mandate in Syria which stated: 'Free France . . . holds that there can be no question of legally putting an end to the mandate régime. . . . Free France, which is only recognized—in certain conditions—by Great Britain and the USSR, is not qualified to ask for the discharge of this mandate'.[119]

(iii) *China*. On 20 February 1946 China ratified the Convention on International Civil Aviation, opened for signature at Chicago on 7 December 1944.[120] The Nationalist (Kuomintang) Government of China which had been forced by the Chinese Communists to flee to the island of Formosa on 8 December 1949 withdrew from the Convention on 31 May 1950 and re-acceded on 2 December 1953. This was possible as the depositary of the Convention, the United States, still continued to recognize the Nationalist Government (which in its view was a

[114] See Kim, n. 111 above, 49–50. It may also be argued that the Treaty was void *ab initio*, as the Korean Emperor's consent to the treaty had been procured by coercion. See McNair, n. 78 above, 209. Cf. also Art. 51 of VCLT.

[115] The Munich Agreement had been signed by France, Germany, Italy, and the UK: Parl. Pap. Misc. No 8 (1938), Cmd. 5848.

[116] For the statement of the CNF, see (1942) 2 *Inter-Allied Review* 248–9. See also Ripka, *The Repudiation of Munich* (1943), 13–16; *Four Fighting Years* (1943), 190. Compare the CNF statement with the letter of the British Foreign Secretary, Mr Eden, dated 5 Aug. 1942: 204 LNTS 377. On the annulment of the Munich Agreement by the various powers in general, see Marek, n. 10 above, 320–4; Pergler, 'The Munich "Repudiation"' (1943) 37 *AJIL* 308–10.

[117] For the text of the statement, see (1944) 4 *United Nations Review* 228; Langer, *Seizure of Territory* (1947), 240.

[118] On the treaty character of mandates, see *South West Africa Cases (Preliminary Objections)*, ICJ Rep. 1962, 319 at 330–2.

[119] [1941] III FRUS 790–1. On the incompetence of Free France to terminate the French mandate in the Levant States, see also *ibid*., at 801–3; De Gaulle, n. 16 above, i, 412; and on the termination of the mandate in general, see Bleckmann, *Das französische Kolonialreich und die Gründung neuer Staaten* (1969), 50–71.

[120] 15 UNTS 295.

government in exile)[121] as the Government of China. The British Government, which had recognized the Communist Government of China in Peking on 6 January 1950, did not attribute any legal effect to these actions by the (no longer recognized) Nationalist Government. The General Index to the United Kingdom Treaty Series for the period 1952–4[122] thus appended the following Note to the various entries made under the heading of the Convention on International Civil Aviation: 'The Nationalist Government of China withdrew from the Convention on 31st May, 1950, and re-acceded on 2nd December, 1953. Neither the withdrawal nor the re-accession was recognized by Her Majesty's Government.'[123]

(iv) *Algeria*. The Provisional Government of the Algerian Republic (GPRA) was not recognized by any Western State as the Government of Algeria. On 19 September 1960 the GPRA denounced the North Atlantic Treaty, which according to Article 6 was applicable to the 'Algerian Departments of France'.[124] No legal significance was thus attached by Members of NATO to that denunciation by the GPRA.[125] In a communiqué published on 24 January 1963 the NATO Council observed that the North Atlantic Treaty was 'without object' with regard to Algeria as from 3 July 1962.[126]

On the basis of these precedents, it is argued that in view of the universal non-recognition of the Tibetan Government in exile as the Government of Tibet, the Dalai Lama, as head of the Tibetan Government in exile, by his declaration of 20 June 1959 could not validly denounce the Sino–Tibetan Agreement of 23 May 1951.[127] However, this does not rule out that the Sino–Tibetan Treaty may have been invalid *ab initio* if, as is claimed by the Dalai Lama, it was in fact accepted by the Tibetan representatives only under pressure.[128]

In contrast, authorities in exile recognized as governments have regularly

[121] See the statement of Secretary of State John Foster Dulles on 7 Feb. 1955: US Congress, Senate, Committee on Foreign Relations, *Executive Sessions of the Senate Foreign Relations Committee (Historical Series)* (1978), vii, 309–56 at 317. For the view that the Nationalist Government at least until 1952 was a government in exile, see also Crawford, *The Creation of States in International Law* (1979), 147, 286 *Contra* Perfall, *Die völkerrechtliche Vertretung Chinas* (1967), 166–8.

[122] Cmnd. 368.

[123] Cmnd. 368, 7. See also (1958) 7 *ICLQ* 523.

[124] Signed in Washington, on 4 Apr. 1949: 34 UNTS 243.

[125] See Bedjaoui, n. 19 above, 180, 183, 200–6; Chikh, *L'Algérie en armes ou le temps des certitudes* (1981), 435–6. See also (1961) 6 *Deutsche Außenpolitik [GDR]* 236–44.

[126] Rousseau, 'Chroniques des faits internationaux' (1963) 67 *RGDIP* 118–87 at 129, n. 23*bis*. On the continuation in force of the North Atlantic Treaty with respect to Algeria, see also [1958–60] XIII FRUS 706.

[127] *Contra* International Commission of Jurists, *The Question of Tibet and the Rule of Law* (1959), 99. For the text of the Sino-Tibetan Agreement, see 158 BFSP 731.

[128] Cf. Art. 51 of VCLT.

exercised the right to terminate or suspend existing treaties either in conformity with the provisions of the treaty[129] or with the consent of the other party to the treaty.[130] For example, on 13 March 1915 the Governments of France and Belgium (in exile at Le Havre) signed an agreement suspending for the duration of the war the Franco–Belgian Convention of 30 July 1891 subjecting children of Belgian parents born in France to Belgian national service,[131] and on 6 April 1994 Mr Aristide, the Haitian President in exile, formally denounced the US–Haitian Agreement on Migrants-Interdiction of 23 September 1981.[132] Whether a recognized government in exile may invoke other grounds for terminating or suspending an existing treaty depends upon the circumstances of each case. The fact that a government is in exile alone constitutes neither a supervening impossibility of performance[133] nor a fundamental change of circumstances.[134] It may, however, be pleaded as a justification exonerating the State from liability for non-performance of the treaty in the context of State responsibility.[135] Recognized governments in exile have also continued to act as depositaries of multilateral treaties.[136]

Recognized governments in exile, however, are not merely entitled by

[129] Cf. Arts. 54(a), 57(a) of VCLT.

[130] Cf. Arts. 54(b), 57(b) of VCLT.

[131] Cf. (1917) 44 *JDI* 1905.

[132] The agreement provided that it 'shall continue in force until six months from the date either government gives notice of its intention to terminate the agreement' (33 UST 3559; TIAS No 10241). This agreement had provided the legal basis for the US policy of intercepting Haitian refugees on the high seas and forcibly repatriating them to Haiti. Cf. *Sale* v. *Haitian Centers Council*, 113 S.Ct. 2549 (1993). For the denunciation of the treaty, see *WP*, 7 Apr. 1994, Sec. A., 16; *ibid.*, 10 Apr. 1994, Sec. A, 26; *Guardian*, 7 Apr. 1994, 13; *ibid.*, 8 Apr. 1994, 12; *NY Times*, 10 Feb. 1994, Sec. A, 13; *ibid.*, 22 Apr. 1994, Sec. A, 26. It should be noted that this denunciation has not been listed in the US Department of State's list concerning 'Recent Actions Regarding Treaties to Which the United States is a party' reproduced in ILM. But the agreement has been treated by writers as in abrogation since Oct. 1994, i.e. 6 months after President Aristide's denunciation. Cf. Chivvis, 'US Immigration Law as Applied to Haiti' in Preeg, *The Haitian Dilemma* (1996), 116–26 at 116.

[133] Cf. Art. 61(1) of VCLT. The (temporary) absence of a government from its State does not constitute a '*permanent* disappearance or destruction of an object indispensable for the execution of the treaty'. See also [1963] II *ILC Yb.* 78–9, 206–7; [1966] II *ILC Yb.* 39, 256; [1982] II/2 *ILC Yb.* 59.

[134] Cf. Art. 62 of VCLT. According to the ICJ in the *Fisheries Jurisdiction Case* (*UK* v. *Iceland*), ICJ Rep. 1973, 3 at 21, the fundamental change of circumstances 'should have resulted in a radical transformation of the extent of the obligations still to be performed. The change must have increased the burden of the obligations to be executed to the extent of rendering the performance something essentially different from that originally undertaken'. The absence of a government from its State does not transform the extent of the obligations under a treaty but only renders their fulfilment temporarily impossible.

[135] Cf. Art. 73 of VCLT. See also Art. 31(1) of the ILC Draft Arts. on State Responsibility: [1979] II/2 *ILC Yb.* 122. In general, see Jennings and Watts, n. 78 above, i, 1304.

[136] Cf. e.g. *Arrêtés de Londres*, 98, 139. Recognized governments in exile have also been notified by depositaries of the accession, ratification, or denunciation by other States to multilateral treaties to which the State is a party (cf. *ibid.*, at 80–1; *Législation en exil*, 72, 95, 104).

existing treaties; they are bound by them too. This is illustrated by the fact that during the Second World War the US Government continued to send statements of amounts due and payable under inter-governmental Debt Agreements to those authorities in exile which it recognized as governments, which in turn requested deferment of payment.[137] Notably, no such statements were sent to the Provisional Czechoslovak Government in London prior to its recognition by the United States as Government of Czechoslovakia.[138] Apart from inter-State treaties, governments in exile are also bound by treaties and contracts with private individuals. Thus they are under an obligation to pay interest and instalments on national and State guaranteed foreign loans[139] and to meet other State debts.[140] To what extent they are able to fulfil these obligations will, of course, depend on the financial resources available to them.

In order to have their claim to governmental status recognized authorities in exile have even tried to make (token) payments on the State's debts. But authorities in exile not recognized as governments, as a rule, have not been allowed to meet their State's obligations under existing treaties. The League of Nations' Supervisory Commission, for example, decided in June 1943 that the League could not accept membership contributions offered by representatives of the (former) Government of Estonia 'in view of the uncertainty as to the negotiators' authority to act on behalf of a Government and as to the question whether that Government was recognized by the majority of the States Members'. The Treasury was therefore instructed not to enter such contributions in the books of the League. When on 4 August 1943 a consular representative of Estonia paid a sum of money into the League's bank account in New York, he was advised on behalf of the League that the money which had been deposited could be drawn out as

[137] See e.g. the exchange of letters between the US Secretary of State and the Polish Ambassador in Washington of 2 and 14 Dec. 1939: (1939) 1 *DSB* 687–8.

[138] Cf. (1940) 2 *DSB* 647; (1940) 3 *DSB* 565–6. On the Armenian debt to the USA and the decision of the US Government in 1922 not to send a statement of debt either to the Soviet Government at Erivan or to the exiled Dashnak Government at Paris because neither authority was recognized by the USA, see [1922] I FRUS 398, 399.

[139] e.g. on 31 July 1944 the Norwegian Government in London which had a regular income from its mercantile shipping business paid the last instalment on a loan contracted in the USA in 1924 (*NY Times*, 31 July 1944, 20). See also Koht, *Norway. Neutral and Invaded* (1941), 182; Lehmkuhl, *Journey to London. The Story of the Norwegian Government at War* (n.d.), 120; Royal Norwegian Government Information Office, *Norway's Floating Empire* (1942), 30. On the service of sterling loans by the Belgian Government in exile, see Bareau, 'The Finances of Refugee Governments' (1942) 64/201 *Banker* 17–24 at 22.

[140] In an out-of-court settlement the Kuwaiti Government in exile agreed in Nov. 1990 to pay US$14.6 million to a Dutch construction company for a disputed debt incurred on a 10-year-old contract. Cf. (1990) 34/45 *MEED. Middle East Business Weekly* 24. On the financial liabilities of the Belgian Government at Le Havre, see Langenhove, *L'action du Gouvernement belge en matière économique pendant la guerre* (1927), 87–8.

and when he wished, and the bank was instructed accordingly. The money was finally withdrawn in 1944.[141] In contrast, the League Secretariat on 29 April 1938 accepted a cheque for 10,000 Swiss francs from the Ethiopian Government (in exile) as a token payment for Ethiopia's annual contribution for the year 1935.[142] As a consequence of the Italian aggression against Ethiopia, the League Assembly decided in 1939 not to claim any contributions from Ethiopia for that year. Nor was a claim made for the years 1940 to 1941 inclusive.[143]

(2) *Unilateral Acts*

What has been said with respect to treaties applies *mutatis mutandis* to unilateral acts. Only a government, as State organ, is competent to perform such acts on behalf of the State which it purports to represent. It was for this reason that the French National Committee (CNF), which the Allies did not recognize as the Government of the French State, could not associate itself on behalf of France with the Inter-Allied Declaration Regarding Forced Transfers of Property in Enemy-Controlled Territory of 5 January 1943.[144] The Declaration therefore had to be issued in the name of seventeen Allied States, eight of which were represented by their recognized governments in exile, 'and the French National Committee'. Similarly, in the declaration, adopted at the second Inter-Allied meeting in London on 24 September 1941, the 'governments' of nine Allied States (of which eight were in exile) and 'representatives of General de Gaulle, leader of the Free Frenchmen', made known their adherence to the common principles set forth in the 'Atlantic Charter' of 14 August 1941.[145] Although formally these declarations were not made on behalf of France, in view of the intention of the Free French authorities to act on its behalf, it may be argued that they became binding on France once the Provisional Government of the French Republic, as successor of the Free French authorities,[146] succeeded in establishing itself as the Government of

[141] See League of Nations, Board of Liquidation, *Final Report* (Geneva, 31 July 1947), 41: League Doc.C.5.M.5.1947. The same procedure was followed with respect to contributions offered by representatives of Latvia and Lithuania: *ibid.*, at 41–2.

[142] [1938] I *Survey* 149.

[143] See n. 141 above, 38.

[144] (1943) 8 *DSB* 21–2. That the CNF was not regarded as a government becomes clear from a passage in the declaration which said: 'Accordingly the governments making this declaration and the French National Committee' (*ibid.*).

[145] (1941) 5 *DSB* 233–5; Parl.Pap. Misc. No 3 (1941), Cmd. 6315.

[146] Cf. the French statement accompanying a preliminary agreement between the USA and the Provisional Government of the French Republic, signed on 28 Feb. 1945, which provided that benefits given to the USA by the Provisional Government of France were understood to include benefits provided by the Comité National, the Haut Commandement en Chef, and the CFLN (76 UNTS 204).

France.[147] The position of the Free French authorities was in this respect similar to that of a local *de facto* authority which has received some limited recognition and which finally succeeds in establishing itself as the government of the State. It is generally agreed that acts of a (recognized) local *de facto* authority are binding on the State, once it succeeds in establishing its legal order in the whole State, as the 'principe de la survivance des anciennes conventions' also applies to this case.[148] The same, however, may be said for the case that an authority in exile recognized not as the State's government but in some other, lesser capacity, which concludes a treaty with the intention of acting for the State or its people, finally succeeds in establishing itself *in situ* as the State's Government, recognized as such by the other party or parties to the treaty. As a general rule, however, unilateral acts performed by an authority in exile which is not recognized as a government do not affect the legal position of the State it purports to represent or its legal relationships with other (non-recognizing) States.[149] This is evidenced by the decision of the Japanese Prize Court Review Commission of 24 July 1959 in the case of *The Santa Fé* in which the majority of the Commission held that Japan and France were on 'friendly terms' on 13 February 1942, when the Japanese army seized the *SS Santa Fé* in the port of Saigon despite the fact that on 9 December 1941 the CNF, which was not recognized by the Japanese Government, had declared war on Japan.[150] In contrast, Japan regarded itself in a state of war with the

[147] In *Werner* v. *Vve. Rothschild* the Court of Appeal of Paris referred to 'the commitments entered into in the name of France in this official Declaration [of 5 January 1943]' ((1953) 80 *JDI* 875–9 at 879). The Court assumed that the Declaration constituted a Treaty binding on France. On the legal nature of the Declaration and its effect on French municipal law, see the case notes of Sarraute and Tager (1953) 80 *JDI* 879–85, Goldman (1950) 77 *JDI* 172–4; and Francescakis (1948) 37 *RCDI* 315–23, 496–506. On the legal nature of the Declaration see *De Rothschild* v. *Teuscher et al.* (1953), [1955] III Pas.belge 4 at 9–10; and *NV de Bataafsche Petroleum Maatschappij* v. *War Damage Commission* [1956] SLR 65 at 81–2 (*per* Whyatt CJ).

[148] See Gemma, 'Les gouvernements de fait' (1923–III) 4 *RdC* 297–413 at 345; Spiropoulos, *Die de facto-Regierung in Völkerrecht* (1926), 73–5; Guggenheim, *Lehrbuch des Völkerrechts* (1948), i, 199; Wengler, n. 77 above, i, 297; Erdmann, n. 35 above, 76–7.

[149] It is submitted that France continued to be a member of the League of Nations not because of the declaration made on 18 Apr. 1943 by General de Gaulle to the Secretary-General of the League of Nations repudiating the notification of withdrawal by the French Government at Vichy of 19 Apr. 1941 but because of the invalidity of the initial withdrawal by the Vichy Government. For the text of General de Gaulle's telegramme, see Flory, *Le statut international des Gouvernements réfugiés et le cas de la France Libre 1939–1945* (1952), 192–3. See also [1943] *Keesing's* 5769B.

[150] (1964) 8 *JAIL* 253–81. But see also the separate opinion of Mr Yanai, *ibid.*, at 275–7. For the view that the declaration of war by the CNF had no legal effect, see also Oánh, *Die Wandlung der völkerrechtlichen Stellung Vietnams bis zum Pariser Waffenstillstandsabkommen 1973* (1974), 29. On 24 Oct. 1943 the Provisional Government of Free India declared war on the UK and the USA (Giani, *Indian Independence Movement in East Asia* (1947), ii, 72). Both countries, however, attached no legal significance to this declaration. It is of interest to note in this connection that the PCIJ found that there existed no state of war between Germany and Poland despite the fact that the Polish National Council had participated in the

Netherlands as a consequence of the declaration of war of 8 December 1941 by the Dutch Government in London, which Japan continued to recognize as the Government of the Netherlands.[151] Similarly, the Republic of Korea was not invited to sign the Treaty of Peace with Japan at San Francisco on 8 September 1951,[152] although the unrecognized Provisional Korean Government had declared war on Japan in December 1941.[153] In contrast, States, on whose behalf war had been declared by their recognized governments in exile, were represented at San Francisco. Belgium, Greece, Luxembourg, the Netherlands, Norway, and the Philippines signed the Treaty of Peace with Japan on 8 September 1951.[154] Poland and Czechoslovakia, which had declared war on Japan on 11 and 16 December 1941, respectively, were invited to the San Francisco Peace Conference but did not sign the Peace Treaty. Instead they concluded bilateral treaties with Japan which provided for the termination of the state of war between their countries.[155]

Recognized governments in exile are competent to perform the whole range of unilateral acts on behalf of the State which they represent. For example, they may grant permission to other States to carry out certain acts which otherwise would constitute an infringement of the State's (territorial) sovereignty. Thus the United States justified the entry of its warships into Haitian territorial waters as well as the drop of three million leaflets over Haiti by US military aircraft on 11 September 1994 by the fact that permission had been granted by Haiti's government in exile in Washington.[156] Similarly, when the US Coast Guard on 5 July 1989 intercepted a Panamanian-flagged vessel on the high seas on suspicion of drug trafficking and the captain refused permission for a detailed inspection of the ship, the US Department of State sought approval to detain the vessel and escort it

war against Germany with its own autonomous army (*German Interests in Polish Upper Silesia* (1926), PCIJ, Ser. A, No 7, 28).

[151] See the Japanese declaration of 13 Jan. 1942 in response to the Dutch declaration of war: (1941) 25 *ZVR* 357–8. On recognition of the Dutch Government in London, see the statement of Japanese Deputy Foreign Minister Matsumote on 26 Feb. 1945 (Janke, 'Rechtsnatur und Rechtsstellung der Regierung im Exil', doctoral thesis (University of Hamburg, 1954), 94).

[152] 136 UNTS 45.

[153] On 17 Dec. 1941 Mr Syngman Rhee informed the US Department of State that the Korean Provisional Government had formally declared war on Japan in order to qualify for lend-lease aid; the declaration was, however, ignored by the State Department (Oliver, n. 110 above, 177, 175).

[154] 136 UNTS 45 at 126–37.

[155] For the Czechoslovak–Japanese Protocol of 13 Feb. 1957, see 300 UNTS 119; and for the Polish–Japanese Agreement of 8 Feb. 1957, see 318 UNTS 251. Belgium and the Netherlands on 10 Feb. 1947 also signed the Treaty of Peace with Italy (49 UNTS 3 at 4). The Governments in exile of both countries had declared war on Italy on 21 Nov. 1940 and 11 Dec. 1941, respectively. Czechoslovakia, Greece, and Yugoslavia signed the Treaty of Peace with Bulgaria at Paris on 10 Feb. 1947 (41 UNTS 21). On the same day Czechoslovakia and Yugoslavia signed the Treaty of Peace with Hungary (41 UNTS 135). The former also signed the Treaties of Peace with Finland and Romania (48 UNTS 203 and 42 UNTS 3, respectively).

[156] See *WT*, 13 Sept. 1994, Sec. A, 1.

into a US port from the exiled Government of President Delvalle (who at the time resided in Miami, Florida). Permission of the flag State was required, as international law prohibits countries from asserting jurisdiction over foreign vessels on the high seas save in certain exceptional cases of which drug trafficking is not (yet) one.[157] With respect to the incident, Mr Richard Boucher, a Department of State spokesman declared: 'We certainly do recognize the Delvalle government as the government of Panama and we recognize, therefore, that they have the authority to give us permission.'[158] While it is true that, in principle, the Government of Panama has the authority to give the required permission, the fact that (deposed) Panamanian President Delvalle and his followers were recognized as the Government of Panama only by the United States[159] raises serious doubts about the governmental status of the Delvalle group in international law and, consequently, about its competence to grant the required permission. The fact that US courts[160] regarded the permission given by 'then-deposed' Panamanian President Delvalle as valid must be seen against the background of the US domestic law rule that 'what government is to be regarded here as representative of a foreign sovereign State is a political rather than a judicial question, and is to be determined by the political department of the government'.[161] This determination by the executive is binding on all domestic courts.[162] By virtue of this rule, the US Government is thus able to 'make' a group of exiles the government of a foreign sovereign State within the jurisdiction of the US courts simply by recognizing it as such. This, however, is not true within the jurisdiction of international tribunals where recognition by the United States will only be (non-conclusive) evidence among other evidence on the legal status of the authority in exile. In cases such as that of ousted Panamanian President Delvalle, where recognition is based on political rather than legal considerations, US recognition of an

[157] Cf. Arts. 6(1), 22(1) of the Geneva Convention on the High Seas (HSC) 1958 (450 UNTS 11); Arts. 92(1), 110(1) of UNCLOS; and the *Lotus Case* (1927), PCIJ, Ser. A., No 10, 25. See also *United States* v. *Marino-Garcia*, *United States* v. *Cassalins-Guzman*, where the US Court of Appeals held that all nations have jurisdiction to board and seize vessels engaged in universally prohibited activities and that 'there is a growing consensus among nations to include drug trafficking as a universally prohibited crime' (679 F.2d 1373 at 1382, n. 16 (11th Cir. 1982)). For treaty jurisdiction in respect of drug trafficking at sea, see Art. 17 of the 1988 UN Convention against Illicit Traffic in Narcotic Drugs and Psychotropic Substances (UN Doc.E/CONF.82/15; Parl. Pap. Misc. No 14 (1989), Cm. 804).

[158] *WP*, 8 July 1989, Sec. A, 4.

[159] See App. II.

[160] See *United States* v. *Leuro-Rosas*, 952 F.2d 616 at 618–21 (1st Cir. 1991); *United States* v. *Segura Pretel*, 939 F.2d 233 at 236–7 (5th Cir. 1991).

[161] *Guaranty Trust Co. of New York* v. *United States*, 304 US 126 at 137 (1938). In both cases the Court of Appeals expressly referred to this rule.

[162] *Ibid*., at 138; and *Jones* v. *United States*, 137 US 202 at 212 (1890); *Agency of Canadian Car & Foundry Co.* v. *American Can Co.*, 258 F. 363 at 368 (2nd Cir. 1919). In *United States* v. *Leuro-Rosas*, the Court stated: 'the State Department may diplomatically recognize any foreign leader it chooses to recognize, and such a choice, since it is a political question, is made free from judicial review' (952 F.2d 616 at 621 (1st Cir. 1991)).

authority in exile as a government will carry very little evidential weight regarding its governmental status.[163] Moreover, such recognition may give rise to questions of State responsibility. It is suggested that if a State exceeds its discretionary powers by recognizing as a government an authority in exile which does not qualify as such under international law, it may be held responsible for the illegal acts of that authority as if they were its own acts.[164]

Governments in exile may also renounce rights,[165] lodge protests,[166] sever diplomatic relations,[167] recognize new States and governments,[168] consent to the service of their nationals in the military forces of a foreign State,[169] and request assistance against the (illegal) authority *in situ*. The assistance requested may take various forms. Authorities in exile recognized as governments have requested other States as well as regional and international organizations to create a new police force or to modernize their armed forces,[170] to freeze (or order States to freeze) their States' foreign financial assets,[171] to impose trade or economic sanctions on their States,[172] to send

[163] Cf. *Tinoco Arbitration* (1924), 1 RIAA 369 at 381. See in this connection also the finding of the US District Court in *United States* v. *Noriega*: 'Despite this official recognition of Delvalle, the court understands that General Noriega is the *de facto* head of the Panamanian government' (683 F.Supp. 1373 at 1374, n. 3 (SD Fla. 1988)).

[164] Cf. Janke, n. 151 above, 40–2.

[165] e.g. the Belgian Government at Le Havre by declaration of 22 Sept. 1915 renounced the capitulations in the French zone of Morocco ((1917) 44 *JDI* 1633).

[166] For example, the Kuwaiti Government at Taif protested against the decision by the Iraqi authorities in Kuwait that on 6 Oct. 1990 the Kuwaiti dinar would become an illegal tender ((1990) 34/39 *MEED* 17) and declared that the Kuwaiti dinar continued to be the official currency of the State (UN Doc.S/21841). The Government of Democratic Kampuchea, by letter of 3 Aug. 1981 to the Secretary-General of the United Nations, protested against the accession of Viet Nam on 9 June 1981 to the Convention on the Prevention and Punishment of the Crime of Genocide (UN Doc.A/36/417).

[167] For examples see 'Zur diplomatischen Chronik des zweiten Weltkrieges: Abbruch und Aufnahme diplomatischer Beziehungen, Kriegserklärungen, Waffenstillstand und Friedensschluß' (1948–9) 1–2 *JIR* 224–38 *passim*.

[168] On the recognition of the Provisional Czechoslovak Government by the various governments in exile, see App. II.

[169] See n. 68 above.

[170] See the letter dated 24 July 1993 from the President of the Republic of Haiti addressed to the UN Secretary-General: UN Doc.S/26180, annex. The UN Security Council replied to this request in S/RES/867 (1993).

[171] See e.g. the summary of the legislative history to the US Kuwaiti Assets Control Regulations, which read in part: 'the President also issued Executive Order No 12723, at the request of the recognized Government of Kuwait, blocking all property and interests in property of the Government of Kuwait as a protective measure' (55 FR 49856). Cf. also S/RES/661 (1990), para. 9.

[172] See the letter dated 7 June 1993 from the Permanent Representative of Haiti to the UN addressed to the President of the Security Council: 'on instructions from my Government, I request that the Security Council make universal and mandatory the sanctions against the *de facto* authorities adopted at the Ad Hoc Meeting of Ministers for Foreign Affairs of the Organization of American States' (UN Doc.S/25958). The UN Security Council, replying to this letter, on 16 June 1993 imposed a trade embargo on Haiti (S/RES/841). On the importance

civilian missions to their States,[173] or to use military force. For example, on 12 August 1990 the Government of Kuwait in exile notified the President of the UN Security Council pursuant to Article 51 of the UN Charter that: 'In the exercise of its inherent right of individual and collective self-defence[174] . . . [Kuwait] has requested some nations to take such military or other steps as are necessary to ensure the effective and prompt implementation of Security Council resolution 661 (1990).'[175] While there was disagreement whether on the basis of this request and the right of collective self-defence States could institute a naval blockade[176] in order to enforce the economic sanctions imposed upon Iraq by Security Council Resolution 661 (1990),[177] the competence of the almost universally recognized

of the request by the legitimate government in exile, see UN Doc.S/PV.3238, at 8, 12, 17. See also UN Doc.S/PV.3413, 15. On the imposition of economic sanctions against Panama by the USA at the request of President Delvalle, see [1989] *Keesing's* 36683; and (1988) 88/2136 *DSB* 75.

[173] See Resolution MRE/RES.2/91, adopted on 8 Oct. 1991 by the *ad hoc* Meeting of Ministers for Foreign Affairs of the OAS. In that resolution the Ministers resolved 'to accede to the request of President Aristide that a civilian mission be constituted to re-establish and strengthen constitutional democracy in Haiti (OEA-DEMOC), which should go to that country in order to facilitate the re-establishment and strengthening of democratic institutions' (UN Doc.A/46/550–S/23127, annex). See also the letter dated 3 June 1992 from the President of Haiti addressed to the UN Secretary-General: UN Doc.S/24340, annex II.

[174] On the customary international law requirement for collective self-defence of a request by the State which is the victim of an armed attack, see *Military and Paramilitary Activities Case*, ICJ Rep. 1986, 14 at 105.

[175] UN Doc.S/21489. See also the statement by the Press Secretary of US President Bush on 12 Aug. 1990: 'This morning the President received a letter from . . . the Amir of Kuwait, requesting on behalf of the Government of Kuwait and in accordance with Article 51 of the UN Charter and the right of individual and collective self-defence that the US Government take appropriate steps as necessary to ensure that the UN-mandated economic sanctions against Iraq and Kuwait are immediately and effectively implemented' ([1990] AFPCD no 301, at 479; *NY Times*, 13 Aug. 1990, Sec. A, 11). For the Kuwaiti Government's request to the UK, see UKMIL 1990: (1990) 61 *BYBIL* 627. For the Netherlands' request to the USA in Jan. 1942 for assistance in defence of the Islands of Curaçao and Aruba, see [1942] III FRUS 51–2.

[176] The States instituting the blockade referred to their action as naval 'interdiction' of shipping to and from Iraq. The difference between the two, however, seems to be one of semantics rather than substance. As the legal evaluation of an action cannot depend upon the name that is given to it, the different labelling of what in fact constituted a naval blockade is to be seen as diplomatic window-dressing. Interestingly enough, before the 'interdiction' of the shipping was undertaken, officials of the States in question too spoke of a 'blockade'. Cf. e.g. the statement of US Secretary of State Baker: *NY Times*, 11 Aug. 1990, Sec. A, 7.

[177] This view was taken, *inter alia*, by the USA, the UK, and Australia. For the US view, see [1990] AFPCD nos 301, 302, 313; *NY Times*, 13 Aug. 1990, Sec. A, 8. For the British view, see UKMIL 1990: (1990) 61 *BYBIL* 627–31. For the Australian view, see (1992) 13 *AYBIL* 421–4 at 424. The USSR, France, China, Canada, and the UN Secretary-General, Mr Javier Pérez de Cuéllar, on the other hand, argued that such action required authorization by the Security Council under Art. 42 of the UN Charter (*NY Times*, 17 Aug. 1990, Sec. A, 12; *Guardian*, 18 Aug. 1989, 3). The controversy was settled, but not necessarily determined, by S/RES/665 (1990), in which the Security Council 'calls upon *those Member States co-operating with the Government of Kuwait* which are deploying maritime forces to the area to use such measures . . . as may be necessary under the authority of the Security Council to halt all inward and outward maritime shipping in order to . . . ensure strict implementation of the provisions

Government of Kuwait to request assistance against Iraq was not called into question as such.[178] The case of Haiti suggests that an authority in exile recognized as a government is competent to request assistance not only within the framework of collective self-defence against a foreign aggressor that has occupied its State but also against a domestic rival authority that has ousted it in a *coup d'état* or revolution. Although owing to constitutional restraints[179] couched in very general terms, the letter of 29 July 1994 from Fr. Jean-Bertrand Aristide, the recognized President of Haiti in exile, to the Secretary-General of the United Nations may be regarded as a request for the use of force against the (in the constitutional law sense) illegal authority *in situ.*[180] It reads in its final paragraph: 'Therefore, I feel that the time has come for the international community, as a party in the process which led to that [Governors Island] Agreement, to take prompt and decisive action, under the authority of the United Nations, to allow for its full implementation.'[181] Two days later, the UN Security Council, 'taking note' of this letter and a further letter from the Permanent Representative of Haiti to the UN,[182] authorized 'Member States . . . to use all necessary means to facilitate the departure from Haiti of the military leadership, consistent with the Governors Island Agreement'.[183] However, valid requests for military assistance against the usurpers will be very rare indeed,

related to such shipping laid down in resolution 661 (1990)' (italics added). On the interdiction of shipping to and from Iraq and the question of self-defence at the request of the Government of Kuwait in exile, see also El Sayegh, *La crise du golfe: de l'interdiction à l'autorisation du recours à la force* (1993), 334–7, 367–70; Warbrick, 'The Invasion of Kuwait by Iraq' (1991) 40 *ICLQ* 482–92 at 485–7; Schachter, 'United Nations Law in the Gulf Conflict' (1991) 85 *AJIL* 452–73 at 457–61; Weller, 'The legal right to fight surrendered', *The Times*, 6 Sept. 1990, 10.

[178] In S/RES/661 (1990), para. 9, the Security Council, having affirmed the inherent right of individual or collective self-defence decided 'that . . . nothing in the present resolution shall prohibit assistance to the legitimate Government of Kuwait'. See also S/RES/665 (1990), para. 1; S/RES/678 (1990), para. 2; and S/RES/686 (1990).

[179] See Arts. 135–1 and 138 of the Constitution of the Republic of Haiti of 10 Mar. 1987.

[180] For other more explicit requests for assistance by the Haitian Government in exile, see nn. 170, 172, 173 above. On the legal significance attributed by the USA to the 'full consent of the legitimate government' of Haiti in exile to the deployment of US troops in Haiti, see Nash, 'Contemporary Practice of the United States Relating to International Law' (1995) 89 *AJIL* 96–130 at 122–6.

[181] UN Doc.S/1994/905, annex.

[182] In this letter, dated 30 July 1994, the President of the UN Security Council was informed 'of the agreement of the Government of President Aristide with the draft resolution S/1994/904'. It said further: 'The Government considers that this draft resolution provides an appropriate framework for the implementation of the Governors Island Agreement' (UN Doc.S/1994/910). See also the statement of the Haitian Permanent Representative to the UN, Mr Longchamp, in the meeting of the Security Council on 31 July 1994: UN Doc.S/PV.3413, 4.

[183] S/RES/940 (1994). Great importance was attached to these letters by the members of the Security Council when adopting the resolution. Compare UN Doc.S/PV.3413, at 5, 19–20, 21, 23, 24, 25. See also *NY Times*, 31 July 1994, Sec. 1, 10; *The Times*, 1 Aug. 1994, 1. The 10-point Governors Island Agreement, signed on 3 July 1993, provided *inter alia* for the restoration of democracy, the return of President Aristide to Haiti by 30 Oct. 1993, and the resignation of the officers who overthrew him by 15 Oct. 1993 (UN Doc.A/47/975–S/26063, at 2–3).

as elected governments which are forced into exile by a *coup d'état* may continue to be recognized as governments only in exceptional circumstances.[184] In view of the possibility of abuse, by requests for military assistance being made by an exiled government recognized as such only by the requested State or States, only widespread recognition, especially by the United Nations or regional organizations, of the requesting authority in exile as a government will normally secure that a request is regarded as a valid justification of the military intervention to (re-)install the government in exile. Recognition by the intervening State alone usually cannot suffice to legalize or justify an intervention. This is illustrated by the US invasion of Panama on 19 December 1989 which the US Government tried to justify on the ground that it had acted with the (tacit) consent of Mr Guillermo Endara, whom it recognized as the legitimate, i.e. democratically elected, President of Panama. At the time of the consent 'President' Endara, however, was in 'internal exile' on a US military base in Panama and recognized as such only by the United States.[185] The US invasion was 'deplored'—it is submitted correctly—as a 'flagrant violation of international law' by the UN General Assembly in Resolution 44/240, adopted on 29 December 1989.[186] The Organization of American States (OAS) on 22 December 1989 also had 'deeply deplored' the invasion in a resolution opposed only by the United States, with twenty voting in favour (Panama, represented by the ousted Noriega Government, amongst them) and six members abstaining.[187]

2 FOREIGN RELATIONS AND JUDICIAL PROCEEDINGS

(1) *Bilateral Relations*

(a) Formal Diplomatic Relations

Practice shows that States have maintained a wide range of relations with both recognized governments in exile and authorities in exile not recognized as governments but recognized in some other, lesser capacity.[188] The

[184] Following the adoption of S/RES/841 (1993) making universal and mandatory economic sanctions against the *de facto* authorities in Haiti at the request of the Aristide Government, the President of the Security Council stated that 'the adoption of this resolution is warranted by the unique and exceptional situation in Haiti and should not be regarded as constituting a precedent' (UN Doc.S/PV.3238, at 9).

[185] See the remarks by Mr Sofaer, Legal Adviser, US Department of State, (1990) 84 *ASIL Proc.* 182–203 at 185, 187; Professor Moore, *ibid.*, at 191, 197; and, for criticism of this argument, Professor Frankowska, *ibid.*, at 196.

[186] The resolution was adopted by 75 votes to 20, with 40 abstentions.

[187] On the problem of assistance on request in general, see Jennings and Watts, n. 78 above, i, 435–7.

[188] e.g. as a '*de facto* belligerent government', a '*de facto* government', the 'sole legitimate representative of a people', 'the supreme organ of a movement', the 'present trustee of a future government', or 'the supreme organ of the nation, and the first basis of a future government'.

difference between relations with a recognized and an unrecognized government in exile is one of form rather than substance. This may be illustrated by the communication of the Italian Foreign Ministry to the Corte di Cassazione in *Re Arafat and Salah* (1985),[189] which states with respect to the relations between the Italian Republic and the Palestine Liberation Organization (PLO), which had been recognized and in 1993 still was by Italy 'as a National Liberation Organization',[190] that 'these relations, although they are regular and have reached the highest levels . . . retain a "formal character, different from that of normal relations between States"'.[191] States have maintained formal diplomatic relations only with authorities in exile which they recognized *de jure* as governments, i.e. as the representative organs of sovereign States.[192] This may be explained by the fact that only States possess the right of legation (*jus legationis*), i.e. the right to send and receive agents entitled to those diplomatic privileges and immunities recognized by international law.[193] States however exercise the right of legation through their Heads of State and/or Ministers of Foreign Affairs[194] who, as a rule, are members of the government in exile.[195]

The Belgian Government in London which functioned in London during the Second World War seems to have been an exception to that rule. King Leopold III, the Belgian Head of State, had surrendered to the German Army and had become a prisoner of war.[196] The absence of the King, however, did not create any serious constitutional problems. According to Article 82 of the Belgian Constitution of 7 February 1831, as amended, the cabinet of ministers had to assume supreme executive power if the King was unable to govern. On 28 May 1940 the Belgian Government in France issued a declaration stating that the King was unable to rule, being under the power of the invader, and announced that the Government would

[189] (1988) 7 *Ital. YIL* 295–8.

[190] Letter from the Italian Embassy in London, dated 29 Jan. 1993. See App. I, No. II.9.

[191] See n. 189 above, at 296–7.

[192] They may, however, maintain informal relations with authorities in exile not recognized *de jure* as a government. See Hackworth, n. 3 above, iv, 415–9; BDIL VII, 534–5.

[193] By way of exception and for historical reasons the right of legation also belongs to the Holy See. It should be noted that the 'right' of legation is not a right in the strict legal sense but rather an attribute of sovereign statehood. Cf. Hurst, 'Les immunités diplomatiques' (1926–II) 12 *RdC* 119–241 at 121. On the right of legation in general, see Hackworth, n. 3 above, iv, 393; Jennings and Watts, n. 78 above, i, 1056–8; Dahm, Delbrück, and Wolfrum, *Völkerrecht* (2nd edn., 1989), I/1, 262–3.

[194] Cf. Art. 14(1) of VCDR.

[195] For some historical examples of formal diplomatic relations with dethroned sovereigns in exile who continued to be recognized as the legitimate sovereign of their State, see Bonfils, *Lehrbuch des Völkerrechts für Studium und Praxis* (3rd edn., 1904), § 659.

[196] On 28 May 1940 King Leopold III signed the capitulation of the Belgian Armed Forces at Bruges. The Belgian cabinet which had previously left the country met in Paris and declared the capitulation illegal. For the events in May 1940, see Stengers, *Leopold III et le gouvernement: les deux politiques belges de 1940. Aux origines de la question royale* (1980).

continue to prosecute the war.[197] States which carried on to recognize the Belgian Ministers in London as the Government of Belgium continued to send Ambassadors and Envoys Extraordinary and Ministers Plenipotentiary to the Belgian Government.[198] Supplementary notes prepared for the use of the British Secretary of State in Parliament in December 1940 read on this point:

> It is proposed to allow the privilege [of receiving diplomatic envoys] to the Belgian Government, too, although the absence of the Head of the Belgian State places them technically in a different position from the other Allies. It is not proposed that this right of a Sovereign State [i.e. the right of legation] shall be conceded to national movements such as that of General de Gaulle, the representation of other countries to whom will be, as it were, unofficial and carrying with it no diplomatic status.[199]

This statement shows that the presence or absence of the Head of State is to be regarded as a mere technicality which does not affect the competence of a recognized government in exile to exercise the State's right of legation. The contrary view would mean leaving the exercise of the State's right of legation to chance. It is therefore argued that the exercise of the State's right of legation depends only on the recognition of the authority in exile as a government by the host State and the States with which formal diplomatic relations are to be to maintained.

That States maintain formal diplomatic relations only with authorities in exile recognized *de jure* as governments is well illustrated by the case of the Czechoslovak authorities in exile, which during the Second World War were recognized in several different capacities. Formal diplomatic relations with the Czechoslovak authorities in exile, however, were established only on the occasion of or after their recognition as the Government of the Czechoslovak Republic. For example, the British Government on 20 December 1939 recognized the Czechoslovak National Committee under Dr Eduard Beneš as 'qualified to represent the Czecho-Slovak peoples'.[200] Unspecified 'relations' were established on 21 July 1940, on the occasion of 'the recognition of the Czechoslovak National Committee as a Provisional

[197] For text of the declaration, see *Moniteur belge* (Paris), 18–30 May 1940, 6; *The Times*, 31 May 1940, 6; [1940] I FRUS 208–9.

[198] For a list of diplomats accredited to the Belgian Government, see Kerchove d'Exaerde, n. 74 above, 93–151 at 119.

[199] Supplementary Notes for the Use of the Secretary of State in Proposing Second Reading in the House of Lords of the Bill to Confer Immunities and Privileges upon the Allied Administrations, 17 Dec. 1940: FO 371/26 427, 300; quoted in Kerchove d'Exaerde, n. 74 above, 93–151 at 125.

[200] See HL Debs. vol. 356, col. 552, 20 Dec. 1939. See further DAFP IV, no 201, at 272; DCER VII, 26–7 at 27; [1939] *Keesing's* 3848E. For similar recognition by other States, see App. II. See also *Four Fighting Years* (1943), 178; Schwelb, 'Legislation in Exile: Czechoslovakia' (1942) 24 *JCL* 120–4 at 123; Halajczuk, *Los estados conquistados ante el derecho internacional* (1950), 80.

Czechoslovak Government'.[201] These relations found their expression in the appointment of Mr Bruce Lockhart as 'representative' to the Provisional Czechoslovak Government.[202] That these 'relations' did not amount to formal diplomatic relations becomes clear from a special Czechoslovak memorandum which was presented to the British Government on 18 April 1941. It contained, *inter alia*, the request that 'full diplomatic and *de jure* recognition be given to the Czechoslovak Government' and that 'as a result of this recognition a British Plenipotentiary Minister to the Czechoslovak Government be appointed, as well as a Czechoslovak Minister to the British Government'.[203] The British Government finally accredited an Envoy Extraordinary and Minister Plenipotentiary to Dr Beneš as President of the Czechoslovak Republic on 18 July 1941, the day it accorded 'full recognition' to the Czechoslovak Government.[204] It was explained in a note dated 5 August 1942 by the Foreign Secretary, Mr Eden, to the Czechoslovak Foreign Minister that the decision to accredit an Envoy Extraordinary and Minister Plenipotentiary to Dr Beneš as President of the Czechoslovak Republic 'implied that His Majesty's Government in the United Kingdom regarded the juridical position of the President and Government of the Czechoslovak Republic as identical with that of the other Allied heads of States and Governments established in this country'.[205] By the time the

[201] See HC Debs., vol. 363, cols. 614–15, 23 July 1940. On that recognition, see also [1941] II FRUS 26; DAFP IV, no 201, 272–4 at 273–4; [1940] *Keesing's* 4158A. Canada also entered into 'relations' when it recognized the Provisional Czechoslovak Government on 23 Oct. 1940 (DCER IX, no 1496, at 1821–2; *ibid.*, VII, 30–1).

[202] Taborsky, n. 12 above, 89; (1940) 2 *Free Europe* 177.

[203] *Four Fighting Years* (1943), 186. Compare in this connection also the 'relations' between the British Government and the Czechoslovak National Council until the organization of the future Czecho-Slovak Government which was provided for in Art. 1 of the Agreement of 3 Sept. 1918 between the two parties: [1918] I FRUS Supp. 1, 844–5; Taborsky, n. 12 above, 74–5.

[204] See HC Debs., vol. 373, col. 861, 23 July 1941. On the appointment of Mr Nichols as British Minister, see also [1941] *Keesing's* 4703C; (1941) 4 *Free Europe* 116. It is of interest to note that the British Government decided to accord 'full recognition' to the Provisional Czechoslovak Government only after the Government of the USSR had advised Dr Beneš on 9 July 1941 that it recognized him as President of Czechoslovakia and accepted the juridical continuity and frontiers of the pre-war Czechoslovak Republic. On 2 July 1941 the British Government had still only intended to delete the prefix 'provisional' from the references to the Czechoslovak Government in London and to appoint to it a 'British Diplomatic Representative'. See DAFP IV, 692, n. 5.

[205] 204 LNTS 377. See also DCER IX, no 1495, at 1821; *Four Fighting Years* (1943), 187–8, and Korkisch, 'Zur Frage der Weitergeltung des Münchner Abkommens' (1944) 12 *ZaöRV* 83–105 at 83–4. On 9 June 1942 the British and Czechoslovak Governments decided to exchange ambassadors. The announcement by the Canadian Prime Minister on 17 July 1942 to receive Dr Pavlasek as Minister of the Czechoslovak Republic was accompanied by the statement that the Czechoslovak Government in London 'was recognized in a full sense as Government of the Czechoslovak Republic and as being in its juridical position identical with the position of other Allied Heads of States and Governments in United Kingdom' (DCER IX, no 1498, at 1823). See also *ibid.*, at 1821–2 and DCER VII, 30–1. On US recognition and the appointment of an Envoy Extraordinary and Minister Plenipotentiary, see [1941] II FRUS 32, 34; (1941) 4 *Free Europe* 135.

Czechoslovak Government under Dr Beneš left London for Czechoslovak territory in March 1945 it had been recognized by some thirty States and maintained four Embassies, twenty-three Legations, eight Consulates-General, and eight Consulates, as well as two other offices.[206]

The difference in form between relations with authorities in exile recognized as the governments of foreign sovereign States and those recognized only as provisional governments, such as the Provisional Czechoslovak Government, also found expression in the Diplomatic Privileges (Extension) Act 1941,[207] which in section 2 distinguished between the 'envoy of a foreign Power' and the 'representative of any such provisional government'. Both were treated as if they were envoys of a foreign Power accredited to His Britannic Majesty and were accorded the same diplomatic privileges and immunities. This may be explained as follows: at the time the Act became law, on 6 March 1941, the British Government had not yet recognized the Provisional Czechoslovak Government as the Government of the Czechoslovak Republic and therefore did not treat its 'representatives' as envoys of a foreign Power. Some of the fully recognized governments in exile in London had, however, already recognized Dr Beneš' Government as the Government of the Czechoslovak Republic and had exchanged envoys with it.[208] By granting the privileges and immunities of envoys to the representatives of provisional governments the Act attempted to reconcile these two different positions. That representatives of provisional governments not fully recognized as governments normally were not granted diplomatic immunities becomes clear from the fact that the Act did not provide for such immunities with respect to representatives of one provisional government accredited to another provisional government.

That States do not maintain formal diplomatic relations with authorities in exile which they do not recognize as governments is also well illustrated by the case of the various Free French authorities, which all received some limited recognition but none of which was recognized as the Government of France. Thus, General de Gaulle, who resided in London, was recognized 'as the leader of all free Frenchmen, wherever they may be, who rally to him in support of the Allied Cause'.[209] Similarly, the CNF in London was

[206] *Czechoslovak Sources and Documents*, no 28 (1947), 49.

[207] 4 & 5 Geo. 6, c. 7.

[208] Norway (12 Oct. 1940), Poland (27 Nov. 1940), and Belgium (13 Dec. 1940).

[209] The British Government recognized General de Gaulle in this capacity on 28 June 1940. See HC Debs., vol. 374, col. 149, 10 Sept. 1941; Woodward, n. 15 above, i, 330; Cassin, 'Vichy or Free France' (1941) 20 *For. Affairs* 102–12 at 102–3; De Gaulle, n. 66 above, i, 22–3, 72. This recognition was explained by the Dominions Secretary, Viscount Caldecote, in a letter to the Canadian Secretary of State for External Affairs, Mr Mackenzie King, dated 4 July 1940 as follows: '[It] does not mean that General de Gaulle has been recognized as head or organizer of an alternative Government or that we have ceased to have dealings with the French Chargé d'Affaires in London, who still represents the Bordeaux Government' (DCER VIII, 592–3 at 592). See also the statement of the Joint Under-Secretary of State for War, Sir Edward Grigg:

recognized 'as representing all Free Frenchmen wherever they may be who rally to the Free French movement in support of the Allied Cause',[210] and the CFLN in Algiers was recognized, *inter alia*, 'as the body qualified to ensure the conduct of the French effort in the war within the framework of inter-Allied co-operation'.[211] While several States maintained 'relations' with the Free French authorities 'by the informal exchange of representatives',[212] no State entered into formal diplomatic relations with them.[213] Explaining the absence of formal diplomatic relations the British Foreign Secretary, Mr Eden, wrote to General de Gaulle in October 1941 that 'while HM's Government will be happy to maintain their representation with the Free French movement, they could not accredit a diplomatic representative accredited by you since this would involve your recognition as the Head of a sovereign State'.[214]

During the first years of its existence the Provisional Government of the Algerian Republic (GPRA) did not maintain formal diplomatic relations with States that had recognized it *de jure* but only accredited so-called 'Algerian Provisional Government Missions' to those States.[215] This did not,

'we have also recognized in General de Gaulle not a sovereign Government' (HC Debs., vol. 364, col. 1351, 21 Aug. 1940). For the Australian and Canadian recognition, see DAFP IV, no 250, at 334 and DCER VIII, 592–623, respectively. For similar recognition by the Soviet Union, see Soviet For. Pol. I, 99; [1941] I FRUS 189.

[210] For the British recognition, see HC Debs., vol. 376, col. 727, 26 Nov. 1941. For Soviet recognition of the CNF as 'the directing body of Fighting France', see Soviet For. Pol. I, 182.

[211] For the recognition statements of Australia and Canada, see DAFP VI, no 274, at 505 and 670; for that of South Africa, see [1943] *Keesing's* 5971A; for that of the UK, see DAFR VI, 669. The Belgian and Soviet Governments went further by recognizing the CFLN also 'as the representative of the State interests of the French Republic' (Soviet For. Pol. I, 234; DAFR VI, 670; and (1943) 3/34 *News from Belgium and the Belgian Congo* 269). After its formation on 3 June 1943 the CFLN had asked the governments of the United Nations to recognize it 'as the body qualified to ensure the conduct of the French effort in the war within the framework of inter-Allied co-operation as well as the administration and defence of all French interests.' See Woodward, n. 15 above, ii, 442; Funck, 'La "Reconnaissance" du C.F.L.N. (Québec, août 1943)' (1959) 9/33 *RHDGM* 37–48 at 37.

[212] Cf. DCER IX, no. 1379, at 1708–9. On the Canadian representative to the CNF, see *ibid.*, no 38, at 26. On Fighting French representatives in Mexico, see [1942] *Keesing's* 5491. On the US 'representative to consult with the CNF in London on all matters relating to the conduct of the war', see DAFR V, 542; (1942) 7 *DSB* 613.

[213] On the accreditation of 'representatives' of foreign powers to General de Gaulle and by General de Gaulle to foreign powers, see Art. 6(1) of the Ordinance 16 of 24 Sept. 1941 on the organization of the public powers of Free France ((1940–5) 67–72 *JDI* 171–2 at 172), and Art. 3(2) of the Ordinance of 3 June 1943 on the constitution of the French Committee of National Liberation (*ibid.*, 173–4 at 174).

[214] Manning, n. 15 above, 41–54 at 45, n. 6; Flory, n. 149 above, 65.

[215] Cf. Art. 1 of the decree concerning the organization of external missions, adopted by the GPRA on 6 Feb. 1960: 'The Algerian Provisional Government shall be represented in foreign countries by a single permanent delegation, called according to local conditions: "Algerian Provisional Government Mission" or "National Liberation Front Delegation". The Misssion or Delegation shall come under the authority of the Minister for Foreign Affairs' (Bedjaoui, n. 19 above, 125). Missions were accredited to States which had recognized the GPRA while delegations were sent to other States. The GPRA had missions accredited to Tunisia,

however, mean that the States in question had not recognized it as a government but rather that the GPRA, for political reasons, had 'not sought to open formal relations of the traditional type with foreign states'.[216] As has been shown above, recognition does not automatically entail formal diplomatic relations. The establishment of such relations rather requires the consent of both parties to the relations. It was therefore for the GPRA to decide on the form of relations which it wanted to enter into with the States that had accorded it *de jure* recognition.[217] It was for this reason that, at the end of 1961, the GPRA could change its policy and ask several States which had recognized it *de jure* to give legal form to their relations by officially accrediting ambassadors to it.[218] By April 1962, Pakistan, Ghana, and China had done so, while North Vietnam, Outer Mongolia, North Korea, Cuba, the USSR, Czechoslovakia, and Albania had asked the GPRA to establish formal diplomatic relations.[219]

In the same way as a State cannot recognize at the same time both an authority *in situ* and an authority in exile as the government of a State, it cannot maintain formal diplomatic relations at the same time with two authorities, one in exile and one *in situ*, both claiming to be the government of the same State.[220] The whole matter is closely connected with the question of recognition, for the presentation or acceptance of letters of credence implies recognition of the government in question.[221] States may,

Morocco, Libya, Egypt, Saudi Arabia, Jordan, Iraq, Lebanon, Syria, Guinea, Ghana, Mali, China, Indonesia, Pakistan, Yugoslavia, Somalia, Yemen, and Ivory Coast. FLN Delegations were established in London, Rome, Bonn, Madrid, Berne, Stockholm, Prague, Buenos-Aires, Montevideo, Mexico, Havana, Ankara, New Delhi, and Tokyo (Chikh, n. 125 above, 418, n. 3).

216 Bedjaoui, n. 19 above, 123.

217 Cf. Art. 21 of the Provisional Institutions of the Algerian State: 'The GPRA can establish diplomatic relations with other States' and Art. 22: 'The GPRA nominates the chiefs of mission abroad' (*Die Algerische Revolution* (1963), App. (translation supplied)).

218 See para. 2 of the Report of the Ministry of Foreign Affairs of the GPRA, dated April 1962: 'In order to give our established relations with the States that have recognized the GPRA a legal character, we can now request them officially to accredit ambassadors to our government' (ARA no 87, 404–8 at 407 (author's translation)).

219 *Ibid.* The head of the Algerian mission to China, M. Abderrahmane Kiouane, presented his letters of credence to the President of the People's Republic, Liou Chaou Chi, on 19 May 1961 (Chikh, n. 125 above, 449). It was announced in Accra on 10 Mar. 1962 that M. Bu Ashura was appointed Algerian Ambassador in Accra and Mr Tay, Ghanian Ambassador in Tunis, was also accredited as Ambassador to the GPRA (BBC, *SWB*, 2nd series, ME/893/B/5, 13 Mar. 1962). The new Ambassador of the GPRA to Ivory Coast presented his credentials at Bamako on 18 Mar. 1962 (*ibid.*, ME/900/B/2, 21 Mar. 1962). It should also be noted that the States which recognized the GPRA *de jure* normally expressed at the same time their willingness to establish normal diplomatic relations 'between the two countries' (Bedjaoui, n. 19 above, 121, 123–4; [1961] *Keesing's* 18258F; [1962] *Keesing's* 18808; *The Times*, 8 May 1962, 12).

220 Bonfils, n. 195 above, 358, § 659. In this connection, it may also be recalled that Cardinal Mazarin refused to receive the envoys of King Charles II, exiled in France, after he had formally received the envoys of Oliver Cromwell.

221 Cf. Jennings and Watts, n. 78 above, i, 174, 1122.

however, maintain formal diplomatic relations with one authority and official but informal relations with the other or they may maintain informal relations with both authorities. The relations between the USSR and the two Cambodian authorities, the Royal Government of National Union of Cambodia (RGNUC) in Peking and the Government of the Khmer Republic in Phnom Penh, is a good case in point. For five years the USSR tried to evade the question of the Cambodian Government by never fully recognizing either side but never breaking relations with them, either.[222] After the overthrow of Prince Sihanouk on 18 March 1970 the Soviet Government did not formally recognize the Republican Government of President Lon Nol and replaced its ambassador in Phnom Penh with a *chargé d'affaires*.[223] On 23 June 1970 it granted the representative of the RGNUC in Moscow the status of an ambassador[224] but continued to have diplomatic relations with the Lon Nol Government through the Cambodian Embassy in Moscow and the Soviet Embassy in Phnom Penh, which both continued to function. On 9 October 1973 the Soviet Ambassador to China informed Prince Sihanouk that the Soviet Union had never broken off relations with his Government or formally recognized President Lon Nol's Government, and that it regarded the NUFK and the RGNUC as the true representatives of the Cambodian people. Two weeks later it recalled its *chargé d'affaires* and closed its embassy in Phnom Penh.[225] The Lon Nol Government, however, continued to maintain its *chargé d'affaires* in the Cambodian Embassy in Moscow until 28 March 1975, when the Soviet Union finally broke relations with it and informed Prince Sihanouk that 'henceforth, the Government of the USSR will recognize no Government other than the RGNUC as the legal government of all Cambodia'.[226]

That States do not maintain formal diplomatic relations with authorities in exile which they do not recognize as governments is also evidenced by the fact that they do not exchange ambassadors or ministers with such authorities, but representatives with some diplomatic-sounding title such as 'representative with the personal rank of ambassador' or 'representative with

[222] The Soviet Union did not give *de jure* recognition to either side ([1971] *Keesing's* 24810).

[223] See (1970) 25 *EA* Z135; *NY Times*, 6 June 1970, 1, 7.

[224] The granting of the status of an ambassador must be distinguished from the accrediting of an ambassador by a foreign State. Only the latter enjoys formal diplomatic status as of right.

[225] The embassy was scaled down to three lower-level aides as 'caretakers' without diplomatic status and privileges. See [1973] *Keesing's* 26188; *NY Times*, 11 Oct. 1973, 3; *ibid*., 22 Oct. 1973, 4; *ibid*., 26 Oct. 1973, 3. It is of interest to note that other States announced at the time of their recognition of the RGNUC the closure of their diplomatic missions in Phnom Penh ([1970] *AdG* 15504).

[226] BBC, *SWB*, 2nd series, FE/4870/A2/1, 5 Apr. 1975; [1975] *Keesing's* 27152; *NY Times*, 29 Mar. 1975, 3.

ambassadorial status',[227] 'plenipotentiary representative',[228] '*chef de mission*',[229] 'representative',[230] 'delegate',[231] or '*gérant des affaires*'.[232] Similarly, the offices of such authorities are not referred to as Embassies, Legations, or Consulates but as 'Delegations,'[233] 'Commissions',[234] or '*Bureaux Consulaires*'.[235]

[227] For examples of 'representatives with the personal rank of Ambassador' to the CFLN, see (1943) 9 *DSB* 379; RIIA *Chronology of the Second World War*, 22 Nov. 1943; [1943] *Keesing's* 5971A. On the 'personal rank of Ambassador' of the 'representatives' of various governments to the CFLN, see DCER X, no 32, at 19–20. On the distinction between diplomatic rank and personal rank in the diplomatic service, see BDIL VII, 671.

[228] On 25 Aug. 1943 the People's Commissariat for Foreign Affairs communicated the following to the CFLN. 'The Government of the USSR has decided to recognize the French Committee of National Liberation as representing the State interests of the French Republic, and as leading all French patriots fighting Hitlerite tyranny, and to exchange with it plenipotentiary representation' ([1943] *Keesing's* 5971A). For the appointment of Aleksandr Efremovich Bogomolov as Plenipotentiary Representative to the CFLN, see also [1943] III FRUS 582. It was announced on 12 July 1944 that on 23 Apr. 1944 the Soviet Government had agreed to the immediate establishment of relations with the Danish 'Freedom Council' and to receive in Moscow a representative of Fighting Denmark similar to the representative of Fighting Denmark in London. By decision of the 'Freedom Council', Mr Thomas Doessing was appointed plenipotentiary representative of Fighting Denmark in the USSR, with the rights of a Minister (Soviet For. Pol. II, 91–2). On the Netherlands' representation with the French National Committee, see Manning, n. 15 above, 41–54 at 46–7.

[229] The Belgian Government accredited on 9 Sept. 1943 a *Chef de mission* to the CFLN and not a *chargé d'affaires* or Minister Plenipotentiary as it had done with respect to the Czechoslovak, Polish, Luxembourg, Norwegian, Dutch, and Greek Governments in exile (Kerchove d'Exaerde, n. 74 above, 93–151 at 120).

[230] On the 'British Representative' to the Provisional Czechoslovak Government in London, see DCER IV, 692, n. 5. On the Canadian 'Representative' to the CFLN, see DCER X, no 44. According to Art. 8 of the Agreement between the British Government and the Czecho-Slovak National Council of 3 Sept. 1918 the latter 'will appoint a representative in London through whom relations with His Majesty's Government will be maintained' ([1918] I FRUS Supp. 1, 844–5). On 20 Feb. 1984 the new PLO 'representative' to Romania presented his credentials to President Ceausescu (BBC, *SWB*, 2nd series, ME/7579/A/3, 29 Feb. 1984).

[231] For the appointment of a Fighting French delegate in Wellington, New Zealand, see [1942] *Keesing's* 5318A. For appointment of a Fighting French delegate in Teheran, see *ibid.*, 5211B. On the Fighting French delegation in the USA, see De Gaulle, *War Memoirs* (1955), i, 224. Correspondence to the representative of the CFLN in Canada was addressed to the 'French Delegate, Ottawa' (DCER X, no 44). On FLN delegations in countries that did not recognize the GPRA, see Bedjaoui, n. 19 above, 125, 132. On 14 Dec. 1993 the Irish Government approved the establishment of an Israeli embassy in Dublin and also invited the PLO to set up a delegation (*Independent*, 15 Dec. 1993, 10).

[232] In 1958 the new Pope, John XXIII, did not accept the credentials of Mr Pappé, the ambassador of the Polish Government in exile in London to the Holy See. Mr Pappé, who until that time had been the doyen of the diplomatic corps, was thereupon listed only as *gérant des affaires* in the diplomatic list of the Holy See (Gelberg, n. 82 above, 41; *NY Times*, 27 Dec. 1958, 1 and 6 Jan. 1959, 7). After the death of Pope John XXIII (1881–1963) the Vatican finally withdrew its recognition of the Polish Government in London (Iwańska, *Exiled Governments: Spanish and Polish* (1981), 59).

[233] See DCER X, no 44.

[234] For the Belgian Commission to the CFLN, see (1943) 3/36 *News from Belgium and the Belgian Congo* 286.

[235] In the UK and Canada representatives of the CFLN were allowed to perform consular functions and to use the former French consulates under the title 'Bureaux Consulaires':

It must however be added that the absence of formal diplomatic relations has not precluded States from granting in individual cases and as a matter of courtesy (and not of right) such representatives, delegates, etc., and their respective offices diplomatic status or certain diplomatic privileges and immunities.[236]

In States which do not recognize an authority in exile as a government and which are not prepared to grant its representatives certain diplomatic privileges and immunities as a matter of courtesy, representatives of an unrecognized authority in exile may nevertheless benefit from so-called 'borrowed diplomatic status', that is, they may enjoy diplomatic status as members of diplomatic missions of other States. In a certificate submitted in 1985 to the Corte di Cassazione, the Italian Foreign Ministry stated that the PLO office, set up in Rome in 1974:

> has not been recognized as having a diplomatic status in the strict sense but, in practice, it has been arranged in such a way that the directors of the office have been allowed to enjoy such status, allowing them to be accredited by one of the Arab embassies located in the capital among the members of its own staff.[237]

This practice was widely made use of by the GPRA in States which did not recognize it as the Government of Algeria and which, in order not to impair their relations with France, were not prepared to grant diplomatic status to its representatives directly. Thus, members of the GPRA Office in New York were advisers to the Syrian delegation to the United Nations, as those of the Geneva Bureau were members of the Yemeni delegation to the European Office of the United Nations. Members of the FLN delegations installed in Rome, Madrid, Bonn, or London were members of the Tunisian or Moroccan Embassies in these capitals.[238] However, in view of the right of

DCER X, nos 40–2. On 25 Mar. 1943 the Canadian Secretary of State for External Affairs stated: 'we are not ready to do anything which could be regarded as provisional recognition of [General] Giraud's administration [in French North Africa] as a government . . . the opening of consulates . . . of course could not be allowed' (*ibid*., IX, no 1387).

[236] On 13 Dec. 1978 the Foreign Affairs Committee of the Austrian Parliament approved, at the suggestion of the Austrian Government, the granting of full diplomatic status to Dr Husayn in his capacity as the official representative of the PLO in Austria (BBC, *SWB*, 2nd series, ME/5995/A/4, 15 Dec. 1978). On the status of the PLO office in Romania, see Dinu, 'The Role of the United Nations Organization in the Efforts for Finding a Solution to the Problem of the Palestinian People. Romanian Positions and Proposals' (1983) 17 *Rev. Roum. Et. Int.* 271–87 at 283. It is of interest to note that most States that have recognized the 'State of Palestine' after its proclamation on 15 Nov. 1988 have elevated the PLO office in their country to the status of embassy. For example, the Soviet Foreign Minster, Mr Shevardnadze, declared on 10 Jan. 1990 that the Soviet Union had consented to let the PLO 'reorganize' its mission in Moscow into 'the embassy of the state of Palestine in the Soviet Union'. He also declared that the representative of the Soviet Union at the PLO headquarters in Tunis would now be considered an ambassador (*WP*, 11 Jan. 1990, Sec. A, 28).

[237] *Re Arafat and Salah* (1985): (1988) 7 *Ital.YIL* 295–8 at 296–7.

[238] Bedjaoui, n. 19 above, 132. A special case of borrowed diplomatic status is the use of the diplomatic bag (pouche) of friendly States. See ARA no 87, 404–8 at 406.

the receiving State to declare any member of a diplomatic mission *persona non grata*,[239] the enjoyment of borrowed diplomatic status requires, at least, the connivance of the receiving State. With respect to the FLN delegation in Bonn the German Government, which neither recognized the GPRA nor the FLN, on 14 March 1960 issued the following statement:

> Due to its affiliation with the Tunisian embassy this [FLN] bureau enjoyed diplomatic immunity and privileges, i.e. a status which is usually referred to as extraterritoriality. . . . The Federal Government however cannot tolerate any political activity of this bureau, as it does not maintain relations with the so-called FLN Government [author's translation].[240]

The German Government therefore asked the Tunisian Ambassador to remove the FLN delegation from the Tunisian embassy in Bonn.

(b) Diplomatic and Consular Missions to States whose Governments are in Exile

(i) *Belligerent occupation.* When a government is forced into exile by belligerent occupation the question arises whether foreign diplomatic and consular missions may remain in the occupied territory or whether they must follow the government into exile or return to their own country. It appears that in the majority of cases the sending States either instructed their diplomatic agents to follow the government into exile[241] or were requested to recall them by the belligerent occupant.[242] There are, however, some notable exceptions with respect to neutral third States. Thus, during the First World War the Ministers of Spain, the Netherlands, and the United States were allowed by the German Government to reside in Brussels notwithstanding the German occupation of Belgium and the flight of

[239] Cf. Art. 9(1) of VCDR.

[240] [1960] *Bulletin* 499; [1960] *AdG* 8278F.

[241] e.g. the Serb Government was accompanied on its flight (Oct. 1915–Jan. 1916) by the ministers of England, France, Italy, and Russia. See Boppe, *A la suite du gouvernement Serbe, de Nich à Corfu, 20 Octobre 1915–19 Janvier 1916* (1917). The diplomatic corps which had taken up residence at the seat of the Polish Government in exile in Angers, France, on 12 Dec. 1939 comprised the Ambassadors of France, Great Britain, and the USA, the Ministers of Brazil and Czechoslovakia and the Egyptian *Chargé d'affaires* (Cang (ed.), *The Who's Who of the Allied Governments 1942* (1942), 94).

[242] In 1940 Germany requested the recall of the diplomatic and consular agents of neutral States in German occupied territories: [1941] II FRUS 748–9; DDS XIII, no 324, at 783. Similarly, in Feb. 1915 the German Government annulled the exequaturs of the consuls of neutral governments in Belgium (Garner, *International Law and the World War* (1920), i, 51, n. 2). But see the opinion of the US Government on the revocation of the exequaturs of consuls in certain parts of Belgium by the German occupant: *Correspondance diplomatique relatif à la guerre de 1914–1915* (1915), ii, no 112, at 117. On the neutral consuls in Belgium, see also Mérignhac and Lémonon, *Le Droit des Gens et la Guerre de 1914–1918* (1921), i, 395–6.

the Belgian Government to Le Havre.[243] The US vice-consul at Belgrade was required to leave Serbia after its occupation by the Central Powers, but after some correspondence between the Governments of the United States and Austria-Hungary he was allowed to return, subject to certain restrictions.[244] Similarly, during the Second World War the United States was permitted to maintain its diplomatic mission at Brussels after the German occupation and to represent the interests of six States in Belgium.[245] It is argued that, as a rule, diplomatic and consular agents of *neutral* (in contrast to enemy) States may remain in the occupied State and continue to enjoy—subject to general restrictions necessitated by armed conflict[246]—diplomatic or consular status.[247] There is no basis in international law for a general right of the belligerent occupant to terminate diplomatic or consular relations between the occupied and third States. The termination of such relations is a sovereign act of the State under occupation—the belligerent occupant however has *de facto* authority rather than sovereignty.[248] The right to request the recall of individual foreign diplomatic and consular agents may be based on Article 43 of the Hague Regulations Respecting the Laws and Customs of War on Land (HR) 1907.[249] But for the recall request to be warranted under this provision the diplomatic or consular agent to be recalled has to constitute a threat to public order and, especially, to the security of the belligerent occupant. Unlike in the case of enemy States, such a threat cannot generally be assumed. In the case of diplomatic and consular agents of neutral States the recall request must therefore be justified in each individual case.[250] The fact that the receiving State's government is in exile also does not require diplomatic agents to leave the occupied State as diplomatic and consular relations exist between the sending and the receiving State and not between their respective governments. Furthermore, the functions of diplomatic agents are not restricted to deal-

[243] While the majority of members of the *corps diplomatique* followed the Belgian Government to Le Havre in Oct. 1914 (*Le Temps*, 14 Oct. 1914, 4; Jumeau, *Le Refuge du Gouvernement National à l'Etranger* (1941), 78), the US Minister, Mr Whitlock, was instructed only on 23 Mar. 1917 to withdraw the US legation from Belgium and to take up official residence at Le Havre ([1917] FRUS Supp. 1, 655–60). See also Garner, n. 242 above, i, 51–2; Liszt, n. 103 above, 491.

[244] Garner, n. 242 above, i, 51, n. 2.

[245] The USA represented in occupied Belgium the interests of the UK, France, South Africa, the Netherlands, Canada, and Luxembourg. The US Ambassador, Mr Cudahy, remained in Belgium until Nov. 1940 (cf. [1940] I FRUS 217).

[246] Cf. Lee, *Consular Law and Practice* (2nd edn., 1991), 440–2.

[247] Cf. also Jennings and Watts, n. 78 above, i, 1116. *Contra* Dahm *et al.*, n. 193 above, I/1, 295; Hurst, n. 193 above, 119–241 at 230–3.

[248] See Jennings and Watts, n. 78 above, i, 1116, n. 2; Weller, 'The Kuwait Crisis: A Survey of Some Legal Issues' (1991) 3 *RADIC* 1–40 at 17.

[249] 100 BFSP 338.

[250] It is argued that sufficient grounds for espionage, communication of military information to the enemy or other activities incompatible with diplomatic or consular status must exist in order to justify a recall request.

ings with the government of the receiving State, but have a strong territorial connection.[251] This is true even more in the case of consular agents.

In order not to impair their own relations with the foreign occupying State, States have voluntarily ordered their diplomatic agents to return home while leaving them formally accredited to the government in exile, thus moving from resident to non-resident accreditation.[252]

States have also instructed their diplomatic agents to remain in an occupied country and keep their mission open in order to manifest their non-recognition of the purported illegal annexation of the country by the belligerent occupant.[253] The case of the Kuwaiti Government in exile may serve here as an example. Iraq invaded Kuwait on 2 August 1990 and on 8 August 1990 declared the annexation of the country.[254] Consequently, on 10 August 1990 the Iraqi authorities ordered the sixty-eight existing diplomatic missions in Kuwait City to close by 24 August 1990. The UN Security Council on 9 August 1990 declared the annexation 'null and void' and called upon States 'not to recognize that annexation, and to refrain from any action or dealing that might be interpreted as an indirect recognition of the annexation',[255] and on 18 August 1990 demanded 'that the Government of Iraq rescind its orders for the closure of diplomatic and consular missions in Kuwait and the withdrawal of the immunity of their personnel, and

[251] See Art. 3 of VCDR.

[252] The Swiss Minister to Poland, Herr Martin, although residing in Bern during the Second World War remained accredited to the Polish Government in exile (DDS XIII, 654, n. 3; Klarer, n. 19 above, 191, 335–6). In general, considerations for Swiss–German relations influenced the Swiss Government's relations with the Polish Government. See DDS XIII, nos 177, 264, 271. On 12 Dec. 1939 it was announced that the Argentine and Swedish Governments had informed the Polish Government in exile that although their respective diplomatic representatives were unable at present to take up residence at its seat they would nevertheless remain accredited to the new Polish Government ([1939] *Keesing's* 3846B). The Swedish Minister to Norway, Baron Beck-Friis, was not sent to London until May 1943 in order not to endanger the existence of the Swedish Consulate General in Oslo ([1942] III FRUS 357; and [1943] *Keesing's* 5805B).

[253] On 4 May 1936 Emperor Haile Selassie left Ethiopia and on 9 May 1936 Italy announced the annexation of the country. The British and French legations remained open until 21 Dec. 1936 when they were transformed into consulates general. This transformation may be interpreted as *de facto* recognition of the annexation. So also Mattern, n. 71 above, 25. This becomes clear from a statement of the Under-Secretary of State for Foreign Affairs, Mr Butler, in Parliament: 'while it is difficult to fix a specific date on which His Majesty's Government first accorded this measure of [*de facto*] recognition to the Italian position in Abyssinia, it might be said that that position had been reached in the second half of December, 1936' (HC Debs., vol. 333, WA, *col.* 618, 17 Mar. 1938). See also the certificate of the Foreign Office in *Bank of Ethiopia* v. *National Bank of Egypt and Liguori* [1937] 1 Ch. 513 at 515. The US legation remained open until 31 Mar. 1937 ([1937] II FRUS 611). On the foreign diplomatic mission in Ethiopia, see also [1936] III FRUS 184–5.

[254] The Revolutionary Command Council of Iraq (RCC) in response to a request by the Provisional Free Government of Kuwait (PFGK) decided to 'return the part and the branch, Kuwait, to the whole and origin, Iraq, in a comprehensive and eternal merger unity' (RCC Decree 313 of 8 Aug. 1990).

[255] S/RES/662.

refrain from any such actions in the future'.[256] On the occasion of the withdrawal of the Romanian diplomatic staff from Kuwait City the spokesman of the Romanian Foreign Ministry, Mr Chebeleu, stated at a news conference in Bucharest on 30 August 1990:

Romania has not recognized the annexation of Kuwait by Iraq. . . . Therefore, our government decided to maintain our embassy in Kuwait even after the date of 24 August established by the occupying Iraqi authorities to close embassies in Kuwait, and we continue to maintain relations with the legitimate government of Kuwait.[257]

Twenty-four other States (including the United States, Canada, and eight European Union States) also ignored the closure order, but their diplomatic agents were finally forced by unbearable living conditions to leave Kuwait. On 17 December 1990 the British Ambassador, as last diplomatic agent, left for London. However, States insisted that their missions, although temporarily unstaffed, remained open and that they continued to maintain diplomatic relations with Kuwait.[258] In order to avoid any action that might have been interpreted as an indirect recognition of the Iraqi annexation of Kuwait and for the presumedly temporary nature of the state of affairs these relations were however mainly maintained through the over 100 Kuwaiti embassies abroad.[259] Only a small group of States decided to send diplomatic agents to the Kuwaiti Government at Ta'if in Saudi Arabia.[260] The first country to do so was Turkey, which on 7 September 1990 decided to sent its Ambassador to Kuwait, Mr Güner Öztek, to Ta'if to serve as Ambassador to the Kuwaiti Government in exile.[261] France announced on 4 October 1990 that it had charged M Jean Bressot, a former Ambassador to Kuwait, with a *mission de liaison* with the Kuwaiti Govern-

[256] S/RES/664. See also S/RES/667 and S/RES/674. On the forced closure of diplomatic and consular missions in Kuwait City, see Puissochet, 'Relations diplomatiques et protection des nationaux' in Stern (ed.), *Les aspects juridiques de la crise et de la guerre du Golfe* (1991), 93–106 at 97–8.

[257] BBC, *SWB*, 3rd series, EE/0860/A4/1, 4 Sept. 1990.

[258] For the Soviet Russian view, see BBC, *SWB*, 3rd series, SU/0855/A1/1, 29 Aug. 1990, and for the US view, see *WP*, 15 Dec. 1990, Sec. A, 17; [1990] AFPCD no 359, at 554.

[259] (1990) 14 *MECS* 514; *NY Times*, 16 Aug. 1990, Sec. A, 15. The representative character of the Kuwaiti diplomatic agents abroad was not questioned except by Iraq which arrested the diplomatic and consular agents of Kuwait in Baghdad at the outset of the invasion. See UN Doc.S/21654. In cases where no reciprocal diplomatic relations exist continued dealings with the State's consuls may be taken as evidence for the continued recognition of its government in exile. With respect to the Czechoslovak consul in Australia, see *Anglo-Czechoslovak & Prague Credit Bank* v. *Janssen* [1943] VLR 185 at 192, 199.

[260] Only Saudi and US diplomats were allowed to stay permanently at Ta'if. All other western diplomats sent to the Kuwaiti Government in exile had to take their residence in Jiddah (*Le Monde*, 2 Feb. 1991, 6). The Ambassador of New Zealand to Kuwait was received by the Emir on 6 Nov. 1990 (Al Roumi, *The Crime. Iraq's Invasion of Kuwait* (1991), Sect. 1, 155).

[261] See (1990) 4/22 *TR* 100; BBC, *SWB*, 3rd series, ME/0865/A/15, 10 Sept. 1990.

ment in exile.[262] The spokesman of the Quai d'Orsay explained that 'there was no question of France closing its embassy in Kuwait, but that it was indispensable to have someone to guarantee the contact with the Kuwaiti rulers at Ta'if'.[263] Until 29 October 1990, when the French *Chargé d'Affaires*, M Galtier, left Kuwait City, France thus operated both an embassy and a liaison mission. The host State itself established an embassy at the seat of the Kuwaiti Government in exile which 'conducted its business like any other Embassy overseas' and the 'Saudi Ambassador accredited to Kuwait attended the Amir in Taif'.[264] It may be added that while States—especially with regard to UN Security Council Resolution 664—were entitled to maintain their diplomatic and consular missions in Kuwait[265] this was more a political gesture than necessitated by legal considerations as a formal protest would have sufficed to express their non-recognition of the annexation.[266]

(ii) *Coup d'etat.* States which continued to recognize a government forced into exile by internal events, such as a *coup d'état* or revolution, have continued to maintain their diplomatic agents within the country in order to mediate between the ousted government (still recognized by them) and the new rulers or in order to monitor the human rights situation and influence the political developments in the country. It appears that all States kept their diplomatic mission in Haiti after the *coup d'état* on 30 September 1990 despite their continued recognition of exiled President Aristide and their non-recognition of the *de facto* authorities in Port-au-Prince.[267] The United States also maintained its embassy in Panama after President Delvalle was ousted on 26 February 1988 despite the fact that it continued to recognize Mr Delvalle, who took up residence in the United States, as the President

[262] M. Jean Bressot was received by the Emir of Kuwait on 7 Oct. 1990. See Daoudi, 'Les problèmes rencontrés par le Koweit dans ses relations internationales pendant la crise du Golfe' in Stern (ed.), *Les aspects juridiques de la crise et de la guerre du Golfe* (1991), 107–21 at 119, n. 9; Puissochet, n. 256 above, 93–106 at 103; *Maghreb Machrek*, no 131 (1991), 70.

[263] *Le Monde*, 6 Oct. 1990, 3 (translation supplied).

[264] Letter, dated 29 Mar. 1995, of the Saudi Ambassador to the UK, Mr Ghazi Algosaibi, to the author.

[265] See Meron, 'Prisoners of War, Civilians and Diplomats in the Gulf Crisis' (1991) 85 *AJIL* 104–9 at 108–9.

[266] e.g. in the cases of Ethiopia (1936), Austria (1938), Albania (1939), Czechoslovakia (1939), and the Baltic States (1940), States maintained that the closure of their diplomatic missions in these countries did not constitute *de jure* recognition of their annexation. See Jennings and Watts, n. 78 above, i, 1123, n. 4; Allina, *Restoration of Austria* (1942), 6–7; and Langer, n. 17 above, 136–7, 224–7. With respect to Kuwait, see Weller, n. 248 above, 1–40 at 18; *id.*, 'Defiant diplomats in Kuwait establish a point of principle', *The Times*, 24 Aug. 1990, 3.

[267] e.g. the USA in Mar. 1993 appointed Mr Charles Redman as new *chargé d'affaires* in Haiti (*FAZ*, 20 Mar. 1993, 5), and after Robert Malval, the powerless Prime Minister affirmed by President Aristide, had taken up office inside Haiti on 26 Aug. 1993, Mr William Swing took up residence in Haiti on 15 Oct. 1993 as US Ambassador to Haiti (*The Times*, 19 Oct. 1993, 10).

of Panama. Only after the regular elections of 7 May 1989 were declared null and void did the United States on 15 May 1989 recall its Ambassador, Mr Arthur Davis. On the occasion of the expiry of President Delvalle's term of office, on 1 September 1989, US President Bush declared: 'Panama is, therefore as of this date, without any legitimate government. Accordingly, the United States will not recognize any government installed by Gen. Noriega. Our Ambassador will not return, and we will not have any diplomatic contact with the Noriega regime.'[268]

The continued mission of the diplomatic agents of States which continue to recognize a government forced into exile by *coup d'état* is an expression of their legal viewpoint. As long as they continue to recognize the ousted government no change in diplomatic representation with the receiving State is called for and, consequently, their diplomatic agents may remain there. As the functions of a diplomatic mission are not limited to negotiations with the Government of the receiving State,[269] there is also no practical need for the diplomatic agents to follow the recognized government into exile. Diplomatic agents may in particular enter into unofficial and personal dealings with the unrecognized authority *in situ* on behalf of their nationals. The sending States may, however, recall their Ambassadors and replace them by *chargés d'affaires* in order to express their moral condemnation of the *coup d'état* and their non-recognition of the authority *in situ.*[270]

If after a *coup d'état* or revolution the sending State does not recognize the new government *in situ* its diplomatic mission continues, according to international usage, to enjoy diplomatic status and privileges, although, at least formally, due to lack of presentation of new credentials, it has ceased to be a diplomatic mission.[271] If the sending State continues to recognize the ousted government in exile and refuses to recognize the government *in situ* the latter, which, unlike a belligerent occupant, has the right to exercise the State's sovereignty, may break off diplomatic (and consular) relations and/or request the sending State to recall its diplomatic and consular agents and, on its failure on the expiry of a reasonable period to do so, may compel them to withdraw.[272] Thus, in November 1991 the unrecognized *de facto* authorities in Haiti declared the French Ambassador, M. Jean-Raphaël

[268] 'U.S. Severs Diplomatic Contact With Noriega Regime', President's Statement, 1 Sept. 1989: (1989) 89/2152 *DSB* 69. US diplomatic agents, nevertheless, remained in Panama until the invasion of the country by the USA on 20 Dec. 1989.

[269] On the functions of a diplomatic mission, see Art. 3 of VCDR.

[270] This approach was adopted, for example, by Brazil and Spain with respect to the military authorities in Haiti which had ousted President Aristide (UN Doc.A/47/599/Add.1, 2–3 and 7, respectively). It is of interest to note that these Ambassadors did not take up residence at the seat of the recognized Government of Haiti in Washington.

[271] Cf. also Jennings and Watts, n. 78 above, i, 1121–2.

[272] On the right of a *de facto* government to withdraw the *exequatur* of consuls of States failing to grant recognition in general, see Jennings and Watts, n. 78 above, i, 1152; Lee, n. 246 above, 104–11.

Dufour, *persona non grata* and demanded his departure for the 'protection of the national sovereignty'. As a consequence France had to recall him and replaced him by a *chargé d'affaires*.[273] Similarly, the British Government's continued recognition of the Royal Government of Yemen in exile in Jedda, Saudi Arabia, and its refusal to recognize the Republican Government in Sana'a after the latter had been recognized by the majority of States and the United Nations led the Republican Government to request on 10 February 1963 that the British Legation should be closed within seven days. The Legation was accordingly closed on 16 February and the United States *chargé d'affaires* assumed responsibility for British interests in Yemen.[274] The situation is more difficult if the authority *in situ*, for political reasons or for fear of military intervention by the non-recognizing State, decides to tolerate the continued presence of the diplomatic and consular mission of the non-recognizing State. For example, the United States, which did not recognize the military-controlled Solís Palama Government in Panama but continued to recognize exiled President Delvalle as the Government of Panama, maintained nearly 100 diplomats in Panama and was able to move diplomatic personnel into Panama by quietly obtaining visas for them, first from the Panamanian consulate in Tampa, Florida, which remained loyal to the Solís Palma Government, and, later, on the basis of an informal understanding, from Panamanian military officers at the Panama City airport.[275] It is argued that so long as the authority *in situ* tolerates a diplomatic mission, i.e. so long as it does not formally break off diplomatic relations with the non-recognizing State or declares particular members of the staff of the diplomatic mission *non grata* or not acceptable,[276] the authority *in situ* is estopped from denying the members of the mission diplomatic privileges and immunities.

(c) Status of Diplomatic Agents Following the Government into Exile

(i) *Diplomatic status in the host State of the government in exile*. If a head of mission or another diplomatic agent (and his or her staff) follows the government to which he or she is accredited into exile, or if a new

[273] The Ambassador was replaced by a *chargé d'affaires*, M. Hervé Ladsous, and later M. Philippe Selz (*Le Monde*, 14–15 Nov. 1993, 3; *WP*, 16 Nov. 1991, Sec. A, 24).

[274] On British non-recognition and the closure of the British Legation, see Lauterpacht (ed.), *British Practice in International Law 1963* (1965), 5–9; Pattison, 'The International Law of Recognition in Contemporary British Foreign Policy', Ph.D. thesis (University of Virginia, 1981), 174–87; Flory, 'La mission d'observation des Nations Unies au Yémen' (1963) 9 *AFDI* 612–26 at 612–13.

[275] *WP*, 9 Feb. 1989, Sec. A, 30.

[276] e.g. the Solís Palma Government on 15 Mar. 1988 ordered the expulsion within 48 hours of a US diplomat. The State Department, however, refused to comply with the order as it had not been issued by President Delvalle ([1988] *Keesing's* 35819). It is submitted that in this case the Panamanian authorities *in situ* would have been justified, on the expiry of a reasonable time, to deny the US diplomat any privileges and immunities.

diplomatic agent is accredited to the government in exile, the question of his or her diplomatic status in the host State of the government in exile will arise.[277] The question is not expressly addressed by the Vienna Convention on Diplomatic Relations 1961 which applies only to the diplomatic agents accredited to the host government. The Convention, however, provides in Article 5 (1) for multiple accreditation of diplomatic agents. By accrediting the head of mission (and its staff) accredited to the host State concurrently to the government in exile, States may circumvent the question of the diplomatic status of diplomatic agents accredited (only) to a government in exile.[278] The status in the host State of diplomatic agents accredited (only) to the government in exile is thus still governed by customary international law.[279] Host States of recognized governments in exile have, as a rule, accorded the foreign diplomatic agents accredited to the exiled governments the privileges and immunities enjoyed by the diplomatic agents accredited to themselves.[280] No (or only very limited) diplomatic privileges and immunities have, however, been accorded to the diplomatic agents of the host States themselves accredited to the governments in exile. The reason for this is that diplomatic agents always remain under the jurisdiction of the sending State. If the host State's diplomatic agents to the government in exile enjoyed the same status as foreign diplomatic agents in the host State no forum at all would exist for them.[281]

[277] Cf. Flory, n. 149 above, 188–9.

[278] e.g. the Ambassadors of Cuba, Iran, Mexico, and Nicaragua to Algeria were also accredited to the President of the Saharan Arab Democratic Republic (SADR): Barbier, *Le conflit du Sahara occidental* (1982), 292; (1988) 42 *MEJ* 285. On 13 Dec. 1983 Senegal established diplomatic relations with the CGDK and named its Ambassador to China to fill the post concurrently ((1983) 2/4 *Ind. Chron.* 14). Similarly, Japan on 2 May 1985 appointed a minister at the embassy in Bangkok as *chargé d'affaires ad interim* to the CGDK ((1985) 4/2 *Ind. Chron.* 12). During the Second World War the South African High Commissioner in London was also accredited as Minister to the Greek Government in exile (DAFP V, no 25, at 43), and the US Ambassador to Canada was also accredited to the Luxembourg Government in exile in Montreal ((1941) 8 *Monatshefte für Auswärtige Politik* 375).

[279] The Preamble to the VCDR provides that 'the rules of customary international law should continue to govern questions not expressly regulated by the provisions of the present Convention'.

[280] See in this connection also Art. 11(1) of the Law on the Prerogatives of the Highest Pope and of the Holy See and on the relations of the State with the Church of 13 May 1871, which provides that 'The Envoys of foreign Governments to His Holiness shall enjoy, in the Kingdom [of Italy], all the rights and immunities which belong to Diplomatic Agents, in accordance with international law' (65 BFSP 638 at 640). See also Oppenheim, *International Law: A Treatise* (2nd edn., 1912), i, 160.

[281] See Schwelb, 'The Status of Allied Governments under the Diplomatic Privileges (Extension) Act, 1941' [1942] *CYBIL* 201–2 at 202; Dahm, *Völkerrecht* (1958), i, 346. For the similar problem of privileges and immunities of diplomatic agents of the host State of an international organization or conference, see Arts. 37 and 67 of the Vienna Convention on the Representation of States in Their Relations with International Organizations of a Universal Character, 1975 ((1975) 69 *AJIL* 730–59).

It appears that host States felt they had an obligation to accord diplomatic status to the foreign diplomatic agents accredited to the governments in exile. Moving the Second Reading of the Diplomatic Privileges (Extension) Bill in the House of Lords, the Lord Chancellor said on 19 December 1940:

> If a particular foreign State in normal times would have its Diplomatic Envoys accredited to the Belgian Government in Brussels such a person must in existing circumstances be here in this country, because the Belgian Government is here, and we feel we *ought* to give those diplomatic representatives accredited to these Allied Governments a protection which corresponds to the protection we should grant to Diplomatic Envoys to the Court of St James.[282]

As a rule it may thus be stated that, by virtue of customary international law, the host State which recognizes *and* invites a government in exile to establish itself *as such* within its territory is under an obligation to accord to the foreign diplomatic agents accredited to that government in exile the same diplomatic status which it accords to the diplomatic agents accredited to itself.

(ii) *Access of foreign diplomatic agents to the host State.* The question of diplomatic status of foreign diplomatic agents accredited to the government in exile must be distinguished from that whether the government in exile may receive any foreign diplomatic mission or agent it wishes. Delicate problems might arise if the exiled government gave the *agrément* for the diplomatic agent of a State hostile to the host State or to a diplomatic agent who was *persona non grata*. Governments in exile or sending States have, therefore, as a matter of courtesy and in view of immigration procedures, usually consulted the host government before agreeing to a diplomatic mission or to the appointment of a new diplomatic agent.[283] To infer from this practice an obligation of the government in exile to consult the host State or even to obtain (also) the *agrément* of the host State for the foreign diplomatic agents accredited to it would, however, be mistaken, as such an

[282] HL Debs., vol. 118, col. 193, 19 Dec. 1940, italics added. See also the Supplementary Notes for the Use of the Secretary of State in Proposing Second Reading in the House of Lords of the Bill to Confer Immunities and Privileges upon the Allied Administrations, 17 Dec. 1940: 'Although there is no precedent, it is clearly fitting and politically expedient that the Heads of the Allied States in this country should be given facilities for continuing to receive diplomatic representations from foreign States' (FO 371/26 427, 300: reproduced in Kerchove d'Exaerde, n. 74 above, 93–151 at 125). See also BDIL VII, 534–5.

[283] It is of interest to note that the US Government before appointing Mr Schoenfled as *Chargé d'affaires a.i.* to the Governments of Norway and the Netherlands in London informally ascertained whether the British Government had any objection of Mr Schoenfeld's appointment ([1940] I FRUS 181). According to Professor Daoudi, the Saudi authorities accorded all the facilities possible but they were informed of visits and contacts (Daoudi, n. 262 above, 107–21, at 110). On the requirement of consent of the territorial State for the granting of diplomatic status to diplomatic agents accredited to another State, see Art. 40(1) of VCDR.

obligation would be incompatible with the exiled government's status as the representative organ of a sovereign State. It appears that, so far, no problems have arisen between a government in exile and the sending States on the one hand and the host State on the other. When on 5 November 1914 France declared war on the Ottoman Empire the Belgian Government at Le Havre severed diplomatic relations with Turkey the very next day.[284] When Italy on 23 May 1915 declared war on Austria-Hungary a difficulty arose in regard to the diplomatic agents of the Central Powers accredited to the Holy See.[285] In order not to embarrass the Pope it was decided to raise no question on the subject and the diplomatic agents of Prussia, Bavaria, and Austria-Hungary accredited to the Pope 'voluntarily' left Rome together with their colleagues accredited to the Italian King.[286] It is suggested that if problems concerning the reception of a foreign diplomatic agent by the government in exile arise the host State's territorial sovereignty will have to prevail.

(d) Severance of Diplomatic Relations and Withdrawal of Recognition Distinguished

The severance of diplomatic relations with a recognized government in exile (without at the same time recognizing another authority as the State's government) should be sharply distinguished from the question of withdrawal of recognition from an authority in exile (until then) recognized as a government;[287] the latter is concerned with the status of the authority in exile and thus has much more far-reaching consequences than just the termination of diplomatic missions. While withdrawal of recognition automatically means severance of existing diplomatic relations,[288] this is not the

[284] See *Correspondance diplomatique relatif à la guerre de 1914–1915* (1915), ii, nos 62–4; Mérignhac and Lémonon, n. 242 above, i, 71.

[285] Prior to the conclusion of the Lateran Treaty between the Holy See and Italy on 11 Feb. 1929 (130 BFSP 791), the Holy See had no territorial basis and its legal status under the Law of Guarantees of 13 May 1871 (65 BFSP 638) was comparable to that of a government in exile. Cf. Jumeau, n. 243 above, 74; 'Transference of the Belgian Government to Havre' (1914) 137 *LT* 598.

[286] (1916) 21 *DJZ* 960–1; and Dittrich, *Die Preussische Gesandtschaft beim Vatikan* (1917), 48–9. See also the Report on the [British] Mission to the Holy See, dated 25 October 1922: *Anglo-Vatican Relations, 1914–1939* (1972), 1–38 at 27.

[287] On the 'fundamental importance' of the distinction between severance of diplomatic relations and withdrawal of recognition, see DCER IX, no 31, at 19–21.

[288] See the statement of the Canadian Government on the withdrawal of recognition from the French Government at Vichy, published on 11 Nov. 1942: 'the Canadian Government has ceased to recognize the present Government at Vichy as being the *de jure* Government of France and diplomatic relations with Vichy are accordingly terminated' (DCER IX, no 31, 19–21 at 21). Upon its withdrawal of recognition from the Montenegrin Government in exile Great Britain ceased her diplomatic representation at the Court of King Nicholas after 24 Aug. 1920. Similarly, France withdrew her diplomatic representative on 30 Dec. 1920 (Laffan, 'The Liberation of the New Nationalities. Part I. The Yugo-Slavs' in Temperley (ed.), *A History of the Peace Conference of Paris* (1921), iv, 171–212 at 204).

case the other way round. The litmus test to establish whether a State has withdrawn recognition from a government in exile is official third-party protection of the interests of the State of the government in exile in the State concerned. If only diplomatic relations have been broken off as a consequence of war or armed conflict governments in exile have been allowed to entrust the protection of their State's interests to other States.[289] But, if recognition as a government has been withdrawn from an authority in exile no or only 'unofficial' protection of interests in the State withdrawing recognition has been allowed.[290] This may be explained by the fact that the protecting State is chosen by[291] and receives its instructions for the protection of the State's interests from the government of the protected State. Withdrawal of recognition, as a rule, shows that, in the opinion of the derecognizing State, the authority in exile no longer qualifies as the government of the State whose interests are to be protected, and that, consequently, the protection of the State's interests is impossible as there is no government to choose and instruct a protecting State. But, while the interests of the State whose government is not (or no longer) recognized may not be protected in the non-recognizing State, the interests of the non-recognizing State may be protected in the State whose government is not (or no longer) recognized so long as the unrecognized government *in situ* recognizes the non-recognizing government. For example, from 1963 to 1970, first the United States and later Italy were allowed to protect British interests in Yemen, although the United Kingdom refused to recognize the Republican Government in Sana'a and continued to recognize the Royal Government in exile.[292]

The difference between withdrawal of recognition and severance of diplomatic relations is well illustrated by the turbulent relations between the Polish Government in London and the USSR during the Second World War,[293] which are characterized by a sequence of derecognition, rerecognition, severance of diplomatic relations, and definite derecognition. On 17 September 1939, the day the Red Army invaded

[289] For a list of neutral States representing Belgian, Serb and Montenegrin interests in the territories of the Central Powers during the First World War, see (1917) 44 *JDI* 569–70. After the Japanese attack on the USA, on 8 Dec. 1941 the Belgian Government in London severed diplomatic relations with Japan. Belgian interests in Japan were protected by Colombia (*NY Times*, 9 Dec. 1941, 8). The Spanish Government which in 1942 rejected the offer of the Greek Government in exile to establish diplomatic relations, nevertheless agreed to the protection of Greek interests in Spain by Argentina. See Janke, n. 151 above, 93.

[290] e.g. Switzerland was not allowed officially to protect French interests in the Allied States after they had withdrawn recognition from the French Government at Vichy. See DDS XV, no 8, at 19–20; DAFP VI, no 103, at 216; *ibid.*, no 127, at 275; DCER IX, no 35, 24–5 at 25.

[291] Cf. Arts. 45, 46 of VCDR.

[292] See [1963] *Keesing's* 19302; [1970] *Keesing's* 24114C. The USA protected British interests in Yemen from 1963 to 1967 (Newsom (ed.), *Diplomacy Under a Foreign Flag. When Nations Break Relations* (1990), App. A, at 119).

[293] On Polish–Soviet relations during the Second World War in general, see Kacewicz, *Great Britain, the Soviet Union and the Polish Government in Exile (1939–1945)* (1979).

Eastern Poland, the Soviet People's Commissar of Foreign Affairs, Mr Molotov, declared that 'the Polish State and its Government have virtually ceased to exist' and asked the Polish Ambassador, Mr Grzybowski, to leave.[294] The Soviet Government did not consent to the protection of Polish interests by any other State represented in Moscow on the ground that the Polish State had ceased to exist.[295] On 30 July 1941, after the German invasion of the USSR, the Soviet Government concluded an agreement with the Polish Government in London in which it recognized 'the Soviet-German Treaties of 1939 [providing for the partition and annexation of Poland by the Soviet Union and Germany] as having lost their validity' and which provided for the 'resumption' of diplomatic relations between the two Governments upon the signing of the agreement; the USSR thus re-recognized the Polish Government in London.[296] Following a Polish request to the International Red Cross to inquire into German allegations of a Soviet massacre of Polish Officers in the Katyn region, the Soviet Government on 25 April 1943 severed diplomatic relations with the Polish Government in London but did not withdraw recognition from it.[297] Thus, on 22 May 1943 Australia could take over the official protection of Polish interests in the USSR.[298] As a consequence of the exchange of 'representatives' between the Supreme Soviet and the Polish Committee of National Liberation[299] the Soviet Government on 23 August 1944 informed the Australian Government that 'it does not consider it possible any longer for the Legation of the Australian Commonwealth to continue protection of the interests of Poland as this responsibility has been undertaken by representatives of the Polish Committee of National Liberation'.[300] By terminating Australia's protection of Polish interests the USSR implicitly withdrew recognition of the Polish Government in London as the Government of Poland. On

[294] For the text of the note to the Polish Ambassador in Moscow, see DPSR I, no 43, at 46; DAFR II, 361–2. See also [1933–9] FRUS 782, and Fiedorowicz, 'Continuité de l'Etat' (1939) 24 *RDI* 129–75 at 132.

[295] See [1941] I FRUS 207 and Heydon, 'Protecting Polish Interests in the USSR 1943–1944: An Episode in Australian Representation' (1972) 18 *AJPH* 189–213 at 191.

[296] For the text of the agreement, see Soviet For. Pol. I, 81–2. See also [1941] I FRUS 243–4.

[297] For the note from Commissar Molotov to Ambassador Romer, see DPSR I, no 313, at 533–4; Soviet For. Pol. I, 202–3. See also [1943] III FRUS 396–7, 399–400, 404; and [1943] *Keesing's* 5731A. The Polish Ambassador and his staff left Kuibyshev for Teheran on 29 Apr. 1943.

[298] On the protection of Polish interests in the Soviet Union by Australia, see DAFP VI, nos 214, 203, 196, 194; *ibid.*, VII, nos 11, 92, 104, 182, 238, 256. For a historical account, see Heydon, n. 295 above. In June 1943 the following announcement appeared in *Izvestia*: 'The Australian Legation in the USSR informs Polish citizens that, *according to a request of the Polish Government*, it has undertaken the protection of Polish interests in the Soviet Union' (*ibid.*, at 197, italics added).

[299] On the exchange of 'representatives' on 2 Aug. 1944, see [1944] III FRUS 1428, 1430; *NY Times*, 2 Aug. 1944, 9, and 3 Aug. 1944, 7.

[300] DAFP VII, no 256, at 489. See also *The Times*, 25 Aug. 1944, 3.

5 January 1945 the Soviet Union finally recognized the Polish Committee of National Liberation as the Provisional Government of Poland.[301]

The liquidation of the Australian protection of Polish interests in the USSR proved difficult as Australia continued to recognize the Polish Government in London as the Government of Poland until 30 October 1945.[302] Due to the recognition of different 'Polish Governments' by the former protecting State and the receiving State it took more than fourteen months before the Australian Minister in Moscow handed over to the new Polish Ambassador to the USSR the goods and money which were the property of the Polish State in May 1943 and which the Australian Legation subsequently received on its behalf as well as documents and records (birth certificates, passports, etc.) received from the Polish Embassy or from or on behalf of Polish nationals in the Soviet Union.[303]

State practice shows that, as a rule, recognition is not expressly withdrawn from governments in exile. Notable exceptions are the withdrawal of recognition from the Revolutionary Government of Angola in Exile (GRAE) by the OAU in June 1971[304] and from the Government of Democratic Kampuchea (GDK) by the United Kingdom and Australia.[305] Here an announcement of the withdrawal of recognition was necessary as recognition was not 'transferred' to any other government, but for the time being no authority, either in exile or *in situ*, was recognized as the government of the State in question.[306] The withdrawal of recognition is usually implied by the recognition *de jure* of the extinction of the government in exile's State either by voluntary merger into another State[307] or (to the extent that it may still lawfully occur) through annexation,[308] or by the establishment of formal

[301] See DPSR II, nos 291, 292; *NY Times*, 6 Jan. 1945, 1.

[302] See DAFP VIII, no 41.

[303] See DAFP VIII, no 350, at 550, and Heydon, n. 295 above, at 209–10.

[304] See Marcum, *The Angolan Revolution* (1978), ii, 187. Commenting on the withdrawal of recognition, OAU Assistant Secretary-General Mohamed Sahnoun, said that 'far from strengthening the liberation struggle, the recognition of the GRAE had been detrimental to it' (*ibid.*). The withdrawal of recognition was first recommended by the OAU Committee of Five for Angola in June 1968 (*ibid.*, 207). This recommendation was endorsed by the OAU Liberation Committee in July 1968 ([1968] *Keesing's*, 22991 A). See also [1971–2] ACR C19–C21.

[305] The withdrawal of recognition from GDK was announced by the UK on 6 Dec. 1979 (HC Debs., vol. 975, col. 723, 6 Dec. 1979; *Daily Telegraph*, 7 Dec. 1979, 8) and by Australia on 14 Feb. 1981 ((1987) 10 *AYBIL* 286–91). See also [1981] *Keesing's* 30671.

[306] For the Australian and British announcements, see references in n. 305 above. Commenting on the recommendation of the OAU Liberation Committee to withdraw recognition from the GRAE, the OAU Secretary-General, Mr Telli, said that the OAU had for the moment decided not to recognize any government in exile, but rather to recognize only governments formed in a national territory and by the people there themselves ([1968] ARB 971C).

[307] The case of the Montenegrin Government in 1921 may serve as an example. See App. II.

[308] That only *de jure* recognition of annexation implies withdrawal of recognition from a government in exile is well illustrated by the case of the Italian annexation of Ethiopia. So long as it recognized the Italian Government only as the *de facto* government of Ethiopia, the British Government continued to accord recognition to Dr Martin in his capacity of Envoy

diplomatic relations with (and thus recognition of) the authority *in situ*.[309] This becomes clear from the proposals of the British Delegation to the Potsdam Conference concerning Poland which read in the relevant part as follows: 'The establishment by the British and United States Governments of diplomatic relations with the Polish Provisional Government has resulted in the withdrawal of their recognition from the former Polish Government in London'.[310] As a consequence of the (implied) withdrawal of recognition the functions of diplomatic agents accredited and consular officers appointed by the government in exile come to an end, if they are not taken over by a recognized government *in situ*.[311] Thus, when on 29 July 1970 the British Government recognized the Republican Government of Yemen, the Yemeni royalist *chargé d'affaires* in London was informed that recognition of his mission had lapsed with the British Government's decision to recognize the Republican Government.[312] But these diplomatic and consular agents and their families nevertheless continue to be entitled to

Extraordinary and Minister Plenipotentiary from His Majesty the Emperor of Ethiopia at the Court of St James. See the certificates of the Foreign Secretary in *Haile Selassie* v. *Cable and Wireless, Ltd (No 2)* (1938), [1939] 1 Ch. 182 at 183. Diplomatic recognition was withdrawn from the Ethiopian Minister only when the British Government recognized the King of Italy as the *de jure* sovereign of Ethiopia. It is also of interest to note that until 1924, the year the UK accorded *de jure* recognition to the Soviet Government and thus to its rule over Georgia, *Whitaker's Almanack* listed M. Soumassoff as 'Chargé d'Affaires of the National Georgian Government (exiled by Soviet invaders)' (*ibid*., 1923, 784; 1924, 825). For some historical examples, see Holtzendorff (ed.), *Handbuch des Völkerrechts* (1887), iii, 626; Hurst, n. 193 above, 119–241 at 160.

309 After the formation of the Polish Government of National Unity in Warsaw on 28 June 1945 one State after the other recognized it as the Government of Poland (App. II) and established diplomatic relations with it, thereby withdrawing its recognition from the Polish Government in London. The statement of the British Government on the recognition of the Polish Government of National Unity on 5 July 1945, for example does not mention either the Polish Government in London or its derecognition. For the text of the statement, see *The Times*, 6 July 1945, 4; DPSR II, no 377, at 625–6.

310 For the text of the proposal, dated Babelsberg, 19 July 1945, see DPSR II, no 382, 631–2 at 632. See also Point X of the Potsdam Agreement of 2 Aug. 1945 (145 BFSP 864). On the withdrawal of recognition through recognition, see also DPSR II, no 378, at 383; DBPO, 1st ser., VI, no 2, at 6, n. 10; Rozek, *Allied Wartime Diplomacy. A Pattern in Poland* (1958), 397–400; Raczynski, *In Allied London* (1962), 294–9.

311 Recognizing the union of Montenegro with Serbia Great Britain on 17 Mar. 1921 cancelled the exequaturs of Montenegrin consuls (Laffan, n. 288 above, 171–212 at 204). The USA also withdrew recognition from the Montenegrin diplomatic and consular officers on 21 Jan. 1921 by a revocation of Letters of Patent. On the 'Termination of Official Relations Between the United States and the Kingdom of Montenegro', see [1921] II FRUS 945–9. The USA had agreed only on 8 Oct. 1917 to the establishment of a Montenegrin Legation in Washington ([1918] I FRUS Supp. 1, 786). On 23 Dec. 1936 the Swiss Government informed the Consul-General of Ethiopia in Zurich that as a consequence of the Swiss recognition of Italian sovereignty over Ethiopia, the Swiss Federal Council regarded his exequatur as void and the Consulate-General as non-existent ([1937] LNOJ 265).

312 [1970] *Keesing's* 24114C.

their privileges and immunities until they leave the country or on the expiry of a reasonable time to do so.[313]

(2) Multilateral Relations

(a) Representation of Members in Inter-State Forums

It has by and large been acknowledged as 'the ultimate principle for representation' that a State should be represented in Inter-State forums such as (universal or regional) organizations and conferences by the authority which exercises effective control over people and territory, as only the effective authority *in situ* will normally be capable of fulfilling all the responsibilities of membership.[314] Principle would therefore suggest that an authority in exile, albeit continuing to be recognized as the State's government by a number—or even majority—of the member-States, is not entitled to represent the state in question.[315] But strict application of principle disregards the fact that the effective authority *in situ* may have come to power contrary to international law, i.e. as the result of an act of aggression or outside intervention,[316] or that representation by an effective but unconstitutional authority *in situ* may be contrary to the principles of the forum such as the promotion and consolidation of representative democracy.[317]

[313] See Art. 44 of VCDR and Art. 53.3 of the Vienna Convention on Consular Relations (VCCR).

[314] Cf. Higgins, *The Development of International Law through the Political Organs of the United Nations* (1963), 166. See also Greig, *International Law* (2nd edn., 1976), 135, and Dorfman, Hasey, Schmidt, and Weil, 'Cambodian Representation' (1974) 15 *Harv. ILJ* 495–513 at 504–9; Leifer, 'The International Representation of Kampuchea' [1982] *Southeast Asian Affairs* 47–59 at 55. In a memorandum entitled 'Legal Aspects of Problems of Representation in the UN', Secretary-General Trygve Lie on 8 Mar. 1950 expressed the view that the government which exercises effective authority within the territory of the State and is habitually obeyed by the bulk of the population should represent the State in the UN, as the obligations of membership could be carried out only by governments which in fact possessed the power to do so (UN Doc.A/1466). In a communiqué, issued on 6 Apr. 1970, UN Secretary-General U Thant declared that: 'it is the normal policy of the Secretariat [of the UN] to deal with the authorities which are apparently in control of the government of a member state' ((1970) 13/16 *PR* 25).

[315] Cf. Jennings and Watts, n. 78 above, i, 178.

[316] See the opinion of the UK that the principle of effective control does not apply to the representation of States whose governments have changed as a result of aggression from outside: GAOR, 5th Session, Ad Hoc Political Committee, 18th Meeting, 117.

[317] See the Preamble and Arts. 2(b), 3(d) of the OAS Charter. See also Resolution 1080 (AG/RES.1080 (XXI–0/91)), on representative democracy, adopted by the OAS GA at its 21st regular session, held at Santiago, Chile, on 5 June 1991 ((1991) 2/40 *DSD* 750), and the resolution adopted by the Permanent Council of the OAS on the day of the *coup d'état* in Haiti, 30 Sept. 1991 (*ibid.*). In accordance with the Santiago Commitment to Democracy the *ad hoc* meeting of the OAS Ministers of Foreign Affairs on 2 Oct. 1991 resolved 'to demand the immediate reinstatement of President Jean-Bertrand Aristide in the exercise of his legitmate authority' and 'to recognize the representatives designated by the constitutional Government

For legal and, probably more often, for political reasons, Inter-State forums have not always adhered to the 'principle of effective government' when deciding on the representation of member-States. As early as 1814 the French Foreign Minister M. de Talleyrand, wrote in his Instructions for the King's Ambassadors to the Congress of Vienna:[318]

A sovereign whose States are conquered . . . by the conquest only loses *de facto* possession, and consequently retains the right to do everything that does not require that possession. The sending of plenipotentiaries to the Congress does not require possession, as the Congress may have the aim of reclaiming it [author's translation].[319]

It is therefore suggested that, especially in the cases of rival claimants to governmental authority of which one may be in exile, it is not the 'principle of effective government' but the 'principle of recognition *by the forum*' (as distinct from recognition by individual member-States) of one of the rival authorities as the State's government which determines the question of representation of a member-State in Inter-State forums.[320] Thus, General Assembly Resolution 396 (V) of 14 December 1950 was entitled '*Recognition by the United Nations* of the Representation of a Member State'.[321] In this connection it is important to realize that recognition by the forum does not automatically mean collective recognition by all the member-States. This is the logical consequence of international organizations having a separate legal personality from that of the individual member-States.[322] That recognition by the forum does not automatically entail recognition by its member-States is also shown by the fact that international forums which

of President Jean-Bertrand Aristide as the only legitimate representatives of the Government of Haiti to the organs, agencies, and entities of the inter-American system' (MRE/RES.1/91: UN Doc.A/46/231, 3 Oct. 1991).

[318] Sept. 1814–June 1815.

[319] Talleyrand, *Mémoires* (1891), ii, 214–54 at 218. For the view that governments in exile, although not exercising actual sovereignty over their territories which are occupied by a foreign power, may nevertheless claim *de jure* sovereignty and exercise it through various international activities such as participation in conferences, see the decision of the Tribunale Roma in *Sovrano Militare Ordine di Malta* v. *Caccese* (1954), (1955) 22 ILR 1–5 at 2.

[320] See also Schermers, *International Institutional Law* (1980), §§ 203, 204, and 1655.

[321] GAOR 5th Session, Supp. No 20 (UN Doc.A/1775), 24–5, italics added. On the 'recognition' of the RGNUC by the United Nations, see *ibid*., 29th Session, 2300th Plenary Meeting, 27 Nov. 1974, 1115–16 (Mr Giambruno (Uruguay)); *ibid*., 29th Session, 2301st Plenary Meeting, 27 Nov. 1974, 1143 (Mr Richard (UK)). On the 'recognition' of the RGNUC by the Forth Conference of Heads of State or Government of Non-Aligned Countries, meeting in Algiers from 5–9 Sept. 1973, see NAC/AHG/CONF.4/RES.10, 9 Sept. 1973 (UN Doc.A/9330, 48). On recognition of a government by the United Nations in general, see Liang, 'Recognition by the United Nations of the Representation of a Member State: Criteria and Procedure' (1951) 45 *AJIL* 689–707.

[322] When States vote on the credentials of a delegation they do not act in their individual capacity but as part of the competent organ of the forum to which their action is attributable.

recognized a government in exile have called on their member-States also to accord recognition.[323]

The recognition by an international forum is normally the product of the ability of the authority in exile to secure the votes of a majority of individual member-States. In the practice of many member-States voting is determined by their own recognition decision. Thus, the Jordanian representative to the United Nations, Mr. Rifa'i, said on 20 December 1962 in the debate on the question of which of the two authorities claiming to represent Yemen[324] should be seated in the General Assembly 'that the position of each delegation on this matter is determined by whether the Government of that delegation does or does not recognize one or the other authority in Yemen'.[325] On the other hand, a favourable vote on the credentials issued by an authority in exile will normally imply its 'recognition' in the sense that, in the opinion of the approving member-State, the issuing authority in exile qualifies in international law as the government of the member-State in question as only the State's government or, in exceptional circumstances, the authority embodying the State's sovereignty[326] is competent to issue the

[323] e.g. the OAU which had recognized the GRAE in 1963 on several occasions called upon its member-States to grant recognition. Thus, the OAU Council of Ministers, meeting in Dakar on 2–11 Aug. 1963, on 10 Aug. 1963 adopted a resolution requesting 'all Member States to accord recognition to the Revolutionary Government of Angola in exile' (CM/Res.4 (I)). See also AHG/Res.18 (I). See further the Final Declaration of the Extraordinary Session of the Islamic Foreign Ministers' Conference, held in Islamabad on 27–29 Jan. 1980: DPIC XX, 431–40 at 436.

[324] The ousted Government of Iman al Badr in exile in Saudi Arabia or the Government of Brigadier al Sallal in Sana'a.

[325] GAOR 17th Sess., 1201st Plenary Meeting, 20 Dec. 1962, 1220–1. For the connection between (non-)recognition of a government and the vote on the credentials of its delegation, see also *ibid.*, 17th Sess., 1202nd Plenary Meeting, 20 Dec. 1962, 1225 (Mr Barrington (Burma)); 1229 (Mr Primelles (Cuba)); 1232 (Mr Mencia Lister (Dominican Republic)). On the relation between representation and recognition, see also *ibid.*, 5th Session, Ad hoc Political Committee, at 121, 373; and UN Doc.A/AC.38/L.6 (para. 3); A/AC.38/L.21 (para. 4), and A/AC.38/L.45 (para. 4). See also Ghobashi, 'The United Arab Republic and the United Nations' (1959) 15 *Rev. égypt.* 152–62 at 153. For the view that a favourable vote on the report of the Credentials Committee as a whole does not prejudice, in one way or the other, the position of the government regarding the question of recognition, see GAOR, 17th Sess., 1202nd Plenary Meeting, 20 Dec. 1962, 1232 (Mr Crowe (UK)); 1227 (Mr Okazaki (Japan)).

[326] For the transitional period from 1991–3 (i.e. prior to the installation of an elected government) Cambodia's seat at the UN was occupied by the Supreme National Council (SNC) of Cambodia which the UN Security Council described as the 'unique legitimate body and source of authority in which, during the transitional period, the independence, national sovereignty and unity of Cambodia is embodied' (S/RES/668 (1990)). On the status of the SNC, see also Art. 3 of the Agreement on a Comprehensive Political Settlement of the Cambodian Conflict, signed at Paris on 23 Oct. 1991 ((1991) 31 ILM 183). Art. 5 of that Agreement provides that the SNC will represent Cambodia externally during the transitional period, including by occupying Cambodia's seat at the United Nations. On the SNC in general, see Ratner, 'The Cambodia Settlement Agreements' (1993) 87 *AJIL* 1–41 at 2–8. It should, however, be noted that the Cambodian factions regarded the SNC as a 'super government', above the two rival Cambodian 'Governments', the Government of the SOC and the NGC, which continued to exist ([1991] *Keesing's* 38293).

credentials for its representatives. That, however, does not mean that the approving member-State also 'recognizes' that government, in the sense of expressing a willingness to maintain formal official relations with it. The two different meanings of the term 'recognition' may thus explain the practice of States to vote for the acceptance of credentials while at the same time maintaining that they do not 'recognize' the issuing authority.[327] It is argued that if States in fact vote for the seating of a delegation nominated by an authority in exile which, in their opinion, does not qualify in international law as the government of the member-State, i.e. which they do not and could not recognize, the question of state responsibility may arise both towards the forum and the (wrongly) represented member-State. One might think of the situation that a representative nominated by an authority in exile not qualifying as the member-State's government under international law invites the forum or another member-State authorized by the forum to intervene militarily in the member-State, consents to a disproportional increase in the member-State's contributions to the forum, or performs other acts contrary to the interests of the member-State.

It may be added that, as the recognition decision of individual member-States is very often motivated by political rather than legal considerations, the representation of a member-State in an Inter-State forum should always be seen before the background of the political interests involved in a particular case. Thus, it may, for example, be argued that the continued recognition of GDK and CGDK by ASEAN States and their support for their credentials at the UN was based on a mixture of concerns with legal principle and with the balance of power in Indochina.[328]

International practice abounds in examples of a member being represented in an Inter-State forum by its recognized government in exile. The Belgian Government at Le Havre and the Serbian Government at Corfu, which were both recognized even by the Central Powers, took part in the Economic Conference of the Allied States held at Paris in June 1916.[329]

[327] From 1979 to 1990 the USA voted in favour of the credentials issued by the Government of Democratic Kampuchea (GDK) and by the CGDK, while at the same time maintaining that it did not recognize those governments. On 12 Sept. 1990 Robert Kimmitt, Under Secretary for Political Affairs, declared before the House Foreign Affairs Subcommittee on Asian and Pacific Affairs: 'We, along with the vast majority of UN members, supported the coalition's UN credentials in the past because we did not—and do not—see the Vietnam-installed Hun Sen regime as a superior claimant to the seat . . . we do not now—and never have—recognized, supported, or otherwise dealt with the resistance coalition as a whole, precisely it includes the Khmer Rouge' ((1990) 1/37 *DSD* 102–4 at 102–3). On US practice with respect to Cambodian representation in the UN, see also (1991) 2/42 *DSD* 780; [1990] AFPCD nos 458, 474. Several countries of the EU also did not recognize the governments of DK but voted for the seating of their representatives in the UN. See also the Memorandum by Secretary-General Trygve Lie, 'Legal aspects of problems of representation in the United Nations', 8 Mar. 1950: UN Doc.A/1466, at 5.

[328] Cf. Leifer, n. 314 above, 47–59 at 52–3.

[329] See (1916) 43 *JDI* 1363–9.

The Polish Government at Angers, which in 1939 was still recognized by all States with the exception of Germany and the USSR, represented Poland in the Assembly of the League of Nations in December of that year.[330]

In 1944 the United Slav Committee lodged an objection to the Royal Yugoslav Government in London nominating delegates to the Twenty-sixth Session of the International Labour Conference and requested the Conference to invite a delegation nominated by the Yugoslav National Committee of Liberation instead. Since the Royal Yugoslav Government in exile was generally recognized by the other members of the International Labour Organization (ILO), and the opposing National Committee of Liberation had not been recognized by any State as the Government of Yugoslavia, the ILO had little difficulty in rejecting the objection and in seating the delegates nominated by the exiled government.[331]

The Government of the Emir of Kuwait at Ta'if, recognized by all States with the exception of Iraq, represented Kuwait at the United Nations,[332] the League of Arab States, the Gulf Co-operation Council, the Organization of Islamic Conference (OIC),[333] and the Organization of Petroleum Exporting Countries (OPEC) meeting in Vienna on 12 December 1990.[334]

The Government of President Aristide at Washington, which was recognized by the large majority of States, represented Haiti at the UN,[335]

[330] League of Nations, *Records of the Twentieth Ordinary Session of the Assembly* (11–14 Dec. 1939), Plenary Meetings, X, 5. See also Gelberg, n. 82 above, 32–3.

[331] See the Second Report of the Credentials Committee: International Labour Conference, *Records of Proceedings*, 26th Session, 1944, 292. See also Schermers, n. 320 above, § 203; Perfall, n. 121 above, 95.

[332] The credentials of the Kuwaiti Delegation were accepted by the Credentials Committee on 24 Oct. 1990 (UN Doc.A/45/674). In a *Note verbale*, dated 18 Dec. 1990, Iraq claimed that as a consequence of the merger of Kuwait and Iraq since 9 Aug. 1990, the two countries could be represented by only one delegation. Iraq therefore formulated a reservation concerning the powers of the so-called delegation of Kuwait (UN Doc.A/45/891). For the reply of the Government of Kuwait, dated 26 Dec. 1990, see UN Doc.A/45/909–S/22036. See also UN Docs.A/45/912, A/45/914, A/45/915, A/45/916.

[333] DPIC VI, 223, 226. During the Iraqi occupation the Emir of Kuwait was chairman of OIC.

[334] Both an Iraqi and a Kuwaiti delegation were present at the meeting. The deputy oil minister of Iraq, Mr Ramzi Salman, when asked about the presence of the Kuwaiti delegation declared: 'We represent all of Iraq.' (*NY Times*, 13 Dec. 1990, Sec. D, 1).

[335] 'On 21 September 1992, the spokesman for the Secretary-General reported that the Secretary-General had received communication from the so-called Haitian Government, which included purported credentials for a delegation to the forty-seventh session of the General Assembly. He stated that, since by its resolution 46/7 of 11 October 1991 the General Assembly had affirmed as unacceptable any entity resulting from the attempted illegal replacement of the constitutional President of Haiti and had demanded the immediate restoration of the legitimate Government of President Aristide, the purported credentials from the so-called Government of Haiti in Port-au-Prince were not receivable from the legal point of view and were of no legal consequences to the United Nations' (The Situation of Democracy and Human Rights in Haiti. Report of the Secretary-General, 3 Nov. 1992: UN Doc.A/47/599, at 13).

OAS,[336] and the International Conference on Population and Development (ICPD), held in Cairo on 5–13 September 1994.[337]

The representation of Ethiopia at the League of Nations from 1936 to 1939, generally given as an example for the representation of members in Inter-State forums by their governments in exile,[338] must be treated with caution. While it is true that Ethiopia, despite Italian occupation and annexation on 9 May 1936, formally never ceased to be a member of the League of Nations,[339] the last delegation sent by Emperor Haile Selassie, who resided at Bath, England,[340] was seated at the seventeenth Assembly of the League in September 1936.[341] In view of the report of the credentials committee of the seventeenth Assembly which had expressed doubts 'whether the Head of State from whom the credentials under examination emanate was exercising his legal title effectively enough to make those credentials perfectly in order'[342] and the subsequent recognition by numerous States of the Italian conquest of Ethiopia, Emperor Haile Selassie felt that there was a danger that his authority to grant the necessary credentials might be definitely denied by the credentials committee in 1937, and that their report to this effect might be accepted by the Assembly. If the Assem-

[336] On 3 Oct. 1991 the *ad hoc* meeting of Ministers of Foreign Affairs of the OAS resolved *inter alia* 'to recognize the representatives designated by the constitutional Government of President Jean-Bertrand Aristide as the only legitimate representatives of the Government of Haiti to the organs, agencies, and entities of the inter-American system' (MRE/RES.1/91).

[337] See the report of the credentials committee: UN Doc.A/CONF.171/13, 18 Oct. 1994, 152–3 at 153.

[338] See Leifer, n. 314 above, 47–59 at 48; Dorfman *et al.*, n. 314 above, 495–513 at 511–12. On Ethiopian representation, see Lauterpacht, 'The Credentials of the Abyssinian Delegation to the Seventeenth Assembly of the League of Nations' (1937) 18 *BYBIL* 184–6; Gretschaninow, 'Der Mitgliederbestand des Völkerbundes Anfang 1939' (1939) 9 *ZaöRV* 80–109 at 102–8; and Sandford, *Ethiopia under Haile Selassie* (1946), 100–1.

[339] The Final Report of the Board of Liquidation (C.5.M.5.1947) does not list Ethiopia, which had become a member of the League on 28 Sept. 1923, as a member 'whose membership was terminated prior to 18 April 1946'. See also the Assembly resolution of 12 Apr. 1946: LNOJ Spec. Supp. No 194, at 277.

[340] Though Emperor Haile Selassie had taken up residence in England, he was regarded by the British Foreign Office merely as a private person, not as the head of a government in exile (Woolbert, 'The Future of Ethiopia' (1942) 20 *For. Affairs* 535–51 at 539).

[341] See LNOJ Spec. Supp. No 155, at 36, 40–2.

[342] *Ibid.*, at 40. The credentials committee proposed 'that the Assembly should consider the credentials submitted by the Ethiopian delegates, despite the doubt as to their regularity, as sufficient to permit that delegation to sit *at the present session*' (*ibid.*, at 41, italics added). A proposal to ask the PCIJ for an advisory opinion whether, in view of the present position of H. M. Haile Selassie I, the credentials in question meet the requirements of Rule 5(2) of the Rules of Procedure of the Assembly, so as to enable the holders of those credentials to be regarded as the representatives of a member of the League within the meaning of Art. 3(1) of the Covenant was not followed, as the question would have been settled, according to Rule 5(4) of the Rules of Procedure of the Assembly, in favour of the sitting of the Ethiopian representatives before the court could have given a ruling, because Rule 5(4) provides that any representative to whose admission objections have been raised shall sit provisionally with the same rights as other representatives, unless the Assembly decides otherwise.

bly had adopted a resolution rejecting the credentials issued by the Emperor this would practically have amounted to the expulsion of Ethiopia from the League of Nations and the Emperor would have lost the one remaining right of some value which membership of the League conferred—that of addressing letters of protest to the Secretary-General and having these and accompanying documents circulated to the governments of all member-States and printed in the Official Journal.[343] The Emperor, deciding not to put the issue to the test, therefore did not send a delegation to the Assembly of the League from 1937 to 1939 but only maintained a permanent delegation at Geneva.[344] On the occasion of an Ethiopian delegation, headed by the Emperor himself, addressing the Council of the League of Nations on 12 May 1938 on the question of 'the consequences of the present situation in Ethiopia', the President of the League Council, M. Munters, expressly stated that '[i]t was the desire of the Council to assure the participation of delegates of the Emperor Haile Selassie in the Council's session ... *without prejudice to questions of principle and irrespective of the precise character of their full powers*.'[345] It is argued that formal representation of Ethiopia at the League of Nations after the seventeenth Assembly in September 1936 could be maintained only because Emperor Haile Selassie refrained from sending delegations to the Assembly and because the Covenant of the League did not make provision for the termination of membership of the League except in cases of violation of the Covenant.[346] While in September 1936 no State had yet recognized *de jure* the Italian conquest of Ethiopia, during the succeeding months one country after the other accorded *de jure* recognition to the Italian conquest and, at the same time, withdrew recognition from the Emperor's Government.[347] In view of these recognitions it seems highly unlikely that Ethiopian credentials issued by the Emperor would have been accepted by the Assembly, if put to the test.

In the debate on the representation of Cambodia in the United Nations the Government of the Khmer Republic regularly argued that the Government of National Union of Cambodia (RGNUC) of Prince Sihanouk was not entitled to represent Cambodia in the United Nations *because* it was

[343] Sandford, n. 338 above, 100–1.

[344] See LNOJ Spec. Supp. No 169, at 35–6. See also the letter dated 8 Sept. 1938 of Emperor Haile Selassie to the Secretary-General of the League of Nations, Joseph Avenol: 'The Ethiopian Government, in the name of Ethiopia, a Member of the League of Nations, is abstaining provisionally from sending its representatives to the next session of the Assembly of the League of Nations, the agenda of which does not include any question directly relating to Ethiopia' ([1938] LNOJ 669). For the permanent delegation of Ethiopia to the League, see [1939] LNOJ 8.

[345] [1938] LNOJ 333, italics added.

[346] See Art. 16(4) of the Covenant of the League of Nations. Of a violation of the Covenant Ethiopia could, of course, not be accused.

[347] For a list of countries recognizing the Italian conquest of Ethiopia, see App. II.

'nothing more or less than a Government in exile'.[348] This led Prince Sihanouk to claim on several occasions that his was not a 'government-in-exile',[349] while at the same time arguing, alternatively, that during the Second World War, *inter alia*, 'Her Majesty the Queen of the Netherlands sent her government out of the country' and that 'this did not prevent the freedom- and justice-loving governments from continuing to recognize her legitimacy and that of her government in exile'.[350] Some of the States sponsoring the RGNUC's claim to Cambodia's seat in the United Nations also expressly referred to historical precedents of States being represented in international forums by their governments in exile.[351] As has been shown above, there is no legal rule preventing a government in exile from representing a member-State in an international forum.[352] It is therefore argued that the RGNUC did not fail to occupy Cambodia's seat in the United Nations because it was, in fact, a government in exile but because it was not recognized as the Government of Cambodia (in exile) by a majority of the member-States. This view is supported by the fact that the United States, which did not recognize the RGNUC and, consequently, opposed its claim to Cambodia's seat, argued (consistently) that 'Prince Sihanouk does not head a government in exile; he is a non-government in

[348] GAOR, 28th Session, 2188th Plenary Meeting, 4 Dec. 1973, 4 (Mr Long Boret). See also Mr Long Boret's statement that 'The admission of the Sihanouk Government-in-exile to the United Nations—a Government domiciled in a foreign country—would amount to giving that foreign country two votes' (*ibid.*, 28th Session, General Committee, 212th Meeting, 16 Oct. 1973, 22). See also UN Doc.A/9230, annex, at 1. For the view that the RGNUC is a government in exile, see also the speech of Mr Panyarachun (Thailand): *ibid.*, 28th Session, 2189th Plenary Meeting, 4 Dec. 1973, at 5, 7. On the question of Cambodian representation in the United Nations, in general, see Leifer, n. 314 above, 47–59; Dorfman *et al.*, n. 314 above; Douc Rasy, *La question de la représentation Khmère à l'ONU: droit ou politique?* (1974).

[349] See e.g. (1970) 13/20 *PR* 12–13, 15; (1970) 13/21 *PR* 19, 21–2; (1970) 13/35 *PR* 8–15; and [1972] *Keesing's* 25547 and [1973] *Keesing's* 26187. Prince Sihanouk argued in 1972 that the RGNUC administered over 80 per cent of the country ([1972] *Keesing's* 25547). To sustain this argument, it was announced on 22 Nov. 1973 that the Ministers in the RGNUC, with the exception of Prince Sihanouk and the Prime Minister, had moved their seat to liberated areas on 9 Nov. 1973 (UN Doc.A/9344, annex I).

[350] See 'Letter of Samdech Norodom Sihanouk, Head of State of Cambodia, to Their Majesties and Their Excellencies The Heads of State and Heads of Government of Non-Aligned Countries, August 1970': (1970) 13/35 *PR* 8–15 at 12. In this letter Prince Sihanouk also asked the non-aligned States 'to recognize *de jure*' the RGNUC (*ibid.*, at 15).

[351] GAOR, 28th Session, 2188th Plenary Meeting, 4 Dec. 1973, 1–2 (Algeria); 11 (China); *ibid.*, 28th Session, 2190th Plenary Meeting, 5 Dec. 1973, 7 (Syria).

[352] Cf. the statement of Mr El Hassan (Mauritania): GAOR, 29th Session, 2301st Plenary Meeting, 27 Nov. 1974, 1149. See also the statement of Mr Koh (Singapore) with respect to the right of the (Coalition) Government of Democratic Kampuchea to represent Cambodia in the United Nations General Assembly: *ibid.*, 37th Session, 42nd Plenary Meeting, 25 Oct. 1982, 749.

exile'.[353] Of the 139 member-States of the United Nations in December 1973 only forty-three had recognized the RGNUC.[354] On the other hand, the Government of the Khmer Republic still had formal diplomatic relations with more than fifty member-States.[355] The number of recognitions received by the two authorities found its expression in the decisions of the General Assembly on the question of Cambodian representation. On 5 December 1973 the Assembly decided by fifty-two votes to fifty, with twenty-two abstentions, to postpone discussion of the agenda item 'Restoration of the lawful rights of the RGNUC in the United Nations'. Twelve days later, on 17 December 1973, a motion to amend the General Assembly's approval of the report of the credentials committee to provide for the substitution of the RGNUC delegation for that of the Khmer Republic was rejected by fifty-five votes to fifty, with seventeen abstentions. In November 1974 when the next challenge to the credentials of the Khmer Republic was mounted the ratio of member-States to member-States recognizing the RGNUC was 142 to forty-five. The attempt to seat the RGNUC was thus again defeated on 29 November 1974 by fifty-six votes to fifty-four, with twenty-four abstentions.[356]

Practice is not always consistent as regards the representation of member-States in international forums. Governments in exile have been allowed to represent member-States in one forum but not in another.

The delegations of the RGNUC, for example, were seated from 1972 to 1974 at the conferences of the Non-Aligned Movement[357] but not at the United Nations.[358] Conversely, the Government of Democratic Kampuchea (GDK) and its successors—CGDK and NGC—represented Cambodia

[353] GAOR, 28th Session, 2190th Plenary Meeting, 5 Dec. 1973, 11 (Mr Bennett). On US support for the Lon Nol Government's claim to Cambodia's seat in the UN, see Rovine 'Contemporary Practice of the United States Relating to International Law' (1974) 68 *AJIL* 309–24 at 318–20. On US recognition policy with respect to Cambodia, see Barnes, 'United States Recognition Policy and Cambodia' (1970) 50 *Boston ULR* Special Issue, 117–29.

[354] See App. II. Cf. also the statement of the Syrian representative, Mr Kelani, in the General Assembly: GAOR, 28th Session, 2190th Plenary Meeting, 5 Dec. 1973, 8.

[355] See the statement of Mr Long Boret (Khmer Republic): GAOR, 28th Session, General Committee, 212th Meeting, 16 Oct. 1973, 22.

[356] For the debates on the 'Restoration of the lawful rights of the RGNUK in the United Nations', see the 2188th–2191st Plenary Meeting of the General Assembly on 4–5 Dec. 1973 and the 2298th–2302nd Plenary Meeting of the General Assembly on 26–29 Nov. 1974.

[357] [1972] *Keesing's* 25465A and [1973] *Keesing's* 26118. It should be noted that the 4th Conference of the Heads of State or Government of Non-Aligned Countries, meeting in Algiers from 5 to 9 Sept. 1973, 'considering that by its collective recognition of the Royal Government of National Union of Cambodia it has provided the Cambodian people with the most valuable support in their rightful struggle for independence, sovereignty and neutrality' called upon 'all peace and justice-loving countries to give official recognition to the Royal Government of National Union of Cambodia as the sole legal Government of Cambodia'. See NAC/AHG/CONF.4/RES.10 (UN Doc.A/9330, at 48).

[358] See Dorfman *et al.*, n. 314 above, 495–513. See also [1974] *Keesing's* 26343.

from 1979 to 1989 at the United Nations and in United Nations sponsored conferences[359] as well as in the Group of 77[360] but not in the Non-Aligned Movement, which left the Cambodian seat vacant.[361]

On the initiative of Saudi Arabia[362] the eighteenth Islamic Conference Organization (ICO) Foreign Ministers' conference, held in Riyadh on 13–16 March 1989, in its final communiqué on 16 March 1989 offered the seat of Afghanistan, which had been vacant since January 1980,[363] to the Interim Government of Afghan Mojahedin (AIG) with its seat in Peshawar, Pakistan.[364] Afghanistan's seat in the United Nations and in the Non-Aligned

[359] e.g. the GDK represented Cambodia at the 8th Session of the 3rd UN Conference on the Law of the Sea (UNCLOS) in Geneva, 19 Mar.–27 Apr. 1979 (BBC, *SWB*, 2nd series, FE/6089/A3/9, 10 Apr. 1979), in the UN Conventional Weapons Conference in Geneva, 15 Sept.–10 Oct. 1980 (UN Docs.A/CONF.95/10 and A/CONF.95/SR.11, 4–7), in meetings of the UN Economic and Social Commission for Asia and the Pacific (ESCAP), held in Bangkok on 17 Apr. 1984 ((1984) 3/2 *Ind. Chron.* 10) and 23 Apr. 1987 ((1987) 6/2 *Ind. Chron.* 13), and at the Conference on UN Decade for Women in Nairobi in July 1985 ((1985) 4/3 *Ind. Chron.* 9). On Cambodian representation in the United Nations system, see also Nash (ed.), *Cumulative Digest of United States Practice in International Law 1981–1988* (1994), i, 412–14; Klintworth, *Vietnam's Intervention in Cambodia in International Law* (1989), 8 and 85, n. 1; and Sciso, 'La questione delle credenziali cambogiane all'Assemblea generale delle Nazioni Uniti' (1981) 64 *Riv. DI* 83–95.

[360] The CGDK represented Kampuchea at the 5th ministerial meeting of the Group of 77 at Buenos Aires on 1 Apr. 1983 ((1983) 2/2 *Ind. Chron.* 8).

[361] While the delegation of the GDK was initially seated, although without the right to speak and vote, at the meetings of the Co-ordinating Bureau of the Non-Aligned Movement in Mobutu, Mozambique, at the end of Jan. 1979, and in Colombo, Sri Lanka, in June 1979 ([1979] *Keesing's* 29843; Leifer, n. 314 above, 47–59 at 53), since the Havana summit meeting in Sept. 1979 the seat of Cambodia remained 'vacant'. The Conference of Heads of State or Government of Non-Aligned States, held at Havana, from 3 to 9 Sept. 1979, decided that 'as long as there is no decision on which of the parties has the right to the vacant seat [of Cambodia], neither of the parties shall claim its alleged rights in any organ of the Movement' (UN Doc.A/34/542, annex, at 98). See [1980] *Keesing's* 30041; [1983] *ibid.* 31890; [1984] *ibid.* 32671; [1987] *ibid.* 34969. See also Chakraborti, *India and Kampuchea. A Phase in their Relations, 1978–81* (1985), 67–8. On Cambodian representation in general, see Warbrick, 'Kampuchea: Representation and Recognition' (1981) 30 *ICLQ* 234–46 at 236–40.

[362] Saudi Arabia had been the first country to recognize the Afghan Interim Government on 9 Mar. 1989, i.e. four days before the start of the ICO Foreign Ministers' Conference to be held in Riyadh, in a move apparently timed to put pressure on other Islamic nations to follow suit. See *The Times*, 10 Mar. 1989, 11; *Le Monde*, 11 Mar. 1989, 4; BBC, *SWB*, 3rd series, ME/0405/i, 10 Mar. 1989.

[363] After the Soviet invasion of Afghanistan an Extraordinary Session of the Islamic Foreign Ministers' Conference, held in Islamabad on 27–29 Jan. 1980, 'decided to suspend the membership of Afghanistan in the Organization of the Islamic Conference' and 'invited member-States to withhold recognition to the illegal regime in Afghanistan and sever diplomatic relations with that country until the complete withdrawal of Soviet troops from Afghanistan'. For the text of the Final Declaration, see DPIC XX, 431–40 at 436. But in subsequent years Mojahedin delegates had attended ICO meetings as official guests or observers. See also Moinuddin, *The Charter of The Islamic Conference and Legal Framework of Economic Co-operation among its Member States* (1987), 101.

[364] The AIG was admitted to occupy the Afghan seat in the ICO by a vote of 35 in favour, 5 against (Syria, Libya, North Yemen, South Yemen, Iraq) and two abstentions (Iran, Pakistan). See (1989) 13 *MECS* 181; *The Times*, 17 Mar. 1989, 10; [1989] *Keesing's* 36538; BBC, *SWB*, 3rd series, ME/0412/A1, 18 Mar. 1989. For the Final Communiqué of the 18th ICO

Movement,[365] on the other hand, continued to be occupied by the Najibullah Government at Kabul.

These inconsistencies are due not so much to a controversy over the principle that a government in exile is entitled to represent a member-State in international forums but to the fact that each forum decides for itself whether or not to recognize an authority in exile as the State's government. In this connection it should be noted that it is a widespread solecism, in cases in which two authorities (one in exile and one *in situ* or both *in situ*) claim to represent the State, to ask which of the two 'governments' is entitled to represent the State in the international forum, thereby giving the wrong impression that a State may have two 'governments'. As a State can have only one government at a time and as States are, as a rule, represented in international forums by their governments the question must be which of the two rival authorities qualifies as the State's government in international law. This question, however, is answered by each forum for itself (and independently of its individual members) when it is called upon to decide which of two rival delegations to admit. The admission of a delegation may thus be interpreted as constituting recognition of the sending authority both in the sense that, in the opinion of the forum, the sending authority qualifies as the government of the member-State and in the sense that it expresses the willingness of the forum to enter into official relations with it as such. As international practice shows this recognition decision of a forum may differ not only from the decisions of other fora but also from the individual recognition decisions of its member-States.[366]

As the decision of the forum on which of two rival claimants may occupy the seat of a member-State is usually a collective act of all the member-States of the forum, problems may arise if member-States are split over the question of which authority is to be recognized as the government of the member-State. For example, the nineteenth OAU Summit Meeting, held in Tripoli on 15–26 November 1982, which failed to reach an agreement on the question which of the two authorities claiming to represent Chad—the Habré Government in N'djamena, which received an invitation, or the Goukouni Government in exile—should be seated, was obliged to close

Foreign Ministers' Conference held in Riyadh on 13–16 Mar. 1989, see BBC, *SWB*, 3rd series, ME/0413/A1–9 at A5, 20 Mar. 1989. Commenting on the decision to seat the AIG, the Soviet Foreign Ministry spokesman, Mr Perfilyev, told a press briefing on 20 Mar. 1989: 'As earlier, the Soviet Union proceeds and will proceed from the fact that Afghanistan has only one legitimate government recognized by most countries in the world. This government alone has legal powers to represent the Afghan State and the Afghan people in the international arena and at international forums' (*ibid.*, 3rd series, SU/0415/A1/5, 22 Mar. 1989). On the seating of the AIG, see also [1989] *Nahost Jahrbuch* 174–6 at 175.

365 *Munzinger. Zeitarchiv*, Afghanistan, Chronik, 1989, 54.

366 e.g. the Government of ousted Panamanian President Delvalle continued to be recognized as the Government of Panama by the USA, a member of the UN, but not by the UN which recognized the Government of President Solís Palma. Cf. UN Doc.A/43/PV.6, at 2–25.

even before an agenda could be established.[367] The seating of one of the claimants on the basis of a majority vote may also often not be practical, as the walkout of the member-States recognizing the other claimant may lead to the lack of quorum.[368] In order to avoid such negative consequences and in the interests of unity, international forums have adopted the 'empty chair policy', whereby neither of the rival claimants is allowed to take the member-State's seat.[369] This, however, does not mean that the member-State has no government, but only that the member-States of a forum cannot agree on who to recognize as the government of the member-State.

(b) Admission to Membership of Inter-State Forums

The representation of a member-State in an Inter-State forum must be distinguished from the question of admission to membership of such a forum. The latter arises in particular if an authority in exile applies on behalf of its (newly proclaimed) State for admission to a forum open only to sovereign independent States. While representation of a member-State requires recognition by the forum of the authority in exile as the government of the member-State, admission to membership, in addition, requires that the entity on whose behalf the application for admission is made is recognized as a sovereign and independent State by the forum. This is well illustrated by the case of Montenegro. The reason given for the fact that the Montenegrin Government at Neuilly-sur-Seine, as one of the Allied and Associated Powers, had not been invited to take part in the Paris Peace Conference was that 'the majority of the Great Powers have assumed that Montenegro would be absorbed by the Kingdom of the Serbs, Croats and Slovenes'.[370] Similarly, its application for membership of the League of Nations in November 1920 was rejected, *inter alia*, on the ground that 'the question of the current existence of an independent State of Montenegro has never been decided'.[371] While admission to Inter-State forums is often

[367] See [1982] *West Africa* 3127, 3129, 3130–1.

[368] When the representative of the GDK addressed the session of the UN Conference on Trade and Development (UNCTAD) in Manila in May 1979, the Soviet representative led a walkout of 13 delegations. See Leifer, n. 314 above, 47–59 at 53.

[369] For example, Cambodia's seat at the Non-Aligned Movement Summit meeting, held in Lusaka (Zambia) on 16–17 May 1970, was left vacant ([1972] *Keesing's* 25465A). But on 10 Aug. 1972 the Conference of Foreign Ministers of non-aligned countries in Georgetown, Guyana, decided to give Cambodia's seat to the RGNUC (*ibid.*).

[370] See the statement of the President of the credentials committee of the Paris Peace Conference made on 10 May 1919: Kiss, *Répertoire de la Pratique française en matière de droit international public* (1969), vi, no. 1105, at 577 (translation supplied).

[371] Proposition of M. Paul Mantoux, Director of the Political Department of the League Secretariat: Jumeau, n. 243 above, 150. With respect to Montenegro's application for membership of the League, Mr Cecil Harmsworth, the British Under-Secretary of State for Foreign Affairs, stated in Parliament that Montenegro had applied for admission to the League of Nations but that 'until the future status of the country was settled, the question of her becoming a member of the League would not arise' (HC Debs., vol. 135, col. 1736, 6 Dec. 1920; *The Times*, 7 Dec. 1920, 16).

determined by political rather than legal considerations, and much also depends on the particular rules and procedures for admission of the forum in question, it is argued that a precondition for a successful membership bid is double recognition by the forum, namely, recognition as a State of the entity on whose behalf the application is made and recognition of the applying authority in exile as its government. As practice shows, if one recognition is missing, the application will fail.

The requirement of recognition by the forum of the applying authority in exile as a State government can best be illustrated by the admission to the United Nations Conference on International Organization (UNCIO), held in San Francisco from 25 April to 26 June 1945. During UNICO the Korean Provisional Government (KPG) at Chungking, China, requested on several occasions that Korea[372] be admitted to the Conference.[373] The request was declined on the ground 'that by agreement among the sponsoring powers invitations to the San Francisco Conference were extended only to those nations which were United Nations on 1 March 1945. Provision is not being made for observers from other nations.'[374] This, however, was not the real ground as is shown by the fact that Argentina, Denmark, Lebanon, and Syria, which were admitted to the Conference, also had not adhered to the Declaration by United Nations on 1 March 1945. That the KPG's request was declined because it had not been recognized by any of the United Nations as the Government of the State of Korea[375] becomes clear from a letter dated 5 June 1945 from the US Acting Secretary of State Joseph Grew to the Chairman of the Korean Commission in the United States, Mr Syngman Rhee, explaining the reasons for the non-admission of the Korean Provisional Government to the San Francisco Conference:

> The United Nations which are represented at the San Francisco Conference all have legally constituted governing authorities, whereas the 'Korean Provisional Government' and other Korean organizations do not possess the qualifications requisite for obtaining recognition by the United States as a governing authority. The 'Korean Provisional Government' has never had administrative authority over any part of Korea nor can it be considered representative of the Korean people of today.[376]

[372] Korea had been annexed by Japan on the basis of a Treaty concluded between the Emperors of Korea and Japan on 29 Aug. 1910 and at the time of the San Francisco conference was still governed by Japan. For the text of the Treaty of Annexation, see (1910) 4 *AJIL* Supp., 282–3.

[373] See [1945] VI FRUS 1028–9. See also Choong-Sik, n. 110 above, 229–30.

[374] [1945] VI FRUS 1025. The KPG was also denied participation in the Paris Peace Conference (Choong-Sik, n. 110 above, 141) and in the conference on Limitations of Armament in the Pacific and the Far East, held in Washington in Nov. 1921. For the latter, see Cong. Rec., 67th Cong, 2nd Sess, vol. 62, pt. 3, 3057–8 (26 Feb. 1922), and vol. 62, pt. 2, 1747–8 (26 Jan. 1922). See also Oliver, n. 110 above, 151–4.

[375] See Henderson, *Korea: The Politics of the Vortex* (1968), 86. On *de facto* recognition by several States, see App. II.

[376] [1945] VI FRUS 1029–30 at 1030. See also Acting Secretary Grew's statement on 'Review of Policy regarding Korea', released on 8 June 1945: (1945) 12 *DSB* 1058–9 at 1058; also DAFR VII, 230–1. See further Choong-Sik, n. 110 above, 229–30.

Not non-recognition but the inability of the United Nations to agree on which of the two Polish authorities (the Provisional Government in Warsaw or the Government in London) to recognize as the Government of Poland was the reason that Poland was not participating in UNCIO.[377]

The role which recognition plays in the admission to membership of an Inter-State forum is also well illustrated by the admission of the Saharan Arab Democratic Republic (SADR) to the OAU which almost led to the disintegration of the organization.[378] The OAU was first confronted with the question of recognition with respect to the Western Sahara conflict at the twenty-sixth Council of Ministers' meeting in Addis Ababa on 23 February to 1 March 1976 where the question before the organization was the recognition of the Polisario Front as the legitimate liberation movement in the Sahara.[379] However, the question of recognition of the Polisario Front as a liberation movement was overtaken by events, when on 26 February 1976 an independent and sovereign State, the SADR, was proclaimed. Recognition of a sovereign and independent State was a more serious matter for the Council of Ministers' meeting since it entailed membership of the OAU and therefore posed a direct challenge to Morocco and Mauritania which were occupying the Western Sahara. The Council compromised on the divisive issue of recognition of the SADR by voting on 1 March 1976 that recognition of the SADR as an independent and sovereign State was the prerogative of individual member-States.[380] By the time of the seventeenth OAU

[377] US Secretary of State Stettinius wrote on 28 May 1945: 'Poland is a United Nation and should be here. But there are two Polish Governments—the London Government and the Warsaw "Provisional Government"' ([1945] VI FRUS 438). While the Polish Government in London was almost universally recognized the Provisional Polish Government in Warsaw was recognized in Apr. 1945 by 4 States only. On the question of Polish representation at the San Francisco conference, see DUNCIO I, 168, 346–8, 350; V, 93–6, 305; and DPSR II, nos 323, 339, 344, 349, 373.

[378] On SADR membership of the OAU in general, see Pazzanita, 'Legal Aspects of Membership in the Organization of African Unity: The Case of Western Sahara' (1985) 17 *CWRJIL* 123–58; Pazzanita and Hodges, n. 29 above, 318–26; Damis, 'The OAU and Western Sahara' in El-Ayouty and Zartman (eds.), *The OAU After Twenty Years* (1984), 273–96; Naldi, 'The Organization of African Unity and the Saharan Arab Democratic Republic' (1982) 26 *JAL* 152–62; Bennouna, 'L'admission d'un nouveau membre à l'Organisation de l'Unité Africaine' (1980) 26 *AFDI* 193–8; Vance, 'Recognition as an Affirmative Step in the Decolonization Process: The Case of Western Sahara' (1980) 7 *Yale JWPO* 45–87 at 74–5.

[379] 17 members reportedly favoured the recognition of Polisario as a liberation movement, 9 were against, and 21 abstained (*Le Monde*, 4 Mar. 1976, 2; [1976] *Keesing's* 27747).

[380] The Council of Ministers on 1 Mar. 1976 adopted the following three points: '(1) The people of the Western Sahara have the right to self-determination the same as all other peoples are entitled to freedom and independence; (2) The Council understands that by exercising this right, the people of the Western Sahara have declared an independent and sovereign state designated the "Saharan Arab Democratic Republic" and consequently, the recognition of the Polisario Front in the Sahara is no longer valid; (3) the recognition of an independent and sovereign state is an act of sovereignty pertaining each member of the international community, an act to be taken individually and, it is, therefore, up to member states and each individual OAU power [to decide] whether to recognize or not the newly independent state' (BBC, *SWB*, 2nd series, ME/5149/A/9, 3 Mar. 1976).

Summit in Freetown, Sierra Leone, on 1–4 July 1980, twenty-six African States had recognized the SADR.[381] Although the SADR now had the support of the majority of the fifty OAU member-States, the summit postponed a decision on the question of SADR membership in face of the threat by several members to leave the organization over the admission of the SADR.[382] At the thirty-eighth Council of Ministers' meeting in Addis Ababa on 28 February 1982 the SADR was seated for the first time, thus becoming the fifty-first member of the organization. OAU Secretary-General Edem Kodjo termed his action to seat the SADR an 'administrative decision', based on the formal notification by a majority of OAU member-States of their recognition of the SADR.[383] Morocco and several other member-States walked out of the meeting and threatened to boycott the organization as long as the SADR was seated.[384] The admission of the SADR thus split the OAU. Several meetings of the organization had to be adjourned *sine die* because they were boycotted by either group and thus lacked a quorum.[385] Only after the decision of the SADR 'temporarily' not to attend OAU meetings, the OAU was able to hold its nineteenth summit in Addis Ababa on 8–12 June 1983.[386] But when the SADR took its seat at the twentieth summit in Addis Ababa on 12–15 November 1984 Morocco and Zaïre announced their withdrawal from the OAU.[387] The SADR has since attended all OAU summits and other meetings without substantial opposition, and as a gesture of the OAU's determination that the membership issue should henceforth be closed, the SADR's president in exile, Mohammed Abdelaziz, was elected to the vice-presidency of the organization at the twenty-first OAU summit in 1985.[388]

[381] For the 26 member-States of the OAU recognizing the SADR, see App. II.

[382] See [1980] ARB 5874A. See also Naldi, n. 378 above, at 153. On 3 June 1980 the Polisario Front had officially asked the OAU to recognize the SADR and to admit it to membership (Bennouna, n. 378 above, at 195, n. 4). For the Moroccan response to this request, see *ibid.*, at 195–6. On 3 July 1980 8 States (amongst which were Morocco, Tunisia, Egypt, Sudan) said they would withdraw from the OAU if the SADR was admitted ((1980) 34 *MEJ* 480).

[383] Damis, n. 378 above, 280. For the attitude of the USA toward the seating of the SADR delegation, see [1984] AFPCD 943–4.

[384] UN Doc.A/AC.109/667, 3 Aug. 1981, at 7; [1982] *Keesing's* 31487.

[385] At a meeting of Ministers of Information held at Dakar on 16 Mar. 1982, 13 States were said to have walked out when Senegal refused to allow the SADR delegates to attend. Subsequently at a meeting of Ministers of Labour, held at Salisbury on 5 Apr. 1982, 9 countries were said to have boycotted the meeting to protest the presence of representatives of the SADR. The OAU Charter (Arts. 10, 14) requires two-thirds of the members, i.e. then 34 States, for a quorum. Thus, the 19th summit scheduled to be held in Tripoli on 5–8 Aug. 1982 had to be adjourned as 19 member-States stayed away in protest against the admission of the SADR.

[386] (1983) 37 *MEJ* 242, 663. The SADR also did not attend the 40th Council of Ministers' meeting in Addis Ababa on 27 Feb.–5 Mar. 1984 ([1985] *Keesing's* 33324).

[387] [1984] ARB 7428A; [1985] *Keesing's* 33324. While Morocco at the end of 1996 still has not returned to the OAU, Zaïre resumed its membership at the 44th Council of Ministers' meeting in Addis Ababa in July 1986 ([1986] ARB 8139C/8140A).

[388] Pazzanita and Hodges, n. 29 above, 325–6. The OAU Council of Ministers' meeting on 22–27 June 1992 discussed the possibility of suspension of the SADR pending the UN

A 'State' may be admitted to one forum but not to another. In spite of an initiative by the Casablanca group of States[389] to extend an invitation to Algeria, the GPRA was not invited to the second conference of African Heads of State and Government, held in Lagos in January 1962, as Algeria was not (yet) a fully independent State.[390] Algeria, represented by the GPRA, also was not admitted to full membership of the League of Arab States.[391] Similarly, Angola, represented by the GRAE, was not admitted to membership of the OAU.[392] In both cases a different approach was followed by the Non-Aligned Movement which counted both 'States' as its full members (prior to their factual achievement of independence) and admitted the leaders of their respective governments in exile as 'Heads of State or Government' to its conferences in 1961 and 1964. This may be explained by the fact that in 1961 the GPRA was recognized *de facto* or *de jure*, by seventeen of the twenty-four non-aligned States[393] and that in 1964 the GRAE was recognized *de facto* or *de jure* by nineteen (or, according to

organized referendum on self-determination in the West Sahara, but no final decision was taken ([1992] *Keesing's* 38992). A motion to expel the SADR from the OAU was defeated at the 39th summit, held in Tunis on 13–15 June 1994 ([1994] *Nahost Jahrbuch* 173).

389 The Casablanca group of States consisted of Morocco, the UAR, Ghana, Guinea, and Libya. The GPRA was recognized by these States as 'the sole authority empowered to represent and undertake obligations for Algeria' (Bedjaoui, n. 19 above, 114, n. 11). The GPRA (but not Algeria) participated as a full member in the Conference of African Heads of State and Government at Casablanca from 3–6 Jan. 1961. This becomes clear from the African Charter of Casablanca which speaks of His Excellency Ferhat Abas as 'President of the Provisional Government of the Algerian Republic' and not as President of the Republic of Algeria. Cf. *ibid*., at 129.

390 See Elias, 'The Charter of the Organization of African Unity' (1965) 59 *AJIL* 243–67 at 244–5. On GPRA participation in the Lagos conference, see also Favrod, *Le FLN et l'Algérie* (1962), 344–5.

391 Only on 16 Aug. 1962 Algeria was admitted to membership of the Arab League by a decision of the Arab League Council (166 BFSP 890). However, on 6 Feb. 1960 the GPRA had nominated a permanent Algerian representative to the Arab League and participated in the various Councils of the League. See Bedjaoui, n. 19 above, 133, who misleadingly speaks of 'the adherence of Algeria to the Arab League'. The GPRA had enjoyed the status of an 'observer' since 7 Sept. 1959. See BBG, 'Le GPRA et la Ligue Arabe' (1960) 16 *Rev égypt*. 68–9 at 68. On 19 Oct. 1958 the Council of the Arab League had included a title in its budget called 'the payment of an annual subsidy of 12 million sterling to *the Government of Free Algeria*' (Favrod, n. 390 above, 328, italics added, translation supplied).

392 Cf. [1964] *West Africa* 858. The People's Republic of Angola, represented by the MPLA Government, became the 47th Member of the OAU on 11 Feb. 1976. On OAU membership, see Arts. 4 and 28 of the Charter of the OAU ((1963) 2 ILM 766). On membership of the OAU of governments in exile of dependent territories, see Akwensioge, *Die Organisation für Afrikanische Einheit—Entstehungsgeschichte und Entwicklung seit 1963* (1974), 107.

393 'Algeria' was represented by the GPRA at the conference of 25 non-aligned States, held in Belgrade on 1–6 Sept. 1961. The final communiqué of the conference, issued on 6 Sept. 1961, stated with respect to Algeria: 'The Heads of State and Government are particularly gratified that Algeria is represented at this conference by its rightful representative, the Prime Minister of the Provisional Government of Algeria' ([1961–2] *Africa Diary* 124). For a list of States recognizing the GPRA in 1961, see App. II.

statements of its officials, even by twenty-six)[394] of the forty-six member-States of the Non-Aligned Movement.[395]

Authorities in exile which are not recognized by the majority of the member-States of a forum as the governments of States may, by way of exception, be allowed limited participation or even full participation as non-State members in that forum. Inter-State forums have granted unrecognized authorities in exile 'observer'[396] or 'guest' status,[397] thus permitting them to participate in the work of the forum without a right to vote. They have also allowed them to participate as full members in their own right (as distinct from the organ of an independent State). For example, the GPRA (not Algeria) was admitted as a member with full rights to the various conferences of Nine (later Eleven) Independent African States,[398] and the GRAE (not Angola) was admitted, *inter alia*, to the OAU Conference of Foreign Ministers, held at Lagos on 24 February–1 March 1964.[399]

(3) Judicial Proceedings

The question of representation of a State by an authority in exile does not arise only with respect to international political fora but also with respect to judicial fora. The principle of representation in national and international

[394] For the 19 non-aligned States recognizing the GRAE, see App. II. At a press conference in Dar-es-Salaam on 22 Oct. 1964 Sr Roberto explained that so far 29 countries (of which at least three were not members of the non-aligned movement) had recognized the GRAE but did not name these countries. ([1964] *Africa Diary* 2045).

[395] 'Angola', listed as one of 47 non-aligned States, was represented by Sr Holden Roberto, the President of the GRAE, at the second conference of heads of State or government of the non-aligned States, held in Cairo on 5–10 Oct. 1964. See the Final Declaration of the Conference: BBC, *SWB*, 2nd series, ME/1681/E/2–9, 13 Oct. 1964. See also [1964] *West Africa* 814.

[396] e.g. the Provisional Government of Free India attended the Assembly of Greater Asiatic Nations in Tokyo on 5–6 Nov. 1943 as an 'observer' (Giani, n. 150 above, ii, 73). The GPRA was represented as an observer at the Preparatory Meeting for the Conference of the Uncommitted Countries, held at Cairo from 5–12 June 1961 (*The Conference of Heads of State or Government of Non-Aligned Countries, Belgrade, September 1–6, 1961* (n.d.), 15). India adopted the position that for 'judicial' reasons a representative of the GPRA should not be seated at all at the Cairo conference: see Misra, 'Recognition of the "Provisional Government of the Algerian Republic": A Study of the Policy of the Government of India' (1962) 10 *Pol. Stud.* 130–45 at 136.

[397] Sr Holden Roberto, Prime Minister of the GRAE, attended the 2nd Assembly of the Heads of State and Government of the OAU, held in Cairo on 17–21 July 1964, as a 'guest' ([1964] *Keesing's* 20253A). Representatives of the GPRA attended sessions of the UN General Assembly as guests of friendly delegations (Bedjaoui, n. 19 above, 133).

[398] The Conferences of Nine Independent African States (Ethiopia, Ghana, Guinea, Liberia, Libya, Morocco, Sudan, Tunisia, and the United Arab Republic) were held in Monrovia on 4–8 Aug. 1959 and in Accra on 7–10 Apr. 1960. The Conference of Eleven Independent African States (the former plus Nigeria and Somalia) was held in Addis Ababa on 14–24 June 1960. See Bedjaoui, n. 19 above, 128, 129; Favrod, n. 390 above, 166; [1959] *Keesing's* 17066A; [1960] *ibid.* 17554A.

[399] The GRAE delegation was headed by the Foreign Minister, Mr Jonas Savimbi. See [1964] ARB 21C.

courts has been clearly stated by the Court of Appeal of Brussels in *Estado da India* v. *Société anonyme Kredietbank et Verbruggen* (1965) as follows: 'A State which has been invaded contrary to the United Nations Charter can validly appear in court represented by its government in exile or by the legal representatives of that government.'[400] The question, however, remains whether a particular authority in exile qualifies as the State's government (in exile). Recognition of an authority in exile as a government has been treated by courts as strong or, depending on the forum, even as conclusive evidence as to the governmental status of an authority in exile. Thus, at least in national courts, authorities in exile which were formally recognized by the forum State as governments or with which the forum State's government had government-to-government dealings have, as a rule, been allowed to bring an action,[401] to intervene,[402] or to be sued[403] on behalf of their State. On the other hand, authorities in exile which were not recognized as governments were regarded as lacking competence to instruct counsel to act on behalf of the State. In *Republic of Somalia* v. *Woodhouse Drake & Carey* (1992),[404] the solicitors had been instructed by a Mr Qalib, who was based in Riyadh, Saudi Arabia, and who described himself as the 'Prime Minister of [the interim Government of] the Somali

[400] [1966] II Pas.belge 19 (translation supplied). See also (1967) 3 *RBDI* 565–6. In this case the 'Portuguese State of India' was represented by its Government in exile in Lisbon.

[401] In *Republic of Haiti* v. *Duvalier*, the Supreme Court of New York, allowing an appeal by the Republic of Haiti, pointed out that 'during most of the pendency of this litigation . . . and specifically, during the pendency of this appeal, the democratically elected legitimate government was in exile' (626 NYS2d 472 at 474 (AD 1st Dept. 1995)). In *Republic of Panama* v. *Republic National Bank of New York*, 681 F.Supp. 1066 (SDNY 1988) and *Republic of Panama* v. *Citizens and Southern International Bank*, 682 F.Supp. 1544 (SD Fla. 1988) the plaintiff was represented by the Government of exiled President Delvalle. On a claim brought by the Montenegrin Government in exile on behalf of Montenegro, see Clunet, 'La plainte en Justice du Monténégro et l'exterritorialité diplomatique' (1920) 47 *JDI* 490–3. But see also *Badan Persatuan RMS et al.* v. *Mayor of The Hague and Municipality of The Hague*, where the District Court of The Hague held that the 'Badan Persatuan RMS', the unrecognized Government in exile of the Republic Maluku Seletan, could act as a party to legal proceedings, not as the representative of the Republic of Maluku Seletan but as an 'independent person' ([1975] NJ No 220).

[402] See e.g. *Anderson* v. *NV Transandine Handelmaatschappij*, 289 NY 9 (CA NY 1942); affirming 31 NYS2d 194 (1941), and 28 NYS2d 547 (1941); *In re Kahn's Estate*, 38 NYS2d 839 (1942). In both cases the State of the Netherlands, as represented by the Royal Dutch Government in London, intervened in the proceedings.

[403] In the *Republic of Latvia Case* the Kammergericht held that 'the Republic of Latvia, as represented by the Government in exile in London, has the requisite *locus standi* and is the defendant liable in these proceedings' (KG, 25 Feb. 1955: (1957) 7 *JIR*, 397–400 at 400). The Court of Appeal affirmed the decision of the Restitution Chamber of Berlin (WK Berlin, 3 Oct. 1953: [1953] RzW 368). It must be noted, however, that Latvia was represented not by a (non-existent) government in exile in London but by the Minister of the (former) Latvian National Government in London. See also *Dessaulles* v. *Republic of Poland* [1944] SCR 275, affirming *Republic of Poland* v. *Dessaulles and Bar of Montreal* [1943] Qu.BR 224. In this case a Canadian lawyer sued the Republic of Poland, represented by the Polish Government in London, for professional fees.

[404] [1992] 3 WLR 744.

Republic'.[405] Hobhouse J, taking note of a Foreign Office communication which stated that 'there have been no dealings on a government to government basis' with the Interim Government of the Somali Republic, concluded that the solicitors did not have the authority of the Republic of Somalia as 'the instructions and authority they have received from the interim government are not instructions and authority from the Government of the Republic [of Somalia]'.[406]

3 STATE PROPERTY ABROAD

(1) Access to State Property Abroad

Although most authorities in exile have, at least partly, been financed by their host State or other States,[407] the access to the property abroad of the State which they claimed to represent has played a vital role in their struggle to regain control over the national territory by enabling them to organize an effective administration in exile, to pay lobbyists and public relations firms to advance their cause, to maintain diplomatic missions with regional and international organizations as well as influential States, to equip and pay armed forces, and, last but not least, to conduct military operations against the authority *in situ*. Access to State property has also allowed authorities in exile a certain independence of their host State. It is therefore not surprising that it is usually one of the first actions of authorities in exile to secure control of their State's assets and sources of revenue abroad.[408] In this, however, they usually are not alone, as the authorities *in situ* will likewise try to lay hands on the State's property abroad.[409]

[405] *Ibid.*, at 748. Mr Qalib, who had become Prime Minister of Somalia's Interim Government in Feb. 1991, lived in exile in Riyadh as a guest of the Saudi Government throughout 1991 from where he bombarded UN Secretary-General Boutros Boutros-Ghali with letters on stationery that said 'Office of Prime Minister-Mogadishu', demanding formal recognition of his government. See *WP*, 7 Dec. 1992, Sec. A, 26; [1991] *Keesing's* 38323.

[406] [1992] 3 WLR 744 at 757.

[407] A notable exception is the exiled Government of Kuwait which had at its disposal foreign assets estimated at US$ 90 to 100 billion (*NY Times*, 25 Sept. 1990, Sec. D, 6). On Kuwaiti funds abroad, see also Daoudi, n. 262 above, 107–21 at 113–16.

[408] After the *coup d'état* in Qatar on 27 June 1995 in which Emir Khalifa was deposed by his son, the exiled Emir, claiming to be the legitimate ruler of Qatar, had the country's foreign assets, estimated by experts to amount to US$ 6 to 8 billion, transferred to his private bank accounts and claimed to administer the money for the people of Qatar (*FAZ*, 9 Apr. 1996, 6). A legal battle between the new and the exiled Emir of Qatar, fought in 8 countries, started on 31 July 1996 with a closed hearing at London's High Court. All actions however were dropped after an agreement between the old and the new Emir on 21 Oct. 1996.

[409] On 13 Sept. the acting Iraqi Finance Minister warned against the disposal of Kuwaiti assets in foreign countries as these had become the property of the Republic of Iraq on 8 Aug. 1990, the date of the Iraqi annexation of Kuwait (BBC, *SWB*, 3rd series, ME/0870/A/6, 15 Sept. 1990).

The Syrian representative to the United Nations, Mr Kelani, referring to Prince Sihanouk's RGNUC in Peking said on 5 December 1973 that 'a Government which leaves its territory is not merely a *de facto* body. It is not a private entity unable to dispose of national property abroad',[410] thereby implying that a government in exile is entitled to dispose of its State's property abroad.[411] While the principle as such is well established, the problem is to determine in each individual case whether the government that has left its territory retains its status as a government or becomes, what Mr Kelani called, a mere *de facto* body. The answer to this question which each State normally decides for itself finds its expression in the continued recognition or non-recognition of the authority in exile as the State's government. The right to dispose of State property abroad thus largely depends on recognition of the authority in exile as a government by the State in whose territory the property is situated.

Authorities in exile which were recognized as the governments of certain States by the government of the *situs*, as a rule,[412] have been allowed to use the funds of those States deposited with local banks[413] or held in trust by the recognizing government.[414] Thus, after having recognized the Spanish Republican Government in exile as the Government of Spain on 30 August 1945, the Mexican Government in September 1945 turned over to representatives of the Spanish Republican Government in exile the assets of the Junta de Auxilio a los Republicanos Españoles (JARE), a refugee agency established in mid-1939 and operating with funds of the old Spanish Republic, which since March 1943 had been administered under its control.[415] Authorities in exile recognized as governments have also been allowed to sell national property.[416] This is well illustrated by the case of the Chinese

410 GAOR, 28th Session, Plenary Meetings, Plenary Meetings, 2190th Meeting, 5 Dec. 1973, 7.

411 On the financial activities of governments in exile in general, see Bareau, n. 139 above, 17–24.

412 In a notable exception, the Government of Brazil on 4 May 1944 refused to pay some US$ 950,000 of Yugoslav State funds to the Yugoslav Government in exile, although it still recognized that Government as the Government of Yugoslavia ((1944) 38 *AJIL* 483).

413 Cf. *Republic of Panama* v. *Republic National Bank of New York*, 681 F.Supp. 1066 (SDNY 1988); *Republic of Panama* v. *Citizens and Southern International Bank*, 682 F.Supp. 1544 (SD Fla. 1988). On the attempts of the Belgian Government in exile to recover gold deposited by the Banque Nationale de Belgique with the Banque de France, see [1941] *Keesing's* 4644A and [1942] *ibid.* 5067A. See also *De Gorter* v. *Banque de France*, 29 NYS2d 842 (1941), 30 NYS2d 815 (1941); and *Banque de France* v. *Supreme Court of the State of New York*, 287 NY 483 (1942).

414 On the negotiations between the Polish Government in exile and the Free French authorities for the release of some US$64 million worth of gold deposited with the Bank of France, which, on the eve of the German occupation of France, had been removed to French West Africa, see [1943] III FRUS 443–4, 454, 495–6 and [1944] III FRUS 1266–7. See also [1941] *Keesing's* 4889B.

415 See Smith, *Mexico and the Spanish Republicans* (1955), 275, 289; Tusell and Alted, 'The Government of the Spanish Republic in Exile: 1939–1977' in Shain (ed.), *Governments-in-Exile in Contemporary World Politics* (1991), 145–65 at 151.

416 In Nov. 1936 the Ethiopian Government in exile sought to transfer shares given as compensation to Ethiopia in exchange for the grant of concessions by Ethiopia to foreign

aircraft in Hong Kong. On 12 December 1949 the Nationalist Chinese Government, which according to the Supreme Court of Hong Kong at the time of the transaction 'was established outside Chinese territory',[417] sold forty civil aircraft belonging to the Chinese State grounded in Hong Kong to two American citizens. The sale was upheld by the Privy Council in *Civil Air Transport Incorporated* v. *Central Air Transport Corporation* (1952) on the ground that, at the time of the transaction, the Nationalist Government was still recognized by the United Kingdom as the *de jure* Government of China.[418] Recognized governments in exile have also been permitted to draw upon credits granted to their States,[419] to manage State-owned or controlled companies,[420] to occupy State property such as diplomatic and consular premises,[421] and to recover sums due to their States.[422]

companies. See in this connection the Public Notice of the Italian Government warning against transactions 'with individuals claiming to be representatives of the ex-Ethiopian Empire' who are seeking to transfer State property, published in the advertisement columns of *The Times*, 12 Nov. 1936, 3.

417 See [1953] AC 70 at 90.

418 *Ibid.*

419 e.g. the Polish Government at Angers was allowed to draw upon credits granted to Poland by France and the UK prior to the German invasion of that country. See Fiedorowicz, n. 294 above, at 174.

420 Cf. *Republic of Panama* v. *Air Panama Internacional*, 745 F.Supp. 669 (SD Fla. 1988). The Kuwaiti Government in exile relied, *inter alia*, on the revenue received from Kuwait Petroleum International, the overseas marketing and refining arm of Kuwait's oil company, in order to maintain cash flow. On the control exercised by the Belgian Government at Le Havre over the funds of the National Bank of Belgium, a private bank, deposited with the Bank of England, see Fauchille, 'Chronique des faits internationaux' (1919) 26 *RGDIP* 310–29 at 320; Feilchenfeld, *The International Economic Law of Belligerent Occupation* (1942), 100.

421 On 9 Oct. 1945 the building and archives of the Spanish Embassy in Mexico, which had been under the care of the Portuguese Legation, were given over to the newly recognized Republican Government in exile (Smith, n. 415 above, 289). After the rupture of relations between (Vichy) France and the USSR on 30 June 1941 ([1941] I FRUS 178), the French Embassy in Moscow was taken care of by the Turkish Ambassador (De Gaulle, n. 231 above, i, 295). However, on 14 May 1944, i.e. prior to Soviet full recognition, the French Embassy in Moscow was handed over to a representative of the CFLN (RIIA *Chronology of the Second World War* (1947), 14 May 1944). On 14 September 1944 the UK and the USA gave the representatives of the CFLN 'the use' of the former French Embassies in these countries. Canada followed on 15 Sept. (DCER X, no. 49).

422 See *Haile Selassie* v. *Cable and Wireless, Ltd (No 2)* (1938), [1939] 1 Ch. 182 (CA). English courts have jurisdiction to decide the title to State property claimed by the government in exile and the authority *in situ*, even if the authority *in situ* is a foreign sovereign State. See the judgment of the Court of Appeal in *Haile Selassie* v. *Cable and Wireless, Limited* [1938] 1 Ch. 839, reversing the judgment of Bennett J [1938] 1 Ch. 545. But compare the decision of the Tribunal civil de la Seine in *Haïlé Sélassié* v. *Gouvernement italien*, GP 1937. II. 924; affirmed by the Cour d'appel de Paris *sub nom. Haïlé Sélassié* v. *Etat italien*, GP 1939.I.640. Compare also *Lehigh Valley Railroad Co.* v. *State of Russia*, 21 F.2d 396 (2nd Cir. 1927). In that case the Provisional Russian Government, recognized *de jure* by the USA in Mar. 1917, was permitted to maintain a tort claim in the name of the Russian State, although almost a decade before it had in fact been overthrown by the Bolsheviks. On a rebate of US$ 350,000 to the Haitian Government of exiled President Aristide from a contract concluded by an earlier Haitian Government, see *Miami Herald*, 8 Dec. 1993, Sec. C, 1.

Furthermore, they have been regarded as entitled to their States' property taken abroad by the illegal authority *in situ*.[423] It should however be added that, if the illegal authority *in situ* is a foreign State, as in the case of belligerent occupation, and the property taken abroad is in its possession, claims to the property by the State's recognized government in exile may be barred by sovereign immunity of the occupying State.[424]

Some authorities in exile not recognized as governments have not even attempted to get access to their States' property. According to estimates at the time of the Second World War there were French assets worth more than one billion dollars in US banks, which had been frozen by the US Government.[425] In view of the fact that they had not been recognized by the US Government as the Government of France, the various Free French authorities did not even try to get these funds released.[426] In this connection it is interesting to note that only on 25 October 1944, i.e. two days after the United States had 'recognized the *de facto* authority established under the leadership of General de Gaulle as the Provisional Government of the French Republic'[427] the US Treasury proposed the 'unfreezing' of French assets in the United States.[428]

Authorities in exile which, in spite of their non-recognition as governments, have tried to get access to State property have either failed on the ground that they were not 'entitled' to the State property[429] or that they lacked capacity to sue on behalf of the State.[430]

[423] Between 6 and 8 Aug. 1990 Iraqi authorities removed 15 Kuwaiti aircraft from Kuwait to Iraq. On 26 Oct. 1990 the ICAO Assembly adopted RES.4/1 on the Aeronautical Consequences of the Iraqi Invasion of Kuwait which requested 'all States in whose territory any of these aircraft are found to hand them over to the legitimate Government of Kuwait' (UN Doc.S/21923, annex). See also *NY Times*, 27 Oct. 1990, Sec. 1, 5, and S/RES/661 (1990), para. 9(a); S/RES/670 (1990), para. 9. See also Art. 2(2) of the Kuwaiti Decree–Law 3/A/1990 concerning the Holding in Trust by the State of Kuwait of Property Belonging to Kuwaitis or Residents of Kuwait, issued on 18 Oct. 1990: UN Doc.S/21887, annex, at 3.

[424] Cf. *Kuwait Airways Corporation* v. *Iraq Airways Company and Republic of Iraq* (1993), [1994] 1 Lloyd's Rep. 276 (CA). See also Talmon, 'War Booty of "Separate Entity" Protected by Sovereign Immunity' (1995) 15 *OJLS* 295–307.

[425] Funk, 'La "Reconnaissance" du C.F.L.N. (Québec, août 1943)' (1959) 9/33 *RHDGM* 37–48 at 38.

[426] See [1943] II FRUS 186. On 30 Aug. 1943 the US Secretary of State, Cordell Hull, said that the frozen money of the French Government in the USA would be kept in trust for the French Government when it was restored in proper form ([1943] II FRUS 188).

[427] See (1944) 11 *DSB* 491; and [1944] V FRUS 777, n. 15.

[428] RIIA *Chronology of the Second World War* (1947), 25 Oct. 1944.

[429] In *Re an Application by Ernst Jaakson and Aarand Roos* (1990), the English High Court held that two Estonian Consuls in the USA, with which the British Government did 'not have dealings . . . as the representatives of Estonia or the Government thereof', were not entitled to the proceeds of sale of the (former) Legation of the Republic of Estonia in London, and that the proceeds were to be lodged in court (85 ILR 53).

[430] Cf. *Bela Varga* v. *Crédit-Suisse*, 162 NYS2d 80 at 82 (1957); reversed on other grounds, 171 NYS2d 674 at 676 (1958); affirmed *per curiam*, 182 NYS2d 17 (1958). See also *Haile Selassie* v. *Cable and Wireless, Ltd (No 2)* (1938), [1939] 1 Ch. 182 at 198 (CA).

(2) The Role of the State of situs

(a) The Practice of Freezing Foreign Assets

The property of States whose governments are forced into exile either by belligerent occupation or *coup d'état* has usually been blocked or frozen by the State of *situs*, either as a measure called for by war or neutrality[431] or in response to the request by an international or regional organization.[432] The purpose of these measures is not to deprive recognized governments in exile of their right to dispose of their States' property but to prevent the authority *in situ* from gaining access to it.[433] This becomes clear from a message to the US Congress in which President Bush stated on 3 August 1990: 'in order to protect the property of the legitimate Government of Kuwait from possible seizure, diversion, or misuse by Iraq, and with the approval of the Kuwaiti Government, we are blocking Kuwaiti assets within the jurisdiction of the United States'.[434] Special machinery is therefore usually set up under national legislation allowing the authority in exile recognized by the State of *situs* to dispose of its State's frozen assets.[435] Thus, on 26 August 1990 the Finance Minister of the Kuwaiti

[431] For an overview of the freezing of funds of governments in exile in the USA during the Second World War, see Cong. Rec., 77th Cong., 1st Sess., vol. 87, pt. 6, 2687–8 (27 Mar. 1941). See also Executive Orders 12723 of 2 Aug. 1990, 12725 of 9 Aug. 1990 (Kuwait). On 2 Aug. 1990 the USA, the UK, Germany, and Japan froze all Kuwaiti funds (Al Roumi, n. 260 above, Sect. 1, 13, 14). On the freezing of Kuwaiti assets in the UK, see Richards Butler, *MEED Gulf Crisis Report. The Legal Implications of the United Nations Embargo for Businesses* (1990), 39–46.

[432] On 8 Oct. 1991 the *ad hoc* meeting of Ministers for Foreign Affairs of the OAS resolved 'to urge the member States to proceed immediately to freeze the assets of the Haitian State' (MRE/RES.2/91: UN Doc.A/46/550–S/23127, 9 Oct. 1991). For a call by the UN Security Council to freeze Haitian assets abroad, see S/RES/841 of 16 June 1993. Similarly, on 6 Aug. 1990 the UN Security Council called upon all States 'to take appropriate measures to protect assets of the legitimate Government of Kuwait and its agencies' (S/RES/661).

[433] On the protective purpose of the worldwide freezing of Kuwaiti assets, see e.g. Arts. 1, 2, 4 of the Decree on the Protection of Assets of the State of Kuwait in Switzerland of 10 Aug. 1990: Campbell and Newcomb (eds.), *The Impact of the Freeze of Kuwaiti and Iraqi Assets on Financial Institutions and Financial Transactions* (1990), 286–7. See also EC Council Regs. 2340/90 [1990] OJ L213/1–2, and 3155/90 [1990] OJ L304/1–4.

[434] [1990] AFPCD no 284, at 463. See also the joint statement of the European Community and its Member States of 4 Aug. 1990: 'In order to safeguard the interests of the legitimate Government of Kuwait they have decided to protect all assets belonging directly or indirectly to the State of Kuwait' ([1990] 7–8 *EC Bull.* 122).

[435] In the UK the Department of Trade and Industry permitted a large number of Kuwaiti owned institutions to operate normally once their control by the legitimate Government of Kuwait had been established (Richards Butler, n. 431 above, 44). For the announcement of the Japanese Finance Ministry cancelling the freeze of Kuwaiti assets on a case-by case basis if that does not run counter to the interests of the exiled Government of Kuwait, see BBC, *SWB*, 3rd series, FE/0847/A4/4, 20 Aug. 1990. See also Craig, Polkinghorne, and Moghaizel, 'French Policy concerning Financial and Commercial Relations with Kuwait and Iraq' (1991) 19 *Int. Bus. Lawyer* 158–62.

Government in exile could announce that Europe and Japan had permitted the legitimate Government of Kuwait to manage again Kuwaiti assets abroad.[436]

(b) US Legislation: The Edge Act 1941

Banks holding property for the account of a foreign State may face conflicting claims by an authority in exile and an authority *in situ*, both claiming to be the government of the same State. In this case banks may make either payments or deliveries at their peril or refuse to do so until the title to the property is decided by the courts. Resort to the latter alternative makes funds unavailable until a decision is reached. By claiming the property the authority *in situ* may thus, at least temporarily, effectively 'block' the State's property with respect to the authority in exile recognized as the State's government by the forum State. In order to avoid time-consuming litigation and to give the recognized governments forced into exile during the Second World War effective control over their States' property the United States in April 1941 enacted section 25(b) of the Edge Act, which is still in force[437] and which provides that any federal reserve or insured banks shall be conclusively presumed to have acted lawfully in delivering foreign State property and shall be completely discharged and released of any liability with respect to such property, if the property is delivered to a person who is recognized by the Secretary of State as the accredited representative of the foreign State to the United States, and if the authority of the person to act with respect to the property is recognized by the Secretary of State and certified by him to the bank.[438]

(c) The Case of Panamanian Property in the United States

On 26 August 1988 the Legislative Assembly of Panama, at the instigation of General Noriega, resolved to dismiss President Eric Arturo Delvalle and Vice-President Roderick Esquivel and installed the Minister of Education, Manuel Solís Palma, as Minister in charge of the Presidency. International reactions to this action were mixed. While some States recalled their ambassadors as a sign of disapproval, only the United States continued to recog-

[436] Al Roumi, n. 260 above, Sect. 1, 45.

[437] 12 USC § 632 (1994).

[438] On the purpose of this provision, see the statements of the Senator from Michigan, Mr Brown: Cong. Rec., 77th Cong., 1st Sess., vol. 87, pt. 6, 2686, 2690, 2691 (27 Mar. 1941). See also Marks, 'Protective Expropriatory Decrees of the Governments in Exile—Their Application in the United States' (1941) 41 *Col. LR* 1072–87 at 1086–7; American Law Institute, *Restatement of the Law (Second). The Foreign Relations Law of the United States* (1965), § 111, Reporter's Note, at 351; Whiteman, n. 2 above, ii, 713. See also *Republic of Panama* v. *Republic National Bank of New York*, 681 F.Supp. 1066 at 1070, 1071–3 (SDNY 1988).

nize President Delvalle as the legitimate President of Panama.[439] During the first week of March lawyers instructed by ousted President Delvalle identified the location of Panamanian State assets in the United States. The bulk of the money, amounting to about US$ 60 million was held in four New York banks.[440] Letters were sent to the chairmen of these banks asserting the Delvalle Government's claim to those assets.[441] The letters, however, did not have the desired effect. One of the banks, Republic National, which had been asked on 1 March 1988 by the Solís Palma Government to transfer US$ 10 million to Panama planned to comply the next day. The Embassy of Panama at Washington, loyal to President Delvalle, thereupon sent a diplomatic note, dated 2 March 1988, to the State Department, stating that Ambassador Sosa was the sole person having authority to receive, control, or dispose of any Panamanian financial assets in the United States. On the same date Acting Secretary of State, John C. Whitehead, certified pursuant to the Edge Act, 12 USC section 632 (1982), that Ambassador Juan B. Sosa 'is recognized by me as being the accredited representative of the Republic of Panama to the Government of the United States' and that he 'is the sole person having authority to receive, control or dispose of any property held in any . . . Federal Reserve bank or insured bank from or for the account of the Republic of Panama . . . and that his authority with respect of such property is accepted and recognized by me'.[442] Equipped with this certificate counsel representing the Delvalle Government instituted proceedings in several jurisdictions in the United States and successfully established title to Panamanian bank deposits and prevented banks holding those deposits from transferring them to the Solís Palma Government. The US$ 10 million were transferred by Republic National Bank into Account No 1 at the Federal Reserve Bank of New York for use by the Delvalle Government.[443] On 8 April 1988, President Reagan ordered all property and interests in property of the Government of Panama in the United States to be blocked, prohibited all payments or transfers of funds from the United States to the Solís Palma Government, and ordered that all such payments or transfers owed to the Government of Panama be made into an escrow account at the Federal Reserve Bank of New York, 'to be held for the benefit of the

[439] See Scranton, *The Noriega Years. U.S.–Panamanian Relations, 1981–1990* (1991), 131; *Guardian*, 29 Feb. 1988, 8. Cf. also the statement by the Panamanian Foreign Minister, Sr Ritter, on 31 October 1988: 'I want to state something very clearly. The only country that does not recognize the Panamanian Government [of Solis Palma] is the USA' (BBC, *SWB*, 3rd series, ME/0298/D/1–D/2, 2 Nov. 1988).

[440] The banks were Republic National, Chase Manhattan, Irving Trust, and City Bank.

[441] See Nash, n. 359 above, i, 316–22; Scranton, n. 439 above, 134–9.

[442] See *Republic of Panama* v. *Citizens and Southern International Bank*, 682 F.Supp. 1544 at 1551 (SD Fla. 1988); *Republic of Panama* v. *Republic National Bank of New York*, 681 F.Supp. 1066 at 1069 (SDNY 1988).

[443] Scranton, n. 439 above, 135; *WP*, 4 Apr. 1989, Sec. A, 18.

Panamanian people'.[444] Property was, however, not to be deemed blocked 'with respect to which transactions are authorized by, or on behalf of, the recognized representative of the Government of Panama as certified by the Secretary of State', or are otherwise authorized in certain regulations.[445] The access of the Delvalle Government to Panamanian property in the United States was thus based on two crucial points: the Edge Act of 1941 and its application on behalf of governments forced into exile during the Second World War combined with recognition of the exiled Delvalle Government as the lawful Government of Panama and of Ambassador Sosa as its representative in the United States.[446]

The fact that the so-called 'Delvalle Government', which consisted of ousted President Delvalle, several members of the Washington Embassy headed by Ambassador Juan B. Sosa, and the members of some consular offices, was recognized as the legitimate government of Panama only by the United States raises serious doubts about its competence to dispose of Panamanian State property. By recognizing a group of exiles politically acceptable to the United States as the Government of Panama and thereby giving them access to Panamanian property in the United States, the US Government in fact disposed of Panamanian State property.[447] In *Republic of Panama* v. *Republic National Bank of New York* (1988), MacMahon DJ correctly pointed out that there was a real threat that Panamanian funds 'would be dissipated and irretrievably lost if disbursed to persons other than the lawful representative of the Republic of Panama'.[448] However, the question of who is the lawful representative of the Republic of Panama cannot, at least in the international sphere, depend on the view of the US Government alone. It is submitted that while States may have a wide discretion in recognizing or withholding recognition of a government,[449] questions of State responsibility may arise if a State in whose territory foreign State property is situated recognizes (for political reasons) an individual or group of exiles as the government of the foreign State and thereby

[444] See Executive Order 12635 of 8 Apr. 1988 (53 FR 12134). As at 17 July 1989 Government of Panama Account No 2 contained US$ 136.4 million (Scranton, n. 439 above, 177, n. 141). It should be noted that Ambassador Sosa had to give an irrevocable instruction that no payments be made from that account, unless the US Secretary of State or his lawful delegate had first notified the Bank in writing that 'constitutional order has been restored in Panama,' (Nash, n. 359 above, i, 320). In late 1990 these funds were finally released to the US-installed Endara Government.

[445] See Executive Order 12635 of 8 Apr. 1988 (53 FR 12134). On the blocking of Panamanian State property in the USA, see also Nash, n. 359 above, ii, 2738–41; *ibid.*, iii, 2985–91.

[446] Scranton, n. 439 above, 135.

[447] Cf. the address of Mr Solís Palma, President of the Republic of Panama, to the UN General Assembly on 27 Sept. 1988: UN Doc.A/43/PV.6, 2–25 at 19–20.

[448] 681 F.Supp. 1066 at 1070 (SDNY 1988).

[449] For the (wide) discretion of States in according or withholding recognition, see Janke, n. 151 above, 22–8.

enables it to dispose of that State's property. In this case recognition as a government may amount to *de facto* dispossession or expropriation of the foreign State's property and give rise to an obligation to pay compensation.[450] Furthermore, if the exiled group contends with a rival political group *in situ* for control of the government of the State, recognition of the exiled group as the State's government may also amount to interference in the internal affairs of the State as the group that controls the State property 'will have a decisive advantage over the other for effective control of the government'.[451] Such interference is facilitated by legislation such as the Edge Act 1941 and judicial deference to the Executive branch of government in regard to questions of status of foreign governments which in fact make recognition the 'key' to the property of foreign States situated in the United States. As early as during the discussion of Senate Bill 390 (which later became section 25(b) of the Edge Act) Senator Danaher pointed out the possibility of misuse of the powers given by that Bill. He stated: 'But if we pass this bill . . . the President . . . may utilize the funds in this country to play power politics anywhere with reference to the disposition of the funds or their use'.[452] That the US Government might not be totally above such accusations may be illustrated by the practice followed with respect to some US$50 million of Haitian State funds on deposit in the United States. These funds were frozen after President Aristide had been deposed by a military *coup d'état* on 29 September 1991[453] and were controlled by the Treasury Department which had to release them when so ordered by the State Department. According to the Treasury spokesman, Peter O'Brien, before issuing such an order, the State Department determined whether exiled President Aristide's request was '*consistent with US foreign policy goals*'.[454]

(3) Succession to Property Abroad Controlled by Authorities in Exile

It is important to recall that a 'government' is not a legal person but that it is the (executive) organ of the legal person called 'State'. A government therefore, as a rule, does not own property but holds in trust the property owned by its State. As has been shown above, the right of an authority to administer State property abroad depends on its recognition as the State's

[450] On the international responsibility of States for their recognition decisions, see also *ibid.*, at 40–2.

[451] *Republic of Panama* v. *Republic National Bank of New York*, 681 F.Supp. 1066 at 1070 (SDNY 1988).

[452] Cong. Rec., 77th Cong., 1st Sess., vol. 87, pt. 6, 2689 (27 Mar. 1941). See also *ibid.*, at 2688.

[453] See Executive Orders 12775 of 4 Oct. 1991 (56 FR 50641) and 12779 of 28 Oct. 1991 (56 FR 55975).

[454] *Chicago Tribune*, 23 Nov. 1993, 13, italics added. On access to Haitian State funds in US banks by exiled President Aristide, see *WP*, 15 Jan. 1994, Sec. A, 18; *Daily Telegraph*, 24 Oct. 1993, 23; *NY Times*, 5 Mar. 1993, Sec. A, 3.

government by the State of *situs*. Once recognition as the State's government is transferred by the State of *situs* from one authority (either in exile or *in situ*) to another authority the right to administer the State's property automatically passes to the newly recognized government.[455] Point IX of the Potsdam Agreement of 2 August 1945 on Poland may illustrate this:

> The establishment by the British and United States Governments of diplomatic relations with the Polish Provisional Government has resulted in the withdrawal of their recognition from the former Polish Government in London, which no longer exists. The British and the United States Governments have taken measures to protect the interests of the Polish Provisional Government as the recognized Government of the Polish State, in the property belonging to the Polish State located in their territories and under their control, whatever the form of the property may be. They have further taken measures to prevent alienation to third parties of such property. All proper facilities will be given to the Polish Provisional Government for the exercise of the ordinary legal remedies for the recovery of any property belonging to the Polish State which may have been wrongfully alienated.[456]

Thus, when the British Government on 5 July 1945 ceased to recognize the Polish Government in London as the Government of Poland and instead recognized the Polish Provisional Government of National Unity in Warsaw, the former was, at that date, denied control of Polish property in the United Kingdom.[457] All assets of the Polish State came under the complete control of the Interim Treasury Committee for Polish Questions.[458] Upon the conclusion of an Agreement for the Settlement of Outstanding Financial Question on 24 June 1946[459] these assets were finally transferred by the British Government to the Provisional Government of National Unity.[460]

[455] Cf. *Haile Selassie* v. *Cable and Wireless, Ltd (No 2)* (1938), [1939] 1 Ch. 182 at 194–9 (CA). For an (unsuccessful) attempt to safeguard the title of the exiled Ethiopian Emperor to Ethiopian State property within the jurisdiction of the UK after British *de jure* recognition of Italian rule over Ethiopia, see Haile Selassie Emperor of Ethiopia (Property) Bill: HC Debs., vol. 337, cols. 1089–93, 22 June 1938; *ibid.*, vol. 341, cols. 1534–5, 22 Nov. 1938.

[456] 145 BFSP 864–8.

[457] On 6 July 1945 it was announced that the Provisional Government of National Unity in Warsaw had appointed a commission 'to take over and secure' all property of the Polish State in the UK ([1945] *Keesing's* 7301). See also DBPO, 1st ser., VI, no 2, at 6–8; DPSR II, no 382, at 631–2. Polish assets included, *inter alia*, about £20 million of gold in the Polish National Bank (Bank Polski) in London ([1945] *Keesing's* 7301), Polish merchant ships chartered to the British Government (DBPO, 1st ser., VI, no 8, at 29), and the buildings used as embassy and consulates.

[458] On 4 July 1945 Count Edward Raczynski, the Polish ambassador to Great Britain, signed at the Foreign Office a document whereby the buildings and other property belonging to the Polish State were made over to the Interim Treasury Committee (Raczynski, n. 310 above, 297). On the handing over of the embassy, see also *ibid.*, at 297–9. On the Interim Treasury Committee, see *The Times*, 6 July 1945, 4; HC Debs., vol. 414, cols. 663, 15 Oct. 1945; *ibid.*, vol. 420, col. 181, 5 Mar. 1946; DBPO, 1st ser., VI, no 2, at 7; Flory, n. 149 above, 255–6.

[459] 11 UNTS 59.

[460] Kacewicz, n. 293 above, 50–1.

Similarly, upon recognition of the Provisional Government of National Unity on 30 October 1945, the Australian Government, which had represented Polish interests in the Soviet Union on behalf of the Polish Government in London from 25 May 1943 to 23 August 1944, handed over to the Provisional Government of National Unity (i) goods and money which were the property of the Polish State in 1943 and which it subsequently received on its behalf; (ii) documents and records (birth certificates, passports, etc.) received from the Polish Embassy or from or on behalf of Poles.[461]

The situation is different with respect to property controlled by an authority in exile not recognized by the State of *situs* as the government of a certain State. In this case problems of succession will not arise with respect to State property (which due to lack of recognition the authority in exile will not be allowed to control) but with respect to property originally acquired by the authority in exile. As unrecognized 'governments' in exile, as a rule, do not possess legal personality their property has been vested or registered, according to the law of the *situs*, in the names of private individuals.[462] It is argued that due to lack of title such property usually cannot be claimed by the recognized government of the State which the authority in exile purported to represent. As the authority in exile has not been recognized as the government of a certain State it cannot be regarded as the predecessor of any subsequently recognized government of that State. The fact alone that the authority in exile claimed to represent the State also gives no title paramount to its property abroad. This may be illustrated by the Irish funds in the United States. On 21 January 1919 25 members of the Sinn Féin party elected to the British House of Commons met in Dublin and constituted themselves a Parliament for the Irish Republic called the Dáil Eireann. On 1 April 1919 they elected a Government with Eamonn de Valéra as President and then went underground. Mr de Valera left for the United States in June 1919 where he stayed for eighteen months in order to secure recognition of the Irish Republic from the Government of the United States[463] and

[461] DAFP VIII, no 350, at 550. See also the memorandum on Polish gold in Canada dated 23 July 1946 which stated that the 'recognized Polish Government is entitled to Polish gold in Canada' (DCER XII, no 1232 and also no 1233). In 1960 the last Polish art treasures, which had been deposited in Canada in 1940 by the Polish Government in London, were returned to Poland against the will of the (no longer recognized) Polish Government in London. On the Polish art treasures in Canada, see Williams, 'The Polish Art Treasures in Canada, 1940–60' (1977) 15 *CYIL* 146–72; and DCER XII, nos 1230, 1234, 1239; [1952] *Keesing's* 12189C.

[462] e.g. the buildings of the unrecognized Polish Government in exile in London (1945–90) were administered by the Polish National Fund, a non-profit organization under English law, and were registered privately in the names of certain Polish exiles (Iwańska, n. 232 above, 86). The funds of the 'Irish Republic' in the USA were vested in Eamonn de Valéra, President of the Republic, and two others as trustees (Dickinson, 'The Case of the Irish Republic's Funds' (1927) 21 *AJIL* 747–53 at 747).

[463] On the quest for US recognition, see *The Times*, 12 Aug. 1920, 9 ('De Valera's Bid for Recognition'); *NY Times*, 26 Nov. 1920, 2; and Ward, 'Can the United States of America

to float the Dáil Eireann External Loan. Bond certificates were issued to subscribers to the loan by 'Eamonn De Valéra, President of the elected government of the Republic of Ireland'.[464] In 1927 the Irish Free State, contending to be 'the successor of the original *de facto* government which raised the money', claimed some US$ 2.5 million still on deposit in New York. In *Irish Free State* v. *Guarantee Safe Deposit Co.* (1927),[465] Peters J, noting that 'the Dáil organization was never recognized by any foreign country'[466] found that the Irish Free State neither was the successor to 'the revolutionary organization known as Dáil Eireann' nor could show paramount title to the funds.[467]

It may be added that, while recognized governments *in situ* may not claim, by way of succession, the property of unrecognized authorities in exile which purported to represent their State, they are also not obliged to meet their obligations: In contrast, governments *in situ* have been held responsible for the acts of their recognized predecessors in exile.[468]

4 PROTECTION OF NATIONALS

The protection of their nationals abroad is one of the most noble tasks of States. It is a corollary of the State's personal sovereignty over its nationals. While authorities in exile may be prevented from exercising the State's territorial sovereignty due to their lack of control over national territory, they are able to exercise the State's personal sovereignty over its nationals[469]

Recognize the Republic of Ireland Without Committing Any Breach of International Law in Reference to Great Britain?' (1922) 5 *Bi-Monthly LR* 129–38. On the Irish Republic in general, see Bell, 'The Transcendental Irish Republic: The Dream of Diaspora' in Shain (ed.), *Governments-in-Exile in Contemporary World Politics* (1991), 202–18.

[464] The Australian Government forbade entry into the country of pamphlets entitled 'Bond Certificate for the First Loan of the Elected Government of the Republic of Ireland' (*NY Times*, 8 May 1920, 17).

[465] 222 NYS 182. On this case, see Dickinson, n. 462 above, 747–53; Garner, 'A Question of State Succession' (1927) 21 *AJIL* 753–7; Brown, 'Loans to Unrecognized Insurgents' (1927) 7 *Boston ULR* 312–15; and Hackworth, n. 3 above, v, 679–81. But, *contra*, see *Fogarty* v. *O'Donoghue* (1925), [1926] IR 531.

[466] 222 NYS 182 at 188.

[467] 222 NYS 182 at 202.

[468] In *Jackson* v. *Royal Norwegian Government*, 177 F.2d 694 (2nd Cir. 1949) the Royal Norwegian Government at Oslo was held liable for a breach of contract by the Royal Norwegian Government in London.

[469] Moving the Second Reading of the Allied Powers (Maritime Courts) Bill, the Secretary of State for the Home Department, Mr Herbert Morrison, said that the British Government recognized the foreign Governments in London as 'sovereign Governments, with sovereign powers in respect of their own people and citizens' (HC Debs., vol. 371, col. 1106, 13 May 1941). See also KG, 25 Feb. 1955: [1955] RzW 211 at 212; *Gdynia Ameryka Linie* v. *Boguslawski* (1952), [1953] AC 11 at 41 (*per* Lord Reid); *Delany* v. *Moraitis*, 136 F.2d 129 at 131 (4th Cir. 1943). Cf. also *Lee Wei Fang* v. *Kennedy*, 317 F.2d 180 (DC Cir. 1963).

and hence to protect them and their interests abroad.[470] A precondition, however, is that they are recognized as the governments of the States whose nationals require protection. This becomes clear from *In re Graud's Estate* (1943), where the Surrogate's Court of New York County held that 'so long as that recognition [as a valid subsisting government by the United States] continues and so long as it remains our governmental policy to deny recognition to forcible occupations of countries with which this country is at peace the right of the original government of any seized territory to protect the interests of its nationals must be recognized by the courts'.[471] Similarly, in a series of decisions concerning compensation for maltreatment suffered by nationals of German-occupied States abroad during the Second World War, the (West) German courts held that it was the government in exile of the occupied State or (in countries which no longer maintained diplomatic relations with the government in exile but still recognized it as such) the State that protected its interests[472] and not the German Reich, as occupying power, that had the right and, dependent on its municipal law, the duty to protect its nationals abroad as neither the occupation nor the purported annexation by Germany affected the nationality of the inhabitants of the occupied State.[473] Nationality was held to be the only prerequisite for the right of diplomatic protection, the effectiveness of the protection in a particular case being irrelevant.[474] A recognized government in exile also remains entitled to protect the nationals of other States if its State has undertaken their protection by international agreement. Thus the (West)

470 Verdross, *Völkerrecht* (4th edn., 1959), 245; Flory, n. 149 above, 207–8; Sperduti, n. 100 above, at 408. On the possible withdrawal of consular protection by a government in exile, see HC Debs, vol. 353, cols. 229–30, 8 Nov. 1939.

471 41 NYS2d 263 at 268 (Surr.Ct. NY Co 1943).

472 On the protection of the interests of the Polish Government in London in the USSR by Australia, see Heydon, n. 295 above. On the possibility of a protecting power acting for a government in exile, see in general Guggenheim, n. 148 above, ii, 802, n. 106.

473 BGH, 2 Mar. 1966 [1966] RzW 367; BGH, 13 Feb. 1963 [1963] RzW 368; BGH, 12 July 1963: LM § 2 BEG 1956, No 28; BGH, 18 Mar. 1959 (1961–2) 9 AVR 215–17, reversed OLG Koblenz, 8 July 1958 [1958] RzW 398. The last case concerned the internment of a Polish national in Shanghai. In a note on the decision of the BGH Professor Wengler argued that Germany had a right (and a duty) to protect Polish nationals against measures of States, such as Japan, that had recognized the German annexation of (parts of) Poland: [1960] RzW 24–5. However, that argument was not followed by the courts. See BGH, 13 Apr. 1960 [1960] RzW 380 at 381; BGH, 29 June 1966 [1966] RzW 557 at 559. Mr Tadeusz Romer served as Polish Ambassador to Japan until 4 Oct. 1941. On the protection of Polish nationals in Japan, see DAFP IV, no 392. On the protection of Polish nationals, see also [1943] III FRUS 314, 327; and Hecker, 'Diplomatischer Schutz der Staatsangehörigen des geteilten Polens und Danzigs durch Besatzungsmacht oder Exilregierung von 1939–1945, insbesondere in Ostpolen, Shanghai und Mauritius' (1984) 22 *AVR* 172–94. See also the decision of the US Court of Appeals in *Delany* v. *Moraitis*: '[Governments in exile] are true governments set up and organized to protect the interests of their nationals' (136 F.2d 129 at 131 (4th Cir. 1943)).

474 OLG Düsseldorf, 30 Apr. 1964 [1964] RzW 467 at 467, affirmed by BGH, 2 Mar. 1966 [1966] RzW 367. See also BGH, 12 July 1963 [1964] RzW 79. On the relation between nationality and diplomatic protection in general, see Brownlie, n. 71 above, 402–3.

German courts held that the diplomatic protection of the nationals and residents of the Free City of Danzig outside the territory of the Axis Powers rested solely with the Polish Government in exile, which in some cases in fact granted such protection.[475]

In order to protect their nationals abroad recognized governments in exile have, *inter alia*, provided consular representation, lodged protests,[476] made arrangements for their deportation,[477] and concluded amnesty agreements.[478]

Once, and so long as, an authority in exile is recognized as the State's government the authority *in situ* has no *locus standi* to protect the State's nationals in the recognizing State. The case of the French puppet government at Sigmaringen, Germany, may serve as an example. On 20 October 1944 Germany refused to consent to the protection of French interests in Germany by Switzerland on behalf of the Provisional Government of the French Republic in Paris on the ground that it still recognized Marshal Pétain (who was, in fact, a prisoner at Sigmaringen) as Head of State of France.[479] Conversely, so long as the authority *in situ* is recognized as the government of the State it may, in principle, protect the State's nationals abroad even against actions of the authority in exile.[480]

Due to the strong Algerian community in Tunisia, the question of consular protection of Algerian nationals in Tunisia by the Provisional Revolutionary Government of the Algerian Republic (GPRA) was discussed with

[475] BGH, 17 Oct. 1962 [1963] RzW 228; KG, 6 Jan. 1975 [1979] RzW 16 at 18. On the latter case, see Lichtenstein, 'Der Fall Mauritius. Ein Nachspiel' [1979] RzW 204–7. By Art. 2(1) of the Convention between Poland and the Free City of Danzig, signed at Paris on 9 Nov. 1920, Poland had undertaken the conduct of the foreign relations of the Free City of Danzig as well as the protection of its nationals abroad (6 LNTS 187). See also Art. 104(6) of the Treaty of Peace between Allied and Associated Powers and Germany, signed at Versailles, 28 June 1919 (112 BFSP 1). See also Hecker, n. 473 above, at 190–3.

[476] On 15 May 1916 the Belgian Government in Le Havre sent a note to the Government of Spain, which was representing Belgian interests with the German authorities, and the Government of the USA protesting against the forced call-up of Belgian nationals resident in Germany ((1916) 43 *JDI* 1448).

[477] Cf. *Delany* v. *Moraitis*, 136 F.2d 129 (4th Cir. 1943). On the deportation of nationals to their government in exile, see also the note on the reversed judgment *Moraitis* v. *Delany*, 46 F.Supp. 425 (1942), in (1942) 42 *Col. LR* 1343–6.

[478] See e.g. the Protocol attached to the Agreement between the USSR and Poland, signed in London on 30 July 1941, which provides for an 'amnesty to all Polish citizens now detained on the territory of the Union of Soviet Socialist Republics, either as prisoners of war or on other sufficient grounds' (Soviet For. Pol. I, 81–2). This agreement freed about 1.5 million Poles detained in the Soviet Union after the occupation of the eastern part of Poland by Soviet troops (*NY Times*, 10 Mar. 1992, Sec. D, 24). See also Marek, n. 10 above, 445–6.

[479] DDS XV, nos 222, 238, 264.

[480] For the consular protection of a French national detained on a Free French Ship in Sydney Harbour by the acting Consul-General of the French Government at Vichy in Australia, see *In re Captain Ortoli* (1942) 59 WN 146. On (Vichy) French consular representation in Australia, see DAFP IV, nos 191, 250, 369, 463. Australia withdrew the exequatur of the (Vichy) French Consul on 7 Dec. 1942 (*ibid.* VI, no 107).

the Tunisian Government on several occasions.[481] In these discussions the GPRA held the view that 'the recognition of the GPRA imposed on us a consular duty towards our compatriots'.[482] It may have been for this reason that the Government of Tunisia, which on 19 September 1958 had recognized the GPRA, in February 1959 at first objected to any contact between the French Consul-General and two detainees which it regarded as Algerian nationals. Tunisia finally rescinded its decision and authorized the French Consul-General to visit the two detainees, but only after it had allowed them to 'choose' between French and Algerian nationality and they had opted for French nationality.[483]

Recognized Governments in exile have regularly furnished those of their nationals who applied for them with passports and other identity documents, thereby protecting them from being treated as if they were stateless.[484] Such documents, however, have validly been issued or extended not only by authorities in exile recognized as governments but also by authorities in exile recognized in some other, lesser capacity.[485] Thus, on 10 July 1941 the British Dominions Secretary, Viscount Caldecote, wrote to the Canadian Secretary of State for External Affairs, Mr Mackenzie King:

His Majesty's Government in the United Kingdom have now decided to accept as valid passports issued by Free French Headquarters in London and by Free French Naval Mission at Brazaville. Though renewals of existing French passports by Free French representatives abroad will be recognized, only two authorities mentioned

[481] In Aug. 1960 some 300,000 Algerian refugees lived in Tunisia and Morocco ((1962) 5/1–2 *Freies Algerien* 1).

[482] ARA no 95, 447–58 at 454 (translation supplied).

[483] See Bedjaoui, n. 19 above, 106–9; *NY Times*, 20 Feb. 1959, 2, 15 Feb. 1959, 24, and 27 Feb. 1959, 6. On problems with Tunisia in the field of consular relations, see ARA no 86, 394–404 at 398. It is also of interest to note that with the establishment of the Government of Free India, all non-resident Indians in Burma, as elsewhere in Southeast Asia, became subjects of that Government, i.e. came under the jurisdiction of that Government (Becka, 'Subhas Chandra Bose and the Burmese Freedom Movement' in Bose (ed.), *Netaji and India's Freedom* (1975), 54–68 at 60).

[484] On passports issued by governments in exile, see Engers, 'The United Nations Travel and Identity Document for Namibians' (1971) 65 *AJIL* 571–8 at 571–2. On passports issued by the GPRA, see Bedjaoui, n. 19 above, 103–5; Favrod, n. 390 above, 166. On the need of Belgian refugees in France to obtain passports from the Belgian Government at Le Havre in order to leave France, see (1916) 43 *JDI* 106.

[485] The Entente Powers accepted passports and identity certificates issued by the Polish National Committee. See Mattern, n. 71 above, 37; Jumeau, n. 243 above, 120; Sperduti, n. 100 above, at 405. See also Art. 7 of the Agreement of 3 Sept. 1918 between the British Government and the Czecho-Slovak National Council: 'His Majesty's Government will recognize the passports issued by the Czecho-Slovak National Council or by its duly authorized representatives' ([1918] I FRUS Supp. 1, 844–5 at 845). On the (alleged) acceptance of a diplomatic passport issued by the 'Spanish Republican Government in exile' by British, French, and US authorities in spite of the fact that none of those countries had recognized that 'government', see Alvarez del Vayo, *The Last Optimist* (1950), 364. On the acceptance by Belgium of travel documents issued by various unrecognized 'governments in exile', see (1968) 4 *RBDI* 293–4.

will be regarded as competent to issue new passports, as they are in a position to ensure that these will be issued only after adequate scrutiny.[486]

However, this was only justified because the French Government at Vichy, which was still recognized by most States including the United Kingdom as the Government of France,[487] refused to protect French nationals who had rallied to the Free French Movement[488] and had even formally deprived some of them of their French nationality.[489] If there is a recognized government *in situ* which maintains diplomatic or consular relations with the accepting State and which is willing to accord protection to its nationals the acceptance of passports issued or extended by an authority in exile will constitute interference in the internal affairs of the foreign State. States, thus, did not accept passports and other documents issued or prolonged by the Polish Government in London after they had recognized the Polish Provisional Government of National Unity at Warsaw.[490]

[486] DCER VIII, no 445, at 614–15. See also *ibid.*, nos 444, 446. On 17 Aug. 1942 it was announced that the validity of Fighting French passports had been recognized by all Governments of the British Commonwealth, Belgium, China, Costa Rica, Cuba, Egypt, Guatemala, Haiti, Iceland, the Netherlands, Panama, Persia, Salvador, the USSR, the USA, and Uruguay, and that special travel facilities to holders of Fighting French credentials would be given by Chile, Columbia, Mexico, and Peru ([1942] *Keesing's* 5318A). On 27 Mar. 1943 Ecuador announced the acceptance of Fighting French passports but stressed that this was not to imply diplomatic recognition of Fighting France ([1943] *Keesing's* 5696B).

[487] On the UK, see Woodward, n. 15 above, i, 327 and 402, n. 1. Australia and New Zealand terminated consular relations with the French Government at Vichy only on 2 Dec. 1942 and 17 Nov. 1942, respectively (RIIA *Chronology of the Second World War* (1947), 2 Dec. 1942 and 17 Nov. 1942). On 8 Nov. 1942 the French Government at Vichy and the US Government severed diplomatic relations ([1943] II FRUS 88).

[488] These nationals thereby becoming '*de facto* stateless'. See in this connection also Decree 45–766 of 15 Mar. 1946 of the Provisional Government of the French Republic which provided for the issuing by French authorities of identity documents to Spanish Republican refugees 'with regard to whom it is established, that in law or in fact they do not enjoy the protection of the Spanish State' ((1940–6) 35 *RCDI* 340–1, translation supplied).

[489] See Art. I of the 'Act on the forfeiture of French nationality', published in the *Journal Officiel* at Vichy on 24 July 1940, which provided that every Frenchman who left the French metropolitan territory between 10 May and 30 June 1940 'without regular instructions issued by the competent authority or without a legitimate motive, will be considered as having intended to escape his obligations and duties towards the national community and consequently as having renounced French nationality'. According to Art. II the expatriation may include women and children (Oppenheimer, 'Governments and Authorities in Exile' (1942) 36 *AJIL* 568–95 at 573). See also Flory, n. 149 above, 209–11. This decree was, however, given no effect by the US courts. See *Bollack* v. *Société Générale*, 33 NYS2d 986 (1942), reversing 30 NYS2d 83 (1941). It is also of interest to note in this connection that after France had capitulated French nationals resident in the UK which did not adhere to the Free French Movement lost their privileged status as allies and became aliens (Cassin, n. 209 above, at 104).

[490] See Marek, n. 10 above, 537; Iwańska, n. 232 above, 60.

5

Jurisdiction

1 INTRODUCTION

In the present context jurisdiction refers to particular aspects of the general legal authority[1] of States usually referred to as sovereignty. It denotes the legislative, judicial, and executive authority of States under international law over persons, property, and events.[2] As jurisdiction refers to the legal authority of *States*, only authorities in exile recognized as representative of the State's sovereign authority, i.e. as governments, may exercise the State's jurisdiction in the recognizing State. The importance of recognition for the exercise of jurisdiction was emphasized by the Court of Appeal of Rome in *In re Savini* (1927).[3] The Court which had to decide the legality of a dentist's diploma signed by the 'Interior Minister' of the unrecognized Montenegrin Government at Rome[4] stated:

> The Government of such a State, however, in order to be able to exercise the rights of sovereignty derived from the principle of extraterritoriality with regard to its political and administrative functions, free from interference on the part of the judicial authorities of the foreign State, must enjoy *full and formal recognition*.[5]

However, while full recognition of an authority in exile as a government is the basic precondition for the exercise of jurisdiction within the recognizing State, recognition does not establish that jurisdiction. In *State of the Netherlands* v. *Federal Reserve Bank of New York* (1951), Goddard DJ held that 'the mere fact that our [i.e. the US] government recognized The Netherlands Government-in-exile does not confer upon the Netherlands Government-in-exile jurisdiction which did not exist',[6] and *In re Amand* (1941) Viscount Caldecote CJ held that the Netherlands Government did

[1] The terms 'authority', 'competence', and 'power' are used interchangeably by courts and writers.

[2] Cf. Brownlie, *Principles of Public International Law* (4th edn., 1990), 298; Akehurst, *A Modern Introduction to International Law* (6th edn., 1987), 104. See also the *Lotus Case* (1927), PCIJ, Ser. A, No 10, at 19.

[3] (1927–8) 4 AD No 106, at 166–7.

[4] After the death of King Nicholas in Mar. 1921 the seat of the no longer recognized Montenegrin Government in exile was transferred from France to Italy.

[5] N. 3 above.

[6] 99 F.Supp. 655 at 660 (SDNY 1951), reversed on other grounds, 201 F.2d 455 (2d Cir. 1953).

not by its recognition 'acquire any powers over Netherlands subjects not otherwise possessed by it according to Netherlands law'.[7] It is therefore important to distinguish in the following between the *existence* of jurisdiction, which depends on the governmental status of an authority in exile under international law, and the *exercise* of jurisdiction in a foreign State, which depends upon recognition of the authority in exile as a government by that State.[8] Thus, an unrecognized government in exile that qualifies as a government in international law possesses jurisdiction by virtue of its governmental status, but for lack of recognition of that status it will not be able to exercise that jurisdiction in the non-recognizing States. This becomes clear from the fact that authorities in exile have been able to exercise jurisdiction in one State but not in another, depending on their recognition by the respective State as governments. As there is little State practice of authorities in exile not recognized as governments attempting to exercise jurisdiction in a foreign State, the following examination will mainly concentrate on the question to what extent authorities in exile recognized as governments have been allowed to exercise jurisdiction in their host State. By establishing what jurisdiction recognized governments in exile have been allowed to exercise the extent of the existing jurisdiction is hoped to emerge. Unless otherwise indicated, in this Chapter the term 'government in exile' therefore refers to *authorities in exile recognized as governments*.

ANC?

2 EXERCISE OF JURISDICTION IN THE HOST STATE

(1) *Existence of Jurisdiction*

Governments in exile do not exercise jurisdiction derived from the host State but exercise their (State's) *own* jurisdiction in the host State.[9] This becomes clear in the *Allied Forces (Czechoslovak) Case* (1942), where the Czechoslovak Military Court of Appeal in London emphasized that '[A] Czechoslovak court cannot derive its power to exercise jurisdiction *as a Czechoslovak court* from any source other than one of Czechoslovak law.'[10] The wording of some British Acts and Orders concerning the jurisdiction of the military and maritime courts of the Allied Governments in exile in the

[7] [1941] 2 KB 239 at 252.

[8] See also Janke, 'Rechtsnatur und Rechtsstellung der Regierung im Exil', doctoral thesis (University of Hamburg, 1954), 36.

[9] Reut-Nicolussi, 'Exilregierung' in *Staatslexikon* (6th edn., 1959), iii, 209–12 at 211; Drucker, 'The Legislation of the Allied Powers in the United Kingdom' [1942] *CYBIL* 45–59 at 53; Schwelb, 'The Competence of Foreign Governments Instituted in Great Britain over Civil Persons, In Particular the Allied Powers (Maritime Courts) Act, 1941' [1942] *CYBIL* 198–201 at 198.

[10] (1941–2) 10 AD No 31, 123–8 at 124, italics added. See also s. 1(1) of the Allied Forces Act 1940, which provides that the service courts and authorities of any foreign Powers allied with His Majesty may 'exercise . . . within the United Kingdom . . . all such powers as are conferred upon them by the law of that Power' (3 & 4 Geo. 6, c. 51).

United Kingdom during the Second World War is misleading in so far as they speak of 'conferred powers' or 'conferred jurisdiction'.[11] This legislation was not intended to confer British jurisdiction on these courts but to confer on them the right to exercise their State's own jurisdiction in the United Kingdom.[12] This becomes clear from a parliamentary statement of the Lord Chancellor. Moving the Second Reading of the Allied Powers (Maritime Courts) Bill, Viscount Simon stated: 'We are not setting up a new jurisdiction. We are making arrangements by which the old jurisdiction of the Netherlands Court, which they ought to exercise but cannot for practical reasons exercise in the Netherlands capital, may be exercised in this country.'[13] However, this is true only for recognized governments in exile. Authorities in exile not recognized as the government of another State can only exercise the jurisdiction conferred by the host State. This may be illustrated by the following examples.

(i) *Free French.* The Free French authority in the United Kingdom, i.e. General de Gaulle,[14] was not recognized by the British (or any other) Government as the Government of France.[15] Its disciplinary jurisdiction over the members of the Free French volunteer force in the United Kingdom which had been referred to on occasions as 'the private army of General de Gaulle'[16] or even as a 'private club'[17] therefore could not, unlike that of the recognized governments in exile, be based on the personal sovereignty of the French State over its nationals but only on British territorial sovereignty. Indeed, the

[11] Cf. s. 1(1) of the Allied Powers (Maritime Courts) Act 1941 (4 & 5 Geo. 6, c. 21); and s. 1(5) of the Schedule to the Allied Forces (Application of 23 Geo. 5, c. 6) (No 1) Order 1940 (S.R. & O. 1940 No 1818).

[12] Wolff, 'The International Position of Dispossessed Governments at Present in England' (1943) 6 *MLR* 208–15 at 210; Mattern, *Die Exilregierung* (1953), 60. But *contra*, King, 'Jurisdiction over Friendly Foreign Armed Forces' (1942) 36 *AJIL* 539–67 at 557; and Schwelb, 'The Status of the United States Forces in English Law' (1944) 38 *AJIL* 50–73 at 56–8, who therefore criticize the British legislative acts on this point.

[13] HL Debs., vol. 119, cols. 289–90, 21 May 1941. See also the statements of the Attorney-General, Sir Donald Somervell (HC Debs., vol. 371, col. 1316, 15 May 1941) and of the Secretary of State for the Home Department, Mr Herbert Morrison (*ibid.*, vol. 371, col. 1105, 13 May 1941).

[14] Cf. the preamble to the Allied Forces (Application of 23 Geo. 5, c. 6) (No 2) Order 1941: S.R. & O. 1941 No 47.

[15] During the debate on the Allied Forces Bill, the Joint Under-Secretary of State for War, Sir Edward Grigg, said: 'we have also recognized in General de Gaulle not a sovereign Government, but an authority recognized as representing the feeling and faith of free Frenchmen outside occupied France' (HC Debs., vol. 364, col. 1351, 21 Aug. 1940). On the British recognition of General de Gaulle, as 'leader of all Free Frenchmen wherever they may be', see also *ibid.*, vol. 374, col. 149, 10 Sept. 1941.

[16] See the judgment of Sir Gervais Rentoul, sitting as magistrate in *In re Scellier* (1945) 9 *J.Crim. Law* 169–72 at 172.

[17] HC Debs., vol. 364, col. 1400, 21 Aug. 1940. On the status of the French Volunteer Forces in 1940, see also De Gaulle, *War Memoirs* (1955), i, 94; Cassin, 'Vichy or Free France' (1941) 20 *For. Affairs* 102–12 at 104. According to Dr. Janke General de Gaulle was to be regarded as 'Commander of a British unit' (n. 8 above, 61, 64).

question was whether the members of the Free French volunteer force were still French nationals. Point III.6 of the Agreement of 7 August 1940 between the British Prime Minister, Mr Churchill, and General de Gaulle concerning the organization, employment, and conditions of service of the French Volunteer Force provided that 'His Majesty's Government in the United Kingdom will use their best endeavours, at the time of conclusion of peace, to help the French volunteers to regain any rights, including national status, of which they may have been deprived as a result of their participation in the struggle against the common enemy'.[18] It is therefore argued that the jurisdiction exercised by the Free French military courts in the United Kingdom was in fact conferred British and not French jurisdiction. This becomes clear from the British Allied Forces Act 1940,[19] which makes provision for the exercise of disciplinary jurisdiction over foreign armed forces in the United Kingdom. The Act distinguishes in section 1 between the forces of a foreign 'government' in exile and those of a foreign 'authority' such as the Free French. While the military courts and authorities of the recognized governments in exile were allowed to exercise the disciplinary powers conferred upon them by the law of their country, the Free French military courts were not allowed to exercise disciplinary powers conferred by French law but only those conferred upon them by order of the Free French authority '*made with the concurrence of the British Admiralty or a Secretary of State*'.[20] While several Orders made after the British recognition of the CFLN as 'the body qualified to ensure the conduct of the French effort in the war within the framework of inter-Allied co-operation'[21] on 26 August 1943 referred to the '*forces of France* under the control of that Committee',[22] it is argued that, despite this politically motivated change in terminology, the CFLN legally still exercised British territorial (and not French personal) sovereignty over the members of the French volunteer force in the United Kingdom, as the British Government was not prepared to allow the CFLN to exercise French personal sovereignty which could have been exercised only by an authority recognized as the Government of France. Thus, on 19 June 1943 the British Foreign Secretary,

[18] Parl. Pap. France No 2 (1940), Cmd. 6220. Point II.1 of the Agreement said: 'The force will, as far as possible, retain the character of a French force.'

[19] 3 & 4 Geo. 6, c. 51.

[20] See s. 1(2) of the Act. On the military courts of the Allied Governments in exile in the UK in general, see Kuratowski, 'International Law and the Naval, Military and Air Force Courts of Foreign Governments in the United Kingdom' (1942) 28 *Grot. Soc.* 1–25.

[21] Woodward, *British Foreign Policy in the Second World War* (1971), ii. 459.

[22] See the French Visiting Forces (United Kingdom) Order of 24 Sept. 1943 (S.R. & O. 1943 No 1379). See also the Allied Forces (French Air Force) Order of 24 Sept. 1943 (S.R. & O. 1943 No 1381) modifying the Allied Forces (Free French Air Force) Order 1941 (S.R. & O. 1941 No 260).

Mr Eden, wrote in a minute to Prime Minister Churchill with respect to possible dealings with the newly formed CFLN: 'we should take care that we do not invest the Committee with attributes belonging only to the fully recognized Governments of sovereign States'.[23] This view is also supported by the following passage in a paper, dated 13 July 1943, written by Prime Minister Churchill for his Cabinet colleagues: 'we passed an Act of Parliament [in 1940] *investing* de Gaulle with powers of discipline over the Free French forces in British territory, and certainly these powers must now be vested in the new Committee'.[24]

(ii) *Czechoslovak National Committee.* The military courts of the autonomous Czechoslovak Army which was reconstituted by the Czechoslovak National Committee on French territory in 1939–40 were in the same position as the Free French courts. As the Czechoslovak National Committee in Paris was not recognized by the French Government as the Government of Czechoslovakia, but only as 'qualified to represent the Czecho-Slovak peoples',[25] these military courts could exercise only conferred French territorial and not Czechoslovak personal jurisdiction over the members of the Czecho-Slovak volunteer force.[26] Dr Fisher, Judge, Public Prosecutor, and President of the Military Court of the Czechoslovak Army during the Second World War, has pointed out that 'the Czechoslovak Military Courts in France in 1940 were Czechoslovak only in respect to language and the circumstances that the judges were Czechoslovak military persons'.[27] Thus, the French Military Code was applied to members of the Czechoslovak volunteer force, appeals were to be decided by superior French courts, and the right to mercy was reserved to the appropriate French authorities.[28]

In view of the legal principle *nemo plus iuris transferre potest quam ipse habet* (no-one can transfer a greater right than he himself has), the conferring of jurisdiction by the host State on an authority in exile not recognized as a government finds its limit in the host State's own jurisdiction. Thus

[23] N. 21 above, ii, 444.

[24] Churchill, *The Second World War* (1954), v, 136–7 at 136. See also the view of the Foreign Secretary, Mr Eden, that British recognition of the CFLN did not give much more in the way of recognition than had been given to the former Fighting French National Committee (Woodward, n. 21 above, ii, 447).

[25] *Four Fighting Years* (1943), 178; Schwelb, 'Legislation in Exile: Czechoslovakia' (1942) 24 *JCL* 120–4 at 123.

[26] See Art. IV(b) of the Military Agreement Regarding the Reconstruction of the Czechoslovak Army in France, signed at Paris, 2 Oct. 1939; and the Decree on the organization of the administration of justice with regard to the Czechoslovak military authorities in France of 1 Apr. 1940.

[27] Fisher, 'Czechoslovak Military Courts in France and Great Britain During World War II' in Ewing and Fisher (eds.), *Czechoslovak Military Justice Abroad During the Second World War* (1975), 7–14 at 8–9.

[28] *Ibid.*, 8.

actions which are within the exclusive jurisdiction of a foreign State can only be performed by that State's government. Some of these actions may be identified by comparing the jurisdiction exercised by the various Free French authorities[29] which were not recognized as governments and thus could exercise only jurisdiction conferred by their host State with the jurisdiction exercised by recognized governments in exile.

(i) *Call up of nationals*. The Free French authorities, unlike authorities in exile recognized as governments,[30] were not allowed to call up or conscript French nationals into a French Army. While the legal position is not at all clear on the question whether States may require aliens to serve in their own armed forces,[31] it seems impossible that a State can make, by its law, a foreign national a member of a foreign armed force. In *Re de Bruijn* (1941), Fisher J pointed out that 'it is the law of the foreign Power alone that can make a man a member of the military forces of a foreign Power'.[32] According to Article I.1 of the Exchange of Letters between the British Prime Minister and General de Gaulle of 7 August 1940 the latter was 'engaged in raising a French force composed of volunteers'. Only on 5 July 1944, i.e. after the CFLN had adopted on 3 June 1944 the name 'Provisional Government of the French Republic', two decrees of 24 January and 21 April 1944 were made public, whereby all Frenchmen and Frenchwomen resident abroad were made liable to call up for service with the French Armed Forces.[33] These decrees were (indirectly) given effect in the United Kingdom by The Allied Powers (War Service) (No 3) Order of 10 August 1944, which was to apply as at 1 September 1944, section 1 of the Allied Powers (War Service) Act 1942 (which imposed on allied nationals to whom the section applied liability for service under the British National Service Acts 1940 to 1941, in default of service in their own countries' forces) to French nationals.[34] That effect was given to the call up decrees of the CFLN by the United Kingdom prior to its recognition of the Committee as the 'Provisional Government of France'[35] on 23 October 1944 may be explained by the fact that on

[29] i.e. the Free French authority of General de Gaulle (June 1940–Sept. 1941), the CNF (Sept. 1941–June 1943), and the CFLN (June 1943–June 1944).

[30] For the various call-up decrees by the recognized governments in exile, see Janke, n. 8 above, 110–11.

[31] Cf. Brownlie, n. 2 above, 520–1; Jennings and Watts (eds.), *Oppenheim's International Law* (9th edn., 1992), i, 908–9.

[32] [1942] 1 DLR 249 at 257. See also *In re Amand* [1941] 2 KB 239 at 255.

[33] [1944] *Keesing's* 6568.

[34] On the previous non-application of this Act to the Free French authorities, see HC Debs., vol. 380, cols. 2198, 2199, 25 June 1942. On the voluntary service of members of the Free French movement in the USA in the forces of Fighting France, see *In re Bonchage's Petition*, 177 F.Supp. 887 at 895–6 (SDNY 1959).

[35] [1944] *Keesing's* 6767A.

10 August 1944 when the Order in question was made, the British Government had already decided to accord recognition and thought that the announcement of that decision was imminent. As the British Government, however, wanted to accord recognition in concert with the United States the announcement of British recognition was unduly delayed as US President Roosevelt felt unable to recognize any Government of France until the people of France had had their free choice in the matter.[36]

(ii) *Maritime courts.* Although with ninety-two merchant vessels under their control the Free French authorities had at least as much need for maritime courts as, for example, Belgium with fifty-four or Poland with thirty-two merchant vessels under their control.[37] But as the United Kingdom itself could not establish *French* courts it also could not confer that power on the Free French authorities. By section 1 of the Allied Powers (Maritime Courts) Act 1941,[38] the British Government could by Order in Council enable foreign 'Powers' to establish in the United Kingdom their own maritime courts for the trial and punishment of certain offences committed by persons other than British subjects on board their merchant ships. By Orders in Council the British Government enabled in 1941 all the seafaring recognized Governments in exile (with the exception of Yugoslavia) to establish such courts.[39] That the British Government prior to its recognition of the CFLN as the Provisional Government of France, by Order in Council on 29 June 1944,[40] finally allowed that authority to establish French maritime courts in the United Kingdom may again be explained by the fact that the British Government had been willing to recognize the CFLN as the Provisional Government of France since early June 1944 but delayed that recognition in order to act in concert with the United States.[41] It may be added in this connection that the merchant ships under the control of Free French authorities even had to be added to the British ship register, as the Free French

[36] See Woodward, *British Foreign Policy in the Second World War* (1962), 264.

[37] (1941) 4 *Free Europe* 195. The figures given for the Allied Governments are: Norway (719), the Netherlands (480), Greece (240), Belgium (54), Poland (32). To these must be added Yugoslavia (48). See Oppenheimer, 'Governments and Authorities in Exile' (1942) 36 *AJIL* 568–95 at 594, n. 137. On the Norwegian merchant fleet 1939–42, see Royal Norwegian Government Information Office, *Norway's Floating Empire* (1942), 26–30.

[38] 4 & 5 Geo. 6, c. 21.

[39] See S.R. & O. 1941 Nos 797–801. For the non-application of the Act to the Free French authorities, see the parliamentary statements of British Government officials: HC Debs., vol. 371, cols. 1292, 1295, 15 May 1941. For the view that only a sovereign power and not General de Gaulle could establish maritime courts, see also Schwelb, n. 9 above, at 199.

[40] Order in Council Applying s. 1(2) of the Allied Powers (Maritime Courts) Act to France, 1941: S.R. & O. 1944 No 824.

[41] Cf. Woodward, n. 36 above, 260–70.

authorities, not being recognized as a government, could not, unlike the recognized governments in exile, keep the French ship register.[42]

(iii) *Issue of currency*. As, apart from a belligerent occupant, only the government of a State may issue the national currency, unlike the recognized governments in exile for their State,[43] the Free French authorities were not allowed to authorize the printing of French franc notes for the use of the Allied liberating forces in metropolitan France. It was pointed out on 14 May 1944 by the Acting US Representative to the CFLN at Algiers that the issuance of currency was a sovereign privilege to be exercised by the State's government.[44] As the United States was not prepared to recognize the CFLN as the Government of France, the United States itself printed 80 billion 'supplementary francs' (without imprimatur of any French authority) for the use of the Allied forces. By a currency proclamation of the Commander-in-Chief of the Allied Expeditionary Forces, General Eisenhower, these supplementary francs were declared legal tender in liberated France.[45] That only recognized governments in exile have jurisdiction to authorize the printing of currency was also confirmed more recently by the United States Court of Appeals in *United States* v. *Grosh* (1965), where the defendant was found guilty of counterfeiting Cuban peso notes despite his claim of having printed the notes with the authority of the Cuban Government in exile, an authority not recognized as such by the United States.[46]

The exercise of jurisdiction by a recognized government in exile in the host State may give the impression that it has 'more' jurisdiction than if it were *in situ*. However, an exiled government does not possess more powers abroad than it has at home, it may only be allowed by the host State to

[42] The seafaring governments in exile, on the other hand, had retained their own national registers. Only in Dec. 1943 were the French ships on the British register allowed to fly their own flag by virtue of the Registration of Government Ships (Minister of War Transport) (Provisional) Order, amending the existing law which required all ships on the British register to fly the Red Ensign ([1943] *Keesing's* 6178C; S.R. & O. 1943 (vol. I, 621)). Cf. also Art. 5 of the Geneva Convention on the High Seas (HSC) 1958 and Art. 91 of UNCLOS 1982.

[43] e.g. the Soviet–Czechoslovak Monetary Agreement of 14 July 1944 provided that, at the request of the Czechoslovak Government, the Soviet authorities were printing a limited sum of new Czechoslovak currency for use by the Soviet liberating forces. See [1944] *Keesing's* 6618C; (1944) 10 *Free Europe* 14. For the printing of currency by the Belgian Government in exile, see *Daily Telegraph*, 29 June 1944, 6.

[44] [1944] III FRUS 683–5 at 684.

[45] On the issue of French francs for the Allied liberation forces, see also [1944] III FRUS 699–714, and Woodward, n. 36 above, 267, n. 1.

[46] 342 F.2d 141 at 143 (2nd Cir. 1965), cert. denied 85 S.Ct. 1767. On US non-recognition of the 'Government of Cuba in Arms-in-Exile', see Whiteman (ed.), *Digest of International Law* (1968), vi, 354–5; and *The Times*, 9 Oct. 1961, 10.

exercise in its territory, by way of comity, more of these existing powers than usual, because of the special circumstances.[47] Thus it was pointed out by Wrottesly J in *In re Amand (No 2)* (1942) that the recognized Dutch Government in London could not legislate for Great Britain or for persons living in Great Britain 'to any greater extent than it could do when in the Kingdom of Holland'.[48]

(2) *Consent of the Host State*

It follows from the principle of territorial sovereignty that a State may exercise jurisdiction in the territory of another State only with the latter's consent.[49] In *Boguslawski* v. *Gdynia-Ameryka Linie* (1950) Denning LJ, referring to the Polish Government in London, observed, obiter, that 'no other government can exercise acts of sovereignty here except with our consent'.[50] This consent may be either express or implied. According to a principle of customary international law, the permission given by a State for the armed forces of a friendly foreign State to enter its territory implies its consent to the exercise of jurisdiction over members of the armed forces by their own military courts and authorities in matters concerning discipline and internal administration.[51] It is argued by analogy that the invitation of a recognized government of a foreign State to establish its seat within the host State's territory or the recognition of a group of exiles that has already established its seat there as the government of a foreign State implies the consent of the host State to the exercise by that government of its State's

[47] Mattern, n. 12 above, 63; Schwelb, n. 9 above, 198–201 at 198.

[48] [1942] 1 All ER 236 at 242 (KBD).

[49] Cf. *Corfu Channel Case*, ICJ Rep. 1949, 4 at 35 and 76 (dissenting opinion of Judge Krylov); *Island of Palmas Arbitration* (1928), 2 RIAA 829–71 at 838; *The Lotus* (1927), PCIJ, Ser. A, No 10 at 18–19. On the requirement of consent, see also *United States* v. *Deutsches Kalisyndikat Gesellschaft et al.*, 31 F.(2d) 199 at 203 (SDNY 1929); *Kingdom of Belgium* v. *Albrecht and Willem Wannijn* (1953) 20 ILR 28–31 at 29; BVerfG, 22 Mar. 1983, BVerfGE 63, 343 at 372–3.

[50] [1951] 1 KB 162 at 180 (CA). See also the statement of Wrottesley J in *In re Amand (No 2)*: 'No one can doubt that a foreign legislature could not function here in the United Kingdom against the will of the Government, even as foreign courts could not function here in the like case' ([1942] 1 All ER 236 at 242 (KBD)). Cf. also McNair and Watts, *The Legal Effects of War* (4th edn., 1966), 425; Dahm, *Völkerrecht* (1958) i, 252; Oppenheimer, n. 37 above, at 594; Wolff, n. 12 above, at 209; Travers, *Le droit pénal international et sa mise en œuvre en temps de paix et en temps de guerre* (1920), i, 245.

[51] Barton, 'Foreign Armed Forces: Immunity from Supervisory Jurisdiction' (1949) 26 *BYBIL* 380–413 at 412; King, n. 12 above, at 547. See in this connection also HC Debs., vol. 364, col. 1395, 21 Aug. 1940; *ibid.*, vol. 364, col. 1405, 21 Aug. 1940. On jurisdiction over the members of the Allied Armed Forces in Great Britain, in general, see Schwelb, 'The Jurisdiction over the Members of the Allied Forces in Great Britain' [1942] *CYBIL* 147–71. It should, however, be noted that foreign forces *serving with a unit of the host State* may be subjected to the military jurisdiction of the host State. See the Allied Forces (Norwegian Air Force) Order 1941 (S.R. & O. 1941 No 918) and the Allied Forces (Polish Air Force) Order 1941 (S.R. & O. 1941 No 438).

jurisdiction within the host State.[52] Otherwise the invitation or recognition would be of no effect, as the government could not function as such. In the *Amand* cases which concerned the exercise of legislative authority by the Dutch Government in the United Kingdom the Attorney-General stated that the Dutch Government was recognized as such by the British Government and that 'it is established and exercising its [legislative, administrative, and other] functions in the United Kingdom with the assent and on the invitation of His Majesty's Government'.[53] When in 1940 the British Government recognized Dr Beneš' Czechoslovak National Council in London as the (Provisional) Government of Czechoslovakia it did so subject, *inter alia*, to the condition that the Czechoslovak Government relinquished any claim to exercise legislative authority over certain Czechoslovak nationals (in particular Sudeten Germans) and their property in the United Kingdom.[54] This condition would not have been necessary if the recognition had not, by a rule of customary international law, implied the British Government's consent to the exercise of legislative jurisdiction by the Czechoslovak Government in the United Kingdom. However, the recognition as a government or the invitation of a recognized government implies only the host State's consent to the exercise by the government of its legislative and not of its enforcement (i.e. judicial and arrest) jurisdiction in the host State. Thus, without the express consent of the host State, governments in exile have not been allowed to enforce their legislative jurisdiction in the host State by way of executive action, such as arrest of persons and seizure of property or by way of judicial action through their own courts.[55] Referring to the provisions for conscientious objectors in the laws of the Allied governments in exile, the Attorney-General, Sir Donald Somervell, said in the debate on the Allied Powers (War Service) Bill:

[52] Cf. Jumeau, *Le Refuge du Gouvernement National à l'Etranger* (1941), 72. Cf. also *In re Savini* (1927–8) 4 AD No 106, at 166–7. For the view that the offer to a recognized government to establish its seat temporarily within the host State and the acceptance of such an offer constitute an 'international accord' which entails that the government in exile is granted the right to carry out the sovereign rights of its State in the host State, see Drucker, n. 9 above, at 53. It seems, however, questionable whether the host State has the intention of binding itself by an international agreement and, if so, for what time and to what extent.

[53] *In re Amand (No 2)* [1942] 1 All ER 236 at 240 (KBD); *In re Amand* [1941] 2 KB 239 at 240. For a similar statement with respect to the Greek Government in the UK, see *Royal Hellenic Government* v. *Vergottis* (1945) 78 Ll. LR 292 at 297.

[54] See DAFP IV, no 201, 272–4 at 273–4; 692, n. 5; and DCER IX, no 1495, at 1821. This condition was maintained when in July 1941 the British Government accorded full diplomatic recognition to the Czechoslovak Government and was revoked in the second half of 1942 only after Sudeten German representatives had taken their seats in the Czechoslovak State Council, the provisional Czechoslovak parliament in exile.

[55] Cf. Wolff, n. 12 above, at 209; Oppenheimer, n. 37 above, at 586–7. See also the statement of the Under-Secretary of State for Foreign Affairs, Mr Butler: 'The Polish Government have no powers of compulsion over their nationals resident in this country' (HC Debs., vol. 352, cols. 229–30, 8 Nov. 1939).

If in any document that they send out to their nationals or any approaches they may make to them they provide for the operation here of any machinery for dealing with conscientious objectors—which would, of course, be informal because it could not be a court—it would be a matter for them.[56]

As no host State is obliged to consent to the exercise of (judicial) jurisdiction by the courts of a government in exile within its territory,[57] a host State doing so may determine how far the courts of the government in exile may exercise their jurisdiction. With respect to the fact that in certain cases in which Czechoslovak courts on Czechoslovak territory would have had jurisdiction they were not allowed to exercise this jurisdiction while on British soil, the Czechoslovak Military Court of Appeal in London stated 'This does not cause any infringement of the sovereignty of the Czechoslovak Republic since it is evident that the sovereignty of any State is unrestricted on its own territory only, while on foreign territory it naturally yields to the sovereignty of the foreign State.'[58] The British Government, by the Allied Powers (Maritime Courts) Act 1941,[59] allowed the Allied Governments in exile to set up maritime courts in the United Kingdom. The Act provided, *inter alia*, that only certain offences could be tried by these courts and only if they were committed within a certain period of time,[60] that certain sentences such as capital punishment could not be imposed, and that British subjects were excluded from their (criminal) jurisdiction.[61] In addition,

[56] HC Debs., vol. 380, col. 2201, 25 June 1942. See also the statement of the Lord Chancellor, Viscount Simon: 'It would be intolerable, of course, that the emissaries of even the most friendly Allied Power should be allowed to go about the country and summon, or it may be arrest, somebody inside our borders' (HL Debs., vol. 119, col. 288, 21 May 1941). And the Foreign Secretary, Mr Eden, said: 'In this country our own law *operates* except in so far as we have given special rights to other Governments under the Act of Parliament' (HC Debs., vol. 389, col. 1715, 27 May 1942, italics added).

[57] Cf. Menzel, 'Anerkennung' in *Staatslexikon* (6th edn., 1959), ix, 77–90 at 89; Schwelb, n. 12 above, at 58; Drucker, n. 9 above, at 53.

[58] *Allied Forces (Czechoslovak) Case* (1941–2) 10 AD No 31, 123–8 at 124. On the restrictions on the jurisdiction of the Czechoslovak military courts in Great Britain, see Hartmann, 'Restrictions on Jurisdiction of Czechoslovak Military Courts in Great Britain' in Ewing and Fisher (eds.), *Czechoslovak Military Justice Abroad During the Second World War* (1975), 15–18. See also Lord Wright's speech in *Amand* v. *Home Secretary and Minister of Defence of Royal Netherlands Government* (1942): 'this jurisdiction [of Dutch service courts] is only possible so far as it is authorized by the British legislature and can only be exercised in accordance with the statutory provisions referred to and subject to the conditions and safeguards specified by statute' ([1943] AC 147 at 159).

[59] 4 & 5 Geo. 6, c. 21. On the extent of the jurisdiction of the maritime courts, see ss. 2, 3, 4, 9.

[60] See also the Note of the British Foreign Office, dated 21 Apr. 1942, to the Czechoslovak Government in London in which it was intimated that the British Government did not permit the prosecution in the UK of members of the Czechoslovak Army for offences committed prior to 22 Aug. 1940. See Hartmann, n. 58 above, at 18; and *Allied Forces (Czechoslovak) Case* (1941–2) 10 AD No 31, 123–8 at 126–7.

[61] See the statement of the Parliamentary Secretary to the Ministry of Transport, Colonel Llewellin: 'we have excluded British citizens from their jurisdiction although, formerly, if they had been on a ship they would have been within the jurisdiction' (HC Debs., vol. 371, col. 1131, 13 May 1941). On the restrictions on the jurisdiction of the maritime courts in general, see *ibid.*, vol. 371, cols. 1110–11: 13 May 1941.

British courts were given the power to review whether in a particular case an allied maritime court had exceeded the jurisdiction which it was allowed to exercise by the Act.[62] However, the decision by the maritime courts of any question within their jurisdiction as defined by the Act was not subject to review by the British courts[63] as this would have been incompatible with the Allied State's sovereignty.

While the host State may determine how far the courts of a government in exile may exercise their jurisdiction in its territory it may not prescribe *how* that jurisdiction is to be exercised. For example, the host State may not prescribe what sentences the courts of the exiled government are to impose or what procedure they are to follow. Amendments to this effect to the Allied Powers (Maritime Courts) Bill were rejected by the Attorney General, Sir William Jowitt, who said:

> These Governments are recognized by us as sovereign Governments, and they are perhaps, all the more because of the circumstances, not unnaturally jealous to preserve their status and their privileges. It is impossible that we should ask them to submit to us a code of procedure or of sentences or anything of that sort, as though they were asking for our approval. We are enabling them to administer in our territory their laws before courts just the same way as they would have administered them in their own territories . . . Therefore, there cannot be anything which enables this House to exercise a check on these Governments as it properly does on its own Executive.[64]

The host State may, however, through diplomatic channels, ask for assurances from the government in exile that, so far as it lies within its power, certain laws are not applied or certain sentences are not imposed before consenting to the exercise of jurisdiction by its courts.[65]

3 LEGISLATIVE JURISDICTION

Legislative jurisdiction may be defined as the authority of the State under international law to regulate, usually in the form of legislation, the conduct of people or the consequences of acts and events and to define the

[62] See s. 11(2) of the Act. Limited review jurisdiction was also exercised with respect to the jurisdiction of military courts and authorities. See, e.g., *Katz* v. *Officer Commanding the Polish Forces in Palestine* (1944) 11 PLR 355.

[63] See s. 11(1) of the Act.

[64] HC Debs., vol. 371, cols. 1340–1, 15 May 1941. See also the statement of the Attorney-General, Sir Donald Somervell: 'it would be wrong and contrary to the recognized principles of comity between nations, on which this Bill is based, if we thought to dictate to these foreign countries that in the matter of the death penalty they must follow the precise provisions of our code in this year 1940' (*ibid.*, vol. 364, col. 1406, 21 Aug. 1940). For further statements to this effect by various government officials, see *ibid.*, vol. 371, col. 1112, 13 May 1941; *ibid.*, vol. 371, cols. 1282, 1287, 1339, 15 May 1941; *ibid.*, vol. 380, col. 2201, 25 June 1941. Cf. also Shaw, *International Law* (3rd edn., 1991), 397.

[65] See HC Debs., vol. 371, cols. 1154, 1287, 1339, 15 May 1941.

legal status of persons and property.[66] The State's authority to legislate must be distinguished from its authority to enforce its legislation. While a government in exile may be competent to exercise the State's legislative authority it may, due to the circumstances of its exile, temporarily be incompetent or be limited in its competence to exercise the State's enforcement authority. As there is no enforcement authority unless there is authority to legislate,[67] it is first to be examined whether and, if so, to what extent a government in exile is competent to exercise its State's legislative authority.[68] It is suggested that this depends upon two factors: the situs of the object subject to the State's legislative authority and the legal status of the authority *in situ*.

(1) Legislative Authority Inside National Territory

(a) National Territory under Belligerent Occupation

While in principle the following considerations apply to belligerent occupation in general,[69] in practice governments in exile will, as a rule, be established, and more importantly will be recognized as such only if the belligerent occupation is the result of the illegal use of force by the occupant.[70] The question whether, during occupation, the State's government in exile is competent to legislate with immediate effect for the territory under belligerent occupation by an aggressor must be distinguished from the question whether it is competent to enact laws during its exile which are to take effect only on its return home. No rule of international law impedes a government in exile in doing the latter.[71] With respect to the former, however, there seems to be no settled rule of international law. State practice is

[66] See also Jennings and Watts, n. 31 above, i, 456.

[67] See Bowett, 'Jurisdiction: Changing Patterns of Authority over Activities and Resources' (1982) 53 *BYBIL* 1–26 at 1.

[68] On the legislative activities of the various governments in exile during the Second World War, see Lachs, 'Polish Legislation in Exile' (1942) 24 *JCL* 57–60; Schwelb, n. 25 above, 120–4; Official of the Royal Norwegian Ministry of Justice and Police, 'Legislation in Exile: Norway' (1942) 24 *JCL* 125–30; Fayat, 'Legislation in Exile: Belgium' (1943) 25 *JCL* 30–40; Zeeman, 'Legislation in Exile: The Netherlands' (1944) 26 *JCL* 4–11; Oppenheimer, n. 37 above, at 584–6; Landheer, 'The Legal Status of the Netherlands' (1943) 41 *Mich. LR* 644–64 at 654–64.

[69] On the concept of belligerent occupation in general, see Bothe, 'Occupation, Belligerent' in Bernhardt (ed.), *Encyclopedia of Public International Law* (1982), iv, 64–7.

[70] The exiled government's claim to legitimacy will normally be based on the illegality of the occupation.

[71] Cf. *Public Prosecutor* v. *Reidar Haaland* (1945), (1943–5) 12 AD No 154, 444–5 at 445. See also McDougal and Feliciano, *The International Law of War* (1994), 773, n. 101. Thus, governments in exile may abrogate even the lawful legislation of the occupant with effect from the liberation of their territory. See, e.g., Art. 1 of the Luxembourg Decree of 13 July 1944: 'The measures taken by the occupant will *ipso jure* be regarded as abrogated with the liberation of the territory' (*Luxembourg. Bull.* No 20/21 (Sept./Oct. 1944), 157, translation supplied). See also Cohn, 'Legislation in Exile: Luxembourg' (1943) 25 *JCL* 40–6 at 45–6.

far from being uniform. While, for example, the Belgian Governments in exile during the First and Second World Wars claimed full legislative competence for occupied Belgian territory,[72] that claim was denied by the German occupation authorities.[73] The British colonial Government of Burma in exile at Simla, India, also claimed legislative competence for Burmese territory occupied by Japan,[74] while, at the same time, the British Government denied that competence to the Italian Government with respect to the British-occupied Italian colony of Tripolitania.[75] The opinion of writers is equally divided. While some advocate the exiled government's unrestricted legislative competence for territory under belligerent occupation by an aggressor,[76] others reject it.[77] The value of the (often inconsistent) decisions of courts is limited by the fact that the competence of a government in exile to legislate for the occupied territory is usually decided only for the specific enactment in question. In this connection it should be noted

[72] See the Report of the Belgian Ministers for King Albert I concerning the Decree-law of 8 Apr. 1917: Langenhove, *L'action du Gouvernement belge en matière économique pendant la guerre* (1927), 91–2; Drucker, n. 9 above, at 56, n. 1. See also Art. 2 of the Belgian Decree–law of 10 Jan. 1941 determining the effect of the legislative measures taken by the Belgian Government in exile: *Arrêtés de Londres*, 16–17.

[73] See the legal opinion, dated 8 Apr. 1915, of the German Secretary of State for Internal Affairs for the German Governor-General of Belgium: 'It only seems to be incompatible with the recognition of the legal effects resulting from the factual situation according to the Hague Regulations to admit the exercise of legislative authority in the occupied territory by the ousted power and its sovereign' (Ettle, 'Zur staatsrechtlichen Stellung des Königs der Belgier während der deutschen Okkupation' (1915) 20 *DJZ* 805–6 at 805, translation supplied). It is of interest to note that Germany, on the other hand, claimed legislative competence for the occupied Rhineland. See Silberschmidt, 'Über die Geltung der deutschen Gesetze in besetzten rheinischen Gebiete' (1923) 12 *RZfZuP* 211–15. See also RFH, 7 Dec. 1926 ((1927) 32 *DJZ* 232–4); RG, 29 Sept. 1921 (RGSt 56, 194); RG, 24 Oct. 1921 (RGSt 56, 196); BayVGH, 5 Dec. 1928 ((1927–8) 4 AD No 80, 119). On the Rhineland occupation after the First World War, see Zieger, 'Rhineland Occupation After World War I' in Bernhardt (ed.), *Encyclopedia of Public International Law* (1982), iv, 190–3; Fraenkel, *Military Occupation and the Rule of Law: Occupation Government in the Rhineland, 1918–1923* (1944).

[74] Cf. Schwelb, 'Legislation for Enemy-Occupied Territory in the British Empire' (1944) 30 *Grot. Soc.* 239–59 at 247–8, 250–2.

[75] Cf. Stein, 'Application of the Law of the Absent Sovereign in Territory Under Belligerent Occupation: The Schio Massacre' (1948) 46 *Mich. LR* 341–70 at 354–5.

[76] Schwelb, n. 74 above, at 258; Wold, 'Legislation Promulgated by the Norwegian Government' (1943) 1 *Norseman* 430–8 at 431; Langenhove, n. 72 above, 90; Hall, *A Treatise on International Law* (8th edn., 1924), 570–1.

[77] Schaumann, 'Exilregierung' in Strupp and Schlochauer (eds.), *Wörterbuch des Völkerrechts* (1960), i, 498–9 at 499; Sundberg, 'The War of Laws' (1958) 28 *Nord. TIR* 268–309 at 308; Charpentier, *La reconnaissance internationale et l'évolution du droit des gens* (1956), 173; Guggenheim, *Lehrbuch des Völkerrechts* (1951), ii, 925, n. 466; Hyde, *International Law* (2nd edn., 1947), iii, 1883, 1886; Spanner, 'Fragen der Verwaltung besetzer Gebiete. Unter besonderer Berücksichtigung der besetzten niederländischen Gebiete' (1944) 34 *AöR* 96–114 at 106–8; Drucker, n. 9 above, at 54; Köhler, *Die Staatsverwaltung der besetzten Gebiete,* I: *Belgien* (1927), 6; Strupp, 'Occupatio bellica' in Strupp (ed.), *Wörterbuch des Völkerrechts und der Diplomatie* (1925), ii, 154–71 at 162; Kohler, 'Review of *Das Moratoriumsrecht in Belgien* by Ernst Cohnitz' (1917–18) 10 *ZVR* 229–30 at 229; Meene, 'Die Gesetzgebungstätigkeit der verdrängten Staatsgewalt' (1917) 22 *DJZ* 825–7 at 825; Laband, *Die Verwaltung Belgiens während der kriegerischen Besetzung* (1916), 9; Dove, 'Der Rechtszustand in den okkupierten Gebieten Belgiens und Russisch-Polens' (1915) 44 *JW* 425–30 at 427.

that most cases cited by writers in support of the proposition that a government in exile has full legislative authority within its occupied national territory concerned the Belgian Decree–Law of 26 October 1914 which suspended the running of the statute of limitations for the duration of the war. In addition, the decisions of municipal courts usually deal only with the question whether the State's government in exile is competent to legislate under its constitutional law, not whether it is competent to do so under international law.[78]

It is submitted that, as there is no uniformity, either in State practice, court decisions, or the opinion of writers, the question whether and, if so, to what extent a government in exile is competent to legislate with immediate effect for the occupied territory is to be decided on principle. The government's right to exercise legislative authority rests in its State's sovereignty.[79] Since the adoption of the Hague Regulations Respecting the Laws and Customs of War on Land (HR) in 1907[80] it has generally been agreed that occupation does not transfer sovereignty over the occupied territory,[81] but, by virtue of Article 43 of HR 1907, confers upon the occupying State (only) the right to exercise provisionally some of the occupied State's authority.[82] According to the large majority of writers and the practice of States Article 43 of HR 1907 also applies in favour of an aggressor State.[83] The distinction between the retention of sovereignty by the occupied State and the

[78] Thus, the Norwegian Supreme Court stated in *Public Prosecutor* v. *Lian* (1945): 'In any case a Norwegian decree [issued by the Norwegian Government in exile during the German occupation] will as a rule be binding for Norwegian citizens even if it is at variance with international law' ((1943–5) 12 AD No 155, 445–6 at 446). Cf. also Feilchenfeld, *The International Economic Law of Belligerent Occupation* (1942), 137. See also *Re de Baudringhien* [1919] I Pas.belge 153 at 154.

[79] Cf. the *Lotus Case* (1927), PCIJ, Ser. A, No 10 at 19. In particular with respect to legislative authority, see RG, 29 Sept. 1921 (RGSt 56, 194); RG, 24 Oct. 1921 (RGSt 56, 196) See also the argument of the chief public prosecutor, M. Terlinden, in the *Geubelle* case [1919] I Pas.belge 9 at 11.

[80] 'Regulations Respecting the Laws and Customs of War on Land', annexed to the Fourth Hague Convention of 18 Oct. 1907: 100 BFSP 338.

[81] See, e.g., *Re Geubelle* [1919] I Pas.belge 9 at 15; Court of Appeal of Thrace, Judgment 21/1947 (1948) 1 RHDI 379–80; *State of the Netherlands* v. *Federal Reserve Bank of New York*, 99 F.Supp. 655 at 661 (SDNY 1951), reversed in part on other grounds, 201 F.2d 455 (2d Cir. 1953).

[82] Sauser-Hall, 'L'occupation de guerre et les droits privés' (1944) 1 *Schw. JIR* 58–125 at 70; Liszt, *Das Völkerrecht* (12th edn., 1925), 490; Huber, 'Die Fortbildung des Völkerrechts auf dem Gebiete des Prozess- und Landkriegsrechts durch die II internationalen Friedenskonferenzen im Haag 1907' (1908) 2 *JöR* 470–611 at 570–1. See also the Second protest of the Bar at the Brussels Court of Appeal, 22 Feb. 1915: 'It is hardly necessary to state that the decision taken is not a hostile act directed against the exercise by the occupant of the powers which international law and the Hague Convention confer on it' (*La Guerre de 1914–1918. Cahiers Documentaires* (1915), xx, 3–6 at 3, translation supplied). See further Court of Appeal of Thrace, Judgment 21/1947 (1948) 1 RHDI 379–80; *Procureur Général près de la Cour d'Appel de Liège* v. *Marteux, Michaux et Consorts* (1916), [1915–16] I Pas.belge 375 at 417. For the view that the occupant's position is a legal one, see also Oppenheim, *International Law. A Treatise*(7th edn., 1952), ii, 434, 436.

[83] On the application of the laws of belligerent occupation to an aggressor, see Brownlie, *International Law and the Use of Force by States* (1963), 406–8, and the references there given.

occupant's right to exercise, by virtue of international law, some of the occupied State's sovereign powers has not always been appreciated. Thus, Dutch and Belgian courts in particular have (in their post-occupation decisions)[84] regularly inferred the unlimited competence of their governments in exile to legislate for their occupied territories from the fact that their occupied States had not lost their sovereignty. For example, in *Agrocide* v. *Arsocid* (1946) the Court of Appeal of The Hague held that 'the Crown had never lost its lawful sovereignty over occupied Holland, and had undoubtedly continued to be entitled to legislate for the whole of the country',[85] and in *Re Hoogeveen et Consorts* (1944) the Belgian Court of Cassation rejected the argument that a government in exile could no longer exercise sovereign legislative authority when the territory of the State was entirely occupied by the enemy by stating that 'this claim does not find support in the principles of international law; that, on the contrary, it is a principle that the occupation of a territory by the enemy leaves intact the sovereignty of the invaded State' (author's translation).[86] While this is true in principle this view neglects that the occupying State has the right to exercise *de facto*[87] some (of the occupied State's) authority in the occupied territory and that the occupied State's authority cannot be exercised by two opposing authorities at the same time. Thus, the view advanced by Goddard DJ in *State of the Netherlands* v. *Federal Reserve Bank of New York* (1951) that 'though remaining the sovereign, the absent government may, nevertheless, be limited in its further authority to govern the subjugated areas',[88] seems to be preferable. Reconciling the legislative authority of the government in exile with the authority of the occupant, it is submitted that the State's government in exile is competent to exercise legislative authority in the occupied territory in so far as this does not conflict with the *lawful* exercise of authority by the occupant.[89] The borderline must thereby be the occupant's right to exercise authority and not whether it has actually exercised

[84] For a notable exception, see *De Nimal* v. *De Nimal* [1919] II Pas.belge 83. It is of interest to note that after the First World War, in which the Netherlands had been neutral, the District Court of Rotterdam held that the German Governor-General of Belgium, by virtue of his authority under Art. 43 of HR 1907, could lawfully 'repeal' a decree of the Belgian Government in exile introducing a moratorium for the payment of debts until the end of the war. See *Cillekens* v. *De Haas* (1919), (1919–22) 1 AD No 336, 471.

[85] (1946) 13 AD No 142, 349–50 at 350. See also *La Belgique industrielle* v. *Desmaele* (1920), [1921] I Pas.belge 177 at 178; *Re de Baudringhien* [1919] I Pas.belge 153.

[86] [1945] I Pas.belge 23 at 24.

[87] The *de facto* as the 'in fact' in Art. 43 of HR 1907 indicates that the (exercise of) authority is not based on sovereignty.

[88] 99 F.Supp. 655 at 660 (SDNY 1951), reversed in part on other grounds, 201 F.2d 455 (2d Cir. 1953).

[89] Cf. Castrén, *The Present Law of War and Neutrality* (1954), 215; Flory, *Le statut international des Gouvernements réfugiés et le cas de la France Libre 1939–1945* (1952), 113–14. For the view that the exiled government is incompetent to legislate for the occupied territory only in so far as the occupant may lawfully legislate, see McNair, 'Municipal Effects of Belligerent Occupation' (1941) 57 *LQR* 33–73 at 73; McNair and Watts, n. 50 above, 446;

authority, as otherwise the government in exile might wage a 'war of laws' against the occupant. The contrary view that the exiled government may legislate even in respect of those matters for which the occupant may lawfully legislate unless and until the latter actually does legislate in respect of them[90] fails to realize that the occupant usually implicitly 'endorses' the laws in force at the time of the occupation, thereby precluding any alteration of them by the exiled government.[91] This view is also supported by the decision in *State of the Netherlands* v. *Federal Reserve Bank of New York* (1953), where the US Court of Appeals for the Second Circuit held:

> Obviously, absentee legislation intended to interfere with the occupant's *legitimate* rule should not be given effect. Otherwise the authority vested in the occupying power by Article 43 of the Hague Regulations would become nugatory. Mere hostility to the occupant should not, however, invalidate the absent sovereign's enactments. To have such an effect the hostile legislation must be directed against those aspects of governmental control which international law vests in the occupant. In short, the legitimate sovereign should be entitled to legislate over occupied territory insofar as such enactments do not conflict with the legitimate rule of the occupying power.[92]

The question to what extent a government in exile is competent to exercise legislative authority over the occupied territory thus depends on the scope of the occupant's 'legitimate rule'. This must be determined for each individual case by reference to the relevant provisions of the international humanitarian law instruments.[93] As, for example, the occupying State has the right to regulate commercial intercourse in the occupied territory[94] a decree of an exiled government which prohibits and invalidates contracts with the enemy becomes effective in the occupied territory only on its

Feilchenfeld, n. 78 above, 135–6. This view seems too narrow, as the occupant may lawfully exercise not only legislative but also executive and judicial authority which the exiled government ought not to be entitled to interfere with by legislation.

[90] McNair and Watts, n. 50 above, 446, n. 3; Feilchenfeld, n. 78 above, 135.

[91] See e.g. the proclamation of the Commander-in-Chief of the Japanese occupation army in the Philippines of 3 Jan. 1942 that 'all the laws now in force in the Commonwealth . . . shall continue to be effective for the time being as in the past' (Perkins, 'Enemy Legislation and Judgments in the Liberated Countries: The Philippines' (1948) 30 *JCL* 17–27 at 17).

[92] 201 F.2d 455 at 462 (2d Cir. 1953), reversing in part 99 F.Supp. 655 (SDNY 1951), and affirming with different reasoning 79 F.Supp. 966 (SDNY 1948). See also the decision of the Court of Appeal of Brussels in *De Nimal* v. *De Nimal*: 'the new laws enacted by the legal authority in order to combat the occupier and to undermine its power are not applicable in the territories under belligerent occupation' ([1919] II Pas.belge 83 at 84, translation supplied).

[93] Cf. especially Arts. 42–56 of HR 1907 and Arts. 47–78 of the Fourth Geneva Red Cross Convention (GRCC) 1949. The occupant's obligation under Art. 43 of HR 1907 to 'ensure . . . public order and safety' confers upon him broad powers of regulation with respect to the occupied territory.

[94] According to Westlake the phrase 'public order and safety' used in the English translation of Art. 43 of HR 1907 does not adequately represent the meaning of 'l'ordre et la vie publique' which describes the entire social and commercial life of the country (*International Law*, Part II: *War* (2nd edn., 1913), 95).

liberation. This was confirmed in a rare decision by an international court in this area. In *Herwyn* v. *Müller* (1922) the Belgian–German Mixed Arbitral Tribunal stated:

In consideration of the fact that, on the other hand, one cannot put forward as a defence that the treaty between the parties has been annulled by the royal decree of 10 December 1916 and that, consequently, the defendant has no contractual liability;

That the contract could only be annulled at the time of the liberation of the Belgian territory in November 1918, as the royal decree was not in force in the occupied territory before that time [author's translation].[95]

The question from which date the decree of a government in exile becomes effective in the occupied territory also arose with respect to Decree No E.133 enacted on 20 October 1944 by the Dutch Government in London. Article 3 of that decree provided that all property of the enemy or of a subject of the enemy in Holland reverted to the State as from 25 October 1944. While the Court of Appeal of The Hague held that the decree came into operation in the occupied part of Holland on 25 October 1944[96] both German[97] and Canadian courts[98] held, it is submitted correctly, that the decree came into force in the Netherlands on the withdrawal of the German army. On the other hand, decrees that do not conflict with the 'legitimate rule' of the occupant are effective *ab initio* in the occupied territory, even though they can normally be implemented there only on the liberation of the territory. This will usually be the case with decrees providing for the protection of private property interests of the occupied State's nationals as the occupant, as a rule, has no right to destroy or confiscate private

[95] (1923) 2 Recueil TAM 368–71 at 370. See also OLG Cologne, 18 Feb. 1959, where the court held with respect to the Dutch Decree No A.6 of 7 June 1940, prohibiting and invalidating contracts with the enemy, that 'even if the decree was applicable to the foundation of the X-Bank in the Netherlands during the war it must be regarded as repealed for the time of its foundation as Germany exercised the territorial jurisdiction in the Netherlands from the start of the German campaign in the West to the revival of Netherlands sovereignty in 1945' ([1961] WM 183 at 184, author's translation). But, with respect to that Decree, see the contrary decisions of the Dutch courts in *Handelstrust West NV* v. *Shell-Nederland NV* [1948] NJ No 681; *Damhof* v. *State of the Netherlands* (1949) 16 AD No 155, 429–30; *Landelijke Hypotheekbank Ltd* v. *Receiver of Taxes for Amsterdam* (1950), (1949) 16 AD No 156, 430–1; *Rotterdam Bank Ltd* v. *Nederlandsch Beheers-Instituut* (1948) 15 AD No 174, 530–1, and the decision of the Dutch Supreme Court in this case, rendered in 1950(1949) 16 AD No 154, 428–9. It is of interest to note that in the different cases organs of the Dutch State contended both that the decree had no validity in occupied Holland and that it was valid there. Only in the *Nederlandsch Beheers-Instituut* cases was the question of Art. 43 of HR 1907 addressed (obiter).

[96] *Agrocide* v. *Arsocid* (1946) 13 AD No 142, 349–50 at 350.

[97] LG Düsseldorf, 14 June 1952 ([1957] RIW 225); OLG Cologne, 18 Feb. 1959 ([1961] WM 183 at 185), and BVerwG, 7 July 1977 (BVerwGE 54, 159 at 166–8).

[98] See the decision of the Ontario High Court in *Brown, Gow, Wilson et al.* v. *Beleggings-Societeit NV* (1961), 42 ILR 409.

property.[99] Thus, in *Ammon* v. *Royal Dutch Company* (1954) the Swiss Federal Tribunal held with respect to Dutch Decree No E.100 of 17 September 1944, which was aimed at protecting private property of inhabitants of the Netherlands who had lost their assets, and in particular securities, as a result of the German occupation, that 'enactments by the Head of State of the Netherlands who was resident in the United Kingdom during the war . . . applied *ab initio* to the territory occupied by the German army even though they could not be effectively implemented there until the liberation of that territory'.[100] In *State of the Netherlands* v. *Federal Reserve Bank of New York* (1953) the US Court of Appeals held that Dutch Decree No A.1 of 24 May 1940, which vested protective title in the State of the Netherlands to claims capable of being transferred outside the occupied Netherlands and belonging to persons domiciled there, to be effective *ab initio* as 'Decree A-1 does not conflict with any legitimate legislation or regulation of the occupant'.[101] The rule that laws which do not conflict with the occupant's lawful exercise of authority are effective *ab initio* in the occupied territory is of special importance with regard to changes of the occupied State's criminal law by its government in exile. Inhabitants of the occupied territory which commit acts which the exiled government is competent to prohibit may thus lawfully be prosecuted by the government on its return home. As a rule, the government in exile may enact laws which make it a criminal offence for the inhabitants of the occupied territory to commit acts which the occupant has no right to require them to do. In its decision in *Public Prosecutor* v. *Reidar Haaland* (1945),[102] the Norwegian Supreme Court stated with respect to the Norwegian decree of 3 October 1941 reintroducing the death penalty for treasonable offences to be judged after the war: 'The occupying power has no legitimate claim that the nationals of the occupied territory shall betray their country for the benefit of the occupant. Over the penalties for treasonable acts the lawful authorities therefore will have free mastery also within the occupied territory.'[103] While the occupant has the right to maintain law and order in the occupied territory, prevent attacks on its interests, and requisition certain goods and services from the inhabitants, it has no right to require them to commit treason, denounce their compatriots, or commit acts which endanger the

[99] Cf. especially Arts. 23(g), 46, 47, 52, 53(2) of HR 1907; Arts. 53, 147 of GRCC IV.

[100] BGE 80 II 53 at 64.

[101] 201 F.2d 455 at 463 (2d Cir. 1953), reversing in part 99 F.Supp. 655 at 661 (SDNY 1951).

[102] (1943–5) 12 AD No 154, 444–5.

[103] Sundberg, n. 77 above, 268–309 at 304, n. 2. On the Norwegian decree of 3 Oct. 1941, see Andenaes, Riste, and Skodvin, *Norway and the Second World War* (1966), 128–9; Official of the Royal Norwegian Ministry of Justice and Police, n. 68 above, 125–30 at 129–30; [1941] *Keesing's* 4826F. On the basis of this Decree Vidkun Quisling, the leader of the Nasjonal Samling, was on 10 Sept. 1945 sentenced to death and on 24 Oct. 1945 executed. See also *Kst. statsadvokat Annæus Schjødt, aktor mot Vidkun Quisling* [1945] Norsk Ret 109–42 at 117.

security of the occupied State. Accordingly, a government in exile may, with immediate effect in the occupied territory, make the punishment of treason more severe or introduce new treasonable offences[104] and make the giving of 'voluntary' assistance to the occupant[105] or the denunciation of compatriots a criminal offence.[106] Such laws are usually justified by the fact that the inhabitants continue to owe allegiance to their occupied State and its government in exile.[107] Other decrees which are as a rule not precluded by the legitimate rule of the occupant are decrees suspending periods of prescription and limitation in civil[108] and criminal matters[109] and decrees altering the legal status of members of a resistance movement fighting the occupant.[110]

In conclusion it may be stated that the government in exile, as the organ through which the occupied State exercises its sovereignty, is in principle

[104] The Belgian Decree–law of 7 Jan. 1943 introduced the death penalty for traitors ([1943] *Keesing's* 5594B). For the various penal law provisions ensuring the security of the State issued by the Luxembourg Government in exile, see *Luxembourg. Bull.* No 10/11 (July/Aug. 1943), 77–9. On the Norwegian Decree of 22 Jan. 1942 making membership of the Nasjonal Samling (regarded as a form of assistance to the enemy) a punishable offence and declaring the party to be a treasonable organization, see Wold, 'The 1942 Enactment for the Defence of the Norwegian State' (1942) 20 *Can. BR* 505–9; Andenaes *et al.*, n. 103 above, 132–3; [1942] *Keesing's* 5142. However, the exiled government may not declare such acts as normal trade with the enemy a treasonable offence.

[105] The Polish Decree 1006, issued by the Polish Government in Angers on 30 Nov. 1939, provided for the punishment of Polish citizens who voluntarily assisted the occupying power. See Drucker, n. 9 above, at 54–5; Lachs, n. 68 above, 57–60 at 58. See also the Burma Act No. XIX of 1943 ('The Defence of Burma (Amendment) Act 1943'), enacted by the Governor of Burma at Simla, India, which provided that any overt act towards or in furtherance of the intent to wage war against His Majesty or to assist any State at war with His Majesty shall be punished with death, or transportation for life, or imprisonment or whipping (Schwelb, n. 74 above, at 252).

[106] The Belgian Decree–law of 17 Dec. 1942, which introduced the death penalty for denunciations which led to the death of the denounced person, was given effect in the cases of *Re Bergmans* (1944), [1945] I Pas.belge 33; *Re Peereboom* (1944), [1945] I Pas.belge 54; and *Re Hoogeveen et Consorts* (1944), [1945] I Pas.belge 23. The Belgian Decree–law of 8 Apr. 1917, which made malicious denunciation to the enemy a criminal offence, was given effect to in the cases of *Re Kauhlen* (1920), [1921] I Pas.belge 99; *Re van Dieren* [1919] I Pas.belge 97, 153, affirming [1919] III Pas.belge 1; and *Re de Baudringhien* [1919] I Pas.belge 153.

[107] See *Moraitis* v. *Delany*, 46 F.Supp. 425 at 432 (D.Md. 1942); *Public Prosecutor* v. *Reidar Haaland* (1945), (1943–5) 12 AD No 154, 444–5 at 445.

[108] This was expressly affirmed for the Belgian Decree–law of 26 Oct. 1914 in *De Nimal* v. *De Nimal* [1919] II Pas.belge 83 at 84. This Decree–law was also given immediate effect, however without reference to the specific international law question, in *Vandevondeele* v. *Boxus* [1919] II Pas.belge 100; *Mutuelle des Syndicats réunis* v. *Génion* [1919] III Pas.belge 112.

[109] The Belgian Decree-law of 29 Apr. 1943 provided for the interruption of prescription in criminal matters: *Moniteur belge* (London), 8 May 1943, 174.

[110] The Netherlands Decree No E.62 of 5 Sept. 1944 gave the members of the 'Netherlands Forces of the Interior' the status of members of the Dutch Army. This Decree was given effect to in *Van Hoeve de Freyter* v. *Fire Insurance Company of 1859 Ltd* (1947) 14 AD No 81, 169–71; *State of the Netherlands* v. *B.* (1954) 21 ILR 431–2.

competent to legislate with immediate effect for the occupied territory. However, in so far as that legislation conflicts with the legitimate rule of the occupant it takes effect in the occupied territory only upon its liberation.[111]

(b) National Territory under Control of a *de facto* Government

In the following the term '*de facto* government' describes an authority which has gained effective control of the State by overthrowing the constitutional government in a *coup d'état* or a revolution but has not (yet) been recognized as legally qualified to represent the State on the international plane.[112] *De facto* governments are to be distinguished from national governments installed by or formed under the auspices of an occupant. The latter are only organs of the occupant to which the same rules apply as to the occupant itself.[113] A *de facto* government, as distinct from an occupation government, is the result of an internal struggle for the (exercise of the) State's sovereign authority.[114] This internal struggle is, as a rule, of no concern to international law, and the *de facto* government is regarded as competent to exercise the State's legislative authority in so far as its control of the State extends.[115] This is evidenced by the fact that foreign courts have regularly applied the laws of *de facto* governments with respect to matters

[111] The contrary finding of the Greek Council of State in its Judgment 54/1945 [*Re XY*], denying any force of law to the legislation of a government in exile inside occupied territory, must be seen against the background of Art. 8 of the Greek Constitutional Law 21 of 1945 which provided: 'In order that such laws and other constitutional acts promulgated by the Greek Governments abroad during the period of foreign occupation may have full legal effect within Greek territory they must be promulgated anew in the Official Gazette [at Athens]. They shall, however, continue in force abroad notwithstanding non-compliance with this requirement' ((1943–5) 12 AD No 147, 431–2 at 432).

[112] Cf. Gemma, 'Les gouvernements de fait' (1924–III) 4 *RdC* 297–413 at 360; *Williams* v. *Bruffy*, 96 US 176 at 185 (1878); *Guaranty Trust Co. of New York* v. *United States*, 304 US 126 at 140 (1938). For a different definition, see Spiropoulos, *Die de facto-Regierung im Völkerrecht* (1926), 1–5. In *Co Kim Cham* v. *Valdez Tan Keh* (1945) the Philippine Supreme Court distinguished three kinds of *de facto* governments: (1) the revolutionary government or 'government *de facto* in a proper legal sense', (2) the military occupation government of paramount force, (3) the secessionist government ((1950–1) 3 *Stanford LR* 7–13). See also US Executive Orders 12775 of 4 Oct. 1991 (56 FR 50641) and 12779 of 28 Oct. 1991 (56 FR 55975): 'The term "de facto regime in Haiti" means those who seized power illegally from the democratically elected government of President Jean-Bertrand Aristide on September 30, 1991'.

[113] On the distinction between a *de facto* and an occupation government, see Greek Consular Tribunal of Alexandria, Judgment 214/1945, (1949) 2 RHDI 305–7 at 306–7. See also McNair and Watts, n. 50 above, 426: 'There is a clear legal distinction between the *de facto* Government of a country and a belligerent occupant'.

[114] See Sauser-Hall, n. 82 above, at 70–3.

[115] See *ibid.*, at 70; Spiropoulos, n. 112 above, 79–87. See also Greek Consular Tribunal of Alexandria, Judgment 214/1945, (1949) 2 RHDI 305–7 at 307.

under their effective control.[116] The courts of some States may, however, require that the *de facto* government is (at least implicitly) recognized *as such* by the government of the forum. For example, in *Autocephalous Greek-Orthodox Church of Cyprus* v. *Goldberg and Feldman Fine Arts, Inc.* (1989) the US Court of Appeals refused to give effect to the decrees of the Turkish Cypriot '*de facto* government north of the Green Line' on the ground that the US Government did not 'recognize that [the Turkish administration] has functioned as a *de facto* or quasi government . . . ruling within its own borders'.[117] It is submitted that the *de facto* government's general competence to exercise the State's legislative authority with respect to the territory under its control is not affected by the fact that the constitutional government establishes itself in exile and continues to be recognized as the State's legitimate Government by foreign States. States have continued to recognize governments overthrown in the course of civil strife only in exceptional circumstances. Often it has been controversial whether a government was overthrown in internal events or whether there was outside involvement making the authority *in situ*, in fact, the puppet of a foreign power. The only unambiguous cases of continued recognition of a government ousted in internal events are the continued recognition of Panamanian President Delvalle (ousted by a *coup* on 25 February 1988) by the United States and the continued recognition of Haitian President Aristide (overthrown on 29 September 1991) by a large majority of the international community. The Governments of Prince Sihanouk of Cambodia and of Prince Souvanna Phouma of Laos had been overthrown by local leaders on 18 March 1970 and 9 December 1960, respectively. In both cases, however, the States that continued to recognize these governments during their exile alleged US involvement in their overthrow. Similarly, the States which in 1945 and 1946 recognized the Spanish Republican Government in exile justified their recognition by the fact that the Franco Government, which came to power in the Spanish civil war (1936–9), had been installed with German and Italian help. There are, consequently, no authorities directly on the question whether a *de facto* government may exercise the State's legislative authority if the constitutional government ousted in internal events establishes itself in exile and continues to be recognized as the State's government. There are, however, several decisions dealing indirectly with this question. For instance, in the *Boguslawski*

[116] See *Salimoff* v. *Standard Oil Co.*, 262 NY 220 at 227 (CA NY 1933); *Hausner* v. *Banque Internationale de Commerce de Pétrograd SA* (1924), BGE 50 II, 507 at 511–12. On the application of the laws of *de facto* governments by foreign courts in general, see Stierlin, *Die Rechtsstellung der nichtanerkannten Regierung im Völkerrecht* (1940), 48–111; Rösch, *Die Rechtsstellung der nichtanerkannten Regierung vor Gericht* (1968), 60–89.

[117] 917 F.2d 278 at 291–3 (7th Cir. 1990), affirming 717 F.Supp 1374 (SD Ind. 1989). See also *A.M. Luther* v. *James Sagor and Company* [1921] 3 KB 532 (CA), reversing the judgment of Roche J (1920), [1921] 1 KB 456 (KBD).

cases[118] the English courts were called upon to determine for the period from 28 June to 6 July 1945 the respective spheres of authority of the Polish Government in exile in London (which was recognized by the British Government as 'the Government of Poland' until 6 July 1945) and of the Polish Provisional Government of National Unity in Warsaw (established on 28 June 1945 and regarded by the courts as 'the *de facto* government of metropolitan Poland').[119] By holding that the British recognition on 6 July 1945 of the Warsaw Government as the Government of Poland enabled and required the courts to regard as valid acts done since 28 June relating to matters under its control, the courts indicated that a *de facto* government can, at least in principle, validly act with respect to matters under its effective control even if there is a recognized government in exile. In a series of decisions during and after the Second World War Greek courts, on the incorrect premise that the various Greek puppet governments installed by the German occupation authorities were *de facto* governments,[120] held that these *de facto* governments had full legislative authority for the territory under their effective control.[121] At the same time the courts denied the laws of the Greek Government in exile in Cairo the force of law within Greece.[122] It should also be noted that in civil war situations the State's recognized *de jure* government, even while still holding on to some part of the State's territory, has been regarded as incompetent to legislate for territory under the control of a rival local *de facto* government.[123] It is argued, *a maiori ad*

[118] [1950] 1 KB 157 (KBD), [1951] 1 KB 162 (CA) and [1953] AC 11 (HL).

[119] At least the 'official' British interpretation of events in Poland at the time was that the Government in London was replaced by the Provisional Government of National Unity as a result of an internal Polish agreement rather than as a consequence of the occupation of Poland by the Soviet Union.

[120] Only the Criminal Court of Heraklion in its Judgment 107/1945 [*In re G.*] departed from this premise, stating that 'these Governments cannot even be regarded as *de facto* Governments. Actually they constitute mere organs of the occupant' ((1943–5) 12 AD No 151, 437–40 at 439). For the view that the Greek governments installed by the German occupant were not *de facto* governments, see also Ténékidès, 'La nature juridique des gouvernements institués par l'occupant en Grèce suivant la jurisprudence hellénique' (1947) 51 *RGDIP* 113–33; Lambadarios, 'Pouvoir législatif de l'autorité d'occupation et nature juridique des gouvernements hellénique d'occupation' (1948) 1 *RHDI* 381–4; Pesmazoglou, 'La nature juridique des Gouvernements formés pendant une occupation militaire ennemie' (1949) 2 *RHDI* 168–82.

[121] See Court of Appeal of Athens, Judgment 1554/1946, (1948) 15 AD 562; Areopagus, Judgment 68/1944 [*In re Law 900 of 1943*], (1947) 51 RGDIP 118–19; Council of State (All Chambers Combined), Judgment 132/1942 [*In re G.D.*], (1919–42) 11 AD No 153, 276–7; Council of State (All Chambers Combined), Judgment 353/1942 [*Marika Eliadi Maternity Home Case*], (1919–42) 11 AD No 152, 275–6, affirming Council of State (All Chambers Combined), Judgment 97/1942, (1945) 56 Thémis 41.

[122] See Council of State, Judgment 54/1945 [*Re XY*], (1943–5) 12 AD No 147, 431–2.

[123] In *Civil Air Transport Incorporated* v. *Claire Lee Chenault and Others*, the Supreme Court of Hong Kong said: 'His Majesty's Government recognized that the Central People's Government was the *de facto* government of various parts of China. . . . It follows that any acts done by the Nationalist Government [which was still recognized by the British Government as

minus, that the same holds good if the *de jure* government no longer controls any State territory. Support for the rule that the recognized government in exile is incompetent to exercise the State's legislative authority with respect to territory under the control of the *de facto* government may also be drawn from the decision of Clauson J in *Bank of Ethiopia* v. *National Bank of Egypt and Liguori* (1937).[124] In this case, as in the Greek cases above, an occupation authority again was wrongly treated as a *de facto* government. Clauson J, who in his treatment of the Italian occupant of Ethiopia as the *de facto* government of that country deferred to the decision of the British Government, which for political reasons had recognized it as such,[125] applied the rules governing *de facto* governments to the question whether exiled Emperor Haile Selassie, who was still recognized by the British Government as the *de jure* sovereign of his country, could counteract an Italian decree liquidating the Bank of Ethiopia by issuing a decree on his part empowering all companies incorporated under Ethiopian law to hold valid meetings and to carry on business outside Ethiopia. In view of the fact that the seat of the Bank was Addis Ababa, which was under the control of the Italian *de facto* government, Clauson J refused to pay any attention to the Emperor's decree.[126] The rule that a recognized govern-

the *de jure* Government of China] as regards that part of China under *de facto* control of the Central People's Government are to be regarded as a mere nullity in that area' ((1950) 34 HKLR 386–414 at 412). See also *Banco de Bilbao* v. *Sancha; Same* v. *Rey* [1938] 2 KB 176 at 195–6 (KBD). Compare also OLG Frankfurt a.M., 18 Mar. 1938 ([1938] JW 1122 (14)); Hanseatisches OLG, 4 Jan. 1939 (HRuGZ XXII, B, 91 at 96). The German courts held that as the German Reich recognized the Nationalist Government of General Franco as the only legal Government of Spain the authorities of 'Red Spain' (i.e. the Republican Government) were to be regarded as mere 'insurgents' without standing in international law and without competence to legislate for the territory under their control. The courts therefore applied the laws of the Franco government to the territory under control of the Republican Government. These decisions are not in conflict with the above submission, as they are based on the denial of the status of *de facto* government to the Spanish Republican authorities. In a situation of secession rather than in a struggle for the State's government, the English Court of Appeal recognized the (banking) laws of the Government of the (unrecognized) Turkish Republic of Northern Cyprus (TRNC) which it regarded as in '*de facto* control of its territory since about 1974' and not the laws of the Government of the Republic of Cyprus which the British Government recognized 'as the Government of the whole of Cyprus' (HC Debs., vol. 199, col. 259, 20 Nov. 1991). See *Polly Peck International* v. *Nadir (No 2)* [1992] 4 All ER 769. See also the judgment of Lord Denning MR in *Hesperides Hotels Ltd* v. *Aegean Turkish Holidays Ltd* (1977), [1978] QB 205 at 217–28 (CA).

[124] [1937] 1 Ch. 513.

[125] For valid criticism of the (politically and strategically motivated) British recognition of the Italian occupant as the *de facto* government of Ethiopia, see Sauser-Hall, n. 82 above, at 72.

[126] See [1937] 1 Ch. 513 at 521–2. Cf. also the decision of O'Bryan J in *Anglo Czechoslovak & Prague Credit Bank* v. *Janssen* [1943] VLR 185 at 193. In this connection it is of interest to note that in *Haw Pia* v. *China Banking Corporation* (1948) the Philippines Supreme Court held that even an occupation government had the authority under international law to order the liquidation of banks ((1951) 18 ILR No 203, 642–61 at 643). *Contra* McNair, n. 89 above, at 52–3.

ment in exile is not competent to legislate with immediate effect for the territory under the control of a *de facto* government is not called into question by the recent practice of US nationals residing in Panama, who refrained from making payments to the Panamanian *de facto* government controlled by General Noriega, as they were not so much complying with a Decree enacted on 2 March 1988 by ousted President Delvalle, which provided that all payments of debts, taxes, or fees to the Noriega-installed government of Panama would not be recognized as payments to the Government of Panama,[127] as with Executive Order 12635 of 8 April 1988 by which US President Reagan had ordered US persons in Panama to suspend payments to the Government of Panama and instead pay them into an account at the Federal Reserve Bank of New York to be held for the benefit of the Panamanian people.[128] The US Order was based on the continued recognition by the United States of Mr Delvalle as the President of Panama[129] and the non-recognition of the Noriega-installed Solís Palma Government (which, however, was acknowledged by the United States as a *de facto* government). In view of the fact that the Solís Palma Government was internationally recognized (except by the United States) as the Government of Panama, this unilateral action which was intended to starve the Noriega regime of cash and force its ouster must be regarded as an unlawful intervention by the United States in the internal affairs of Panama.[130]

In conclusion it may be stated that the constitutional government in exile which continues to be recognized as the State's (legitimate) government is not competent to exercise the State's legislative authority with immediate effect for the territory under the control of the (rival) *de facto* government. It may, however, on its return home modify or revoke the laws of the *de facto* government in the same way as this may be done by one government *in situ* following another.[131]

(2) Extraterritorial Legislative Authority

As a general rule the State's legislative authority, especially over its nationals and their property, is not limited to its own territory but extends abroad

[127] The decree was broadcast on 2 Mar. 1988 from Costa Rica: BBC, *SWB*, 3rd series, ME/0091/iii, 4 Mar. 1988.

[128] 53 FR 12134. See also [1988] *Keesing's* 35872. A similar Order (No 12775 of 4 Oct. 1991) was made, although under different legal conditions, after the overthrow of President Aristide of Haiti (56 FR 50641).

[129] Cf. s. 4 of the Order.

[130] See the address of the President of Panama to the UN General Assembly on 27 Sept. 1988 (UN Doc.A/43/PV.6, 28 Sept. 1988, 2–25 at 13, 19–20) and on 3 Oct. 1989 (UN Doc.A/44/PV.17, 10 Oct. 1989, 2–25 at 5). On the US Order and its consequences see also *WP*, 4 Apr. 1989, Sec. A, 18.

[131] Cf. Spiropoulos, n. 112 above, 85–6.

and is limited only by the territorial sovereignty of other States.[132] In international and civil war situations a considerable number of the State's nationals is usually fleeing either the occupant or the political opponent.[133] One of the major aims of any government in exile will be to make use of these refugees as well as of other expatriates and their property abroad in the struggle against the occupation or *de facto* authority *in situ*, or at least to remove them from the control of the authority *in situ*. This is usually done in the form of legislation as the government in exile, to which the State's nationals continue to owe allegiance,[134] is competent to exercise the State's legislative authority over them.[135] Thus, Wrottesley J felt bound to say in *In re Amand (No 2)* (1942) that 'the Government of the Netherlands [in London] can legislate here . . . for Dutchmen wherever they may be. Generally speaking it . . . can legislate [for persons in Great Britain] as fully as when it was within the territory of [its] Kingdom'.[136] This is true irrespec-

[132] See *The Lotus* (1927), PCIJ, Ser. A, No 10 at 19; *The Apollon* (1824) 9 Wheat. 362 at 370; *Blackmer* v. *United States of America*, 284 US 421 at 436, 438 (1932); BSG, 11 Oct. 1973, BSGE 36, 209 at 215. The State's extraterritorial legislative authority may be founded on one or more of the following principles of jurisdiction: nationality principle, protective principle, passive personality principle, or universality principle.

[133] In the first months of the war 1914 about one million Belgians fled to France, England, and the Netherlands. Many returned to Belgium, but about 500,000, that is about 6.5 per cent of the Belgian population, settled in foreign countries during the war. See Langenhove, n. 72 above, 33. For the number of refugees from countries under Axis occupation in the UK during the Second World War, see (1942) 5 *Free Europe* 92. The Iraqi occupation of Kuwait forced about half the 680,000 native Kuwaitis to flee the country. About 160,000 found refuge in Saudi Arabia and 60,000 in other Gulf States: see *NY Times*, 17 Nov. 1990, Sec. 1, 5; US Information Service, London, *The Gulf Crisis. A Chronology, July 1990–July 1991* (1991), 7.

[134] See Lord Wright's speech in *Sovfracht (V/O)* v. *Van Udens Scheepvaart en Agentuur Maatschappij* (1942), [1943] AC 203 at 299 (HL). See also *Moraitis* v. *Delany*, 46 F.Supp. 425 at 432 (D.Md. 1942), overruled on other grounds 136 F.2d 129 (4th Cir. 1943); *In re Amand (No 2)* [1942] 1 All ER 236 at 240. On the allegiance owed by Indians to the Provisional Government of Free India, see Toye, *The Springing Tiger* (1959), 91–2.

[135] See Lord Reid's speech in *Gdynia Ameryka Linie* v. *Boguslawski* (1952): 'The Polish Government [in London] . . . was recognized . . . as the government of Poland and it exercised sovereign powers over Polish subjects who were outside enemy occupied territory. By virtue of . . . decrees made by it during the war it had certain powers with regard to the Polish merchant navy' ([1953] AC 11 at 41–2 (HL)). See also Lord Porter's speech: '[the Polish Government in London] was recognized . . . as the *de jure* government of all Poland and of all Polish citizens and their property and as the *de jure* and *de facto* authority over all Polish citizens, their property and ships outside Poland itself' (*ibid.*, at 29). See further the decision of the US Tax Court in *Jamvold* v. *Commissioner of Internal Revenue*: 'a citizen of Norway, remained subject to the jurisdiction, authority, and orders of the Norwegian Government in exile' (11 TC 122 at 125 (1948)), and the decision of the WK Berlin of 3 Oct. 1953: 'The present Latvian Government in exile thus exercises from abroad personal sovereignty over Latvian nationals resident in the countries of the Western bloc' ([1953] RzW 368, author's translation, affirmed by the KG, 25 Feb. 1955, [1955] RzW 211 at 212). Moving the Second Reading of the Allied Powers (Maritime Courts) Bill the Secretary of State for the Home Department, Mr Herbert Morrison, said that the British Government recognized the foreign Governments in London as 'sovereign Governments, with sovereign powers in respect of their own people and citizens' (HC Debs., vol. 371, col. 1106, 13 May 1941).

[136] [1942] 1 All ER 236 at 242. See also *In re Amand* [1941] 2 KB 239 at 254.

tive of whether the authority *in situ* is a *de facto* or an occupation government, as in any case its competence to exercise the State's legislative authority is restricted to the territory under its control.[137] This was confirmed by the Greek Consular Tribunal of Alexandria in its judgment 214 of 1945.[138] Denying any legal effect in Greek courts abroad to Decree–law 35 of 15 May 1941 of the (German-installed) Government at Athens, which adjourned *sine die* the entry into force of the new Greek Civil Code which had been enacted but not yet entered into force prior to the German occupation, the Tribunal said:

> In consideration of the fact that even if one were to regard the Government . . . as a *de facto* government, one must admit that the authority which it exercised during the occupation did not cross the frontiers of our country occupied by the enemy, because abroad there existed a Greek Government . . . which alone was recognized by the United Nations and which abroad alone exercised all legitimate authority over the Greeks abroad and over all diplomatic, consular, military and other services [author's translation].[139]

The government in exile is competent to legislate not only for the State's nationals in its host State but for all nationals abroad.[140] However, the effect that the legislation of the exiled government has in a particular State will depend upon the State's willingness to enforce it.

By virtue of the State's legislative authority over its nationals abroad (on the basis of the nationality principle) governments forced into exile by a military occupant have enacted decrees introducing conscription of labour, seafaring duties, and compulsory military service for their nationals in the host State and other States.[141] They have also levied taxes on their

[137] Cf. Feilchenfeld, n. 78 above, 131, 134. On the 'spheres' in which a *de jure* government in exile and a *de facto* government *in situ* are entitled to exercise acts of sovereignty, see *Gdynia Ameryka Linie* v. *Boguslawski* (1952), [1953] AC 11 at 38–9 (*per* Lord Oaksey).

[138] (1949) 2 RHDI 305–7.

[139] *Ibid.*, at 307.

[140] In *Haak and Others* v. *Minister of External Affairs* the Supreme Court of South Africa, Cape Provincial Division, stated with respect to the Dutch Decree providing for the conscription of Dutch nationals abroad, that 'decrees when made by the [Dutch] Sovereign while in England, setting out the duties of the subjects of the country of that Sovereign were binding on such subjects even though they were not resident in that country but resident in another country' ((1942) 59 SALJ 313–14 at 314, affirmed SALR [1942] AD 318).

[141] e.g. the Belgian Decree–laws of 1 Mar. 1915 and 21 July 1916 subjected to military service all Belgian adults up to the age of 40 outside the occupied territory (HC Debs., vol. 75, col. 1173, 10 Nov. 1915; Meene, n. 77 above, at 826), the Dutch Decrees A.5 of 6 June 1940 and C.19 of 11 Mar. 1942 introduced a seafaring duty for Dutch nationals (Zeeman, n. 68 above, at 9, 10), and the Norwegian Decrees of 12 July 1940 and 12 Dec. 1941 provided for the registration of Norwegian nationals abroad and the introduction of conscription of labour (Official of the Royal Norwegian Ministry of Justice and Police, n. 68 above, at 126; Wold, n. 76 above, at 432). The right of a government in exile to impose services on its nationals abroad was affirmed *In re Amand* [1941] 2 KB 239; *In re Amand (No 2)* [1942] 1 All ER 236; *Re de Bruijn. Re Romeijnsen* (1941), [1942] 1 DLR 249; *Haak and Others* v. *Minister of External Affairs*, SALR [1942] AD 318; and *Assendelft* v. *Minister of External Affairs*, PH 1942 (1), K.46.

incomes[142] and have imposed restrictions on their commercial freedom.[143] For example, on 10 December 1916 the Belgian Government at Le Havre passed a Decree–law which prohibited, for the duration of the war, every Belgian subject outside the territory of the enemy from concluding or from executing an agreement whatsoever with an enemy subject or a person resident within enemy territory and declaring null and void all acts done or contracts concluded in violation of that prohibition.[144] While a government in exile is competent, in principle, to prohibit its nationals abroad from trading with the enemy, it is argued that it is not competent to prohibit such conduct in so far as it conflicts with, for example, the right of neutral States to require foreign nationals within their territory to execute existing contracts with enemy subjects or residents in enemy-occupied territory, as such a prohibition would infringe upon the territorial sovereignty of the neutral States.[145] It is also of interest to note the competence of a government in exile to requisition the merchant ships owned by the State's nationals (both resident at home and abroad) flying the State's flag.[146] It is submitted that the same is not true for foreign-owned

[142] Dutch Royal Decree B.78 of 18 Sept. 1941 instituted compulsory taxation on Dutch nationals outside their national territories. The decree was abolished by Decree C.33 of 30 Apr. 1942 (Zeeman, n. 68 above, at 10–11; *NY Times*, 2 Oct. 1941, 10). On taxes levied by the Norwegian Government in London, see Koht, *Norway. Neutral and Invaded* (1941), 182; *Jamvold* v. *Commissioner of Internal Revenue*, 11 TC 122 at 124 (1948). The Allied Governments in London were not allowed to set up their own systems of tax collection but were allowed to make deductions at source from payments to government officials and soldiers which were exempt from British taxation. See Bareau, 'The Finances of Refugee Governments' (1942) 64/201 *The Banker* 17–24 at 18 and HC Debs., vol. 371, col. 1149, 13 May 1941. The Provisional Government of Free India set up 'Boards of Management for Raising Funds' to which from the beginning of 1944 Indians (living in Japan or Japanese occupied countries) had to declare their assets upon which levies from 10 to 25 per cent were imposed and collected (Toye, n. 134 above, 95).

[143] e.g. by Decree–law of 23 Feb. 1915 the Belgian Government at Le Havre made for the duration of the war the sale of Belgian merchant vessels to foreigners subject to its consent: see (1917) 44 *JDI* 1919; Langenhove, n. 72 above, 61. By Decree–law of 19 Feb. 1942 the Belgian Government in London suspended the powers of stockholders, directors, and officers residing in occupied Belgian with respect to all corporate properties and affairs outside Belgium. This Decree–law was given effect to in *Chemacid, SA* v. *Ferrotar Corporation*, 51 F.Supp. 756 (SDNY 1943). See also Dutch Decree A.6 of 7 June 1940 suspending the power of acting on behalf of any Dutch corporations or individuals within enemy-occupied territory, in so far as such purported action related to assets outside such territory. The decree was given effect to in *Amstelbank* v. *Guaranty Trust Co.*, 31 NYS2d 194 (S.Ct. NY 1941).

[144] See (1917) 44 *JDI* 1920; Langenhove, n. 72 above, 75–6. For the similar Decree–law, enacted by the Belgian Government in London on 10 Apr. 1941, see Fayat, n. 68 above, at 38.

[145] Cf. Oppenheim, *International Law. A Treatise* (8th edn., 1955), i, 296, n. 1.

[146] On the charter of the requisitioned ships to the British Government, see (1942) 19 *Bulletin of International News* 544. The competence of the Dutch Government to requisition vessels of its nationals was recognized in *Ex parte Sulman*, SALR [1942] CPD 407. The Governments of Belgium and Norway issued decrees requisitioning all merchant ships flying their State's flags while still in their country on 17 and 18 May 1940, respectively. On the basis

ships flying the State's flag (only for reasons of convenience) as the State has no authority to requisition the property of foreign nationals outside its own territory.[147] All the authorities on this subject concern ships of nationals flying the flag of their State.[148] The situs of the ships, while of importance to the enforcement of their requisition, is thereby of no relevance to the competence of a government in exile to order their requisition.[149] This competence was taken advantage of in late April 1940 when the British Government suggested to the Greek Government on Crete that it 'take steps, through the promulgation of a legislative decree to ensure that every [Greek] ship and the ownership thereof shall pass under the control and jurisdiction of Free Greece'.[150] By requisitioning the ships of its nationals the Greek Government was to obviate the adverse legal effects resulting from the fact that the British Government on 29 April 1941 declared Greece to be enemy-occupied territory. According to the British Trading with the Enemy Act 1939,[151] this meant that insurance policies issued by Lloyds of London to shipowners resident in Greece became automatically terminated as they were contracts with the enemy. In order to safeguard the property abroad of natural and legal persons domiciled in the occupied territory, and more importantly to prevent the property from falling into the hands of the occupant, exiled governments have also regularly vested

of these decrees the two governments then requisitioned ships while in exile. On the Norwegian Government, see *Lorentzen* v. *Lydden* (1941), [1942] 2 KB 202; *The Solgry* (1919–42) 11 AD No 82, 153–4; *The Rigmor* (1941–2) 10 AD No 63, 240–7. On the Belgian Government, see *The Kabalo* (1940) 67 Ll.LR 572; *The Laurent Meeus*, 1941 AMC 991 (SD Cal. 1940), affirmed 43 F.Supp. 807 (SD Cal., Centr.Div. 1942), modified 133 F.2d 552 (9th Cir. 1942), cert. denied 318 US 781; and [1941] II FRUS 1–4 at 3. In addition, the Belgian Government, by Decree–law of 1 July 1942, provided for the requisitioning of all seamen and fishermen (Fayat, n. 68 above, 30–40 at 37). On the requisition of merchant ships in general, see McNair, 'Problems Connected with the Position of the Merchant Vessel in Private International Law, with particular Reference to the Power of Requistion' (1945) 31 *Grot. Soc.* 30–46 (and discussion, 46–58); *id.*, 'The Requisitioning of Merchant Ships' (1945) 27 *JCL* 68–78.

[147] Cf. Beitzke, 'Probleme der Enteignung im internationalen Privatrecht' in Ipsen (ed.), *Festschrift für Leo Raape zu seinem siebzigsten Geburtstag 14. Juni 1948* (1948), 93–111 at 94–5.

[148] By Decree–law of 2 Feb. 1916 the Belgian Government at Le Havre requisitioned all Belgian merchant ships (Langenhove, n. 72 above, 55–8). By Decree C.17 of 5 Mar. 1942 the Dutch Government in London requisitioned all Dutch merchant ships for the duration of the war and six months thereafter (Zeeman, n. 68 above, at 9).

[149] Carpmael, in McNair, *Grot. Soc.*, n. 146 above, 49.

[150] See *Royal Hellenic Government* v. *Vergottis* (1945) 78 Ll. LR 292 at 297, 313. Cl. 1 of the Agreement between the Royal Greek Government and the British Government of 20 May 1941 provided that: 'All Greek ships not already under requisition shall forthwith be requisitioned by the Royal Greek Government'. By Law 3140 of 11 Jan. 1943 the Greek Government in exile declared all merchant ships flying the Greek flag requisitioned as from 7 Dec. 1941. The competence of the Greek Government in exile to requisition the ships of its nationals abroad was also recognized in *American Tobacco Co.* v. *The Ioannis P. Goulandris*, 1941 AMC 1797 (SDNY 1941); *The Margaret-Tassia*, 1941 AMC 1742 (SDNY 1941); *The Maliakos*, 1941 AMC 1737 (SDNY 1941).

[151] 2 & 3 Geo. 6, c. 89.

protective title[152] to, or the administration of the property in, themselves.[153] For example, Article 1 of the Emeri Decree–Law 3/A/1990 of 18 October 1990 concerning the Holding in Trust by the State of Kuwait of Property Belonging to Kuwaitis or Residents of Kuwait vested title to all assets of Kuwaiti citizens and residents in the State of Kuwait as represented by its lawful Government. The introductory note to this law emphasized that:

> The *purpose* of this law is to enable the State of Kuwait, represented by its lawful Government . . . , to take all necessary and appropriate measures *to protect* property belonging to Kuwaitis or residents of Kuwait and to establish the right of the lawful Government to have recourse to foreign administrative and judicial authorities for the purpose of protecting such property.[154]

This emphasis on the protective purpose of the Decree was not so much necessitated by any restriction in international law on the competence of governments in exile to vest title to property abroad of their nationals in their State but by the conditions on which foreign courts have recognized and enforced such decrees.[155] In *State of the Netherlands* v. *Federal Reserve Bank of New York* (1951), Goddard DJ pointed out that 'from the standpoint of international law theory, The Netherlands Government-in-exile had the status to legislate in connection with assets of its nationals situated in foreign countries whether or not such countries chose to apply the law within their respective jurisdiction.'[156] Similarly, the Commercial Counsellor of the Dutch Legation in Washington stated in *Anderson* v. *NV Transandine Handelmaatschappij* (1942)[157] that 'the British Government has stated that so far as it is within their province they recognize the

[152] See § 1(3) of the Dutch Decrees A.1 of 24 May 1940 and C.18 of 6 Mar. 1942, as amended by Decree C.34 of 7 May 1942, which vested protective title in the State of the Netherlands to claims capable of being transferred outside the occupied Netherlands and the Netherlands East Indies and belonging to persons domiciled there. On these decrees, see the statement by the Government of the Netherlands: DCER VIII, no 765, at 930. The Belgian and Norwegian Governments (the latter while still in Norway) had promulgated decrees similar in general purport to the Dutch Decrees (DCER IX, no 1511, at 1833). See also Lourie and Meyer, 'Governments-in-Exile and the Effect of Their Expropriatory Decrees' (1943) 11 *U.Chicago LR* 26–48.

[153] e.g. by Decree of 5 Feb. 1941 the Luxembourg Government vested the administration of the National Savings Bank of Luxembourg in the Treasury (Cohn, n. 71 above, at 44). See also the Decree of the President of the Polish Republic, made at Angers on 26 Feb. 1940, which provided for the appointment by the Polish Government of persons called 'curators' to administer and dispose of the property of Polish corporations and citizens outside the territory of occupied Poland. The Decree was given effect in *Gdynia Ameryka Linie* v. *Boguslawski* (1952), [1953] AC 11 (HL).

[154] UN Doc.S/21887, 22 Oct. 1990, annex, at 2 (italics added). Art. 2 provided that the 'lawful Government shall have the right as trustee . . . to protect the aforementioned property of which it is the rightful owner'.

[155] On these conditions, see 5 below.

[156] 99 F.Supp. 655 at 660 (SDNY 1951).

[157] 289 NY 9 (CA NY 1942), affirming 31 NYS2d 194 (S.Ct., App. Div., 1st Dept. 1941), affirming 28 NYS2d 547 (S.Ct. NY Co. 1941).

Netherlands Royal Decree of 24 May 1940, as a legitimate exercise of the legislative power of the Netherlands'.[158] While Allied governments recognized the competence of the governments in exile to enact vesting decrees, in principle, they were reluctant to give full effect to them, especially insofar as they conflicted with their own Trading with the Enemy Acts which vested in the Custodian of Enemy Property title to property in their territory belonging to persons residing in enemy-occupied territory.[159] Limited effect was given to the vesting decrees by provision being made that the property was held by the Custodian on behalf of the exiled governments[160] or by the appointment of advisers to the Custodian of Enemy Property by the exiled government which advised on all questions concerning property belonging to their nationals.[161] After the liberation of their countries once the property was no longer subject to the custodianship of the Custodian of Enemy Property full effect was given by the British Government to the Vesting Decrees of the Dutch and Belgian Governments in exile with respect to the property of their nationals in the United Kingdom on the understanding that the decrees 'are intended to preserve the property in question, and that it will eventually be returned to the persons entitled'.[162] In addition, by virtue of the passive personality and universality principles, governments in exile have passed laws extending their courts' criminal jurisdiction by providing, *inter alia*, for the prosecution of nationals

[158] Quoted in the Brief for the Netherlands Government: McNair and Watts, n. 50 above, 432. See also the letter of the Canadian High Commissioner in Great Britain to the Secretary of State For External Affairs dated 6 June 1940: 'Present View of the United Kingdom authorities is that the Netherlands Decree does not affect the duties of the Custodian or of any persons holding or managing enemy property. Decree appears to authorize the Netherlands Government to intervene in specific cases (such as attempts to sell in neutral countries bearer bonds owned by Netherlands citizens) but not to take general initiative' (DCER VIII, no 769, at 933).

[159] On 31 July 1943 Assistant Secretary of State Berle wrote in a memorandum: 'The Netherlands Government claims title to this property under a decree of 1940 which requisitions such property. The Department has been cautious about giving extraterritorial effect to that decree . . . Mr Hackworth [the legal adviser] and I came to the conclusion that it was dangerous to give unlimited recognition to such a decree since this might easily create an embarrassing precedent' ([1943] II FRUS 462–3). See also [1943] II FRUS 465. On the question whether full force and effect should be given to Dutch Vesting Decree A.1 of 24 May 1940 in Canada, see DCER VIII, no 767; *ibid.*, IX, nos 1510–15, 1522–3; *ibid.*, XII, nos 113–15.

[160] See the Agreement between the Government of the UK and the Government of Belgium concerning Property within the UK belonging to Persons resident in Belgium, effected by Exchange of Notes on 6 Oct. 1944: 145 BFSP 446. The agreement provided, *inter alia*, that 'Belgian property' is to be vested in the Custodian of Enemy Property 'on behalf of the Belgian Government' and that 'when the Belgian Government have resumed the administration of the whole of Belgium, all Belgian property as defined in the Agreement shall be at the free disposal of the Belgian Government.' A similar Agreement was concluded between the UK and the Netherlands on 2 Oct. 1944: 231 UNTS 317.

[161] See DCER IX, no 1512, at 1838; no 1522, at 1848.

[162] See 145 BFSP 446 at 455 (Anglo-Belgian Agreement) and 231 UNTS 317 at 332 (Anglo-Dutch Agreement).

and foreigners who commit war crimes and other serious offences against the State's nationals abroad.[163]

These examples, apart from showing that a government in exile has full competence to exercise the State's legislative authority abroad, well illustrate a more general and often underestimated point, viz., that States (whose authority governments in exile are only exercising) possess far-reaching extraterritorial legislative authority. What they do not have, however, is a right under international law to have their laws given extraterritorial effect by other States.

4 ENFORCEMENT JURISDICTION

Enforcement jurisdiction may be defined as the legal authority of a State under international law to enforce its legislation, either by way of executive action such as arrest or seizure or by way of judicial action through the courts. It follows from the territorial sovereignty of States that jurisdiction to enforce is exclusively territorial and that, as a rule, a government must not exercise enforcement jurisdiction within the territory of another State without its consent.[164] A government in exile may, however, continue to exercise enforcement jurisdiction on the ships flying the State's flag on the high seas.[165] It may also continue to exercise enforcement jurisdiction abroad under pre-existing arrangements.[166]

Not every executive action taken by a government in exile requires the prior consent of the territorial sovereign. There are certain executive acts,

[163] The Belgian Decree–law of 5 Aug. 1943 conferred 'exceptional competence on Belgian jurisdictions with regard to certain crimes and offences committed in wartime outside Belgian territory' (*Arrêtés de Londres*, 123–5). See also (1943) 3/47 *News from Belgium and the Belgian Congo* 372. On convictions on the basis of the similar Dutch Decree D.61 of 22 Dec. 1943, see *In re Gerbsch* (1948) 15 AD No 155, at 491–3, and (1949) 16 AD No 143, at 399; *In re Zuhlke* (1948) 15 AD No 122, at 415–16.

[164] Cf. *The Lotus* (1927), PCIJ, Ser. A, No 10 at 18–19. See also Verdross and Simma, *Universelles Völkerrecht* (3rd edn., 1984), § 456; Akehurst, n. 2 above, at 148; Wold, n. 76 above at 432.

[165] Cf. Arts. 5, 6 of the HSC 1958; Arts. 27, 28, 92(1), 94(1) of UNCLOS 1982. With respect to the requisition of a ship by the Yugoslav Government in exile Callahan J declared in *Fields* v. *Predionica i Tkanica AD*: 'In any event, when the steamship . . . reached the high seas it was freed from any restraint concerning the exercise of sovereign power' (37 NYS 2d 874 at 882 (S.Ct., App.Div., 1st Dept. 1942). On the exercise of jurisdiction by a government in exile over ships on the high seas, see also *Radovcic* v. *The Princ Pavle*, 45 F.Supp. 15 at 16 (SDNY 1942); *Delany* v. *Moraitis*, 136 F.2d 129 at 131 (4th Cir. 1943); *Gdynia Ameryka Linie* v. *Boguslawski* (1952), [1953] AC 11 at 38 (HL). It is of interest to note that the alleged assassin of two senior PLO members who had been sentenced to death in March 1991 by a Palestinian military tribunal sitting in Sana'a, Yemen, was executed by the PLO 'in international waters' in Nov. 1991 ([1991] *Keesing's* 38595).

[166] e.g. the Greek consular courts in Egypt under the capitulation regime continued to exercise jurisdiction under the authority of the Greek Government in exile during the Second World War. It is also of interest to note that US courts regularly declined jurisdiction with

such as calling up its nationals,[167] which not only a government in exile but governments in general may, under existing international practice, perform in the territory of another State without the prior consent of the territorial sovereign. Thus, on 1 May 1943 the Polish press in London carried the following announcement:

The Consul General of the Polish Government in London calls for the enlistment of all Polish citizens residing in Great Britain, born in the years 1902–1925 inclusive, who have not yet come forth. They are to register between May 10 and May 28. Individuals in the above-mentioned group who do not enlist will be considered as avoiding service and will be treated according to precepts of Polish law.[168]

Referring to this notice the British Foreign Secretary, Mr Eden, declared on 27 May 1943: '[This is] a perfectly legitimate exercise of the right of the Allied Polish Government to call upon their citizens of military age in this country to perform military service in accordance with the law of Poland. It is recognized even in peace that a friendly State has the right to call up its nationals for military service who are residing in the territory of another friendly State'.[169] This was confirmed by *In re Amand (No 2)* (1942), where Wrottesley J stated with respect to a call up notice of the Netherlands Government in London:

Never . . . has it been thought to be any trespass on the sovereignty of this country that foreign governments should acquaint their nationals, either through the medium of the post or through the medium of their accredited representatives and consuls, that it is the duty of such nationals to join the forces of those countries.[170]

While a government in exile may thus (without prior consent) send out call-up notices to its nationals in the host State as well as in other States and may even threaten sanctions if they do not comply with the call up it may not exercise any compulsion in order to enforce the call up The Canadian Prime Minster, Mr King, stated on 1 May 1941:

respect to claims for personal injury brought by seamen serving on the vessels of the various Allied governments in exile as the libellants had not yet exhausted all the remedies available to them under the laws of the governments in exile and administered by special arbitration boards in the USA. See e.g. *Miluton* v. *Steamship Princ Pavle*, 1942 AMC 259 (D.Md. 1941); *The Memas*, 35 F.Supp. 837 (EDNY 1940); *Lura* v. *M/S Ivaran*, 121 F.2d 445 (2nd Cir. 1941); *Radovcic* v. *The Princ Pavle*, 45 F.Supp. 15 (SDNY 1942).

[167] For other acts which heads of State may perform abroad without the consent of the territorial sovereign, see Verdross and Simma, n. 164 above, § 456 at 277.

[168] *Poland in the British Parliament 1939–1945* (1948), ii, 202.

[169] HC Debs., vol. 389, cols. 1743–4, 27 May 1943. See also *ibid.*, vol. 352, cols. 229–30, 8 Nov. 1939; *ibid.*, vol. 381, col. 972, 9 July 1942; *ibid.*, vol. 390, col. 1896, 1 July 1943. The Swiss Government, responding to a German protest against the call up of Polish nationals in Switzerland by the Polish Government in France, stated that the toleration (in contrast to the active support) of the Polish call up was in conformity with its neutrality. See DDS XIII, no 193, 448–9. On the call up of Belgian nationals in Great Britain during the First World War, see HC Debs., vol. 75, col. 1173, 10 Nov. 1915.

[170] [1942] 1 All ER 236 at 240. See also *Re de Bruijn* (1941), [1942] 1 DLR 249 at 252.

A foreign government, which has a legal system imposing compulsory military service on its nationals abroad, can, under existing international practice, provide for calling them up. Its representatives can bring the call to the attention of the nationals. They cannot exercise any compulsion within Canada in order to induce them to respond to the call.[171]

In general, States anxious to protect their territorial sovereignty have been extremely reluctant to consent to the exercise of enforcement jurisdiction by a government in exile within their territory. They have, however, tolerated the informal administration by governments in exile of procedures which normally would have been administered by the State's courts *in situ*. Thus, governments in exile, calling up their nationals, have informally operated machinery for dealing with conscientious objectors[172] and have even rendered decisions in divorce cases.[173] The only example of a State consenting to the limited exercise of enforcement jurisdiction by exiled governments within its territory seems to be the Allied Powers (Maritime Courts) Act 1941.[174] This Act authorized Allied governments in the United Kingdom to exercise there, through their own maritime courts, limited jurisdiction over persons other than British nationals with respect to offences committed on board their merchant ships and over persons who are both their nationals and seamen with respect to acts and omissions in contravention of their merchant shipping law and mercantile marine conscription law.[175] This (exceptional) authorization was necessitated by the fact that in the absence of a special connection between a State and the offence only the flag State has jurisdiction over offences committed by foreign nationals on board its ships on the high seas.[176] This had led to the situation that prior to the enactment of the Allied Powers (Maritime Courts) Act 1941 some 30,000 Allied seamen were removed from any kind of enforcement jurisdiction and this had threatened discipline on the merchant ships of the Allied governments in exile which had been chartered to

[171] (1942) 20 *Can. BR* 167–70 at 169–70. On the calling up of Belgian and Dutch nationals in Canada by their consuls, see DCER VIII, nos 690–700, 788.

[172] See HC Debs., vol. 380, col. 2201, 25 June 1942.

[173] The Norwegian Decree of 15 Apr. 1942 provided that the Ministry of Justice may make decisions in divorce cases (Official of the Royal Norwegian Ministry of Justice and Police, n. 68 above, at 128–9).

[174] 4 & 5 Geo. 6, c. 21. On the Act, generally, see HC Debs., vol. 371, cols. 1105–57, 13 May 1941; cols. 1281–1357, 15 May 1941; cols. 1482–1516, 20 May 1941; HL Debs., vol. 119, cols. 286–90, 21 May 1941. See also Chorley, 'Allied Powers (Maritime Courts) Act, 1941' (1941) 5 *MLR* 118–20; Schwelb, n. 9 above, 198–201; Jessup, 'Norwegian Maritime Courts in England' (1942) 36 *AJIL* 653–7; and the speeches delivered on the occasion of the opening of the Netherlands Maritime High Court in London on 3 Nov. 1941: (1942) 58 *LQR* 41–52.

[175] See s. 2(1) of the Act.

[176] O'Connell, *The International Law of the Sea* (1984), ii, 800; Churchill and Lowe, *The Law of the Sea* (2nd edn., 1988), 168–9. See also Arts. 6(1), 11(1) of HSC 1958 and Arts. 92(1), 97(1) of UNCLOS 1982.

the British Government.[177] However, this exercise of enforcement jurisdiction was limited to the actual proceedings before the maritime courts. Summonses and warrants of arrest requiring any person (the charged or witnesses) to attend or to be brought before these courts had to be issued by British courts and executed by British officials.[178] The Lord Chancellor, Viscount Simon, moving the Second Reading of the Allied Powers (Maritime Courts) Bill said with respect to the question how anybody could be brought before these Courts:

> It would be intolerable, of course, that the emissaries of even the most friendly Allied Power should be allowed to go about the country and summon, or it may be arrest, somebody inside our borders and hale him before a tribunal. That, therefore, must be done through the ordinary machinery of a British justice of the peace.[179]

The maritime courts also relied on the British authorities for the detention of persons sentenced and for the recovery of fines imposed.[180] Beside maritime courts exiled governments have regularly established in the host State of their armed forces their own military service courts which, by virtue of a rule of international law, have been authorized to exercise enforcement jurisdiction in matters concerning discipline and internal administration.[181] The exercise of enforcement jurisdiction over armed forces abroad is not peculiar to governments in exile. What is, however, peculiar to them is the fact that prison sentences imposed by their military service courts will usually have to be served in the prisons of the host State as prisoners cannot be sent home and the host States, as a rule, have not consented to the

[177] See the statement of the British Secretary of State for the Home Department, Mr Morrison: HC Debs., vol. 371, cols. 1105–9, 13 May 1941. See also *ibid.*, cols. 1147–8 (The Solicitor-General, Sir William Jowitt); and HL Debs., vol. 119, col. 286, 21 May 1941. See further Baer, 'Belgian Justice in Great Britain', *Message*, No 5 (Mar. 1942), 33–4 at 33.

[178] See ss. 5–7 of the Allied Powers (Maritime Courts) Act 1941. See also the Allied Powers (Maritime Courts) Regulations 1941 (S.R. & O. 1941 No 872), the Allied Powers (Maritime Courts) Rules 1941 (S.R. & O. 1941 No 873/L.14), and the Allied Powers (Maritime Courts) (Scotland) Rules 1941 (S.R. & O. 1941 No 966/S.31).

[179] HL Debs., vol. 119, col. 288, 21 May 1941.

[180] See s. 8 of the Allied Powers (Maritime Courts) Act 1941. The Lord Chancellor, Viscount Simon, said: 'Who is to carry out the sentence? The only person authorized to carry out the sentence would be our British officials. The only sentences which under the Bill can be thus carried out are sentences of detention . . . and sentences of fine. If the sentence is one of imprisonment, then it will be in a British prison and under the custody of a British gaoler that the offending individual will be detained' (HL Debs., vol. 119, cols. 288–9, 21 May 1941).

[181] During the debate on the Allied Forces Bill, the Joint Under-Secretary of State for War, Sir Edward Grigg, said: 'The principle of the Bill of allowing the Forces of a foreign Government to be under their own discipline is a principle recognized by international law' (HC Debs., vol. 364, col. 1395, 21 Aug. 1940). Under Art. 1(1) of the Allied Forces Act 1940, the discipline and internal administration of Allied forces in the UK was regulated by their own laws and offenders under those laws were to be tried and punished by their own courts and authorities. See also Art. 1 of App. IV of the Anglo-Dutch Agreement concerning the organization and employment of the Dutch Armed Forces in the UK of 5 May 1942 (147 BFSP 931 at 936). See further the Franco-Belgian Declaration on Military Criminal Jurisdiction of Jan. 1916: (1916) 43 *JDI* 726–7.

running in their territory of detention camps or prisons by governments in exile.[182] A notable exception constitutes the 'civil re-education centres' in Morocco run by the Algerian Government in exile. On 31 May 1960 the Government of Morocco and the GPRA, which had been recognized by Morocco as the Government of Algeria, concluded an Agreement which in Article VI provided that 'the Algerians, arrested by the Moroccan authorities at the request of the GPRA's chief of mission in accordance with articles I, II, III of the present accord, will be taken to one of the two civil re-education centres, which the GPRA will be authorized to open, in order to be interned there' (author's translation).[183] While the GPRA was responsible for the operation and financing of these internment and re-education centres the Moroccan security forces, however, remained responsible for guarding them.[184]

As governments in exile normally are not allowed to enforce their laws themselves within the territory of another State they have to look to the courts and authorities of that State for their enforcement.[185] The authorities of territorial States which have enforced the laws of exiled governments, however, did not (and could not) act on the basis of these foreign laws but on the basis of special national laws giving effect to these laws.[186] This may be illustrated by the statement of Mr Attlee, the Lord Privy Seal, on 18 September 1940:

His Majesty's Government intend to submit to Parliament in due course legislation to confer the necessary authority upon the Allied Governments in this country to call up their nationals for military service. . . . *Until this legislation has been passed* the position remains that the Allied Governments have the right to call upon their

[182] Art. 2 of the Belgian Decree–law of 8 June 1940 on Belgian Military Justice in France provided that sentences imposed by Belgian service courts were to be served in French prisons (*Arrêtés de Londres*, 5–6). See also s. 2(1) of the Allied Forces (Penal Arrangements) (No 1) Order 1940 (S.R. & O. 1940 No 1817) and the Allied Forces (Penal Arrangements) (No 2) Order 1941 (S.R. & O. 1941 No 49). See further Art. 6 of the two French Decrees of 31 May 1918 organizing military justice in the Czechoslovak and Polish Armies in France (JORF 3 June 1918, 4788, 4789).

[183] ARA no 96, 458–61. On the civil reeducation centres, see Ch. III, Arts. 6–9, of the Agreement.

[184] See Art. 8 of the Agreement.

[185] Cf. Oppenheimer, n. 37 above, at 586–7.

[186] e.g. the South African War Measure 1 of 2 Jan. 1942, headed 'Regulations to compel Conscripted non-Union Nationals to render war service', provided for the rendering of assistance to Allied States by arresting and delivering their conscripts to their representatives: see *Haak and Others* v. *Minister of External Affairs*, SALR [1942] AD 318 at 324; *Assendelft* v. *Minister of External Affairs*, PH 1942 (1), K.46, and *Ex parte Sulman*, SALR [1942] CPD 407 at 408. See also the speech of the Lord Chancellor, Viscount Simon, in *Amand* v. *Home Secretary and Minister of Defence of Royal Netherlands Government* (1942), setting out the statutory basis for the arrest by British authorities of a deserter from the Dutch forces in the UK ([1943] AC 147 at 152–5 (HL)). See also the judgment of Fisher J in *Re de Bruijn* (1941): 'to justify the applicant's arrest and detention on Canadian soil authority must be found in the law of this country' ([1942] 1 DLR 249 at 250).

nationals in this country for military service in accordance with their own national laws, but that *our own Courts and authorities have no power to assist the Allied Governments in enforcing such obligations* for military service upon any of their nationals who may be unwilling to respond voluntarily.[187]

The enforcement of the conscription laws of the exiled Allied Governments proved a very delicate subject indeed, and it took the British and exiled Allied Governments more than two years to reach agreement on how to proceed in this matter. The main concern of the British Government was to prevent a situation in which foreign nationals who had fled their country for political, racial, or religious reasons, as well as foreign nationals living in the United Kingdom for many years, could be forced to serve in the armed forces of their exiled governments against their will.[188] The conscription laws of the governments in exile were finally enforced by the Allied Powers (War Service) Act 1942.[189] It provided that foreign nationals of military-age resident in the United Kingdom who had not by a specific date joined the armed forces of their government in exile could be rendered liable for national service in the British forces as if they were British subjects.[190]

5 RECOGNITION AND ENFORCEMENT OF LEGISLATION IN EXILE BY FOREIGN COURTS

(1) General Rule

As has been shown above, a government in exile may validly legislate for its State's nationals and their property within the territory of another State but may not enforce its laws there.[191] Governments in exile have therefore

[187] HC Debs., vol. 365, col. 149, 18 Sept. 1940, italics supplied. See also *ibid.*, vol. 364, cols. 1355, 1356, 1385, 21 Aug. 1940; vol. 367, cols. 398–9, 3 Dec. 1940; vol. 369, col. 911, 5 Mar. 1941; vol. 373, col. 1785, 5 Aug. 1941.

[188] However, once those nationals had joined the forces of the exiled government they were fully subject to its (disciplinary) jurisdiction. The following case may illustrate that. On 8 June 1945 Dr Jan Jagodzinski, chief of the London bureau of Polpress, the official newsagency of the (rival) Polish Provisional Government at Warsaw was arrested at the request of the Polish Government in London by the City of London police under authority of the Allied Forces Act 1940 and was turned over to the military authorities of the Polish Government in London as a deserter from the Polish army. On the Jagodzinski case, see *NY Times*, 9 June 1945, 8 and 10 June 1945, 9.

[189] 5 & 6 Geo. 6, c. 29. On this Act in general, see HC Debs., vol. 380, cols. 2174–204, 25 June 1942; vol. 381, cols. 967–1003, 9 July 1942. See also Hartmann, 'The Allied Powers (War Service) Act' (1942) 6 *MLR* 72–5. The Act was applied by the Allied Powers (War Service) Order 1943 as from 1 Apr. 1943 to the nationals of Belgium, Czechoslovakia, Greece, the Netherlands, Norway, Poland, and Yugoslavia (S.R. & O. 1943 No 381). See also Allied Powers (War Service) (No 3) Order 1944 (S.R. & O. 1944 No 992).

[190] See s. 1 of the Act. For the different approach followed in the First World War, compare the Military Service (Conventions with Allied States) Act 1917 (7 & 8 Geo. 5, c. 26).

[191] See also Collins (ed.), *Dicey and Morris on the Conflict of Laws* (12th edn., 1993), 991: 'In public international law the jurisdiction of a State extends to its nationals and their property wherever they are.'

regularly tried to get their laws recognized and enforced in the local courts. In the following it is to be examined under what conditions such attempts have been successful. The effect given by the local courts to the laws of governments in exile is but part of the more general question under what conditions extraterritorial effect is given by courts to foreign laws affecting persons and property within the forum.[192] It follows from the principle of territorial sovereignty of States that a State is under no obligation to recognize and enforce the laws of another State within its territory. Each State may thus, in principle, lay down its own (conflict of laws) rules[193] prescribing under what conditions foreign laws are to be recognized and enforced by its courts. It seems, however, that States have adopted more or less the same general rule, viz. that, by comity, the valid laws of a government in exile concerning its nationals and their property in the forum are given effect unless this would conflict with the State's public policy. In *Anderson* v. *NV Transandine Handelmaatschappij* (1942) the Court of Appeals of New York stated with respect to the enforcement of Dutch Decree No A.1 of 24 May 1940, which vested the title to assets of Dutch nationals in the United States in the State of the Netherlands as represented by the Royal Netherlands Government in London:

> By comity of nations, rights based upon the law of a foreign State to intangible property which has a situs in this State, are recognized and enforced by the courts of this State, unless such enforcement would offend the public policy of this State. *That rule is part of the law of this State, as it is, in general, the law of all countries which accept the reign of law.*[194]

Similarly, in *Kingdom of Belgium* v. *EMJCH* (1953), which concerned the enforcement by the Dutch courts of the Belgian Decree–law of 2 June 1944 by which the Belgian Government in London ordered that any person who had received compensation out of the Belgian Treasury from the German occupant must refund it, the Court of Appeal of The Hague stated:

> By entertaining the action of the Belgian State, the Court below in fact applied the accepted principle of international law, necessitated by the requirement of international intercourse, under which States *ought* to assist each other in securing extra-territorial effect to their legislation which concerns their subjects,

[192] See *Anderson* v. *NV Transandine Handelmaatschappij*, 289 NY 9 at 15 (CA NY 1942); *Estate of Oei Tjong Swan* v. *Commissioner of Internal Revenue*, 24 TC 829 at 869 (1955).

[193] On the variety of private international law rules, see North and Fawcett, *Cheshire and North's Private International Law* (12th edn., 1992), 9.

[194] 289 NY 9 at 19, italics supplied (CA NY 1942), affirming 28 NYS2d 547 at 552 (S.Ct., NY Co. 1941). This statement of the law was expressly endorsed by the US Court of Appeals in *State of the Netherlands* v. *Federal Reserve Bank of New York*, 201 F.2d 455 at 460 (2d Cir. 1953). In *Lorentzen* v. *Lydden* (1941), Atkinson J expressly followed the judgment of the Supreme Court of New York in the *Anderson* case ([1942] 2 KB 202 at 216). See also *Republic of Panama* v. *Citizens and Southern International Bank*, 682 F.Supp. 1544 at 1547 (SD Fla. 1988).

unless such legislation conflicts with ordre public or established national legal concepts.[195]

The general rule that the valid laws of a government in exile concerning its nationals and their property are recognized and enforced by foreign courts *unless this would be contrary to their State's public policy* seems to have been applied in all cases but one. Only in *Bank voor Handel en Scheepvaart NV* v. *Slatford* (1951)[196] did Devlin J state the general rule to be that 'property in England is subject to English law and to none other'.[197] He also dismissed the notion that, as an exception to the general rule, extraterritorial effect should be given to a special category of laws, including those of the Allied governments in exile, for reasons of public policy.[198] Accordingly, Devlin J declined to give any extraterritorial effect to Dutch Decree No A.1 of 24 May 1940 vesting the title to a quantity of gold deposited by a Dutch company in London in the State of the Netherlands.[199] Apart from the fact that extraterritorial effect has been given to this and similar decrees of governments in exile by the English courts,[200] it is submitted that if the general rule were indeed as stated by Devlin J, the invocation by the English courts of the fact that a foreign law affecting property in England was penal or confiscatory or that it was contrary to English public policy in

[195] (1953) 20 ILR 26–8 at 28, italics added.

[196] [1953] 1 QB 248. The appeals in this case, *ibid.*, and [1954] AC 584 (HL), did not deal with the question of giving extraterritorial effect to the laws of a government in exile.

[197] [1953] 1 QB 248 at 260. See, in favour of this rule (1951) 4 *LQR* 492–5 at 495; North and Fawcett, n. 193 above, 128; Collins, n. 191 above, Rule 122, at 991, 993–4. But for criticism of the general denial of extraterritorial effect to foreign property legislation, see Bartol's case note (1952) 65 *Harv. LR* 1463–6 at 1464; Oppenheim, n. 145 above, i, 328, n. 4.

[198] [1953] 1 QB 248 at 263–7.

[199] Devlin J could have reached the same result by holding that the enforcement of the Dutch Decree would be contrary to the public policy of the UK as it was in direct conflict with the Trading with the Enemy Act 1939, to which the property had become subjected prior to the enactment of the Dutch Decree. Cf. Bartol, n. 197 above, at 1464–5.

[200] Effect was given to Dutch Decree A.1 by Morris J in *O/Y Wasa Steamship Co.* v. *Newspaper Pulp & Wood Export, Ltd* (1949) 82 Ll. LR 936 at 961. Effect was also given to the similar Norwegian Decree of 18 May 1940 by Atkinson J in *Lorentzen* v. *White Shipping Co.* (1942) 74 Ll.LR 161 at 162, and *Lorentzen* v. *Lydden* (1941), [1942] 2 KB 202. With respect to the latter case Devlin J stated in the *Bank voor Handel* case: 'If Atkinson J is to be taken as deciding that the general rule was otherwise, I respectfully prefer the decision in *The El Condado* [1939 SC 413]' ([1953] 1 QB 248 at 263). It is of interest to note that Devlin J had unsuccessfully advanced the *lex rei situs* rule as counsel for the losing party in the case *Lorentzen* v. *Lydden*. The contrary rule of Atkinson J was endorsed, obiter, by Denning LJ in *Boguslawski* v. *Gdynia-Ameryka Linie* (1950): 'When the Norwegian Government made a decree requisitioning choses in action [in England], the English courts gave effect to it' ([1951] 1 KB 162 at 180). It should also be noted that in *Gdynia Ameryka Linie* v. *Boguslawski* (1952) the House of Lords gave effect to the Decree of 26 Feb. 1940 of the Polish Government in France providing for the appointment of so-called curators to take in charge the property of Polish corporations and of Polish citizens outside Poland. These curators were, by Regulation 27 of 1 May 1940, entitled to dispose of Polish property abroad ([1953] AC 11 at 31). While these laws did not vest title to property in England in the Polish Government they had practically the same effect.

order to exclude its recognition and enforcement would be superfluous.[201] It is also difficult to understand why English courts should give extraterritorial effect to the laws of a government in exile affecting the legal position of its nationals in England[202] but not their property.

Courts which, as a general rule, give extraterritorial effect to the laws of governments in exile usually have to decide two main questions: whether the law in question is valid and, if so, whether its recognition and enforcement would be contrary to the public policy of their State.[203]

(2) Validity of the Law

As a rule, foreign law is a question of fact to be proved by evidence.[204] With respect to Dutch Decree No A.1 of 24 May 1940 vesting title to property of Dutch nationals in the United States in the State of the Netherlands, Shientag J stated in *Anderson* v. *NV Transandine Handelmaatschappij* (1941): 'The statement of the duly accredited Envoy Extraordinary and Minister Plenipotentiary of the Netherlands to the United States to the effect that the "Decree is a valid and binding act of the Royal Netherlands Government . . ." is conclusive in our courts as to the law of the Netherlands.'[205] Courts, such as the English courts, which do not accept the statements of the accredited diplomatic agents of foreign governments (irrespective of whether they are in exile or *in situ*) as conclusive evidence of the constitutional validity of a law face the problem whether they should examine that validity of the law. It is submitted that there is no rule of international law which prevents a court that is asked to give extraterritorial effect to the decree of a government in exile from examining (incidentally)

[201] See Beitzke, n. 147 above, 93–111 at 108 and the references there given. In favour of the Atkinson rather than the Devlin rule, also Lachs, 'Allied Governments in Exile. The Effect of Allied Legislation in Britain' (1942) 92 *Law Journal* 275–6 at 276; McNair, n. 89 above, at 36.

[202] e.g. in *In re Amand* Viscount Caldecote CJ held that the effect of Dutch Decree A.10 of 8 Aug. 1940 and the calling up notices was to change the applicant's civilian status to that of a member of the Dutch Army ([1941] 2 KB 239 at 254–5 (KBD)).

[203] Cf. *Ammon* v. *Royal Dutch Company* (1954), BGE 80 II 53.

[204] With respect to Dutch Decree A.10 of 8 Aug. 1940 providing for the call up of Dutch nationals in the UK, the USA, and Canada, Viscount Caldecote CJ said in *In re Amand*: 'Evidence is required to prove what is a question of fact, namely the foreign law' ([1941] 2 KB 239 at 253 (KBD)). For Canada, see *Re de Bruijn* (1941), [1942] 1 DLR 249 at 253. See also Táborský, 'The Constitutionality of Official Acts of Allied Governments and International Law' [1942] *CYBIL* 190–5 at 192.

[205] 28 NYS2d 547 at 551 (S.Ct., NY Co. 1941). The statement of the exiled government's diplomatic agent was also regarded as conclusive in *Amstelbank* v. *Guaranty Trust Co.*, 31 NYS2d 194 at 199 (S.Ct., NY Co. 1941); *Fields* v. *Predionica i Tkanica A.D.*, 35 NYS2d 408 at 412 (S.Ct., NY Co. 1942); *In re Black's Estate*, 150 P.2d 567 at 569 (CA, 2nd Dist., Div. 3, Cal. 1944). See also Kuhn, 'The Effect of a State Department Declaration of Foreign Policy upon Private Litigation—the Netherlands Vesting Orders' (1942) 36 *AJIL* 651–3.

whether it has properly been made in accordance with the constitution of the State which the exiled government represents.[206] Indeed, courts have on several occasions entered upon such an examination.[207] The question, however, is whether it is judicially expedient to do so. Practice shows that most exiled governments did not and, indeed, could not comply with their constitutional provisions concerning legislation.[208] Thus, courts which examined the constitutional validity of the laws of governments in exile had to have recourse to such dubious notions as expediency, emergency, and necessity, to the concept of inherent powers or to the principle of *impossibilium nulla obligatio* in order to uphold the constitutionality of the laws in question.[209] In *Boguslawski* v. *Gdynia-Ameryka Linie* (1950) Denning LJ stated with respect to the decrees of the governments in London imposing compulsory military service and requisitioning the ships of their nationals:

I do not know that our courts would ever embark on an inquiry whether those decrees were constitutionally valid according to the pre-war constitution of the country concerned.[210] If the exiled government was to exercise the functions of government, it must have the powers to make decrees, and if the old machinery could not be operated in exile, the exiled government must be able to adapt the

[206] Cf. Meyer and Torczyner, 'Corporations in Exile' (1943) 43 *Col. LR* 364–75 at 368–9; the case note by E. on the *El Condado* case, (1944) 21 *BYBIL* 188–94 at 190; McNair and Watts, n. 50 above, 440. For the examination of the 'formal validity' only see Wolff, n. 12 above, at 212. For further qualifications of the right to examine the constitutionality of foreign laws, see Mann, 'The Sacrosanctity of the Foreign Act of State' (1943) 59 *LQR* 155–71 at 157. On the examination of the constitutionality of foreign laws by English courts in general see *Dubai Bank Ltd* v. *Galadari and Others (No 5)* [1990] TLR 490; *Buck and Others* v. *Attorney-General* [1965] 1 Ch. 745 at 770 (CA). *Contra* the examination of the validity of the laws of exiled governments on grounds of the act of State doctrine, see King, 'Sitting in Judgment on the Acts of Another Government' (1948) 42 *AJIL* 811–31 at 822–30.

[207] Cf. *In re Amand (No 2)* [1942] 1 All ER 236 at 242–3, 248–50, 251; *In re Amand* [1941] 2 KB 239 at 252–3; *Lorentzen* v. *Lydden* (1941), [1942] 2 KB 202 at 204. In *Haak and Others* v. *Minister of External Affairs*, Jones J was inclined to the view that it did not fall within the jurisdiction of the Court to inquire into and determine the [constitutional] legality of the Royal [Netherlands] Decree, but nevertheless considered the validity of the decree and came to a conclusion in favour of it (SALR [1942] AD 318 at 326). The constitutionality of the Dutch Decree was also examined in *Assendelft* v. *Minister of External Affairs*, PH 1942 (1), K.46.

[208] Cf. Wolff, n. 12 above, at 213. See also the rather dubious attempt of M. Tschoffen, a Belgian Government official, to prove the 'constitutional validity' of the legislative acts of the 4-member Belgian Government in exile: 'The Exceptional Powers Exercised by the Belgian Government', *Message*, No 9 (July 1942), 23–7.

[209] See *In re Amand (No 2)* [1942] 1 All ER 236 at 244–6. See also the statement of an Official of the Royal Norwegian Ministry of Justice and Police: 'The authority of the King to enact provisions having legal power, without the constitutional sanction of the legislative body is, under the present circumstances, by virtue of the *principles of constitutional emergency*, amplified to embrace legal provisions of every kind' (n. 68 above, at 125, italics added). See further Drucker, n. 9 above, at 48–52; Jovičić, 'Le gouvernement en exil — Son statut légal. Ses pouvoirs — (Commentaires)' (1959) 6 *JRMP* 102–4 at 103.

[210] Denning LJ was mistaken as the English courts had on several occasions examined the constitutional validity of the decrees of governments in exile. See n. 207 above.

machinery so far as necessary for it to exercise its functions here. Otherwise our recognition of it might be rendered valueless to them and to us.[211]

Recognition of an authority in exile as a government by the executive, as a rule, entails the recognition of its exclusive competence to perform the legislative, administrative, and other functions appertaining to its State.[212] In order to avoid the risk of counteracting the executive's recognition by denying effect to the decree of the government in exile on the ground of its being unconstitutional, it is suggested that the courts should show judicial restraint and abstain from any examination of the constitutional validity of the laws of governments in exile and should, instead, examine only the international validity of these laws, i.e. whether they are a valid exercise of the State's legislative authority.[213]

(3) Public Policy

Courts recognize or enforce the decrees of governments in exile only if this is not contrary to the public policy of their State.[214] Public policy (*ordre public*) is not a uniform concept but is determined by the legal, political, social, and economic systems of each State. Nevertheless, the public policy of most States is opposed to the recognition or enforcement of foreign laws of a public law nature, such as confiscatory or penal laws, laws which adversely affect the rights of nationals or residents of the forum, or laws which conflict with laws of the forum. Thus, the decrees of the various Allied governments in exile during the Second World War which vested in their States title to the property of their nationals abroad could be given effect only in so far as they were not 'confiscatory or otherwise against the public policy of the forum'.[215] For example, in *Anderson* v. *NV*

[211] [1951] 1 KB 162 at 180. This may explain why, in all cases in which the constitutional validity of a decree was in fact examined, the decree was found to be constitutional.

[212] See the statements to this effect in *In re Amand (No 2)* [1942] 1 All ER 236 at 240; *Royal Hellenic Government* v. *Vergottis* (1945) 78 Ll. LR 292 at 297. See also *Anderson* v. *NV Transandine Handelmaatschappij*, 289 NY 9 at 15 (CA NY 1942).

[213] See also Táborský, n. 204 above, at 194; Beneš, 'Review of "McNair: Municipal Effects of Belligerent Occupation"' [1942] *CYBIL* 218–21 at 221; Hartmann, 'Conscription in the Allied Armies' (1941–2) 5 *MLR* 256–61 at 260–1. In *Fields* v. *Predionica i Tkanica AD*, the Supreme Court of New York stated: 'even if we assume that, because the requisition took place in Brazil [i.e. abroad], the Yugoslav Government must show that it acted in conformity with law. . . . The law applicable would be the rules of international law relating to the sovereign powers of governments, not any particular statutory authority of Yugoslavia' (37 NYS 2d 874 at 882 (S.Ct., App.Div., 1st Dept. 1942)).

[214] Cf. Rule 2 in Collins, n. 191 above.

[215] *NV Suikerfabriek 'Wono-Aseh'* v. *National Bank of City of New York*, 111 F.Supp. 833 at 846 (SDNY 1953).

Transandine Handelmaatschappij (1942)[216] the Court of Appeals of New York stated with respect to the Dutch vesting Decree No A.1 of 24 May 1940:

> Argument may be made that confiscatory decrees of foreign countries offend fundamental rules upon which our economic and social system rests, that no person may be deprived of his property without due process of law and upon payment of fair compensation. Here the challenged decree does not in purpose or effect violate that rule. Under its terms the State becomes in effect trustee for its subjects and their property which might otherwise be without protection and perhaps subject to seizure by a ruthless enemy.[217]

From this emphasis on the conservatory or protective purpose of the Dutch vesting Decree[218] it may be concluded that vesting decrees the (sole) purpose of which it is to raise funds for the maintenance of the government in exile or for the struggle against the authority *in situ* rather than to protect the interests of the State's nationals, as a rule will not be given effect to by foreign courts.[219] The same holds good in so far as these decrees exclude local creditors of a foreign debtor from resort to its property within the forum for the satisfaction of the debt[220] or prevent the imposition and collection of a tax by the forum State.[221] However, it seems that in some States, such as the United States, where public policy is used as a more

[216] 289 NY 9 (CA NY 1942). The decision in the *Anderson* case was expressly followed in *Duestervald* v. *Ladewig*, NYLJ (15 Jan. 1942), 215, col. 2 (S.Ct., NY Co. 1942); *Gruenebaum* v. *NV Oxyde Maatschappij Voor Ertsen En Metalen*, 57 NYS2d 152 (S.Ct., NY Co. 1942).

[217] 289 NY 9 at 19 (CA NY 1942). See also the judgment of Shientag J at first instance: 28 NYS2d 547 at 554 (S.Ct., NY Co. 1941).

[218] Art. 1(3) of Decree A.1 provided: 'The proprietary rights vested in the States of the Netherlands, by virtue of the provisions of the preceding paragraphs, shall only be exercised for the conservation of the rights of the former owners.' The protection of private interests was also stressed in *Ammon* v. *Royal Dutch Company* (1954) 21 ILR 25–9 at 25–6; *Rothschild* v. *NV Gebroeders Pappenheim's Tabakshandel*, 88 NYS2d 157 at 160 (S.Ct., NY Co. 1949); *Estate of Oei Tjong Swan* v. *Commissioner of Internal Revenue*, 24 TC 829 at 872, 874 (1955).

[219] It is probably for this reason that the explanatory note to the Kuwaiti Vesting Decree of 18 Oct. 1990 expressly stated that 'the purpose of this law is to enable the State of Kuwait . . . to take all necessary and appropriate measures to protect property belonging to Kuwaitis or residents of Kuwait' and that Art. 2 of the Decree referred to the Kuwaiti Government in exile as 'trustee' with the right to protect the aforementioned property of which it is the rightful owner (UN Doc.S/21887, 22 Oct. 1990, annex, at 2–3).

[220] Cf. *Anderson* v. *NV Transandine Handelmaatschappij*, 28 NYS2d 547 at 555–7 (S.Ct., NY Co. 1941), and 289 NY 9 at 19–20 (CA NY 1942); *In re Kahn's Estate*, 38 NYS2d 839 at 842 (Surr.Ct., NY Co. 1942); *NV Transandine Handelmaatschappij* v. *Massachusetts Bonding & Insurance Co.*, 40 NYS2d 499 at 502 (S.Ct., NY Co. 1943); *State of the Netherlands* v. *Federal Reserve Bank of New York*, 99 F.Supp. 655 at 662 (SDNY 1951); and 201 F.2d. 455 at 463 (2nd Cir. 1953). On the position of foreign creditors, see Domke, 'Dutch War-Time Legislation Before American Courts 1953' (1953–4) 1 *Ned. TIR* 365–73 at 366.

[221] With respect to Dutch Vesting Decree A.1 of 24 May 1940, see the decision of the US Tax Court in *Estate of Oei Tjong Swan* v. *Commissioner of Internal Revenue*, 24 TC 829 at 873–4 (1955).

political instrument, the executive or legislative branch of government may formulate an overriding public (or rather foreign) policy to the effect that the support for a government in exile or a common war effort requires that the vesting decrees of a government in exile are to be recognized or enforced by the courts, despite the fact that they are confiscatory or have adverse effects on the rights of local creditors, and that, as such, their recognition or enforcement would normally be contrary to the public policy of the State (or its federal States).[222] This use of public policy has been criticized on the ground that it attributed positive rather than restrictive force to public policy.[223] However, this is not correct. The overriding public or political policy does not make enforceable an otherwise unenforceable law but only 'overrides' the (general) public policy which would normally prevent the enforcement of an otherwise enforceable law.

[222] The question of two conflicting public policies, viz., the public policy to give effect to the Dutch Vesting Decree and the public policy to protect the rights of domestic creditors, arose *In re Kahn's Estate*, 38 NYS2d 839 at 842 (Surr.Ct., NY Co. 1942). The question, however, did not have to be decided as the Netherlands Government withdrew its claim to title to the property in question. See also *Anderson* v. *NV Transandine Handelmaatschappij*, 289 NY 9 at 17, 20 (CA NY 1942). See further Marks, 'Protective Expropriatory Decrees of the Governments in Exile—Their Application in the United States' (1941) 41 *Col. LR* 1072–87 at 1085. On the overriding public policy of the United States, as expressed in the Litvinov assignment, of giving effect to Russian confiscation decrees concerning property in the USA, see Jessup, 'The Litvinov Assignment and the Pink Case' (1942) 36 *AJIL* 282–8 at 285–6.

[223] See Wolff, *Private International Law* (2nd edn., 1950), 528. See also Devlin J in *Bank voor Handel en Scheepvaart NV* v. *Slatford* (1951), [1953] 1 QB 248 at 263–4. This criticism was based on Atkinson J's statement in *Lorentzen* v. *Lydden* (1941) that 'England and Norway are engaged together in a desperate war for their existence, and that *public policy demands* that effect should be given to this decree' ([1942] 2 KB 202 at 215–16, italics added). In favour of the idea that public policy demanded that effect be given to the decree of the Norwegian Government in exile, see Mann, 'Extraterritorial Effect of Confiscatory Legislation' (1941–2) 5 *MLR* 262–3 at 263.

6

Privileges and Immunities

1 INTRODUCTION

The question which is perhaps of greatest significance to the individual members of an authority in exile is whether and, if so, to what extent they enjoy privileges and immunities in the host State. While host States have accorded certain privileges and immunities to both recognized governments in exile and authorities in exile not recognized as governments,[1] only authorities in exile recognized as governments have claimed and enjoyed privileges and immunities *as of right*. Thus, a report of the Ministry of North-African Affairs to the Minister of External Affairs of the Provisional Government of the Algerian Republic (GPRA) on Algero–Tunisian relations, dated April 1960, reads:

> Ever since the proclamation of the GPRA the Tunisian Government has been unwilling to draw the juridical and diplomatic conclusions resulting from its recognition of the [Algerian] State or of the Algerian Government.
>
> On the practical level the recognition of our government, with all its juridical and diplomatic consequences, would have contributed considerably to the Algerian revolution in the sense that it would have entailed:
>
> 1. diplomatic status of the GPRA officials including immunity from civil and criminal jurisdiction, but, on the contrary, several of them have been arrested;
> 2. inviolability of GPRA premises;
> 3. inviolability of the correspondence of the GPRA;
> 4. exemption from customs duties for goods imported by the official services of the GPRA [author's translation].[2]

The GPRA's claim to certain privileges and immunities in Tunisia[3] as a consequence of Tunisian recognition of the State of Algeria and of the GPRA as its government[4] may be explained by the fact that an authority in exile recognized as the government of a State is, as organ of the State,

[1] e.g. France accorded diplomatic status to the members of the 'Spanish Republican Government' in exile in Paris from 1946 to 1961, although it did not recognize the 'Republican Government' as the Government of Spain (Iwańska, *Exiled Governments: Spanish and Polish* (1981), 2 and 35).

[2] ARA no 95, 447–58 at 455.

[3] Tunis was the political and diplomatic capital of the GPRA from 1960 to 1962 (Chikh, *L'Algérie en armes ou le temps des certitudes* (1981), 489).

[4] President Habib Bourguiba said during a press conference on 18 Feb. 1959: 'We have recognized the Algerian Government as the representative of the Algerian people, nation and State' (Bedjaoui, *Law and the Algerian Revolution* (1961), 113, n. 9).

entitled to benefit from the jurisdictional immunity of the State under international law.[5] Further, for an authority (irrespective of whether in exile or *in situ*) to qualify under international law as the government of a State and not just as the subsidiary organ of the government of another State, i.e. the host State, it must have a certain independence. A prerequisite of the independence of a government in exile however is its exemption and that of its officials from the jurisdiction of the host State.[6] While the Tunisian Government was not prepared to conclude an agreement with the GPRA clearly defining the latter's status in Tunisia, in practice, the GPRA on the whole enjoyed the above mentioned privileges and immunities.

The following examination will concentrate on the question to what extent authorities in exile which were recognized by their host State as a government have enjoyed privileges and immunities *as of right*. At the outset, however, a distinction must be drawn between the recognized government in exile as organ of the State, representing the State and its property, and individual members of the recognized government in exile and its army. The former, like its counterpart *in situ*, enjoys State or sovereign immunity, while the latter, as a rule, enjoy certain personal privileges and immunities within the host State. Only if legal proceedings are brought against them in their capacity as State representatives, will the question of immunity have to be determined in accordance with the rules of State immunity.[7]

2 GOVERNMENT IN EXILE

(1) *Jurisdictional Immunities*

(a) Action *in personam*

A State is generally represented by its government in judicial proceedings. Therefore an action against an authority in exile recognized by the forum as the government of a certain State *eo nomine* is not distinguishable from a

[5] On the jurisdictional immunity of States and their organs, see Jennings and Watts (eds.), *Oppenheim's International Law* (9th edn., 1992), i, 341–55; Verdross and Simma, *Universelles Völkerrecht* (3rd edn., 1984), §§ 1027, 1177.

[6] See *Ministère public* v. *D* (1915): 'the rights of inviolability and extraterritoriality accorded in one country to the representatives of another country derive, if no law expressly defines them, from traditional usage and are based on the necessity of making them independent of the head of State near whom they reside' ((1915–16) 11–12 RDIP 215–16 at 215, author's translation). See also Clunet, 'La présence des Alliés en France et "l'exterritorialité"' (1918) 45 *JDI* 514–17 at 515; Hurst, 'Les immunités diplomatiques' (1926–II) 12 *RdC* 119–241 at 144; King, 'Sitting in Judgment on the Acts of Another Government' (1948) 42 *AJIL* 811–31 at 818, 820–1.

[7] Cf. Art. 2.1(b)(i) and (v) of the ILC Draft Articles 1991 on jurisdictional immunities of States and their property 1991 (ILC Draft Articles 1991) and the commentary on these provisions: [1991] II–2 *ILC Yb*. 15, 18–19.

direct action against that State. Courts have long recognized the practical effect of an action against a foreign government (whether *in situ* or in exile) as identical to an action against the State.[8] As long as the State continues to be recognized as in existence the authority in exile recognized as its government shares its immunity from the jurisdiction of foreign courts. Thus, the Tribunal civil du Havre held in *Charron* v. *Evans et gouvernement belge* (1915) that the Belgian Government in exile at Sainte Adresse, which continued to be recognized by France as the Government of Belgium, was immune from suit on the ground that 'Belgium had not ceased to exist, that it was still a foreign State and that, as such, it was exempt from our jurisdiction'.[9] The immunity enjoyed by authorities in exile recognized as governments is, however, subject to the generally accepted exceptions to State immunity[10] and may be waived by them either expressly or by implication.[11] As not only the State as such but also its political sub-divisions (which are entitled to perform acts in the exercise of sovereign authority of the State) may enjoy jurisdictional immunity under certain conditions[12] so may authorities in exile recognized as the governments of such sub-divisions.[13]

[8] See the commentary on Art. 2.1(b)(i) of the ILC Draft Articles 1991: [1991] II–2 *ILC Yb.* 15. See also the commentary on Art. 6.2(a) ILC Draft Articles 1991: *ibid.*, at 24. See further s. 14(1)(b) of the UK State Immunity Act (SIA) 1978 which provides that 'references to a State include references to the government of that State'. Cf. also *Republic of Poland* v. *Dessaulles and Bar of Montreal* [1943] Qu. BR 224 at 232, affirmed *sub nom. Dessaulles* v. *Republic of Poland* [1944] SCR 275, and the declaration of the Foreign Office in *The Kabalo* that 'the British Government recognized the Belgian Government [at the time in exile in France] as an independent Sovereign State' ((1940) 67 Ll. LR 572 at 572).

[9] (1915–16) 11–12 RDIP 208–14 at 214, translation supplied. See also the statement of the Conseil de guerre belge at Le Havre, 21 July 1918, that 'another irrefutable proof of the coexistence of the Belgian and French sovereignties may be found in the fact that the French courts have generally refused to recognize their jurisdiction with respect to cases brought before them against the Belgian Government [at Le Havre]' (Travers, *Le droit pénal international et sa mise en œuvre en temps de paix et en temps de guerre* (1920), i, 241–5 at 244).

[10] It must be borne in mind that the cases decided during the First and Second World Wars were decided on the rule of absolute immunity. Nowadays the majority of States adhere to the rule of restrictive immunity whereby immunity is granted only for *acta jure imperii.* On the exceptions to jurisdictional immunity, see Jennings and Watts, n. 5 above, i, 355–63.

[11] *Charron* v. *Evans et gouvernement belge* (1915–16) 11–12 RDIP 208–14 at 214. Cf. also Arts. 7, 8 of ILC Draft Articles 1991; Arts. 1–3 of the European Convention on State Immunity (ECSI) 1972; s. 2 SIA 1978; § 1605(a)(1) of the US Foreign Sovereign Immunities Act (FSIA) 1976.

[12] Cf. Art. 2.1(b)(iii) of the ILC Draft Articles 1991; Art. 27 of the ECSI 1972; s. 14 of the SIA 1978; and § 1603(a) of the FSIA 1976.

[13] In *Grangemouth & Forth Towing Co.* v. *Government of the Netherlands East Indies* the Scottish Court of Session on 20 Mar. 1942 in an admiralty action *in personam* granted immunity to the Netherlands East Indies Government which had been in exile in Australia since 9 Mar. 1942 on the ground that it was a 'Sovereign State'. Lord Robertson thought that 'the designation under which the defenders are called is sufficient by itself to establish that point' ((1942) 72 Ll. LR 216 at 217). See in this connection also *Van Heyningen* v. *Netherlands-Indies Government* [1949] ST.R.Qd. 54 (FC), affirming [1948] QWN 19; and *Isbrandtsen* v. *Netherlands East Indies Government*, 75 F.Supp. 48 (SDNY 1947).

(b) Action *in rem*

Recognized governments in exile have successfully invoked State immunity not only in actions *in personam* but also in actions *in rem* against property under their control on the ground that such actions indirectly implead the State.[14] Thus during the Second World War the exiled Allied governments successfully invoked immunity in admiralty actions[15] seeking the seizure, arrest, or detention of ships and/or their cargo or freight which they had requisitioned in foreign territorial waters in order to further their war effort. However, the conditions on which immunity was granted by the various courts were not uniform. The only basic conditions required by all courts were that the authority in exile claiming immunity was recognized as a government by the government of the forum and that it was in factual possession of the ship.[16] If possession had been acquired within the limits of the territorial waters of the forum some courts further required that it had been acquired without compulsion or violence and without any other arbitrary interference in the earlier possession.[17] The requisition without compulsion of a ship flying the State's flag by its recognized government in exile, as an act of State sovereignty, was not regarded as an arbitrary interference with the earlier possession if the decree on which the requisition was based was in accordance with the public policy of the forum.[18] In contrast the validity of the requisition decree in the law of the exiled government was regarded as immaterial if the ship was in the possession of the government

[14] The immunity from jurisdiction of a vessel requisitioned by a government in exile may, however, not only be invoked in an action *in rem* against the vessel. See *Ex parte Sulman*, SALR [1942] CPD 407.

[15] On the extent of the Admiralty jurisdiction of the English High Court, see s. 20 of the Supreme Court Act (SCA) 1981.

[16] According to the judgment of Sir Boyd Merriman P in *The Kabalo* (1940) 67 Ll. LR 572 at 574, it is immaterial whether the ship is held by its master for named ministers of the government in exile or for the government in exile itself. On the condition of possession, see *The Anghyra*, 1941 AMC 1495 (ED Va. 1941); *The Margaret-Tassia*, 1941 AMC 1742 (SDNY 1941); *The Laurent Meeus*, 1941 AMC 991 (SD Cal. 1940), affirmed 43 F.Supp. 807 (SD Cal. 1942), modified 133 F.2d 552 (CA 9th Cir. 1942), cert. denied 318 US 781 (1943). US courts accepted as conclusive statements of fact by the diplomatic representatives of the government in exile concerning possession if they had been accepted 'as true' by the Department of State. See *American Tobacco Co.* v. *The Ioannis P. Goulandris*, 1941 AMC 1797 (SDNY 1941); *The Maliakos*, 1941 AMC 1737 (SDNY 1941).

[17] See the decisions of the Supreme Court of Sweden in *The Rigmor* (1942), (1943) 37 AJIL 141–51 at 148–9; and *The Solgry* (1942), (1919–42) 11 AD No 82, 153–4 at 154. But compare Lord Wright's speech in *The Cristina*: 'It is unnecessary to consider by what mode the respondent (i.e. the Spanish Republican Government) obtained possession. It is enough to ascertain that it had possession at the time when the claim to immunity was made' ([1938] AC 485 at 506). To the same effect see also the supplementary opinion in *The Janko (The Norsktank)*, 54 F.Supp. 241 at 243–4 (EDNY 1944).

[18] On these cases see also Jägerskiöld, 'The Immunity of State-Owned Vessels in Swedish Judicial Practice During World War II' (1948) 42 *AJIL* 601–7. For further background information on these cases, see Roskill, 'The Norwegian Ships in Sweden 1941/42' (1993) 109 *LQR* 59–65; and [1943] II FRUS 739–51.

in exile.[19] But the facts of requisition, i.e. that the ship had actually been requisitioned and that the government in exile was in actual possession of the ship, had to be proved by evidence.[20] With regard to the evolving rule of restrictive immunity some courts emphasized that the requisitioned ship was used for public purposes.[21] Although nowadays much depends on the immunity legislation enacted in a number of countries, as a general rule it may be stated that under the prevailing rule of restrictive immunity an authority in exile recognized as a government by the forum may invoke State immunity in an action *in rem* against a (validly) requisitioned ship and/or its cargo or freight if, at the time when the cause of action arose, it was used for government non-commercial purposes.[22]

(c) Action Against a Third Party

A State may be indirectly impleaded not only by an action *in rem* against its property but also by an action against a third party imperilling property in which it has a proprietary, possessory, or other interest.[23] Thus recognized governments in exile have successfully invoked immunity, for example, in actions against their nationals or natural and legal persons domiciled within their State's territory[24] wherein the plaintiff attached or seized certain property[25] alleged to belong to the defendant, the title to which had for

[19] *The Kabalo* (1940) 67 Ll. LR 572 at 574, 575. See also *Fields* v. *Predionica i Tkanica AD*, 37 NYS2d 874 at 882 (S.Ct., App.Div., 1st Dept. 1942), reversing 35 NYS2d 408 at 412 (S.Ct., NY Co. 1942), where the Appellate Division of the Supreme Court of New York held that even if, because the requisition had taken place abroad, the requisitioning government had to show that it had acted in conformity with the law 'the law applicable would be the rules of international law relating to the sovereign powers of governments, not any particular statutory authority' of the requisitioning State. The validity of the requisition in the law of the exiled government may, however, be relevant as regards the government's *right to possession*. See *Government of Kingdom of Belgium* v. *The Lubrafol*, 43 F.Supp. 403 at 407–8 (ED Tex. 1941).

[20] Cf. *The Anghyra*, 1941 AMC 1495 (ED Va. 1941).

[21] *The Rigmor* (1942), (1943) 37 AJIL 141–51 at 147–8; and *The Solgry* (1942), (1919–42) 11 AD No 82, 153–4 at 154. See also *The Janko (The Norsktank)*, 54 F.Supp. 240 and 241 (EDNY 1944). On the latter case see also the 'Representations to the United States by Norway, the UK, and the Netherlands Regarding Immunity from Suit of the MV "Norsktank"' [1944] V FRUS 1198–1205.

[22] Cf. Art. 16 ILC Draft Articles 1991. The Art. is phrased in general terms and does not expressly refer to proceedings *in rem* as such proceedings are peculiar to the common law jurisdictions. See commentary on Art. 16: [1991] II–2 *ILC Yb*. 51. Cf. also Arts. 1–3 of the International Convention for the Unification of Certain Rules Concerning the Immunity of State-owned Vessels 1926; s. 10 of the SIA 1978; and § 1605(b) of the FSIA 1976. A ship requisitioned by the government in exile to further its effort to oust the authority *in situ* will normally be in use for governmental purposes.

[23] See Art. 6.2(b) of the ILC Draft Articles 1991; Art. 13 of the ECSI 1972; and s. 6(4) of the SIA 1978.

[24] The same is true in garnishee proceedings.

[25] Both chattels and choses in action (such as bank accounts and securities).

protective purposes been vested by decree in the government in exile[26] or had been requisitioned by it.[27] However, a recognized government in exile claiming immunity with respect to property which is the subject of an action between private parties on the ground of its proprietary interest in the property will normally have the burden of proving its title by a preponderance of evidence if the *prima facie* evidence put forward is challenged by one of the parties.[28]

(2) Inviolability of Seat of Government in Exile

The seat of a government in exile, as a rule, is not extraterritorial in the sense that it is deemed to be outside the territory of the host State.[29] Only in exceptional circumstances have buildings used by members of recognized governments in exile temporarily been removed from the territorial sovereignty of the host State. For example, Ottawa Civic Hospital was declared extraterritorial and temporarily 'Dutch territory within Canada' by the Canadian Government in order to ensure that the heir to the throne was born on Dutch territory,[30] and in 1945 the Mexican President declared the building in Mexico City in which the Spanish Republican Cortes met to elect a new President temporarily Spanish territory as, according to the Spanish Constitution of 1931, the Cortes had always to meet on Spanish territory.[31] It is submitted that States which agree to the establishment of

[26] Cf. *Anderson* v. *NV Transandine Handelmaatschappij*, 289 NY 9 (CA NY 1942), affirming 31 NYS2d 194 (S.Ct., App.Div., 1st Dept. 1941), affirming 28 NYS2d 547 (S.Ct., NY Co. 1941). On immunity of expropriated property from the jurisdiction of the US courts, see Lourie and Meyer, 'Governments-in-Exile and the Effect of Their Expropriatory Decrees' (1943) 11 *U.Chicago LR* 26–48 at 35–8; and Marks, 'Protective Expropriatory Decrees of the Governments in Exile—Their Application in the United States' (1941) 41 *Col. LR* 1072–87 at 1076.

[27] Cf. *Fields* v. *Predionica i Tkanica AD*, 37 NYS2d 874 (S.Ct., App.Div., 1st Dept. 1942), reversing 35 NYS2d 408 (S.Ct., NY Co. 1942).

[28] In *Fields* v. *Predionica i Tkanica AD*, Shientag J held that (where the claim of immunity was not recognized by the State Department) the 'only course open to the movant [the Royal Yugoslav Government in exile] was to come into this court and establish its title to property in question and thereby have the attachment vacated' (35 NYS2d 408 at 411 (S.Ct., NY Co. 1942), reversed on other grounds, 37 NYS2d 874 (S.Ct., App.Div., 1st Dept. 1942)). See also *Fields* v. *Predionica i Tkanica AD*, 31 NYS2d 739 at 744 (S.Ct., App. Div. 1st Div. 1941). See in this connection also *Shearson Lehman Brothers* v. *Maclaine Watson & Co. Ltd (No 2)* in which the House of Lords held that where a foreign sovereign asserted a right of property it was open to a party to challenge the *prima facie* evidence and the legal burden of proving its case rested upon the sovereign who was seeking to assert it ([1988] 1 WLR 16 at 30–1).

[29] See *Ministère public* v. *D* and the note on that case: (1915–16) 11–12 RDIP 215–16. See also Jumeau, *Le Refuge du Gouvernement National à l'Etranger* (1941), 72; Langenhove, *L'action du Gouvernement belge en matière économique pendant la guerre* (1927), 30; Flory, *Le statut international des Gouvernements réfugiés et le cas de la France Libre 1939–1945* (1952), 20–1.

[30] *The Times*, 19 Jan. 1943, 6. On the extraterritoriality of the birthplace of the Dutch heir to the throne, see also *DCER* IX, nos 1516–17.

[31] Smith, *Mexico and the Spanish Republicans* (1955), 286; and Iwańska, n. 1 above, 94.

the government of a sovereign State on their territory must, in accordance with the legal principle *cuicunque aliquis quid concedit concedere videtur et id sine quo res ipsa esse non potuit*,[32] be deemed to have granted to the premises of that government the same inviolability and privileges as enjoyed by diplomatic premises, as only then will the government in exile be able to function as such.[33] Thus the Polish communiqué issued on 22 November 1939, on the occasion of the transfer of the Polish Government to Angers, reads in part as follows:

> The Government of the French Republic, which recognizes the full sovereignty of the Polish Government, has agreed to the establishment of the seat of the Polish Government in France at Angers, and for that purpose has granted all extraterritorial rights to the buildings occupied by the Polish organs and authorities.[34]

Problems may arise with respect to the archives and documents of a government in exile if the host State for political reasons withdraws its consent to the establishment of the seat of government in its territory but continues to recognize the exiled authority in question as a government. The situation is comparable to that of a special mission the function of which has come to an end. It is therefore suggested that the host State must grant the recognized government in exile facilities for removing its archives and documents from the host State.[35] If, however, the host State withdraws its recognition as the government of a certain State from an authority in exile it must preserve its premises, archives, and documents, as far as they concern State property, and turn them over to the newly recognized government of the State. Thus, when the British Government on 6 July 1945 withdrew recognition from the Polish Government in London, it announced the setting up of an Interim Treasury Committee for Polish Questions to administer the affairs and liquidate the machinery of the former Polish Government, and to negotiate with the Commission appointed by the Polish Provisional Government in Warsaw the orderly transfer to it of Polish State property.[36]

[32] Whoever grants a thing to any one is deemed also to grant that without which the grant itself would be of no effect.

[33] Cf. Arts. 22–24 of the Vienna Convention on Diplomatic Relations (VCDR) 1961. For the definition of 'premises', see Art. 1(i) of the VCDR 1961. Such premises also benefit from rules relating to State immunity: s. 16(1)(b) of the SIA 1978 and Art. 32 of the ECSI 1972.

[34] Gelberg, *Die Entstehung der Volksrepublik Polen* (1972), 30 (translation by the author). No special announcement to this effect was made by the French Government.

[35] In so far the situation of the government in exile is comparable with that of a special mission whose function has come to an end. Cf. Art. 45.2 of the Convention on Special Missions (CSM) 1969.

[36] See [1945] *Keesing's* 7301; DBPO, 1st ser., VI, no 2, at 6–8; DPSR II, no 382, 631–2 at 632. On the activities of the Interim Treasury Committee for Polish Questions, see also HC Debs., vol. 414, cols. 663–4, 15 Oct. 1945; *ibid*., vol. 420, col. 181, 5 Mar. 1946.

3 INDIVIDUAL MEMBERS OF THE GOVERNMENT IN EXILE AND ITS ARMY

(1) General Principle: Qui in territorio meo est, etiam meus subditus est

Territorial sovereignty has been defined as the exclusive and impenetrable authority of the State to regulate all conditions concerning persons, property, or events within the State's territory. Accordingly, whenever a person, whether as a private individual or as a member of a foreign government (either in exile or *in situ*) or its armed forces, enters a State's territory, it *ipso facto* subjects itself to the territorial jurisdiction of that State and to the possibility of civil suit and criminal prosecution in its courts.[37] States are, however, free to grant immunity from their territorial jurisdiction to whomever they like. Thus (host) States have accorded jurisdictional immunities as well as other privileges to members of both recognized governments in exile and authorities in exile not recognized as a government. For example, section 1(1) of the Diplomatic Privileges (Extension) Act 1941[38] extended diplomatic immunities and privileges to members of the governments, provisional governments, national committees, and other foreign authorities established in the United Kingdom. Similarly, members and officials of the Allied governments in London and certain leading members and officials of authorities in exile not recognized as governments were exempt from the obligation to register in the United Kingdom under the International Labour Force (Registration of Foreign Nationals) Orders 1941 and 1943.[39] The discussion below concerns which individual members of a recognized government in exile and its armed forces may claim (personal) immunity from the jurisdiction of the host State and certain other privileges *as of right*. In the absence of an international convention governing this question any such claim can be based only on customary international law.[40]

[37] See Jennings and Watts, n. 5 above, i, 384, 904–5; Ipsen, *Völkerrecht* (3rd edn., 1990), § 23, No 4, 249. Cf. also Art. 15 of the OAS Charter and Lord Macmillan's speech in *The Cristina*: 'It is an essential attribute of the sovereignty of this realm, as of all sovereign independent States, that it should possess jurisdiction over all persons and things within its territorial limits' ([1938] AC 485 at 496 (HL)). With respect to members of the armed forces of a government in exile, see the *Allied Forces (Czechoslovak) Case* (1942), where the Czechoslovak Military Court of Appeal in London held that 'all members of the Czechoslovak Army, who are for the time being in Great Britain . . . are . . . subject to the territorial sovereignty of the British constitutional authorities as long as they stay on this territory' ((1941–2) 10 AD No 31, 123–8 at 124).

[38] 4 & 5 Geo. 6., c. 7. S. 5 of the Diplomatic Privileges (Extension) Act 1944 (7 & 8 Geo. 6, c. 44) provided for the continued extension of these immunities and privileges to members of such governments and authorities even when no longer established in the UK.

[39] See S.R. & O. 1941 Nos 719–24; S.R. & O. 1943 No 381.

[40] The members of a government in exile are covered neither by the VCDR 1961 nor the Vienna Convention on Consular Relations (VCCR) 1963 or the CSM 1969. All three Conventions affirm in their preamble that 'the rules of customary international law (should) continue to govern questions/matters not (expressly) regulated by the provisions of the present Conven-

(2) Heads of State

Customary international law has long recognized the general exemption of a Head of State,[41] whether in exile or only on a visit abroad, from the jurisdiction of the host State if he or she is staying with the consent of its government.[42] This is affirmed in a letter dated 3 May 1941 from the Canadian Secretary of State to the Minister of the Netherlands which reads in the relevant part: 'I am pleased to inform you that the Canadian Government is prepared to recognize the Grand Duchess [of Luxembourg] as a reigning sovereign provisionally abroad and as such enjoying, as of right under international law, the generally accepted immunities from civil and criminal jurisdiction and from taxation'.[43] It was for this reason that the British Diplomatic Privileges (Extension) Act 1941 did not provide for privileges and immunities for the Heads of State of the Allied Governments in London.[44] However, the basic precondition for personal immunity is that the exiled head of State is recognized as such.[45] Thus on 22 January 1991 the Tribunal de Paris ordered Prince Norodom Sihanouk, the 'President [in exile] of Cambodia', who was not recognized as such by the French Government, to pay the Foreign Minister of the ruling State of Cambodia (SOC) Hor Nam Hong 20,000 francs in a defamation suit.[46] In an early precedent,

tion'. It is interesting to note, however, that the Lord Chancellor, Viscount Simon, compared the situation of the members of governments and authorities in exile as regards privileges and immunities with that of a 'Special Envoy who may enjoy what corresponds to diplomatic privilege in certain cases' (HL Debs., vol. 118, col. 191, 19 Dec. 1940).

[41] Head of State is often understood to include the head of government. See, e.g., *Saltany* v. *Reagan* where Head of State immunity was granted to the Prime Minister of the UK (702 F.Supp. 319 at 320 (DDC 1988), order affirmed in part, reversed in part (on other grounds), 886 F.2d 438 (DC Cir. 1989), cert. denied, 495 US 932 (1990)).

[42] e.g. in 1688 James II, the last Stuart King, fled to France where he lived for the next 13 years at St Germain. Louis XIV, who continued to recognize the exiled King as *chef d'Etat*, accorded him all the privileges attaching to this quality. Cf. 'Transference of the Belgian Government to Havre' (1914) 137 *LT* 598. See also the judgment of Marshall CJ in *The Schooner Exchange* v. *M'Faddon* (1812) 7 Cranch 116 at 137–8. For a more recent pronouncement to this effect, see BGH, 14 Dec. 1984 [*In re Honnecker*]: BGHSt 33, 97 at 98. On head of State immunity in general, see Jennings and Watts, n. 5 above, i, 1036–7.

[43] DCER VIII, no 762, at 925–6. On exemption of the Grand Duchess, her family and suite from customs duties, see *ibid.*, no 763, 927–8 at 928.

[44] i.e. the Kings of Norway, Greece, and Yugoslavia, the Queen of the Netherlands, and the Presidents of Poland and Czechoslovakia. Speaking in the debate on the Diplomatic Privileges (Extension) Bill, the Lord Chancellor, Viscount Simon, said: 'The legal position is undoubtedly . . . that the Sovereigns or heads of States of the foreign Governments as such already enjoy immunity, which is secured by rules of International Law and recognized in our own Courts' (HL Debs., vol. 118, cols. 191–2, 19 Dec. 1940). For a similar statement, see also HC Debs. vol. 369, col. 330, 20 Feb. 1941. See nowadays s. 20(1) and (5) of the SIA 1978.

[45] See *Lafontant* v. *Aristide*, 844 F.Supp. 128 at 131–3 (EDNY 1994). The continued recognition of an exiled head of State by the government of the forum may also preclude immunity of the *de facto* head of State. See *United States* v. *Noriega*, 746 F.Supp. 1506 at 1519–20 (SD Fla. 1990).

[46] (1991) 10/1 *Ind. Chron.* 10. For further information, see (1990) 9/1 *Ind. Chron.* 12, and (1990) 9/4 *Ind. Chron.* 14. The case is briefly reported as *X* v. *Y*. [1991] Recueil Dalloz Sirey N.

immunity was denied by the Cour de Paris in 1872 to Isabella of Spain, who had been deposed in 1868 and had settled in France, on the ground that she had acted as a private person and not as a head of State.[47] In addition to personal immunities, recognized exiled heads of State are entitled by virtue of customary international law to exemption from military and other services[48] and special protection as regards their personal safety and dignity. This was confirmed in an opinion of the Political Department of the Swiss Confederation (EPD) on the question whether Queen Wilhelmina of the Netherlands, despite the fact that she was in exile, was covered by Article 296 of the Swiss Criminal Code (StGB) which provided for the special protection of foreign Heads of State against insults. In its opinion of 15 June 1943 for the Higher Court of Zurich the EPD pointed out:

> the fact that the Royal Netherlands Government no longer resides in its own country but in England, does not alter that position, as the Swiss Confederation continues to recognize that Government and maintains diplomatic relations with it. . . . This must be binding for the Swiss criminal judge who has to apply Art. 296 StGB. . . . If Switzerland recognizes a foreign State and its government, it will also have to grant its head of State and its diplomatic representative the protection of its criminal law, which international law and the comitas gentium demand.[49]

In conclusion it may be stated that, as far as privileges and immunities are concerned, the legal position of an exiled head of State does not differ from

12 (21 Mar. 1991), Informations Rapides (IR), 77. On 17 July 1991 Prince Sihanouk was elected President of the Supreme National Council (SNC) of Cambodia and on 20 Nov. 1991 he was recognized by the SOC Government as the 'legitimate head of State'. See also *Re Arafat and Salah* (1985), in which the President of the PLO, Mr Yasser Arafat, was denied Head of State immunity from Italian criminal jurisdiction by virtue of customary international law on the ground that the PLO did not qualify as a State ((1988) 7 Ital. YIL 295–8).

[47] See *Mellerio* v. *Isabelle de Bourbon, ex-reine d'Espagne* (1872), (1874) 1 JDI 32–3.

[48] The question of militia service arose in 1795 with respect to William V of the Netherlands who took refuge in England upon the overrunning of the Netherlands by France and continued to be recognized by England as the Head of State of the Netherlands. See BDIL VII, 106–8, and McNair, *International Law Opinions* (1956), i, 108–10.

[49] The opinion of the EPD and related material is reproduced in Klarer, *Schweizerische Praxis der völkerrechtlichen Anerkennung* (1981), 194–5 (translation by the author). The defendant had argued that his insult to Queen Wilhelmina was not covered by Art. 296 StGB, as the Queen, being in exile, could no longer be regarded as a Head of State. See in this connection also *Public Prosecutor* v. *TJ* [1954] NJ No 649, 1207. In this case the defendant was prosecuted under Art. 117 of the Dutch Criminal Code for in 1951 insulting the Head of State of Spain, General Franco. The defence submitted that the defendant had no intention of insulting a Head of State, as it was his opinion that the Head of the legitimate Spanish Government was outside Spain. This submission, however, was dismissed by the court on the ground that it was a well known fact that the Dutch Government recognized the Franco Government and not the Republican Government in exile. Exiled Heads of State (irrespective of whether or not they are recognized as such) may, of course, also avail themselves of ordinary criminal or civil procedures to protect themselves against libel and slander. See e.g. *Haile Selassie* v. *Evening Standard Company, Limited*, *The Times*, 28 July 1938, 4; *Zog, King of the Albanians* v. *Sunday Pictorial Newspapers (1920), Limited*, *The Times*, 28 May 1943, 8.

that of a head of State on a (temporary) visit abroad. In both cases the enjoyment of privileges and immunities under customary international law depends solely on the (continued) recognition of the head of State as such and (with regard to the host State) the consent of the host government to his or her presence in its territory.

(3) Members of Government and Senior Staff

While exiled heads of State may, without doubt, claim personal immunities and privileges by virtue of customary international law, the legal position of the members of a government in exile and their senior staff seems less clear. The British Under-Secretary of State for Foreign Affairs, Mr Butler, stated in Parliament on 20 February 1941: 'The legal position of the sovereigns or heads of States is covered by international law and recognized in our own courts, but the individual members of Allied Governments and their official staffs are not so covered.'[50] Accordingly, the British Government considered it necessary to pass the Diplomatic Privileges (Extension) Act 1941[51] to confer upon the individual members of the Allied Governments and their senior staff personal privileges and immunities.[52] But the United Kingdom is the only host State of a recognized government in exile that has passed such legislation.[53] One reason for this may be that in the view of other host

[50] HC Debs., vol. 369, col. 330, 20 Feb. 1941. The Canadian Secretary of State for External Affairs, Mr King, wrote on 3 May 1941: 'The position of individual members of allied governments and their official staffs is one of some difficulty. Unlike sovereigns, or heads of states, their status is not covered by international law, recognized in the courts. . . . Briefly, therefore, the position is that members of the Luxembourg Government, not having diplomatic status, are not entitled, under international law, to rights of extra-territoriality' (DCER VIII, no 762, at 926).

[51] 4 & 5 Geo. 6, c. 7. See also s. 5 of the Diplomatic Privileges (Extension) Act 1944 (7 & 8 Geo. 6, c. 44). For instructive statements by members of the British Government in the debates on the Diplomatic Privileges (Extension) Bill in Parliament, see HC Debs., vol. 369, cols. 329–35, 20 Feb. 1941; HL Debs., vol. 118, cols. 190–4 19 Dec. 1940. See also Schwelb, 'The Status of Allied Governments under the Diplomatic Privileges (Extension) Act, 1941' [1942] *CYBIL* 201–2; and Kerchove d'Exaerde, 'Quelques questions en droit international public relatives à la présence et à l'activité du gouvernement belge en exil à Londres (Octobre 1940–Septembre 1944)' (1990) 23 *RBDI* 93–151 at 122–7.

[52] The Lord Chancellor, Viscount Simon, said: 'legislation is needed to enable us to confer upon individual members of the Allied Governments and their official staffs the privileges and immunities to which their position and standing rightly entitles them' (HL Debs., vol. 118, col. 192, 19 Dec. 1940).

[53] For France in 1914–18 and 1939–40, compare the issues of the JORF for these years, and (1915–16) 11–12 *RDIP* 216, n. 1. For Egypt in 1943–4, compare Chlala, 'Législation égyptienne en matière de Droit international de 1936 à 1946' (1946) 2 *Rev. égypt.* 73–97. For Saudi Arabia 1990–1, compare Al Roumi, *The Crime* (1991). However, the existing legislation on diplomatic privileges and immunities of the host State may be phrased in broad enough terms to cover under certain circumstances also members of a government in exile and their senior staff. Compare, e.g., Arts. 22, 23 of the Regulations of the People's Republic of China on Diplomatic Privileges and Immunities 1986; and § 20(1) of the German Judicature Act (GVG). On the latter, see Kissel, *Gerichtsverfassungsgesetz* (2nd edn., 1994), § 20, No 32.

States the members of a government in exile and their senior staff already enjoy immunity recognized by their courts by virtue of customary international law. This view is supported by the decisions of the French courts with respect to the members of the Belgian Government at Sainte Adresse during the First World War. For example, the Tribunal civil du Havre held in *Charron* v. *Evans et gouvernement belge* (1915) that 'the rules of international law oppose any act of judicial sovereignty which is incompatible with the inviolability of their ministers and of the dignity of the state which they represent'.[54] For such a rule of customary international law to exist according to the predominant view two elements are necessary: constant and uniform State practice, and *opinio juris vel necessitatis*, i.e. the conviction that the practice conforms to a legal obligation.[55] A review of State practice since the First World War shows that all host States, with the exception of Canada,[56] have granted to the members of recognized governments in exile and some or all of their (senior) staff what were formerly called 'rights of extra-territoriality', such as personal immunities and certain other privileges: on 11 October 1914 the French President, M. Poincaré, informed King Albert of the Belgians that 'the Government of the Republic . . . will immediately take the necessary measures in order to guarantee in France the stay of Your Majesty and of his Ministers in full independence and sovereignty'.[57] Similarly, in 1939 the French Government granted 'all extraterritorial rights to . . . the members of the [Polish] Government and their official staff'[58] and in 1940 it assured the Belgian Government of the exercise of its full independence and granted the Belgian

[54] (1915–16) 11–12 RDIP 208–14 at 213, translation supplied. See also the decision of the Tribunal correctionnel du Havre in *Ministère public* v. *D* (1915): 'the members of the Belgian Government, who are at present residing in France, enjoy all the rights of inviolability and extraterritoriality, without it being necessary to determine these rights in a written act or decree' (*ibid.*, 215–16 at 215, author's translation). See also the note on these cases: *ibid.*, at 216.

[55] Bernhardt, 'Customary International Law' in Bernhardt (ed.), *Encyclopedia of Public International Law* (1992), i, 898–905 at 899. See also *Military and Paramilitary Activities Case*, ICJ Rep. 1986, 14 at 108–9.

[56] Cf. DCER VIII, no 762, at 926. However, it must be noted that the Luxembourg Prime Minster had stated in an *aide mémoire* that he asked for no privileges or derogations not enjoyed by Canadians. But the Canadian Government issued members of the Luxembourg Government in Montreal with identification cards granted to the heads of diplomatic missions, granted them diplomatic visas, and exempted them from national registration, customs duties, and income tax. See *ibid.*, no 763, at 928.

[57] *Correspondance diplomatique relatif à la guerre de 1914–1915* (1915), ii, no 56, at 49 (author's translation); Langenhove, n. 29 above, 232. See also Strisower, 'L'exterritorialité et ses principales applications' (1923) 1 *RdC* 233–87 at 269. Similar assurances were given in Jan. 1916 to the King and Government of Montenegro. It is of interest to note in this connection that during the negotiations between the Governments of Russia and Romania in July–Aug. 1917 on the establishment of the Romanian Government at Kerson in Russia the Russian Government guaranteed the extraterritoriality of the Romanian Government in Russia (Jumeau, n. 29 above, 154).

[58] Gelberg, n. 34 above, 30. On 20 Sept. 1939 the French Prime Minister, M. Daladier, wrote to the Polish Ambassador in Paris that 'the hospitality of allied France is guaranteed to the

officials diplomatic immunities.[59] By the Diplomatic Privileges (Extension) Act 1941 the British Government granted diplomatic privileges and immunities to the members and senior officials of the seven Allied Governments in London.[60] The Egyptian Government also announced in June 1943 that it 'granted, on temporary and exceptional terms, diplomatic status to all members of the Greek Government and Greek Foreign Office officials'.[61] In order to surround the French puppet governmental authority in exile in Sigmaringen (southern Germany) with all the trappings of a 'genuine' government in exile the German Government decided at the end of September 1944 to accord the privilege of extraterritoriality to the 'Commission gouvernementale française pour la Défense des Intérêts nationaux'.[62] Owing to the short lived exile of the Government of Kuwait at Taif, the Saudi Government did not specially issue a list of diplomatic privileges of the members and high officials of the Kuwaiti Government. But in principle, the Kuwaiti Government at Taif was treated as the legal government of Kuwait[63] and 'the Amir of Kuwait and his Crown Prince and Ministers were . . . treated with the utmost of dignity and respect'.[64] It is submitted that this settled practice raises a strong presumption of *opinio juris*[65] to the effect that members of an authority in exile recognized as a government and their senior staff are legally entitled to personal immunities and certain other privileges in the recognizing host State. This presumption is supported by the following statement of the British Under-Secretary of State for Foreign Affairs, made on the occasion of moving the Second Reading of the Diplomatic Privileges (Extension) Bill: 'I feel confident that the House will wish to honour these Allied Governments by giving to them the independent and dignified status to which their position

President of the Republic and to the Polish Government and that the French Government is ready to take all measures safeguarding the sovereign rights of the Head of the Polish State in order to guarantee the extraterritorial exercise of His powers and those of His Government' (Fiedorowicz, 'Continuité de l'Etat' (1939) 24 *RDI* 129–75 at 167, author's translation).

[59] Halajczuk, *Los estados conquistados ante el derecho internacional* (1950), 126.

[60] On this Act, see n. 51 above. For the fact that the Act was only to cover 'the members and senior officials of the Allied Governments', see HC Debs., vol. 369, col. 331, 20 Feb. 1941 (Mr Butler).

[61] (1943) 8 *Free Europe* 14. The Greek Government, except for the Ministries of Finance, Mercantile Marine, and Information, was transferred from London to Cairo on 24 Mar. 1943. With respect to the Netherlands Indies Government to be established in Camp Columbia, Brisbane, the Australian Minister for External Affairs, Dr Evatt, wrote on 5 Apr. 1944 to the Dutch Minister to Australia: 'The Australian authorities will be glad to extend to the Lieutenant-Governor-General and his Council all appropriate courtesies and facilities' (DAFP VII, no 107, at 225–6).

[62] See the letter of M. de Brinon to Marshal Pétain of 30 Sept. 1944: Noguères, *La dernière étape: Sigmaringen* (1956), 68; Brissaud, *Pétain à Sigmaringen (1944–1945)* (1960), 231.

[63] Exchange of letters between the Saudi Ambassador to London, M. Ghazi Algosaibi, and the author.

[64] Rashid and Shaheen, *Saudi Arabia and the Gulf War* (1992), 203.

[65] Cf. Brownlie, *Principles of Public International Law* (4th edn., 1990), 8.

and Sovereign powers *entitle* them.'[66] In conclusion it may thus be stated that, as a rule, the members of an authority in exile recognized as a government and their senior staff enjoy personal privileges and immunities in the recognizing host State on the basis of a rule of customary international law.[67] These privileges and immunities are normally granted not only for the period of the actual exile but also for a limited period after the return of the government to its State in order to allow it to wind up its affairs in the host State.[68]

The significance of recognition by the host State for the enjoyment of diplomatic privileges and immunities is well illustrated by the case of the Polish Government in London. Upon withdrawal of recognition by the British Government on 6 July 1945 the members of the Polish Cabinet and other high officials, including President Raczkiewicz, lost their diplomatic privileges and immunities and had to register as aliens,[69] despite the fact that some twenty other States continued to recognize the Polish Government in London as the Government of Poland.[70] On 29 January 1946, at a time when some ten States still recognized the London Polish Government,[71] Mr Noel-Baker, the Minister of State for Foreign Affairs, wrote: 'No diplomatic privileges are granted to any members of the Polish Government formerly established in this country'.[72]

Who is a 'member of the government' will normally depend on the use of the term in the domestic law of the host State. Thus 'member of the government' in the Diplomatic Privileges (Extension) Act 1941 was used in

[66] HC Debs., vol. 369, col. 329, 20 Feb. 1941, italics added. For a similar statement by the Lord Chancellor, Viscount Simon, see n. 52 above. But see also the statement of the Solicitor-General, Sir William Jowitt, that 'the Bill . . . is designed as *a matter of courtesy* to the people whom we desire to shelter' (*ibid.*, vol. 369, col. 333, 20 Feb. 1941, italics supplied).

[67] So also Dahm, *Völkerrecht* (1958), i, 308. See also Blumenwitz, 'Genieβt der Vorsitzende des Staatsrates der DDR in der Bundesrepublik Immunität nach den allgemeinen Regeln des Völkerrechts' [1985] *JZ* 614–18 at 615. Doubtful about any clear rule of customary international law are Jennings and Watts, n. 5 above, i, 1125, n. 2. The fact that the members of governments in exile and their senior staff are not expressly included in Art. 3.2 of the ILC Draft Articles 1991 does not prejudice the extent of privileges and immunities granted to them by host States under customary international law. Cf. commentary on Art. 3.2 of the ILC Draft Articles 1991: [1991] II–2 *ILC Yb*. 22.

[68] The UK accorded diplomatic privileges and immunities to members of the Allied Governments and their senior staff still operating in London after the liberation of their States. See [1945] III Lond. Gaz. 3563–5 (10 July 1945), 4026 (7 Aug. 1945), 4708 (21 Sept. 1945); [1945] IV Lond. Gaz. 5481 (9 Nov. 1945), 5950–1 (7 Dec. 1945). See also s. 5 of the Diplomatic Privileges (Extension) Act 1944 (7 & 8 Geo. 6, c. 44).

[69] See Rozek, *Allied Wartime Diplomacy* (1958), 400. See also [1945] III Lond. Gaz. 3564 (10 July 1945).

[70] See DBPO, 1st ser., VI, no 70.i, at 273.

[71] See Charpentier, *La reconnaissance internationale et l'évolution du droit des gens* (1956), 226.

[72] HC Debs., vol. 418, WA, *col.* 188, 29 Jan. 1946. See also the statement of the Canadian Secretary of State for External Affairs, Mr King: 'it will be feasible to exempt from income tax the members of the Government, staff and retinue of Her Royal Highness in Canada while . . . they remain in this country *under their present status* of a Government in exile' (DCER VIII, no 763, 927–8 at 928, italics added).

the British sense as meaning (only) one of the cabinet ministers.[73] Difficulties may arise in drawing the line between the senior staff and the more numerous junior clerical and subordinate staff of a member of the government in exile. Section 1(1) of the Diplomatic Privileges (Extension) Act 1941 defined the senior staff of a member of the government as persons 'recognized by His Majesty to be performing duties no less responsible than those of a Diplomatic Secretary'. By section 1(2) the Secretary of State was to compile (and keep up-to-date) a list of persons to whom immunities and privileges were extended, the list being conclusive evidence whether a certain person enjoys privileges and immunities at any one time.[74] It is suggested that nowadays the proper point of reference is the 'member of the diplomatic staff' of a diplomatic mission.[75] As it may sometimes be difficult for the courts and authorities of the host State to compare the responsibilities of a (senior) government official with those of a member of the diplomatic staff it is suggested that in the interest of legal certainty the host government follows the example of the British Government during the Second World War and compiles a list of the senior staff to whom privileges and immunities are extended.[76] The host government may thereby keep the number of senior staff within limits which it considers as reasonable and normal.[77]

It was pointed out by Mr Butler, the British Under-Secretary of State, that the Diplomatic Privileges (Extension) Bill proposed to 'confer a

[73] Cf. the statement of the Lord Chancellor, Lord Simon: HC Debs., vol. 118, col. 192, 19 Dec. 1940.

[74] The number of members of the Allied Governments in London and their senior staff to whom diplomatic privileges and immunities were extended varied according to the total number of officials of the respective governments. According to the 'List of persons to whom immunities and privileges are extended under s. 1(2) of the Diplomatic Privileges (Extension) Act, 1941', published in The London Gazette from 26 Aug. 1941 to 10 July 1945, the following picture emerges. The figures given under I. refer to the number of 'Members of the Government' and the ones under II. refer to the number of 'Official Staffs of the Members of the Government' to which diplomatic privileges and immunities were accorded at any one time during the above mentioned period:

Belgium	I. 3–7,	II. 74–115	Czechoslovakia	I. 10–14,	II. 38–60
Greece	I. 2–5,	II. 7–22	Luxembourg	I. 1–4,	II. 1–4
Netherlands	I. 9–14,	II. 63–97	Norway	I. 12–13,	II. 44–88
Poland	I. 10–15,	II. 56–111	Yugoslavia	I. 3–13,	II. 12–32
(Free France	I. 3–9,	II. 6–20)			

It is of interest to note that in Aug. 1941 the Belgian Government in London had about 700 staff (Kerchove d'Exaerde, n. 51 above, at 127).

[75] See Art. 1(d) of the VCDR 1961.

[76] See in this connection § 20(1) of the German Judicature Act (GVG) which provides that the representatives of foreign States and their staffs ('Begleitung'), who stay in Germany at the official invitation of the German Government, enjoy diplomatic privileges and immunities. According to parliamentary materials staff means only such personnel included in a 'list of delegation' accepted by the German Government. See BT–Drs. 10/1447, at 14.

[77] Cf. Art. 11 of the VCDR 1961. The British Government refused governments with a lot of personnel the inclusion in the list of persons with a rank equivalent to third secretary while it included such person in the case of governments with less staff (Kerchove d'Exaerde, n. 51 above, at 123).

position corresponding to that of members of the Diplomatic Corps upon the members and senior officials of the Allied Governments. . . . Such privileges were accorded to the Government of Belgium during the last war by the French Government;[78] while in this war, before the fall of France, privileges similar to those suggested here were afforded by France to the Poles.'[79] The privileges and immunities accorded to the members of those governments in exile and their senior staff include, *inter alia*, personal inviolability, immunity from criminal and, with certain exceptions, civil and administrative jurisdiction, freedom from taxation, rating, and fiscal regulations,[80] and exemption from registration[81] and visa requirements.[82] In so far as the Vienna Convention of Diplomatic Relations 1961 codifies customary international law it may thus be applied, *mutatis mutandis*, to the members and senior officials of a government in exile. Furthermore, by virtue of their position equal to that of diplomatic agents the members of a government in exile and their senior staff also come within the scope of the Convention on the Prevention and Punishment of Crimes Against Internationally Protected Persons, including Diplomatic Agents.[83]

(4) Junior and Subordinate Staff

While junior and subordinate government officials have been treated by the host State as friendly aliens and have been granted certain privileges and immunities on the basis of special legislation[84] they have, unlike senior officials, not been granted immunity *ratione personae*.[85] This may be

[78] In *Charron* v. *Evans et gouvernement belge* (1915), the Tribunal civil du Havre held that 'the immunity attached to the situation of this government and of the ministers forming it is the same which for example the Belgian ambassador to Paris enjoys' ((1915–16) 11–12 RDIP 208–14 at 213, translation supplied).

[79] HC Debs., vol. 369, cols. 330–1, 20 Feb. 1941, italics added. For a similar statement by the Lord Chancellor, Viscount Simon, see HL Debs., vol. 118, col. 192, 19 Dec. 1940.

[80] *Ministère public* v. *D* (1915), (1915–16) 11–12 RDIP 215–16. Cf. also Arts. 29, 31(1), 34 of the VCDR 1961. See also Clunet, n. 6 above, at 514–15.

[81] See s. 3 of the International Labour Force (Registration of Foreign Nationals) Order 1941 (S.R. & O. 1941 Nos 719–724).

[82] The reason given for the exemption of the members and senior officials of the Belgian Government from visa requirements was 'the rights of sovereignty which were granted to the Belgian Government on French territory'. See the statement of the French Minister of the Interior in the Senate on 18 Nov. 1915: [1915] JORF 607, col. 2 (author's translation).

[83] Cf. Art. 1(1)(b) of the Convention in connection with Art. 29 of the VCDR 1961. The Convention was opened for signature on 14 Dec. 1973. For text, see (1974) 13 ILM 41. See also s. 1(5)(b) of the UK Internationally Protected Persons Act 1978.

[84] By s. 3 of the various International Labour Force (Registration of Foreign Nationals) Orders 1941 and 1943, all officials of the Allied Governments in exile engaged upon official business in Great Britain were exempt from the obligation to register. On the immunities and privileges enjoyed by the members of the Allied maritime courts established in the UK during the Second World War, see s. 1(5) of the Allied Powers (Maritime Courts) Act 1941 (4 & 5 Geo. 6, c. 21).

[85] Statements on the granting of privileges and immunities to the officials of governments in exile have regularly spoken only of ministers, members of the government, or senior govern-

explained by the fact that personal privileges and immunities for the more numerous clerical and subordinate staff does not seem necessary to safeguard the independence of the government in exile in the same way as in the case of senior, responsible government officials. Junior officials should, however, enjoy immunity *ratione materiae*.[86] As government officials they are, irrespective of their seniority, State representatives, and as such their official acts may be attributed to the State. Subjecting the official acts of junior officials of the government in exile to the jurisdiction of the host State would mean subjecting their State itself to that jurisdiction. This, however, would be inconsistent with the concept of State or of sovereign immunity.[87] It is for this reason that, for example, members of the non-diplomatic staff of permanent and *ad hoc* missions,[88] as well as consular officers and staff,[89] enjoy (limited) immunity in respect of acts performed in the exercise of their official functions. The same, however, must be true for the junior and subordinate officials of governments in exile.

(5) Members of the Armed Forces of the Government in Exile

The question of immunity of the individual members of foreign armed forces from the civil and criminal jurisdiction of the host State is a general question,[90] not restricted to the armed forces of a government in exile, although it regularly arises when a government goes into exile, as it is usually accompanied by (the remains of its defeated) armed forces or raises such forces in the host State. As in the case of visiting armed forces which

ment officials. In the only case that concerned the responsibility of a junior government official, viz. the General Prosecutor of the Czechoslovak Military Court of Appeal, for a libel contained in an official communication, the question of immunity was not argued. Cf. *Szalatnay-Stacho* v. *Fink* (1945), [1946] 1 All ER 303 (KBD), affirmed (with different reasoning) [1947] KB 1 (CA).

[86] So King, n. 6 above, at 822. But see *Szalatnay-Stacho* v. *Fink* (1945), [1946] 1 All ER 303 (KBD), where no immunity *ratione materiae* was granted to a junior official of the Czechoslovak Government in London for his official acts. On this case, see Kuhn, 'Civil Responsibility for Communications by Officials of a Friendly Foreign Government' (1948) 42 *AJIL* 108–11; Mann, 'Libellous Communications by a Foreign State Official' (1945) 9 *MLR* 179–82.

[87] Cf. Art. 2.1(b)(v) of the ILC Draft Articles 1991 and the commentary on that provision: [1991] II–2 *ILC Yb.* 18. See also *Guillot* v. *Colonel Vinckier* (1916). In this case, which concerned an action against the Commander of the Belgian troops at Ruchard in France for damages caused by Belgian soldiers, the Tribunal civile of Chinon held that 'in terms of assignment, Colonel Vinckier is the commander of the Belgian troops in camp Ruchard; that he is thus the representative of the Belgian State and consequently the Belgian State itself is implicated in the case; that it follows from this that the tribunal must declare itself to have no jurisdiction on this point' ((1918) 14 RDIP 430–1 at 431, translation supplied).

[88] Cf. Art. 37.2 of the VCDR 1961 and Arts. 36, 37 of the CSM 1969.

[89] Cf. Art. 43 of the VCCR 1963.

[90] See e.g. Barton, 'Foreign Armed Forces: Immunity from Supervisory Jurisdiction' (1949) 26 *BYBIL* 380–413 and *id.*, 'Foreign Armed Forces: Immunity from Criminal Jurisdiction' (1950) 27 *BYBIL* 186–234; Wijewardane, 'Criminal Jurisdiction over Visiting Forces With Special Reference to International Forces' (1965–6) 41 *BYBIL* 122–97.

come to and sojourn on the territory of the host State with its consent, personal 'immunity from jurisdiction can only flow from the [express or] tacit renunciation of the exercise of local sovereignty.'[91] The fact that the host State has recognized the authority in exile directing the armed forces as a government does not imply a general exemption of the members of these forces from its jurisdiction. In *Shipanga* v. *Attorney-General* (1976), the Attorney-General of Zambia submitted that the Government of Zambia had recognized SWAPO as a government in exile, and that therefore its military units should be accorded the status of a visiting force which was outside the jurisdiction of the Zambian courts.[92] A similar submission was made by counsel for the defendant in *R.* v. *Navratil* (1942).[93] In neither case was the submission accepted by the court. The members of the armed forces of the Allied Governments in the United Kingdom during the Second World War were liable to be tried by the British civil courts for any act or omission constituting an offence against its law.[94] A member of the armed forces of a government in exile, like any other State representative, may, however, enjoy immunity *ratione materiae* when acting as such.[95] Furthermore, in cases where an action has little effect outside the armed forces of the government in exile, as where one member of the force commits an offence against a fellow member of the force within the quarters of the force, the courts of the host State may find it inexpedient to try the offence, even though it falls within its formal jurisdiction.[96]

[91] *Manuel* v. *Minstère Public* (1943), (1943–5) 12 AD No 42, 156–62 at 157. According to the Regional Court of Appeal of Nuremberg there is no rule of customary international law exempting visiting armed forces from the (criminal) jurisdiction of the host State. See OLG Nuremberg, 12 Aug. 1975, [1975] NJW 2151 at 2152.

[92] [1976] ZLR 224 at 233, 243.

[93] (1919–42) 11 AD No 85, 161–5 at 162.

[94] See e.g. Art. 2 of Annex III of the British–Czechoslovak Military Treaty of 25 Oct. 1940 (Ewing and Fisher (eds.), *Czechoslovak Military Justice Abroad during the Second World War* (1975), App. IV, 42); and Art. 3 of App. IV of the Anglo–Dutch Agreement of 5 May 1942 (147 BFSP 931 at 936). See also s. 2(1) of the Allied Forces Act 1940 (3 & 4 Geo. 6, c. 51). On this Act, see 'Allied Forces in England' (1940) 190 *LT* 175–6; and HC Debs., vol. 364, cols. 1352–4, 1395–6, 1405–6, 21 Aug. 1940; HL Debs., vol. 117, cols. 195–7, 246, 13 Aug. 1940. Generally, see Schwelb, 'The Jurisdiction over the Members of the Allied Forces in Great Britain' [1942] *CYBIL* 147–71. For a case in which an English court tried a Czechoslovak soldier for the attempted murder of a fellow soldier, see *R.* v. *T*, reported in Němec, 'Czechoslovak Military Prosecutors during World War II in Great Britain and in Territories under its Control' in Ewing and Fisher (eds.), *Czechoslovak Military Justice Abroad during the Second World War* (1975), 19–25 at 23–5. Cf. also *Allied Forces (Polish Court of Honours) Case* (1941), (1941–2) 10 AD No 32, 128–9.

[95] See *Guillot* v. *Colonel Vinckier* (1916), (1918) 14 RDIP 430–1. See also Art. 2.1(b)(v) ILC Draft Articles 1991.

[96] See the statement of the Attorney-General, Sir Donald Somerville, in the debate on the Allied Forces Bill: 'although . . . we do claim complete jurisdiction over all offences, in practice it is not, of course, claimed where an offence is committed within the lines and the life or property of one of our own subjects is not involved' (HC Debs., vol. 364, col. 1405, 21 Aug. 1940). For such a case of judicial restraint with respect to soldiers of the Belgian Government in exile, see *R.* v. *Garrett, ex parte de Dryver* (1917), 34 TLR 13; *R.* v. *Aughet* (1918), 34 TLR 302.

Conclusion

I do not intend in these final pages to give a detailed summary of the findings contained in the preceding chapters. It is rather intended to draw some general conclusions from these findings.

In Part I it was established that the term recognition and its variants, in the sense of recognition of governments, may be used in at least two different ways: they may indicate the recognizing State's willingness to enter into certain relations and/or express its opinion on the legal status of the authority recognized. With which meaning recognition is used in a particular case depends solely on the intention of the recognizing State. States may, however, indicate their willingness to enter into certain relations or express their opinion on the legal status of an authority, not only by making a formal announcement containing the term recognition but also by other actions clearly expressing this willingness or opinion, such as the formal sending and receiving of diplomatic agents. The institution of recognition of governments in international law is thus much more than simply the term recognition. Recognition of governments denotes the *act* through which it becomes apparent that a State is willing to enter into certain relations with an authority as the government of a State and/or that, in the opinion of the State, the authority qualifies as a government in international law. By no longer making formal announcements of recognition States have thus only abandoned one mode of recognition but have not (and could not) abolish the institution of recognition of governments in international law. Recognition as an *action* thus also differs from cognition in the Kantian sense ('Er-kenntnis'), i.e. the conscious knowledge of the facts, in so far as according to Fichte it requires, in addition, the taking of a deliberate action on those facts ('willentliche Stellungnahme').

With respect to States which still make formal announcements on the recognition of governments the essential question which must be asked at the beginning of each investigation into a recognition problem is therefore in what meaning the term recognition has been employed. Courts will have to determine in what meaning 'recognition' has been used by a State in a declaration that it does or does not 'recognize' a certain government in order to assess its evidential value in the particular case. Thus, a non-recognition statement expressing an unwillingness to enter into diplomatic relations will be worth very little in an international tribunal. On the other hand recognition statements by several States, expressing that, in their opinion, an authority qualifies as a government will be of great evidential value regarding the authority's legal status as a government. The different meanings of recognition must also be borne in mind when examining the criteria for recognition, the actions implying recognition, and the legality or illegality of the granting or withholding of recognition, as the answers to all these questions will differ depending on whether recognition refers to the willingness to maintain relations or to legal status. The use of recognition in the above two different meanings may also explain the rule of retroactivity of recognition. Thereby it should be noted that the question of retroactivity of recognition has arisen only in States in which the courts regard the recognition of a foreign authority by the executive as conclusive evidence on the question of the authority's legal status. Courts which establish the legal status of a foreign authority for themselves have no need for the rule of retroactivity of recognition. In cases in which the executive's prolonged 'non-recognition' of an authority (which, in fact, qualifies as a government under international law) indicates its unwillingness to maintain relations with it, rather than expressing the executive's opinion that the authority does not qualify as a government, the rule of retroactivity enables the courts to treat the authority as a government from the date on which it actually qualifies as a government in international law once the executive has finally recognized it, i.e. once it has expressed its willingness to maintain relations with it.

With respect to States which have adopted the policy of formally recognizing only States, not governments, earlier State practice and authorities have not become obsolete. On the contrary, under the new policy they are the only guidance for courts which defer to the executive on questions of legal status of foreign authorities. By establishing how their own State or other States have dealt with and only have dealt with authorities which they formally recognized as governments courts may be able to infer their government's opinion on the legal status of an authority from their State's dealings with that authority. This may be illustrated by the following example. If it can be established on the basis of State practice that States have formally accredited ambassadors or ministers only to an authority which they had formally recognized in the sense that, in their opinion, it qualified as a government, then, as a rule, it will be safe for courts to conclude from the accreditation of an ambassador to an authority that, in the opinion of the accrediting government, the authority in question qualifies as a government under international law. The display of State practice with respect to recognized governments in exile in Part II of the study may thus be of some help to courts and practitioners.

The fact that the term recognition may be used by States in two meanings also has repercussions on the question of the legal effects of recognition and on the debate whether recognition is a constitutive or a declaratory act.

The two main theories are normally tested with respect to effective but unrecognized governments *in situ*, and in this setting it is obvious that it is not recognition that makes the government a government in the sense of international law but that the government is a government in international law because it is effective, i.e. fulfils the main criterion for governmental status. Recognition, it is argued by writers, can therefore only be declaratory of the existence of the government and of all the rights and duties following from that existence. However, if the theories are tested in the setting of recognized but ineffective governments in exile and against the background of the different meanings of recognition, i.e. the expression of the willingness to enter into relations and/or the manifestation that, in the opinion of the recognizing State, the government recognized qualifies as such, the answer to the question of the legal effects of recognition is different. Recognition as the expression of a willingness to enter into relations is constitutive of the ensuing relations—nothing more. Recognition as the manifestation of a subjective opinion on the legal status of an authority can be neither constitutive of its objective legal status under international law nor declaratory of government status if the authority in question does not qualify for government status under international law in the first place. An authority that does not otherwise qualify as a government in international law can be neither authoritatively declared to be a government with legal effect on the international plane nor constituted as a government simply by a certain State recognizing it as such, i.e. by expressing its view that the authority is a government. However, while recognition cannot have such an effect on the international plane it may have it on the national plane. In States where courts and administration are bound by the government's view on the legal status of a foreign authority the government may authoritatively declare an authority to be a government by recognizing it as such. The recognition as the government of a State of an authority in exile that does not qualify as such in international law shows that while the recognizing State can neither authoritatively declare nor constitute the exiled authority as the State's government in international law it can treat it as such within its jurisdiction. Recognition of an authority in exile as a government is in this respect constitutive of the right to exercise governmental functions and to enjoy governmental privileges and immunities within the jurisdiction of the recognizing State. The fact that writers have focused on the question whether recognition has a constitutive or a declaratory effect rather than on its meaning has led them to argue that the question of recognition of governments arises only in cases of an unconstitutional change of government as only unconstitutional authorities do or do not (depending on the theory) 'require' recognition to exist as the State's government. The question of recognition, i.e. whether a State is willing to maintain relations with a government or whether it regards (or in the case of exiled governments still regards) an authority as the government of a certain State, however, arises with respect to every government all the time. While it is true that States have chosen, as a rule (but not without exceptions), formally to announce their recognition only in problematic cases such as the unconstitutional change of government it is equally true that in other (unproblematic) cases their recognition can be inferred from their conduct. Thus, the accrediting of an ambassador to a government (or, more precisely, to its head) implies recognition, i.e. expresses the willingness to maintain diplomatic relations and indicates that, in the view of the accrediting State, the authority to which the ambassador is accredited qualifies as a government. This is true irrespective of whether the government has come to power by constitutional or unconstitutional means. The fact that recognition of governments is not restricted to unconstitutional changes of governments is well illustrated by the formal recognition of the various constitutional governments in exile and the reiteration of their recognition from time to time in the face of changing circumstances. Thus, most States formally announced their continued recognition of the Kuwaiti Government in exile on the occasion of the (forced) closure of their embassies in Kuwait City. After the Soviet Union had recognized the Polish Provisional Government at Lublin, the United Kingdom and the United States announced almost weekly (and in June 1945 almost daily) their continued recognition of the Polish Government in London.

In Part II of the study the treatment of authorities in exile recognized as a government was examined and their treatment was compared with the treatment of authorities in exile not recognized as governments (but in some other, lesser capacity). The comparison shows that recognition of an authority in exile *as a government* has certain legal consequences, which become apparent in the different treatment of recognized and unrecognized governments in exile in the recognizing State. At the same time Part II shows that the legal effects of recognition are mainly limited to the jurisdiction of the recognizing State and inter-governmental relations. A comparison of the treatment of recognized governments in exile with that of recognized governments *in situ* shows that with the exception of legislative authority inside national territory recognized governments in exile have the same representative and jurisdictional competence and enjoy the same privileges and immunities in foreign States as if they were residing in their State's capital.

The fact that the treatment of recognized and unrecognized governments in exile differs and that all authorities in exile recognized as governments have been accorded the same rights and privileges by the recognizing States shows that recognition is a 'legal act' (understood in the sense of an act-in-law or juridical act), and not just a political act, since it is intended to produce and in actual fact produces legal effects. Depending on the circumstances recognition may, however, also be or become an illegal act. In the case of recognition as a government of an authority in exile which does not qualify as such in international law recognition may combine the characteristics of both a juridical act and an international delict which entails the responsibility of the recognizing State *vis-à-vis* the State as whose government the authority in exile is recognized. In the sphere of optional relations and voluntary obligations no problem arises. States may recognize the authority in exile, i.e. express their willingness to maintain relations with it and accord its members diplomatic privileges and immunities. This may be an unfriendly act towards the State and its actual government which the authority in exile claims to represent; it is, however, not an international delict entailing the responsibility of the recognizing State. Matters are different in cases in which the recognizing State hands over to the authority in exile the State's assets in the recognizing State and allows it the protection of the State's nationals and the representation of the State's interests in legal proceedings to the exclusion of the State's government *in situ*. Recognition of an authority in exile as a government (which does not qualify as such) may also be part of a policy of aggression, especially if the consent of the recognized 'government' in exile is relied on as a justification of the use of force against the State which the authority in exile purports to represent.

Appendix I
Questionnaire on the Recognition of Governments and Answers Received

NOTE: On 22 January 1993 the author sent out a questionnaire on the recognition of governments to 158 diplomatic and consular missions accredited to the United Kingdom. Within the next ten months some fifty replies were received, of which only thirteen contained substantial answers. These answers vary considerably in length and quality. The author is aware that no general conclusions on the recognition of governments can be drawn from such a limited number of replies. Nevertheless, some of the replies are very interesting on their own as statements of the recognition practice of the particular State and it is for this reason that they are reproduced here.

I. QUESTIONNAIRE

1.1. Which of the policies described, (A), (B), or (C), does your country follow?

(A) In the event of an unconstitutional change of regime in a recognized State an official statement announcing the decision to recognize or not to recognize the regime as the government of the State in question is issued. The 'recognition statement' may take the form of a declaration in Parliament or a press release, an explicit confirmation of recognition in reply to a question in Parliament or a press conference, a formal notification of recognition by means of a diplomatic note, a joint communiqué of recognition or an oral confirmation of recognition to a representative of the regime in question by a diplomatic representative.

(B) As a general rule, when an unconstitutional change of regime occurs in a recognized State no official statement announcing the decision to recognize or not to recognize the regime as the government of the State concerned is issued, though it may be in exceptional cases. (For the possible forms of these recognition statements in exceptional cases see under (A).)

(C) In the event of an unconstitutional change of regime in a recognized State no official statement announcing the decision to recognize or not to recognize the regime as the government of the State in question is issued. On the question whether your government recognizes a regime as the government of a certain State your government regularly answers 'we recognize States, not governments'.

1.2. If your country's policy is not adequately described by (A), (B), or (C), please give a description of your country's policy.

2.1. If your country follows policy (A), what criteria are taken into consideration by your government when deciding whether formally to recognize a regime as the State's government?

2.2. If your country follows policy (C) or (B), what criteria are taken into account by your government when deciding on the nature of its relations with a new regime and, especially, when deciding whether to deal with it as the State's government?

2.3. If your country follows policy (B), under which exceptional circumstances or for what reasons does your government officially announce its decision to recognize or not to recognize a new regime as the State's government?

3. From what date has your country followed its present policy, and which policy did it follow previously?

4.1. If in legal proceedings before your country's national courts the question of status of a foreign regime arises (i.e. whether a regime is the *de facto* or *de jure* government of a recognized State), do the courts

(A) refer to your government for information on the regime's status and treat this information as conclusive, or do they

(B) determine the regime's status for themselves on all the evidence put before them by the parties?

4.2. If your country's national courts follow practice (A) in question 4.1., which of the policies described does your government follow?

(A) When asked whether a regime is the (*de facto* or *de jure*) government of a certain State, your government issues a certificate stating whether the regime is recognized as such or not.

(B) When asked whether a regime is the (*de facto* or *de jure*) government of a certain State, your government describes the nature of the dealings it has with the regime, from which the courts then infer your government's attitude on the question of the regime's status.

5. Under which circumstances does your government continue formally to recognize or deal with a government which has had to flee its country as the lawful government (in exile) of that country?

6. Did your government continue to recognize the government of the Emir of Kuwait (in exile in Saudi Arabia) as the Government of Kuwait during the occupation of Kuwait by Iraqi forces (02 August 1990–26 February 1991)?

II. ANSWERS

1. The Bahamas

[To 1.1] 'In the event of an unconstitutional change occurring in a recognized State, the Government of the Commonwealth of The Bahamas would follow the course described at (B), that is not to issue an official statement as to whether the Government recognizes or does not recognize the new regime.'

[To 2.2] 'The Government of the Commonwealth of The Bahamas would take into account the position adopted by regional and international organizations the Constituent Instruments of which The Bahamas subscribes to. In the contemporary case of Haiti, the situation may arise when The Bahamas in its national interest may have to deal with the *de facto* government on a specific issue. The issue being the presence in The Bahamas of an estimated 40,000 illegal Haitian nationals, all of whom are economic refugees. Any discussions with the *de facto* authorities in Haiti would have as their sole objective repatriation.'

[To 2.3] 'The Commonwealth of The Bahamas since its independence in July 1973 has not had the experience where exceptional circumstances would dictate that the Government officially announce its decision to recognize or not to recognize the new regime.'

[To 3.] 'The Commonwealth of The Bahamas has followed the present policy from July, 10, 1973, the date of its independence from the United Kingdom.'

[To 4.1] 'Since independence, the scenario described here has not arisen. In the event that it does, the courts would follow the practice which obtains in the United Kingdom, that is to request a statement of fact from the Ministry of Foreign Affairs. The courts will treat this statement as conclusive.'

[To 4.2] 'The Commonwealth of The Bahamas would follow (A), that is to issue a Certificate.'

[To 5.] 'Following the overthrow of President Aristide of Haiti in September of 1991 and his subsequent exile The Bahamas continued to recognize his government because it was the constitutionally and democratically elected government of Haiti. Further, the Organization of American States of which The Bahamas is a member recognizes him as the President of Haiti. The opportunity to deal with the Government in exile, per se has not arisen. However, at both the OAS and the UN, Bahamian representatives conducted interchanges with the representatives of the Government in exile.'

[To 6.] 'Yes. But no official announcement in this regard was made.'[1]

2. *Belgium*

[To 1.1.] '(C).'

[To 2.2.] 'Cette question soulève deux problèmes distincts, d'une part celui de la "nature" des relations établies avec un nouveau régime et d'autre part celui du choix de traiter avec un nouveau régime en tant que représentant de l'Etat.

a. S'agissant du premier problème, étant donné que la Belgique ne reconnaît que des Etats, un changement de régime ne conduit pas la Belgique à notifier une quelconque reconnaissance de Gouvernement. L'on peut éventuellement considérer qu'il y a là quelque forme de reconnaissance implicite découlant du maintien des relations avec ces nouveaux gouvernements.

b. Quant au problème du choix de l'autorité publique qui représente l'Etat,

[1] Letter from the High Commission of the Commonwealth of the Bahamas in London, dated 4 Mar. 1993.

celui-ci se pose en cas de guerre civile, lutte pour l'indépendance. . . . Dans cette hypothèse, il est vrai que la position "traditionnelle" de la Belgique doit être nuancée car il faut bien opérer un choix entre plusieurs autorités concurrentes. A titre d'exemple, l'on peut observer que le Ministre belge des Affaires étrangères déclara en 1969 que la Belgique avait expressément "reconnu le droit de la Chine continentale d'occuper le siège permanent du Conseil de Sécurité", ce qui pourrait être analysé comme un forme tacite de reconnaissance. De même, l'attitude adoptée depuis 1979 à propos de la question du Cambodge démontre que dans certains cas, la doctrine "traditionnelle" souffre certaines exceptions.[2] Cela dit, il serait présomptueux de croire que l'on dispose à ce propos de critères "scientifiques". Il s'agit plutôt d'un dosage subtil entre l'effectivité de l'autorité concernée et une appréciation politique de la situation.'

[To 3.] 'La position actuelle de la Belgique fut expressément affirmée en 1965 en étant qualifiée de "position traditionnelle de la Belgique". Quant à la position antérieure adoptée par la Belgique, celle-ci n'est pas parfaitement claire. La pratique belge témoigne sans doute de l'existence de reconnaissances de nouveau régime (p. ex., la reconnaissance en 1848 et en 1871 du nouveau gouvernement de la France ou la reconnaissance en 1909 du prince Ferdinand comme Tsar de Bulgarie). Mais la différence entre la reconnaissance d'Etat et celle de Gouvernement n'est pas toujours perceptible (p. ex. dans le cas de la Bulgarie). De plus la situation se complexifie à cette époque par l'utilisation de la distinction entre la reconnaissance de iure et de facto.'

[To 4.1] '(B).'

[To 5.] 'Globalement, même réponse que pour 2.2.b.'

[To 6.] 'Oui, cela découlait d'ailleurs des termes des résolutions adoptées par le Conseil de Sécurité (voy. par ex. la rés. 662 (1990) demandant à tous les Etats de ne pas reconnaître l'annexion du Koweït par l'Irak et de s'abstenir de tout acte qui pourrait être interprété comme une reconnaissance implicite de cette annexion).'[3]—Author's translation:

[To 2.2] This question raises two different problems; on the one hand the "nature" of the relations established with a new regime and on the other hand the decision to deal with a new regime as representing the State.

a. As far as the first problem is concerned, given that Belgium recognizes only States, a change of government does not lead Belgium to notify any recognition of government. One may perhaps consider that there is some form of implicit recognition in the maintenance of relations with the new governments.

b. As far as the question of the selection of the public authority which represents the State is concerned, which arises in case of civil war, liberation struggle. . . . In this case it is true that the "traditional" position of Belgium must be nuanced because one has to choose expressly between several competing authorities. For example, one may observe that the Belgian Minister of Foreign Affairs declared in 1969 that Belgium had expressly "recognized the right of continental China to occupy the permanent seat on the Security Council", which could be analysed as a form of tacit

[2] On the Belgian recognition practice with respect to Cambodia, see Maes, 'België erkent geen regeringen, enkel staten. Het geval Cambodia 1979–1991' (1991) 33/2 *Res Publica* 255–302.

[3] Letter from the Belgian Embassy in London, dated 3 Mar. 1993.

recognition. Also, the attitude adopted since 1979 with respect to Cambodia demonstrates that in certain cases, the "traditional" doctrine allows certain exceptions. That said, it would be presumptuous to believe that one has scientific criteria in this respect. It is rather a subtle dosage between the effectiveness of the authority concerned and a political evaluation of the situation.

[To 3.] Belgium's current position was expressly affirmed in 1965, being characterized as "traditional position of Belgium". As far as Belgium's earlier position is concerned, this is not perfectly clear. The Belgian practice undoubtedly shows the recognitions of new regimes (e.g. the recognition in 1848 and 1871 of the new Government of France and the recognition in 1909 of Prince Ferdinand as Tsar of Bulgaria). But the difference between recognition of State and that of Government is not always perceptible (e.g in the case of Bulgaria). Moreover the situation is complicated in that period by the utilization of the distinction between *de jure* and *de facto* recognition.

[To 4.1] (B)

[To 5.] Same response as for 2.2.b.

[To 6.] Yes, this followed in any case from the resolutions adopted by the Security Council (see e.g. resolution 662 (1990) calling on all States not to recognize the annexation of Kuwait by Iraq and to refrain from any act which could be interpreted as tacit recognition of that annexation).

3. *Bolivia*

[To 1.1] 'Bolivia used to follow policy described in 1.1 (A) of the questionnaire until the 1992 meeting of Ministers of Foreign Affairs of the Organization of American States (OAS), held in Santiago, Chile, in October 1992. [Previously] Bolivia followed the policy of an oral confirmation of recognition to a representative of the regime in question by a diplomatic representative, once the Bolivian Government was satisfied that the regime had complete control and authority and normal public and private activities were restored.'

[To 4.1] 'The Supreme Court refers to the Government for information as to the status of recognition of the government of a country and considers this information conclusive.'

[To 4.2] 'Bolivia follows the practice described in (A).'

[To 5.] 'Governments in exile.—The recent experience of the Government of Haiti has moved the OAS to continue recognition of the elected president M. Aristide as the legitimate head of government, suspending relations with Haiti until the restoration of legitimacy. This is an OAS resolution.'

[To 6.] 'The Kuwait experience.—Yes, Bolivia rejected the annexation of Kuwait by Iraq and continued to recognize the Emir of Kuwait as Head of State.'[4]

4. *Dominica*

[To 1.1.] 'The Commonwealth of Dominica follows policy (A).'

[To 2.1] 'When deciding whether to formally recognize a regime, Government considers:

[4] Letter from the Bolivian Embassy in London, received 4 Feb. 1993.

—The record of the ousted Government in relation to its treatment of its citizens; neighbouring States and the international Community; its respect for international law, and its practices in relation to Human Rights.
—Whether the ousted Government owned its position to popular support as expressed through free and fair elections.
—The record of the new regime, or the persons and groups comprising that new regime; the perception of their legitimacy in the eyes of the citizens of the State concerned, and their declared and/or perceived intentions as regards legitimizing their status by way of free and fair elections and the establishment/consolidation of democratic practices and processes.
—The impact of the new regime on matters of regional and international security would also be taken into account.'

[To 3.] 'The Commonwealth of Dominica has followed this policy from the date of independence in November, 1978 . . .'

[To 4.1] 'If in legal proceedings before our courts, the question of the status of a foreign regime arises, the courts would refer to government for information on the regime's status and treat this information as conclusive.'

[To 4.2] 'When asked whether a regime is the (*de facto* or *de jure*) government of a certain state, government issues a certificate stating whether the regime is recognized as such, or not.'

[To 5.] 'If the government had been recognized by the Government of the Commonwealth of Dominica prior to its ouster and the Government of the Commonwealth of Dominica does not recognize the new *de facto* government, it is likely to sustain recognition of the ousted government, as it did in the case of Haiti.'

[To 6.] 'Yes.'[5]

5. *Finland*

[To 1.1.] 'Finland follows the policy of recognizing States not governments.'

[To. 2.2.] 'There are no particular criteria for deciding upon the character of relations with a new government. These matters are decided *ad hoc*, in the course of normal diplomatic intercourse. The general principles of Finland's foreign policy—particularly its aim to keep itself outside the conflicts of interest between the Great Powers—have, in the past, provided a general guideline. With the end of the cold war, as Finland's foreign policy seeks to adjust itself to the new environment, other factors (such as whether the new government has attained general recognition or acceptance, what its human rights record might be etc.) might gain some relevance. But no general and even less legal rules apply.'

[To 3.] 'This policy has been followed throughout the post-war period.'

[To 4.1] 'The rules of evidence applicable in Finnish courts do not fix conditions under which legal effect should be given for acts of foreign governments or States. In accordance with the applicable principle of free appreciation of evidence courts may use governmental views as basis for decision but they are not legally compelled

[5] Letter from the Ministry of External Affairs and OECS Unity at Roseau, dated 5 Feb. 1993.

to defer to such views. In one recent case a certificate issued by the legal department of the Ministry Foreign Affairs regarding the position of a Eastern European State was accepted as *de facto* conclusive evidence on that State's international position. It would, however, be inappropriate to prejudge the behaviour of courts in future cases.'

[To 5. and 6.] 'The only relevant example would be the Government of Kuwait, exiled at Taif, Saudi Arabia from 3 August 1990–3 April 1991. This would not be a matter of recognition but rather of non-recognition of the illegal occupation of Kuwait by Iraq, in accordance with binding Security Council resolutions. The relevant criterion is the existence of a legal duty not to recognize which has the consequence of endowing legitimacy on the exiled government. (But note, it is not a question of express recognition to the exiled government.)'[6]

5. Ghana

'The Fourth Republic began on 7th January 1993, so the answer may relate mainly to the pre 1993 era. . . .'

[To 1.1.(A)] 'No [official recognition] statement is issued.'

[To 1.1. (B and C)] 'As a general rule, when an unconstitutional change of a regime occurs in a recognized State no official statement announcing the decision to recognize or not to recognize the regime as the government of the State concerned is issued. The commonest form of recognition is by action or conduct that is when the Ghana Government deals with the new regime when it gains *de facto* legitimacy . . . the government does business with the new regime once it is in effective control of the State. For example, during the recent Commonwealth Summit in Limmasol, Cyprus, Ghana, like the majority of the delegations to the Summit did not object to the presence of the delegation sent by the Transitional Government of Nigeria whose legitimacy has become a subject of controversy in Nigeria following the annulment of the Presidential elections believed to have been won by Abiola. Indeed reports indicate that the Summit did not recognize the delegation sent by Abiola.'

[To 4.1] 'Such issues [concerning the status of a foreign regime] have not been the experience of the Courts. But presumably as a common law country, the courts may follow the English Judicial pronouncements on the subject, that is to say, they will refer the matter to the Government on the grounds that recognition is essentially a political act. However, where the interest of Justice and the merits of the case demand the courts may not hesitate to [determine the regime's status for themselves on all the evidence put before them by the parties].'

[To 5.] 'Usually if it is a Liberation Movement recognized by Sub or Regional Organization such as ECOWAS, and the OAU or the UN, e.g. the PLO, and ANC. Ghana for example supported the Kuwaiti Government-in-exile during the Iraqi invasion and will no doubt support the Burundi Government-in-exile.'

[To 6.] [Ghana continued to recognize the government of Kuwait in exile.]

[6] Letter from Dr Martti Koskenniemi, Legal Counsellor at the Ministry for Foreign Affairs at Helsinki, dated 8 June 1993. Dr Koskenniemi stressed 'the extent to which these matters are decided on the basis of the principle of guaranteeing maximum freedom of action'.

'Indeed there was a press release, an oral confirmation to that effect during a visit by a Kuwaiti Minister of State in the wake of the crisis to rally international opinion against Iraq. During the visit the Kuwaiti delegation stated that promises made to Ghana before the invasion for general assistance will be honoured despite the invasion.'[7]

7. Greece

[To 1.1] 'Greece follows policy C.'

[To 2.2] 'If the Greek Government considers that the new regime of a recognized country has come to power by unconstitutional means, as a general rule it will probably tend to limit relations to the minimum necessary for an indeterminate period. This is a simple guiding principle, there being no hard and fast rules in the matter. Since the majority of governments in the world have not come to power as a result of elections or constitutional change, the Greek Government maintains a pragmatic approach and employs additional criteria in order to decide the nature of its relations with these States, such as historical ties with the nation in question, political and economic interests, the size of the local Greek community, if any, moves toward greater democracy and respect for human rights in the country in question, etc.'

[To 3.] 'Policy (C) is traditional Greek policy.'

[To 4.1] 'Greece does not distinguish between *de facto* and *de jure* governments in the case of recognized States. In the case of military occupation, Greece applies the rules of international law pertaining to the (illegal) occupation of foreign territories and their administration by the occupying power.'

[To 5.] 'When the legitimate government of a recognized State has been forced to flee as a result of a foreign invasion.'

[To 6.] 'Yes.'[8]

8. Iran

'We would draw your attention to the following points:—

* There is no specific procedure regarding the recognition in the Iranian Constitution or ordinary laws.
* The method used for this purpose is generally in accordance with the international code of practice i.e a letter of congratulations is sent to the Head of State concerned or when actual Diplomatic Relations are established.
* Voting favourably for admission of a newly established State in the U.N. is also a means of recognizing a State, by joint action.

In a nutshell, it is the actual establishment of Diplomatic Relations which is an

[7] Letter from Mr Ebenezer Appreku, Legal and Consular Counsellor at the Ministry of Foreign Affairs at Accra, dated 1 Nov. 1993. The letter, although written on the official stationery of the Ghanaian Ministry of Foreign Affairs, contained the proviso that the 'views expressed herein do not necessarily reflect the official position of the Government of Ghana'.

[8] Letter from the Second Secretary at the Greek Embassy in London, Dr Constantine A. Papadopoulos, dated 1 Feb. 1993.

indication of recognition. Friendly messages are also a means of expressing a desire to recognize and establish relations with the State concerned.'[9]

9. *Italy*

[To 1.1] 'The answer is (C).'

[To 2.2] 'Importance of the relations in the framework of regional, economic and trade interest, consistency of Italian immigration, level of human rights respect.'

[To 3.] 'Italy has followed this policy specially since it became a Republic, in 1946.'

[To 4.1] 'The answer is (A).'

[To 5.] 'Since the end of World War Two there has not been such a case.'

[To 6.] 'Yes.'[10]

10. *New Zealand*

[To 1.1] '(B) is probably closest.'

[To 1.2] 'Generally speaking (but not always), recognition (or non-recognition) is not a matter of public or express declaration but is left to be inferred from the nature and level of dealings with the new government.'

[To 2.2] 'It is not possible to lay down strict criteria; each situation gives rise to different considerations and needs to be looked at case by case.'

[To 2.3] 'Again, no hard and fast rules apply; but the significance of the change at issue, the extent of public interest or concern, and the immediacy of the need for the government to make a declaration, may well have a bearing on the decision to do so.'

[To 3.] 'Current practice has been followed for many years.'

[To 4.1] 'There is little enough New Zealand case law on this subject. In one recent case (1988)[11] a certificate that included comment on the question of recognition was provided by the Minister of Foreign Affairs, at the request of the Court, under the Diplomatic Privileges and Immunities Act.'

[To 4.2] 'Neither alternative fully reflects the situation in the case referred to in para. 4.1 above, although (B) is closest. In that case, the certificate set out New Zealand's general practice on recognition questions, noted that no declaration was made in respect of the Government of the country in question (Fiji), and provided some general comment on diplomatic and other relations with that country. The Court accepted the position on recognition set out in the certificate that no declaration had been made, and examined the nature and level of Government to Government dealings.'

[To 5.] 'No general comment can be made; the circumstances would need to be considered case by case (see also para 2.2 above).'

[To 6.] 'The lawful government of Kuwait was that in power prior to the Iraqi

[9] Letter from the Iranian Embassy in London, dated 2 Feb. 1993.

[10] Letter from the Italian Embassy in London, dated 29 Jan. 1993.

[11] The case referred to is *Attorney General for Fiji* v. *Robt. Jones House Ltd* [1989] 2 NZLR 69.

occupation and subsequently restored, and no Iraqi or other (local Kuwaiti) regime was recognized during the period of occupation.'[12]

11. Solomon Islands

[To 1.1] 'Until, 1988, Solomon Islands followed the practice that it recognized Governments. Accordingly each time there was a unconstitutional change in Government of a country with which we enjoyed diplomatic ties, we had to consider the pressing question of whether we would recognize it or not. This presented us with problems . . . each time there is an unconstitutional change in Government there are invariably two governments both claiming to be the legitimate Government, namely the *de facto* Government and the *de jure* Government. In order to circumvent this problem and to avoid the necessity of having to consider whether or not to recognize a Government in the event of its unconstitutional change Solomon Islands adopted the policy of recognizing states rather than Governments.'

[To 4.1] '. . . Our courts have not yet had occasion to consider the status of a foreign government, but in the event that it does, we would follow British practice, namely, that the court will take judicial notice of a certificate from the Ministry of Foreign Affairs certifying the Governments recognition of a foreign regime.'

[To 6.] 'During the Kuwait crisis, we voted in favour of the UN resolutions denouncing the Iraqi invasion and reaffirming the right of the Government of the Emir as the legitimate Government of Kuwait. That was however consistent with our policy in that we continued to recognize the state of Kuwait while agreeing only to deal with the *de jure* government which was in Saudi Arabia.'[13]

12. Sri Lanka

'The policy of the Government of Sri Lanka is to recognize States which satisfy the legal criteria for such recognition. It does not extend formal recognition of new Governments, once a State itself has been recognized.

The Sri Lankan Courts have, in practice, taken judicial notice of foreign office certificates that a particular State is or is not recognized by Sri Lanka.'[14]

13. Switzerland

[To 1.1] 'Switzerland follows the policies described under C.'

[To 2.2] 'Effective control over a substantial part of the state's territory.'

[To 3.] 'Present policy since 1945; before formal recognition of governments.'

[To 4.1] 'If in legal proceedings before Swiss courts the question as to the status of a foreign regime arises the Swiss courts refer to the government for information on the regime's status and treat this information as conclusive.'

[12] Letter from the New Zealand High Commission, dated 2 Apr. 1993, transmitting a reply from the Ministry of External Relations and Trade.

[13] Letter from Mr Transform Aqorau, the Legal Adviser to the Ministry of Foreign Affairs and Trade Relations at Honiara, dated 9 Mar. 1993.

[14] Letter from the High Commission of Sri Lanka in London, dated 1 Mar. 1993.

[To 4.2.] 'Swiss government communicates information to requesting court in one form or another (no formal certification).'

[To 5.] 'Answers given under 2.2 [are] also determinative here, exceptions are made on a case by case basis.'

[To 6.] 'Yes, our government continued to recognize the government of the Emir of Kuwait (in exile in Saudi Arabia) as the government of Kuwait during the occupation of Kuwait by Iraqi forces (2nd August 1990–26th February 1991).'[15]

[15] Letter from the Swiss Embassy in London, dated 12 May 1993.

Appendix II
Authorities in Exile Claiming to be 'Governments': Profiles

NOTE: The following are seventy short profiles of authorities in exile claiming to be or calling themselves the 'government' of a State. Some of these 'governments' had a rather ephemeral existence while others existed for more than fifty years. While some received almost universal recognition others were totally ignored by States. Emphasis has been put on the recognition of these authorities by States. Wherever possible the exact date of recognition has been given. The dates of recognition have been compiled from a variety of sources such as *Keesing's*, *Archiv der Gegenwart*, *Le Monde*, *New York Times*, *The Times*, *Frankfurter Allgemeine Zeitung*, and historical works on the respective governments in exile and the conflicts in which they were established. Whenever the dates of recognition given in those sources differed—and they often did—the earliest recorded date has been given. Profiles such as the following are necessarily unsatisfactory, in that they isolate the respective authority in exile from its context in national and international politics. It must however be recalled that this book is not a history of the various governments in exile but an examination of the effects of recognition on authorities in exile claiming to be governments. All entries are listed in chronological order under the country of which the authority in exile claimed to be the government.

Belgium (13 October 1914)

Name: Government of the Kingdom of Belgium
Establishment: Flight of existing Government from Ostende to Le Havre
Head of Government: King Albert I (head of State)
Seat or headquarters: Sainte Adresse near Le Havre, France
Context: War
Return to/establishment in national territory: Reoccupation of those portions of Belgium that had been occupied by Germany since 1914 on 17 November 1918—return of King Albert to Brussels on 22 November 1918
Recognition: The Belgian Government in exile continued to be recognized by all States including the Central Powers.

Serbia (30 November 1915)

Name: Government of the Kingdom of Serbia
Establishment: Flight of existing Government to Albania
Head of Government: King Peter I (head of State), Nicolas Pašić (Prime Minister)
Seat or headquarters: Brindisi, Italy (15 January 1916); Corfu, Greece—occupied by the Entente Powers (19 January 1916); Salonika, Greece (April 1917)

Context: War/annexation
Return to/establishment in national territory: Return to Belgrade in November 1918
Recognition: The King's Government continued to be recognized as the Government of Serbia by all States with the sole exception of Bulgaria, which annexed the parts of Serbia occupied by its troops and officially declared the Serbian State to have ceased to exist.

Montenegro (18 January 1916)

Name: Government of the Kingdom of Montenegro
Establishment: Flight of existing Government to Albania
Head of Government: Head of State: King Nikolas I (until his death on 1 April 1921), King Danilo, King Michael
Seat or headquarters: Lyons, Bordeaux, Neuilly-sur-Seine, and Antibes, France; Rome, Italy
Context: War
Return to/establishment in national territory:
Recognition: Throughout the war King Nicholas and his Government continued to be recognized as the Government of Montenegro by all States including the Central Powers. After a 'National Assembly' at Podgorica on 24 November 1918 had proclaimed the deposition of King Nicholas and the union of Montenegro with Serbia and after these acts had implicitly been confirmed by the general elections to the Serb–Croat–Slovene Constituent Assembly on 28 November 1920, one State after the other withdrew its recognition from the Montenegrin Government in exile: United Kingdom (24 August 1920); France (30 December 1920); USA (21 January 1921); Italy (September 1921).

Czechoslovakia (14 October 1918)

Name: Provisional Czechoslovak Government
Establishment: Notification of the Allied Governments of a decision of the Czechoslovak National Council taken on 26 September 1918 to form a Provisional Government
Head of Government: Professor Thomas Masaryk (President)
Seat or headquarters: Paris (France)
Context: War/secession
Return to/establishment in national territory:
Recognition: Recognition of the Provisional Government must be distinguished from recognition of its predecessor, the Czechoslovak National Council. The latter had been recognized by several States, not as a Government but only 'as the supreme organ of the general interests and policy of the future Czechoslovak Government'. The following States recognized the Masaryk Government as the Provisional Government of the Czecho-Slovak State: France (15 October 1918), Serbia, Belgium (22 October 1918), Greece (23 October 1918), Italy (24 October 1918). The United Kingdom and the USA only acknowledged the receipt of the notification.

Irish Republic (21 January 1919)

Name: 'Provisional Government of the Irish Republic'
Establishment: Election by the Dáil Eireann
Head of Government: President Eamonn De Valéra
Seat or headquarters: 'Internal exile'—President Eamonn De Valéra: United States (June 1919–December 1920)
Context: Secession
Return to/establishment of control in national territory:
Recognition: Neither during the internal exile of the Provisional Government of the Irish Republic nor during De Valéra's 'exile with a purpose' in the United States did the Irish Republic receive any official recognition by other States.

Korea (1 March 1919)

Name: Provisional Government of the Republic of Korea (KPG)[1]
Establishment: Proclamation of independence of the Republic of Korea at Seoul and formation of KPG whose members immediately upon its formation fled the country
Head of Government: Dr Syngman Rhee and Kim Koo
Seat or headquarters: Shanghai and Chungking, China
Context: Secession
Return to/establishment in national territory: Members of the KPG were allowed to return to the area of Korea under American occupation in October 1945, but only as private individuals and not as representatives of the KPG
Recognition: In all its history no State recognized the KPG as the Government of Korea. But the KPG was recognized *de facto* in 1944 by China and in February 1945 by France.

Ukraine (December 1919 and December 1920)

Name: Directorate of the Democratic (People's) Republic of Ukraine
Establishment: Flight of existing *de facto* Government to Ukrainian territory occupied by Polish troops and later to Poland proper
Head of Government: President: Symon Petlyura (until assassination on 25 May 1926), Andrei Livytsky
Seat or headquarters: Exile I: Warsaw and Kamenets Podolskiy (under Polish occupation); exile II: Tarnóv (Poland), Paris
Context: Secession/civil war/intervention
Return to/establishment in national territory:
Recognition: During its exile the Petlyura Government received two notable recognitions: on 21 April 1920 Poland formally 'recognized the Directorate of the

[1] Korea had become part of Japan by the Treaty between Japan and Korea of 29 August 1910 in which the Emperor of Korea made complete and permanent cession to the Emperor of Japan of all rights of sovereignty over the whole of Korea.

independent Ukrainian People's Republic, with Ataman Symon Petlyura as the Head of the Government of the Ukrainian People's Republic' and by decree of 5 March 1921 Argentina recognized the Ukrainian People's Republic as 'Etat libre'. States that had recognized the Ukrainian People's Republic[2] ceased relations with its Government in exile when they recognized the Soviet Government in Kiev. In treaties concluded with Soviet Ukraine those States especially undertook not to lend support to or to tolerate in its territory 'organisations which claim to represent the Government of the opposite Party.'[3]

Western Ukraine (25 July 1920)

Name: Government of the Western Ukrainian National Republic[4]
Establishment: Proclamation in Vienna in reaction to the Peltyura–Pilsudski agreement of 21 April 1920 by which western Ukraine was ceded to Poland
Head of Government: Dr Evhen Petrušzewyčz
Seat or headquarters: Vienna, Austria
Context: Secession/annexation
Return to/establishment in national territory:
Recognition: No State recognized the Petrušzewyčz Government as the Government of western Ukraine. The Conference of Ambassadors in Paris decided on 8 July 1921 that the so-called 'West Ukrainian Government' headed by Evhen Petrušzewyčz did not constitute a government either *de facto* or *de jure* and therefore did not have the right to speak on behalf of any of the former Austrian territories.

Georgia (17 March 1921)

Name: National (Menshevik) Government of the Democratic Republic of Georgia[5]
Establishment: Flight of existing Government from Batum to Constantinople
Head of Government: Noë Jordania (President)
Seat or headquarters: Paris
Context: Invasion/civil war

[2] The Ukrainian People's Republic had been recognized *de jure* by Soviet Russia, Latvia, Lithuania, Estonia, Finland, Georgia, Azerbaijan, Germany, Austria-Hungary, Bulgaria, Turkey, Romania, Czechoslovakia, and the Holy See. *De facto* recognition had been accorded by Switzerland, Sweden, Denmark, and Iran.

[3] See e.g. 4 LNTS 7 at 35–6, 6 LNTS 52 at 131 (Poland); Soviet Treaty Series I, 86–7 (Lithuania); 17 LNTS 318 at 347 (Latvia); 11 LNTS 122 at 135 (Estonia); 20 LNTS 154 at 171 (Austria); Soviet Treaty Series I, 160–1 (Turkey).

[4] The Western Ukrainian National Republic was proclaimed on 19 October 1918 by the Ukrainian National Council on the territory of eastern Galicia, north-western Bukovina, and Transcarpathia (all territories of the former Austro-Hungarian Empire). The Western Ukrainian National Republic was united on 22 January 1919 with the independent Ukrainian Democratic Republic.

[5] The independence of the Democratic Republic of Georgia was proclaimed on 26 May 1918 and affirmed on 12 March 1919.

Return to/establishment in national territory:
Recognition: The question of continued recognition of the Georgian National Government arose only for States that had recognized the independence of Georgia *de jure* before that Government had had to flee its country.[6] But Liberia (28 March 1921) and Mexico (12 May 1921) recognized the independence and sovereignty of the Democratic Republic of Georgia when its Government was already in exile. The Georgian National Government continued to be recognized for some time as 'the legitimate Government of Georgia' by Belgium, the United Kingdom, and France. A Georgian legation existed in Paris until 1933 when it was closed as a consequence of the Franco–Soviet Non-Aggression Pact of 29 November 1932, which provided in Article 5 that 'Each of the High Contracting Parties undertakes in particular not to create, protect, equip, subsidise or admit in its territory . . . organizations assuming the rôle of government or representing all or part of its territories.'[7]

Ethiopia (4 May 1936)

Name: Government of Ethiopia
Establishment: Flight of existing Government
Head of Government: Negus (Emperor) Haile Selassie I (head of State)
Seat or headquarters: Bath (July 1936–June 1940), Karthoum, Sudan (July 1940–January 1941)
Context: War/annexation
Return to/establishment in national territory: Haile Selassie re-entered Ethiopia from Sudan in January 1941 and re-established his Government in Addis Ababa in May 1941
Recognition: By October 1936 Haile Selassie was still recognized as the sovereign of Ethiopia by all countries except Italy and Germany. But subsequently, one by one, States recognized Italian sovereignty over Ethiopia and, consequently, withdrew recognition from the Negus' Government.[8] At the outbreak of the Second World War the only States which had not recognized Italian sovereignty over Ethiopia were: USA, USSR, Mexico, New Zealand, and China. But even those States did not formally continue to recognize the Government of Haile Selassie as the Government of Ethiopia. States which had recognized Italian sovereignty had to re-recognize the independence and sovereignty of Ethiopia and its Government after the liberation of Ethiopia. For example, the United Kingdom re-recognized Ethiopian independence and sovereignty on 31 January 1942 and Switzerland on 8 January 1946. The USA, on the other hand, in 1942 had only to re-establish diplomatic relations with Ethiopia.

[6] The following States had recognized Georgian independence *de jure* prior to 17 March 1921: Argentina (13 Sept. 1919), RSFSR (7 May 1920), Germany (24 Sept. 1920), Belgium, France, Great Britain, Italy, Japan (26 Jan. 1921), Poland (28 Jan. 1921), Austria (17 Feb. 1921), Romania (18 Feb. 1921), Luxembourg (25 Feb. 1921), Haiti (9 Mar. 1921).

[7] 157 LNTS 411. See also [1933] JORF, Débats parl., Chambre, 2383, cols. 2–3; 2395, col. 2; 2441, col. 2.

[8] For an incomplete list of countries recognizing Italian sovereignty over Ethiopia, see HC Debs., vol. 337, col. 1890, 29 June 1938.

Poland (17 September 1939)

Name: 'Polish Government of Unity and National Defence'
Establishment: Proclamation by the Polish President, Professor Ignacy Moscicki, on the transfer of 'the seat of the President of the Republic and of the Highest Office of the State to the territory of one of our Allies'
Head of Government: President: Professor Ignacy Moscicki (until 30 September 1939); Wladyslaw Raczkiewicz (30 September 1939–6 June 1947); August Zaleski; General Kazimierez Sosnkowski; Count Edward Raczynski; Ryszard Kaczorowski
Seat or headquarters: Paris: 30 September–22 November 1939; Angers (France): 23 November–14 June 1940; Bordeaux (France): 15 June–20 June 1941; London: 21 June 1941–22 November 1990[9]
Context: War/annexation
Return to/establishment in national territory:
Recognition: The Polish Government in exile continued to be recognized 'as the legal Government of Poland' by all States, except Germany, the Soviet Union, and their puppet States. The following States made express statements of continued recognition: France (30 September 1939), USA (2 October 1939), Mexico (3 October 1939), United Kingdom, Turkey, Sweden (4 October 1939), Argentina (5 October 1939), Vatican (7 October 1939), Brazil (15 October 1939), Uruguay (18 October 1939). The USSR on 17 September 1939 withdrew recognition from the Polish Government on the ground that 'the Polish State and its Government factually have ceased to exist'. However, after the German invasion of the Soviet Union it re-recognized the Polish Government in London on 30 July 1941. The following Axis States subsequently recognized the German annexation of Polish territory and thus withdrew their recognition from the Polish Government in exile: Italy (12 June 1940); Japan (4 October 1941). After the transformation of the Polish Committee of National Liberation at Lublin ('Lublin Committee') into the 'Provisional Government of the Polish Republic' on 31 December 1944 the following States recognized the Lublin Committee as the Provisional Government of Poland and, consequently, withdrew their recognition from the Polish Government in London: USSR (4 January 1945—recognition already withdrawn: 2 August 1944), Czechoslovakia (31 January 1945), Bulgaria (3 February 1945), Yugoslavia (30 March 1945), Italy (2 May 1945). After the formation of the 'Polish Provisional Government of National Unity' on 28 June 1945 the following States recognized that authority as the Government of Poland and as a consequence withdrew their recognition from the Polish Government in London: France, Sweden (29 June 1945), United Kingdom, USA, (5 July 1945), Norway, China, Switzerland (6 July 1945), Canada, Denmark (8 July 1945), Netherlands (9 July 1945), Belgium (13 July 1945), Finland (17 July 1945), Turkey (6 August 1945), Mexico (26 October 1945), Australia (30 October 1945), Colombia, Venezuela, Peru, Bolivia (12 November 1945). The last countries which continued to recognize the Polish Government in London were Cuba, Ireland, Lebanon, Spain, and the Vatican, the latter being the last State to withdraw its recognition in December 1958.

[9] Between 1954 and 1972 there were two rival Polish Governments in London usually referred to as 'The Castle' and 'The Union' which 1972 reunited in a 'Government of National Reunification'.

Luxembourg (10 May 1940)

Name: Government of the Grand Duchy of Luxembourg
Establishment: Flight of existing Government to France
Head of Government: Grand Duchess Charlotte (head of State)
Seat or headquarters: The Government fled first to France (11 May 1940), thence via Spain and Portugal to London (29 June 1940) and Montreal (13 November 1940), both cities being the official seat of Government
Context: War/annexation
Return to/establishment in national territory: On 21 September 1944 three cabinet ministers returned and on 15 April 1945 the Duchess arrived in Luxembourg
Recognition: The Grand Ducal Government continued to be recognized by all States with the exception of the Axis States.

Netherlands (13 May 1940)

Name: Government of the Kingdom of the Netherlands
Establishment: Flight of existing Government to London
Head of Government: Queen Wilhelmina (head of State)
Seat or headquarters: London (13 May 1940–23 May 1945)
Context: War
Return to/establishment in national territory: On 23 May 1945 the Dutch Government was officially re-established in The Hague
Recognition: The Dutch Government in exile continued to be recognized as the Government of the Netherlands by all States, including the Axis countries, which only severed diplomatic relations with it.

Belgium (20 May 1940)

Name: Government of the Kingdom of Belgium[10]
Establishment: Flight of existing cabinet from Ostende to France
Head of Government: Hubert Pierlot (Prime Minister)[11]
Seat or headquarters: Poitiers, Bordeaux, Vichy (26 June–21 September 1940), and London (22 October 1940)
Context: War
Return to/establishment in national territory: On 8 September 1944 the Government returned to Brussels
Recognition: The rump Government of four Ministers headed by Prime Minister Pierlot continued to be recognized as the legal Government of Belgium by all States including the Axis States, which only terminated diplomatic relations with it. The USSR, which on 9 May 1941 had withdrawn recognition 'owing to the country's loss

[10] From July to Oct. 1940 two authorities in exile claimed to be the Government of Belgium: the Government headed by Prime Minister Pierlot and the Huysmans-Jaspar Government, both in London.

[11] King Leopold III remained in Belgium, signed the capitulation of the Belgian army on 28 May 1940, and became a prisoner of war.

of sovereignty', after the German invasion of the Soviet Union re-recognized the Belgian Government on 20 July 1941.

Norway (7 June 1940)

Name: Government of Norway
Establishment: Flight of existing Government to England
Head of Government: King Haakon VII (head of State)
Seat or headquarters: London (10 June 1940–31 May 1945)
Context: War
Return to/establishment in national territory: Return of first Minister to liberated territory on 18 November 1944; return of the cabinet to Oslo on 31 May 1945; arrival of the King on 7 June 1945
Recognition: The Norwegian Government in London continued to be recognized as 'the *de jure* government of the entire Kingdom of Norway' by all States with the exception of the Axis States and their Allies, some of which continued to recognize the Norwegian Government in exile until 1942. The USSR, which had withdrawn its recognition on 9 May 1941 'owing to the country's loss of sovereignty' after the German invasion of the Soviet Union on 20 July 1941, re-recognized the Norwegian Government in London.

Czechoslovakia (21 July 1940)

Name: 'Provisional Government of the Czechoslovak Republic'
Establishment: Formation abroad by 'presidential' decree
Head of Government: Dr Eduard Beneš (President)
Seat or headquarters: London (until the beginning of March 1945)[12]
Context: War/annexation
Return to/establishment in national territory: Establishment of the seat of Government at Kosice in Slovakia on 3 April 1945—the Government arrived in Prague on 16 May 1945
Recognition: Recognition of the 'Provisional Government' must be distinguished from recognition of the 'Czechoslovak National Committee', which had been formed in Paris on 13 November 1939. The latter had not been recognized by any State as the Government of Czechoslovakia but only 'as qualified to represent the Czecho-Slovak peoples'.[13] It should be noted that only States that had not or no longer recognized *de jure* the German annexation of Bohemia and Moravia and the independence of the State of Slovakia could recognize the Provisional Government in London as the Government of the Czechoslovak Republic. In the case of States that had recognized German sovereignty over Bohemia and Moravia or the State of Slovakia recognition of the Provisional Czechoslovak Government resulted in the withdrawal of such recognition. The following States accorded full or *de jure*

[12] The Czechoslovak National Committee had moved to London in June 1940.
[13] Recognition in that capacity was accorded, e.g., by France (17 Nov. 1939), United Kingdom (20 Dec. 1939), South Africa (12 Feb. 1940), New Zealand (19 Feb. 1940), Australia (10 May. 1940).

recognition to the Czechoslovak Government in London as the Government of the Czechoslovak Republic: Norway (12 October 1940), Canada (12 October 1940, confirmed: 17 July 1942), Poland (27 November 1940), Belgium (13 December 1940), Egypt (13 March 1941), Yugoslavia (19 May 1941), United Kingdom (18 July 1941, *de facto*: 21 July 1940),[14] Australia (18 July 1941, *de facto*: 20 November 1940), South Africa, New Zealand, USSR (18 July 1941), Eire (28 July 1941), USA (31 July 1941), Netherlands (25 August 1941, *de facto*: 15 March 1941), China (2 September 1941), Luxembourg (27 February 1942), Mexico (26 March 1942), Iran (27 May 1942), Bolivia (5 June 1942), Uruguay (29 June 1942), Cuba (4 July 1942), Peru (6 July 1942), Dominican Republic (10 July 1942), Greece (19 August 1942), Brazil (16 September 1942), Colombia, Venezuela, Ecuador (9 January 1943), Chile (31 March 1943), Turkey (4 September 1944), Switzerland (27 February 1945), Italy (8 March 1945), Sweden (5 April 1945).

Yugoslavia (17 April 1941)

Name: Royal Yugoslav Government in exile
Establishment: Flight of existing Government to Jerusalem
Head of Government: King Peter II (head of State)
Seat or headquarters: Jerusalem (Palestine): 21 April 1941; London: 21 June 1941; Cairo (Egypt): 29 September 1943; London: 26 June 1944–5 March 1945
Context: War/annexation
Return to/establishment in national territory: February/March 1945 (but only nominally, and not King Peter)
Recognition: The Allies and those (neutral) countries which had not recognized the independence of Croatia continued to recognize King Peter's Government 'as the legal Government of the Kingdom of Yugoslavia'. The USSR, which had withdrawn its recognition on 9 May 1941, re-recognized the Royal Government after the German invasion of the Soviet Union on 20 July 1941.

Greece (23 May 1941)

Name: Royal Government of Greece
Establishment: Flight of existing Government from Crete to Cairo
Head of Government: King George II (head of State)
Seat or headquarters: Cairo (Egypt): 25 May 1941; Capetown (South Africa): 17 July 1941; London: 22 September 1941; Cairo: 15 March 1943; Caserta (Italy): 9 September 1944
Context: War
Return to/establishment in national territory: The Government returned to Athens on 17 October 1944
Recognition: The Royal Government continued to be recognized as the Government of Greece by the Allies and neutral States. The USSR, which had withdrawn

[14] On 21 July 1940 the British Government had recognized the Provisional Czechoslovak Government only 'as representing the Czech and Slovak peoples and to facilitate its activities'.

its recognition on 3 June 1941 on the ground that it no longer recognized Greece as an independent State, re-recognized the Royal Government after the German invasion of the Soviet Union on 20 July 1941.

Philippines (March 1942)

Name: 'Philippine Commonwealth Government in exile'[15]
Establishment: Flight of existing Government to Australia
Head of Government: President: Manuel Quezon (until his death on 1 August 1944), Sergio Osmeña (former Vice-President)
Seat or headquarters: Washington, DC, since 13 May 1942
Context: War
Return to/establishment in national territory: Establishment of the temporary seat of the Philippine Commonwealth Government in the capital of Leyte, Tacloban, on 23 October 1944—re-establishment of the Government in Manila on 27 February 1945
Recognition: The Philippine Government in exile continued to be recognized by both the Allies and neutral States. On 4 February 1944 the Chief of the Division of Philippine Affairs, Frank P. Lockhart, stated that 'the Commonwealth Government is still recognized as the Government of the Philippine Islands'.[16] The Japanese-installed Government of the 'Republic of the Philippines' was recognized only by Japan and implicitly by some of the Axis States.

Burma (4 May 1942)

Name: Government of Burma[17]
Establishment: Flight of existing Government to India
Head of Government: Sir Reginald Dorman-Smith (Governor of Burma)
Seat or headquarters: Simla (British India)
Context: War
Return to/establishment in national territory: 16 October 1945
Recognition: The British Government decided that the Burma Government should be maintained in order to show the world that it regarded the loss of Burma as only temporary. The Governor's administration continued to be recognized as the Government of Burma by the Allies. The Burmese Government installed by the Japanese occupant, on the other hand, was recognized by Japan, Nanking-China, Manchukuo, Vichy-France, Thailand, Germany, Italy, Croatia, and Slovakia.

[15] The Philippines were under the sovereignty of the USA. However, in 1935 an autonomous form of government, known as the Commonwealth of the Philippines had been established.
[16] [1944] V FRUS 1299.
[17] Burma, like India, was not a colony, but enjoyed self-government in her internal affairs (although not Dominion status).

India (21 October 1943)

Name: 'Provisional Government of Azad Hind (Free India)'
Establishment: Proclamation by the Indian Independence League in Shonan (Singapore)
Head of Government: Netaji Subhas Chandra Bose (Prime Minister, Minister of Foreign Affairs and War)
Seat or headquarters: Singapore: 21 October 1943–January 1944; Rangoon (Burma): 7 January 1944–28 April 1945; Bangkok (Thailand)
Context: War
Return to/establishment in national territory: On 6 November 1943 Japan handed over to the Azad Hind Government the Japanese-occupied Indian islands of Andaman and Nicobar
Recognition: The Bose Government was recognized by the following Axis States and their Allies: Japan (23 October 1943), Burma (24 October 1943), Croatia (27 October 1943), Germany (28 October 1943), Philippines (29 October 1943), Fascist Italy, Manchukuo, Nanking-China (1 November 1943), Thailand (18 November 1943).

Bulgaria (11 September 1944)

Name: Bulgarian National Government in exile
Establishment: Formation on German order in Vienna
Head of Government: Professor Alexander Tsankoff (President and Minister of War)
Seat or headquarters: Vienna (Austria—at the time part of Germany)
Context: War
Return to/establishment in national territory:
Recognition: Only Germany recognized the Tsankoff Government.

Netherlands East Indies (14 September 1944)

Name: Netherlands East Indies Government (NEIG)[18]
Establishment: Netherlands Royal Decree of 14 September 1944
Head of Government: Dr H. J. van Mook (Lieutenant-Governor-General)
Seat or headquarters: Camp Columbia, Brisbane (Australia)
Context: War
Return to/establishment in national territory: October 1945
Recognition: The NEIG was recognized by the host State and accorded all appropriate courtesies and facilities due to a government

[18] Successor to the Netherlands Indies Commission which had been established in Melbourne (Australia) after the fall of the Netherlands East Indies. The Commission, however, only administered NEI affairs in Australia and did not have the status of a government.

France (30 September 1944)

Name: 'Délégation gouvernementale française pour la Défense des Intérêts nationaux'
Establishment: Forced evacuation of existing Government to Germany
Head of Government: Marshal Philippe Pétain (head of State); Fernand de Brinon (head of the Délégation gouvernementale)
Seat or headquarters: Sigmaringen (Germany)
Context: War
Return to/establishment in national territory:
Recognition: In consequence of Marshal Pétain's declaration that he was compelled by force to leave Vichy and was thus no longer in a position to wield effective power as head of the French State, on 23 and 24 August 1944 the States that had continued to recognize the Pétain Government as the Government of France[19] withdrew their recognition. Only Germany formally maintained its recognition of the Pétain Government.

Serbia (4 October 1944)

Name: Serbian Government in exile
Establishment: Flight of existing (German puppet) Government to Vienna
Head of Government: Milan Neditch (Prime Minister)
Seat or headquarters: Vienna (Austria—at the time part of Germany)
Context: War
Return to/establishment in national territory:
Recognition: Only Germany continued to recognize the Neditch Government in exile.

El Salvador (10 November 1944)

Name: Salvadoran Government in exile
Establishment: Proclamation in Guatemala City
Head of Government: Miguel Tomás Molina
Seat or headquarters: Guatemala City (Guatemala)
Context: Political opposition
Return to/establishment in national territory:
Recognition: Although at the time of the proclamation of the 'Salvadoran Government in exile' the Government of Colonel Osmín Aguirre y Salinas, which had come to power by *coup d'état* in El Salvador on 21 October 1944, was recognized only by Nicaragua and Honduras (24 Oct. 1944), no State accorded recognition to the 'Government in exile'. The United States informed Guatemala on 17 November 1944 that 'while the decision . . . regarding the recognition of the regime now controlling El Salvador and the regime in exile in Guatemala is obviously one within Guatemala's sole competence' it believed that 'the Salvadoran regime in exile does

[19] e.g. Portugal, Spain, Sweden, Switzerland, Turkey, and the Vatican.

not appear to have the attributes commonly recognized by international law as prerequisites for recognition. Under these circumstances such recognition might give grounds for allegations that Guatemala is interfering in Salvadoran internal politics.'[20]

Spain (17 August 1945)

Name: Government of the Spanish Republic in exile[21]
Establishment: Election of a new President by ninety-six out of 470 former members of the Spanish Republican *Cortes* in Mexico City
Head of Government: President: Diego Martínez Barrio (17 August 1945–1 January 1960),[22] Luis Jimenez de Asúa (31 January 1969–17 November 1970), José Maldonado (20 November 1970–7 July 1977)
Seat or headquarters: Mexico City, Paris (February 1946 until dissolution in July 1977)
Context: Civil war/intervention/political opposition
Return to/establishment in national territory:
Recognition: The Spanish Republican Government in exile was recognized by the following States 'as the only legitimate Spanish Government': Mexico (28 August 1945), Panama, Venezuela, Guatemala (March 1946), Poland (5 April 1946), Yugoslavia (13 April 1946), Romania (21 May 1946), Hungary (28 July 1946), Czechoslovakia (22 August 1946), Bulgaria (30 November 1946), Albania (December 1946). Of these countries only two, Mexico and Yugoslavia, maintained their recognition until the end of the Francoist regime. Mexico terminated relations with the Republican Government in exile on 18 March 1977 and established diplomatic relations with the Suárez Government in Spain on 28 March 1977.

Slowakia (1947)

Name: Slovak Government in exile
Establishment: 1947
Head of Government: FerdinandĎurčanský
Seat or headquarters: New York
Context: Political opposition
Return to/establishment in national territory:
Recognition: The question of recognition of a Slovak Government in exile could arise only for States that had recognized the State of Slovakia *de jure* during its

[20] [1944] VII FRUS 1109.
[21] At the end of the civil war in Spain on 5 Feb. 1939 the Republican Government fled to France where it continued to function. After the Franco-German armistice on 22 June 1940 it was dispersed. Beside the Spanish Republican Government there existed two other Spanish Governments in exile from 1939 to 1979: the Catalan Autonomous Government in exile (Generalidad de Cataluna) and the Basque Autonomous Government in exile, both in Paris. It is submitted that the Basque and Catalan Governments are to be regarded as autonomous divisions of the Spanish Republic.
[22] President of the Spanish Republican *Cortes*.

existence from 1939 to 1944. Of the twenty-nine States that had recognized the State, Belgium and the United Kingdom had accorded only *de facto* recognition. However, none of those States reacted to a letter sent to them requesting recognition. Switzerland, one of the States that had recognized Slovakia *de jure*, only noted on the letter: 'There is no question of recognizing the Slovak Government in exile. Receipt not to be acknowledged.'[23]

China (8 December 1949)

Name: Nationalist Government of the Republic of China
Establishment: Flight of existing Government to Taiwan
Head of Government: Tshiang Kai shek
Seat or headquarters: Taipeh (Taiwan)[24]
Context: Civil war
Return to/establishment in national territory: With the acquisition of title over Taiwan by China the Nationalist Government became a local *de facto* government in Chinese national territory
Recognition: By 1952 about thirty-five States still continued to recognize the Nationalist Government at Taipeh as the Government of China, while the following twenty States had recognized the Communist Government of the People's Republic of China as the Government of China: USSR (2 October 1949), Bulgaria, Romania (3 October 1949), Albania, Czechoslovakia, Hungary, Poland (4 October 1949), Yugoslavia (5 October 1949), Burma (9 December 1949), India (30 December 1949), Pakistan (4 January 1950), Ceylon, Israel, Norway, Sweden, Switzerland, United Kingdom (6 January 1950), Denmark (9 January 1950), Afghanistan, Finland (13 January 1950).

Estonia (12 January 1953)

Name: 'Estonian Government in exile'
Establishment: Proclamation at Oslo
Head of Government: Alfred Rei (President), John Sikkar (Prime Minister)
Seat or headquarters: Sweden
Context: Annexation
Return to/establishment in national territory:
Recognition: No State accorded recognition but some States continued to recognize the diplomatic representatives of Estonia accredited by the last independent Estonian Government prior to August 1940.

[23] Klarer, *Schweizerische Praxis der völkerrechtlichen Anerkennung* (1981), 197.

[24] The question whether or not the Nationalist Government was in exile depends upon the legal status of Taiwan. It is argued that China, at the earliest, could have gained sovereignty over Formosa and the Pescadores islands on 8 Sept. 1951, on the day the Peace Treaty with Japan was concluded in which the latter, in Art. 2, renounced 'all right, title and claim' to these islands. On the legal status of Taiwan, see O'Connell, 'The Status of Formosa and the Chinese Recognition Problem' (1956) 50 *AJIL* 405–16.

Estonia (2 March 1953)

Name: 'Estonian Government in exile'
Establishment: Proclamation at Detmold (Germany)
Head of Government: Alfred Maurer (Acting President), Johan Holberg (Prime Minister)
Seat or headquarters: Germany
Context: Annexation
Return to/establishment in national territory:
Recognition: No State accorded recognition but some States continued to recognize the diplomatic representatives of Estonia accredited by the last independent Estonian Government prior to August 1940.

Algeria (19 September 1958)

Name: 'Gouvernement Provisoire de la République Algérienne (GPRA)'
Establishment: Proclamation simultaneously at Cairo, Tunis, and Rabat
Head of Government: Prime Minister: Ferhat Abbas and, from August 1961, Youssef Ben Khedda
Seat or headquarters: Cairo, Tunis
Context: Decolonization
Return to/establishment in national territory: 3 July 1962
Recognition: The first action of the GPRA was to notify all diplomatic missions in Cairo of its formation and to request recognition.[25] The day after the announcement of the constitution of the GPRA France declared that it would consider recognition of the GPRA by any government to be an 'unfriendly act',[26] and on 30 April 1959 General de Gaulle declared that 'France would immediately sever its diplomatic relations with any serious State which would recognize the GPRA'.[27] Despite these threats, by 3 July 1962, the following States had accorded (unless otherwise indicated) formal *de jure* recognition:[28] Iraq, UAR,[29] Libya, Tunisia, Morocco (19 September 1958), Saudi Arabia, Jordan (20 September 1958), Yemen (21 September 1958), PR China, Sudan (22 September 1958), North Korea (25 September 1958), North Vietnam (26 September 1958), Indonesia (27 September 1958), Guinea (30 September 1958),[30] Mongolia (15 December 1958), Lebanon (14 January 1959), East Germany (*de facto*: March 1959); Yugoslavia (*de facto*: June 1959,[31] *de jure*: 5 September 1961); Ghana (*de facto*: 9 July 1959, *de jure*: 5 September 1961),

[25] Recognition by several States had already been secured prior to the announcement of the GPRA. See ARA no. 45, 213–19 at 213.
[26] [1958] *Keesing's* 16410A.
[27] Favrod, *Le FLN et l'Algérie* (1962), 166 (translation supplied).
[28] For the text of recognition statements, see Bedjaoui, *Law and the Algerian Revolution* (1961), 113–21.
[29] i.e. Egypt and Syria.
[30] Recognition was confirmed on 6 Aug. 1959.
[31] *De facto* recognition as at June 1959 was confirmed on 12 Apr. 1961: ARA no. 109, 506–16.

Hungary (*de facto*: 1959, *de jure*: 19 April 1962), Liberia (6 June 1960), Togo (17 June 1960), USSR (*de facto*: 3 October 1960,[32] *de jure*: 19 March 1962), Mali (18 February 1961), Congo-Stanleyville (19 February 1961), Czechoslovakia (*de facto*: 2 March 1961, *de jure*: 19 March 1962), Bulgaria (*de facto*: 29 March 1961,[33] *de jure*: 3 October 1961), Cuba (28 June 1961), Pakistan (3 August 1961), Afghanistan (1 September 1961), Cambodia (5 September 1961), Cyprus (6 September 1961), India (*de facto*: September 1961), Somalia (1961), Ethiopia (*de facto*: 28 February 1962, *de jure*: 19 March 1962), Romania (19 March 1962), Ivory Coast (18 March 1962), Albania (19 March 1962), Poland (2 May 1962).

Tibet (31 March 1959)

Name: 'Government of Tibet in exile'
Establishment: Flight of the Dalai Lama and his followers to India
Head of Government: The Dalai Lama Ngawang Lobsang Tenzin Gyatso
Seat or headquarters: Dharamsala (India)
Context: Autonomy/secession
Return to/establishment in national territory:
Recognition: Although the Dalai Lama is regularly received by world leaders in his capacity as a spiritual leader or Nobel laureate, his government in exile has not been recognized by any State. On the contrary, from time to time, States feel obliged expressly to state that they do not recognize the 'self-styled Tibetan Government in exile'.[34]

Sanwi/Ivory Coast (May 1959)

Name: 'Provisional Sanwi Government in exile'
Establishment: Formation abroad
Head of Government: King Amon N'Douffou III, Armand Kadio Attié (Prime Minister)
Seat or headquarters: Accra (Ghana)
Context: Secession
Return to/establishment in national territory:
Recognition: No State accorded recognition. Ghana, which was both the seat of the 'Provisional Government' and its main supporter, on several occasions expressly denied that it had officially recognized that 'Government'.

[32] On Soviet *de facto* recognition, see ARA no. 110, 517–19 at 518.

[33] On Bulgarian *de facto* recognition, see ARA no. 115, 529–32.

[34] For a statement of the German Government, see BT Sten.Ber., 13. Legislative period 113. Session, 20 June 1996, 10097. For a similar statement of the US Government, see (1987) 87/5 *DSB* 49. For a statement by the Indian Government, see Singh and Nawaz, 'The Contemporary Practice of India in the Field of International Law' (1959–60) 1 *Int.Stud.* 281. On 17 March 1980 32 MPs urged Prime Minister Indira Gandhi, 'to recognize the Tibetan Government in exile as the *de facto* and *de jure* government of Tibet' (1980) 12/1 *Tibet. Bull.* 11).

Laos (9 December 1960)

Name: (Neutralist) Government of Laos
Establishment: Flight of Prime Minister and six cabinet ministers from Vientiane to Phnom Penh
Head of Government: Prince Souvanna Phouma (Prime Minister)
Seat or headquarters: Phnom Penh (Cambodia)
Context: Civil War/intervention
Return to/establishment in national territory: Re-establishment of Cabinet inside Cambodia at Xieng Khouang on 31 January 1961
Recognition: The Souvanna Phouma Government, which on 20 December 1960 declared on Radio Hanoi that it had not resigned but was only temporarily absent from Vientiane and would return to Laos as soon as the circumstances permitted, continued to be recognized by Burma, Cambodia, India, North Vietnam, the PR China, the USSR, Yugoslavia, and other Communist countries, which made express statements to that effect.[35] The reason given for the continued recognition of the Souvanna Phouma Government was that its rival at Vientiane, the Government under Prince Boun Oum, had been installed by US intervention. Not surprisingly, the Boun Oum Government was recognized by the United States, Thailand, South Vietnam, and the Western States.

Cuba (6 October 1961)

Name: 'Government of Cuba in Arms-in-Exile'
Establishment: Election by one of the Cuban exile organization in the USA
Head of Government: Dr Julio Carceran de Vall y Souza (Provisional President)
Seat or headquarters: Miami, Florida (USA)
Context: Political opposition
Return to/establishment in national territory:
Recognition: No State granted recognition to this 'Government'. On 7 October 1961 Acting Assistant Secretary of State Coerr wrote to Dr Julio Carceran de Vall y Souza: 'I must inform you that for another government to establish itself within the territory of the United States, without the consent of the Government of the United States, would violate the sovereignty and territory of the United States under international law. I should also mention that the consent of the Government of the United States to the establishment of a government in exile would imply recognition by the United States of such a government. The government of the United States, of course, cannot permit itself to be forced into such a decision. I am constrained to inform you that the Government of the United States does not consent to the pretended or assumed existence of the Government of Cuba in Arms in Exile within its sovereign domain.'[36]

[35] See *The Times*, 23 Dec. 1960, 3; *ibid.*, 26 Dec. 1960, 1 and 7; *ibid.*, 6 Jan. 1961, 1; *ibid.*, 12 Jan. 1961, 3. See also (1961) 4/1 *PR* 19–20; and Renmin Ribao's Comment of 10 Feb. 1961: 'The Chinese Government recognizes only the lawful Phouma Government' (1961) 4/7 *PR* 20).

[36] Whiteman (ed.), *Digest of International Law* (1968), vi, 354–5. See also *The Times*, 9 Oct. 1961, 10. It is of interest to note that in 1959–60 President Eisenhower had planned to recognize a Cuban Government in exile.

Portuguese State of India (17 February 1962)

Name: Government for the Portuguese State of India[37]
Establishment: Promulgation of Law No. 2112 providing that 'for so long as the Portuguese territory of the State of India remains withdrawn from the full and effective exercise of Portuguese sovereignty, the Government of the province, with its organs and services of provisional administration, shall function in Lisbon'.[38]
Head of Government: Governor-General of the Portuguese State of India
Seat or headquarters: Lisbon (Portugal)
Context: Annexation
Return to/establishment in national territory:
Recognition: No formal recognition was found. Some States, however, recognized the Government of India until 1974 only as the *de facto* government of the Portuguese territories in India.[39]

Angola (5 April 1962)

Name: 'Government of the Angolan Republic in Exile', later renamed the 'Revolutionary Government of Angola in Exile' (GRAE)
Establishment: Proclamation in Léopoldville (Kinshasa), Zaïre
Head of Government: Holden Roberto (President)
Seat or headquarters: Léopoldville (Kinshasa), Zaïre
Context: Decolonization
Return to/establishment in national territory:
Recognition: Of vital importance to the GRAE was the recommendation of its recognition by the OAU Liberation Committee in July 1963.[40] Acting upon this recommendation the OAU Council of Ministers, meeting in Dakar on 2–11 August 1963, requested 'all Member states to accord recognition to the Revolutionary Government of Angola in exile'.[41] This call for recognition was repeated by the Assembly of Heads of State and Government, meeting in Cairo on 17–21 July 1964.[42] However, the OAU in June 1971 formally withdrew 'the recognition of the status of government in exile' from the GRAE for its lack of effectiveness in the armed liberation struggle. Equally important to the GRAE was its *de jure* recognition on 29 June 1963 by its host State, Congo–Léopoldville (Zaïre).[43] In response to this recognition Portugal recalled its *chargé d'affaires* in Léopoldville but diplomatic

[37] The Portuguese State of India consisted of several small enclaves on the west coast of the Indian subcontinent: Goa, Damão, and Diu and their still smaller appendages, Dara and Nagar Haveli.

[38] Whiteman, n. 36 above, ii, 486, 1144. See also [1962] *Keesing's* 18662.

[39] For the British statement, see HC Debs., vol. 708, WA, *col.* 31, 8 Mar. 1965.

[40] Although it is not totally clear in what capacity the GRAE was recognized by the Liberation Committee. Some accounts speak of recognition as 'the sole legitimate representative of the Angolan people', some of recognition as 'the legal Government of Angola', and some of recognition as 'the only viable representative of the Angolan liberation movement'.

[41] See CM/Res.4(I), adopted on 10 Aug. 1963.

[42] See AHG/Res.18(I).

[43] For the text of the declaration of *de jure* recognition, see Marcum, *The Angolan Revolution* (1978), ii, 78–9.

relations were not broken off. The Congolese Government later explained that its recognition meant that it recognized Portugal only as a European State and that it recognized the GRAE as the legitimate Government of Angola.[44] The number of States which recognized the GRAE varies from account to account. In the literature the numbers given range from nineteen[45] to twenty-five[46] States, while the GRAE itself claimed to have been recognized by about thirty African and Asian States.[47] Recognition was accorded with high probability by the following twenty-two States. Unless otherwise indicated, *de jure* recognition was accorded:[48] Congo–Léopoldville (29 June 1963), Tunisia (8 August 1963), Algeria (August 1963), Morocco (21 August 1963), Dahomey (August 1963), Mauritania (August 1963), Senegal (13 September 1963), Niger (October 1963), UAR (12 October 1963), Nigeria (*de facto*: 26 October 1963, *de jure*: 4 April 1964), Mali (17 January 1964),[49] Iraq (*de facto*: 3 February 1964), Libya (April 1964), Rwanda (April 1964), Guinea (1964), Liberia (*de facto*: 2 June 1964), Tanzania (8 June 1964), Kenya (24 June 1964), Togo (27 June 1964), CAR (14 August 1964), Ivory Coast (3 August 1964), Cameroon (September 1964).

Iran (22 April 1962)

Name: 'National Government of Iran in Exile'
Establishment: Formation announced on the Voice of Free Iran
Head of Government: Dr Mosaddeq (proposed head of Government)
Seat or headquarters:
Context: Political opposition
Return to/establishment in national territory:
Recognition: No State accorded recognition.

Yemen (5 October 1962)

Name: 'Royal Government in exile'
Establishment: Formation in Saudi Arabia by (legal successor of) deposed sovereign
Head of Government: Imam Mohammed el Badr

[44] Herrich, *Area Handbook for Angola* (1967), 231–2. The Portuguese Foreign Ministry on 9 July 1963 accused the Congo of having withdrawn recognition of the Portuguese Government as the 'legitimate representative of Angola' (*NY Times*, 10 July 1963, 5).

[45] Marcum, 'Government-in-Exile Versus Government-in-Insurgency: The Case of Angola' in Shain (ed.), *Governments-in-Exile in Contemporary World Politics* (1991), 42–51 at 50, n. 4.

[46] Moser, *La Révolution angolaise* (1966), 120.

[47] Press release published by the Angola Information Bureau, Geneva, 20 Sept. 1971: 'GRAE is recognized by about 30 African and Asian states' ([1971–2] ACR C21). Mr Roberto at a press conference in Dar-es-Salaam airport on 22 Oct. 1964 explained that 29 countries had so far recognized the GRAE ([1964] *Africa Diary* 2045; BBC, *SWB*, 2nd series, ME/1692/B/5, 26 Oct. 1964).

[48] For examples of exchanges of formal letters and press releases concerning recognition of the GRAE, see *Angola: Bulletin d'information*, 1/4–5 (15–31 Oct. 1963), 4–6.

[49] The establishment of diplomatic relations was announced on 23 Oct. 1964 (BBC, *SWB*, 2nd series, ME/1692/B/5, 26 Oct. 1964).

Seat or headquarters: Jedda (Saudi Arabia), and Ketaf, a mountain village about thirty miles from the Saudi Arabian border inside Yemen
Context: Coup d'état/civil war/intervention
Return to/establishment in national territory:
Recognition: The Republican Government of Colonel Sallal which was formed in Sana'a on 26 September was recognized by the USSR (28 September 1962), the UAR (29 September 1962), Syria, Tunisia, Algeria, Iraq (9 October 1962), Sudan, Lebanon, Czechoslovakia, Bulgaria, Hungary, the PRC, Poland, East Germany, Cuba, North Vietnam, Pakistan, Ceylon, Indonesia, Mali, Afghanistan, and Somalia. On 23 October 1962 India and West Germany[50] recognized the Republican Government. On 19 December 1962 Italy and the United States followed, the latter being the thirty-sixth State to do so. Australia (20 December 1962), and Canada (21 December 1962) followed. On 21 December 1962 the UN General Assembly accepted the credentials of the Sallal Government by seventy-four votes to four, with twenty-three abstentions.[51] The following States did not recognize the Republican Government until the date given, but continued to recognize the Royal Government in exile: Morocco (18 March 1963), Libya (25 March 1963), Jordan (22 July 1964),[52] Saudi Arabia (22 July 1970), United Kingdom (29 July 1970).[53]

Saudi Arabia (13 November 1962)

Name: 'Arabian Republican Government-in-Exile'
Establishment: Announcement by radio Sana'a
Head of Government: Sayed Nasser El Sayed
Seat or headquarters: Sana'a (Republic of Yemen)
Context: Political opposition
Return to/establishment in national territory:
Recognition: No State, not even the Republic of Yemen, formally recognized the Arabian Republican Government.

South Moluccas (June 1966)

Name: Government in exile of the Republik Maluku Selatan (RMS)[54]
Establishment: Proclamation at a conference of the Unity Front of the South

[50] Germany established diplomatic relations, however, only on 15 July 1969.

[51] GAOR, 17th Session, 1202nd Plenary Meeting, 20th Dec. 1962, 1232. See also the report of the credentials committee: UN Doc.A/5395, paras. 19–25 on Yemen adopted by A/RES/1871 (XVII).

[52] The Jordanian Government announced on 18 Feb. 1967 that it had withdrawn recognition from President Sallal's Republican Government on 19 Jan. 1967.

[53] The UK continued to recognize the Royalist Government, which maintained a legation in London; it was stated that the Yemeni (royalist) *chargé d'affaires* had been told that recognition of his mission had lapsed with the British Government's decision to recognize the Republican Government ([1970] *Keesing's* 24114C).

[54] The RMS, which consisted of several islands of the Indonesian archipelago, proclaimed its independence form the Republic of the United States of Indonesia (RUSI) on 25 Apr. 1950, and for a short period maintained its factual independence. By Jan. 1951 the new Republic was crushed by Indonesian troops, but guerrilla warfare continued on the island of Ceram until at least the early 1960s.

Moluccan People (*Badan Persatuan*)
Head of Government: J. A. Manusama (President)[55]
Seat or headquarters: Rotterdam
Context: Secession
Return to/establishment in national territory:
Recognition: No recognition by other States was received, but the RMS received some unspecified recognition by the Polish anti-communist Government in exile on 30 November 1955.

South Moluccas (17 May 1969)

Name: (Rival) Government in exile of the Republik Maluku Selatan (RMS)
Establishment: Announcement at a conference in Nimwegen
Head of Government: Isaac J. Tamaela (Acting President and Foreign Minister)
Seat or headquarters: Nijverdal (Netherlands)
Context: Secession
Return to/establishment in national territory:
Recognition: No State accorded recognition.

Cambodia (5 May 1970)

Name: 'Royal Government of National Union of Cambodia' (RGNUC)
Establishment: Proclamation at a press conference in Peking
Head of Government: Prince Norodom Sihanouk (head of State), Penn Nouth (Prime Minister)
Seat or headquarters: Peking (China)
Context: Coup d'état/intervention/civil war
Return to/establishment in national territory: Transfer of ministries from Peking to Cambodian territory announced on 9 November 1973—fall of Phnom Penh on 17 April 1975—(temporary) return of Prince Sihanouk to Cambodia on 9 September 1975
Recognition: While the United States and other western States as well as the ASEAN States[56] immediately recognized the Republican Government under General Lon Nol in Phnom Penh, the Soviet Union, Bulgaria, Czechoslovakia, East Germany, Hungary, and Poland did not give *de jure* recognition to either Government. By the time the transfer of the ministries from Peking to Cambodia was announced, on 9 November 1973, the following States had recognized the RGNUC 'as the only legitimate and legal Government of Cambodia': PR China,[57] North Korea, Cuba, Romania, Albania, Syria (5 May 1970), North Vietnam, PRG of South Vietnam, Yugoslavia (6 May 1970), Iraq, Algeria (7 May 1970), UAR,[58] Sudan (13 May 1970), Libya, Guinea (14 May 1970), Mauritania (May 1970), South Yemen

[55] The first President of the RMS, Dr Christian Soumokil, who had led the armed resistance against the Indonesian army inside national territory, was captured and, in Apr. 1966, executed.
[56] i.e. Thailand, Malaysia, Singapore, Indonesia, and the Philippines.
[57] For the Chinese recognition statement, see (1970) 13/20 *PR* 14.
[58] i.e. Egypt.

(May 1970), Congo–Brazzaville (May 1970), Tanzania (19 June 1970), CAR (22 July 1970), Yemen (August 1970), Somalia (4 September 1970), Equatorial Guinea (21 July 1971), Senegal (7 August 1971), Malaysia (4 September 1971), Cameroon (October 1972), Gabon (October 1972), Burundi (November 1972), Madagascar (December 1972), Pakistan (January 1973), Chile (10 January 1973), Dahomey (28 February 1973),[59] Chad (10 March 1973), Mali (April 1973), Morocco (May 1973), Upper Volta (12 July 1973), Togo (14 August 1973), Malta (15 August 1973), Guyana (5 September 1973), UAE (8 September 1973), Oman (September 1973), Uganda (9 September 1973), Zaïre (9 September 1973), Tunisia (11 September 1973), Afghanistan (20 October 1973). After the transfer of the ministries inside Cambodia the following States recognized the RGNUC: Ghana (8 August 1974), Bangladesh (30 July 1974), Soviet Union (28 March 1975), India (1 April 1975), Sri Lanka (4 April 1975), Liberia (5 April 1975), France (12 April 1975), Sweden (15 April 1975), Turkey (16 April 1975)—fall of Phnom Penh—Australia, Iran, Portugal (17 April 1975), Argentina, Jordan, Laos, Malaysia, Nepal, Indonesia, Philippines, Singapore, Thailand, Switzerland (18 April 1975), Japan (19 April 1975), New Zealand (21 April 1975), Canada (25 April 1975), United Kingdom (2 April 1975).

Bangladesh (10 April 1971)

Name: 'Provisional Government of Bangla Desh (Bengal Nation)'
Establishment: Election by a Constituent Assembly on Indian territory
Head of Government: Sheikh Mujibur Rahman (President—in prison), Tajuddin Ahmed (Prime Minister)
Seat or headquarters: Calcutta (India)
Context: Secession
Return to/establishment in national territory: December 1971
Recognition: India, which maintained *de facto* relations with the Provisional Government, did not think it fit formally to recognize a Provisional Government of Bangla Desh in exile.[60] Neither did any other State.[61]

Madagascar (26 February 1975)

Name: 'Malagasy Provisional Democratic Government'
Establishment: Announcement in Paris
Head of Government: Richard Raherivelo
Seat or headquarters: Paris (France)
Context: Political opposition
Return to/establishment in national territory:

[59] i.e. Burkina Faso.

[60] See Tripathi, *India's Foreign Policy on Diplomatic Recognition of States and Governments* (1990), 104–5, 117–20. India was the first country to recognize Bangladesh on 6 Dec. 1971.

[61] The British Government on 28 June 1971 declined to accord recognition on the ground that 'there is no State of Bangla Desh which fulfils our normal criteria for recognition' (HC Debs., vol. 820, WA, *col.* 26, 28 June 1971).

Recognition: No State accorded recognition. The French Foreign Ministry, however, found it necessary to declare that it will 'have relations only with the lawful Government of Madagascar'.[62]

Western Sahara (4 March 1976)

Name: 'Government of the Saharawi Arab Democratic Republic (SADR)'
Establishment: Announcement simultaneously in Algiers, Tripoli, Tananarive, Conakry, and Bujumbura[63]
Head of Government: President (post created 16 October 1982): Mohamed Abdelazziz; Prime Minister: Mohamed Lamine Ould Ahmed (4 March 1976–16 August 1988), Mahmoud Ali Beiba (16 August 1988–19 September 1993), Bouchraya Bayoune (19 September 1993–)
Seat or headquarters: Tindouf and Algiers (Algeria)
Context: Decolonization/annexation by Morocco
Return to/establishment in national territory:
Recognition: The following States have announced their recognition of the SADR (proclaimed on 27 February 1976) and its government:[64] Madagascar (28 February 1976), Burundi (1 March 1976), Algeria (6 March 1976), Benin (10 March 1976), Angola, Mozambique (11 March 1976), North Korea (15 March 1976), Togo, Guinea-Bissau (16 March 1976), Rwanda (31 March 1976), South Yemen (2 February 1977), Seychelles (5 October 1977), Congo (3 June 1978), Sao Tomé, and Príncipe (20 June 1978), Panama (20 July 1978), Equatorial Guinea (3 November 1978), Tanzania (9 November 1978), Ethiopia (24 February 1979), Vietnam (2 March 1979), PR Kampuchea (9 April 1979), Laos (9 May 1979), Afghanistan (20 May 1979), Cape Verde (4 July 1979), Grenada (20 August 1979), Ghana (24 August 1979), Guyana (1 September 1979), Dominica, Saint Lucia (1 September 1979), Jamaica (4 September 1979), Uganda, Nicaragua (6 September 1979), Mexico (8 September 1979), Lesotho (9 October 1979), Zambia (12 October 1979), Cuba (20 January 1980), Iran (27 February 1980), Sierra Leone (27 March 1980), Syria, Libya, (PLO) (15 April 1980), Zimbabwe (16 April 1980), Swaziland (28 April 1980), Botswana (14 May 1980), Mali (4 July 1980), Costa Rica (30 October 1980), Vanuatu (27 November 1980), Papua New Guinea, Tuvalu, Kiribati, Nauru, Solomon Islands (12 August 1981), Mauritius (1 July 1982), Venezuela (3 August 1982), Surinam (11 August 1982), Bolivia (14 December 1982), Ecuador (14 November 1983), Mauritania (27 February 1984), Burkina Faso (4 March 1984), Peru (16 August 1984), Chad (21 August 1984), Nigeria (11 November 1984), Yugoslavia (28 November 1984), Colombia (27 February 1985), Liberia (31 July 1985), India (1 October 1985), Guatemala (10 April 1986), Dominican Republic (24 June 1986), Trinidad and Tobago (1 November 1986), Belize (18 November 1986), St Kitts and Nevis (25 February 1987), Antigua (27 February 1987), Albania (26 December 1987), Barbados (27 February 1988), El Salvador (31 July 1989), Honduras

[62] BBC, *SWB*, 2nd series, SU/4842/A5/2, 28 Feb. 1975.
[63] For the text of the announcement, see BBC, *SWB*, 2nd series, ME/5153/A/2–A/3, 8 Mar. 1976.
[64] Cf. the statement of Ibrahim Hakim, the SADR's Foreign Minister, on 23 Apr. 1980 that 22 African States had so far recognized his Government ([1980] ARB 5634A).

(8 November 1989), Namibia (11 June 1990), Malawi (16 November 1994), South Africa (1995). Of these seventy-seven States the following have subsequently withdrawn their recognition: Equatorial Guinea (5 May 1980), Solomon Islands (3 January 1989), Santa Lucia (17 March 1989), and Dominica (17 April 1989). Caution must however be urged—in most cases it is not clear in what capacity the SADR has been recognized. Only a few States, such as Burkina Faso, Sierra Leone, Tanzania, and Venezuela, have expressly recognized the SADR as 'a sovereign and independent State'. Similarly, only a few States, such as Laos, Nigeria, and Vietnam, have expressly included the Government of the SADR in their announcements of recognition. It may however be presumed that recognition of the SADR also comprises recognition of its Government, at least in the case of the some eighteen States which maintain formal diplomatic relations at ambassadorial level with it.[65]

Nicaragua (17 June 1979)

Name: 'Provisional Junta of National Reconstruction (PJNR)'
Establishment: Announcement by the Sandinista National Liberation Front (FSLN) from Costa Rica
Head of Government: The members of the five-person junta were Sr Sergio Ramírez Mercado, Sr Daniel Ortega Saavedra, Sra Violeta Barrios de Chamorro, Dr Moises Hassan Morales, and Sr Alfonso Robelo Callejas
Seat or headquarters: San José (Costa Rica)
Context: Civil war
Return to/establishment in national territory: After the flight of interim President Dr Urcuyo[66] to Guatemala on 19 July the PJNR arrived in Managua on 20 July from Costa Rica
Recognition: Prior to its installation in Nicaraguan territory the PJNR was recognized as the Government of Nicaragua by the following States: Panama (22 June 1979), Grenada (23 June 1979), Costa Rica (18 July 1969). In a rare case of recognition of belligerency in modern history, the members of the Andean Group (Bolivia, Colombia, Ecuador, Peru, and Venezuela) declared on 17 June 1979 that they had recognized both sides in the Nicaraguan conflict as 'belligerents'.

Cambodia (January 1979)

Name: 'Government of Democratic Kampuchea' (GDK): until 22 June 1982, 'Coalition Government of Democratic Kampuchea' (CGDK):[67] 22 June 1982–3 February

[65] These States are Angola, Benin, Costa Rica, Cuba, El Salvador, Guinea-Bissau, India, Iran, Madagascar, Mexico, Nicaragua, Panama, Seychelles, Togo, Uganda, Venezuela, Vietnam, Zimbabwe.

[66] Dr Urcuyo had succeeded President Somoza on 17 July 1979.

[67] For the text of the Agreement on the formation of a CGDK, signed at Kuala Lumpur on 22 June 1982, see BBC, *SWB*, 2nd series, FE/7057/A3/1–3, 21 June 1982. The CGDK consisted of the communist Khmer Rouge Government of Democratic Kampuchea (GDK), led by Khieu Samphan, and the two non-communist factions, the Khmer People's National Liberation Front (KPNLF), led by Son Sann and the Mouvement pour la Libération Nationale du Kampuchea (Moulinaka), later referred to as Front Uni National pour un Cambodge Indépendant, Neutre, Pacifique, et Coopératif (FUNCINPEC), headed by Prince Sihanouk.

1990, and 'National Government of Cambodia' (NGC): 3 February 1990–10 September 1990
Establishment: After the fall of Phnom Penh on 7 January 1979
Head of Government: GDK: Pol Pot (Prime Minister until December 1979), Khieu Samphan (Prime Minister from December 1979)—CGDK and NGC: Prince Norodom Sihanouk (President), Son Sann (Prime Minister), and Khieu Samphan (Vice President for Foreign Affairs)
Seat or headquarters: Despite claims that they were established in national territory, the various governments had no permanent base inside Cambodia, but operated out of Beijing, Pyongyang, or Bangkok
Context: Invasion/civil war
Return to/establishment in national territory: On 23 November 1991 Prince Sihanouk returned to Phnom Penh from thirteen years' exile as President of the Supreme National Council of Cambodia (SNC)
Recognition: The GDK, CGDK, and NGC continued to be recognized as the Government of Cambodia by some eighty countries of which the following States maintained formal diplomatic relations at ambassadorial level trough their embassies in Beijing and Bangkok with them: Bangladesh, PR China, Egypt, Guinea, Malaysia, Mauritania, North Korea, Pakistan, Senegal, Sierra Leone, Somalia, Sudan, and Yugoslavia. Japan on 2 May 1985 appointed a minister at its Embassy in Bangkok as *chargé d'affaires ad interim* for CGDK. The Government of the People's Republic of Kampuchea (PRK)[68] headed by Heng Samrin as President was recognized as the sole legitimate government of Cambodia by the following States: Vietnam, Laos, USSR, Poland, Hungary, Bulgaria, GDR, Czechoslovakia, Afghanistan (9 January 1979), PR Mongolia, Ethiopia (10 January 1979), Cuba (11 January 1979), Angola (1 February 1979), Mozambique (12 February 1979), Congo (10 March 1079), Libya (12 March 1979), Jamaica, Nicaragua, Grenada, Panama (4 September 1979), Madagascar (1979), India (7 July 1980), Albania (5 October 1983), Guinea-Bissau (22 March 1984), Cape Verde (March 1984), South Yemen (September 1985), Costa Rica (29 July 1989). The following States recognized neither of the two authorities as the government of Cambodia: USA, Germany which had never recognized the GDK, and the United Kingdom and Australia which withdrew their recognition from the GDK on 6 December 1979 and 14 February 1981, respectively

Iran (1 October 1981)

Name: Provisional Iranian Government in exile
Establishment: Announcement in Paris
Head of Government: Abolhassan Bani-Sadr (Provisional President), Massoud Radjani (Prime Minister)
Seat or headquarters: Auvers-sur-Oise (France)
Context: Political opposition
Return to/establishment in national territory:
Recognition: No recognition was accorded.

[68] The PRK on 30 Apr. 1989 was renamed the State of Cambodia (SOC).

Laos (July 1982)

Name: 'Alliance Government for National Liberation' or 'Democratic Government of the Kingdom of Laos'
Date of establishment/proclamation: Formation reported in July 1982
Head of Government: Prince Khamhing (head of State), Thao In-Nge Suriyathai (Prime Minister)
Seat or headquarters: Yunnan Province (Southern China) and Bangkok (Thailand)
Context: Civil war/political opposition
Return to/establishment in national territory:
Recognition: No State formally recognized the 'Alliance Government'. Thailand on 6 December 1982 issued the following communiqué: 'Following the takeover of a communist government in Vientiane, a group of Lao sought political asylum in Thailand. Out of humanitarian considerations, some of these exiles have been allowed to stay in Thailand. . . . As a nation abiding by the UN Charter and international law, Thailand categorically denies the allegations that it has condoned attempts to set up a Lao government in exile. On the contrary, the Thai Government values the good and friendly relations which exist with the Lao Government in Vientiane. . . . The Thai authorities would not allow anyone under whatever pretext to use Thai territory for the purpose of undermining the security and stability of any legitimate foreign government, particularly the Government in Vientiane, which the Thai Government fully recognizes.'[69]

Chad (October 1982)

Name: 'Gouvernement du Paix National (GPN)' and later 'Gouvernement de Salvation Nationale (GSN)'
Establishment: Formation in the Libyan-occupied Aouzou strip
Head of Government: Goukouni Oueddeï (President)
Seat or headquarters: Bardai (Libyan occupied)
Context: Intervention/civil war
Return to/establishment in national territory: With Libyan aid the GSN had re-established itself at Abéché inside Chad by mid-1983
Recognition: Goukouni's Government was recognized only by Libya.

Zaïre (17 January 1983)

Name: Zaïrean Government in exile
Establishment: Announcement in Brussels
Head of Government: Nguza Karl-I-Bond (President)
Seat or headquarters: Brussels (Belgium)
Context: Political opposition
Return to/establishment in national territory:
Recognition: No recognition was accorded.

[69] BBC, *SWB*, 2nd series, FE/7243/A3/4, 9 Dec. 1982.

Central African Republic (10 December 1984)

Name: 'Provisional Government of National Salvation'
Establishment: Announcement by the Mouvement de Libération du Peuple Centrafricain (MLPC)
Head of Government: General Alphonse M'Baikoua (President)
Seat or headquarters:
Context: Political opposition
Return to/establishment in national territory:
Recognition: No recognition was accorded.

Gabon (9 August 1985)

Name: Gabonese Government in exile
Date of establishment/proclamation: Announcement by the Mouvement de redressement national (MORENA) on 12 August 1985
Head of Government:
Seat or headquarters: Paris (France)
Context: Political opposition
Return to/establishment in national territory:
Recognition: No recognition was accorded. In response to the protest of the Gabonese Interior Minister on 13 August 1985 against the announcement of the creation of a Gabonese 'phantom' government in exile in Paris, the French Minister for Foreign Affairs, M. Roland Dumas, went on 18 August 1985 to Libreville and reassured President Bongo, declaring that , 'the French Government does not attach any standing and even less juridical value' to the Gabonese Government in exile which had been established in Paris and that the presence of the Gabonese on French territory had to be 'compatible with the legal rules on asylum'.[70]

Zaïre (8 September 1987)

Name: Zaïrean Government in exile
Establishment: Announcement by the Parti Démocratique et Socialiste Congolais (PDSC) in Geneva
Head of Government: Jerry Mahele (Prime Minister)
Seat or headquarters: 'In an African country'
Context: Political opposition
Return to/establishment in national territory:
Recognition: No recognition was accorded.

Panama (25 February 1988)

Name: Government of Panama
Establishment: Dismissal of President Delvalle by Legislative Assembly
Head of Government: Eric Arturo Delvalle (President)
Seat or headquarters: US military base inside Panama and Miami, Florida (USA)

[70] *Le Monde*, 20 Aug. 1985, 20 (translation supplied).

Context: *Coup d'état*
Return to/establishment in national territory:
Recognition: While States expressed their deep concern about recent developments in Panama and some recalled their ambassadors, only the United States continued to recognize (ousted) President Delvalle as the President of Panama. However, the United States discontinued recognition on 1 September 1989 when President Delvalle's term of office under the Panamanian Constitution expired.

Chad (1 May 1988)

Name: 'Transitional Government of National Unity'
Establishment: Formation reported by Libyan news agency JANA
Head of Government: Goukouni Oueddeï (President)
Seat or headquarters: Aouzou Strip (Libyan occupied)
Context: Libyan intervention/civil war
Return to/establishment in national territory:
Recognition: No formal recognition was reported.

Haiti (8 July 1988)

Name: 'Haitian Government Overseas'
Establishment: Announcement in New York
Head of Government: Nicolas Estiverne (President)
Seat or headquarters: New York (USA)
Context: Political opposition
Return to/establishment in national territory:
Recognition: No recognition was accorded.

Madagascar (17 February 1989)

Name: 'Malagasy Government in exile'
Establishment: Announcement by the Madagascar Committee For Democracy and Development (CMDD) in Paris
Head of Government: Ranaivo-Rahamefy Andrianony (President)
Seat or headquarters: Paris (France)
Context: Political opposition
Return to/establishment in national territory:
Recognition: No recognition was accorded.

Afghanistan (23 February 1989)

Name: 'Afghan Interim Government (AIG)'[71]
Establishment: Election at a *Shura* (council) of the Islamic Union of Mujahidin of Afghanistan (IUAM), the 'Peshawar Resistance Alliance', held in Rawalpindi (Pakistan)

[71] It should be noted that the AIG was the third government in exile proclaimed by the IUAM. The first two interim 'governments' were headed by Ahmed Shah.

Head of Government: Sibghatullah Modjaddidi (President), Rasul Sajjif (Prime Minister)
Seat or headquarters: Peshawar (Pakistan)
Context: Soviet intervention/civil war
Return to/establishment in national territory:
Recognition: The AIG was recognized as the Government of Afghanistan by four Islamic States: Saudi Arabia (9 March 1989), Sudan (11 March 1989), Bahrain (13 March 1989), and Malaysia (12 April 1989). The main sponsors of the AIG, the United States and Pakistan, refrained from according 'formal' or 'full' recognition and continued to recognize the Najibullah Government in Kabul. But the United States in June 1989 sent a special representative with the rank of ambassador to the AIG. It was however explained that this constituted neither 'a formal recognition of the interim government' nor 'the establishment of diplomatic relations'.[72] Pakistan stated that it did 'everything short of formal recognition'.[73]

Laos (10 December 1989)

Name: 'Government for the Liberation of the Lao Nation' or 'Revolutionary Government of Laos' (RGL)
Establishment: Announcement by emigré resistance leader Vang Pao
Head of Government: Pha-Gna Ounghong Souvannavong (Prime Minister)
Seat or headquarters: Thai–Laos border area
Context: Political opposition/civil war
Return to/establishment in national territory:
Recognition: No recognition was accorded.

Somalia (28 January 1991)

Name: Interim Government of Somalia
Date of establishment/proclamation: Appointment by international conference held in Djibouti on 29 January 1991 (with effect from 28 January 1991)
Head of Government: Ali Mahdi Mohamed (President), Omer Arteh Ghalib (Prime Minister)
Seat or headquarters: The Prime Minister's headquarters were in Riyadh (Saudi Arabia) throughout 1991
Context: Civil war
Return to/establishment in national territory:
Recognition: No State accorded recognition to the Government of Ali Mahdi Mohammed.

Kuwait (2 August 1990)

Name: Government of Kuwait
Establishment: Flight of existing Government to Saudi Arabia

[72] *Le Monde*, 8 Apr. 1989, 8; *WP*, 26 June 1989, Sec. A, 9.
[73] *WP*, 22 May 1989, Sec. A, 13.

Head of Government: Sheik Jaber al-Ahmad al-Jaber al-Sabah (Emir of Kuwait)
Seat or headquarters: Ta'if (Saudi Arabia)[74]
Context: Armed conflict/Iraqi occupation and annexation of Kuwait
Return to/establishment in national territory: Liberation of Kuwait on 26 February 1991—on 4 March 1991 Kuwait informed the UN Secretary-General that its Government was resuming its functions of the State and directing the nation's affairs from Kuwait City—on 14 March 1991 the Emir returned
Recognition: All States, with the exception of Iraq, continued to recognize the Emir Al-Sabah Government as the Government of Kuwait, many making formal statements to that effect.

Burma/Myanmar (18 December 1990)

Name: 'National Coalition Government of the Union of Burma (NCGUB)'
Establishment: Proclamation at the Karen National Union base at Manerplaw in the Burmese-Thai border area
Head of Government: Dr Sein Win (Prime Minister)
Seat or headquarters: Some of the members of the NCGUB including the Prime Minister established their headquarters in the United States, others in Thailand
Context: Coup d'état/democratization
Return to/establishment in national territory:
Recognition: No State has recognized the NCGUB although it is made up of elected representatives and has a strong claim to legitimacy; instead all States continue to recognize the country's ruling military junta, the State Law and Order Restoration Council (SLORC). Norway, which in December 1991 gave *de facto* recognition to the NCGUB, stated that it 'would continue to recognize Burma's military rulers as long as they controlled the territory'.

Haiti (30 September 1991)

Name: Government of Haiti
Establishment: Departure for Caracas of deposed President Aristide
Head of Government: Fr Jean-Bertrand Aristide (President), Robert Malval (Prime Minister)
Seat or headquarters: Washington, DC (USA)—Cabinet under Prime Minister Malval resided since 31 August 1993 in Port-au-Prince side by side with the military junta, however, was forced into hiding after the assassination of its Justice Minister. *The Times* called Mr Malval 'probably the world's most powerless . . . prime minister'.[75]
Context: Coup d'état
Return to/establishment in national territory: 15 October 1994

[74] Art. I of the Decree by the Emir of Kuwait concerning the temporary seat of the government of Kuwait, 3 Aug. 1990, provided that 'the Government of the State of Kuwait shall temporarily convene in the Kingdom of Saudi Arabia or any other place chosen by the Emir' (UN Doc.S/21666, 29 Aug. 1990).
[75] *The Times*, 22 Oct. 1993, 12.

Recognition: Exiled President Aristide and his government continued to be recognized by the international community as the legitimate President and Government of Haiti, with the sole exception of the Vatican which accorded formal recognition to the *de facto* government.

Georgia (6 January 1992)

Name: 'President of the Republic of Georgia in Exile'
Establishment: Flight from Tbilisi to Idzhevan in north-eastern Armenia (whose government had offered him temporary asylum)
Head of Government: Zviad Gamsakhurdia (President)
Seat or headquarters: Grosnyj (Chechenia)[76]
Context: Civil war
Return to/establishment in national territory:
Recognition: President Gamsakhurdia was overthrown at a time when most States had not yet recognized his government, although some countries had recognized the independence of Georgia.[77] Thus, for most States the question of the continued recognition of the democratically elected President of Georgia did not arise.

Togo (22 March 1993)

Name: 'Government of Togo in exile'
Establishment: Election by a conference of leading politicians of the opposition of Togo in exile
Head of Government: Jean-Lucien de Trouve (Prime Minister)
Seat or headquarters: Cotonou (Benin)
Context: Political opposition
Return to/establishment in national territory:
Recognition: No State accorded recognition.

Burundi (21 October 1993)

Name: 'Government of Burundi in exile'[78]
Establishment: Announcement on Radio Rwanda
Head of Government: Sylvie Kinigi (Prime Minister)
Seat or headquarters: Prime Minister and several cabinet ministers were in 'internal exile' in the French embassy in Bujumbura—on 23 October 1993 the Ministers of Health and Justice, Dr Jean Minani and Mr Fulgence Bakana, transferred the seat of 'the legally-recognized Government temporarily in exile' to Kigali, the capital of

[76] Grosnyj is the capital of the Russian autonomous republic of Chechen Ingushetia, which on 1 Nov. 1991 had declared its independence.

[77] At the time of the overthrow of President Gamsakhurdia the independence of Georgia had been recognized, *inter alia*, by the USA (25 Dec. 1991), Vietnam and China (27 Dec. 1991), and Laos (31 Dec. 1991).

[78] In a statement issued from the French Embassy Prime Minister Kinigi stated that 'as the government is in exile, the Prime Minister appointed two Ministers who represent the government in foreign countries'.

Rwanda
Context: Coup d'état/ethnic conflict
Return to/establishment in national territory: On 7 November 1993 after the arrival of French soldiers for the protection of the government, Prime Minister Sylvie Kinigi and her cabinet left the French Embassy
Recognition: No formal statements of recognition were issued but the Government of Rwanda supported the Government of Burundi in exile.

Rwanda (17 July 1994)

Name: (Hutu) Provisional Government of Rwanda
Establishment: Flight of exisitng Hutu Government to Zaïre together with some 30.000 troops and militiamen and some 1.4 million Hutu refugees
Head of Government: Theodore Sindikubwabo (President), Jean Kambande (Prime Minister)
Seat or headquarters: Ngosho camp, some ten kilometres from Goma (Zaïre)
Context: Civil war/ethnic conflict
Return to/establishment in national territory:
Recognition: The Hutu Government in exile did not receive any recognition. In response to activities of the government in exile the Government of Zaïre stated on several occasions that 'there was no Rwandan government-in-exile in Zaire, but only some senior officials of the defeated regime who had been given provisional exile'.

Qatar (27 June 1995)

Name: Government of Qatar
Establishment: A statement was issued in Geneva saying Sheikh Khalifa was still the legitimate ruler of his country
Head of Government: Sheikh Khalifa al-Thani
Seat or headquarters: London (June–December 1995), and Abu Dhabi, UAE
Context: Coup d'état
Return to/establishment in national territory:
Recognition: Foreign States were quick in recognizing Emir Hamad after the coup.[79] Although during a journey through the Gulf States at the beginning of 1996, the deposed Emir, Sheikh Khalifa, was welcomed everywhere with the honours due only to a foreign head of State, no State continued formally to recognize him as the legitimate Emir of Qatar during his exile. However, in February 1996, after an unsuccessful *coup* in Qatar, the US Government let the Government of Qatar know that it was 'the wish' of the United States that Sheikh Khalifa return to the throne and that Sheikh Hamad become crown prince.

[79] Sheikh Hamad's Government was recognized on 27 June 1995 e.g., by Jordan, Yemen, Oman, and the USA. The British Foreign Office on 27 June 1995 said that the matter was an internal affair and it would look forward to working with the new government (*Guardian*, 28 June 1995, 11).

Appendix III
List of Treaties Concluded by Authorities in Exile Recognized as Governments

NOTE: Recognized Governments in exile have concluded a large number of treaties relating to military, economic, and political matters. The duration of these treaties varies. Some have been limited to the time of exile while others have bound the State for up to twenty years. Often the only reference to a treaty has been found in a newspaper report on its conclusion. The following list must therefore necessarily be incomplete. But such a list may nevertheless give a good overview of the variety of the treaty-making activities of recognized governments in exile. All entries are listed according to the country which the government in exile claimed to represent and in chronological order. Unless stated otherwise, dates are those of signature or those on which an instrument was declared open for signature. The date of entry into force of a treaty is given only if it is not the same as the date of signature. Wherever possible reference has been made to a full text source.

Belgium (1914–18)

30 November 1914: Agreement with France concerning the search for and arrest of Belgian deserters in French territory. Done at Bordeaux: (1915) 42 *JDI* 236–7.

15–19 December 1914: Additional agreement to the convention of 18 January 1912 with Portugal relating to the establishment of telegraphic connections between the colony of the Belgian Congo and the province of Angola.

3 February 1915: Agreement with Great Britain respecting boundaries between Belgian and British territories in East Africa (Mount Sabinio to the Congo–Nile Watershed). Signed at London (entry into force: 20 October 1919): 110 BFSP 487.

13 March 1915: Agreement with France suspending for the duration of the war the application of the Franco–Belgian convention of 30 July 1891 subjecting to Belgian military service minors born in France of Belgian parents of whom one or the other was born outside France. Signed at Le Havre (instruments of ratification exchanged: 22 March 1915).

23 May 1915: Agreement supplementing the agreement of 14 August 1914 with France concerning military jurisdiction. Signed at Le Havre.

22 July 1915: Convention with Uruguay relating to custom duties on national emblems destined for the consulates of the two countries. Signed at Montevideo (instruments of ratification exchanged: 17 September 1916).

25 July 1915: Supplementary agreement with France concerning the search and arrest of Belgian deserters in France. Signed at Paris: Fauchille, *La guerre de 1914* (1915), i, no 33.

22 September 1915: Declaration with France renouncing the capitulations in the French zone of Morocco. Signed at Le Havre (entry into force: 2 October 1915).

9 November 1915: Agreement with Russia concerning the application to Belgian citizens of the special regime established in the railway zone of eastern China. Effected by exchange of notes at Peking (entry into force: 4 January 1916).

29 December 1915: Declaration with Spain renouncing the capitulations in the Spanish zone of Morocco. Signed at Le Havre (entry into force: 8 January 1916).

29 January 1916: Franco–Belgian declaration on military criminal jurisdiction completely withdrawing from the otherwise unlimited jurisdiction of the French and Belgian military courts in Belgium and France, respectively, all persons, whether civilian or not, who did not belong to the French or Belgian army. Signed at Le Havre: (1916) 43 *JDI* 726.

25 March 1916: Agreement with France on requisitions and compensation. Signed at Le Havre (entry into force: 8 April 1916).

28 March 1916: Resolutions unanimously adopted by the conference of Allies[1] at Paris.

15 April 1916: Anglo–Belgian convention concerning the competence of military tribunals. Signed at Le Havre: 110 BFSP 188.

9 August 1917: Agreement with Great Britain and France concerning British and French military cemeteries in Belgium. Signed at Le Havre: 113 BFSP 779.

4 September 1917: Agreement with Great Britain on requisitions and compensation. Signed at Le Havre.

12 September 1917: Agreement with France concerning the treatment of deserters. Signed at Le Havre.

23 December 1917: Convention with France for the prevention of insults directed against the authorities of the two countries. Signed at Le Havre (the convention never entered into force).

16 February 1918: Agreement with France concerning the exchange of parcels between the Belgian Congo and France and regulating its execution. Signed at Paris (instruments of ratification exchanged: 8 May 1918; entry into force: 1 January 1919).

14 March 1918: Declaration extending the scope of the Franco–Belgian extradition convention of 15 August 1874 to the French zone of Morocco. Signed at Le Havre.

24 April 1918: Declaration with France supplementing the telegraph convention of 23 June 1903 between the Congo Free State[2] and France. Signed at Paris (entry into force: 1 June 1918).

24 April 1918: Convention with France concerning protection against acts by enemy authorities of the property and private interests of the nationals of one State in the territory of the other. Signed at Paris (instruments of ratification exchanged: 19 November 1919).

6 September 1918: Agreement with the USA regarding penal military jurisdiction. Effected by exchange of notes at Washington (extended by exchange of notes on 10 November 1918): [1918] FRUS Supp. 2, 747, 751.

27 September 1918: Declaration with Spain extending the scope of the

[1] Belgium, France, Great Britain, Italy, Japan, Portugal, Russia, and Serbia.

[2] King Leopold II of Belgium had acquired the Congo Free State in 1885 as his private possession. In 1908 the territory became a Belgian colony.

Belgo–Spanish convention for the prevention of crimes and offences of 17 June 1870 to the Spanish zone of Morocco. Signed at Le Havre (entry into force: 7 October 1918).

11 November 1918: Declaration with Portugal relating to the competence of military tribunals. Signed at Le Havre.

Serbia (1915–18)

28 March 1916: Resolutions unanimously adopted by the conference of Allies at Paris.

14 December 1916: Franco–Serbian declaration concerning military criminal jurisdiction. Signed at Paris: (1917) 44 *JDI* 1169.

7/20 July 1917: Declaration of Corfu on the future union of the Serbs, Croats, and Slovenes in a single free and independent Kingdom under the Karageorgević dynasty. Signed by Prime Minster Nicolas Pašić for Serbia and Dr Ante Trumbić for the Yugoslav Committee in London: *Foreign Office Handbook*, No 14, 35.

Ukraine (1920–1)

April 1921: Provisional military agreement with Poland concerning the equipment and supply of the Ukrainian troops at present fighting in the Polish Army. Signed at Warsaw.

21 April 1920: Political, military, and economic convention with Poland in which Poland recognized the Ukraine as an independent State and Ukraine renounced its title to East Galicia, Chomland, Podlackie, and East Wolhynia. Signed at Warsaw.

Poland (1939–45)

19 September 1939: Exchange of notes with France relating to the status of the Polish Government in France. Done at Paris.

21 September 1939: Agreements with France providing for the formation of a Polish division and the creation of a Polish air force in France. Signed at Paris.[3]

25 October 1939: Secret protocol with France and the United Kingdom concerning the utilization of Polish air force personnel evacuated to France and the United Kingdom. Signed at Paris: *DCW* 370.

18 November 1939: Agreement with the United Kingdom placing certain units of the Polish naval forces under British command for the duration of the war and establishing a Polish naval base in Great Britain. Signed at London: (1939) 1 *Free Europe* 39.

25 November 1939: Agreement by exchange of notes with the Government of the United Kingdom regulating in principle the utilization of units of the Polish

[3] It is of interest to note that the agreements were signed by the French Prime Minister Edouard Daladier and General Wladyslaw Sikorski, the latter at the time of signature without office in the Polish Government. Only on 30 Sept. 1939 was General Sikorski appointed Prime Minister of the new Polish Government in exile in France.

mercantile marine in the prosecution of the war against Germany. Done at London: 199 LNTS 65.

2 December 1939: Temporary agreement with the Government of the United Kingdom concerning military co-operation. Signed at London.

4 January 1940: Military convention with France relative to the reconstruction of the Polish army and its high command in France. Signed at Paris: 144 BFSP 407.

4 January 1940: Agreement with France relative to the formation of a Polish air force in France and protocol regarding the carrying out of the military agreements. Signed at Paris: *DCW* 363.

4 January 1940: Protocol with France concerning the organization of Polish military jurisdiction and courts in France. Signed at Paris: *DCW* 365.

17 February 1940: Technical agreement with France concerning the reconstruction of the Polish air force in France. Signed at Paris: *DCW* 367.

11 June 1940: Anglo–Polish air force agreement. Signed at London.

18 July 1940: Agreement with the Government of the United Kingdom reaffirming their political and military co-operation. Signed at London.

5 August 1940: Political and military agreement with the United Kingdom relative to the organization of Polish army and air force units in Great Britain. Signed at London: *DCW* 377.

2 September 1940: Anglo–Polish moratorium treaty. Signed at London.

11 November 1940: Czechoslovak–Polish declaration pledging friendship and co-operation both during the war and in the peace settlement thereafter ('Declaration of Alliance'). Issued at London: 144 BFSP 381.

19 November 1940: Exchange of notes with the United Kingdom concerning death sentences imposed by Polish military tribunals in Great Britain. Done at London on 23 September and 19 November 1940.

22 November 1940: Anglo–Polish protocol on the jurisdiction over Polish forces in the United Kingdom. Signed at London.

3 December 1940: Anglo–Polish protocol concerning the lending of British warships to Poland. Signed at London.

25 February 1941: Anglo–Polish protocol concerning the provision of funds by the British Government for the maintenance of the Polish armed forces to be organized in the United Kingdom in accordance with the Anglo–Polish treaty of 5 August 1940. Signed at London.

5 April 1941: Polish-Canadian declaration announcing the completion of arrangements for constituting a Polish army in Canada for duty overseas. Signed at Ottawa.

12 June 1941: Resolution of the inter-allied meeting, St James's Palace, London: DAFR III, 444.

30 July 1941: Exchange of notes with the United Kingdom relating to the mutual assistance agreement of 25 August 1939. Done at London: 144 BFSP 642.

30 July 1941: Agreement with the USSR annulling the Soviet–German treaty of 28 September 1939 relating to Poland, restoring mutual diplomatic relations, undertaking mutual aid and support in the present war, and formation of a Polish army on the territory of the USSR. Additional protocol on an amnesty to be granted to all Polish citizens on the territory of the USSR deprived of their freedom. Signed at London ('Sikorski–Majski Agreement'): DPSR I, no 106.

5 August 1941: Agreement with the United Kingdom on military co-operation. Signed at London.

14 August 1941: Military agreement with the USSR providing in detail for the formation of Polish army units in Soviet Russia. Signed at Moscow: 144 BFSP 870.

24 September 1941: Czechoslovak–Polish declaration on their intention to co-operate during the war and in the peace settlement thereafter. Issued at London: WPA I, 464.

24 September 1941: Resolutions of the inter-allied meeting, St James's Palace, regarding the Atlantic Charter and the supply of essential requirements to Europe after the war. Adopted at London: WPA I, 3.

29 September 1941: Agreement with the USSR concerning the release of interned Polish troops and the restitution of Polish property in the Polish east provinces occupied by the USSR. Signed at Moscow.

4 December 1941: Russian–Polish declaration of friendship and mutual aid during and after the war, with the announced aim of organizing a just peace through a union of democratic States in Europe. Issued at Moscow: 144 BFSP 873.

31 December 1941: Soviet–Polish agreement for a loan of 100 million roubles to the Polish Government to provide aid for Polish citizens in the Soviet Union. Signed at Kiibyshev: Soviet For. Pol I, 113.

1 January 1942: Signatory to the declaration by United Nations. Signed at Washington: 204 LNTS 381.

13 January 1942: Signatory to the inter-allied declaration on war crimes. Signed at London: *NY Times*, 14 January 1942, 6.

14 January 1942: Joint declaration of the general steering committee, central and eastern European planning board.[4] Issued at New York: WPA I, 8.

22 January 1942: Soviet–Polish agreement for a loan of 300 million roubles to the Polish Government for the upkeep of the Polish army in the Soviet Union. Signed at Kuijbysev: DPSR I, 556.

23 January 1942: Agreement with Czechoslovakia on the principles of the projected Polish–Czechoslovak confederation. Signed at London: (1942) 5 *Free Europe* 43.

12 June 1942: Joint communiqué of the Polish and Czechoslovak Governments on the projected confederation of the two countries. Issued at London: DAFR IV, 275.

1 July 1942: Lend-lease agreement with the USA. Signed at Washington:[5] 103 UNTS 267.

30 October 1942: Exchange of notes with Mexico concerning the question of asylum of Polish nationals on Mexican territory.

17 December 1942: Joint declaration condemning the German policy of extermination of the Jewish population of Europe. Done at Washington and London: WPA I, 14.

5 January 1943: Signatory to the inter-allied declaration against acts of disposition committed in territories under enemy occupation or control: (1943) 8 *DSB* 21.

[4] See n. 10 below.

[5] See also the agreement between the Government of the USA and the Government of the Polish People's Republic on settlement for lend-lease and certain claims, signed at Washington on 28 June 1956: 273 UNTS 79.

25 February 1943: Military service agreement with the USA relating to the service of nationals of one country in the armed forces of the other country. Effected by exchanges of notes, Washington (entry into force: 27 January 1943): 13 UNTS 395.

18 May 1943: Anglo–Polish protocol concerning the care for disabled members of the Polish armed forces. Signed at London.

3 June 1943: Signatory to the final act of the United Nations conference on food and agriculture. Done at Hot Springs: (1943) 37 *AJIL* Supp., 159.

22 July 1943: Exchange of notes with the French Committee of National Liberation (CFLN)[6] concerning the Polish recognition of the Committee. Done at London.

22 July 1943: Agreement with the French Committee of National Liberation (CFLN) providing for the opening of recruiting offices in France for volunteers for the Polish Army (effective as at 28 October 1944).

9 November 1943: Signatory to the agreement for United Nations Relief and Rehabilitation Administration (UNRRA). Signed at Washington (instrument of ratification deposited: 7 March 1945): 145 BFSP 159.

17 December 1943: Agreement with the French Committee of National Liberation (CFLN) concerning the release of gold deposited by the Bank of Poland with the Bank of France. Signed at Algiers.

6 April 1944: Anglo–Polish supplementary protocol on the organization and employment of the Polish air force. Signed at London.

16 May 1944: Signatory to the inter-allied treaty providing for the foundation of the United Nations information organization. Signed at London.

14 June 1944: Exchange of notes with the Provisional Government of the French Republic concerning the recognition of the Provisional Government by Poland. Done at London.

29 June 1944: Military supplies agreement with the Government of Great Britain providing that military supplies to the Polish army, previously paid for from war credits, would in future be supplied on a lend-lease basis. Signed in London (effective retroactively from 1 June 1940).

22 July 1944: Signatory to the final act of the United Nations conference on money and finance. Signed at Bretton Woods.

5 August 1944: Signatory to the agreement on the continuance of co-ordinated control of merchant shipping. Signed at London: Hudson, IX, 129.

31 August 1944: Signatory to the protocol prolonging the international agreement regarding the regulation of production and marketing of sugar of 6 May 1937. Opened for signature at London: 145 BFSP 504.

7 December 1944: Signatory to the convention on international civil aviation. Opened for signature at Chicago (instrument of ratification deposited at Washington: 6 April 1945): 15 UNTS 295.

7 December 1944: Signatory to the interim agreement on international civil aviation. Opened for signature at Chicago (instrument of ratification deposited at Washington: 6 April 1945): 171 UNTS 345.

7 December 1944: Signatory to the international air services transit agreement.

[6] The CFLN had been established in Algiers on 3 June 1943.

Opened for signature at Chicago (instrument of ratification deposited at Washington: 6 April 1945): 84 UNTS 389.

5 January 1945: Signature of the international sanitary convention 1944 modifying the international sanitary convention of 21 June 1926. Opened for signature at Washington on 15 December 1944:[7] 17 UNTS 305.

5 January 1945: Signature of the international sanitary convention for aerial navigation 1944 (with annexes), modifying the international sanitary convention for aerial navigation of 12 April 1933. Opened for signature at Washington on 15 December 1944: 16 UNTS 247.

Czechoslovakia (1939–45)

2 October 1939: Military agreement between the French Government and the Czechoslovak Minister at Paris on behalf of the Provisional Government of the Czechoslovak Republic[8] regarding the reconstruction of the Czechoslovak army in France. Signed at Paris: [1942] *CYBIL* 232.

9 October 1940: Czechoslovak–Polish declaration pledging mutual support and friendship. Issued at London.

25 October 1940: Agreement with the United Kingdom providing for the formation of Czechoslovak armed forces in the United Kingdom. Signed at London: FO 93/119 No 30 (not otherwise published).

11 November 1940: Czechoslovak–Polish declaration pledging friendship and closer political and economic co-operation both during the war and in the peace settlement thereafter. Issued at London: [1939–46] II DIA 314.

10(12) December 1940: Financial agreement with the United Kingdom settling the question of the Czechoslovak gold deposited with the Bank of England before the Munich Agreement and laying down the conditions under which the British Government granted a credit to the Provisional Czechoslovak Government. Signed at London.

12 June 1941: Resolution of the inter-allied meeting, St James's Palace, London:[9] DAFR III, 444.

18 July 1941: Soviet–Czechoslovak agreement concerning the immediate re-establishment of diplomatic representatives, mutual aid, and support in the war against Germany, the establishment and organization of Polish military units in the Soviet Union. Signed at London: 144 BFSP 754.

24 September 1941: Czechoslovak–Polish declaration on the intention of the two countries to co-operate during the war and in the peace settlement thereafter. Issued at London: Parl.Pap. Misc. No 3 (1941), Cmd. 6315.

24 September 1941: Resolutions of the inter-allied meeting, St James's Palace,

[7] It is of interest to note that also on 5 Jan. 1945 the Soviet Government concluded an agreement with the Provisional National Government of Poland (at Lublin) concerning the establishment of diplomatic relations. See CST I, 169.

[8] The Provisional Government of the Czechoslovak Republic in whose name the agreement was signed was not, in fact, recognized as such at the time.

[9] In contrast to the formulation 'the Governments of Belgium, Greece', the resolution speaks of the 'Provisional Government of Czechoslovakia'.

regarding the Atlantic Charter and the supply of essential requirements to Europe after the war. Adopted at London: WPA I, 3.

27 September 1941: Military agreement with the USSR providing for the formation of Czecho-Slovak forces in Soviet Russia. Signed at Moscow.

1 January 1942: Signatory to the declaration by United Nations. Signed at Washington: 204 LNTS 381.

13 January 1942: Signatory to the inter-allied declaration on war crimes. Signed at London: *NY Times*, 14 January 1942, 6.

14 January 1942: Joint declaration of the general steering committee, central and eastern European planning board.[10] Issued at New York: WPA I, 8.

22 January 1942: Agreement with the USSR concerning a loan for maintenance of a Czech brigade in Soviet territory. Signed at Kiibyshev.

23 January 1942: Preliminary agreement with Poland concerning a post-war confederation. Signed at London: (1942) 5 *Free Europe* 43.

11 July 1942: Preliminary lend-lease agreement with the USA. Signed at Washington:[11] 90 UNTS 257.

22 July 1942: Signatory to the protocol to enforce and to prolong after 31 August 1942 the international agreement regarding the regulation of production and marketing of sugar signed in London on 6 May 1937. Signed at London: 144 BFSP 1074.

5 August 1942: Exchange of notes between His Majesty's Government in the United Kingdom and the Government of the Czecho-Slovak Republic concerning the policy of His Majesty's Government in the United Kingdom in regard to Czecho-Slovakia. Done at London: 204 LNTS 377.

28 September 1942: Exchange of notes with the USSR concerning reorganization of diplomatic missions into embassies. Done at London.

17 December 1942: Joint declaration condemning the German policy of extermination of the Jewish population of Europe. Done at Washington and London: WPA I, 14.

5 January 1943: Signatory to the inter-allied declaration against acts of disposition committed in territories under enemy occupation or control: (1943) 8 *DSB* 21.

21 January 1943: Military agreement with the United Kingdom on the organization of the Czechoslovak forces in the war, providing a lend-lease basis for articles and services supplied by the British Government. Signed at London.

28 May 1943: Agreement with the USSR concerning a grant of funds, materials, and services for maintenance of the Czech Brigade on Soviet territory for the duration of the war.

3 June 1943: Signatory to the final act of the United Nations conference on food and agriculture. Done at Hot Springs: (1943) 37 *AJIL* Supp., 159.

21 October 1943: Military service agreement with the USA relating to the service of nationals of one country in the armed forces of the other country. Effected by exchanges of notes, Washington (entry into force: 29 September 1943): 29 UNTS 369.

[10] Czechoslovakia, Greece, Poland, and Yugoslavia had set up the Central and Eastern European Planning Board on 7 Jan. 1942.

[11] On the settlement of the obligations arising under the lend-lease agreement of 11 July 1942, see (1948) 19 *DSB* 413.

9 November 1943: Signatory to the agreement for United Nations Relief and Rehabilitation Administration (UNRRA). Signed at Washington: 145 BFSP 159.

12 December 1943: Soviet–Czechoslovak treaty of friendship, mutual assistance, and post-war collaboration. Signed at Moscow (instruments of ratification exchanged at Moscow: 22 December 1943):[12] Soviet For. Pol. I, 250.

8 May 1944: Agreement with the USSR on relations between the Soviet Commander-in-Chief and the Czechoslovak administration after the entry of Soviet troops into the territory of Czechoslovakia. Signed at London: WPA II, 767.

14 July 1944: Monetary agreement with the USSR concerning the printing of a limited sum of new Czechoslovak currency in notes of various denominations by the Soviet Union.

31 August 1944: Signatory to the protocol prolonging the international agreement regarding the regulation of production and marketing of sugar of 6 May 1937. Opened for signature at London: 145 BFSP 504.

8 September 1944: Economic agreement with Norway. Signed at London.

29 November 1944: Agreement with France concerning the repatriation of Czechoslovak war prisoners, deportees, Jewish and political refugees, and other Czechoslovak citizens living in France and French nationals in Czechoslovakia. Signed at London.

15 January 1945: Signature of the international sanitary convention 1944 modifying the international sanitary convention of 21 June 1926. Opened for signature at Washington on 15 December 1944: 17 UNTS 305.

26 February 1945: Agreement with UNRRA. Signed at London.

1 March 1945: Agreement with Canada whereby Canada provides $15 million in credits to the Czechoslovak Government to be used for purchase in Canada of supplies for rehabilitation and reconstruction after liberation. Signed at Ottawa: 45 UNTS 283.

The Netherlands (1940–5)

14 June 1940: Financial agreement with the United Kingdom. Signed at London: 2 UNTS 251.

14 June 1940: Financial agreement with France. Signed at London: 2 UNTS 263.

15 July 1940: Agreement with Chile relating to trade. Effected by exchange of notes.

20 July 1940: Exchange of notes with Belgium concerning rights to stranded cargo. Done at London.

25 July 1940: Financial agreement with the United Kingdom concerning Curaçao and Surinam. Signed at London: 2 UNTS 275.

1 November 1940: Exchange of notes with the United Kingdom concerning rights to stranded cargo. Done at London.

12 June 1941: Resolution of the inter-allied meeting, St James's Palace, London: DAFR III, 444.

31 July 1941: Trade agreement with Chile. Effected by exchange of notes.

[12] The treaty was to be in force at first for 20 years.

9 August 1941: Lend-lease agreement[13] with the USA. Signed at Washington: [1941] II FRUS 808.

24 September 1941: Resolutions of the inter-allied meeting, St James's Palace, regarding the Atlantic Charter and the supply of essential requirements to Europe after the war. Adopted at London: WPA I, 3.

24 November 1941: Agreement with the USA under which the United States was to send troops to protect the bauxite mines in Surinam (Dutch Guiana).

24 November 1941: Agreement with Brazil for co-operation in the defence of Surinam.

November 1941: Agreement with Venezuela for co-operation in the defence of Surinam.

1 January 1942: Signatory to the declaration by United Nations. Done at Washington: 204 LNTS 381.

13 January 1942: Signatory to the inter-allied declaration on war crimes (pledging to exact a swift postwar retribution from Germany and her satellites for their oppression of occupied countries). Signed at London: *NY Times*, 14 January 1942, 6.

23 April 1942: Agreement with the United Kingdom concerning the exchange of parcels between Curaçao and Trinidad. Effected by exchange of notes (entry into force with retroactive effect form 1 January 1942): 204 LNTS 335.

5 May 1942: Agreement with the United Kingdom concerning the organization and employment of the Dutch armed forces in the United Kingdom, with exchange of notes. Signed at London (amended by protocol of 22 August 1944 as from 1 June 1944): 147 BFSP 931.

23 April 1942: Agreement with the United Kingdom concerning the exchange of parcels between Curaçao and British Guyana. Effected by exchange of notes (entry into force with retroactive effect from 1 March 1942): 205 LNTS 13.

8 July 1942: Lend-lease agreement with the USA. Signed at Washington: 103 UNTS 277.

10 July 1942: Agreement with the USSR concerning the establishment of diplomatic relations between the two countries which had been interrupted since 1917. Signed at London: 241 UNTS 475.

17 July 1942: Agreement with the British Board of Trade and the Cotton Board for the disposal of stocks of Dutch owned cotton frozen in English ports. Signed at London: *Netherlands News*, 4 (11/25 July 1942), 44.

22 July 1942: Signatory to the protocol to enforce and to prolong after 31 August 1942 the international agreement regarding the regulation of production and marketing of sugar signed in London on 6 May 1937. Signed at London: 144 BFSP 1074.

29 July 1942: Agreement with Chile relating to trade. Effected by exchange of notes.

9 September 1942: Agreement with Bolivia, Belgium, and the United Kingdom for the international control of the production and export of tin, with protocol of signature. Signed at London (entry into force: as from 1 January 1942): 205 LNTS 137.

[13] i.e. agreement relating to the principles applying to mutual aid in the prosecution of the war against aggression.

30 September 1942: Military service agreement with the USA relating to the service of nationals of one country in the armed forces of the other country. Effected by exchanges of notes, Washington (entry into force on 8 July 1942): 13 UNTS 151.

4 November 1942: Agreement with the USSR concerning reorganization of diplomatic missions into embassies. Negotiated in London on 22 October and 4 November 1942.

17 December 1942: Joint declaration condemning the German policy of extermination of the Jewish population of Europe. Done at Washington and London: WPA I, 14.

5 January 1943: Signatory to the inter-allied declaration against acts of disposition committed in territories under enemy occupation or control. Approved at London: (1943) 8 *DSB* 21.

3 June 1943: Signatory to the final act of the United Nations conference on food and agriculture. Done at Hot Springs: (1943) 37 *AJIL* Supp., 159.

14 June 1943: Supplementary agreement to the agreement of 8 July 1942 with the USA relating to the principles applying to the provision of aid to the armed forces of the United States. Exchange of notes done at Washington (considered to be effective as from 8 July 1942): 28 UNTS 397.

13 July 1943: Agreement with Chile relating to trade. Effected by exchange of notes on 10 and 13 July 1943.

August 1943: Agreement with the Vatican on the resumption of formal diplomatic relations.

21 October 1943: Monetary convention with Belgium and Luxembourg. Signed at London (entry into force: provisionally on 21 October 1943, definitely on 10 September 1945): 2 UNTS 281.

9 November 1943: Signatory to the agreement for United Nations Relief and Rehabilitation Administration (UNRRA). Signed at Washington: 145 BFSP 159.

22 December 1943: Agreement with the United Kingdom and India relating to rubber. Signed at London.

16 May 1944: Civil affairs agreement with the USA.[14] Signed at London: 132 UNTS 355.

16 May 1944: Civil affairs agreement with the United Kingdom. Signed at London.

11 July 1944: Agreement with Chile relating to trade. Effected by exchange of notes on 10 and 11 July 1944.

5 August 1944: Signatory to the agreement on the continuance of co-ordinated control of merchant shipping. Signed at London: Hudson, IX, 129.

22 August 1944: Protocol with the United Kingdom regarding mutual aid and currency. Signed at London (entry into force: 1 June 1944): 147 BFSP 940.

29 August 1944: Agreement with Belgium concerning the repatriation of their nationals displaced as a result of hostilities. Signed at London.

31 August 1944: Signatory to the protocol prolonging the international agreement regarding the regulation of production and marketing of sugar of 6 May 1937. Done at London: 145 BFSP 504.

5 September 1944: Customs union agreement with Belgium and Luxembourg.

[14] i.e. memorandum of agreement respecting the arrangements for civil administration and jurisdiction in territory liberated by an Allied expeditionary force.

Signed at London (entry into force: provisionally immediately on the reinstallation of the contracting governments in their liberated countries, definitely on 1 January 1948): Hudson, IX, 135, 137.

20 September 1944: Agreement with the Provisional Government of the French Republic concerning the repatriation of their nationals displaced as a result of hostilities.

2 October 1944: Agreement effected by exchange of notes with the United Kingdom concerning property within the United Kingdom belonging to persons resident in the Kingdom of the Netherlands. Done at London:[15] 231 UNTS 317.

2 October 1944: Financial agreement with Sweden.

19 October 1944: Provisional monetary agreement with Belgium. Signed at Brussels.

7 December 1944: Signatory to the convention on international civil aviation. Opened for signature at Chicago: 15 UNTS 295.

7 December 1944: Signatory to the interim agreement on international civil aviation. Opened for signature at Chicago (instrument of ratification deposited at Washington: 11 January 1945; entry into force: 6 June 1945): 171 UNTS 345.

7 December 1944: Signatory to the international air services transit agreement. Opened for signature at Chicago (instrument of ratification deposited at Washington: 12 January 1945; entry into force: 30 January 1945):[16] 84 UNTS 389.

7 December 1944: Signatory to the international air transport agreement. Opened for signature at Chicago (instrument of ratification deposited at Washington: 8 February 1945; entry into force: 8 February 1945): 171 UNTS 387.

2 January 1945: Agreement with Belgium concerning the repatriation of their nationals displaced as a result of hostilities. Signed at London: 19 UNTS 259.

20 March 1945: Agreement for economic consultation with the Provisional Government of the French Republic and the Governments of Belgium and Luxembourg. Signed at Paris (entry into force: 11 October 1945): 2 UNTS 299.

Belgium (1940–4)

7 June 1940: Tripartite agreement between Belgium on the one side and France and the United Kingdom on the other regulating the monetary and financial relations between the three States and fixing the exchange rates between their currencies. Signed at Paris.

6 August 1940: Loan agreement with the Grand Duchy of Luxembourg. Signed at Lisbon.

16 October 1940: Agreement with Chile providing for the prolongation of the provisional commercial agreement between the Belgo–Luxembourg economic

[15] An almost identical agreement was concluded on 6 Oct. 1944 by the UK Government with the Belgian Government which at that time had already returned to Belgium. For the text of that agreement, see 145 BFSP 446.

[16] It is of interest to note that the agreement came into force first between two States whose governments at the time were still in exile. In accordance with Art. VI, the agreement came into force as between the Netherlands and Norway on 30 Jan. 1945, the date on which the Government of the USA received the second notification of acceptance thereof from the Government of Norway, the first such notification having been received from the Governments of the Netherlands on 12 Jan. 1945.

union and Chile of 28 August 1936. Effected by exchange of notes at Santiago de Chile (entry into force: 1 July 1940).

24 December 1940: Second agreement with Chile providing for the prolongation of the provisional commercial agreement between the Belgo–Luxembourg economic union and Chile of 28 August 1936. Effected by exchange of notes at Santiago de Chile (entry into force: 1 January 1941).

21 January 1941: (Two) purchase and finance agreements with the United Kingdom relating to the Belgian Congo and Ruanda-Urundi. Signed at London: UKTS No 1 (1941), Cmd. 6248.

4 April 1941: Trade and payments agreement with the USSR. Signed at Moscow.

12 June 1941: Resolution of the inter-allied meeting, St James's Palace, London: DAFR III, 444.

17 June 1941: (Second) agreement with the Luxembourg Government whereby Belgium advanced to the Luxembourg Government sufficient funds for its operation. Signed at London: *Législation en exil*, 36.

7 August 1941: Agreement with the USSR concerning the re-establishment of diplomatic relations. Signed at London.

24 September 1941: Resolutions of the inter-allied meeting, St James's Palace, regarding the Atlantic Charter and the supply of essential requirements to Europe after the war. Adopted at London: WPA I, 3.

17 December 1941: Accession of Belgium with respect to the Belgian Congo and the mandated territory of Ruanda-Urundi to the international opium convention, signed at Geneva on 19 February 1925, and to the convention on limitation of production and regulation of distribution of narcotic drugs, signed at Geneva on 13 July 1931. Accession registered by the secretariat of the League of Nations: (1941) 5 *DSB* 570.

1 January 1942: Signatory to the declaration by United Nations. Signed at Washington: 204 LNTS 381.

13 January 1942: Signatory to the inter-allied declaration on war crimes. Signed at London: *NY Times*, 14 January 1942, 6.

30 May 1942: Additional agreement with the Luxembourg Government whereby Belgium advanced to the Luxembourg Government sufficient funds for its operation. Signed at London: *Législation en exil*, 108.

4 June 1942: Agreement with the United Kingdom renewing the arrangement of 21 January 1941 for the regulation of purchases of commodities from the Belgian Congo and Ruanda-Urundi, with note. Signed at London: 204 LNTS 363.

4 June 1942: Military agreement with the Government of the United Kingdom concerning the organization and employment of Belgian armed forces in the United Kingdom. Signed at London: Kerchove d'Exaerde, 'Quelques questions en droit international public relatives à la présence et à l'activité du gouvernement belge en exil à Londres (Octobre 1940–Septembre 1944)' (1990) 23 *RBDI* 93–151, 146.

16 June 1942: Lend-lease agreement with the USA. Signed at Washington: 105 UNTS 159.

22 July 1942: Signatory to the protocol to enforce and to prolong after 31 August 1942 the international agreement regarding the regulation of production and

marketing of sugar signed in London on 6 May 1937. Signed at London: 144 BFSP 1074.

25 July 1942: Accession of Belgium with respect to the Belgian Congo and the mandated territory of Ruanda-Urundi to the international opium convention signed at The Hague on 23 January 1912. Letter to the Dutch Government in London: *Législation en exil*, 111.

9 September 1942: Agreement between the Governments of Bolivia, Belgium, the United Kingdom, and the Netherlands for the international control of the production and export of tin, with protocol of signature. Signed at London (entry into force: 1 January 1942): 205 LNTS 137.

15 October 1942: Agreement with the USA concerning US military installations in the Congo. Signed at London (entry into force: 9 November 1942).

16 October 1942: Military service agreement with the USA relating to the service of nationals of one country in the armed forces of the other country. Effected by exchanges of notes, Washington (entry into force: 4 August 1942): 13 UNTS 211.

December 1942: Agreement with the Government of Canada for the supply of wheat as soon as part of the country was liberated.

17 December 1942: Joint declaration condemning the German policy of extermination of the Jewish population of Europe. Done at Washington and London: WPA I, 14.

4 January 1943: Exchange of notes with the Government of the United Kingdom concerning the disposal of property of Belgian and British merchant seamen who died while serving in British and Belgian ships. Done at London: 145 BFSP 120.

5 January 1943: Signatory to the inter-allied declaration against acts of disposition committed in territories under enemy occupation or control: (1943) 8 *DSB* 21.

21 January 1943: Agreement with the USSR concerning the reorganization of diplomatic missions into embassies. Effected by exchange of notes at Kiibyshev.

30 January 1943: Supplementary agreement to the agreement of 16 June 1942 with the USA relating to the principles applying to the provision of aid to the armed forces of the United States by the Government of Belgium. Effected by exchange of notes at Washington (entry into force with retroactive effect as from 16 June 1942): 13 UNTS 371.

3 June 1943: Signatory to the final act of the United Nations conference on food and agriculture. Done at Hot Springs: (1943) 37 *AJIL* Supp., 159.

4 August 1943: Agreement with the USA relating to jurisdiction over criminal offences committed by the armed forces of the United States in the Belgian Congo. Effected by exchange of notes at Washington: 109 UNTS 149.

19 August 1943: Additional agreement with Luxembourg whereby Belgium advanced to the Luxembourg Government sufficient funds for its operation. Signed at London: *Législation en exil*, 154.

20 October 1943: Treaty between the Republic of China and the Belgo–Luxembourg economic union concerning the abolition of the extraterritoriality rights in China and the settlement of questions relating thereto. Signed at Chungking (entry into force: 1 June 1945): 14 UNTS 375.

21 October 1943: Monetary convention between the Netherlands on the one hand

and Belgium and Luxembourg on the other hand. Signed at London (entry into force: provisionally on 21 October 1943, definitely on 10 September 1945): 2 UNTS 281.

22 October 1943: Signatory to the international convention on fisheries policy and measures for the protection of fish (the convention never entered into force).

9 November 1943: Signatory to the agreement for United Nations Relief and Rehabilitation Administration (UNRRA). Signed at Washington: 145 BFSP 159.

20 January 1944: Convention concerning forced labour, adopted by the International Labour Conference during its fourteenth session at Geneva on 28 June 1939. Ratification (20 May 1943) registered: *Arrêtés de Londres*, 145.

30 March 1944: Supplementary protocol to the agreement with the United Kingdom of 4 June 1942 concerning Belgian aviation personnel. Signed at London.

16 May 1944: Civil affairs agreement with the United Kingdom. Done at London: 90 UNTS 283.

16 May 1944: Civil affairs agreement with the USA. Signed at London: [1944] V FRUS 296.

27 May 1944: Protocol with the USA concerning the acquisition of supplies and services. Signed at London.

22 July 1944: Signatory to the final act of the United Nations conference on money and finance. Signed at Bretton Woods.

5 August 1944: Signatory to the agreement on the continuance of co-ordinated control of merchant shipping. Signed at London: Hudson, IX, 129.

22 August 1944: Protocol with the British Government regarding mutual aid. Signed at London (entry into force: 1 June 1944): 90 UNTS 295.

31 August 1944: Signatory to the protocol prolonging the international agreement regarding the regulation of production and marketing of sugar of 6 May 1937. Opened for signature at London: 145 BFSP 504.

31 August 1944: First supplementary and additional protocol to the agreement of 23 May 1935 with the Grand Duchy of Luxembourg concerning financial and monetary questions. Signed at London (entry into force: 15 March 1945).

5 September 1944: Customs union agreement with Belgium and Luxembourg. Signed at London (entry into force: provisionally immediately on the reinstallation of the contracting governments in their liberated countries, definitely on 1 January 1948): Hudson, IX, 135, 137.

13 September 1944: Agreement with the supreme headquarters of the allied expeditionary forces (SHAEF) concerning censorship. Signed at London.

5 October 1944: Monetary agreement with the Government of the United Kingdom. Signed at London: 5 UNTS 227.

6 October 1944: Agreement effected by exchange of notes with the United Kingdom concerning property within the United Kingdom belonging to persons resident in Belgium. Done at London.

Luxembourg (1940–5)

6 August 1940: Agreement with the Belgian Government, acting on behalf of the Belgian Congo, whereby the Luxembourg Government received financial assistance. Signed at Lisbon.

12 June 1941: Resolution of the inter-allied meeting, St James's Palace, London: DAFR III, 444.

17 June 1941: Second agreement with the Luxembourg Government whereby Belgium advanced to the Luxembourg Government sufficient funds for its operation. Signed at London: *Législation en exil*, 36.

24 September 1941: Resolutions of the inter-allied meeting, St James's Palace, regarding the Atlantic Charter and the supply of essential requirements to Europe after the war. Adopted at London: WPA I, 3.

1 January 1942: Signatory to the declaration by United Nations. Signed at Washington: 204 LNTS 381.

13 January 1942: Signatory to the inter-allied declaration on war crimes. Signed at London: *NY Times*, 14 January 1942, 6.

17 December 1942: Joint declaration condemning the German policy of extermination of the Jewish population of Europe. Done at Washington and London: WPA I, 14.

5 January 1943: Signatory to the inter-allied declaration against acts of disposition committed in territories under enemy occupation or control: (1943) 8 *DSB* 21.

3 June 1943: Signatory to the final act of the United Nations conference on food and agriculture. Done at Hot Springs: (1943) 37 *AJIL* Supp., 159.

21 October 1943: Monetary convention between the Netherlands on the one hand and Belgium and Luxembourg on the other hand. Signed at London (entry into force: provisionally on 21 October 1943, definitely on 10 September 1945): 2 UNTS 281.

9 November 1943: Signatory to the agreement for United Nations Relief and Rehabilitation Administration (UNRRA). Signed at Washington: 145 BFSP 159.

27 July 1944: Civil affairs agreement with the USA. Signed at London: [1944] V FRUS 1187.

27 July 1944: Civil affairs agreement with the United Kingdom. Signed at London.

5 September 1944: Customs union agreement with Belgium and Luxembourg. Signed at London (entry into force: provisionally immediately on the reinstallation of the contracting governments in their liberated countries, definitely on 1 January 1948): Hudson, IX, 135, 137.

15 January 1945: Signature of the international sanitary convention 1944 modifying the international sanitary convention of 21 June 1926. Opened for signature at Washington on 15 December 1944: 17 UNTS 305.

15 January 1945: Signature of the international sanitary convention for aerial navigation 1944 modifying the international sanitary convention for aerial navigation of 12 April 1933. Opened for signature at Washington on 15 December 1944: 16 UNTS 247.

Norway (1940–5)

4 April 1941: Trade and payments agreement with the USSR. Signed at Moscow.

28 May 1941: Agreement with the United Kingdom affirming their determination to prosecute the war to a successful end and to re-establish the freedom and independence of Norway and providing for the organization and employment of Norwegian armed forces in the United Kingdom. Signed at London.

12 June 1941: Resolution of the inter-allied meeting, St James's Palace, London: DAFR III, 444.

5 August 1941: Agreement by exchange of letters with the USSR concerning the re-establishment of diplomatic relations and providing for the exchange of ministers. Done at London.

24 September 1941: Resolutions of the inter-allied meeting, St James's Palace, regarding the Atlantic Charter and the supply of essential requirements to Europe after the war. Adopted at London: WPA I, 3.

10 October 1941: Agreement with the United Kingdom whereby the Norwegian Government guaranteed to reserve its mercantile marine for the transport of essential war supplies. Signed at London.

December 1941: Agreement with the United Kingdom providing for Norway and the other continental allies to obtain a share in the British 1941 shipbuilding programme. Signed at London.

1 January 1942: Signatory to the declaration by United Nations. Signed at Washington: 204 LNTS 381.

13 January 1942: Signatory to the inter-allied declaration on war crimes. Signed at London: *NY Times*, 14 January 1942, 6.

11 July 1942: Preliminary lend-lease agreement with the USA. Signed at Washington:[17] 204 LNTS 415.

1942: Agreement by exchange of notes with the USA clarifying provisions relative to the operation of the Norwegian merchant fleet for the allies: (1942) 7 *DSB* 609.

1 August 1942: Exchange of notes with the USSR concerning the reorganization of diplomatic missions into embassies. Done at London.

28 August 1942: Exchange of notes constituting an agreement with the USA relating to the regulation of military relations between armed forces of the two countries in Iceland. Done at London: 139 UNTS 361.

17 December 1942: Joint declaration condemning the German policy of extermination of the Jewish population of Europe. Done at Washington and London: WPA I, 14.

5 January 1943: Signatory to the inter-allied declaration against acts of disposition committed in territories under enemy occupation or control: (1943) 8 *DSB* 21.

16 January 1943: Military service agreement with the USA relating to the service of nationals of one country in the armed forces of the other country. Effected by exchanges of notes, Washington (entry into force: 24 December 1942): 13 UNTS 335.

1943: Agreement with Sweden for the training of Norwegian nationals as an auxiliary police force in Sweden.

3 June 1943: Signatory to the final act of the United Nations conference on food and agriculture. Done at Hot Springs: (1943) 37 *AJIL* Supp., 159.

9 November 1943: Signatory to the agreement for United Nations Relief and Rehabilitation Administration (UNRRA). Signed at Washington: 145 BFSP 159.

[17] On 24 Feb. 1948 Norway and the USA signed an agreement at Washington for the settlement of Norway's lend-lease account: (1948) 18 *DSB* 306.

10 November 1943: Agreement with China providing for the relinquishment of Norwegian extraterritorial rights in China (entry into force: 13 June 1944).[18]

7 February 1944: Signatory to the protocol on the international regulation of whaling. Signed at London (instrument of ratification deposited at London: 31 March 1944; entry into force: 5 October 1945): 145 BFSP 500.

24 February 1944: Exchange of notes constituting an agreement with Sweden relating to the compensation of seamen and survivors for war accidents.

12(13) April 1944: Agreement with Sweden under which the Norwegian Government could order and stock in Sweden various merchandise necessary for the reconstruction of Norway after her liberation. Signed at London.

16 May 1944: Civil affairs agreement with the USA. Signed at London:[19] 67 UNTS 253.

5 August 1944: Signatory to the agreement on the continuance of co-ordinated control of merchant shipping. Signed at London: Hudson, IX, 129.

8 September 1944: Economic agreement with Czechoslovakia. Signed at London.

30 January 1945: Acceptance deposited of the interim agreement on international civil aviation. Opened for signature at Chicago on 7 December 1944 (entry into force: 6 June 1945): 171 UNTS 345.

30 January 1945: Signature of the convention on international civil aviation. Opened for signature at Chicago on 7 December 1944: 15 UNTS 295.

30 January 1945: Acceptance deposited of the international air services transit agreement. Opened for signature at Chicago on 7 December 1944: 84 UNTS 389.

Greece (1941–5)

20 May 1941: Agreement with the Government of the United Kingdom on the employment of Greek ships providing for requisition of all Greek ships by the Greek Government, such ships to be offered on time-charter to the British Government. Signed at London.

12 June 1941: Resolution of the inter-allied meeting, St James's Palace, London: DAFR III, 444.

5 August 1941: Agreement with the USSR concerning the establishment of diplomatic relations. Signed at London.

24 September 1941: Resolutions of the inter-allied meeting, St James's Palace, regarding the Atlantic Charter and the supply of essential requirements to Europe after the war. Adopted at London: WPA I, 3.

1 January 1942: Signatory to the declaration by United Nations. Signed at Washington: 204 LNTS 381.

13 January 1942: Signatory to the inter-allied declaration on war crimes. Signed at London: *NY Times*, 14 January 1942, 6.

14 January 1942: Joint declaration of the general steering committee, central and eastern European planning board.[20] Issued at New York: WPA I, 8.

[18] The agreement had been preceded by a unilateral declaration on 9 Oct. 1942 renouncing Norwegian claims to extraterritoriality in China (WPA I, 486).

[19] Identical agreements were concluded on the same day with the UK and the USSR.

[20] See n. 10 above.

15 January 1942: Agreement with Yugoslavia providing for political, economic, and military co-operation and outlining a constitution for a future Balkan union. Signed at London: (1942) *Yugoslav Documents* No 2, 22.

9 March 1942: Agreement with the United Kingdom whereby Greece received lend-lease aid and whereby arrangements were outlined for the organization and use of Greek land, sea, and air forces in collaboration with British forces. Signed at London.

10 July 1942: Lend-lease agreement with the USA. Signed at Washington: 103 UNTS 289.

17 December 1942: Joint declaration condemning the German policy of extermination of the Jewish population of Europe. Done at Washington and London: WPA I, 14.

5 January 1943: Signatory to the inter-allied declaration against acts of disposition committed in territories under enemy occupation or control: (1943) 8 *DSB* 21.

16 March 1943: Military service agreement with the USA relating to the service of nationals of one country in the armed forces of the other country. Effected by exchange of notes, Washington (entry into force: 2 March 1943): 105 UNTS 227.

14 April 1943: Exchange of notes with the USSR concerning the reorganization of diplomatic missions into embassies. Done at London.

3 June 1943: Signatory to the final act of the United Nations conference on food and agriculture. Done at Hot Springs: (1943) 37 *AJIL* Supp., 159.

9 November 1943: Signatory to the agreement for United Nations Relief and Rehabilitation Administration (UNRRA). Signed at Washington: 145 BFSP 159.

5 August 1944: Signatory to the agreement on the continuance of co-ordinated control of merchant shipping. Signed at London: Hudson, IX, 129.

Yugoslavia (1941–5)

12 June 1941: Resolution of the inter-allied meeting, St James's Palace, London: DAFR III, 444.

24 September 1941: Resolutions of the inter-allied meeting, St James's Palace, regarding the Atlantic Charter and the supply of essential requirements to Europe after the war. Adopted at London: WPA I, 3.

1 January 1942: Signatory to the declaration by United Nations. Signed at Washington: 204 LNTS 381.

13 January 1942: Signatory to the inter-allied declaration on war crimes. Signed at London: *NY Times*, 14 January 1942, 6.

14 January 1942: Joint declaration of the general steering committee, central and eastern European planning board.[21] Issued at New York: WPA I, 8.

15 January 1942: Agreement with Greece providing for political, economic, and military co-operation and outlining a constitution for a future Balkan union. Signed at London: (1942) *Yugoslav Documents* No 2, 22.

14 September 1942: Exchange of notes with the USSR concerning the reorganization of diplomatic missions into embassies. Done at London.

[21] See n. 10 above.

30 September 1942: Military service agreement with the USA relating to the service of nationals of one country in the armed forces of the other country. Effected by exchanges of notes, Washington (entry into force: 18 May 1942): 13 UNTS 199.

24 July 1942: Preliminary lend-lease agreement with the USA. Signed at Washington:[22] 34 UNTS 361.

17 December 1942: Joint declaration condemning the German policy of extermination of the Jewish population of Europe. Done at Washington and London: WPA I, 14.

5 January 1943: Signatory to the inter-allied declaration against acts of disposition committed in territories under enemy occupation or control: (1943) 8 *DSB* 21.

3 June 1943: Signatory to the final act of the United Nations conference on food and agriculture. Done at Hot Springs: (1943) 37 *AJIL* Supp., 159.

9 November 1943: Signatory to the agreement for United Nations Relief and Rehabilitation Administration (UNRRA). Signed at Washington: 145 BFSP 159.

16 June 1944: Agreement between the Royal Yugoslav Government and the Yugoslav National Committee of Liberation on the formation of National Unity Government of Yugoslavia. Signed at Vis: [1939–46] II DIA 334.

25 November 1944: Joint communiqué with the USSR concerning the establishment of a unified Yugoslav Government. Issued at Moscow.[23]

1 December 1944: Agreement between the Royal Yugoslav Government with the Yugoslav National Committee of Liberation on the appointment of a Regency Council and a United Government ('Tito-Sŭbašić Agreement'). Signed at Belgrade: [1939–46] II DIA 340.

Philippine Commonwealth (1942–5)

10 June 1942: Adherence to the declaration by United Nations of 1 January 1942. Done at Washington.[24] 204 LNTS 381.

22 July 1942: Signatory to the protocol to enforce and to prolong after 31 August 1942 the international agreement regarding the regulation of production and marketing of sugar signed in London on 6 May 1937. Signed at London: 144 BFSP 1074.

(19)20 January 1943: Adherence to the inter-allied declaration against acts of disposition committed in territories under enemy occupation or control of 5 January 1943: WPA II, 369.

[22] On 19 July 1948 the USA and Yugoslavia signed agreements settling lend-lease accounts: (1948) 19 *DSB* 137.

[23] It is of interest to note that on 28 Sept. 1944 a press communiqué had been issued in Moscow concerning an agreement between the USSR and the Yugoslav National Committee of Liberation relating to joint military operations in Yugoslavia (CST I, 165). Unlike in the case of Poland the USSR, which at least formally still recognized the Royal Yugoslav Government in London, refrained from concluding a civil affairs agreement with the Yugoslav National Committee of Liberation.

[24] On the adherence by the Commonwealth of the Philippines to the Declaration by United Nations, see [1942] I FRUS 906–8.

3 June 1943: Signatory to the final act of the United Nations conference on food and agriculture. Done at Hot Springs: (1943) 37 *AJIL* Supp., 159.
9 November 1943: Signatory to the agreement for United Nations Relief and Rehabilitation Administration (UNRRA). Signed at Washington: 145 BFSP 159.
31 August 1944: Signatory to the protocol prolonging the international agreement regarding the regulation of production and marketing of sugar of 6 May 1937. Opened for signature at London: 145 BFSP 504.
7 December 1944: Signatory to the convention on international civil aviation. Opened for signature at Chicago (instrument of ratification deposited at Washington: 1 March 1947): 15 UNTS 295.
7 December 1944: Signatory to the international air services transit agreement. Opened for signature at Chicago (instrument of ratification deposited at Washington: 22 March 1946): 84 UNTS 389
7 December 1944: Signatory to the interim agreement on international civil aviation. Opened for signature at Chicago (instrument of ratification deposited at Washington: 22 March 1946): 171 UNTS 345.

Algeria (1958–62)

20 December 1958: Joint communiqué with the Government of the PR China on Algerian independence, nuclear tests, etc. Done at Peking.
26 April 1959: Joint communiqué with the Government of Iraq on the provision by Iraq to the GPRA of weapons and funds. Done at Baghdad.
12 June 1959: Joint communiqué with the Yugoslav Government relating to an official visit to Yugoslavia by the President of the GPRA. Issued at Belgrade:[25] Bedjaoui, *Law and the Algerian Revolution* (1961), 118–19.
20 March 1960: Joint communiqué with the Government of Iraq concerning the provision by Iraq to the GPRA of financial aid amounting to £2 million for 1960 and military aid. Issued at Baghdad.
19 May 1960: Joint communiqué with the Government of the PR China on national liberation movements, Algerian independence, etc. Done at Peking.
May 1960: Protocol with the PR China concerning the provision by China to the GPRA of foreign currency as well as civil and military supplies. Signed at Peking.
31 May 1960: Protocol of agreement between the Government of His Majesty Mohammed V, King of Morocco, and the GPRA relating to the methods to safeguard the unity and authority of the FLN in Morocco within the framework of respect for the public order and sovereignty of Morocco. Signed at Rabat: ARA no 96.
20 June 1960: Instruments of ratification of the four Geneva conventions of 12 August 1949[26] deposited with the Swiss Federal Council, Berne: *NZZ*, 28 July 1960, 3.
5 October 1960: Joint communiqué with the Government of the PR China on peaceful coexistence, national liberation movements, etc. Done at Peking.

[25] As a reaction to this communiqué the Yugoslav ambassador in Paris was summoned to the Quai d'Orsay and, simultaneously, the French ambassador in Belgrade was recalled for consultation (Bedjaoui, *Law and the Algerian Revolution* (1961), 119).
[26] 5 UNTS 31, 85, 135 and 287, respectively.

19 December 1960: Agreement with Tunisia relating to the exemption from customs duties of all supplies and equipment delivered to the GPRA, the ALN, and the Algerian Red Cross. Signed at Tunis.

6 January 1961: Signatory to the African Charter of Casablanca. Signed at Casablanca.

25 March 1961: Agreement between the Government of the Czechoslovak Socialist Republic and the GPRA on the establishment of favourable conditions for the development of economic relations between the Algerian Republic and the Czechoslovak Socialist Republic.[27]

29 March 1961: Aid agreement between the Government of the Bulgarian Socialist Republic and the GPRA. Signed at Sofia.

6 July 1961: Agreement between Morocco and the GPRA, which recognized 'their territorial problem created by the delimitation imposed arbitrarily by France', stated that 'this problem will be resolved through negotiations between the Kingdom of Morocco and the Government of Independent Algeria', and created an Algerian–Moroccan commission to study and solve that problem. Signed at Rabat: *Le Monde*, 23 October 1963, 2.

18 March 1962: Evian accords comprising a cease-fire agreement, a general declaration, and certain special agreements on a referendum, the future of Algeria and French–Algerian relations. Signed at Seran-Les-Bains:[28] Allais, *Les accord d'Evian* (1962), 298–325.

23 March 1962: Agreement with the USSR concerning Soviet *de jure* recognition of the Provisional Government of the Algerian Republic and establishment of diplomatic relations. Effected by exchange of telegrams on 19 and 23 March 1962.

March 1962: Agreement with the Moroccan Government whereby Algerian employees working in the Moroccan administration will return to Algeria at a date to be fixed later.

Angola (1962–75)

26 October 1963: Pact of military collaboration between the Revolutionary Government of Angola in Exile and the South West African People's Organization (SWAPO). Signed at Leopoldville.

15 October 1966: Agreement of reconciliation between the Revolutionary Government of Angola in Exile and the MPLA. Signed at Cairo.

[27] On 11 Apr. 1961 Mr Vaclav David, the Czechoslovak Foreign Minister, declared: 'An agreement was recently signed between the Czechoslovak Socialist Republic and the Algerian Republic, which implies the *de facto* recognition of the Provisional Government of the Algerian Republic by the Socialist Republic of Czechoslovakia' (Bedjaoui, n. 25 above, 182).

[28] The texts of the Evian Accords published by the parties differed only with respect to the preambles of the General Declaration. The preamble published by the French Government speaks of 'The negotiations which have taken place at Evian from 7 March to 18 March 1962 between the Government of the Republic and the FLN' while the preamble published by the GPRA speaks of 'The negotiations which have taken place at Evian from 7 March to 18 March 1962 between the Government of the French Republic and the Provisional Government of the Algerian Republic' (Moureaux, *Les Accords d'Evian et l'avenir de la révolution algérienne* (1962), 155–6 (translation by the author)).

Cambodia (1970–5)

May 1970: Loan agreement with the PR China. Signed at Peking.

17 August 1970: Agreement with the PR China on providing gratuitous military aid by China to Cambodia. Signed at Peking.[29]

1 July 1971: Joint communiqué with Yugoslavia. Issued at Belgrade.

11 February 1972: Agreement with the PR China on economic aid and military supplies by China to Cambodia in 1972. Signed at Peking.

13 January 1973: Agreement with the PR China on gratuitous supply of military equipment and material by China to Cambodia in 1973. Signed at Peking.

13 January 1973: Agreement with the PR China on economic aid by China to Cambodia in 1973. Signed at Peking.

28 February 1973: Agreement with Dahomey (Benin) on the establishment of diplomatic relations at ambassadorial level. Signed at Porto Novo.

29 August 1973: Agreement with Malta on the establishment of diplomatic relations at ambassadorial level.

26 May 1974: Agreement with the PR China on gratis provision of military equipment and supplies by China to Cambodia in 1974. Signed at Peking.

27 May 1974: Joint communiqué with the PR China on the talks during the visit of Cambodian Deputy Prime Minster Khieu Samphan. Issued at Peking.

Western Sahara (1976–date)

March 1984: Economic co-operation agreement and a trade protocol for 1984–5 between Cuba and the Saharan Arab Democratic Republic.[30]

Cambodia (1979–91)

17 October 1980: Signature of the international covenant on civil and political rights. Adopted by the United Nations General Assembly on 16 December 1966.

17 October 1980: Signature of the international covenant on economic, social, and cultural rights. Adopted by the United Nations General Assembly on 16 December 1966.

17 October 1980: Signature of the convention on the elimination of all forms of discrimination against women. Adopted by the United Nations General Assembly on 18 December 1979.

[29] It is of interest to note that three days later, on 20 Aug. 1970, the Lon Nol Government (in Phnom Penh) and the Government of the USA concluded an 'Agreement Relating to the Provision of Defence Articles to Cambodia': 764 UNTS 233. Further agreements relating to economic and military assistance between the USA and the Khmer Republic were concluded on 31 May 1971 (845 UNTS 219) and on 19 June 1974 (961 UNTS 91).

[30] It is of interest to note that the Islamic Republic of Mauritania signed the Peace Treaty of 5 Aug. 1979 with the 'representatives of the Sahrawi people, the Polisario Front' and not with the Government of the Saharan Arab Democratic Republic (SADR), to which there is no reference in the treaty. Mauritania wanted to avoid to recognize the SADR as this would have entailed the rupture of relations with Morocco. For the text of the agreement signed at Algiers, see: UN Doc.A/34/427–S/13503, annex I.

22 June 1982: Agreement between the Government of Democratic Kampuchea, the Khmer People's National Liberation Front (KPNLF), and the Front Uni National pour un Cambodge Indépendant, Neutre, Pacifique, et Coopératifon (FUNCINPEC) on the formation of a Coalition Government of Democratic Kampuchea. Signed at Kuala Lumpur: BBC, *SWB*, 2nd series, FE/7057/A3/1–3, 21 June 1979.

1 July 1983: Signature of the United Nations Convention on the Law of the Sea. Opened for signature at Montego Bay, Jamaica, on 10 December 1982 (entry into force with qualifications: 16 November 1994).

1 August 1984: Joint communiqué with Egypt. Issued in Cairo.

25 March 1987: Agreement with the ASEAN States, Japan, and the PR China providing for the establishment of a co-ordinating committee to develop Kampuchea offshore oil resources. Signed at Bangkok.[31]

5 June 1990: Joint five-point communiqué on the peace process in Cambodia. Signed at Tokyo by Prince Sihanouk for the CGDK and by Hun Sen for the SOC.

Kuwait (1990–1)

November 1990: Agreement with France for the supply of military equipment.

29 December 1990: Agreement of co-operation in information matters with Egypt providing for the installation of Radio Kuwait in Cairo.

January 1991: Contract with the Government of the USA (Corps of Engineers) providing for the reconstruction of infrastructure installations after the departure of Iraqi forces from Kuwait.

Haiti (1991–4)

3 July 1993: Agreement between the President of the Republic of Haiti, Jean-Bertrand Aristide, and the Commander-in-Chief of the Armed Forces of Haiti, Lieutenant-General Raoul Cédras. Signed on Governors Island ('Governors Island Peace Agreement'): UN Doc.A/47/975–S/26063 (12 July 1993), 2–3.

[31] A protest against this agreement was lodged by the PRK on 3 Apr. 1987.

Bibliography

NOTE: The bibliography is divided into two sections. The first contains books and articles—legal, political, and historical—relating to the recognition of governments while the second contains sources of State practice referred to in the book. Such sources comprise, *inter alia*, documents on foreign relations, government information bulletins, foreign policy reports, parliamentary records, digests of international law, treaty series, and law gazettes. Within the State practice section sources are arranged by international organization or individual country. A reference to where a source of State practice may be found in section two is also included in section one if the source was compiled or edited by an individual rather than a government department.

By way of a general comment it may be stated that a lot of the literature on the recognition of governments (as on recognition in general) is repetitive. This is illustrated by the fact that a (by no means exhaustive) list of books and articles on the subject compiled by the author has more than 2,000 entries. A selection was therefore inevitable whenever other views in the literature were discussed in the book.

Books and Articles

ACEVEDO, DOMINGO E., 'The Haitian Crisis and the OAS Response: A Test of Effectiveness in Protecting Democracy' in L. F. Damrosch (ed.), *Enforcing Restraint. Collective Intervention in Internal Conflicts* (New York: Council on Foreign Relations Press, 1993), 119–55.

AKEHURST, MICHAEL, *A Modern Introduction to International Law* (6th edn., London: HarperCollins *Academic*, 1987).

AKINYEMI, A. BOLAJI, 'Organization of African Unity: The Practice of Recognition of Governments' (1975) 36 *Indian JPS* 63–79.

AKWENSIOGE, MOSES NGOLE, *Die Organisation für Afrikanische Einheit—Entstehungsgeschichte und Entwicklung seit 1963. Eine völkerrechtliche und außenpolitische Untersuchung unter besonderer Berücksichtigung der Staatenpraxis* (Munich: Dissertationsdruck Schon, 1974).

ALLAIS, MAURICE, *Les accords d'Evian. Le réferendum et la résistance algérienne: L'autorité, la majorité, le droit* (Paris: L'Esprit Nouveau, 1962).

ALLINA, HEINRICH, *Restoration of Austria* (n.p.: Free Austria Publications, June 1942).

AL ROUMI, HAMAD YOUSSEF, *The Crime. Iraq's Invasion of Kuwait. Events & Documents from Day 1 to Liberation* (Cairo: Kuwait Information Centre in Cairo, 1991).

ALVAREZ DEL VAYO, JULIO, *The Last Optimist* (New York: Viking Press, 1950).

AMBROS, HEINO, 'Nonrecognition: Its Development in International Law and Its Application by the United States with Particular Reference to the Baltic States', Ph.D. thesis (New York, 1965).

AMERICAN LAW INSTITUTE, *Restatement of the Law (Second). The Foreign Relations Law of the United States* (St Paul, Minn.: American Law Institute, 1965).

——*Restatement of the Law (Third). The Foreign Relations Law of the United States* (St Paul, Minn.: American Law Institute, 1987), i.

AMIN, SAYED HASSAN, 'Kuwait. Property Rights. Effect of Kuwaiti Government Declaring Itself Trustee of Property' (1991) 9/7 *OGLTR* D85–6.

ANDENAES, JOHS., RISTE, OLAV, and SKODVIN, MAGNE, *Norway and the Second World War* (Oslo: Johan Grundt Tanum Forlag, 1966).

ANDERSON, E., 'The British Policy Toward the Baltic States 1918–1920' (1959) 19 *J. Cent. Europ. Aff.* 276–89.

ANDERSON, LUIS, *El gobierno de facto* (San José: C. R. Imprenta Lehmann, 1925).

ANDO, NISUKE, 'The Recognition of Governments Reconsidered' (1985) 28 *JAIL* 29–46.

ANZILOTTI, DIONISO, *Lehrbuch des Völkerrechts* (3rd edn., translation by Cornelia Bruns and Karl Schmid, Berlin: Walter de Gruyter, 1929).

AVALISHVILI, ZOURAB, *The Independence of Georgia in International Politics 1918–1921* (London: Headley Brothers, 1940).

BAER, MARCEL DE, 'Belgian Justice in Great Britain', *Message*, No 5 (March 1942), 33–4.

BAKER, 'Woodrow Wilson's Use of the Non-Recognition Policy in Costa Rica' (1965) 22 *Americas* 3–15.

BALEKJIAN, WAHÉ HAGOP, *Die Effektivität und die Stellung nichtanerkannter Staaten im Völkerrecht* (The Hague: Martinus Nijhoff, 1970).

BARBIER, MAURICE, *Le conflit du Sahara occidental* (Paris: L'Harmattan, 1982).

BAREAU, PAUL, 'The Finances of Refugee Governments' (1942) 64/201 *The Banker* 17–24.

BARNES, WILLIAM SPRAGUE, 'United States Recognition Policy and Cambodia', (1970) 50 *Boston ULR* Special Issue 117–29.

BARTLETT, RUHL J.: For *The Record of American Diplomacy* see Sources of State Practice—USA.

BARTON, G. P., 'Foreign Armed Forces: Immunity from Supervisory Jurisdiction' (1949) 26 *BYBIL* 380–413.

——'Foreign Armed Forces: Immunity from Criminal Jurisdiction' (1950) 27 *BYBIL* 186–234.

BAUM, P., 'Full Recognition of Israel' (1948) 8 *LG Rev.* 441–6.

BBG, 'Le GPRA et la Ligue Arabe' (1960) 16 *Rev. égypt.* 68–9.

BECKA, JAN, 'Subhas Chandra Bose and the Burmese Freedom Movement' in S. K. Bose (ed.), *Netaji and India's Freedom* (Calcutta: Netaji Bhawan, 1975), 54–68.

BECKER, AVI, *The United Nations and Israel. From Recognition to Reprehension* (Lexington, Mass.: Lexington Books, 1988).

BEDJAOUI, MOHAMMED, *Law and the Algerian Revolution* (Brussels: International Association of Democratic Lawyers, 1961).

——(ed.), *International Law: Achievements and Prospects* (Paris: UNESCO, and Dordrecht: Martinus Nijhoff, 1991).

BEITZKE, GÜNTHER, 'Probleme der Enteignung im internationalen Privatrecht' in H. P. Ipsen (ed.), *Festschrift für Leo Raape zu seinem siebzigsten Geburtstag 14. Juni 1948* (Hamburg: Rechts- und staatswissenschaftlicher Verlag, 1948), 93–111.

BELKHERROUBI, ABDELMADJID, *La naissance et la reconnaissance de la République algérienne* (Brussels: Etablissements Emile Bruylant, 1972).

BELL, J. BOWYER, 'The Transcendental Irish Republic: The Dream of Diaspora' in Y. Shain (ed.), *Governments-in-Exile in Contemporary World Politics* (New York: Routledge, 1991), 202–18.

BENEŠ, EDUARD, *Memoirs of Dr Eduard Beneš. From Munich to New War and New Victory* (translated by Godfrey Lias, London: Allen & Unwin, 1954).

——*My War Memoirs* (translated by Paul Selver, London: Allen & Unwin, 1928).

BENEŠ, VÁCLAV, 'Review of "McNair: Municipal Effects of Belligerent Occupation" [(1941) 57 *LQR* 33–73]' [1942] *CYBIL* 218–21.

BENNOUNA, MOHAMED, 'L'admission d'un nouveau membre à l'Organisation de l'Unité Africaine' (1980) 26 *AFDI* 193–8.

BENTWICH, NORMAN, 'Legal Aspects of the Restoration of Ethiopian Sovereignty' (1945) 22 *BYBIL* 275–8.

BERBER, FRIEDRICH, *Lehrbuch des Völkerrechts* (2nd edn., Munich: C. H. Beck, 1975), i.

BERGIN, ANTHONY, 'The New Australian Policy on Recognition of States Only' (1988) 42 *Aust. Outlook* 150–4.

BERNHARDT, RUDOLF (ed.), *Encyclopedia of Public International Law* (Amsterdam: North Holland, 1992), 5 vols., and (Amsterdam: North Holland, 1981–1990), 12 inst.

——'Customary International Law' in R. Bernhardt (ed.), *Encyclopedia of Public International Law* (Amsterdam: North Holland, 1992), i, 898–905.

BICKERTON, I. J., 'President Truman's Recognition of Israel' (1968–9) 58 *AJHQ* 173–240.

BIERZANEK, REMIGIUSZ, 'La reconnaissance internationale du Comité Polonais de Libération Nationale et du Gouvernement d'Unité Nationale' (1964–5) 5 *APAI* 41–58.

BINAVINCE, EMILIO S., 'Canadian Perspectives in Matters of Recognition' in R. St J. Macdonald, Gerald C. Morris, and Douglas M. Johnston (eds.), *Canadian Perspectives on International Law and Organization* (Toronto: University of Toronto Press, 1974), 153–83.

BIN CHENG, *General Principles of Law as applied by International Courts and Tribunals* (London: Stevens & Sons, 1953).

BISSCHOP, W. R. (ed.), *International Law Conference London. 10th–12th July, 1943* (Richmond, Surrey: R. W. Simpson, 1943).

BLAY, S. K. N., 'Self-Determination in Cyprus: The New Dimension of an Old Conflict' (1987) 10 *AYBIL* 67–100.

BLECKMANN, ALBERT, *Das französische Kolonialreich und die Gründung neuer Staaten. Die Rechtsentwicklung in Syrien/Libanon, Indochina und Schwarzafrika* (Cologne: Carl Heymanns, 1969).

BLIX, HANS MARTIN, *Treaty-Making Power* (London: Stevens & Sons, 1960).

——'Contemporary Aspects of Recognition' (1970–II) 130 *RdC* 587–704.

Blociszewski, Joseph, 'La restauration de la Pologne et la diplomatie européenne' (1921) 28 *RGDIP* 1–83, (1924) 31 *RGDIP* 89–144, (1926) 33 *RGDIP* 387–483.

Blumenwitz, Dieter, 'Genießt der Vorsitzende des Staatsrates der DDR in der Bundesrepublik Immunität nach den allgemeinen Regeln des Völkerrechts' [1985] *JZ* 614–18.

Bonfils, Henry, *Lehrbuch des Völkerrechts für Studium und Praxis* (3rd edn. by Paul Fauchille, translated and annotated by August Grah, Berlin: Carl Heymanns, 1904).

Boppe, Auguste, *A la suite du gouvernement Serbe, de Nich à Corfou, 20 Octobre 1915–19 Janvier 1916* (Paris: Editions Bossard, 1917).

Bot, Bernard Rudolf, *Nonrecognition and Treaty Relations* (Leiden: A. W. Sijthoff, 1968).

Bothe, Michael, 'Occupation, Belligerent' in R. Bernhardt (ed.), *Encyclopedia of Public International Law* (Amsterdam: North Holland, 1982), inst. 4, 64–7.

Bourquin, Maurice, *Histoire de la Sainte Alliance* (Geneva: Librairie de l'Université, 1954).

Bowers, Claude G., *My Mission to Spain. Watching the Rehearsal for World War II* (London: Victor Gollancz, 1954).

Bowett, Derek W., 'Jurisdiction: Changing Patterns of Authority over Activities and Resources' (1982) 53 *BYBIL* 1–26.

Brandweiler, Heinrich, 'Zur Lehre von den Exilregierungen' (1950–1) 3 *ÖZöR* 497–519.

Brierly, J. L., *The Law of Nations. An Introduction to the International Law of Peace* (6th edn. by Sir Humphrey Waldock, Oxford: Clarendon Press, 1963).

Briggs, Herbert W., 'De Facto and De Jure Recognition: The Arantzazu Mendi' (1939) 33 *AJIL* 689–99.

Brissaud, André, *Pétain à Sigmaringen (1944–1945)* (Paris: Librairie Académique Perrin, 1960).

Brown, A. L., 'Loans to Unrecognized Insurgents' (1927) 7 *Boston ULR* 312–15.

Brown, Philip Marshall, 'The Recognition of Israel' (1948) 42 *AJIL* 620–7.

Brownlie, Ian, *International Law and the Use of Force by States* (Oxford: Clarendon Press, 1963).

——'Recognition in Theory and Practice' (1982) 53 *BYBIL* 197–211.

——*Principles of Public International Law* (4th edn., Oxford: Clarendon Press, 1990).

Brügel, Johann Wolfgang, 'Die Anerkennung der tschechoslowakischen Auslandsregierung 1940–1942' (1983) 24 *Bohemia* 335–47.

Bullock, Alan, *Ernest Bevin. Foreign Secretary, 1945–1951* (London: Heinemann, 1983).

Bünger, K., 'Dokumente zur Entstehung der Vereinigten Staaten von Indonesien—Vorbemerkung' (1950–1) 13 *ZaöRV* 431–52.

Bushe-Fox, P. L., 'The Court of Chancery and Recognition 1804–31' (1931) 12 *BYBIL* 63–75.

——'Unrecognized States: Cases in the Admiralty and Common Law Courts, 1805–26' (1932) 13 *BYBIL* 39–48.

Buza, Ladislaus, 'Die Entstehung der tschechoslowakischen Republik im Lichte des Völkerrechts' (1926) 13 *ZVR* 112–19.

CAMPBELL, BARRY R., and NEWCOMB, DANFORTH (eds.), *The Impact of the Freeze of Kuwaiti and Iraqi Assets on Financial Institutions and Financial Transactions* (London: Graham & Trotman, 1990).

CANG, JOEL (ed.), *The Who's Who of the Allied Governments* (London: Allied Publications, 1942–5).

CANNING, GEORGE, *The Speeches of the Right Honourable George Canning With a Memoir of His Life* (ed. by R. Therry, London: James Ridgway, 1828), 6 vols.

CASSESE, ANTONIO, *International Law in a Divided World* (Oxford: Clarendon Press, 1986).

CASSIN, RENÉ, 'Vichy or Free France' (1941) 20 *For. Affairs* 102–12.

——'La création du Comité national français de Londres, le 24 septembre 1941', *Cah. fr.* (September 1956), 2–5.

CASTRÉN, ERIK, *The Present Law of War and Neutrality* (Helsinki: Suomalaisen Kirjallisuuden Seuran Kirjapainon, 1954).

ČERVENKA, ZDENÊK, *The Unfinished Quest for Unity. Africa and the OAU* (London: Julian Friedman, 1977).

CHAKRABORTI, TRIDIB, *India and Kampuchea. A Phase in their Relations, 1978–81* (Calcutta: Minerva Associates, 1985).

CHANG, HYO SANG, 'International Law in a Divided World: Recent Korean Experiences' in Karl-Heinz Böckstiegel, Hans-Ernst Folz, Jörg M. Mössner, and Karl Zemanek (eds.), *Völkerrecht, Recht der Internationalen Organisationen, Weltwirtschaftsrecht. Festschrift für Ignaz Seidl-Hohenveldern* (Cologne: Carl Heymanns, 1988), 509–25.

CHARLESWORTH, HILARY, 'The New Australian Recognition Policy in Comparative Perspective' (1991) 18 *Melbourne ULR* 1–25.

CHARPENTIER, JEAN, *La reconnaissance internationale et l'évolution du droit des gens* (Paris: A. Pedone, 1956).

——'La reconnaissance du GPRA' (1959) 5 *AFDI* 799–816.

——'La France et le GPRA' (1961) 7 *AFDI* 855–70.

CHATEAUBRIAND, F. A. DE, *De Buonaparte, des Bourbons, et de la nécessité de se rallier à nos princes légitimes, pour le bonheur de la France et celui de l'Europe* (Paris: n.p., 1814).

——*Œuvres complètes* (Paris: n.p., 1862), vii.

CHEN, TI-CHIANG, *The International Law of Recognition. With Special Reference to Practice in Great Britain and the United States* (ed. by L. C. Green, London: Stevens & Sons, 1951).

CHIKH, SLIMANE, *L'Algérie en armes ou le temps des certitudes* (Paris: Economica, 1981).

CHIVVIS, CHRISTOPHER, 'US Immigration Law as Applied to Haiti' in E. H. Preeg, *The Haitian Dilemma* (Washington, DC: Centre for Strategic and International Studies, 1996), 116–26.

CHLALA, JOSEPH, 'Législation égyptienne en matière de Droit international de 1936 à 1946' (1946) 2 *Rev. égypt.* 73–97.

CHOONG-SIK, LEE, *The Politics of Korean Nationalism* (Berkeley, Cal.: University of California Press, 1963).

Chorley, R. S. T., 'Allied Powers (Maritime Courts) Act, 1941' (1941) 5 *MLR* 118–20.

Churchill, Robin R., and Lowe, Alan V., *The Law of the Sea* (2nd edn., Manchester: Manchester University Press, 1988).

Churchill, Winston Spencer, *The Second World War* ('Chartwell' Edition) (London: The Educational Book Company, 1954), 6 vols.

Clunet, Edouard, 'La présence des Alliés en France et «l'exterritorialité»' (1918) 45 *JDI* 514–17.

——'La plainte en Justice du Monténégro et l'exterritorialité diplomatique' (1920) 47 *JDI* 490–3.

Coates, W. P., and Coates, Z. K., *A History of Anglo-Soviet Relations* (London: Lawrence & Wishart, 1943).

Cochran, Charles Leo, 'De Facto and De Jure Recognition: Is There a Difference?' (1968) 62 *AJIL* 457–60.

Cohen, Michael J. (ed.), *The Rise of Israel. A Documentary Record from the Nineteenth Century to 1948*, vol. 39: *The Recognition of Israel, 1948* (New York: Garland Publishing, 1987).

Cohn, Ernst J., 'Legislation in Exile: Luxembourg' (1943) 25 *JCL* 40–6.

Collins, J. F., 'The United Nations and Indonesia', *Int. Conc.*, 459 (March 1950), 115–200.

Collins, Lawrence (ed.), *Dicey and Morris on the Conflict of Laws* (12th edn., London: Sweet & Maxwell, 1993), 2 vols.

Corbett, Percy E., 'The Vietnam Struggle and International Law' in R. A. Falk (ed.), *The International Law of Civil War* (Baltimore, Mld.: The Johns Hopkins Press, 1971), 348–404.

Craig, William Laurence, Polkinghorne, Michael, and Moghaizel, Fadi J., 'French Policy concerning Financial and Commerical Relations with Kuwait and Iraq' (1991) 19 *Int. Bus. Lawyer* 158–62.

Crawford, James, *The Creation of States in International Law* (Oxford: Clarendon Press, 1979).

Dahm, Georg, *Völkerrecht* (Stuttgart: Kohlhammer, 1958–61), 3 vols.

——Delbrück, Jost, and Wolfrum, Rüdiger, *Völkerrecht* (2nd edn., Berlin: Walter de Gruyter, 1989), I/1.

Damis, John, 'The OAU and Western Sahara' in Y. El-Ayouty and I. W. Zartman (eds.), *The OAU After Twenty Years* (New York: Praeger, 1984), 273–96.

Daoudi, Riad, 'Les problèmes rencontrés par le Koweit dans ses relations internationales pendant la crise du Golfe' in B. Stern (ed.), *Les aspects juridiques de la crise et de la guerre du Golfe* (Paris: Editions Montchrestien, 1991), 107–21.

Davidson, J. Scott, 'Beyond Recognition' (1981) 32 *N.Ir.LQ* 22–30.

——'Recognition of Foreign Governments in New Zealand' (1991) 40 *ICLQ* 162–70.

'De Facto and De Jure Governments' (1916–17) 61 *Sol. Jo.* 739–40.

de Gaulle, Charles, *Mémoires de Guerre,* I: *L'Appel 1940–1942* (Paris: Librairie Plou, 1954).

——*War Memoirs,* I: *The Call to Honour 1940–1942* (translated by Jonathan Griffin, London: Collins, 1955).

——For *War Memoirs. Documents* see Sources of State Practice—France.

Degras, Jane, See Sources of State Practice—Russia

Destiny Can Wait. The Polish Air Force in the Second World War (London: William Heinemann, 1949).

DICKINSON, EDWIN DEWITT, 'The Unrecognized Government or State in English and American Law' (1923) 22 *Mich.LR* 29–45 and 118–34.

——'The Case of the Irish Republic's Funds' (1927) 21 *AJIL* 747–53.

Die Algerische Revolution (Stuttgart: Deutsche Verlags-Anstalt, 1963).

DINU, MARCEL, 'The Role of the United Nations Organization in the Efforts for Finding a Solution to the Problem of the Palestinian People. Romanian Positions and Proposals' (1983) 17 *Rev. Roum. Et. Int.* 271–87.

DITTRICH, KURT, *Die Preussische Gesandtschaft beim Vatikan* (Berlin: Paul Zimmermann, 1917).

DOMKE, MARTIN, 'Dutch War-Time Legislation Before American Courts 1953' (1953–4) 1 *Ned. TIR* 365–73.

DONELAN, M. D., and GRIEVE, M. J., *International Disputes. Case Histories 1945–1970* (London: Europa Publications, 1973).

DORFMAN, MARC B., HASEY, MARK S., SCHMIDT, JOHN T., WEIL, JEFFREY G., 'Cambodian Representation' (1974) 15 *Harv. ILJ* 495–513.

DOROSHENKO, DMYTRO, *A Survey of Ukrainian History* (Winnipeg: Trident Press, 1975).

DOUC RASY, *La question de la representation Khmère à l'ONU: droit ou politique?* (Paris: A. Pedone, 1974).

DOVE, HEINRICH, 'Der Rechtszustand in den okkupierten Gebieten Belgiens und Russisch-Polens' (1915) 44 *JW* 425–30, 965–71.

DRUCKER, ALFRED, 'The Legislation of the Allied Powers in the United Kingdom' [1942] *CYBIL* 45–59.

DUNSDORFS, EDGARS, *The Baltic Dilemma. The Case of the de jure Recognition by Australia of the Incorporation of the Baltic States into the Soviet Union* (New York: Speller, 1975).

'Dutch Courts in the United Kingdom' (1941) 192 *LT* 216.

EL-AYOUTY, YASSIN, and ZARTMAN, I. WILLIAM (eds.), *The OAU After Twenty Years* (New York: Praeger, 1984).

ELIAS, T. O., 'The Charter of the Organization of African Unity' (1965) 59 *AJIL* 243–67.

EL SAYEGH, SÉLIM, *La crise du golfe: de l'interdiction à l'autorisation du recours à la force* (Paris: Librairie Générale de Droit et de Jurisprudence, 1993).

ENGERS, J. F., 'The United Nations Travel and Identity Document for Namibians' (1971) 65 *AJIL* 571–8.

ERDMANN, ULRICH, *Nichtanerkannte Staaten und Regierungen: Formen und Grenzen internationaler Beziehungen* (Göttingen: Institut für Völkerrecht der Universität Göttingen, 1966).

ERICH, RAFAEL WALDEMAR, 'La naissance et reconnaissance des Etats' (1926–III) 13 *RdC* 431–507.

ETTLE, 'Zur staatsrechtlichen Stellung des Königs der Belgier während der deutschen Okkupation' (1915) 20 *DJZ* 805–6.

EWING, KEITH, and FISHER, JOHN H. (eds.), *Czechoslovak Military Justice Abroad During the Second World War* (New York: Czechoslovak Society of Arts and Sciences in America, 1975).

EYTAN, WALTER, *The First Ten Years: A Diplomatic History of Israel* (London: Weidenfeld and Nicolson, 1958).

FALK, RICHARD A., 'The New States and International Legal Order' (1966–II) 118 *RdC* 7–103.

——(ed.), *The International Law of Civil War* (Baltimore, Mld.: The Johns Hopkins Press, 1971).

FAUCHILLE, PAUL, 'Chronique des faits internationaux. Belgique—Guerre de 1914—Occupation de la Belgique par les troupes allemandes—La Banque nationale de Belgique sous l'occupation allemande de 1914 à 1918'(1919) 26 *RGDIP* 310–29.

——For *La guerre de 1914* see Sources of State Practice—France.

——*Traité de Droit International Public* (Paris: Librairie Arthur Rousseau, 1922), I/1.

FAVROD, CHARLES-HENRI, *Le FLN et l'Algérie* (Paris: Librairie Plon, 1962).

FAYAT, HENRI, 'Legislation in Exile: Belgium' (1943) 25 *JCL* 30–40.

FEDOZZI, PROSPERO, *Trattato di Diritto Internazionale,* I: *Introduzione al Diritto Internazionale e Parte Generale* (4th edn., Padova: Cedam, 1940).

FEILCHENFELD, ERNST H., *The International Economic Law of Belligerent Occupation* (Washington, DC: Carnegie Endowment for International Peace, 1942).

FELDMANN, MARCUS, *Die Schweiz und Sowjetrußland* (Berne: Verbandsdruckerei, 1944).

FIEDOROWICZ, G. DE, 'Continuité de l'Etat' (1939) 24 *RDI* 129–75.

FISCHER, GEORGES, 'L'indépendance de la Guinée et les accords Franco-Guinéens' (1958) 4 *AFDI* 711–22.

FISHER, JOHN H., 'Czechoslovak Military Courts in France and Great Britain During World War II' in K. Ewing and J. H. Fisher (eds.), *Czechoslovak Military Justice Abroad During the Second World War* (New York: Czechoslovak Society of Arts and Sciences in America, 1975), 7–14.

FITZMAURICE, SIR GERALD, 'The General Principles of International Law. Considered from the Standpoint of the Rule of Law' (1957–II) 92 *RdC* 1–223.

Four Fighting Years: See Sources of State Practice—Czechoslovakia

FLORY, MAURICE, *Le statut international des Gouvernements réfugiés et le cas de la France Libre 1939–1945* (Paris: A. Pedone, 1952).

——'Algérie et le droit international' (1959) 5 *AFDI* 817–44.

——'Algérie algérienne et droit international' (1960) 6 *AFDI* 973–98.

——'Les implications juridiques de l'affaire de Goa' (1962) 8 *AFDI* 476–91.

——'La mission d'observation des Nation Unies au Yémen' (1963) 9 *AFDI* 612–26.

FRAENKEL, ERNST, *Military Occupation and the Rule of Law: Occupation Government in the Rhineland, 1918–1923* (London: Oxford University Press, 1944).

FRENZKE, DIETRICH, 'De-jure-, De-facto- und faktische Anerkennung in der Völkerrechtslehre der DDR und der UdSSR' (1970) 14 *ROW* 181–90.

FRIEDMANN, WOLFGANG G., 'Comment' in J. N. Moore (ed.), *Law and Civil War in the Modern World* (Baltimore, Mld.: The Johns Hopkins Press, 1974), 574–81.

FROWEIN, JOCHEN ABRAHAM, *Das de facto-Regime im Völkerrecht* (Cologne: Carl Heymanns, 1968).

——'Transfer or Recognition of Sovereignty—Some Early Problems in Connection with Dependent Territories' (1971) 65 *AJIL* 568–71.

——'Die Entwicklung der Anerkennung von Staaten und Regierungen im Völkerrecht' (1972) 11 *Der Staat* 145–59.

FUNCK, A., 'La «Reconnaissance» du C. F. L. N. (Québec, août 1943)' (1959) 9/33 *RHDGM* 37–48.

GALLAGHER, CHARLES F., 'Toward a Settlement in Algeria' (1960) 38 *For. Affairs* 273–84.

GALLOWAY, L. THOMAS, *Recognizing Foreign Governments: The Practice of the United States* (Washington, DC: American Enterprise Institute for Public Policy Research, 1978).

GARCIA, LEONIDAS, 'Las Guerras Civiles de Hispano-América y la Doctrina Tobar. Trajo presentado al primer Congreso Cientifico Pan-Americano' (1915) 17 *Revista de Derecho, Historia y Letras* 526–46.

GARNER, JAMES WILFORD, *International Law and the World War* (London: Longmans, Green and Co., 1920), i.

——'A Question of State Succession' (1927) 21 *AJIL* 753–7.

GAULAND, ALEXANDER, *Das Legitimitätsprinzip in der Staatenpraxis seit dem Wiener Kongress* (Berlin: Duncker & Humblot, 1971).

GELBERG, LUDWIK, *Die Entstehung der Volksrepublik Polen. Die völkerrechtlichen Probleme* (translated by Barbara Bönnemann-Wittek, Frankfurt a.M.: Athenäum Verlag 1972).

GEMMA, SCIPIONE, 'Les gouvernements de fait' (1924–III) 4 *RdC* 297–413.

GERNHUBER, HEINZ, 'Der italienisch-abessinische Konflikt und das Völkerrecht', doctoral thesis (University of Königsberg, 1937).

GHOBASHI, OMAR Z., 'The United Arab Republic and the United Nations' (1959) 15 *Rev. égypt.* 152–62.

GIANI, KESAR SINGH, *Indian Independence Movement in East Asia. The Most Authentic Account. The INA and the Azad Hind Movement* (Lahore: Singh Brothers, 1947), 2 parts.

GIBBS, FREDERICK WAYMOUTH, *Recognition: A Chapter from the History of the North American & South American States* (London: William Ridgway, 1863).

GINTHER, KONRAD, 'Die völkerrechtliche Stellung nationaler Befreiungsbewegungen im südlichen Afrika' (1982) 32 *ÖZöRV* 131–57.

GOERDELER, RAINER, *Die Staatensukzession in multilaterale Verträge. Eine Darstellung der Praxis der Gebietsnachfolger Frankreichs in Afrika* (Berlin: Duncker & Humblot, 1970).

GOLAN, GALIA, 'The Soviet Union and the PLO since the War in Lebanon' (1986) 40 *MEJ* 285–305.

GREIG, A. M., 'The Effects in Municipal Law of Australia's New Recognition Policy' (1991) 11 *AYBIL* 33–65.

GREIG, D. W., *International Law* (2nd edn., London: Butterworth, 1976).

GRETSCHANINOW, GEORG VON, 'Der Mitgliederbestand des Völkerbundes Anfang 1939' (1939) 9 *ZaöRV* 80–109.

GUGGENHEIM, PAUL, *Lehrbuch des Völkerrechts. Unter Berücksichtigung der internationalen und schweizerischen Praxis* (Basle: Verlag für Recht und

Gesellschaft, 1948–51), 2 vols.

——For *Répertoire suisse de droit international public* see Sources of State Practice—Switzerland.

——*Traité de Droit international public. Avec mention de la pratique internationale et suisse* (Geneva: Librairie de l'Université, 1953–4), 2 vols.

HACKWORTH, GREEN HAYWOOD: For *Digest of International Law* see Sources of State Practice—USA.

HALAJCZUK, BOHDAN T., *Los estados conquistados ante el derecho internacional* (Buenos Aires: n.p., 1950).

HALL, WILLIAM EDWARD, *A Treatise on International Law* (8th edn. by A. Pearce Higgins, Oxford: Clarendon Press, 1924).

HAMMERBACHER, GERHART, *Die völkerrechtliche Stellung Vietnams. Ein Beitrag zur Problematik der völkerrechtlichen Situation geteilter Staaten* (Augsburg: Verlag Hofmann, 1960).

HARRIS, D. J., *Cases and Materials on International Law* (4th edn., London: Sweet & Maxwell, 1991).

HARTMANN, PAUL, 'Conscription in the Allied Armies' (1941–2) 5 *MLR* 256–61.

——'The Allied Powers (War Service) Act' (1942) 6 *MLR* 72–5.

——'Restrictions on Jurisdiction of Czechoslovak Military Courts in Great Britain' in K. Ewing and J. H. Fisher (eds.), *Czechoslovak Military Justice Abroad During the Second World War* (New York: Czechoslovak Society of Arts and Sciences in America, 1975), 15–18.

HECKER, HELLMUTH, 'Diplomatischer Schutz der Staatsangehörigen des geteilten Polens und Danzigs durch Besatzungsmacht oder Exilregierung von 1939–1945, insbesondere in Ostpolen, Shanghai und Mauritius' (1984) 22 *AVR* 172–94.

HEFFTER, AUGUST WILHELM, *Das europäische Völkerrecht der Gegenwart auf den bisherigen Grundlagen* (4th edn., Berlin: E. H. Schröder, 1861).

HEILBORN, PAUL 'Tobardoktrin' in K. Strupp (ed.), *Wörterbuch des Völkerrechts und der Diplomatie* (Berlin: Walter de Gruyter, 1925), ii, 717–18.

HELD, JOSEPH VON, *Über Legitimität, Legitimitätsprincip* (Würzburg: F. E. Thein, 1859).

HENDERSON, GREGORY, *Korea: The Politics of the Vortex* (Cambridge, Mass.: Harvard University Press, 1968).

HENKIN, LOUIS, 'International Law: Politics, Values and Functions: General Course on Public International Law' (1989–IV) 216 *RdC* 9–416.

HERRICH, ALISON BUTLER, *Area Handbook for Angola* (Washington, DC: United States Government Printing Office, 1967).

HEYDON, SIR PETER, 'Protecting Polish Interests in the USSR 1943–1944: An Episode in Australian Representation' (1972) 18 *AJPH* 189–213.

HEYDTE, FRIEDRICH AUGUST FREIHERR VON DER, *Völkerrecht. Ein Lehrbuch* (Cologne: Verlag für Politik und Wirtschaft 1958–60), 2 vols.

——'Einige Aspekte der Anerkennung im Völkerrecht' in René Marcic, Hermann Mosler, Erik Suy, and Karl Zemanek (eds.), *Internationale Festschrift für Alfred Verdross zum 80. Geburtstag* (Munich: Wilhelm Fink, 1971), 129–51.

HIGGINS, ROSALYN, *The Development of International Law through the Political Organs of the United Nations* (London: Oxford University Press, 1963).

Hobza, Antoine, 'La république Tchécoslovaque et le droit international' (1922) 29 *RGDIP* 385–409.

Hodgson, Sir Robert, *Spain Resurgent* (London: Hutchinson, 1953).

Holborn, Louise Wilhelmine (ed.), *War and Peace Aims of the United Nations* (Boston, Mass.: World Peace Foundation, 1943–8), 2 vols.

Holtzendorff, Franz von (ed.), *Handbuch des Völkerrechts. Auf Grundlage Europäischer Staatspraxis*, 4 vols. (vol. 1: Berlin: Carl Habel, 1885; vols. 2–4: Hamburg: J. F. Richter, 1887).

Horak, Stephan: see Sources of State Practice—Poland.

Hornykiewicz, Theophil, *Ereignisse in der Ukraine 1914–1922 deren Bedeutung und historische Hintergründe* (Philadelphia, Pa.: W. K. Lypynsky Ost-Europäisches Forschungs-Institut, 1969), iv.

Hough, William J. H., 'The Annexation of the Baltic States and its Effect on the Development of Law Prohibiting Forcible Seizure of Territory' (1985) 6 *NYLSJICL* 301–533.

Houghton, Neal D., 'Policy of the United States and Other Nations with Respect to the Recognition of the Russian Soviet Government, 1917–1929', *Int. Conc.*, 247 (February 1929), 83–108.

Hovanisian, Richard G., *The Republic of Armenia,* II: *From Versailles to London, 1919–1920* (Berkeley, Cal.: University of California Press, 1982).

Huber, Max, 'Die Fortbildung des Völkerrechts auf dem Gebiete des Prozess- und Landkriegsrechts durch die II internationalen Friedenskonferenzen im Haag 1907' (1908) 2 *JöR* 470–611.

Hudson, Manley Ottmer (ed.), *International Legislation* (Washington, DC: Carnegie Endowment for International Peace, 1931–50), 9 vols.

Hütten, Helmut J., 'Zur Frage der Anerkennung von Staaten und Regierungen im modernen Völkerrecht' (1951) 3 *SRuSZ* 6–8.

Hurst, Sir Cecil, 'Les immunités diplomatiques' (1926–II) 12 *RdC* 119–241.

Hyde, Charles Cheney, 'The Recognition of Czecho-Slovaks as Belligerents' (1919) 13 *AJIL* 93–5.

——*International Law. Chiefly as Interpreted and Applied by the United States* (2nd revised edn., Boston, Mass.: Little, Brown and Co., 1947), 3 vols.

——'The Status of the Republic of Indonesia in International Law' (1949) 49 *Col. LR* 955–66.

Ibler, Vladimir, 'Prouustavna ratifikacija [Unconstitutional Ratifications]' (1956) 3 *JRMP* 271–86.

Institute of International Law, 'La reconnaissance des nouveaux Etats et des nouveaux gouvernements', Project of Resolutions. Texts adopted by the [eleventh] Commission in session held in Oslo, 19 August 1932: (1934) 38 *Annuaire de l'Institut de droit international* 342–50.

——'La reconnaissance des nouveaux Etats et des nouveaux gouvernements', Resolutions adopted at the Brussels session, 23 April 1936: (1936) 39–II *Annuaire de l'Institut de droit international* 300–5.

International Commission of Jurists, *The Question of Tibet and the Rule of Law* (Geneva: International Commission of Jurists, 1959).

Ion, Theodore P., 'The Hellenic Crisis from the Point of View of Constitutional and

International Law' (1917) 11 *AJIL* 46–73, 327–57, (1918) 12 *AJIL* 312–37, 562–88, 796–812.

Ipsen, Knut, *Völkerrecht* (3rd edn., Munich: C. H. Beck, 1990).

Iwańska, Alicja, *Exiled Governments: Spanish and Polish. An Essay in Political Sociology* (Cambridge, Mass.: Schenkman Publishing Company, 1981).

Jägerskiöld, Stig, 'The Immunity of State-Owned Vessels in Swedish Judicial Practice During World War II' (1948) 42 *AJIL* 601–7.

Jäschke, 'Estland' in K. Strupp (ed.), *Wörterbuch des Völkerrechts und der Diplomatie* (Berlin: Walter de Gruyter, 1924), i, 289.

Janke, Rudolf, 'Rechtsnatur und Rechtsstellung der Regierung im Exil', doctoral thesis (University of Hamburg, 1954).

Jennings, Sir Robert Yewdall, 'Recognition De Jure and De Facto', *Report of the International Law Conference held at London, July 1962* (London: The David Davies Memorial Institute of International Studies, 1962), 21–8.

——and Watts, Sir Arthur (eds.), *Oppenheim's International Law* (9th edn., Harlow: Longman, 1992), i.

Jessup, Philip Caryl, 'Norwegian Maritime Courts in England' (1942) 36 *AJIL* 653–7.

——'The Litvinov Assignment and the Pink Case' (1942) 36 *AJIL* 282–8.

Jovičić, Miodrag, 'Vlada u izbeglištvu—njen pravni status i ovlašćenja (Osvrti i razmatranja)' [Le gouvernement en exil—Son statut légal. Ses pouvoirs—(Commentaires)] (1959) 6 *JRMP* 84–104.

Jumeau, Andrée, *Le Refuge du Gouvernement National à l'Etranger* (Aix-en-Provence: Paul Roubaud, 1941).

Kacewicz, George V., *Great Britain, the Soviet Union and the Polish Government in Exile (1939–1945)* (The Hague: Martinus Nijhoff, 1979).

Kazemzadeh, Firuz, *The Struggle for Transcaucasia (1917–1921)* (Oxford: George Ronald, 1951).

Kelsen, Hans, 'Recognition in International Law: Theoretical Observations' (1941) 35 *AJIL* 605–17.

——*Principles of International Law* (2nd edn. rev. and ed. by Robert W. Tucker, New York: Holt, Rinehart and Winston, 1967).

Kerchove d'Exaerde, François de, 'Quelques questions en droit international public relatives à la présence et à l'activité du gouvernement belge en exil à Londres (Octobre 1940–Septembre 1944)' (1990) 23 *RBDI* 93–151.

Kettle, Michael, *Russia and the Allies,* III: *Churchill and the Archangel Fiasco. November 1918-July 1919* (London: Routledge, 1992).

Kim, Choong-Gu, *Die staatliche Einheit Koreas unter Berücksichtigung des Selbstbestimmungsrechts des koreanischen Volkes* (Würzburg: n.p., 1995).

King, Archibald, 'Jurisdiction over Friendly Foreign Armed Forces' (1942) 36 *AJIL* 539–67.

——'Sitting in Judgment on the Acts of Another Government' (1948) 42 *AJIL* 811–31.

Kiss, Alexandre-Charles: For *Répertoire de la Pratique française* see Sources of State Practice—France.

Kissel, Otto Rudolf, *Gerichtsverfassungsgesetz. Kommentar* (2nd edn., Munich: C. H. Beck, 1994).

KLARER, HEINZ: For *Schweizerische Praxis der völkerrechtlichen Anerkennung* see Sources of State Practice—Switzerland.

KLASEN, KARL, *Die völkerrechtliche Bedeutung der Anerkennung der Tschechoslowaken während des Weltkrieges* (Hamburg: H. Schimkus, 1933).

KLIEMAN, AARON S. (ed.), *American Zionism. A Documentary History,* XIII: *Recognition of Israel: An End and a New Beginning* (New York: Garland, 1991).

KLINTWORTH, GARY, *Vietnam's Intervention in Cambodia in International Law* (Canberra: Australian Government Publishing Service, 1989).

KLÜBER, JEAN LOUIS, *Droit des gens moderne de l'Europe* (Stuttgart: J. G. Cotta, 1819), i.

KOHLER, JOSEF, Review of *Das Moratoriumsrecht in Belgien* by Ernst Cohnitz (1917–18) 10 *ZVR* 229–30.

KÖHLER, LUDWIG VON, *Die Staatsverwaltung der besetzten Gebiete,* I: *Belgien* (Suttgart: Deutsche Verlags-Anstalt, 1927).

KOHT, HALVDAN, *Norway. Neutral and Invaded* (London: Hutchinson, 1941).

KOLAŘ FRANTIŠEK, 'Edouard Beneš et le Conseil national tchécoslovaque de la rue Bonaparte' (1993) 43/169 *GMCC* 9–15.

KORKISCH, FRIEDRICH, 'Zur Frage der Weitergeltung des Münchner Abkommens' (1944) 12 *ZaöRV* 83–105.

KROENER, BERNHARD R., MÜLLER, ROLF-DIETER, and UMBREIT, HANS, *Das Deutsche Reich und der Zweite Weltkrieg* (Stuttgart: Deutsche Verlags-Anstalt, 1988), V/1.

KUHN, ARTHUR K., 'The Effect of a State Department Declaration of Foreign Policy upon Private Litigation—the Netherlands Vesting Orders' (1942) 36 *AJIL* 651–3.

——'Civil Responsibility for Communications by Officials of a Friendly Foreign Government' (1948) 42 *AJIL* 108–11.

KUNZ, JOSEPH L., 'Staatsgewalt de facto' in K. Strupp (ed.), *Wörterbuch des Völkerrechts und der Diplomatie* (Berlin: Verlag Walter de Gruyter, 1925), ii, 605–15.

KURATOWSKI, ROMAN, 'International Law and the Naval, Military and Air Force Courts of Foreign Governments in the United Kingdom' (1942) 28 *Grot. Soc.* 1–25.

LABAND, PAUL, *Die Verwaltung Belgiens während der kriegerischen Besetzung* (Tübingen: J. C. B. Mohr, 1916).

——'Die Staatsgewalt im besetzten feindlichen Gebiet' (1917) 22 *DJZ* 262–5.

LACHARRIÈRE, R. DE, 'Le changement du statut de la Cochinchine', *RJPUF*, April–June 1949, 146–73.

LACHS, MANFRED, 'Polish Legislation in Exile' (1942) 24 *JCL* 57–60.

LACHS, R., 'Allied Governments in Exile. The Effect of Allied Legislation in Britain' (1942) 92 *Law Journal* 275–6.

LAFFAN, R. G. D., 'The Liberation of the New Nationalities. Part I. The Yugo-Slavs' in H. W. V. Temperley (ed.), *A History of the Peace Conference of Paris* (London: Hodder and Stoughton, 1921), iv, 171–212.

LAGONI, RAINER, 'Rechtsmängel springen ins Auge', *Der Spiegel*, 42/47 (21 November 1988), 164.

LAMBADARIOS, B., 'Pouvoir législatif de l'autorité d'occupation et nature juridique des gouvernements hellénique d'occupation' (1948) 1 *RHDI* 381–4.

LANDHEER, BARTHOLOMEW, 'The Legal Status of the Netherlands' (1943) 41 *Mich. LR* 644–64.

LANGENHOVE, FERNAND VAN, *L'action du Gouvernement belge en matière économique pendant la guerre* (Paris: Les Presses Universitaires de France, 1927).

LANGER, ROBERT, *Seizure of Territory. The Stimson Doctrine and Related Principles in Legal Theory and Diplomatic Practice* (Princeton, NJ: Princeton University Press, 1947).

LA PRADELLE, A. DE, 'La Tchécoslovaquie de Versailles à Munich—De la Paix de Versailles à l'Anschluss autrichien (11 mars 1938)' (1938) 22 *RDI* 354–76.

LARNAUDE, F., 'Les gouvernements de fait' (1921) 28 *RGDIP* 457–503.

LASERSON, MAX M., 'The Recognition of Latvia' (1943) 37 *AJIL* 233–47.

LAUTERPACHT, SIR HERSCH, 'Règles générales du droit de la paix' (1937–IV) 62 *RdC* 99–422.

——'The Credentials of the Abyssinian Delegation to the Seventeenth Assembly of the League of Nations' (1937) 18 *BYBIL* 184–6.

——'Implied Recognition' (1944) 21 *BYBIL* 123–50.

——*Recognition in International Law* (Cambridge: University Press, 1947).

LAUTERPACHT, ELIHU: see Sources of State Practice—United Kingdom.

LAWRENCE, T. J., *The Principles of International Law* (7th edn. rev. by Percy H. Winfield, London: Macmillan, 1925).

LEE, LUKE T., *Consular Law and Practice* (2nd edn., Oxford: Clarendon Press, 1991).

LEHMKUHL, DIK, *Journey to London. The Story of the Norwegian Government at War* (London: Hutchinson, n.d.).

LEIFER, MICHAEL, 'The International Representation of Kampuchea' [1982] *Southeast Asian Affairs* 47–59.

LIANG, YUEN-LI, 'Recognition by the United Nations of the Representation of a Member State: Criteria and Procedure' (1951) 45 *AJIL* 689–707.

LICHTENSTEIN, ERWIN, 'Entschädigung für Mauritius-Internierung' [1968] *RzW* 247–9.

——'Der Fall Mauritius. Ein Nachspiel' [1979] *RzW* 204–7.

LISZT, FRANZ VON, *Das Völkerrecht* (12th edn. ed. by Max Fleischmann, Berlin: Springer, 1925).

LLOYD JONES, DAVID, 'Case and Comment [on *Hesperides Hotel Ltd* v. *Aegean Turkish Holidays Ltd* [1977] 3 WLR 656]' (1978) 37 *CLJ* 48–51.

LOCKWOOD, L. D., 'The Philippine Supreme Court and Postwar Problems of International Law' (1950–1) 3 *Stanford LR* 3–34.

LOUDWIN, BERND, *Die konkludente Anerkennung im Völkerrecht* (Berlin: Duncker & Humblot, 1983).

LOURIE, SAMUEL ANATOLE, and MEYER, MAX, 'Governments-in-Exile and the Effect of Their Expropriatory Decrees' (1943) 11 *U.Chicago LR* 26–48.

MACCAS, LÉON, 'La Grèce et l'Entente (1914–1917) [Part II]' (1918) 25 *RGDIP* 154–222.

MAES, MARC, 'België erkent geen regeringen, enkel staten. Het geval Cambodia 1979–1991' (1991) 33/2 *Res Publica* 255–302.

MAKAROV, ALEXANDER N., 'Aufnahme der diplomatischen Beziehungen zwischen

Ungarn und der Sowjetunion' (1934) 4 *ZaöRV* 315–19.
——'Die Anerkennung der Sowjetregierung durch die Vereinigten Staaten' (1934) 4 *ZaöRV* 1–24.
——'Die Eingliederung der baltischen Staaten in die Sowjet-Union' (1940–1) 10 *ZaöRV* 682–707.
MALLOY, WILLIAM M.: For *Treaties* see Sources of State Practice—USA.
MANN, FRITZ ALEXANDER, 'Extraterritorial Effect of Confiscatory Legislation' (1941–2) 5 *MLR* 262–3.
——'Libellous Communications by a Foreign State Official' (1945) 9 *MLR* 179–82.
——*Foreign Affairs in English Courts* (Oxford: Clarendon Press, 1986).
——'The Sacrosanctity of the Foreign Act of State' (1943) 59 *LQR* 42–57, 155–71.
MANNING, A. E., 'Le gouvernement néederlandais à Londres et la "France libre"' (1987) 37/146 *GMCC* 41–54.
MANNING, WILLIAM R.: For *Diplomatic Correspondence of the United States* see Sources of State Practice—USA.
MARCUM, JOHN A., *The Angolan Revolution,* I: *The Anatomy of an Explosion (1950–1962)* (Cambridge, Mass.: The MIT Press, 1969), and II: *Exile, Politics and Guerrilla Warfare (1962–1976)* (Cambridge, Mass.: The MIT Press, 1978).
——'Government-in-Exile Versus Government-in-Insurgency: The Case of Angola' in Y. Shain (ed.), *Governments-in-Exile in Contemporary World Politics* (New York: Routledge, 1991), 42–51.
MAREK, KRYSTYNA, *Identity and Continuity of States in Public International Law* (Geneva: Librairie E. Droz, 1954).
MARKS, MATTHEW J., 'Protective Expropriatory Decrees of the Governments in Exile—Their Application in the United States' (1941) 41 *Col. LR* 1072–87.
MARKUS, VASYL, *L'Ukraine Sovietique dans les Relations Internationales et son statut en Droit International 1918–1923* (Paris: Les Editions Internationales, 1959).
MARTENS, GEORG FRIEDRICH VON, *Précis du droit des gens moderne de l'Europe fondé sur les traités et l'usage* (3rd edn., Göttingen: Dieterich, 1821).
MASARYK, THOMAS GARRIGUE, *The Making of a State: Memories and Observations 1914–1918* (London: Allen & Unwin, 1927).
MATTERN, KARL-HEINZ, *Die Exilregierung. Eine historische Betrachtung der internationalen Praxis seit dem Beginne des Ersten Weltkrieges und deren völkerrechtliche Wertung* (Tübingen: J. C. B. Mohr (Paul Siebeck), 1953).
MCDOUGAL, MYRES S., FELICIANO, FLORENTINO, *The International Law of War. Transnational Coercion and World Public Order* (New Haven, Conn.: New Haven Press, 1994).
MCNAIR, LORD ARNOLD DUNCAN, 'Municipal Effects of Belligerent Occupation' (1941) 57 *LQR* 33–73.
——'Problems Connected with the Position of the Merchant Vessel in Private International Law, with particular Reference to the Power of Requisition' (1945) 31 *Grot. Soc.* 30–58.
——'The Requisitioning of Merchant Ships' (1945) 27 *JCL* 68–78.
——*The Law of Treaties* (Oxford: Clarendon Press, 1961).
——For *International Law Opinions* see Sources of State Practice—United Kingdom.

——with WATTS, SIR ARTHUR D., *The Legal Effects of War* (4th edn., Cambridge: Cambridge University Press, 1966).

MEENE, 'Die Gesetzgebungstätigkeit der verdrängten Staatsgewalt' (1917) 22 *DJZ* 825–7.

MEISSNER, BETTINA JULIANE, *Formen stillschweigender Anerkennung im Völkerrecht* (Cologne: Carl Heymanns, 1966).

MEISSNER, BORIS J., *Die Sowjetunion, die baltischen Staaten und das Völkerrecht* (Cologne: Verlag für Politik und Wirtschaft, 1956).

——'Die staatliche Kontinuität und völkerrechtliche Stellung der baltischen Länder' in B. Meissner (ed.), *Die baltischen Nationen. Estland—Lettland—Litauen* (Cologne: Markus Verlag, 1990), 192–218.

MENON, P. K., 'Some Aspects of the Law of Recognition. Part V: Modes of Recognition' (1991) 69 *RDISDPS* 19–49.

MENZEL, EBERHARD, 'Anerkennung' in Görres-Gesellschaft (ed.), *Staatslexikon* (6th edn., Freiburg: Herder Verlag, 1959), ix, 77–90.

MERKES, MANFRED, *Die deutsche Politik gegenüber dem spanischen Bürgerkrieg 1936–1939* (Bonn: Ludwig Röhrscheid, 1961).

MÉRIC, EDOUARD, 'Le conflit algéro-marocain' (1965) 15 *RFSP* 743–52.

MÉRIGNHAC, A., and LÉMONON, E., *Le Droit des Gens et la Guerre de 1914–1918* (Paris: Librairie de la Société du Recueil Sirey, 1921), i.

MERON, THEODOR, 'Prisoners of War, Civilians and Diplomats in the Gulf Crisis' (1991) 85 *AJIL* 104–9.

MEYER, MAX, and TORCZYNER, HARRY, 'Corporations in Exile' (1943) 43 *Col. LR* 364–75.

MIEHSLER, HERBERT, and SCHREUER, CHRISTOPH, 'Austria' in R. Bernhardt (ed.), *Encyclopedia of Public International Law* (Amsterdam: North Holland, 1992), i, 296–301.

MISRA, KĀŚĪPRASĀDA P., 'Recognition of the "Provisional Government of the Algerian Republic": A Study of the Policy of the Government of India' (1962) 10 *Pol. Stud.* 130–45.

——*India's Policy on Recognition of States and Governments* (Bombay: Allied Publishers, 1966).

MITRA, SARADA, *India and the German Problem. A Case for Recognition of the GDR* (New Delhi: D. P. Sinha, 1966).

MOINUDDIN, HASAN, *The Charter of The Islamic Conference and Legal Framework of Economic Co-operation among its Member States* (Oxford: Clarendon Press, 1987).

MOORE, JOHN BASSETT: For *Digest* see Sources of State Practice—USA.

——For *Arbitrations* see Sources of State Practice—USA.

MOSER, PIERRE A., *La révolution angolaise* (Tunis: Société l'Action d'Edition et de Presse, 1966).

MÖSSNER, JÖRG MANFRED, *Einführung in das Völkerrecht* (Munich: C. H. Beck, 1977).

MOUREAUX, SERGE, *Les Accords d'Evian et l'avenir de la révolution algérienne* (Paris: François Maspero, 1962).

MUGERWA, NKAMBO, 'Subjects of International Law' in M. Sørensen (ed.), *Manual of Public International Law* (London: Macmillan, 1968), 247–310.

Müller, Udo, *Die Neuentstehung von Staaten. Im besonderen: Die Entstehung des Freistaates Thüringen, der Freien Stadt Danzig und der Tschechoslowakischen Republik* (Borna-Leipzig: Universitätsverlag von Robert Noske, 1928).

Murillo-Jimenez, Hugo, 'Wilson and Tinoco. The United States and the Policy of Non-Recognition in Costa Rica, 1917–1919', Ph.D. thesis (San Diego, Cal.: University of California, 1978).

Myres, Denys P., 'Contemporary Practice of the United States Relating to International Law—Recognition of States' (1961) 55 *AJIL* 703–20.

Na, In-Gyun, *Die völkerrechtliche Stellung Koreas* (Darmstadt: Dissertations Druck, 1991).

Naldi, Gino J., 'The Organization of African Unity and the Saharan Arab Democratic Republic' (1982) 26 *JAL* 152–62.

Nash, Marian: For *Cumulative Digest* see Sources of State Practice—USA.

Necatigil, Zaim M., *The Cyprus Question and the Turkish Position in International Law* (2nd edn., Oxford: Oxford University Press, 1993).

Nedjati, Zaim M., 'Acts of Unrecognized Governments' (1981) 30 *ICLQ* 388–415.

Němec, Jaroslav, 'Czechoslovak Military Prosecutors during World War II in Great Britain and in Territories under its Control' in K. Ewing and J. H. Fisher (eds.), *Czechoslovak Military Justice Abroad during the Second World War* (New York: Czechoslovak Society of Arts and Sciences in America, 1975), 19–25.

Newsom, David D. (ed.), *Diplomacy Under a Foreign Flag. When Nations Break Relations* (London: Hurst & Co., 1990).

Nguyen Quoc, Dinh, Daillier, Patrick, Pellet, Alain, *Droit international public* (3rd edn., Paris: LGDJ, 1987).

Noguères, Louis, *La dernière étape: Sigmaringen* (Paris: Librairie Arthème Fayard, 1956).

Nomura, Issei, 'Recognition of Foreign Governments' (1982) 25 *JAIL* 67–72.

North, P. M., and Fawcett, J. J., *Cheshire and North's Private International Law* (12th edn., London: Butterworths, 1992).

Norton, Henry K., *The Far Eastern Republic of Siberia* (New York: Holt, 1923).

Nostitz-Wallnitz, Oswalt von, 'Die Annexion Abessiniens und die Liquidation des abessinischen Konflikts' (1937) 7 *ZaöRV* 38–66.

Noulens, J., 'La reconnaissance du gouvernement soviétique de l'URSS', *Dict.Dipl.* (1933), ii, 532–8.

Oánh, Phan-Huy, *Die Wandlung der völkerrechtlichen Stellung Vietnams bis zum Pariser Waffenstillstandsabkommen 1973* (Bonn: n.p., 1974).

O'Brien, William V., and Goebel, Ulf H., 'United States Recognition Policy Toward the New Nations' in W. V. O'Brien (ed.), *The Yearbook of World Polity*, III: *The New Nations in International Law and Diplomacy* (London: Stevens & Sons, 1965), 98–228 and 284–312.

O'Connell, Daniel Patrick, 'The Status of Formosa and the Chinese Recognition Problem' (1956) 50 *AJIL* 405–16.

——*International Law* (2nd edn., London: Stevens & Sons, 1970), i.

——*The International Law of the Sea* (ed. by I. A. Shearer, Oxford: Clarendon Press, 1984), ii.

Oda, Shigeru, and Owada, Hisashi: See Sources of State Practice—Japan.

Official of the Royal Norwegian Ministry of Justice and Police, 'Legislation in Exile: Norway' (1942) 24 *JCL* 125–30.

Oliver, Robert T., *Syngman Rhee: The Man Behind the Myth* (London: Robert Hale, 1955).

Oppenheimer, F. E., 'Governments and Authorities in Exile' (1942) 36 *AJIL* 568–95.

Oppenheim, Lassa Francis L., *International Law. A Treatise*, vol. 1: 2nd edn. (London: Longmans, Green and Co., 1912), and 8th edn. by Sir Hersch Lauterpacht (London: Longmans, Green and Co., 1955) and vol. 2: 7th edn. by Sir Hersch Lauterpacht (London: Longmans, Green and Co., 1952).

Oppermann, Thomas, 'Die Anwendbarkeit der Genfer Abkommen zum Schutze der Kriegsopfer im Algerien Konflikt' (1961–2) 9 *AVR* 47–59.

——'Die Endphase des Algerienkonfliktes 1959–1962' (1963) 23 *ZaöRV* 1–20.

Padelford, Norman Judson, *International Law and Diplomacy in the Spanish Civil Strife* (New York: The Macmillan Company, 1939).

Panel, 'The Panamanian Revolution: Diplomacy, War and Self-Determination in Panama' (1990) 84 *ASIL Proc.* 182–203.

Patel, Satyavrata Ramdas, *Recognition in the Law of Nations* (Bombay: Tripathi, 1959).

Pattison, Wilfred Keith, 'The International Law of Recognition in Contemporary British Foreign Policy', Ph.D. thesis (University of Virginia, 1981).

——'The Delayed British Recognition of Israel' (1983) 37 *MEJ* 412–28.

Paxson, Frederic Logan, *The Independence of the South-American Republics: A Study in Recognition and Foreign Policy* (reprint of the 1916 edition, New York: Cooper Square, 1970).

Pazzanita, Anthony G., 'Legal Aspects of Membership in the Organization of African Unity: The Case of the Western Sahara' (1985) 17 *CWRJIL* 123–58.

——and Hodges, Tony, *Historical Dictionary of Western Sahara* (2nd edn., Metuchen, NJ: Scarecrow Press, 1994).

Perfall, Eberhard Freiherr von, *Die völkerrechtliche Vertretung Chinas* (Witterschlick bei Bonn: Schwarzbold, 1967).

Pergler, Charles, 'The Munich "Repudiation"' (1943) 37 *AJIL* 308–10.

Perkins, Arthur, E. 'Enemy Legislation and Judgments in the Liberated Countries: The Philippines' (1948) 30 *JCL* 17–27.

Perkins, Dexter, *The Monroe Doctrine 1823–1826* (Cambridge, Mass.: Harvard University Press, 1932).

——*A History of the Monroe Doctrine* (Boston, Mass.: Little, Brown and Co., 1941).

Pesmazoglou, Michel A., 'La nature juridique des Gouvernements formés pendant une occupation militaire ennemie' (1949) 2 *RHDI* 168–82.

Peterson, Martha Jean, 'Political Use of Recognition: The Influence of the International System' (1982) 34 *World Pol.* 324–52.

——'Recognition of Governments Should not be Abolished' (1983) 77 *AJIL* 31–50.

Pflügl, von, 'Sainte-Alliance', *Dict.Dipl.* (1933), ii, 629–30.

Phillimore, Sir Robert, *Commentaries upon International Law* (3rd edn., London: Butterworths, 1882), ii.

Pichlík, Karel, 'Die Entstehung der Tschechoslowakei' (1969) 17 *VZG* 160–80.

PINTO, ROGER, 'Le «GPRA» et les conventions de Genève', *Le Monde*, 13 April 1960, 1 and 2.

PREEG, ERNEST H., *The Haitian Dilemma. A Case Study in Demographics, Development and US Foreign Policy* (Washington, DC: Centre for Strategic and International Studies, 1996).

PUISSOCHET, JEAN-PIERRE, 'Relations diplomatiques et protection des nationaux' in B. Stern (ed.), *Les aspects juridiques de la crise et de la guerre du Golfe* (Paris: Editions Montchrestien, 1991), 93–106.

RACZYNSKI, EDWARD, *In Allied London* (London: Weidenfeld and Nicolson, 1962).

RAESTAD, ARNOLD, 'La reconnaissance internationale des nouveaux Etats et des nouveaux gouvernements' (1936) 17 *RDILC* 257–313.

RASHID, NASSER IBRAHIM, and SHAHEEN, ESBER IBRAHIM, *Saudi Arabia and the Gulf War* (Joplin, Mo.: International Institute of Technology, 1992).

RASMUSSEN, GUSTAVE, 'Danemark (Royaume de)', *Dict.Dipl.* (1947), iv, 302–4.

RATNER, STEVEN R., 'The Cambodia Settlement Agreements' (1993) 87 *AJIL* 1–41.

RAUCHBERG, H., 'Tschechoslowakische Republik' in K. Strupp (ed.), *Wörterbuch des Völkerrechts und der Diplomatie* (Berlin: Walter de Gruyter, 1925), ii, 728–36.

'Recognition of Governments' (1917–18) 62 *Sol. Jo.* 359–60.

REIBSTEIN, ERNST, *Völkerrecht* (Freiburg: Karl Alber, 1963), ii.

REISMAN, W. MICHAEL, and SUZUKI, EISUKE, 'Recognition and Social Change in International Law: A Prologue for Decision-making' in M. S. McDougal and W. M. Reisman (eds.), *International Law Essays: A Supplement to International Law in Contemporary Perspective* (New York: The Foundation Press, 1981), 493–554.

REUT-NICOLUSSI, EDUARD, 'Exilregierung' in Görres-Gesellschaft (ed.), *Staatslexikon* (6th edn., Freiburg: Herder Verlag, 1959), iii, 209–12.

'Rex de facto and Rex de jure' (1919–20) 64 *Sol. Jo.* 631.

RICHARDS BUTLER, *MEED Gulf Crisis Report [September 1990]. The Legal Implications of the United Nations Embargo for Businesses* (London: Middle East Economic Digest, 1990).

RIISMANDEL, VAINO J., 'The Continued Legal Existence of the Baltic States', *Baltic Rev.*, 12 (7 November 1957), 48–68.

RIPKA, HUBERT, *The Repudiation of Munich* (London: Czechoslovak Ministry of Foreign Affairs Information Service, 1943).

ROBERTSON, WILLIAM SPENCE, *France and Latin-American Independence* (Baltimore, Mld: The Johns Hopkins Press, 1939).

RØED, OLE TORLEIF, 'Krig i atomaldern' (1955) 25 *Nord.TIR* 26–41.

ROHR, LUISA, 'El reconocimiento como acto unilateral' (1978) 2 *Derecho Comparado* 107–35.

——'El reconocimiento como acto unilateral' (1979) 3 *Derecho Comparado* 92–124.

ROLIN, HENRI A., 'Conditions and Methods of Recognition of New Governments' in W. R. Bisshop (ed.), *International Law Conference London. 10th–12th July 1943* (Richmond, Surrey: R. W. Simpson, 1944), 40–7.

RÖPER, ERICH, 'Rechtsfragen bei der Entstehung Israels', *APZ*, B18/78, 3–21.

RÖSCH, KLAUS, *Die Rechtsstellung der nichtanerkannten Regierung vor Gericht* (Augsburg: Dissertations-Druck Werner Blasaditsch, 1968).

ROSKILL, LORD, 'The Norwegian Ships in Sweden 1941/42' (1993) 109 *LQR* 59–65.

ROSS, RUSSELL R. (ed.), *Cambodia. A Country Study* (3rd edn., Washington, DC: United States Government Printing Office, 1990).

ROTH, PAUL, *Die Entstehung des polnischen Staates. Eine völkerrechtlich-politische Untersuchung* (Berlin: Verlag von Otto Liebmann, 1926).

ROTTER, MANFRED, 'Government-in-Exile' in R. Bernhardt (ed.), *Encyclopedia of Public International Law* (Amsterdam: North Holland, 1987), inst. 10, 210–14.

ROUGIER, ANTOINE, *Les guerres civiles et le droit des gens* (Paris: L. Larose, 1903).

ROUSSEAU, CHARLES E., 'Le conflit italo-éthiopien—La conquête et ses conséquences' (1938) 45 *RGDIP* 53–123.

——*Droit international public* (Paris: Sirey, 1977), iii.

ROYAL INSTITUTE OF INTERNATIONAL AFFAIRS, *Chronology of the Second World War* (Oxford: Oxford University Press, 1947).

ROYAL NORWEGIAN GOVERNMENT INFORMATION OFFICE, *Norway's Floating Empire* (London: Hodder & Stoughton, 1942).

ROZEK, EDWARD J., *Allied Wartime Diplomacy. A Pattern in Poland* (New York: John Wiley & Sons, 1958).

RUDA, JOSÉ MARIA, 'Recognition of States and Governments' in M. Bedjaoui (ed.), *International Law: Achievements and Prospects* (Paris: UNESCO, and Dordrecht: Martinus Nijhoff, 1991), 449–65.

RUTENBERG, GREGOR, 'Die Anerkennung des Litauischen Staates' (1929) 1–II *ZaöRV* 250–63.

SALMON, JEAN J. A., 'Naissance et reconnaissance du Bangla-Desh. Quelques réflexions sur l'application des principes du droit international touchant les relations amicales entre Etats' in Josef Tittel (ed.), *Multitudo legum ius unum. Festschrift für Wilhelm Wengler zu seinem 65. Geburtstag* (Berlin: InterRecht, 1973), i, 467–90.

SANDFORD, CHRISTINE, *Ethiopia under Haile Selassie* (London: J. M. Dent, 1946).

SASTROAMIDJOJO, ALI, and DELSON, ROBERT, 'The Status of the Republic of Indonesia in International Law' (1949) 49 *Col. LR* 344–61.

SAUSER-HALL, GEORGES, 'L'occupation de guerre et les droits privés' (1944) 1 *Schw. JIR* 58–125.

SCANLON, HELEN LAWRENCE, *European Governments in Exile* (Washington, DC: Carnegie Endowment for International Peace Library, 25 January 1943).

SCELLE, GEORGES, *Manuel de droit international public* (Paris: Editions Domat-Montchrestien, 1948).

SCHACHTER, OSCAR, 'United Nations Law in the Gulf Conflict' (1991) 85 *AJIL* 452–73.

SCHAUMANN, WILFRIED, 'Exilregierung' in K. Strupp and H.-J. Schlochauer (eds.), *Wörterbuch des Völkerrechts* (Berlin: Walter de Gruyter, 1960), i, 498–9.

SCHERMERS, HENRY G., *International Institutional Law* (Alphen aan den Rijn: Sijthoff & Noordhoff, 1980).

SCHEUNER, ULRICH, 'Die Entstehung des indonesischen Staates' (1951–2) 3 *AVR* 44–67.

SCHINDLER, DIETRICH, and TOMAN, JUŘÍ (eds.), *The Laws of Armed Conflict. A*

Collection of Conventions, Resolutions and Other Documents (3rd revised edn., Geneva: Henry Dunant Institute, 1988).

SCHLÜTER, FERDINAND, *De-facto Anerkennung im Völkerrecht* (Würzburg: Verlag Konrad Tiltsch, 1936).

SCHOLZ, MANFRED, *Die Behandlung der Goa-Frage durch die Vereinten Nationen* (Würzburg: n.p., 1970).

SCHWARZENBERGER, GEORG, and BROWN, E. D., *A Manual of International Law* (6th edn., London: Professional Books, 1976).

SCHWELB, EGON, 'Legislation in Exile: Czechoslovakia' (1942) 24 *JCL* 120–4.

——'The Competence of Foreign Governments Instituted in Great Britain over Civil Persons, In Particular The Allied Powers (Maritime Courts) Act, 1941' [1942] *CYBIL* 198–201.

——'The Jurisdiction over the Members of the Allied Forces in Great Britain' [1942] *CYBIL* 147–71.

——'The Status of Allied Governments under the Diplomatic Privileges (Extension) Act, 1941' [1942] *CYBIL* 201–2.

——'Legislation for Enemy-Occupied Territory in the British Empire' (1944) 30 *Grot. Soc.* 239–59.

——'The Status of the United States Forces in English Law' (1944) 38 *AJIL* 50–73.

SCISO, ELENA, 'La questione delle credenziali cambogiane all'Assemblea generale delle Nazioni Uniti' (1981) 64 *Riv. DI* 83–95.

SCRANTON, MARGARET E., *The Noriega Years. U.S.—Panamanian Relations, 1981–1990* (Boulder, Col.: Rienner, 1991).

SELTER, K., 'Zur Rechtslage der baltischen Staaten' [1956] *IRD* 33–51.

SETON-WATSON, R. W., 'The Liberation of the Nationalities. Part III. The Formation of the Czecho-Slovak State' in H. W. V. Temperley (ed.), *A History of the Peace Conference of Paris* (London: Hodder & Stoughton, 1921), iv, 237–77.

SHAW, MALCOLM N., *International Law* (3rd edn., Cambridge: Grotius Publications, 1991).

SHRAGA, DAPHNA, 'Recognition of Governments-in-Exile' (in Hebrew) (1980) 7 *Iyune Mishpat* 681–702.

SILBERSCHMIDT, 'Über die Geltung der deutschen Gesetze im besetzten rheinischen Gebiete' (1923) 12 *RZfZuP* 211–15.

SINGH, NAGENDRA, and NAWAZ M. K.: See Sources of State Practice—India.

SMITH, HERBERT ARTHUR: See Sources of State Practice—United Kingdom.

SMITH, LOIS ELWYN, *Mexico and the Spanish Republicans* (Berkeley, Cal.: University of California Press, 1955).

SPANNER, HANS, 'Fragen der Verwaltung besetzer Gebiete. Unter besonderer Berücksichtigung der besetzten niederländischen Gebiete' (1944) 34 *AöR* 96–114.

SPERDUTI, GIUSEPPE, 'Governi in esilio e comitati nazionali all'estero' [1952] *Com. Int.* 404–13.

SPIROPOULOS, JAN, *Die de facto-Regierung im Völkerrecht* (Kiel: Verlag des Instituts für Internationales Recht an der Universität Kiel, 1926).

STARKE, J. G., 'The New Australian Policy of Recognition of Foreign Governments' (1988) 62 *ALJ* 390–1.

——*Introduction to International Law* (10th edn., London: Butterworths, 1989).

STEED, HENRY WICKHAM, *Through Thirty Years 1892–1922. A Personal Narrative*

(London: William Heinemann, 1924), ii.
——'The Birth of Czechoslovakia' (1943) 8 *Free Europe* 152–3.
STEIN, ERIC, 'Application of the Law of the Absent Sovereign in Territory Under Belligerent Occupation: The Schio Massacre' (1948) 46 *Mich. LR* 341–70.
STEINBERGER, H., 'Sovereignty' in R. Bernhardt (ed.), *Encyclopedia of Public International Law* (Amsterdam: North Holland, 1987), inst. 10, 397–418.
STENGERS, JEAN, *Leopold III et le gouvernement: les deux politiques belges de 1940. Aux origines de la question royale* (Paris-Gembloux: Duculot, 1980).
STIERLIN, PETER, *Die Rechtsstellung der nichtanerkannten Regierung im Völkerrecht* (reprint of the 1940 edition, Nendeln, Liechtenstein: Kraus Reprint, 1977).
STOUPNITZKY, A., *Statut International de l'URRS. Etat Commerçant* (Paris: Librairie générale de droit & de jurisprudence, 1936).
STREBEL, HELMUT, 'Der völkerrechtliche Begriff der Regierung' (1956) 7 *ÖZöR* 309–19.
——'Regierung' in K. Strupp and H.-J. Schlochauer (eds.), *Wörterbuch des Völkerrechts* (Berlin: Walter de Gruyter, 1962), iii, 85–7.
STRISOWER, LEO, 'L'exterritorialité et ses principales applications' (1923) 1 *RdC* 233–87.
STRUPP, KARL, 'Occupatio bellica' in K. Strupp (ed.), *Wörterbuch des Völkerrechts und der Diplomatie* (Berlin: Walter de Gruyter, 1925), ii, 154–71.
——*Grundzüge des positiven Völkerrechts* (5th edn., Bonn: Ludwig Röhrscheid, 1932).
——'Les Règles Générales du Droit de la Paix' (1934–I) 47 *RdC* 263–593.
——'Problèmes soulevés à l'occasion de l'annexion par l'Italie de l'Empire éthiopien' (1937) 44 *RGDIP* 43–50.
SUNDBERG, JACOB, 'The War of Laws' (1958) 28 *Nord. TIR* 268–309.
SUTER, KEITH D., 'The Australian Government's Policy of Recognition and Diplomatic Relations' (1975) 47/3 *Aust.Quart.* 67–79.
SUY, ERIC, *Les actes juridiques unilatéraux en droit international public* (Paris: Pichon & Durand-Auzias, 1962).
SYATAUW, J. J. G., *Some Newly Established Asian States and the Development of International Law* (The Hague: Martinus Nijhoff, 1961).
SYMMONS, C. R., 'United Kingdom Abolition of the Doctrine of Recognition of Governments: A Rose by Another Name?' [1981] *Pub.Law* 249–62.
TÁBORSKÝ, EDVARD, 'The Constitutionality of Official Acts of Allied Governments and International Law' [1942] *CYBIL* 190–5.
——'The Full Recognition of the President of the Czechoslovak Republic and of the Czechoslovak Government by Great Britain and their Recognition by the United States' [1942] *CYBIL* 183–6.
——*The Czechoslovak Cause. An Account of the Problems of International Law in Relation to Czechoslovakia* (London: H. F. & G. Witherby, 1944).
TALLEYRAND, CH. MAURICE DE, *Mémoires* (publiés avec une préface et des notes par le Duc de Broglie, Paris: Calmann Lévy, 1891), 3 vols.
TALMON, STEFAN, 'Recognition of Governments: An Analysis of the New British Policy and Practice' (1992) 63 *BYBIL* 231–97.
——'War Booty of "Separate Entity" Protected by Sovereign Immunity' (1995) 15

OJLS 295–307.

TAYLOR, ALASTAIR M., *Indonesian Independence and the United Nations* (London: Stevens & Sons, 1960).

TEMPERLEY, H. W. V., 'Recognition of New States' in H. W. V. Temperley (ed.), *A History of the Peace Conference of Paris* (London: Hodder & Stoughton, 1921), v, 157–62.

—— *The Foreign Policy of Canning 1822–1827. England, the Neo-Holy Alliance, and the New World* (London: G. Bell and Sons, 1925).

TÉNÉKIDÈS, C. G., 'La nature juridique des gouvernements institués par l'occupant en Grèce suivant la jurisprudence hellénique' (1947) 51 *RGDIP* 113–33.

The Birth of Czechoslovakia: See Sources of State Practice—Czechoslovakia.

'The Recognition of the Czecho-Slovak Armies' (1917–18) 62 *Sol. Jo.* 735–6.

THIERRY, HUBERT, 'La condition juridique du Nord Viet nam' (1955) 1 *AFDI* 169–74.

TIMMERMANS, W. A., 'The Baltic States, the Soviet Union and the Netherlands: A Historical Note' (1985) 32 *Ned. TIR* 288–94.

TOMŠIĆ, IVAN, 'The Identity of the Yugoslav State Under International Law' (1956) 3 *JRMP* 15–27.

TOMMASI DI VIGNANO, ALESSANDRO, 'Note sui governi in esilio' (1958) 25 *RSPI* 479–92.

TOURÉ, SEKOU, *L'Action politique du Parti démocratique de Guinée pour l'emancipation africaine* (Conakry: n.p., 1959), ii.

TOUSCOZ, J., 'Etude de la jurisprudence interne sur les aspects internationaux de l'affaire algérienne' (1963) 9 *AFDI* 953–69.

TOYE, HUGH, *The Springing Tiger. A Study of a Revolutionary* (London: Cassell, 1959).

'Transference of the Belgian Government to Havre' (1914) 137 *LT* 598.

TRAVERS, MAURICE, *Le droit pénal international et sa mise en œuvre en temps de paix et en temps de guerre* (Paris: Sirey, 1920), i.

TRIPATHI, MANJUL RANI, *India's Foreign Policy on Diplomatic Recognition of States and Governments* (Delhi: B. R. Publishing Corporation, 1990).

TSCHOFFEN, PAUL, 'The Exceptional Powers Exercised by the Belgian Government', *Message*, No 9 (July 1942), 23–7.

TUSELL, JAVIER, and ALTED, ALICIA, 'The Government of the Spanish Republic in Exile: 1939–1977' in Y. Shain (ed.), *Governments-in-Exile in Contemporary World Politics* (New York: Routledge, 1991), 145–65.

TWARDOWSKI, JUL. v., 'Ukraine' in K. Strupp (ed.), *Wörterbuch des Völkerrechts und der Diplomatie* (Berlin: Walter de Gruyter, 1925), ii, 753–55.

ULLMAN, RICHARD H., *Anglo-Soviet Relations, 1917–1921*, II: *Britain and the Russian Civil War. November 1918–February 1920* (Princeton, NJ: Princeton University Press, 1968) and III: *The Anglo-Soviet Accord* (Princeton, NJ: Princeton University Press, 1972).

VANCE, R. T., 'Recognition as an Affirmative Step in the Decolonization Process: The Case of Western Sahara' (1980) 7 *Yale JWPO* 45–87.

VATTEL, E. DE, *The Law of Nations or the Principles of Natural Law. Applied to the Conduct and to the Affairs of Nations and Sovereigns* (translation of the edition of 1758 by Charles G. Fenwick, Washington, DC: Carnegie Institution, 1916).

VERDROSS, ALFRED VON, *Völkerrecht* (4th edn., Wien: Springer, 1959).

——Review of *Lehrbuch des Völkerrechts* by Paul Guggenheim (1949–1950) 2 *ÖZöR* 144–5.

——and SIMMA, BRUNO, *Universelles Völkerrecht. Theorie und Praxis* (3rd edn., Berlin: Duncker und Humblot, 1984).

VERHOEVEN, JOE, *La reconnaissance internationale dans la pratique contemporaine. Les relations publiques internationales* (Paris: A. Pedone, 1975).

VERZIJL, J. H. W., *International Law in Historical Perspective*, Part II: *International Persons* (Leyden: A. W. Sijthoff, 1969).

VIRET, JAQUES, *La portée extra-territoriale des actes de souveraineté interne d'un gouvernement non-reconnu* (Montreux: Imprimerie Corbaz, 1951).

VISSCHER, CHARLES DE, 'Les gouvernements étrangers en justice. Reconnaissance internationale et immunités' (1922) 50 *RDILC* 149–70.

VITAS, ROBERT A., *The United States and Lithuania. The Stimson Doctrine of Nonrecognition* (New York: Praeger, 1990).

WARBRICK, COLIN, 'The New British Policy on Recognition of Governments' (1981) 30 *ICLQ* 568–92.

——'Kampuchea: Representation and Recognition' (1981) 30 *ICLQ* 234–46.

——'The Invasion of Kuwait by Iraq' (1991) 40 *ICLQ* 482–92.

WARD, LEO J., 'Can the United States of America Recognize the Republic of Ireland Without Committing Any Breach of International Law in Reference to Great Britain?' (1922) 5 *Bi-Monthly LR* 129–38.

WATERS, MAURICE, *The Ad Hoc Diplomat: A Study in Municipal and International Law* (The Hague: Martinus Nijhoff, 1963).

WEBSTER, CHARLES KINGSLEY: See Sources of State Practice—United Kingdom.

WELLER, MARC, 'Defiant diplomats in Kuwait establish a point of principle', *The Times*, 24 August 1990, 3.

——'The legal right to fight surrendered', *The Times*, 6 September 1990, 10.

——'The Kuwait Crisis: A Survey of Some Legal Issues' (1991) 3 *RADIC* 1–40.

WENGLER, WILHELM, *Völkerrecht* (Berlin: Springer, 1964), 2 vols.

WESTLAKE, JOHN, *International Law*, Part II: *War* (2nd edn., Cambridge: Cambridge University Press, 1913).

WEYR, HANS, 'Der Tschechoslowakische Staat. Seine Entstehung und Verfassung' (1922) 11 *JöR* 351–75.

WHEATON, HENRY, *Elements of International Law* (8th edn. ed. with notes by Richard Henry Dana, Jr., London: Sampson Low, 1866).

WHITEMAN, MARJORIE M.: For *Digest of International Law* see Sources of State Practice—USA.

WIJEWARDANE, D. S., 'Criminal Jurisdiction over Visiting Forces With Special Reference to International Forces' (1965–6) 41 *BYBIL* 122–97.

WILD, PATRICIA BERKO, 'The Organization of African Unity and the Algerian-Moroccan Border Conflict: A Study of New Machinery for Peacekeeping and for Peaceful Settlement of Disputes Among African States' (1966) 20 *Int. Org.* 18–36.

WILDMAN, RICHARD, *Institutes of International Law* (London: William Benning & Co., 1849), i.

WILLIAMS, SHARON ANNE, 'The Polish Art Treasures in Canada, 1940–60' (1977) 15 *CYIL* 146–72.
WILSON, G. G., 'British Recognition De Facto and De Jure of the USSR' (1934) 28 *AJIL* 99–101.
WILSON, HEATHER ANN, *International Law and the Use of Force by National Liberation Movements* (Oxford: Clarendon Press, 1988).
WILSON HARRIS, H., 'The Bolsheviks and Diplomacy' in H. W. V. Temperley (ed.), *A History of the Peace Conference of Paris* (London: Hodder & Stoughton, 1924), vi, 311–34.
WOLD, TERJE, 'The 1942 Enactment for the Defence of the Norwegian State' (1942) 20 *Can. BR* 505–9.
——'Legislation Promulgated by the Norwegian Government' (1943) 1 *Norseman* 430–8.
WOLF, CHARLES, JR., *The Indonesian Story: The Birth, Growth and Structure of the Indonesian Republic* (New York: The John Day Company, 1948).
WOLFF, ERNST, 'The International Position of Dispossessed Governments at Present in England' (1943) 6 *MLR* 208–15.
WOLFF, MARTIN, *Private International Law* (2nd edn., Oxford: Clarendon Press, 1950).
WOODWARD, SIR LLEWELLYN, *British Foreign Policy in the Second World War* (London: Her Majesty's Stationary Office, 1962).
——*British Foreign Policy in the Second World War* (London: Her Majesty's Stationary Office, 1970–5), 5 vols.
WOOLBERT, ROBERT GALE, 'The Future of Ethiopia' (1942) 20 *For. Affairs* 535–51.
WRIGHT, PHILIP QUINCY, 'The British Courts and Ethiopian Recognition' (1937) 31 *AJIL* 683–8.
——'The Goa Incident' (1962) 56 *AJIL* 617–32.
ZEEMAN, J. H., 'Legislation in Exile: The Netherlands' (1944) 26 *JCL* 4–11.
ZIEGER, GOTTFRIED, 'Rhineland Occupation After World War I' in R. Bernhardt (ed.), *Encyclopedia of Public International Law* (Amsterdam: North Holland, 1982), inst. 4, 190–3.

Sources of State Practice

ALGERIA
Algerian Office, New York, *White Paper on the Application of the Geneva Conventions of 1949 to the French-Algerian Conflict* (New York: Algerian Office New York, 1960).
Freies Algerien, ed. by Arbeitskreis der Freunde Algeriens, 1/1 (September 1958)–5/3 (April–May 1962).
Les archives de la révolution algérienne, ed. by Mohammed Harbi (Paris: Les éditions jeune afrique, 1981).

ANGOLA
Angola: Bulletin d'information de libertacao de Angola, issued by the FNLA.

AUSTRALIA

Documents on Australian Foreign Policy 1937–49, ed. by Department of Foreign Affairs, Canberra, 11 vols., 1975–94.

AUSTRIA

Bundesgesetzblatt der Republik Österreich.

BELGIUM

'Arrêtés de Londres'. Législation promulguée par le Gouvernement belge à l'étranger du 17 mai 1940 au 7 septembre 1944 (Brussels: Ferdinand Larcier, n.d.).

Correspondance diplomatique relatif à la guerre de 1914–1915 (Paris: Librairies Hachette, 1914–15), 2 vols.

La Guerre de 1914–1918. Cahiers Documentaires, ed. by Bureau Documentaire Belge, Livraisons 1 à 60 (Le Havre: Imprimerie du 'Havre-Éclair', 1915–18).

Législation promulguée par le Gouvernement belge en exil. Mai 1940–31 Décembre 1943 (Brussels: Etablissements Emile Bruylant, n.d.).

Moniteur belge.

News from Belgium and the Belgian Congo, ed. by Belgian Government Information Centre, New York, 1 (4 April 1941)–5 (29 December 1945).

Répertoire des traités conclus par la Belgique/Repertorium van de door België gesloten verdragen, ed. by I. de Troyer, I: *1830–1940* (Brussels: J. Goemaere, 1973); II: *1941–1986* (Brussels: SMITS, 1988).

CANADA

Documents on Canadian External Relations, ed. by Department of External Affairs, Ottawa, 1 (1909–18)–.

CHINA (PEOPLE'S REPUBLIC)

Bartke, Wolfgang, *The Agreements of the PR China 1949–1975* (Hamburg: Institut für Asienkunde, 1976).

Chiu, Hungdah, *Agreements of the People's Republic of China. A Calendar of Events 1966–1980* (New York: Praeger, 1981).

Johnston, Douglas Millar, and Chiu, Hungdah, *Agreements of the People's Republic of China 1949–1967. A Calendar* (Cambridge, Mass.: Harvard University Press, 1968).

Peking [Beijing] Review. A Weekly Magazine of Chinese News and Views, 1 (1958)–.

CZECHOSLOVAKIA

Czechoslovak Sources and Documents, ed. by Czechoslovak Ministry of Foreign Affairs, Information Service, London and Prague, 1 (1941)–28 (1947).

Four Fighting Years, ed. by Czechoslovak Ministry of Foreign Affairs, Department of Information (London: Hutchinson, 1943).

The Birth of Czechoslovakia, ed. with an introduction by Cestmis Jesina (Washington, DC: Czechoslovak National Council of America, 1968).

EUROPEAN UNION

Bulletin of the European Communities, ed. by the European Commission, 1/1 (January 1968)–26/11 (December 1993), continued as *Bulletin of the European Union*, 1/2 (1994)–.

FRANCE

de Gaulle, Charles, *War Memoirs. Documents*, I: *The Call to Honour 1940–1942*, translated by Jonathan Griffin (London: Collins, 1955).
——*War Memoirs. Documents*, II: *Unity 1942–1944*, translated by Joyce Murchie and Hamish Erskine (London: Weidenfeld and Nicolson, 1959).
——*War Memoirs. Documents*, III: *Salvation 1944–1946*, translated by Joyce Murchie and Hamish Erskine (London: Weidenfeld and Nicolson, 1960).
Fauchille, Paul, *La guerre de 1914. Recueil de documents intéressant le droit international* (Paris: A. Pedone, 1915), i.
Journal Officiel de la Republique Française, Débats parlementaires, chambre des deputés.
Journal Officiel de la République Française.
Kiss, Alexandre-Charles, *Répertoire de la Pratique française en matière de droit international public* (Paris: Editions du Centre National de la Recherche Scientifique, 1962–72), 7 vols.
La politique étrangère de la France. Textes et documents, 1966–70.

GERMANY

Bulletin, ed. by Presse und Informationsamt der Bundesregierung, Bonn, October 1951–.
Bundesgesetzblatt.
Die Bemühungen der Bundesrepublik um Wiederherstellung der Einheit Deutschlands durch Gesamtdeutsche Wahlen. Dokumente und Akten, ed. by Bundesministerium für Gesamtdeutsche Fragen, part 2 (March 1958).
Documents on German Foreign Policy 1919–1945, published jointly by the US Department of State and the British Foreign Office from captured archives of the German Foreign Ministry, 1957–.
Fundstellennachweis B. Völkerrechtliche Vereinbarungen, Verträge zur Vorbereitung und Herstellung der Einheit Deutschlands, ed. by Bundesministerium der Justiz, 1968–.
Texte zur Deutschlandpolitik, ed. by Bundesministerium für Innerdeutsche Beziehungen (Melsungen: A. Bernecker, 1971), vi.
Verhandlungen des Deutschen Bundestages. Drucksachen.
Verhandlungen des Deutschen Bundestages. Plenarprotokolle.

INDIA

Documents on India's Role in Afro-Asian Liberation Movement, I: *Algeria*, compiled and ed. by Man Singh Deora (New Delhi: Discovery Publishing House, 1994).
Singh, Nagendra, and Nawaz M. K., 'The Contemporary Practice of India in the Field of International Law [1958–62]', *Int.Stud.*, 1 (1959–60)–6 (1964–5).

JAPAN

The Practice of Japan in International Law 1961–1970, ed. by Shigeru Oda and Hisashi Owada (Tokyo: Tokyo University Press, 1982).

LEAGUE OF NATIONS
Official Journal, 1921–46.
Official Journal, Spec. Supp., 1921–46.
League of Nations Treaty Series, 205 vols., 1920–46.
Records of the Assembly, 1920–46.

LUXEMBOURG
Luxembourg Bulletin, ed. by Luxembourg Government, Press Section, London, 1 (10 May 1942)–24 (April–May 1945).

NETHERLANDS
Repertorium van door Nederland tussen 1813 en 1950 gesloten Verdragen, ed. by Alexander Maria Stuyt ('s-Gravenhage: Staatsdrukkerij- en Uitgeverijbedrijf, 1953).

PAKISTAN
Documents on Pakistan and International Conflicts, compiled and ed. by Man Singh Deora and R. Grover (New Delhi: Anmol Publications, 1993–).

POLAND
'Chronologie des relations internationales de la Pologne [1944–1967]', *APAI* 1964–5 (1967)–1968 (1971).
Documents on Polish–Soviet Relations 1939–1945 (London: Heinemann, 1961–7), 2 vols.
Poland's International Affairs 1919–1960. A Calendar of Treaties, Agreements, Conventions, and Other International Acts, with Annotations, References, and Selections from Documents and Texts of Treaties, by Stephan Horak (Bloomington, Ind.: Indiana University Press, 1964).
Polish Facts and Figures, published by the Polish Information Centre, New York, 1 (10 March 1944)–17 (25 April 1945).

RUSSIA
A Calendar of Soviet Treaties, I: *1917–1957*, by Robert M. Slusser and Jan F. Triska (Stanford, Cal.: Stanford University Press, 1959), II: *1958–1973*, by George Ginsburgs and Robert M. Slusser (Alphen van deen Rijn: Sijthoff, 1981).
Calendar of Soviet Documents on Foreign Policy 1917–1941, by Jane Degras (London: RIIA, 1948).
Soviet Foreign Policy During the Patriotic War. Documents and Materials [1941–5] (London: Hutchinson, n.d.), 2 vols.
Soviet Treaty Series [1917–39]. A Collection of Bilateral Treaties, Agreements and Conventions, etc., concluded between the Soviet Union and Foreign Powers, ed. by Leonard Shapiro (Washington, DC: The Georgetown University Press, 1950–5), 2 vols.

SWITZERLAND
Documents diplomatiques suisses 1848–1945, ed. by Commission nationale pour la publication de documents diplomatiques suisses (Berne: Benteli Verlag, 1979).

Schweizerische Praxis der völkerrechtlichen Anerkennung, by Heinz Klarer (Zurich: Schulthess Polygraphischer Verlag, 1981).

Répertoire suisse de droit international public. Documentation concernant la pratique de la Confédération en matière de droit international public 1914–1939, ed. by Paul Guggenheim (Basle: Helbing & Lichtenhahn Editions S.A., 1975), 4 vols.

UNITED KINGDOM

A British Digest of International Law, Phase I: *1860–1914*, ed. by Clive Parry, vols. 2b, 5–8 (London: Stevens & Sons, 1965–7).

Anglo-Vatican Relations, 1914–1939: Confidential Annual Reports of the British Minister to the Holy See, ed. by Thomas E. Hachey (Boston, Mass.: G. K. Hall, 1972).

An Index to British Treaties 1101–1968, compiled and annotated by Clive Parry and Charity Hopkins (London: HMSO, 1970), 3 vols.

An Index to British Treaties 1969–1988, compiled and annotated by D. J. Harris and J. B. Shepherd (London: HMSO, 1991).

Britain and the Independence of Latin America 1812–1830. Select Documents from the Foreign Office Archives, ed. by Sir Charles Kingsley Webster (Oxford: Oxford University Press, 1938), 2 vols.

British Practice in International Law [1963–1967], ed. by Elihu Lauterpacht with the assistance of Gilian White (London: The British Institute of International and Comparative Law, 1965–71).

Documents on British Foreign Policy, 1919–1939 (London: HMSO, 1947–86): 1st Series, 27 vols., 1947–86 (covers period 1919–29). 1A Series, 7 vols., 1966–75 (covers period 1925–30). 2nd Series, 21 vols., 1946–84 (covers period 1930–8). 3rd Series, 10 vols., 1949–61 (covers period 1938–9).

Documents on British Policy Overseas (London: HMSO, 1984–): 1st Series, 7 vols., 1984–95. 2nd Series, 4 vols., 1986–91.

Great Britain and the Law of Nations. A Selection of Documents Illustrating the Views of the Government in the United Kingdom upon Matters of International Law, ed. by Herbert Arthur Smith (London: P. S. King, 1932), 2 vols.

International Law Opinions, by Arnold Duncan McNair (Cambridge: University Press, 1956), 3 vols.

Parliamentary Debates. House of Commons. Official Report.

Parliamentary Debates. House of Lords. Official Report.

Parliamentary Papers (House of Commons and Command [Papers laid before Parliament are entitled Command Paper in the case of the Foreign Office]).

Poland in the British Parliament 1939–1945, ed. by Wacław Jędrzejewicz (New York: Jósef Piłsudski Institute of America, 1946–62), 3 vols.

Statutory Rules and Orders Other Than Those of a Local, Personal or Temporary Character for the Year 1890–1947 (London: HMSO, 1890–1948).

'The Contemporary Practice of the United Kingdom in the Field of International Law—Survey and Comment [1956–1959]', compiled by Elihu Lauterpacht, *ICLQ*, 5 (1956)–10 (1961) .

The Contemporary Practice of the United Kingdom in the Field of International Law, 1962, ed. by Elihu Lauterpacht (London: The British Institute of International

and Comparative Law, 1963).
The London Gazette.
United Kingdom Treaty Series.
'United Kingdom Materials on International Law [1978–]'(1968) 49 *BYBIL*–.

UNITED NATIONS

Documents of the United Nations Conference on International Organization San Francisco, 1945, 15 vols., 1945.
General Assembly Official Records, 1946–.
Security Council Official Records, 1946–.
United Nations Treaty Series, 1946–.
Yearbook of the United Nations, 1 (1946–7)–.

UNITED STATES OF AMERICA

A Digest of International Law, ed. by John Bassett Moore (Washington, DC: United States Government Printing Office, 1906), 8 vols.
Congress, Congressional Records.
Congress, House of Representatives, Committee on Foreign Affairs, *Review of US Policy Toward Political Negotiations in Angola*. Hearing. 101st. Cong., 1st sess., 1989.
Congress, House of Representatives, Select Committee on Communist Aggression, *Baltic States: A Study of Their Origin and National Development; Their Seizure and Incorporation into the USSR*. Third Interim Report. 83rd Cong., 2nd sess., 1954.
Congress, Senate, Committee on Foreign Relations, *Executive Sessions of the Senate Foreign Relations Committee (Historical Series)* (1978), vii.
—— *United States Recognition of Foreign Governments*. Hearing. 91st Cong., 1st sess., 1969.
Cumulative Digest of United States Practice in International Law 1981–1988, ed. by Marian Nash (Washington, DC: United States Government Printing Office, 1994–5), 3 vols.
Department of State, *American Foreign Policy: Current Documents*, 1981–.
Department of State, *Bulletin*, 1 (1939)–89 (1989).
Department of State, *Dispatch*, 1 (1990)–.
Department of State, *Establishment of Diplomatic Relations with the Union of Soviet Socialist Republics* (Washington, DC: United States Government Printing Office, 1933).
Department of State, *Foreign Relations of the United States. Diplomatic Papers*, 1933–.
Department of State, *Papers Relating to the Foreign Relations of the United States*, 1862–1932.
Department of State, *Treaties in Force. A List of Treaties and Other International Agreements of the United States in Force on . . .*, 1956–.
Digest of International Law, ed. by Green Haywood Hackworth (Washington, DC: United States Government Printing Office, 1940–4), 8 vols.
Digest of International Law, ed. by Marjorie M. Whiteman (Washington, DC: United States Government Printing Office, 1963–73), 15 vols.

Digest of United States Practice in International Law [1973–80] (Washington, DC: United States Government Printing Office, 1974–89), 9 vols.

Diplomatic Correspondence of the United States Concerning the Independence of the Latin American Nations, ed. by William. R. Manning (Washington, DC: United States Government Printing Office, 1926), iii.

Diplomatic Correspondence of the United States. Inter American Affairs 1831–1860, ed. by William R. Manning (Washington, DC: Carnegie Endowment for International Peace, 1937), ix.

Documents on American Foreign Relations, January 1938/June 1939 (1939)–.

Federal Register.

History and Digest of the International Arbitrations to Which the United States Has Been a Party, ed. by John Bassett Moore (Washington, DC: United States Government Printing Office, 1898), 6 vols.

Information Service, London, *The Gulf Crisis. A Chronology, July 1990–July 1991* (London: Reference Center, United States Information Service, Embassy of the United States of America, 1991).

The Record of American Diplomacy. Documents and Readings in the History of American Foreign Relations, ed. by Ruhl J. Bartlett (2nd edn., New York: Alfred A. Knopf, 1952).

Treaties, Conventions, International Acts, Protocols and Agreements Between the United States of America and Other Powers 1776–1909, ed. by William M. Malloy (Washington, DC: United States Government Printing Office, 1910), 2 vols.

YUGOSLAVIA

The Conference of Heads of State or Government of Non-Aligned Countries, Belgrade, September 1–6, 1961 (Belgrade: 'Yugoslavia', n.d.).

Yugoslav Documents, issued by Yugoslav Government, Information Department, London, 1 (1941)–4 (1943).

Index